Grimgar of Fantasy and Ash

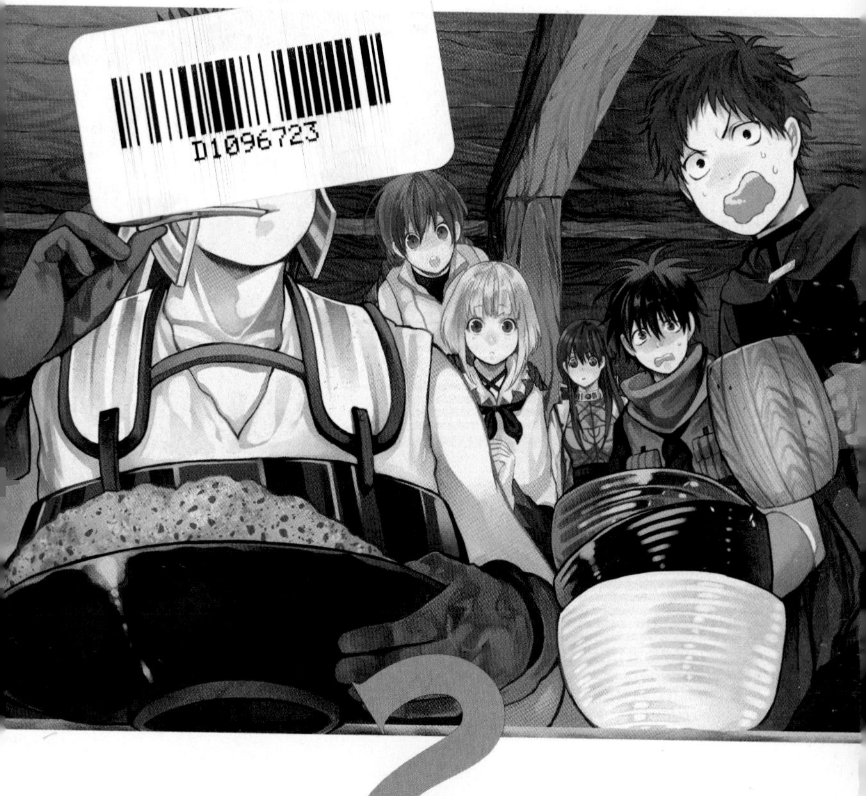

2

LEVEL.2

ORIGINAL STORY
Ao Jyumonji

ART
Mutsumi Okubashi

CHARACTER DESIGN
Eiri Shirai

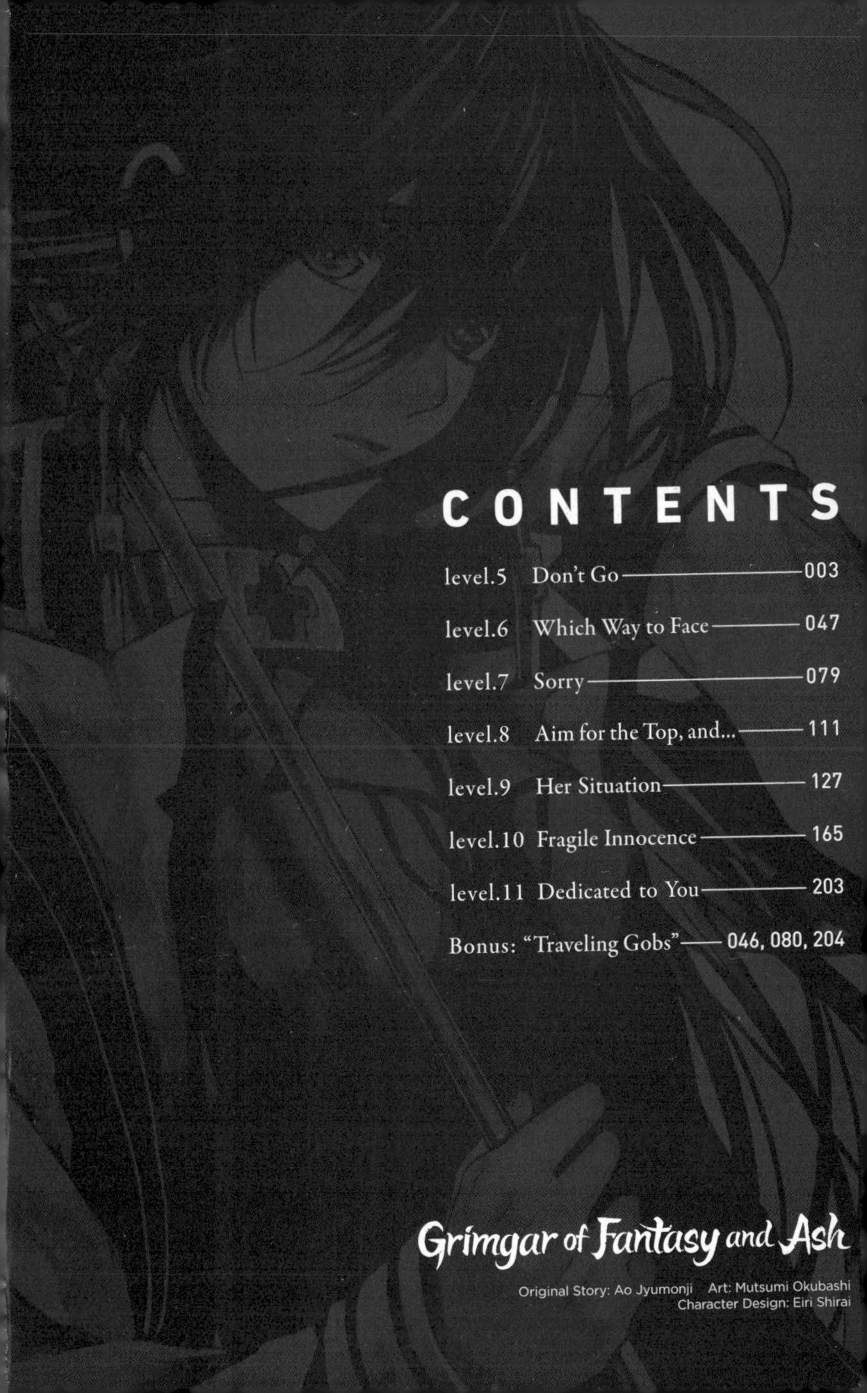

CONTENTS

Grimgar of Fantasy and Ash

Original Story: Ao Jyumonji Art: Mutsumi Okubashi
Character Design: Eiri Shirai

level.5: Don't Go

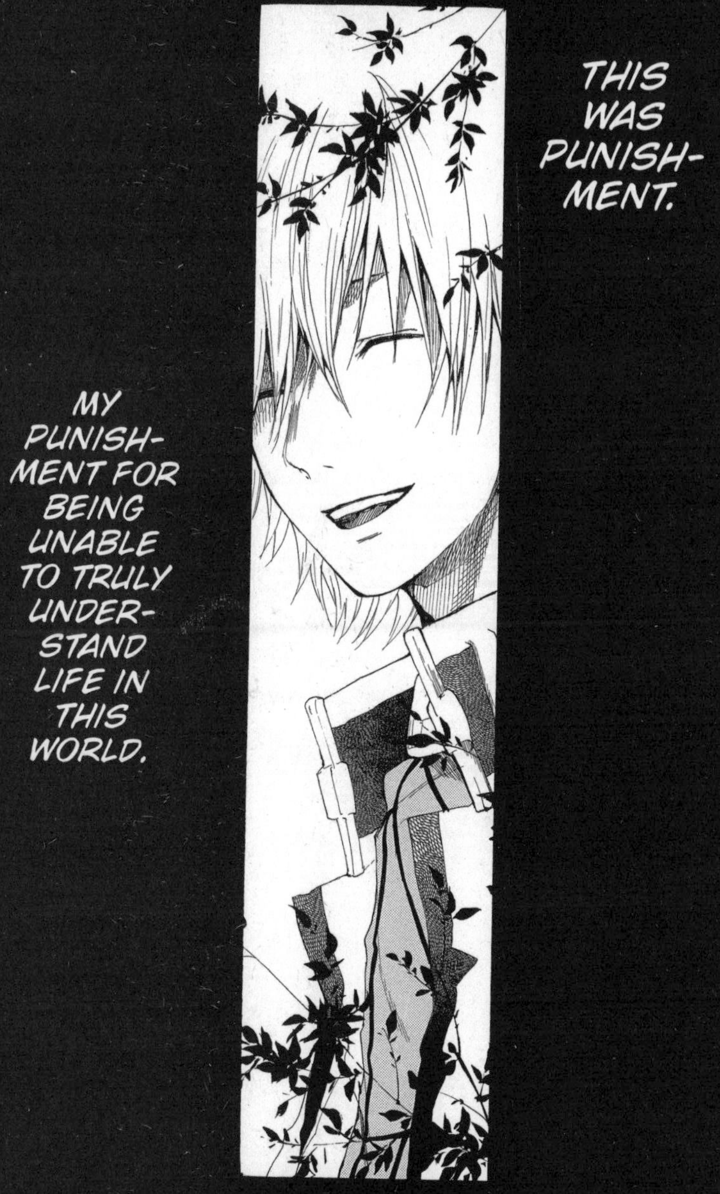
THIS WAS PUNISH-MENT.
MY PUNISH-MENT FOR BEING UNABLE TO TRULY UNDER-STAND LIFE IN THIS WORLD.

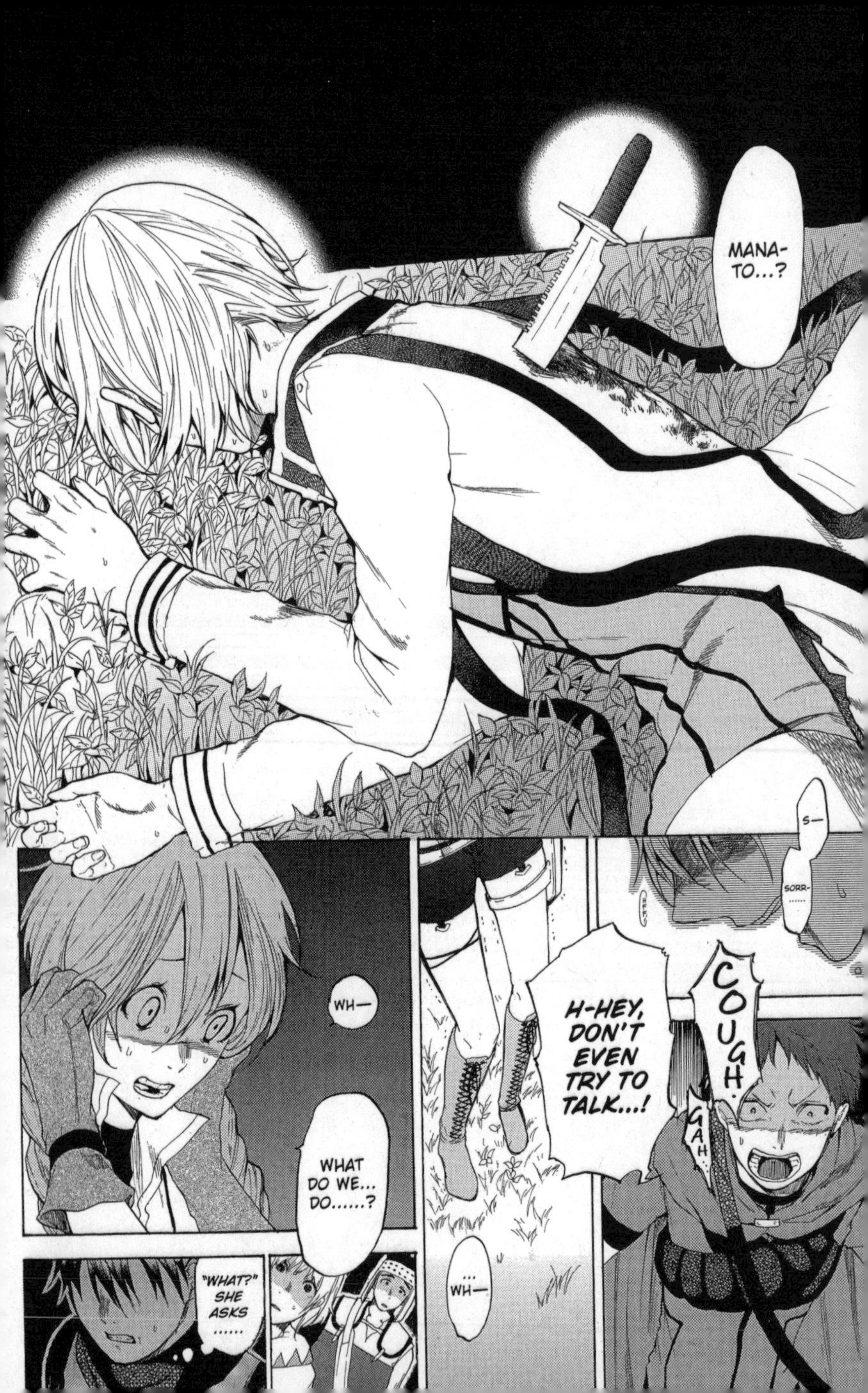
MANA-TO...?
S—
SORR-......
COUGH.
GAH
H-HEY, DON'T EVEN TRY TO TALK...!
...WH—
WH—
WHAT DO WE... DO......?
"WHAT?" SHE ASKS......

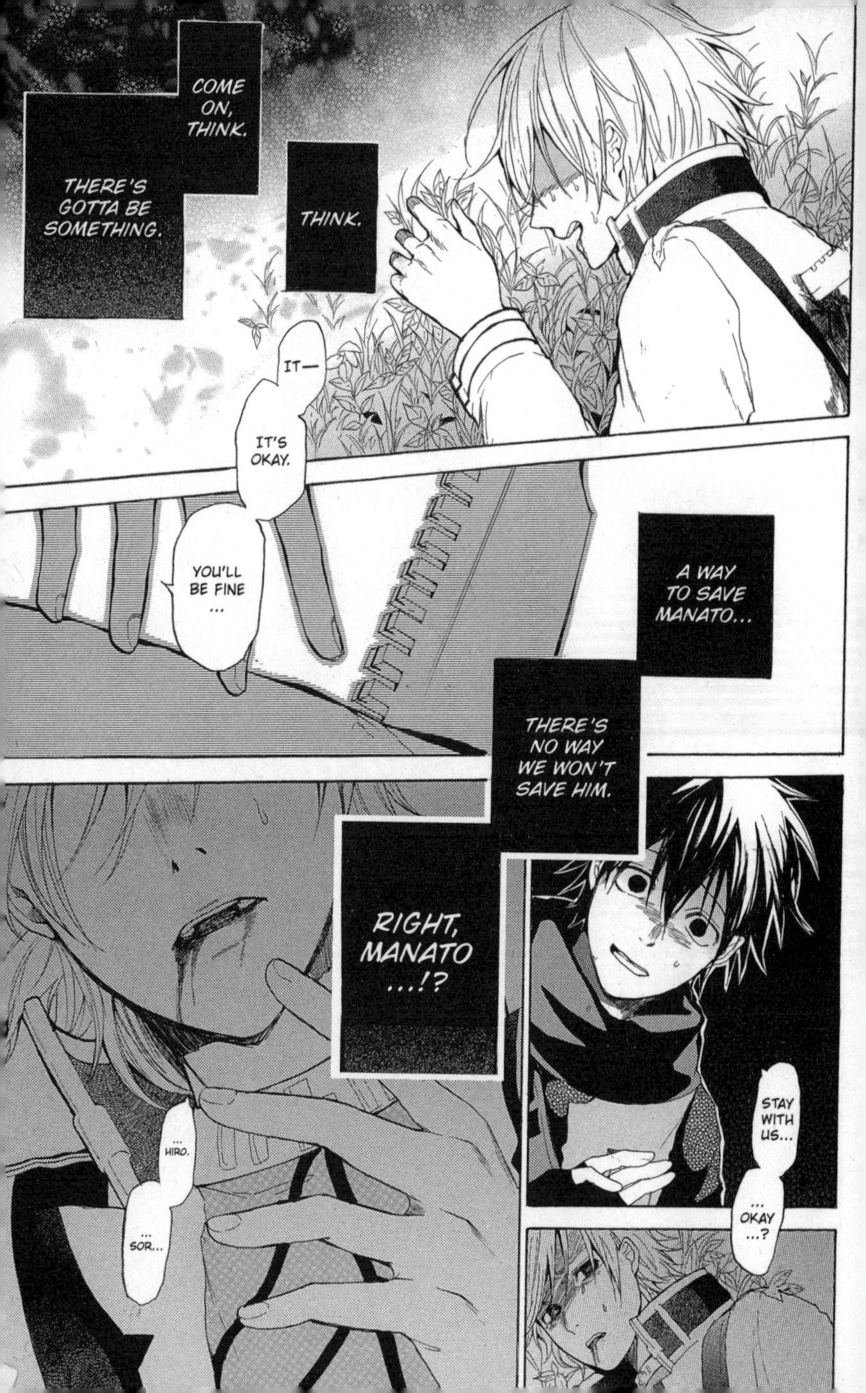
COME ON, THINK.
THERE'S GOTTA BE SOMETHING.
THINK.
IT—
IT'S OKAY.
A WAY TO SAVE MANATO...
THERE'S NO WAY WE WON'T SAVE HIM.
YOU'LL BE FINE ...
RIGHT, MANATO ...!?
STAY WITH US...
... OKAY ...?
... HIRO.
... SOR...

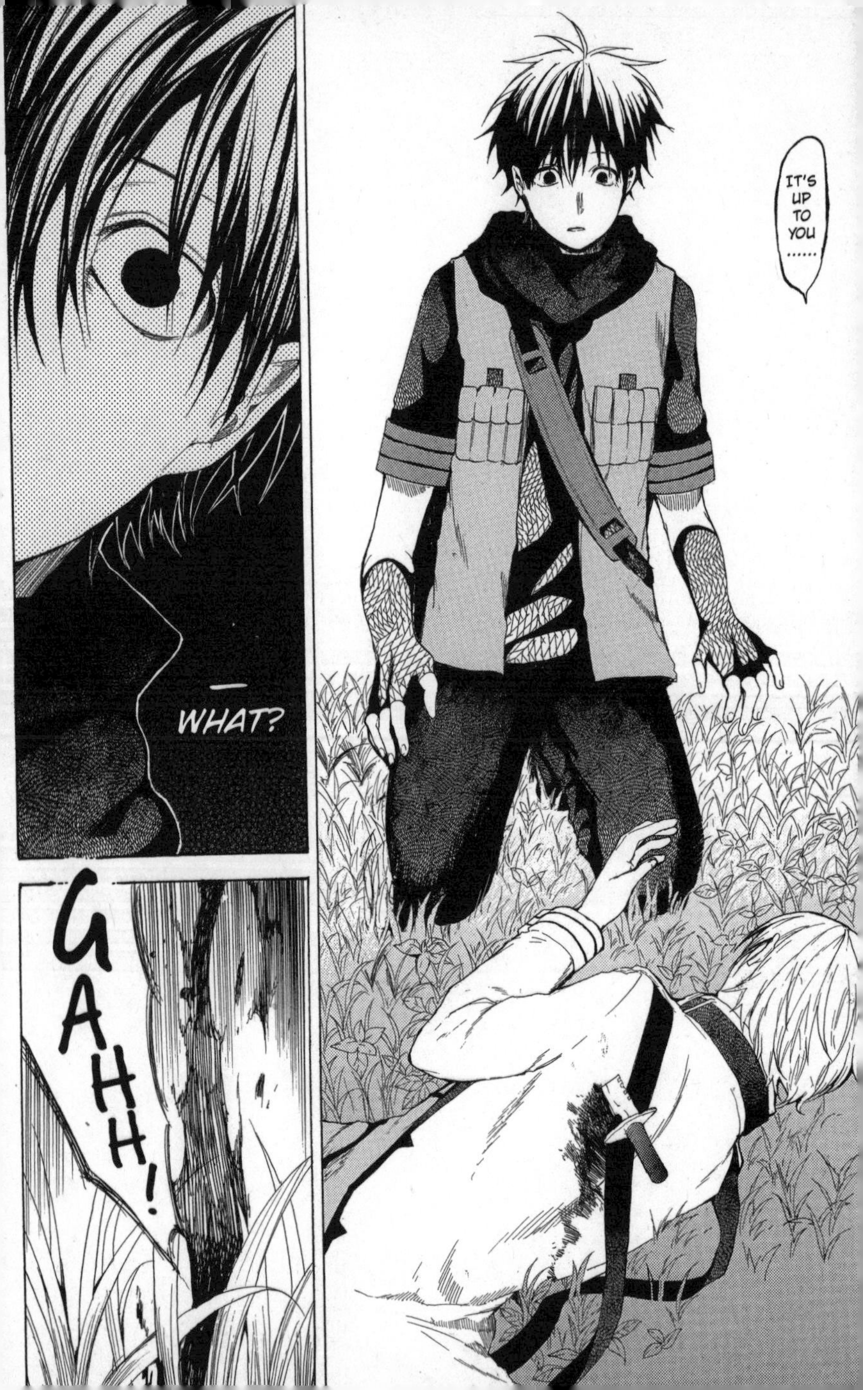
IT'S UP TO YOU......
— WHAT?
GAHH!

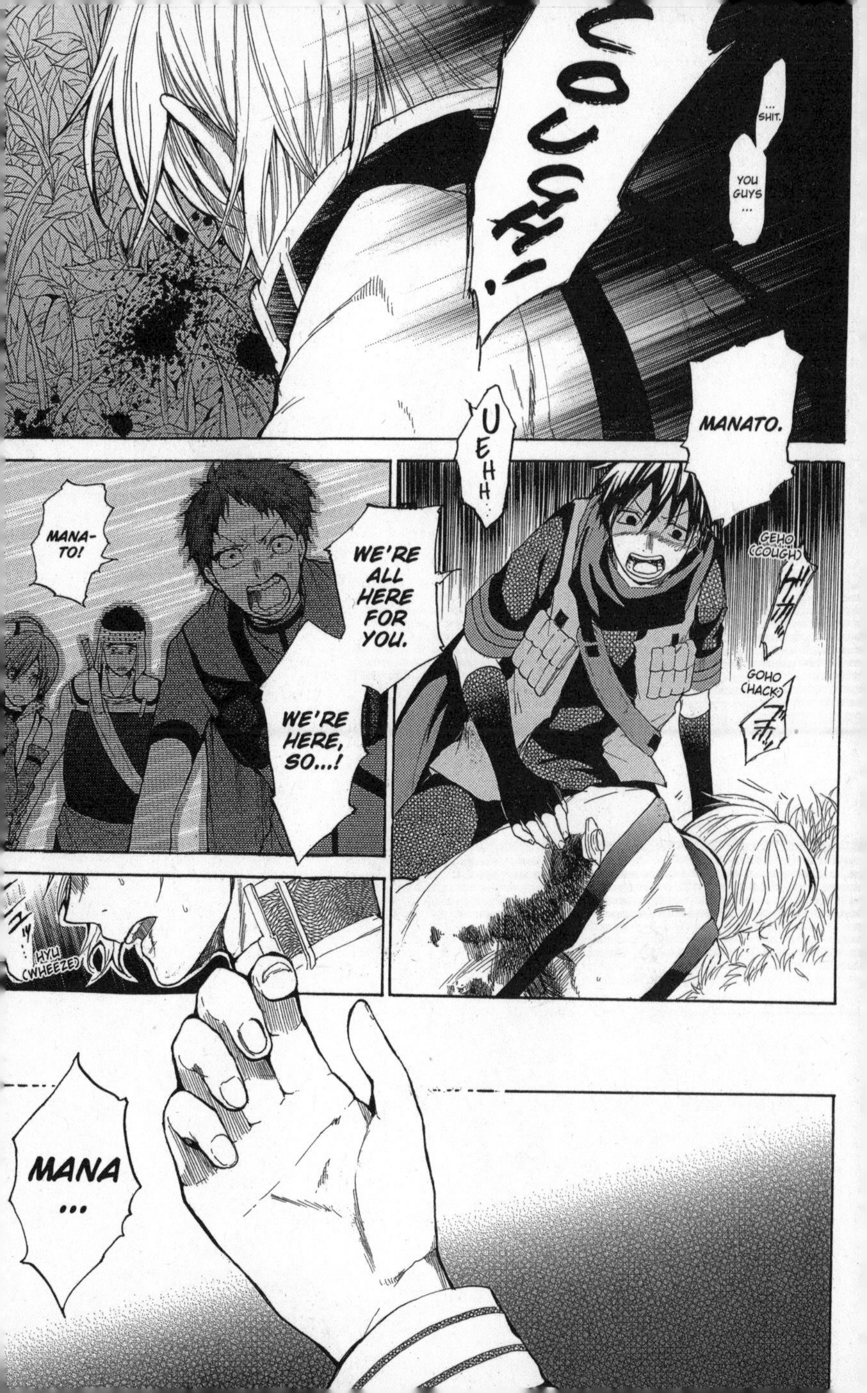
...SHIT.
YOU GUYS...
OUCH!
MANATO.
UEHH...
GEHO (COUGH)
GOHO (HACK)
WE'RE ALL HERE FOR YOU.
MANA-TO!
WE'RE HERE, SO...!
HYU (WHEEZE)
MANA...

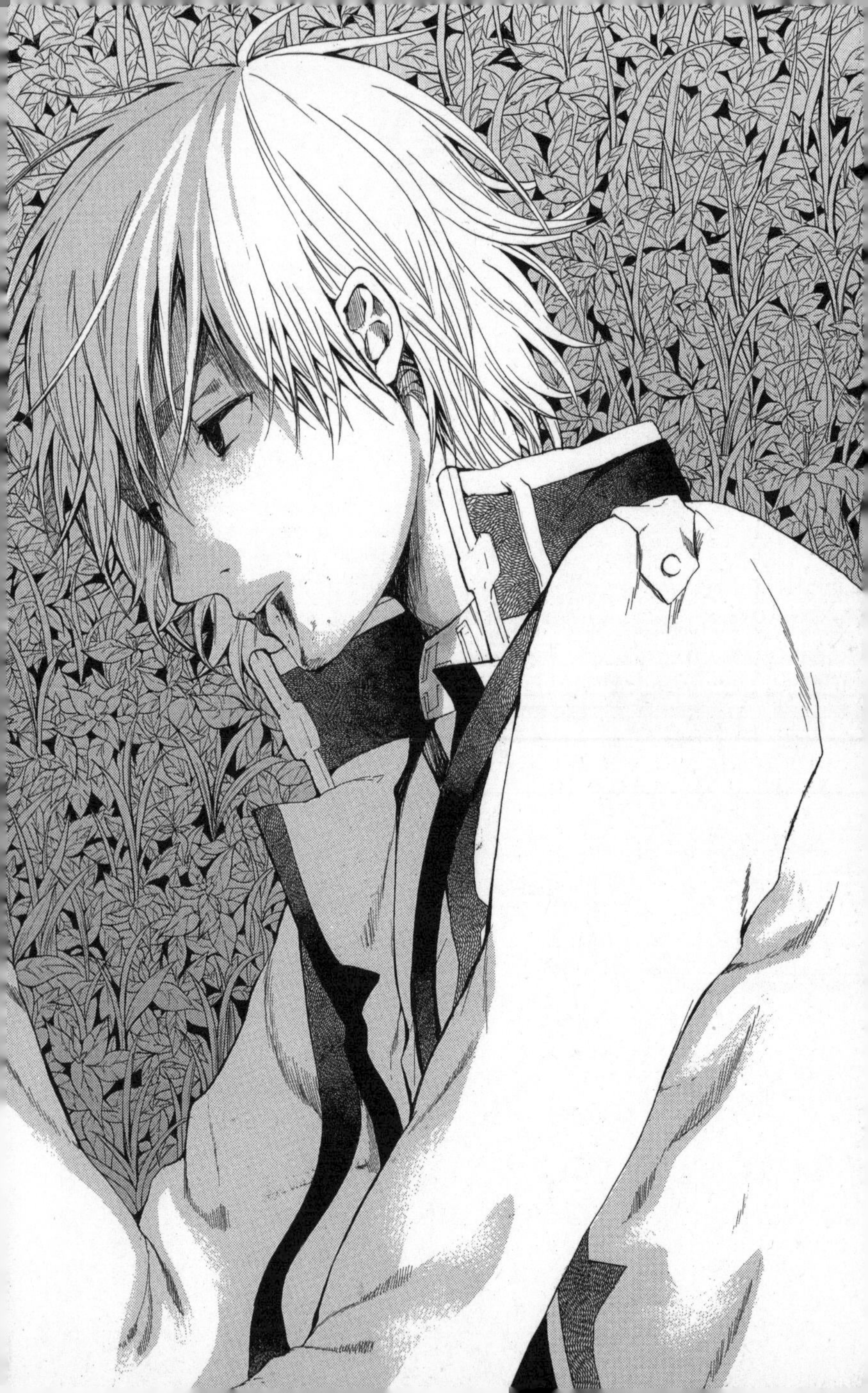

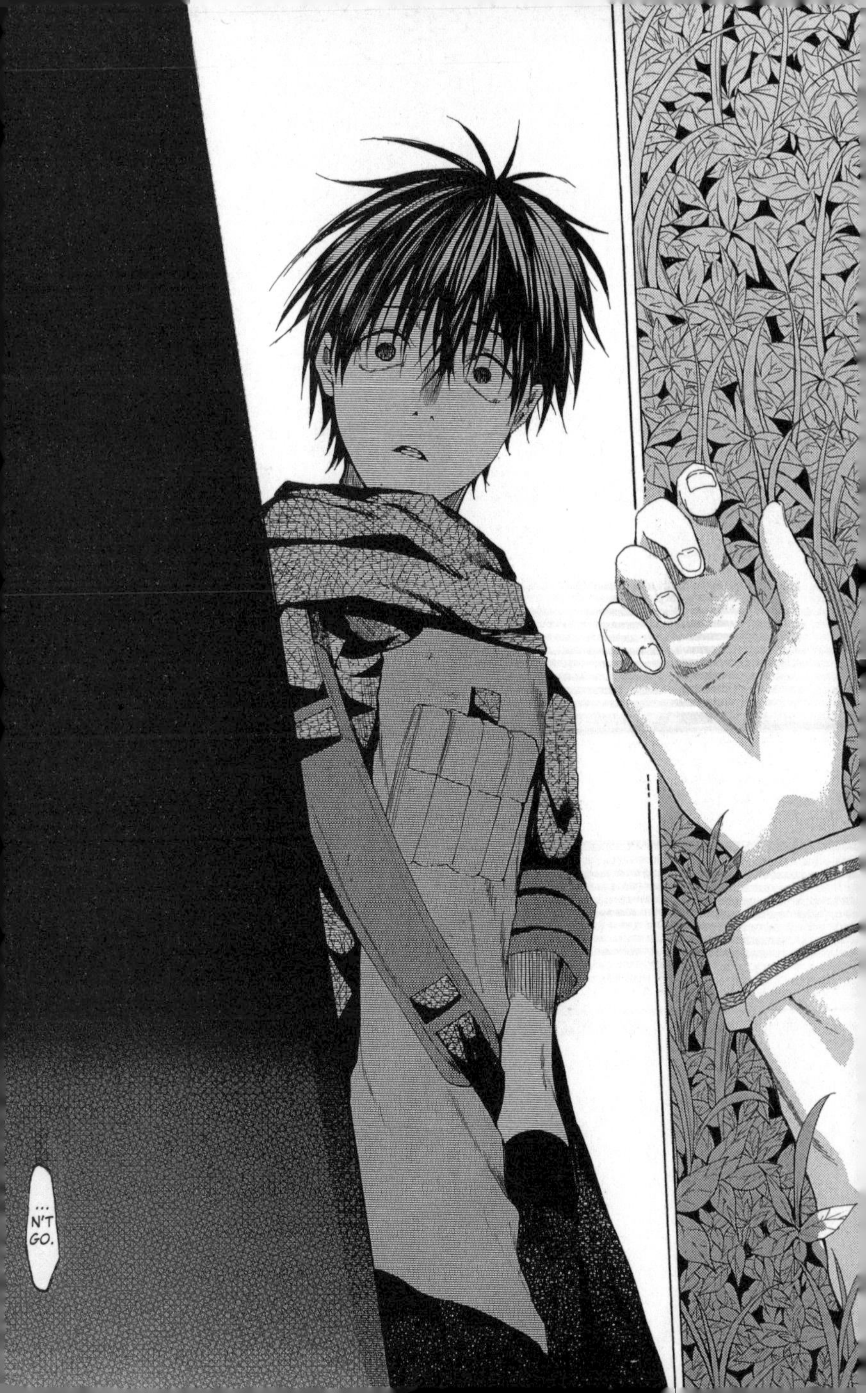
...N'T GO.

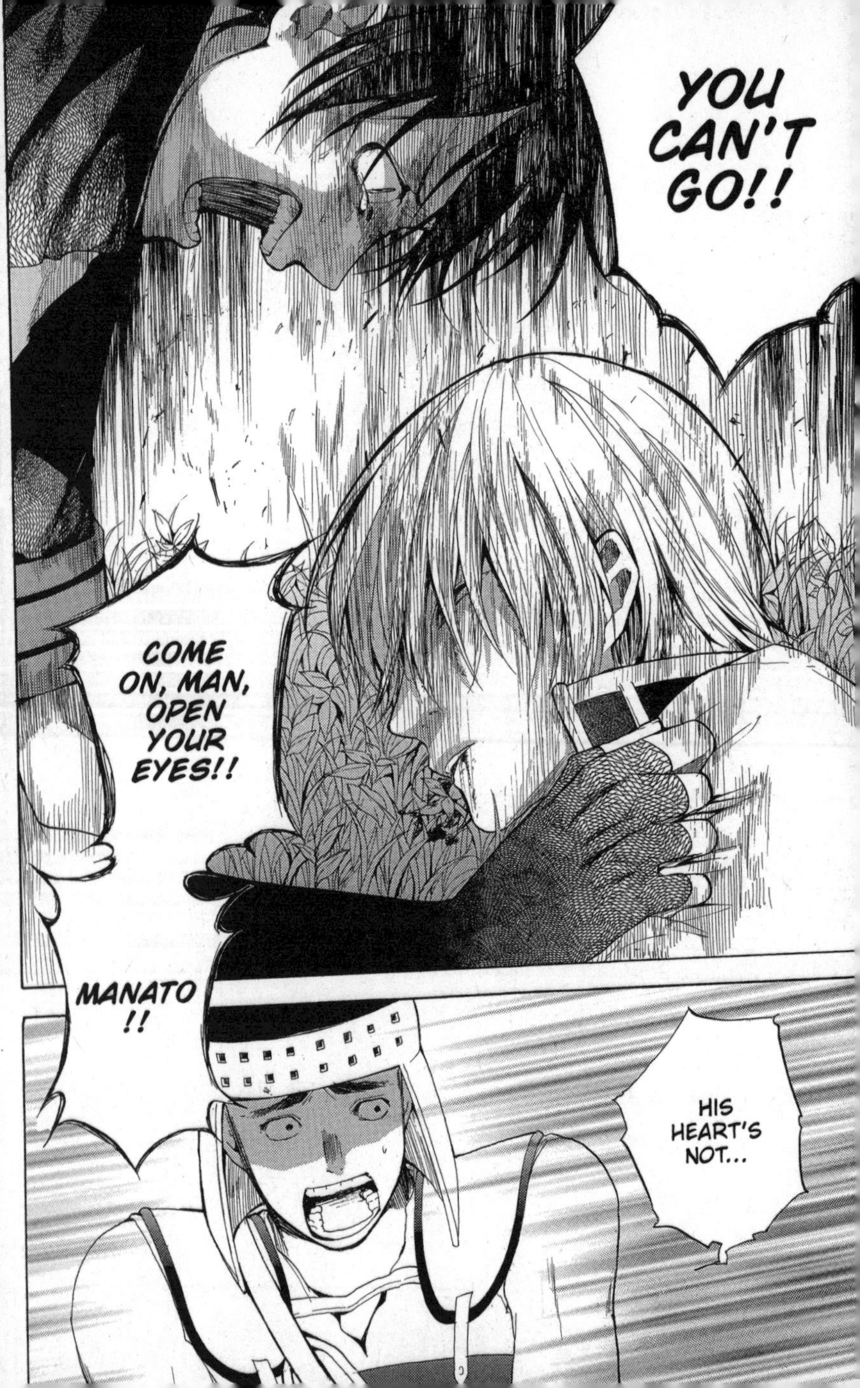
YOU CAN'T GO!!
COME ON, MAN, OPEN YOUR EYES!!
MANATO!!
HIS HEART'S NOT...

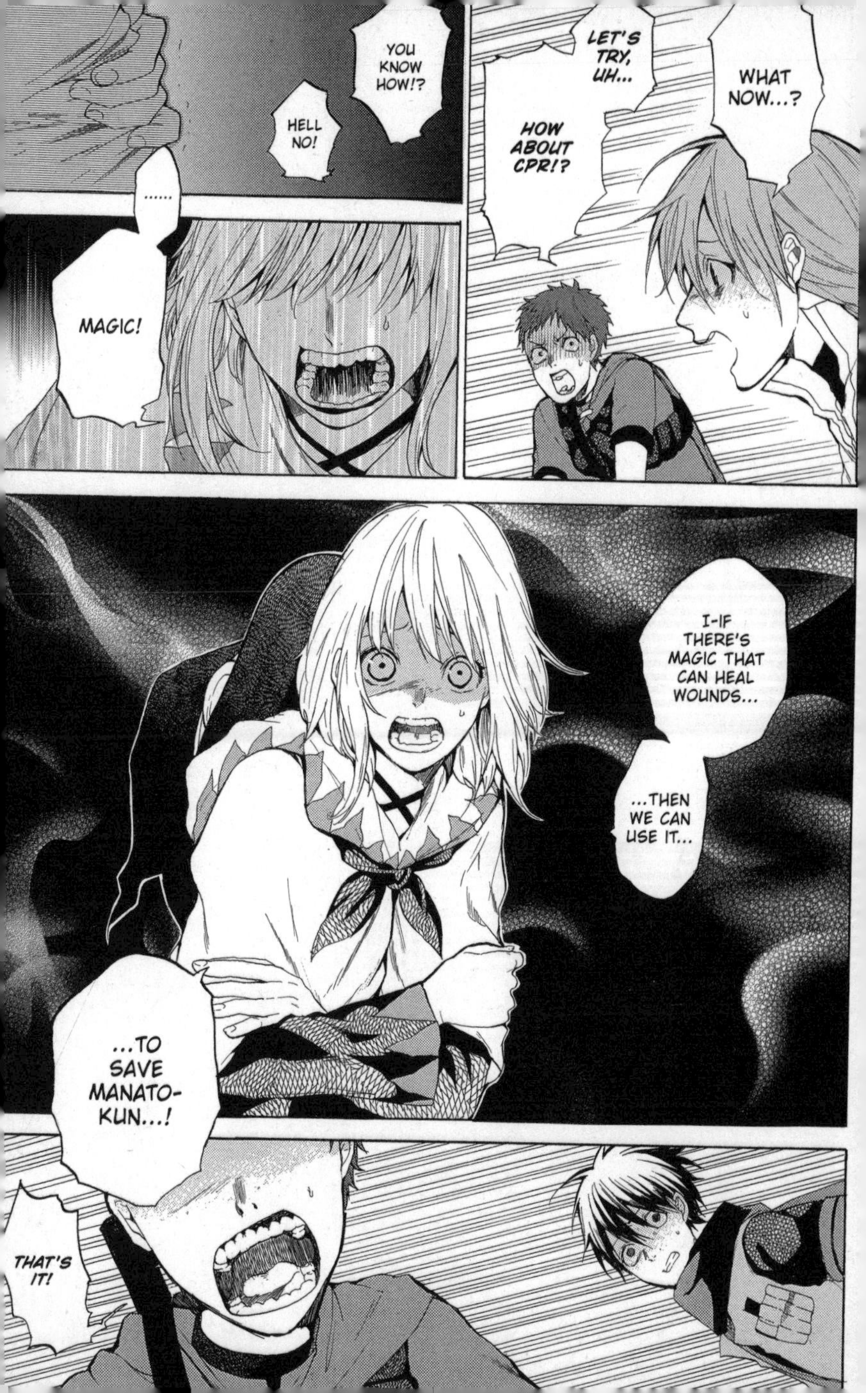
WHAT NOW...?
LET'S TRY, UH...
HOW ABOUT CPR!?
YOU KNOW HOW!?
HELL NO!
......
MAGIC!
I-IF THERE'S MAGIC THAT CAN HEAL WOUNDS...
...THEN WE CAN USE IT...
...TO SAVE MANATO-KUN...!
THAT'S IT!

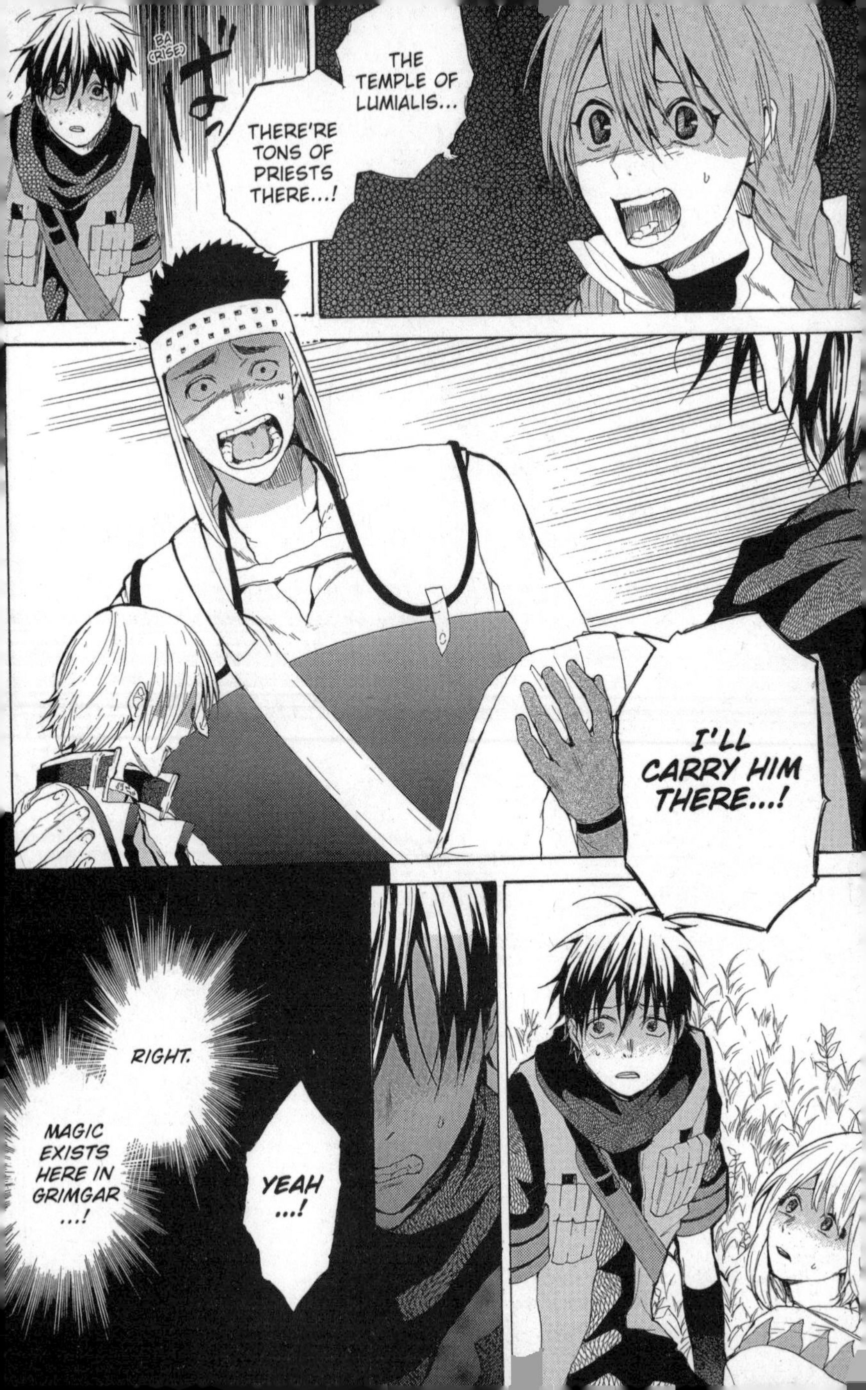
THE TEMPLE OF LUMIALIS...
THERE'RE TONS OF PRIESTS THERE...!
ばっ
BA (RISE)
I'LL CARRY HIM THERE...!
YEAH ...!
RIGHT.
MAGIC EXISTS HERE IN GRIMGAR ...!

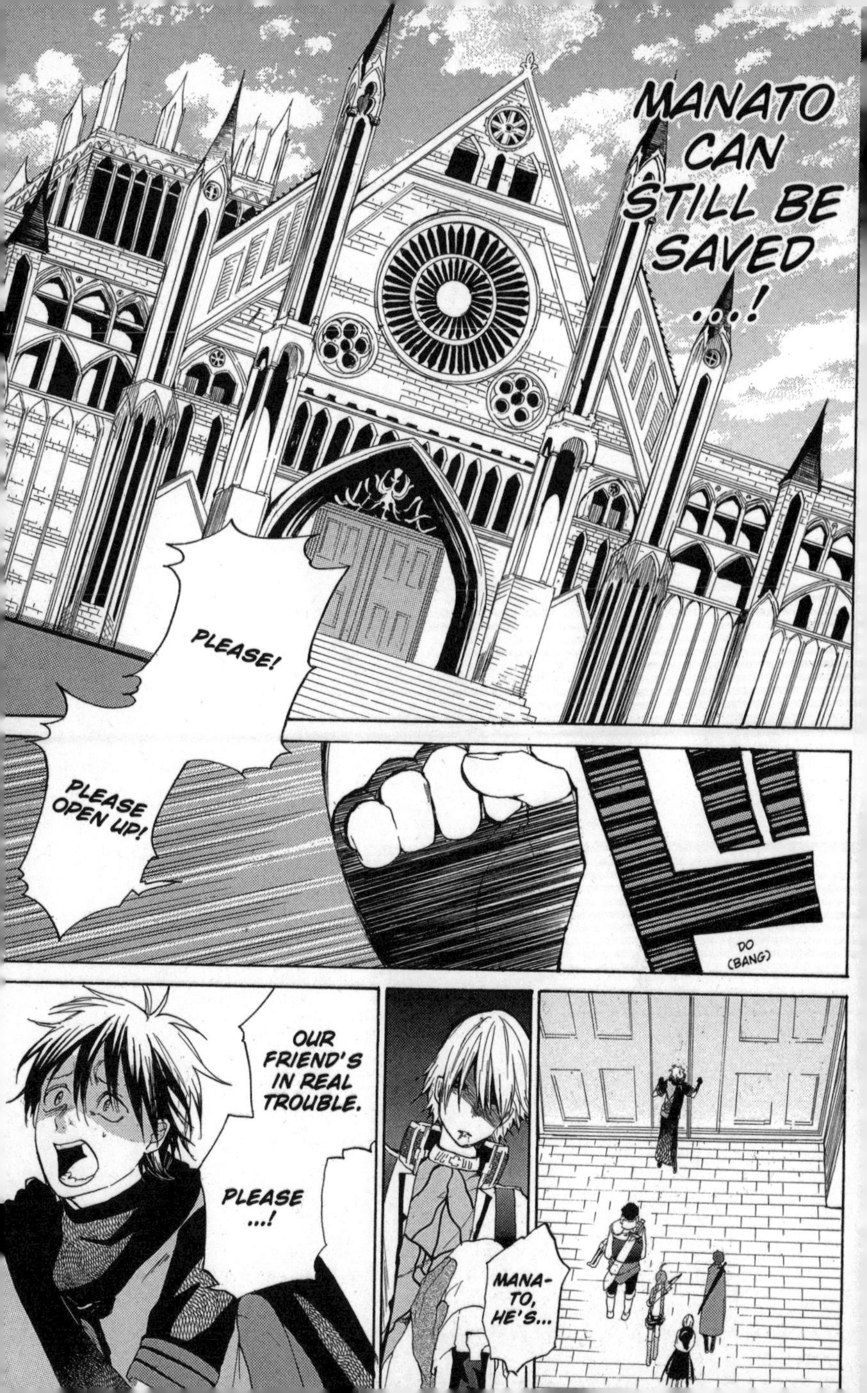
MANATO CAN STILL BE SAVED ...!
PLEASE!
DO (BANG)
PLEASE OPEN UP!
MANA-TO, HE'S...
OUR FRIEND'S IN REAL TROUBLE.
PLEASE ...!

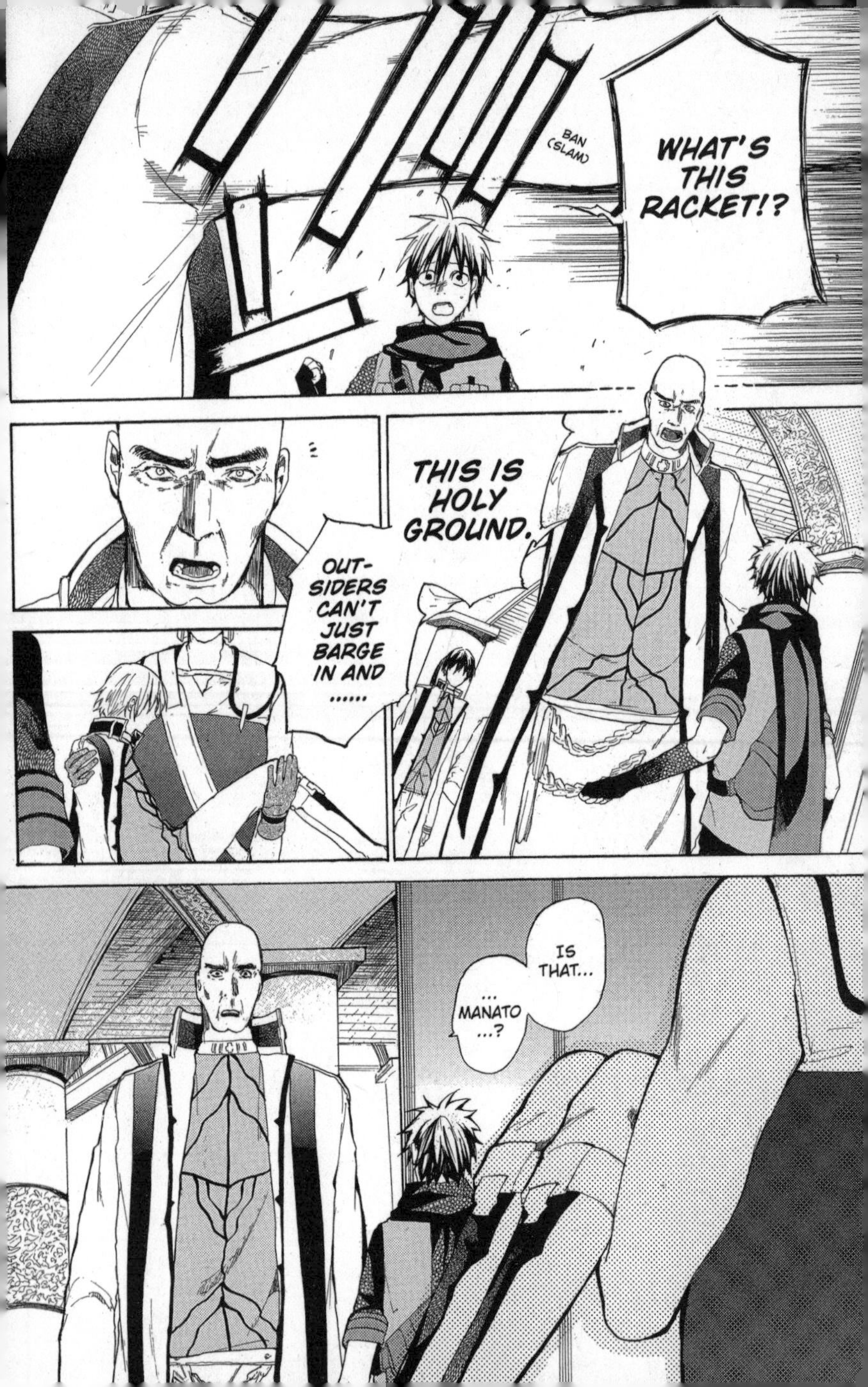
WHAT'S THIS RACKET!?
BAN (SLAM)
THIS IS HOLY GROUND.
OUT-SIDERS CAN'T JUST BARGE IN AND ......
IS THAT...
... MANATO ...?

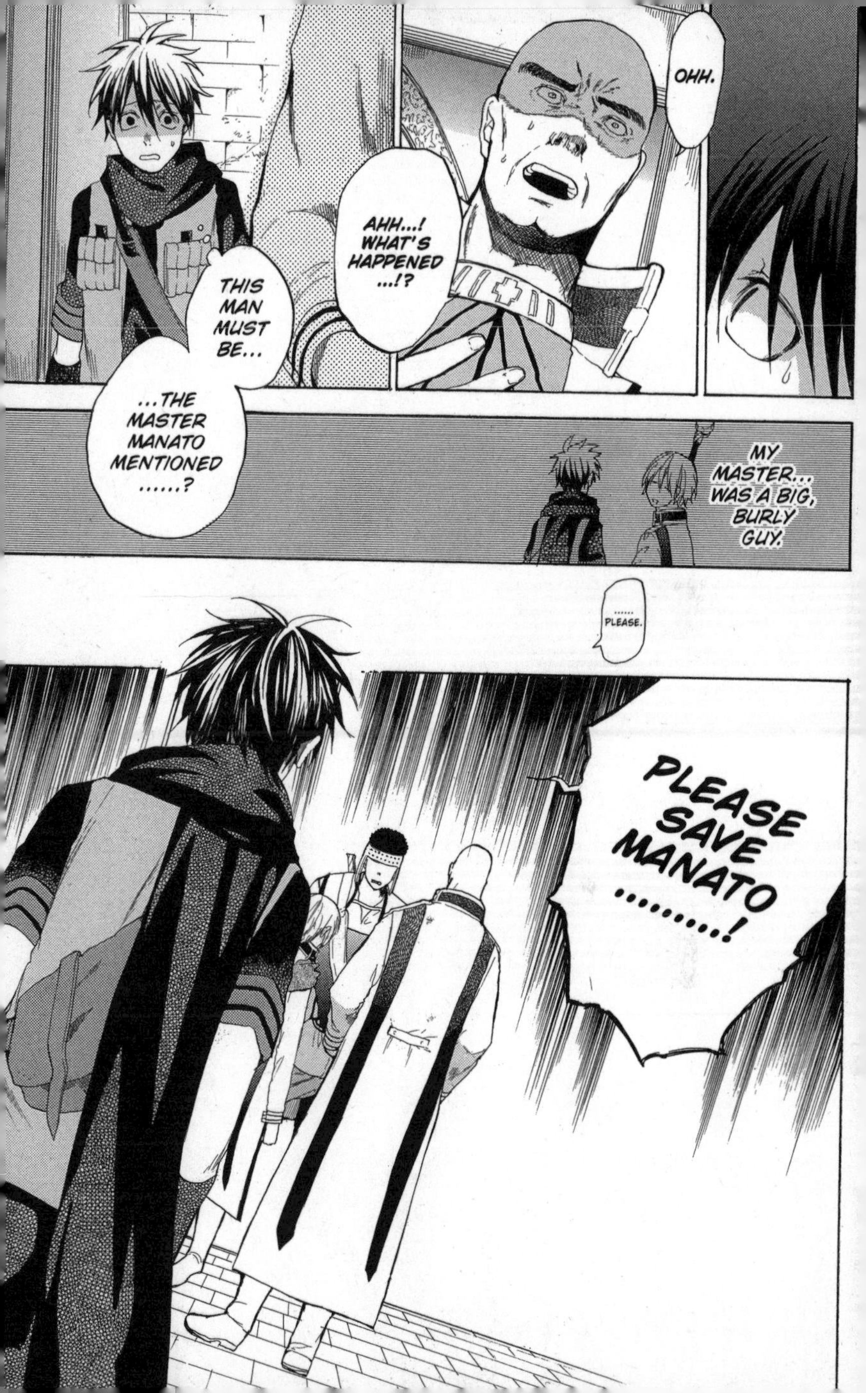
OHH.
AHH...! WHAT'S HAPPENED ...!?
THIS MAN MUST BE...
...THE MASTER MANATO MENTIONED ......?
MY MASTER... WAS A BIG, BURLY GUY.
......PLEASE.
PLEASE SAVE MANATO ....!

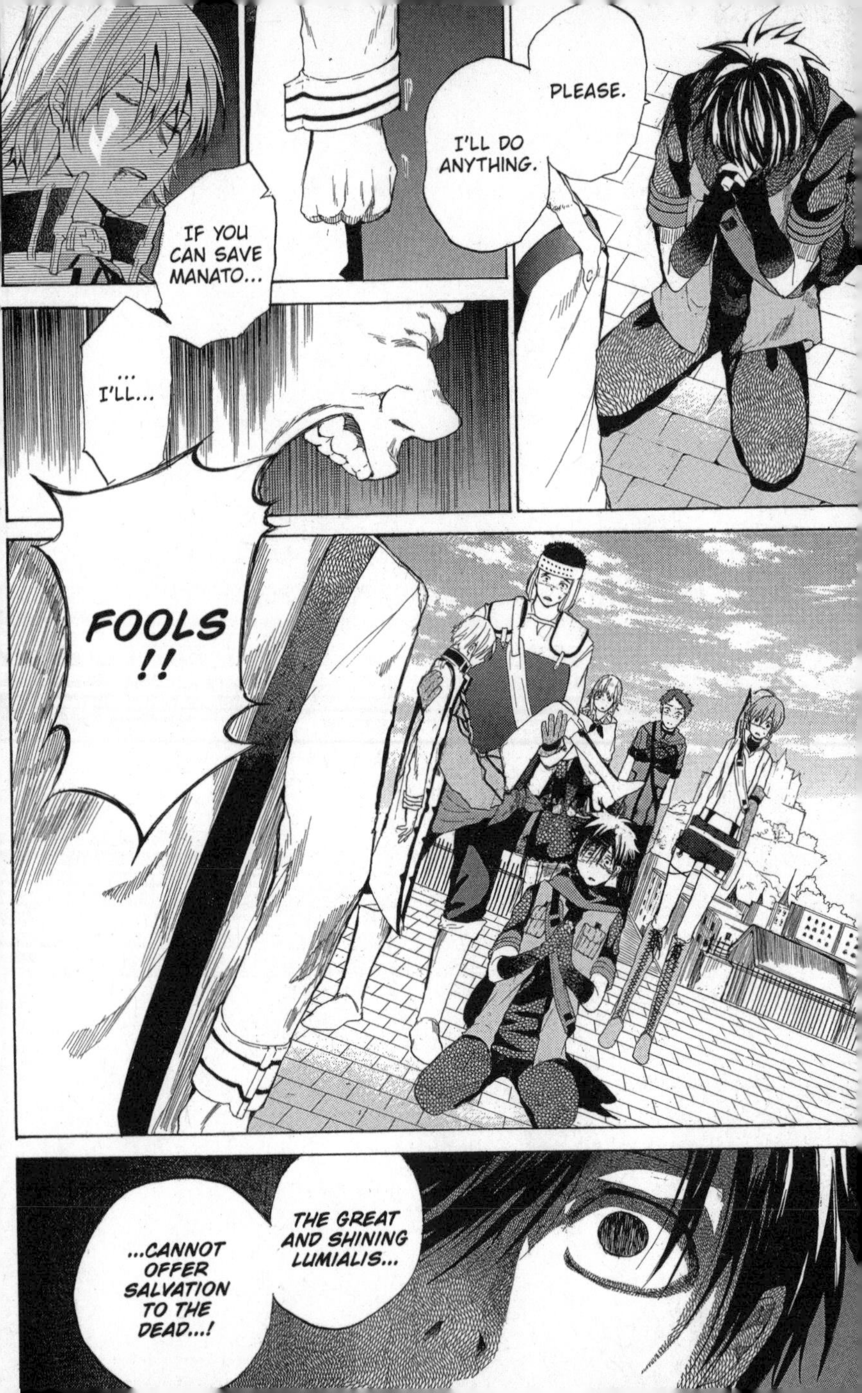
PLEASE.
I'LL DO ANYTHING.
IF YOU CAN SAVE MANATO...
... I'LL...
FOOLS !!
THE GREAT AND SHINING LUMIALIS...
...CANNOT OFFER SALVATION TO THE DEAD...!

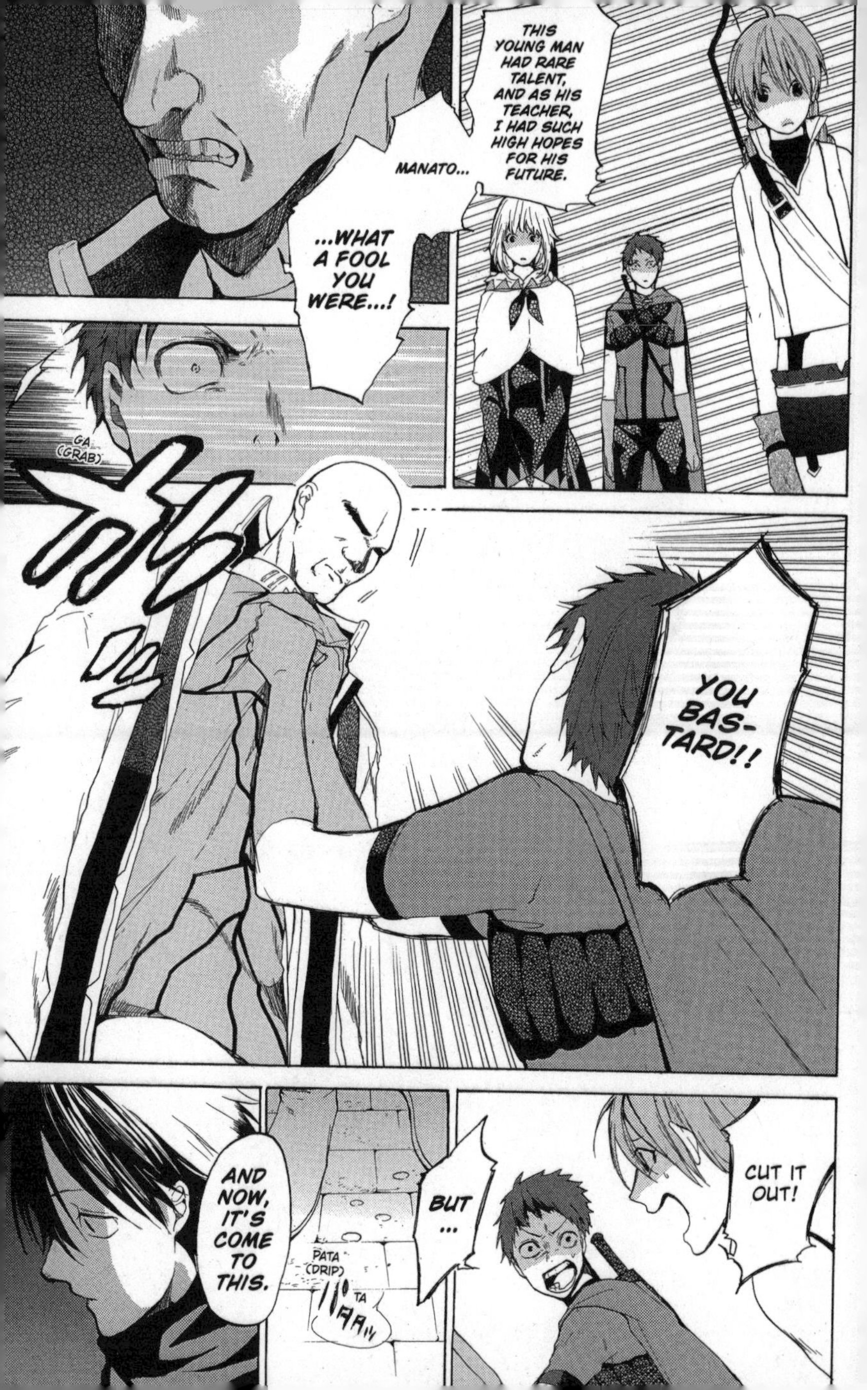
THIS YOUNG MAN HAD RARE TALENT, AND AS HIS TEACHER, I HAD SUCH HIGH HOPES FOR HIS FUTURE.
MANATO...
...WHAT A FOOL YOU WERE...!
GA (GRAB)
YOU BAS-TARD!!
CUT IT OUT!
BUT ...
AND NOW, IT'S COME TO THIS.
PATA (DRIP)
TA

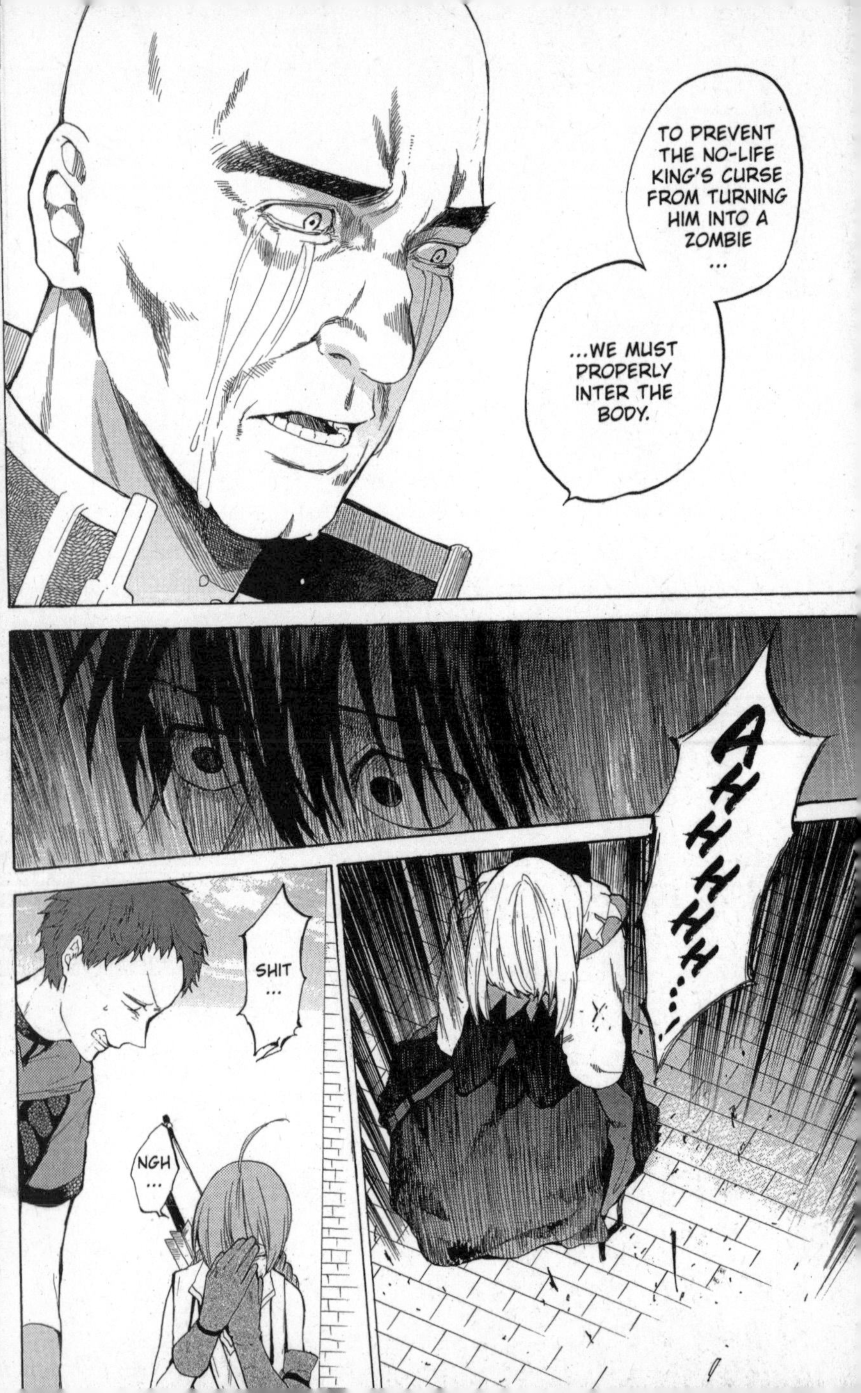
TO PREVENT THE NO-LIFE KING'S CURSE FROM TURNING HIM INTO A ZOMBIE...
...WE MUST PROPERLY INTER THE BODY.
AHHHHHH...!
SHIT...
NGH...

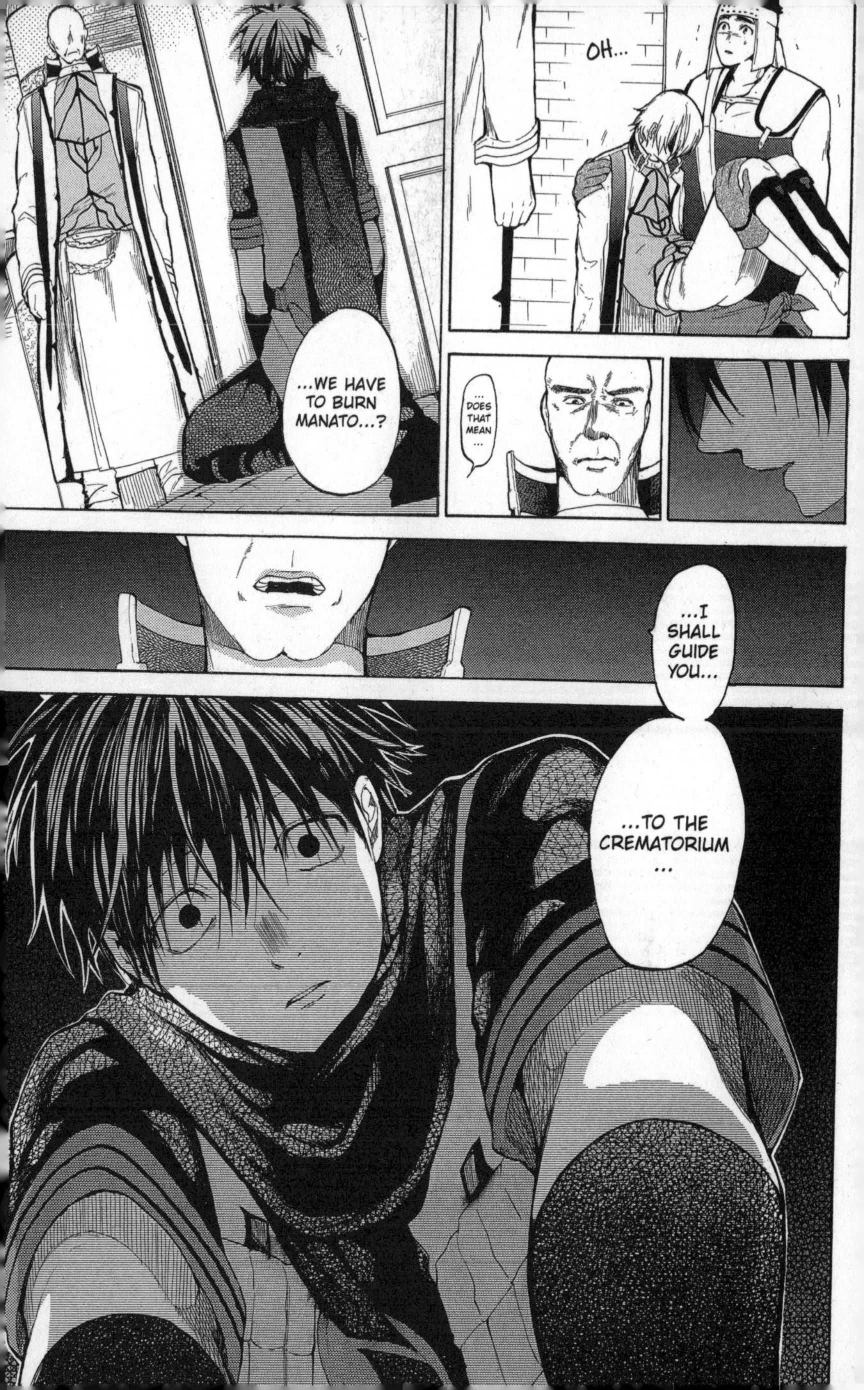
OH...
...DOES THAT MEAN...
...WE HAVE TO BURN MANATO...?
...I SHALL GUIDE YOU...
...TO THE CREMATORIUM...

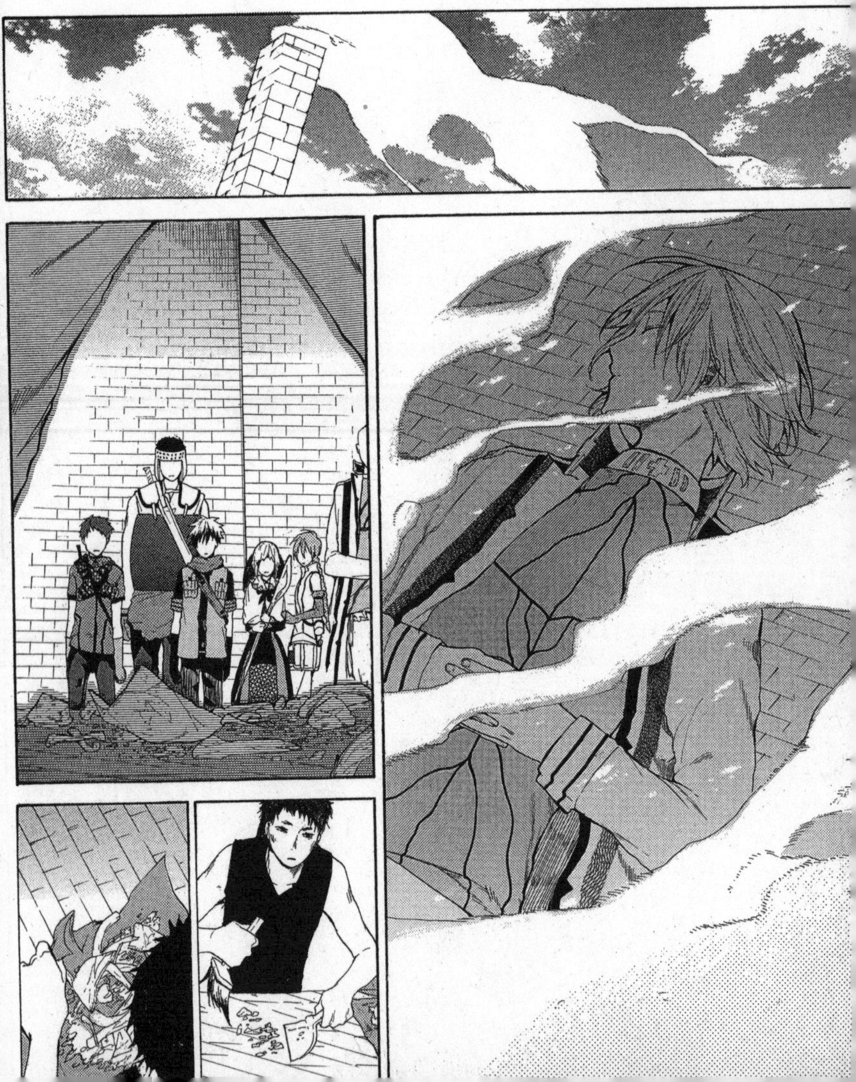

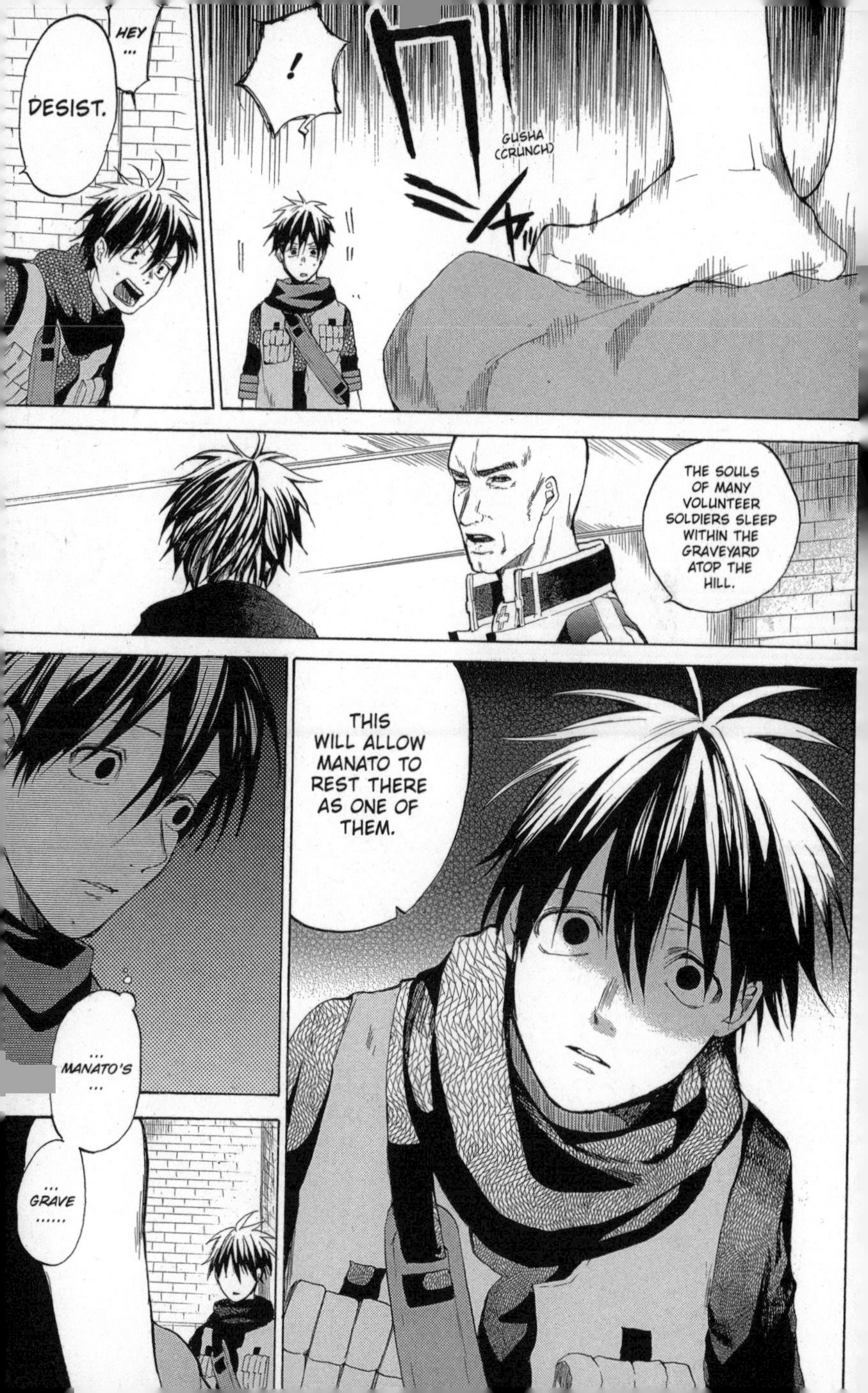
!
GUSHA (CRUNCH)
HEY ...
DESIST.
THE SOULS OF MANY VOLUNTEER SOLDIERS SLEEP WITHIN THE GRAVEYARD ATOP THE HILL.
THIS WILL ALLOW MANATO TO REST THERE AS ONE OF THEM.
... MANATO'S ...
... GRAVE ......

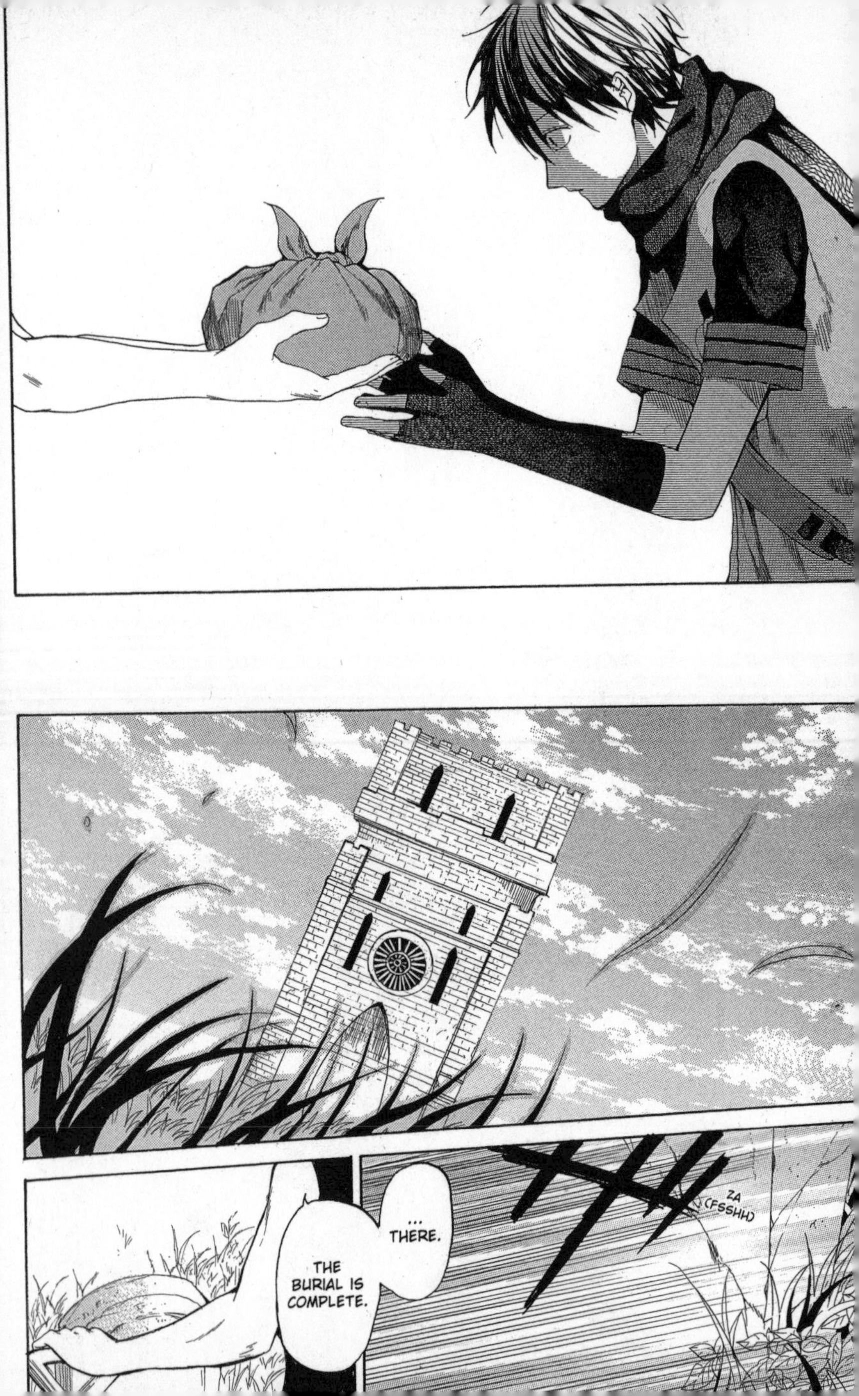

ZA (FSSHH)
... THERE.
THE BURIAL IS COMPLETE.

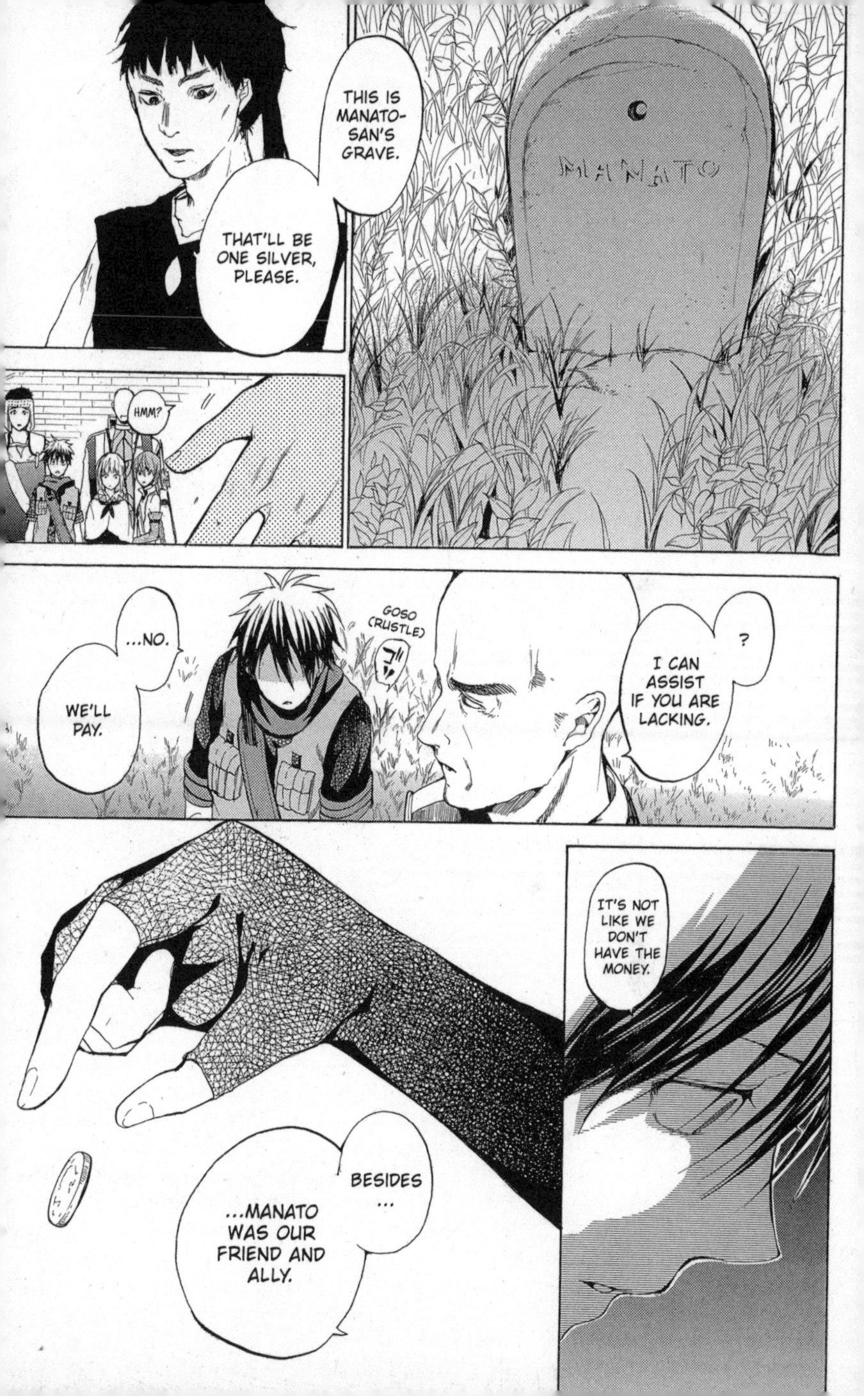
MANATO
THIS IS MANATO-SAN'S GRAVE.
THAT'LL BE ONE SILVER, PLEASE.
HMM?
?
I CAN ASSIST IF YOU ARE LACKING.
GOSO (RUSTLE)
...NO.
WE'LL PAY.
IT'S NOT LIKE WE DON'T HAVE THE MONEY.
BESIDES...
...MANATO WAS OUR FRIEND AND ALLY.

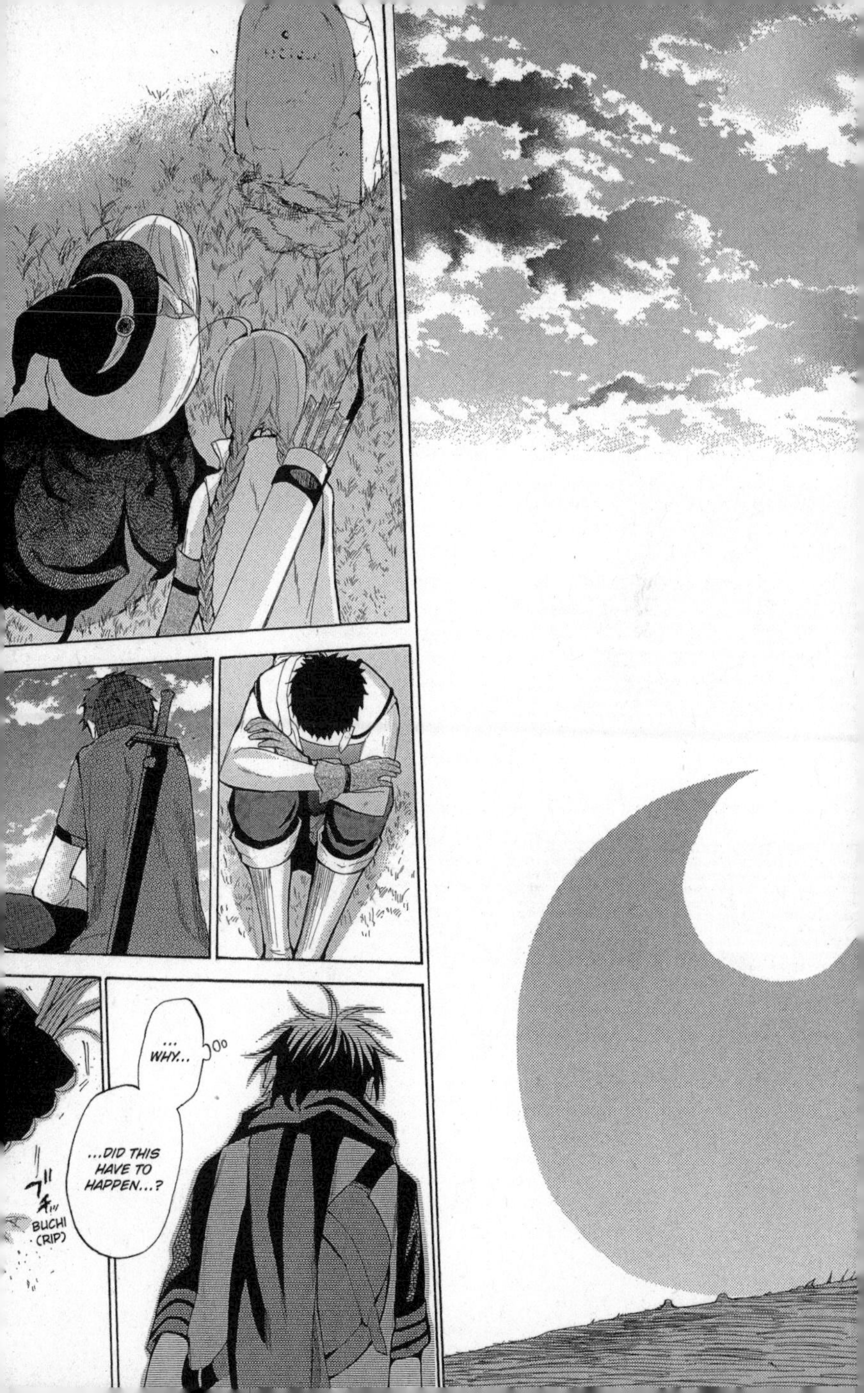
...
WHY...
...DID THIS HAVE TO HAPPEN...?
ブチ
BUCHI (RIP)

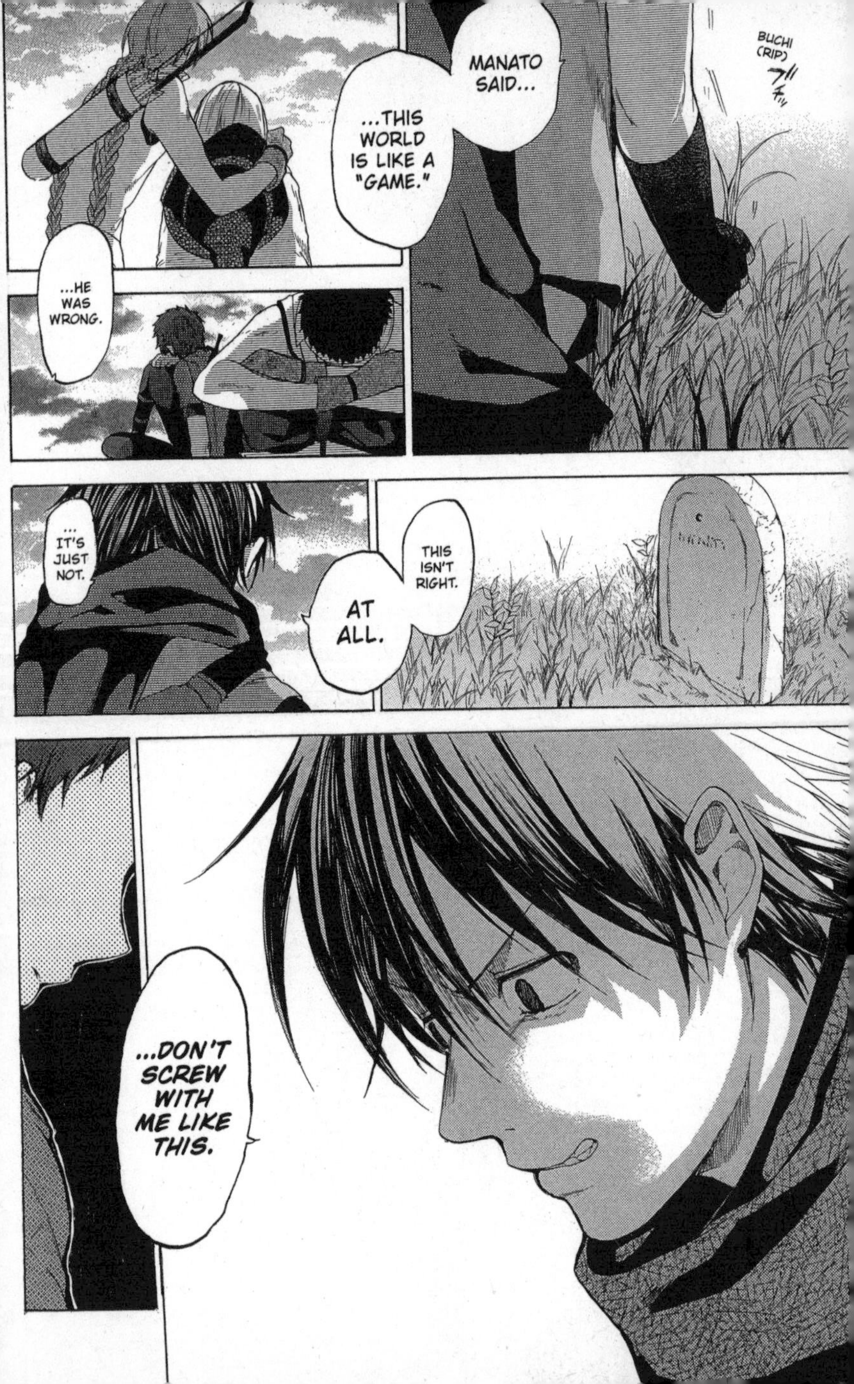
BUCHI (RIP)
MANATO SAID...
...THIS WORLD IS LIKE A "GAME."
...HE WAS WRONG.
THIS ISN'T RIGHT.
AT ALL.
...IT'S JUST NOT.
...DON'T SCREW WITH ME LIKE THIS.

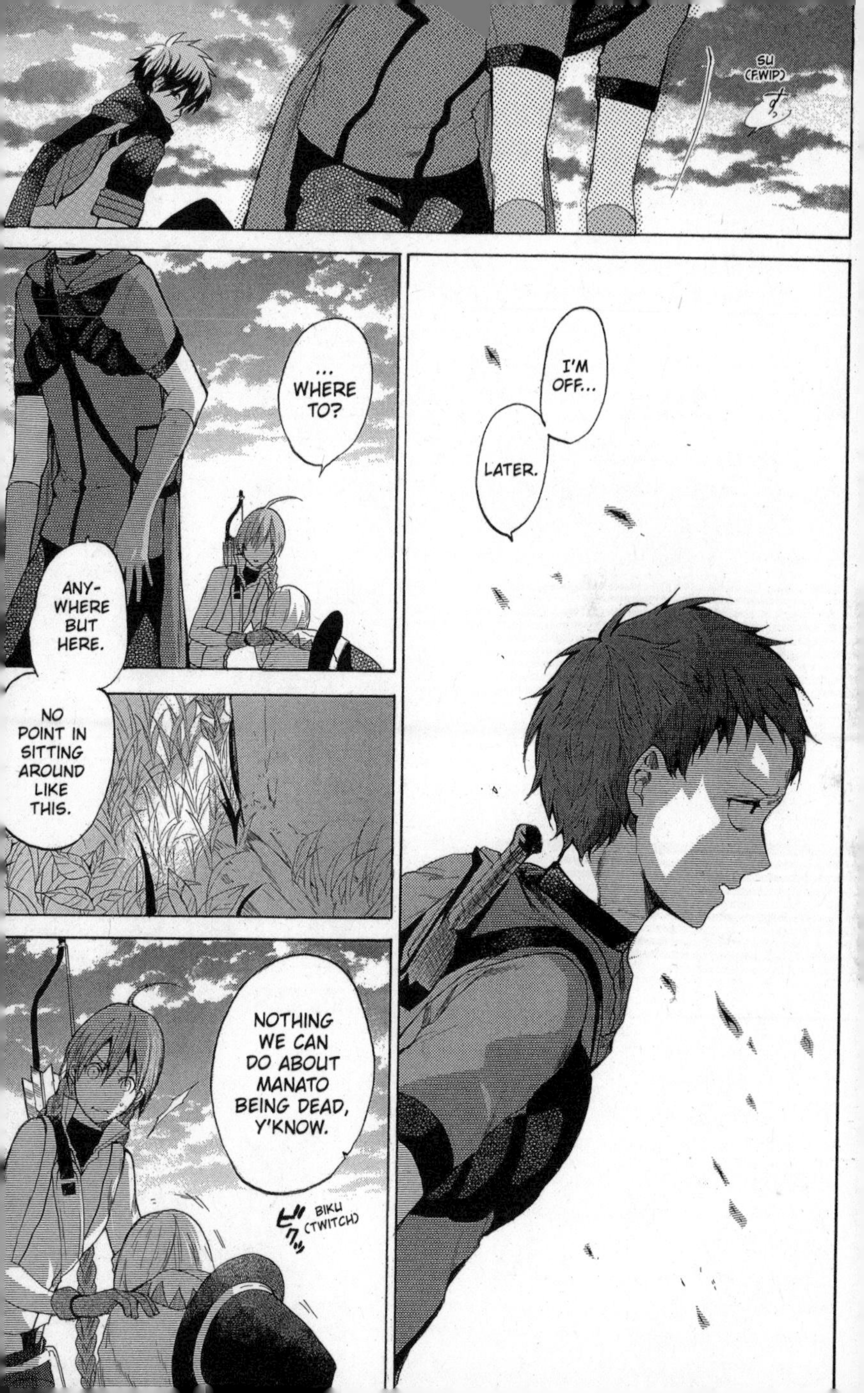
SU (F.WIP)
I'M OFF...
LATER.
...WHERE TO?
ANY-WHERE BUT HERE.
NO POINT IN SITTING AROUND LIKE THIS.
NOTHING WE CAN DO ABOUT MANATO BEING DEAD, Y'KNOW.
BIKU (TWITCH)

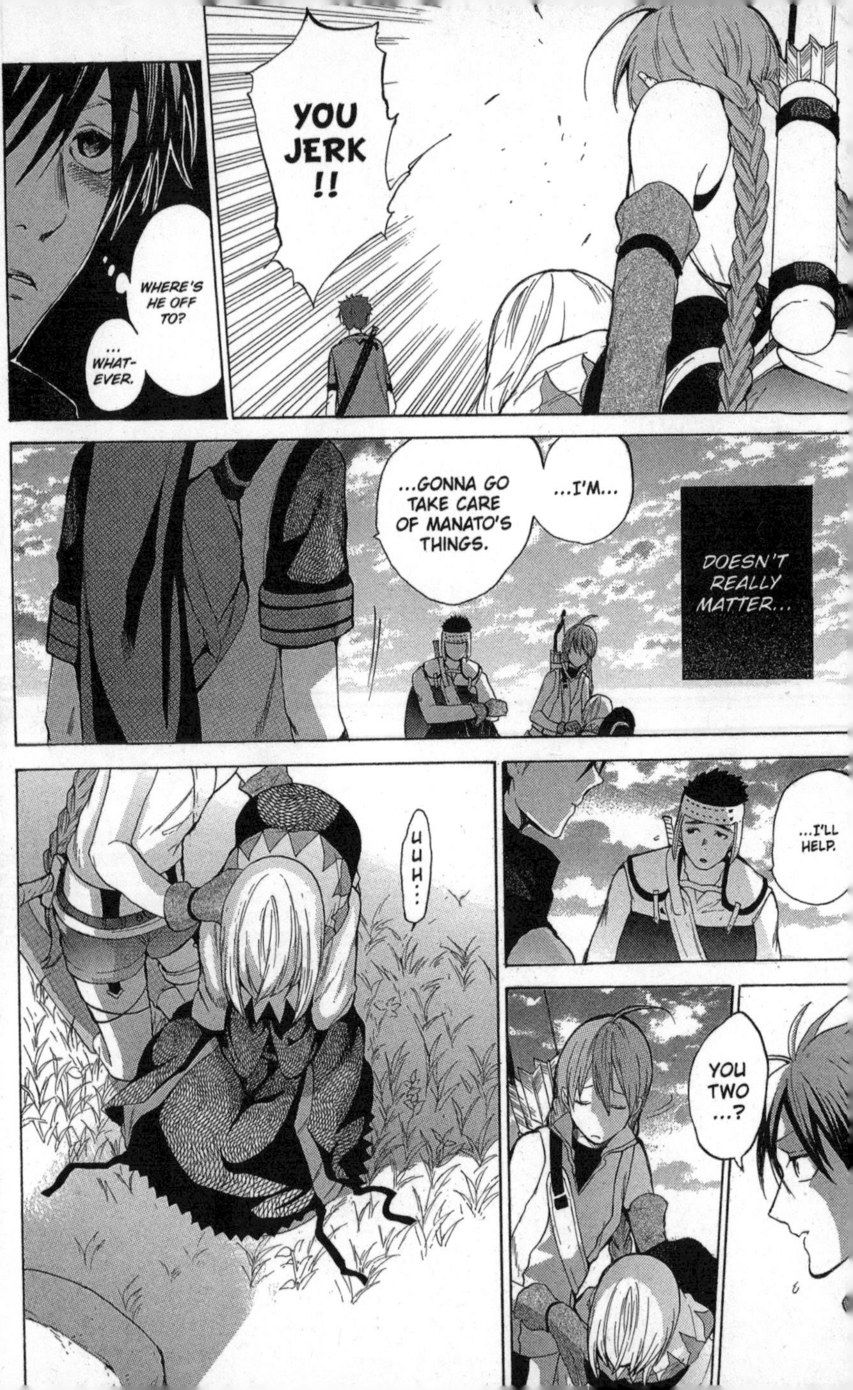
YOU JERK !!
WHERE'S HE OFF TO?
... WHAT-EVER.
DOESN'T REALLY MATTER...
...I'M...
...GONNA GO TAKE CARE OF MANATO'S THINGS.
...I'LL HELP.
YOU TWO ...?
UUH...

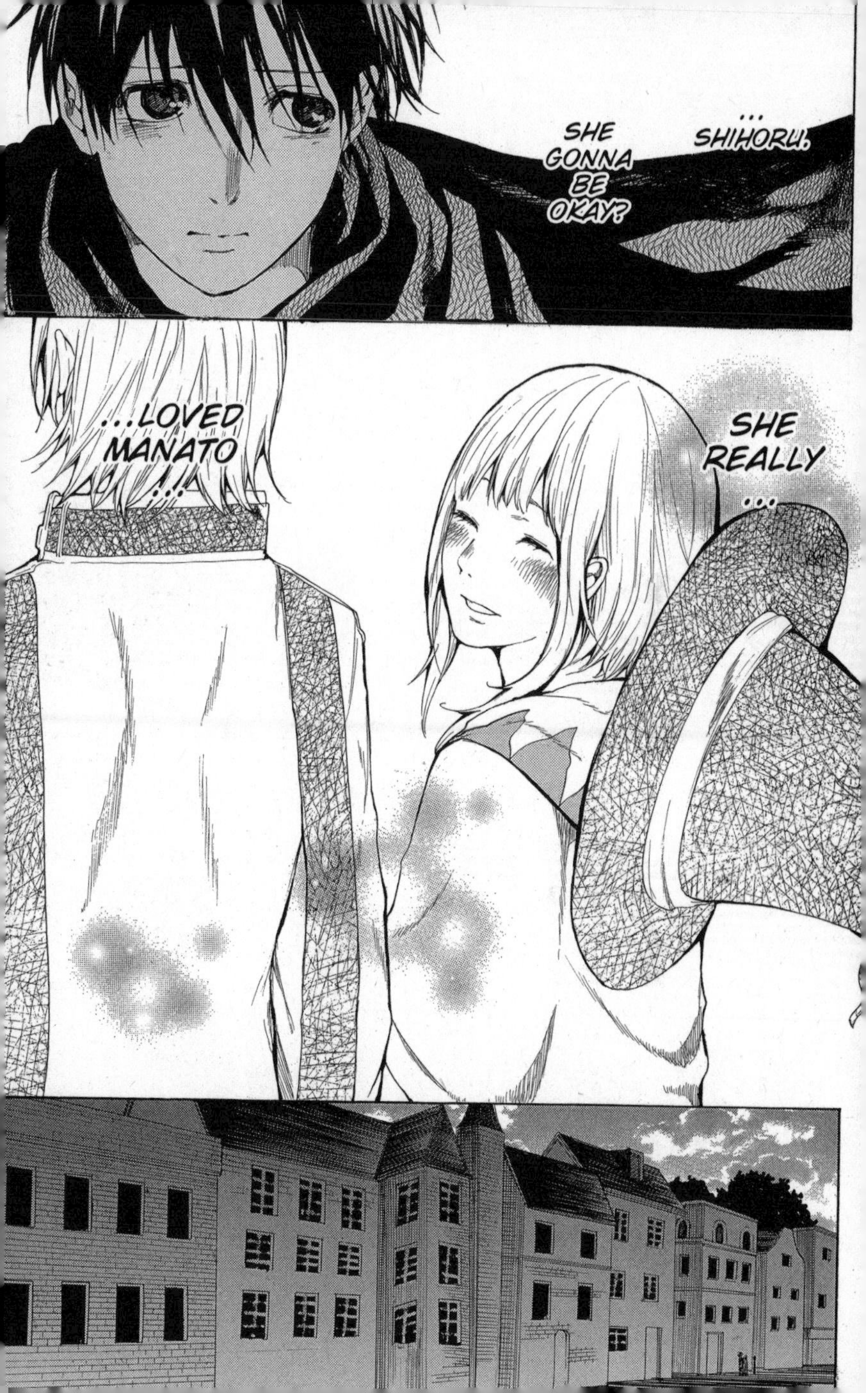
...SHIHORU.
SHE GONNA BE OKAY?
SHE REALLY...
...LOVED MANATO...

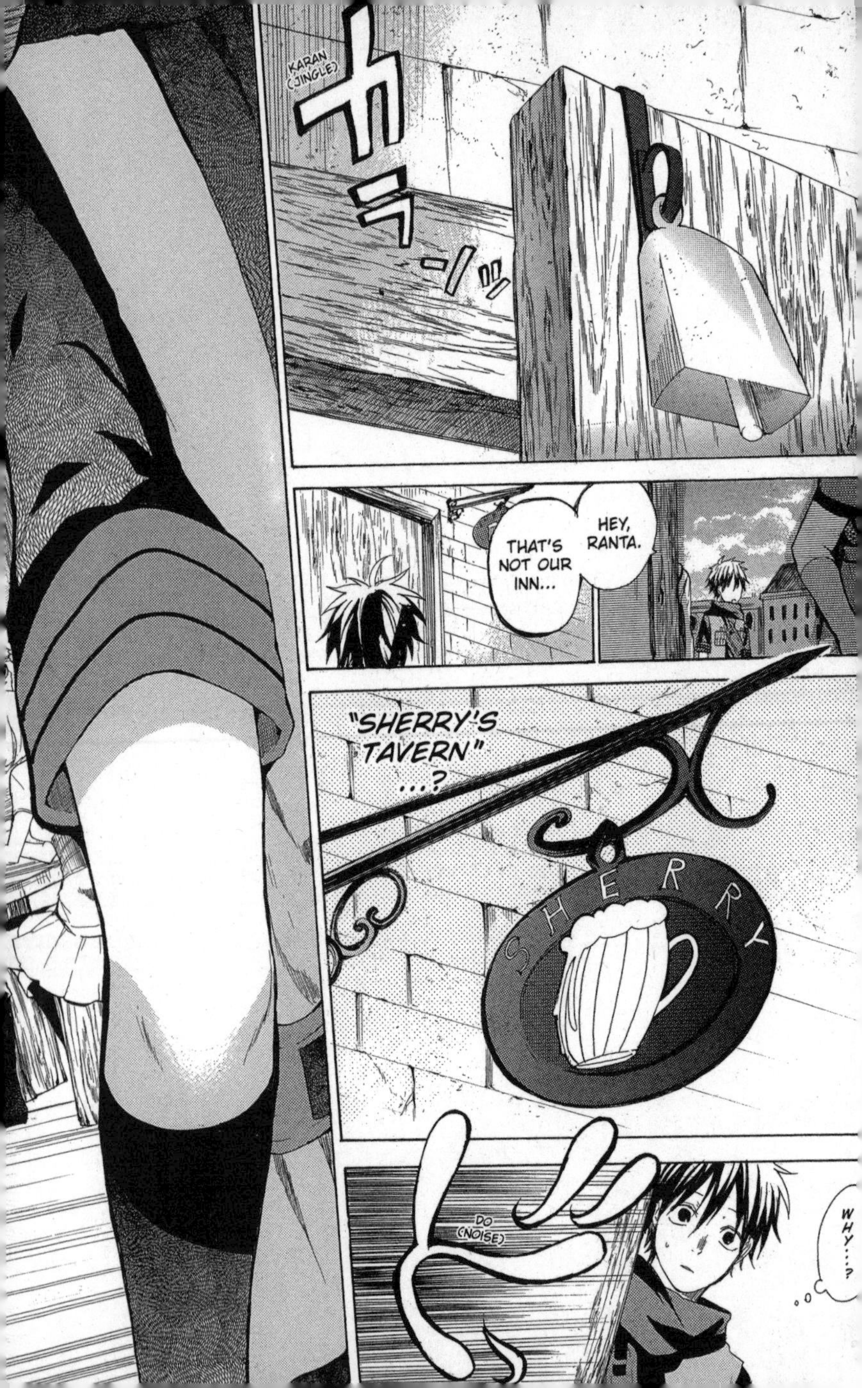

KARAN (JINGLE)
HEY, RANTA.
THAT'S NOT OUR INN...
"SHERRY'S TAVERN" ...?
SHERRY
WHY...?
DO (NOISE)

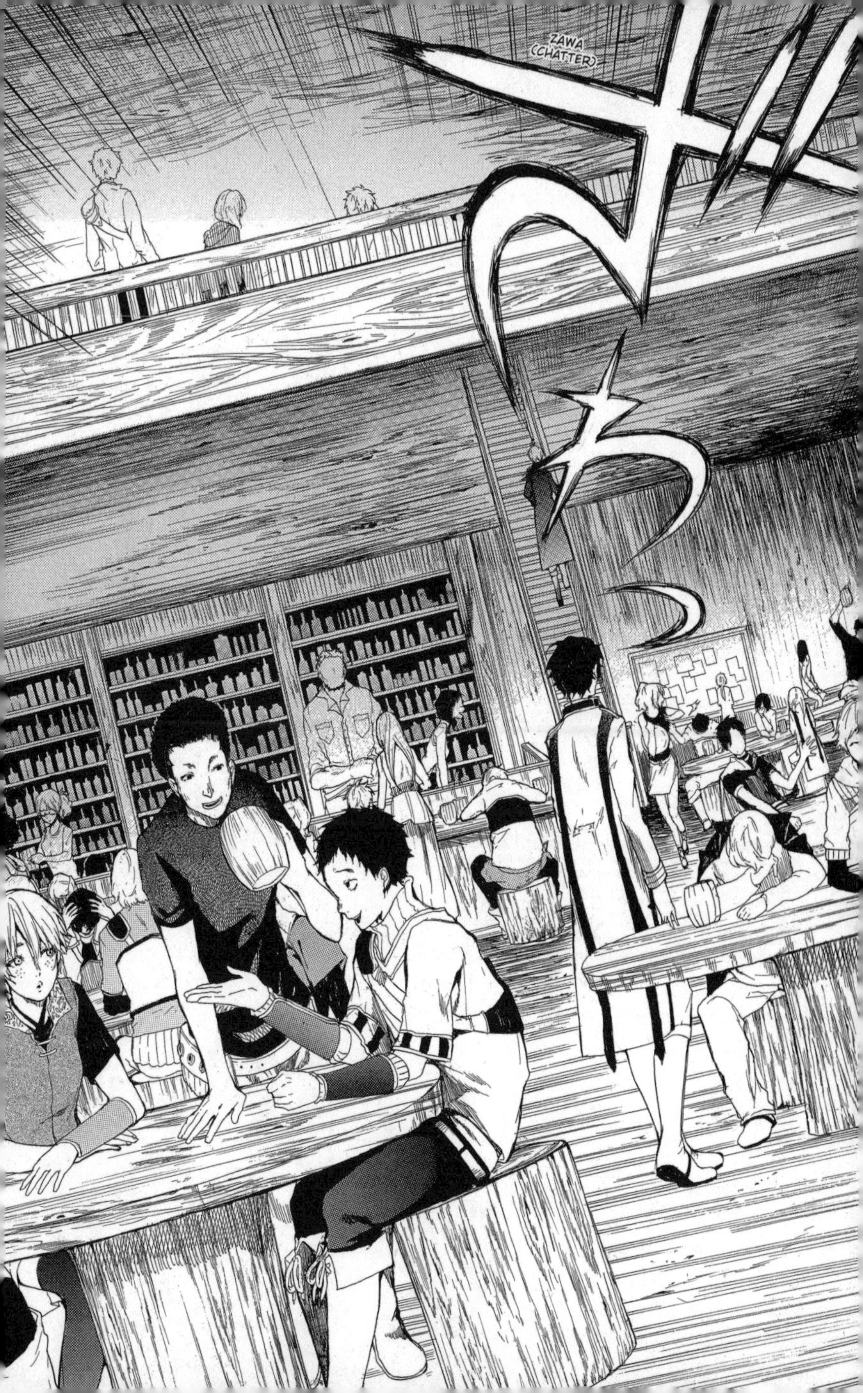
ZAWA
(CHATTER)

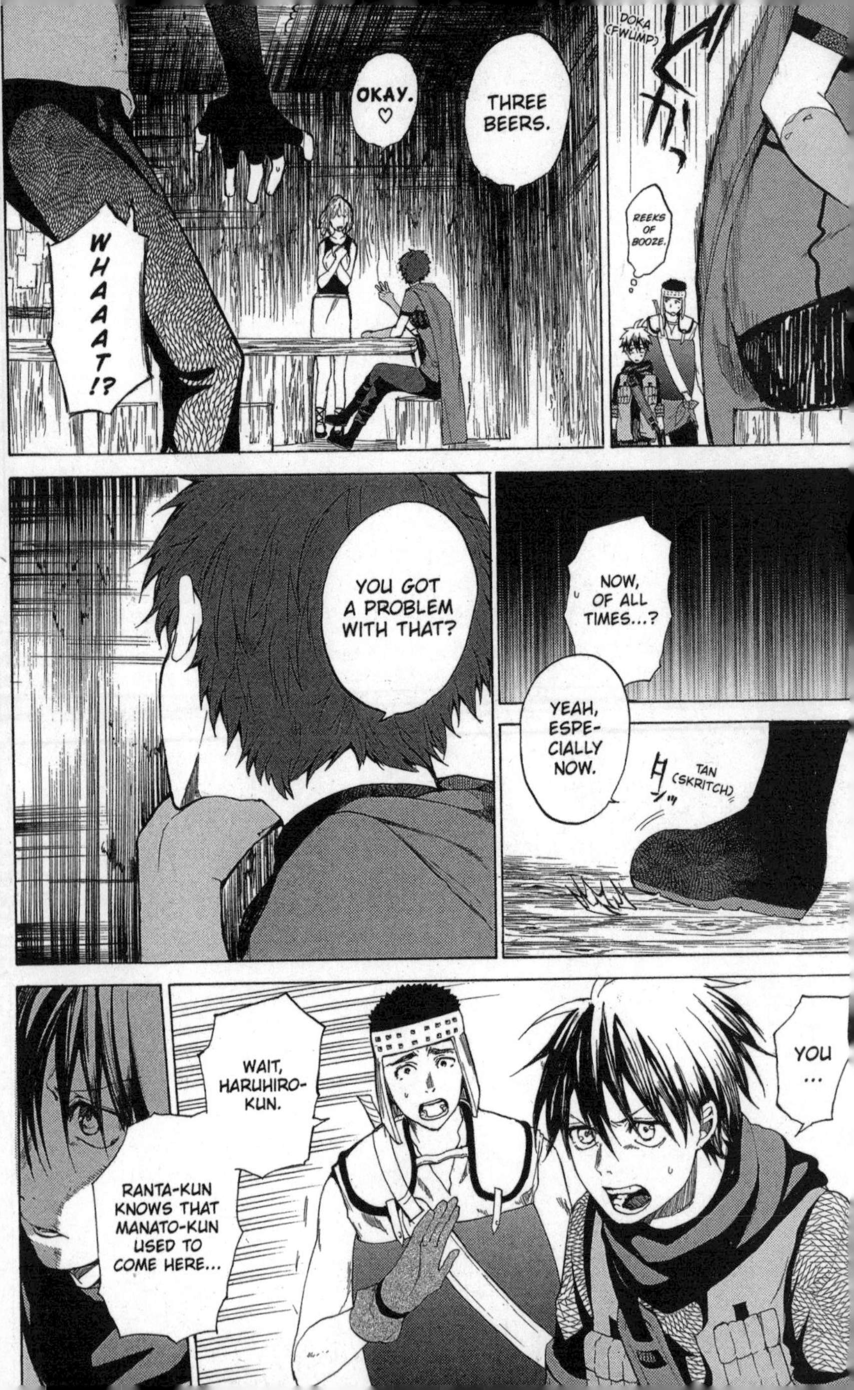
DOKA (FWUMP)
REEKS OF BOOZE.
THREE BEERS.
OKAY. ♡
WHAAAAT!?
NOW, OF ALL TIMES...?
YEAH, ESPECIALLY NOW.
TAN (SKRITCH)
YOU GOT A PROBLEM WITH THAT?
YOU ...
WAIT, HARUHIRO-KUN.
RANTA-KUN KNOWS THAT MANATO-KUN USED TO COME HERE...

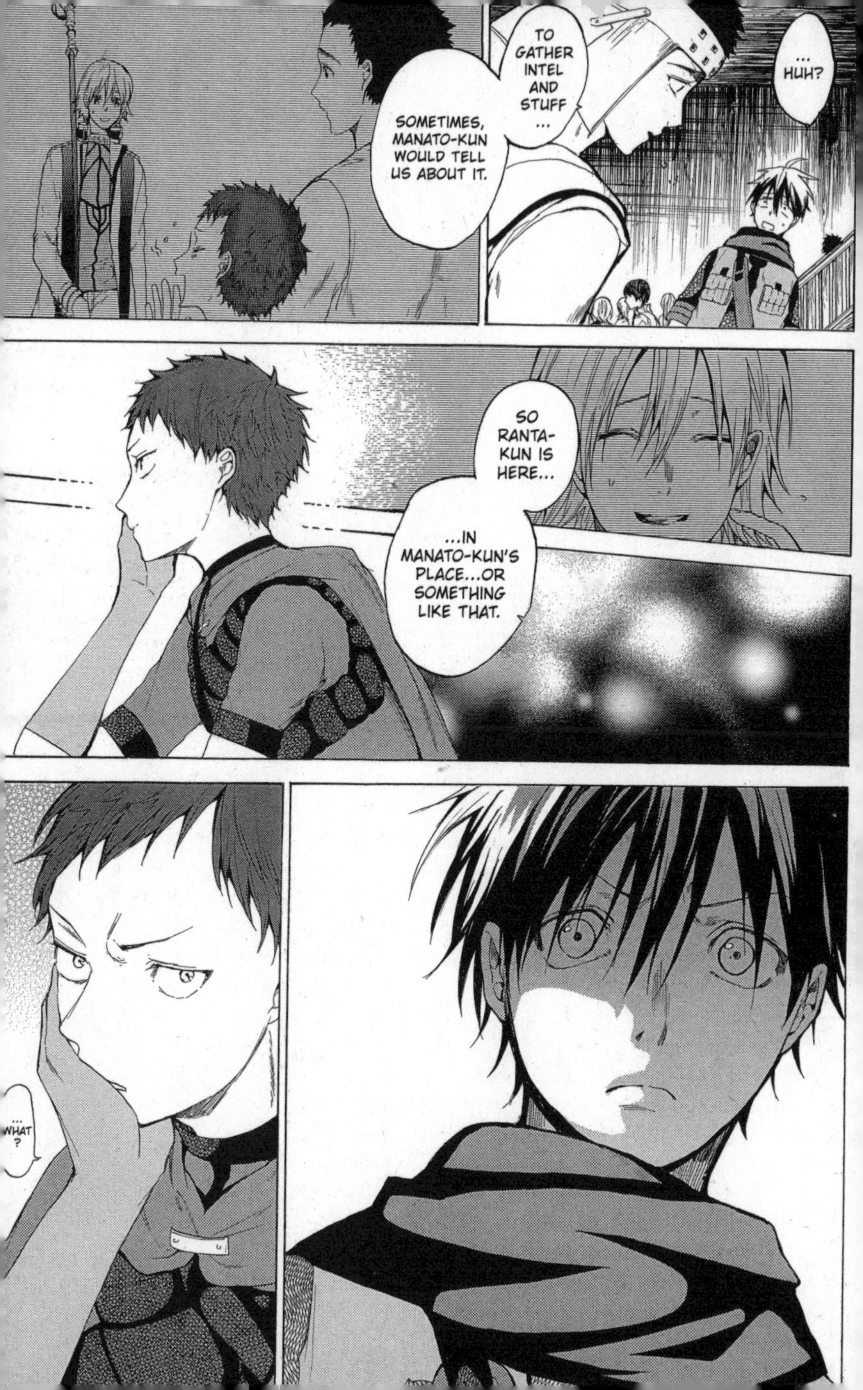
...HUH?
TO GATHER INTEL AND STUFF...
SOMETIMES, MANATO-KUN WOULD TELL US ABOUT IT.
SO RANTA-KUN IS HERE...
...IN MANATO-KUN'S PLACE...OR SOMETHING LIKE THAT.
...WHAT?

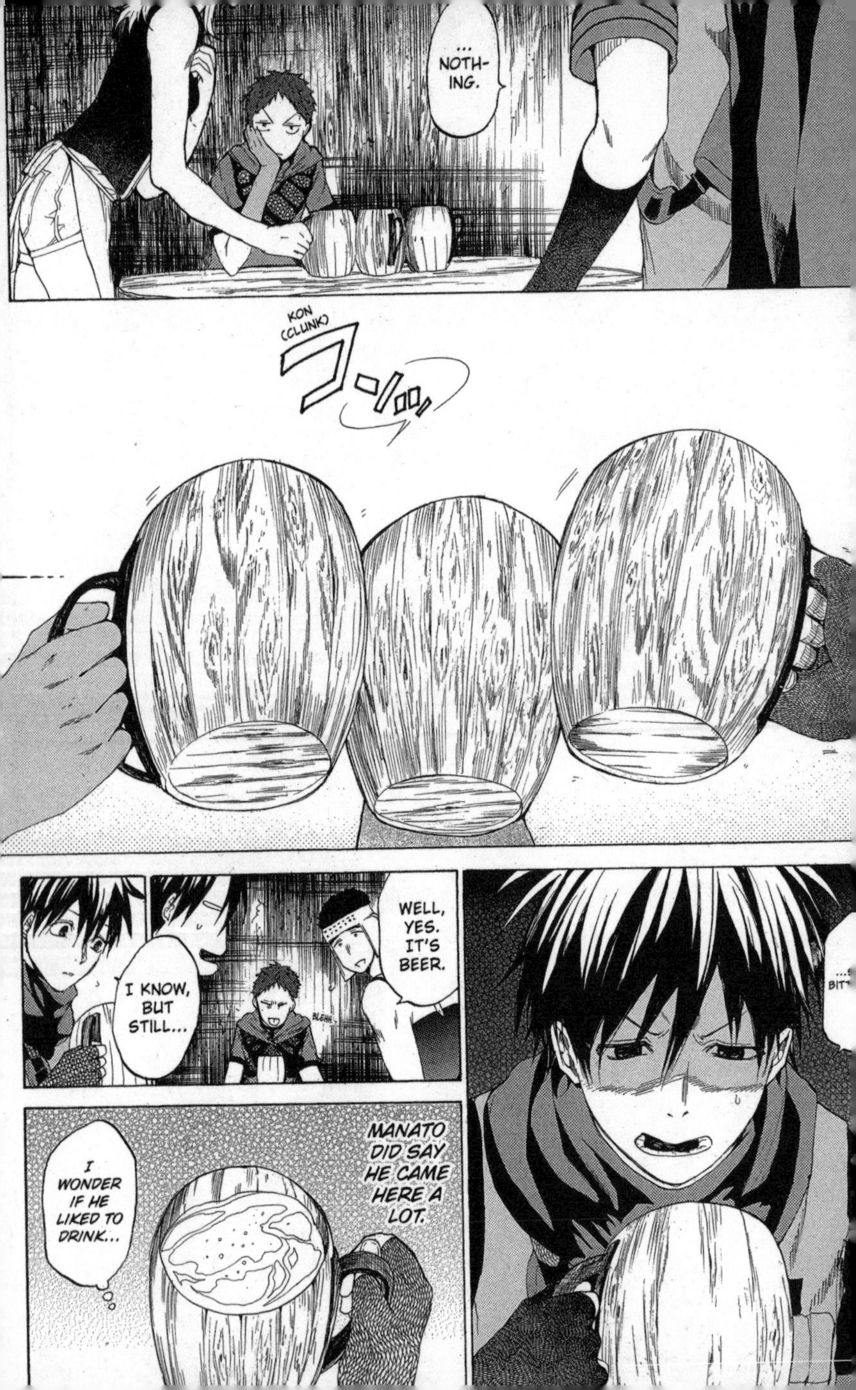
...NOTHING.
KON (CLUNK)
WELL, YES. IT'S BEER.
BLEH
I KNOW, BUT STILL...
MANATO DID SAY HE CAME HERE A LOT.
I WONDER IF HE LIKED TO DRINK...

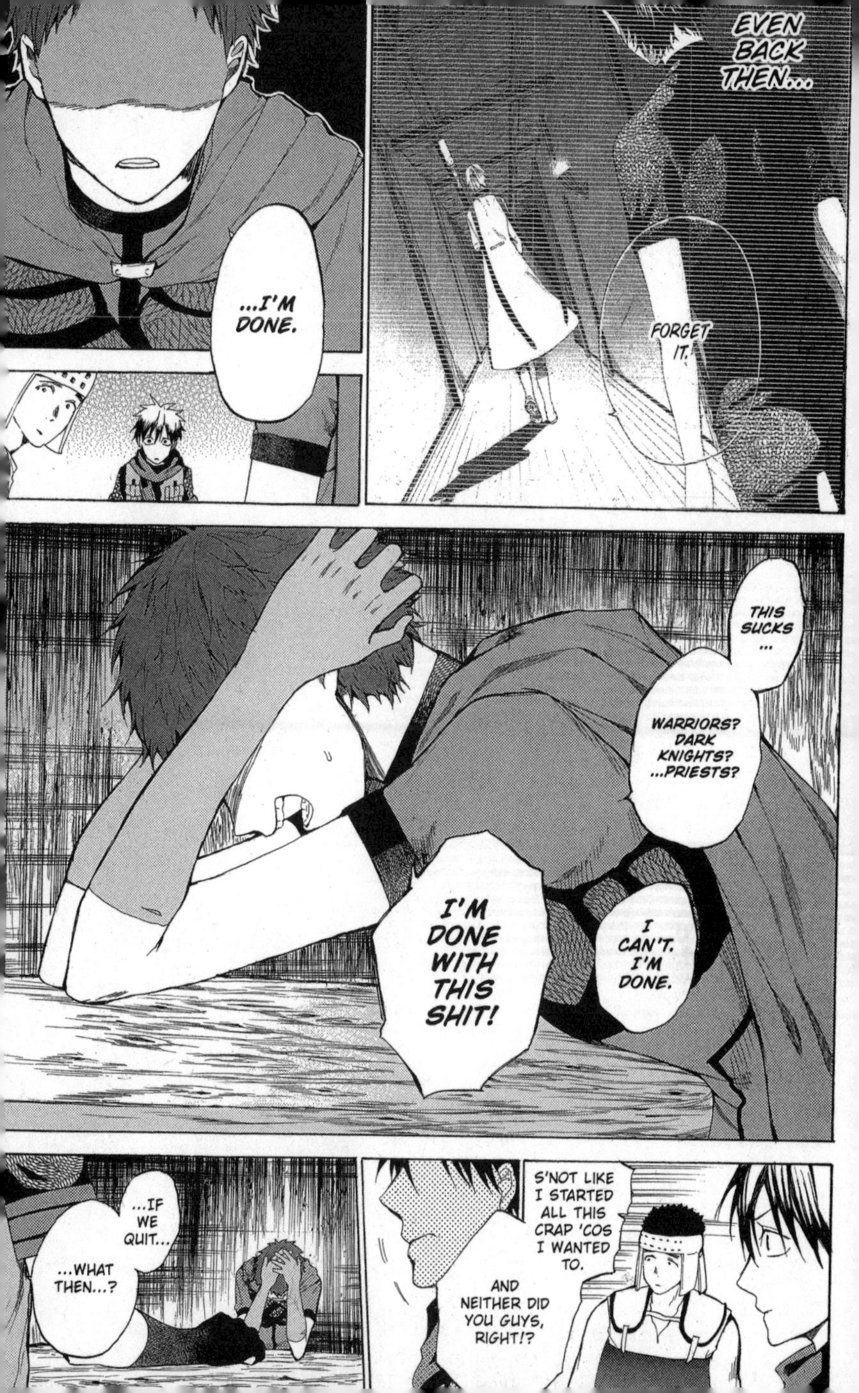
EVEN BACK THEN...
FORGET IT.
...I'M DONE.
THIS SUCKS...
WARRIORS? DARK KNIGHTS? ...PRIESTS?
I CAN'T. I'M DONE.
I'M DONE WITH THIS SHIT!
S'NOT LIKE I STARTED ALL THIS CRAP 'COS I WANTED TO.
AND NEITHER DID YOU GUYS, RIGHT!?
...IF WE QUIT...
...WHAT THEN...?

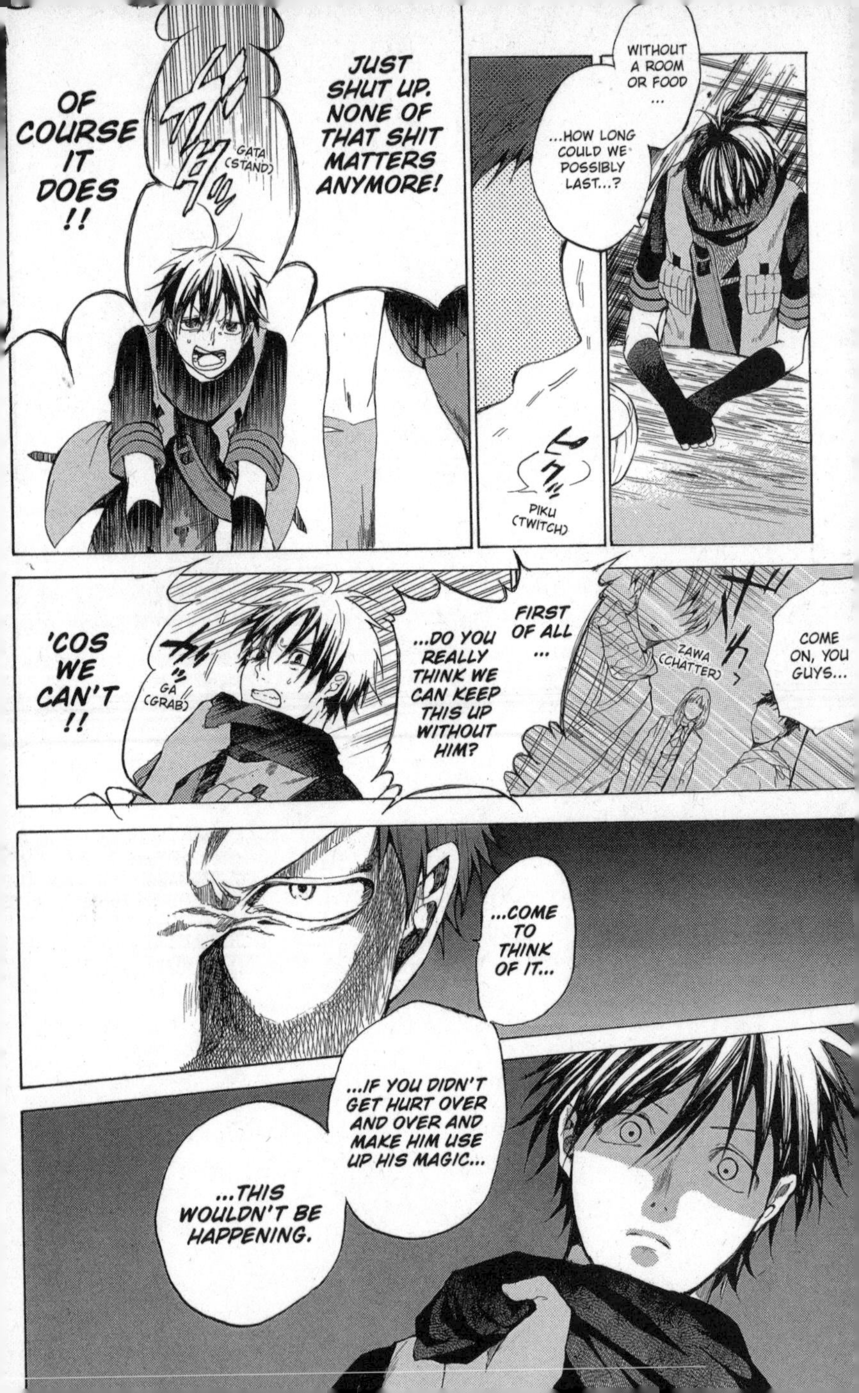
WITHOUT A ROOM OR FOOD ...
...HOW LONG COULD WE POSSIBLY LAST...?
PIKU (TWITCH)
JUST SHUT UP. NONE OF THAT SHIT MATTERS ANYMORE!
GATA (STAND)
OF COURSE IT DOES!!
COME ON, YOU GUYS...
ZAWA (CHATTER)
FIRST OF ALL ...
...DO YOU REALLY THINK WE CAN KEEP THIS UP WITHOUT HIM?
GA (GRAB)
'COS WE CAN'T!!
...COME TO THINK OF IT...
...IF YOU DIDN'T GET HURT OVER AND OVER AND MAKE HIM USE UP HIS MAGIC...
...THIS WOULDN'T BE HAPPENING.

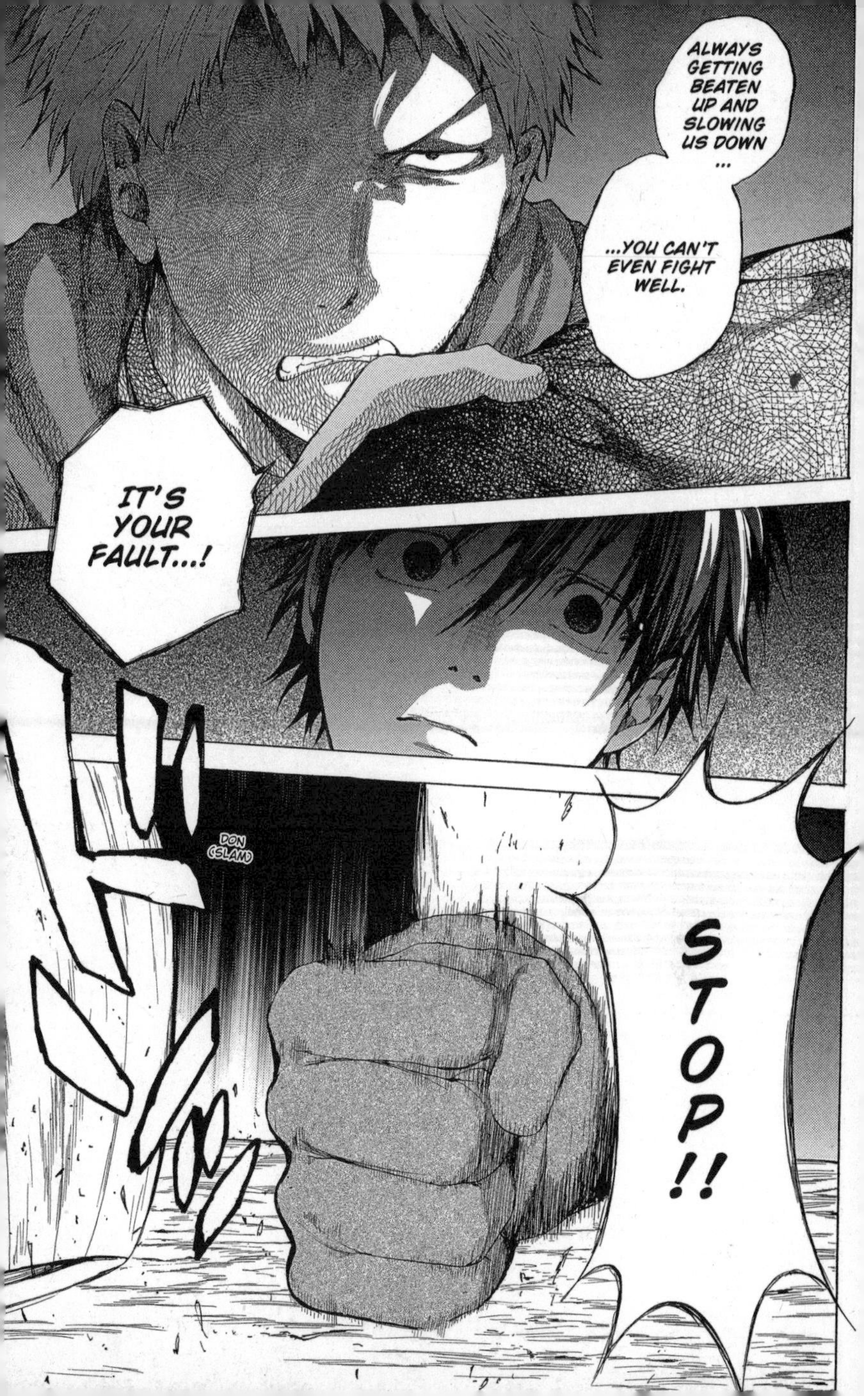
ALWAYS GETTING BEATEN UP AND SLOWING US DOWN ...
...YOU CAN'T EVEN FIGHT WELL.
IT'S YOUR FAULT...!
STOP!!
DON (SLAM)

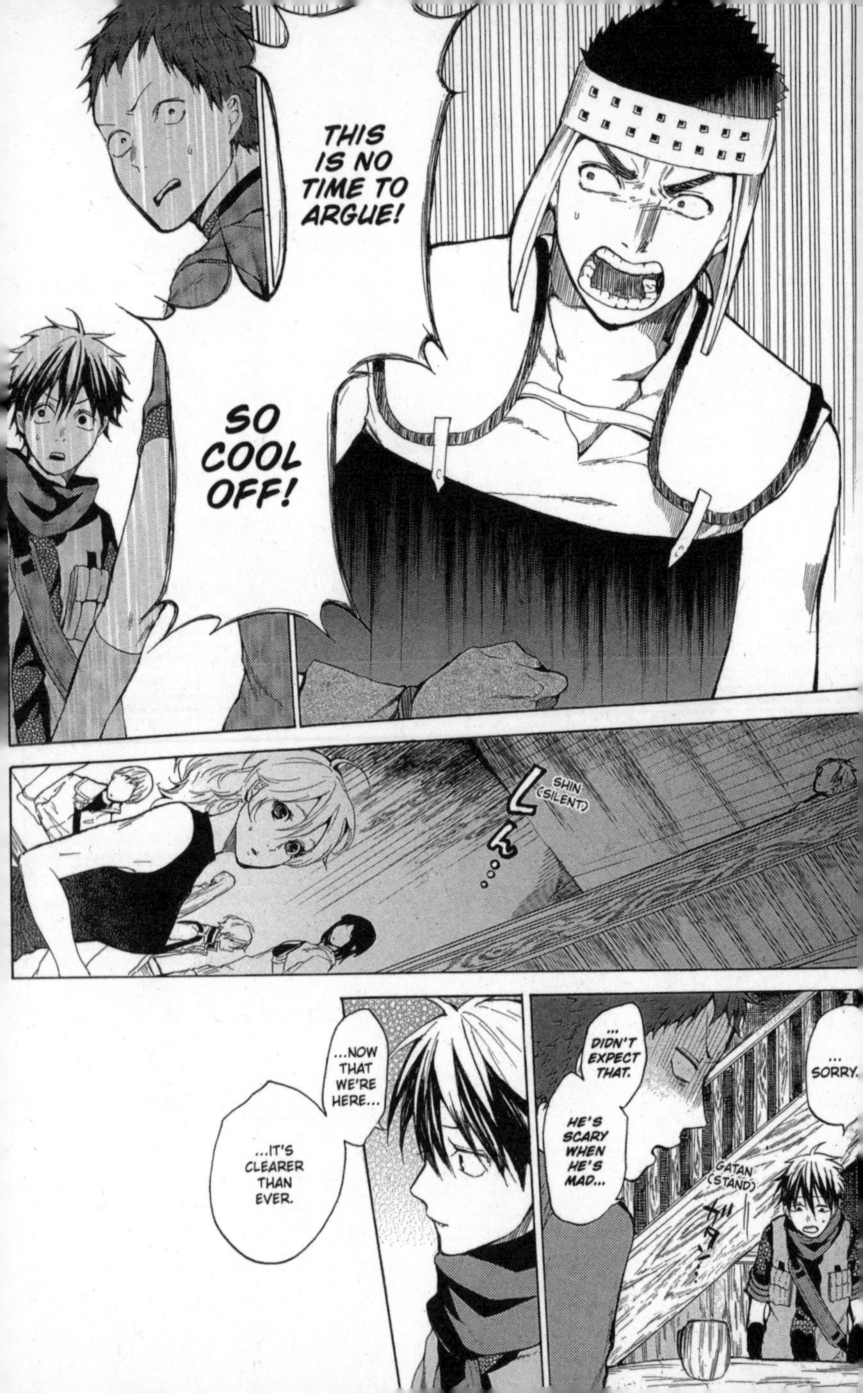
THIS IS NO TIME TO ARGUE!
SO COOL OFF!
SHIN (SILENT)
...SORRY.
...DIDN'T EXPECT THAT.
HE'S SCARY WHEN HE'S MAD...
GATAN (STAND)
...NOW THAT WE'RE HERE...
...IT'S CLEARER THAN EVER.

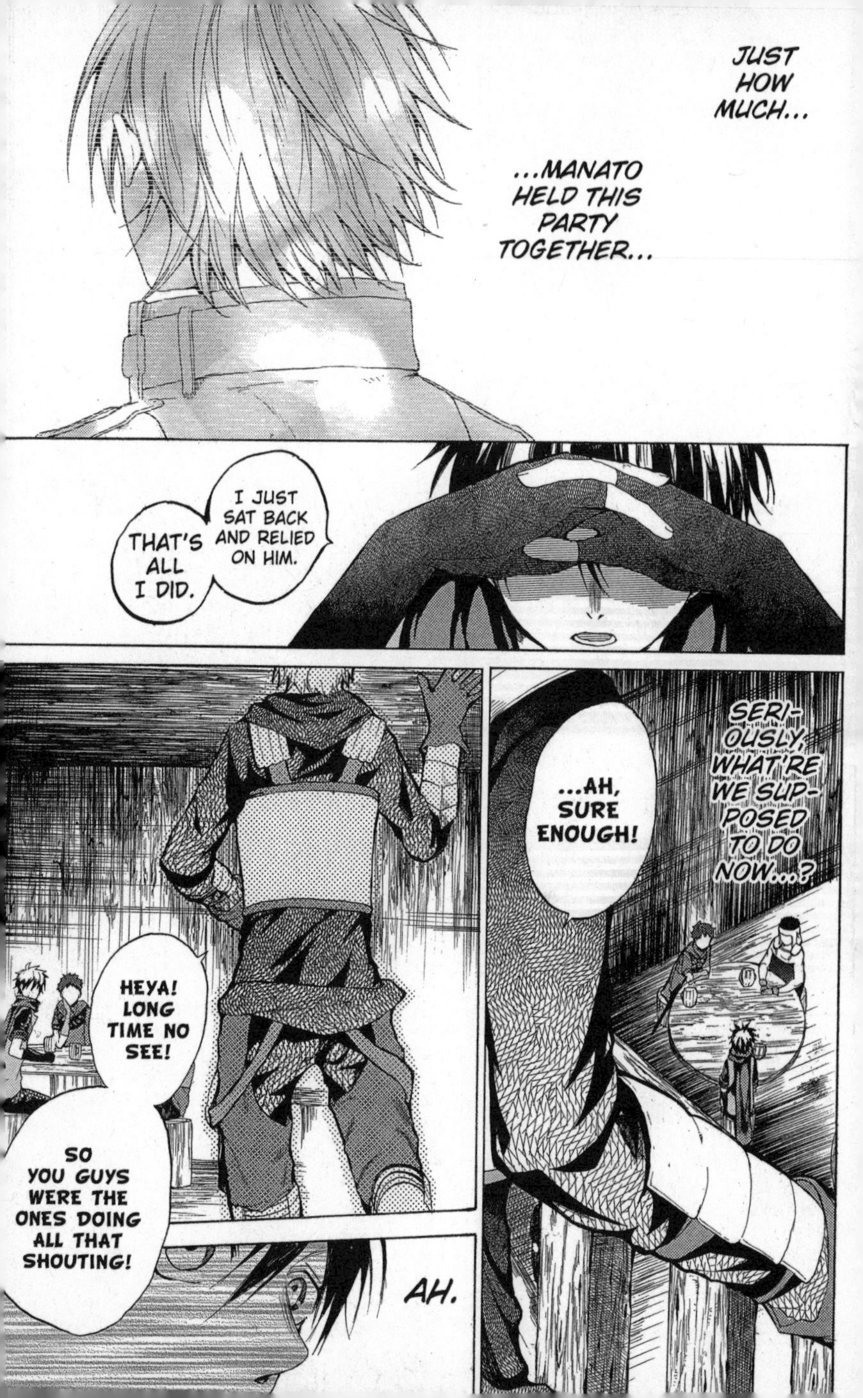
JUST HOW MUCH...
...MANATO HELD THIS PARTY TOGETHER...
I JUST SAT BACK AND RELIED ON HIM.
THAT'S ALL I DID.
SERI-OUSLY, WHAT'RE WE SUP-POSED TO DO NOW...?
...AH, SURE ENOUGH!
HEYA! LONG TIME NO SEE!
SO YOU GUYS WERE THE ONES DOING ALL THAT SHOUTING!
AH.

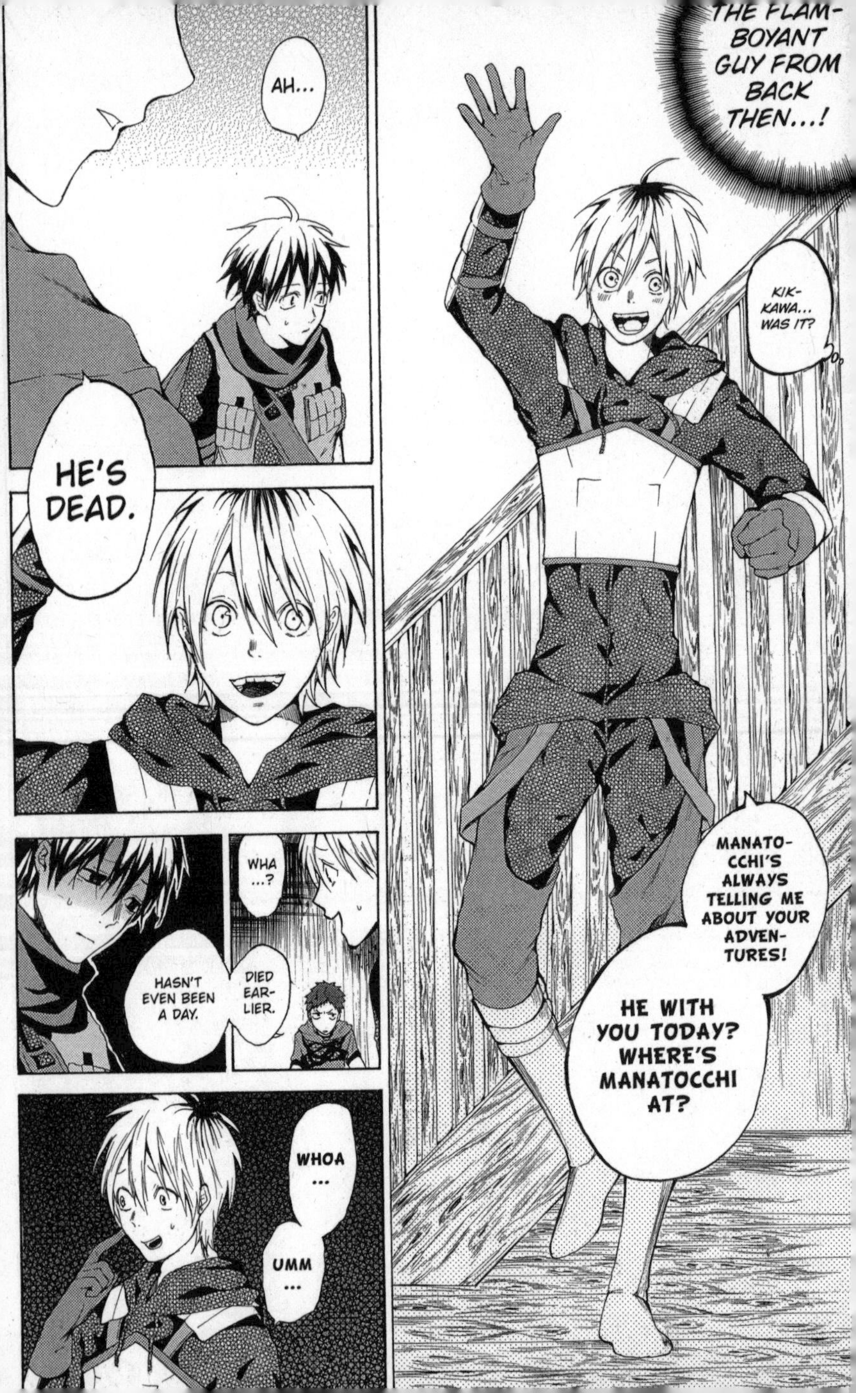
THE FLAM-BOYANT GUY FROM BACK THEN...!
KIK-KAWA... WAS IT?
MANATO-CCHI'S ALWAYS TELLING ME ABOUT YOUR ADVEN-TURES!
HE WITH YOU TODAY? WHERE'S MANATOCCHI AT?
AH...
HE'S DEAD.
WHA ...?
DIED EAR-LIER.
HASN'T EVEN BEEN A DAY.
WHOA ...
UMM ...

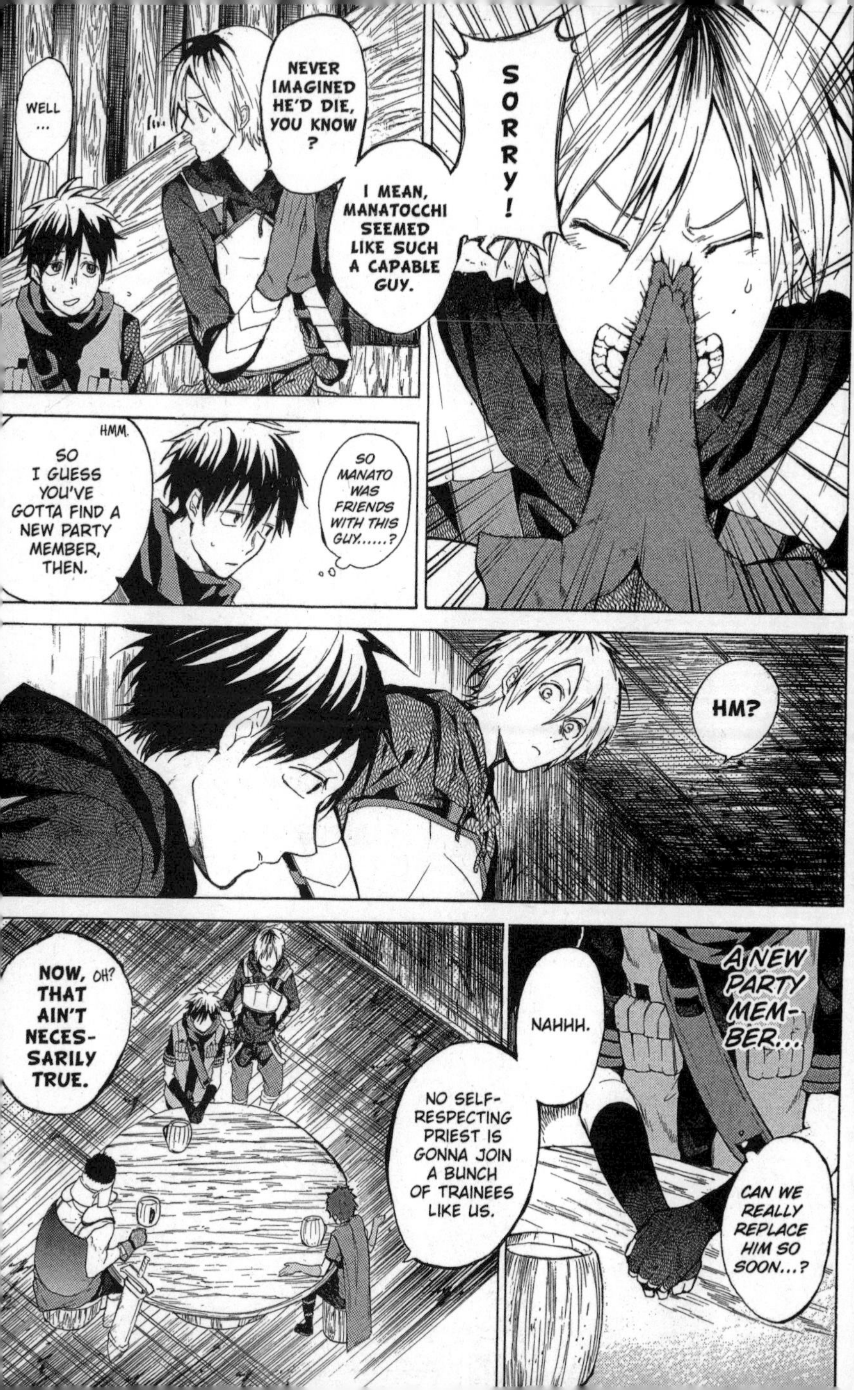
SORRY!
NEVER IMAGINED HE'D DIE, YOU KNOW?
I MEAN, MANATOCCHI SEEMED LIKE SUCH A CAPABLE GUY.
WELL...
SO MANATO WAS FRIENDS WITH THIS GUY......?
HMM.
SO I GUESS YOU'VE GOTTA FIND A NEW PARTY MEMBER, THEN.
HM?
A NEW PARTY MEM-BER...
NAHHH.
NO SELF-RESPECTING PRIEST IS GONNA JOIN A BUNCH OF TRAINEES LIKE US.
CAN WE REALLY REPLACE HIM SO SOON...?
OH?
NOW, THAT AIN'T NECES-SARILY TRUE.

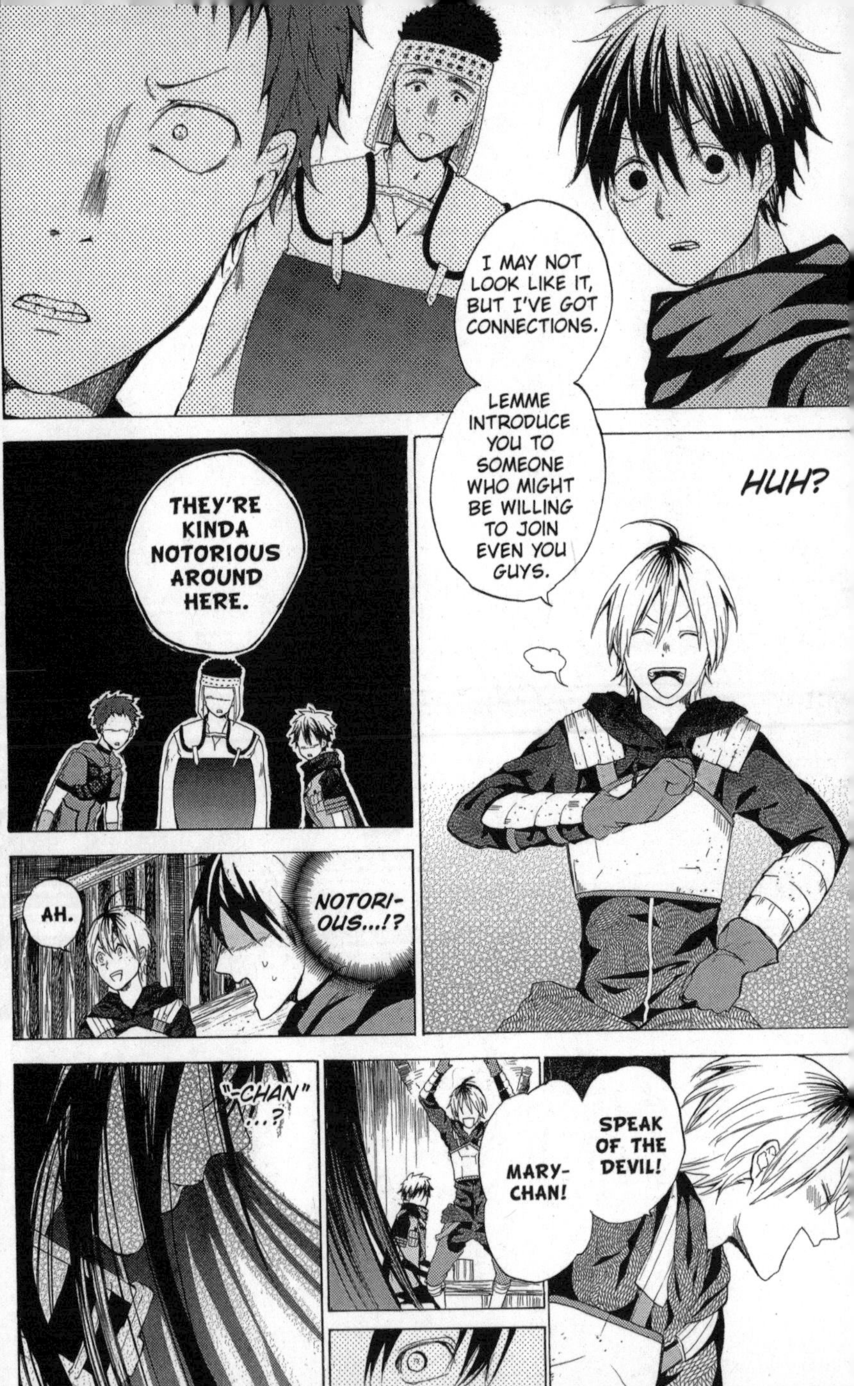
I MAY NOT LOOK LIKE IT, BUT I'VE GOT CONNECTIONS.
LEMME INTRODUCE YOU TO SOMEONE WHO MIGHT BE WILLING TO JOIN EVEN YOU GUYS.
HUH?
THEY'RE KINDA NOTORIOUS AROUND HERE.
NOTORI-OUS...!?
AH.
SPEAK OF THE DEVIL!
MARY-CHAN!
"-CHAN"
...?

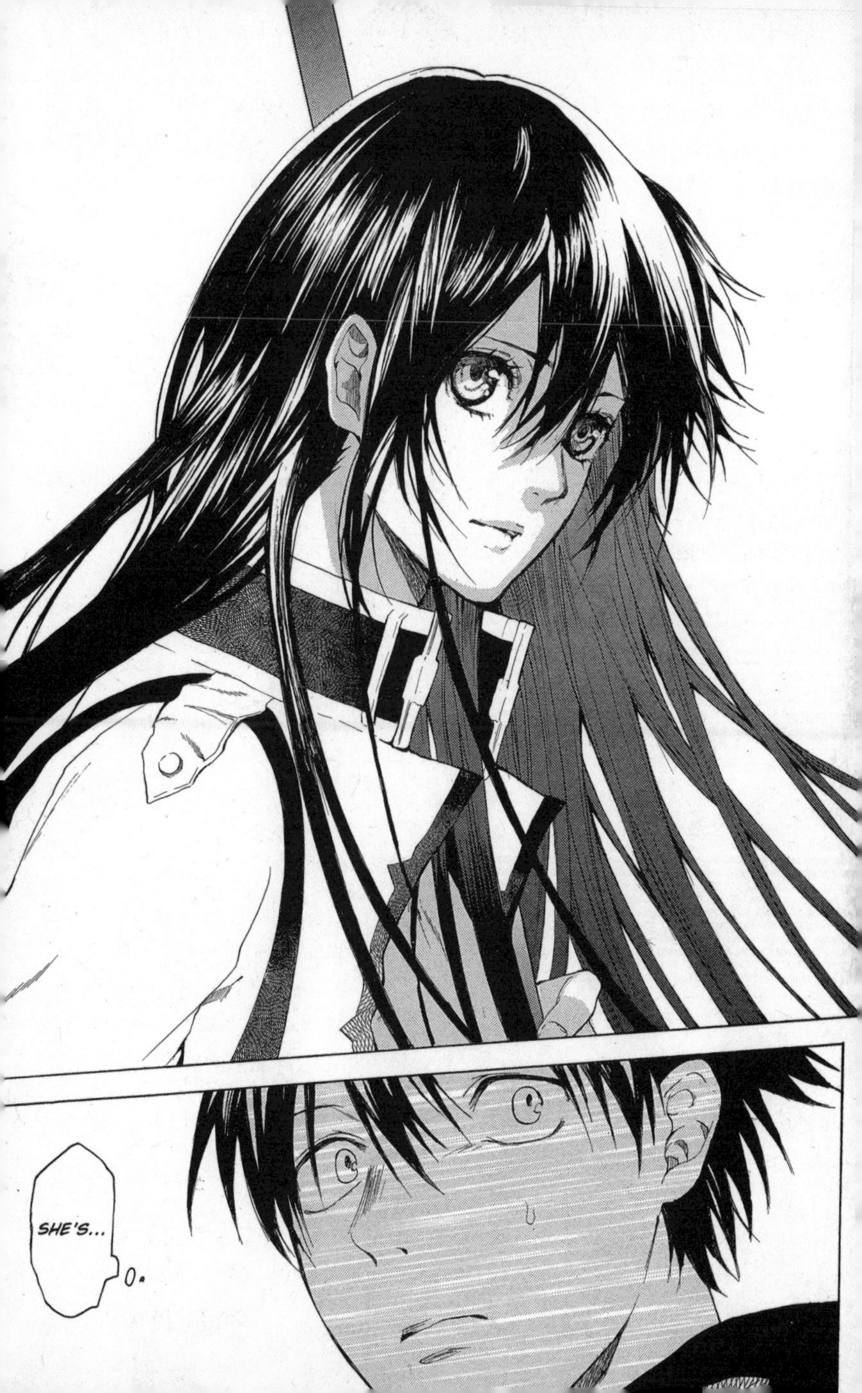
SHE'S...

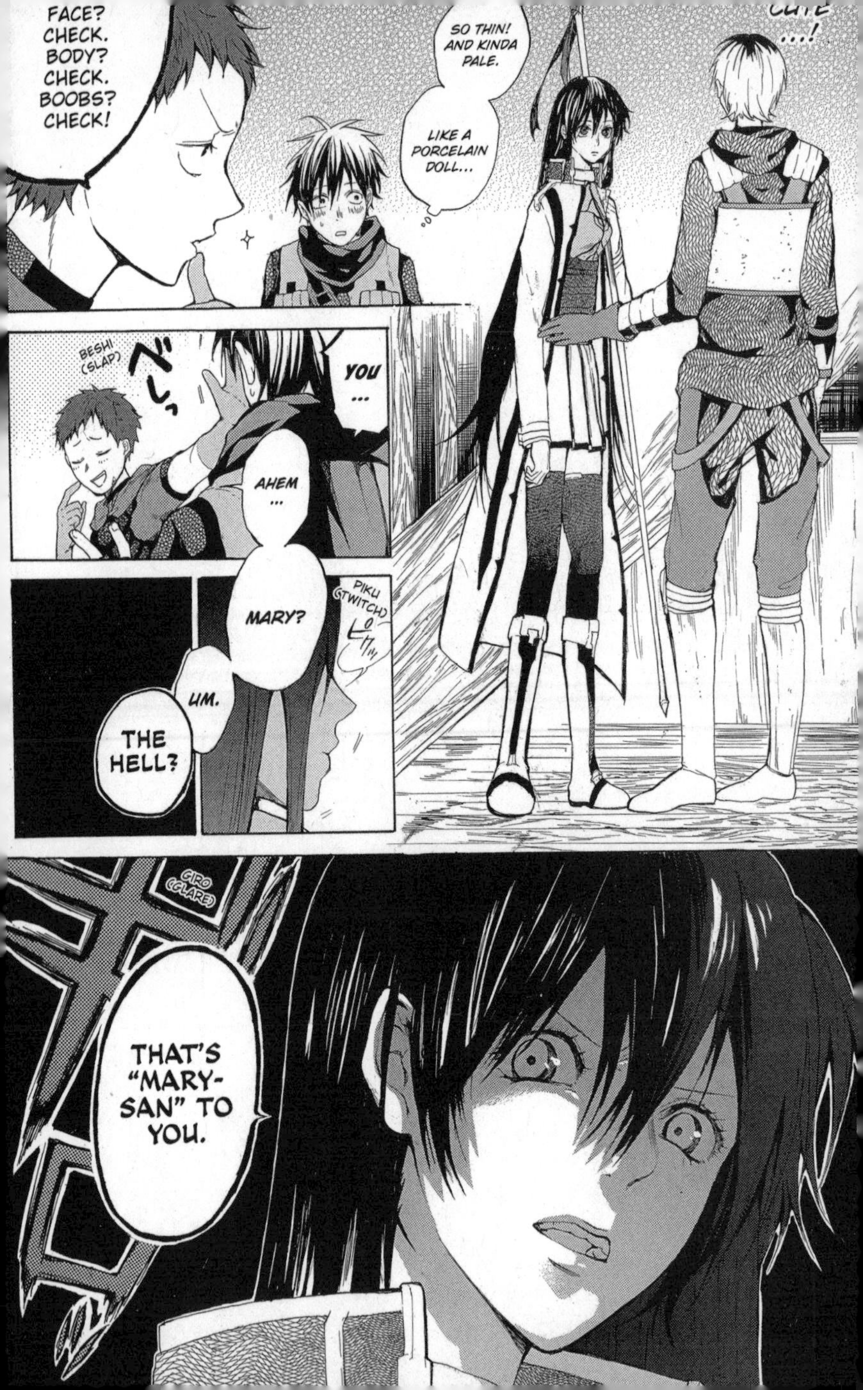

CUTE...!
SO THIN! AND KINDA PALE.
LIKE A PORCELAIN DOLL...
FACE? CHECK. BODY? CHECK. BOOBS? CHECK!
YOU...
BESHI (SLAP)
AHEM...
PIKU (TWITCH)
MARY?
UM.
THE HELL?
GIRO (GLARE)
THAT'S "MARY-SAN" TO YOU.

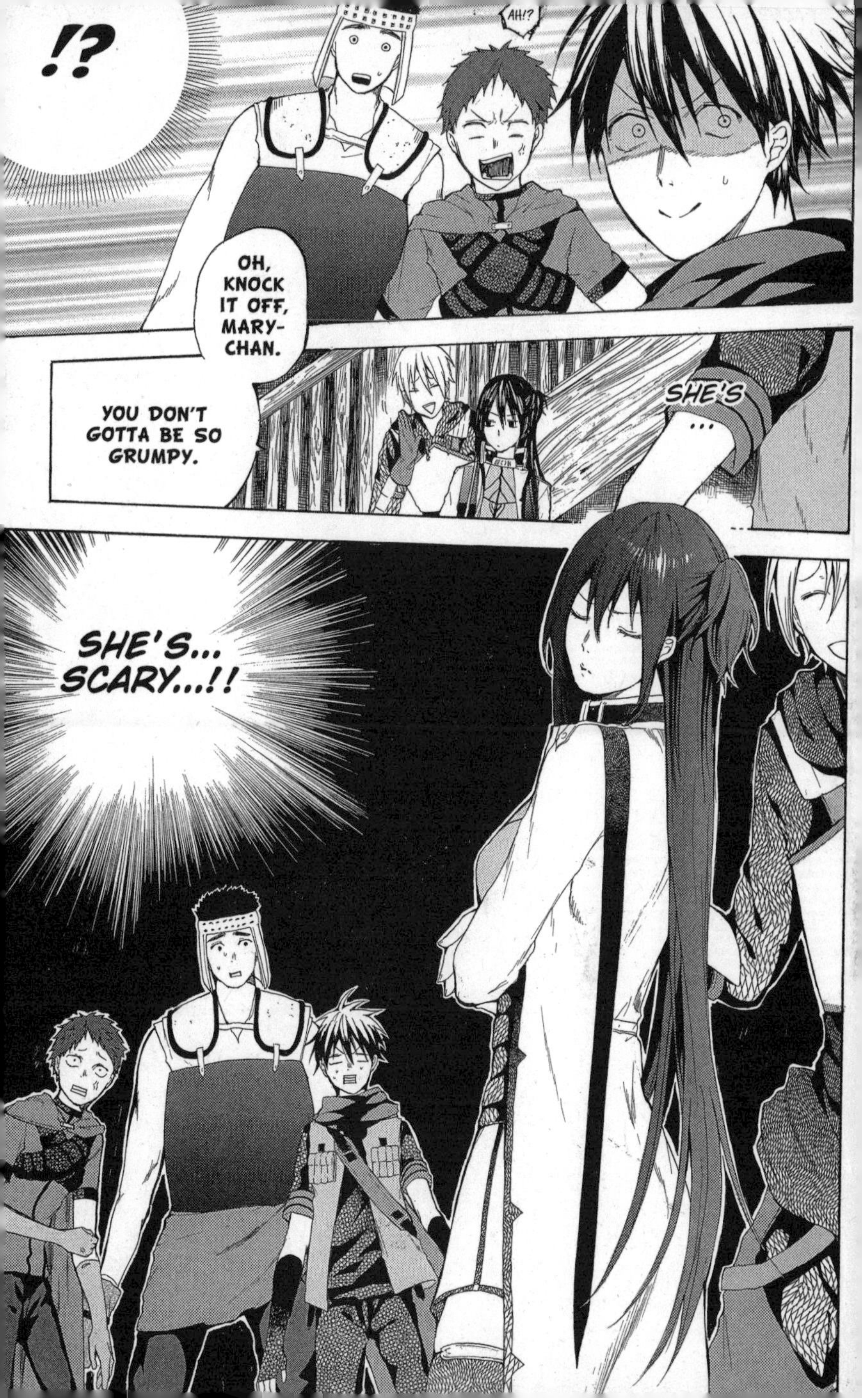
AH!?
!?
OH, KNOCK IT OFF, MARY-CHAN.
SHE'S ...
YOU DON'T GOTTA BE SO GRUMPY.
SHE'S... SCARY...!!

TRAVELING GOBS— STRANGE TALES FROM GRIMGAR OF FANTASY AND ASH GOBLIN DAYS

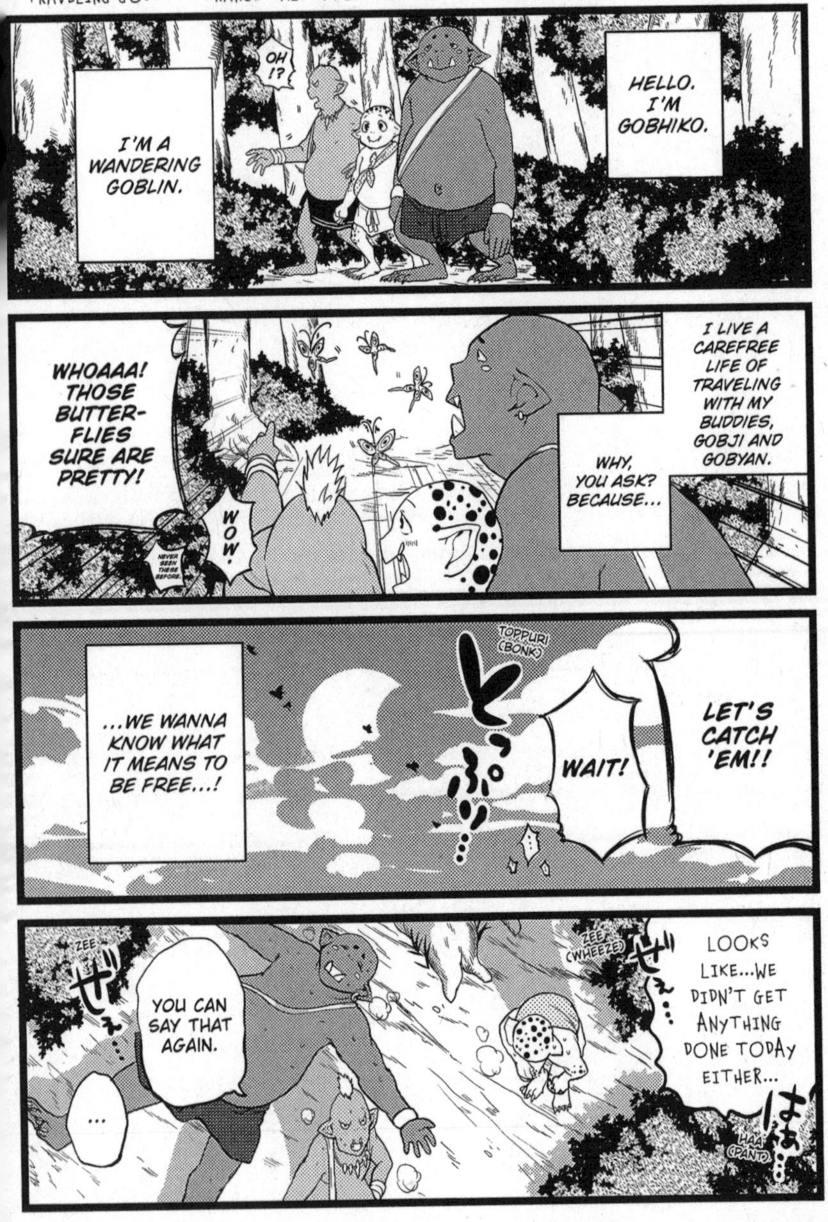
HELLO. I'M GOBHIKO.
OH !?
I'M A WANDERING GOBLIN.
I LIVE A CAREFREE LIFE OF TRAVELING WITH MY BUDDIES, GOBJI AND GOBYAN.
WHY, YOU ASK? BECAUSE...
WHOAAA! THOSE BUTTERFLIES SURE ARE PRETTY!
WOW.
NEVER SEEN THESE BEFORE.
LET'S CATCH 'EM!!
WAIT!
TOPPURI (BONK)
...WE WANNA KNOW WHAT IT MEANS TO BE FREE...!
LOOKS LIKE...WE DIDN'T GET ANYTHING DONE TODAY EITHER...
HAA (PANT)
ZEE (WHEEZE)
YOU CAN SAY THAT AGAIN.
ZEE
...

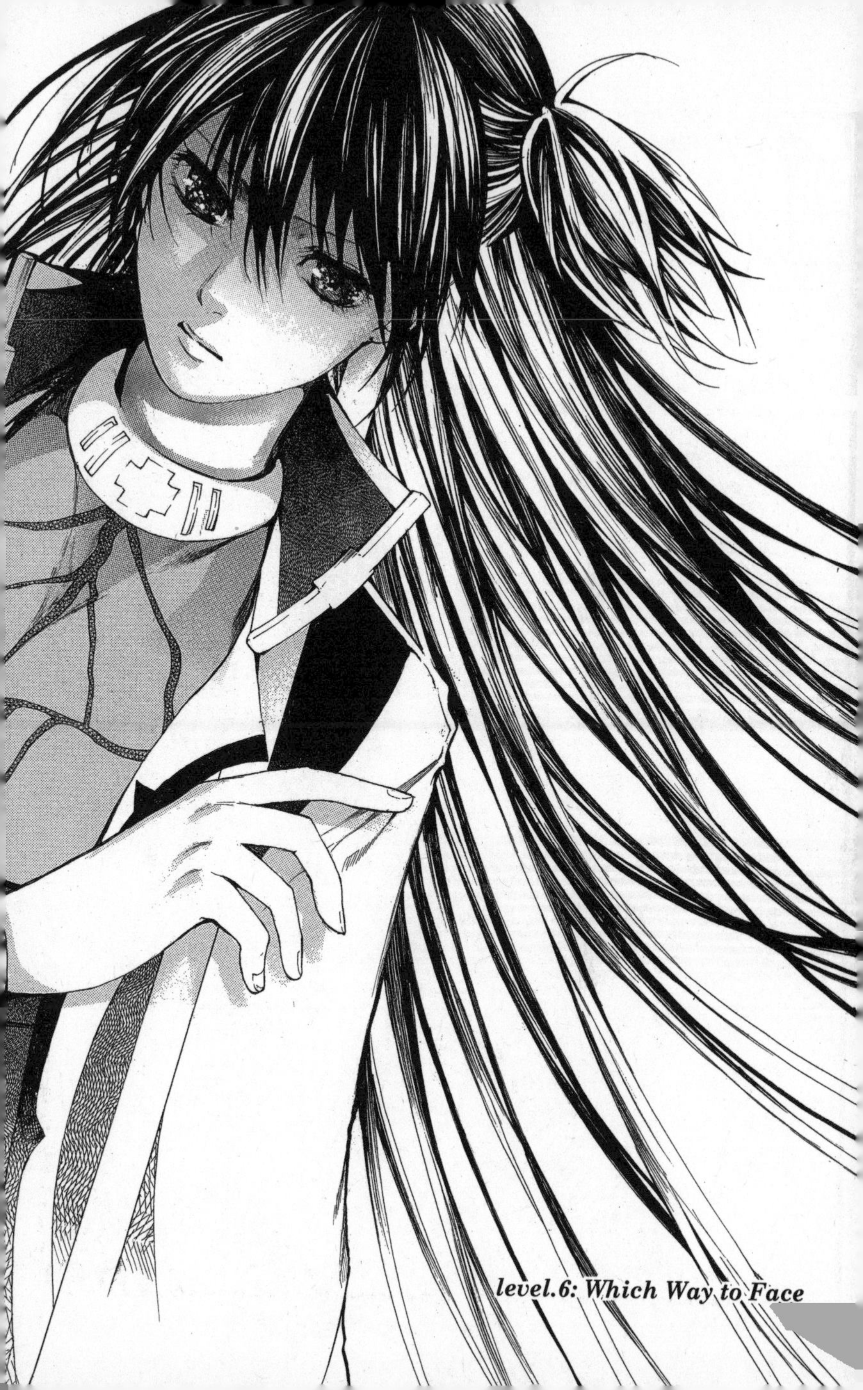

level.6: Which Way to Face

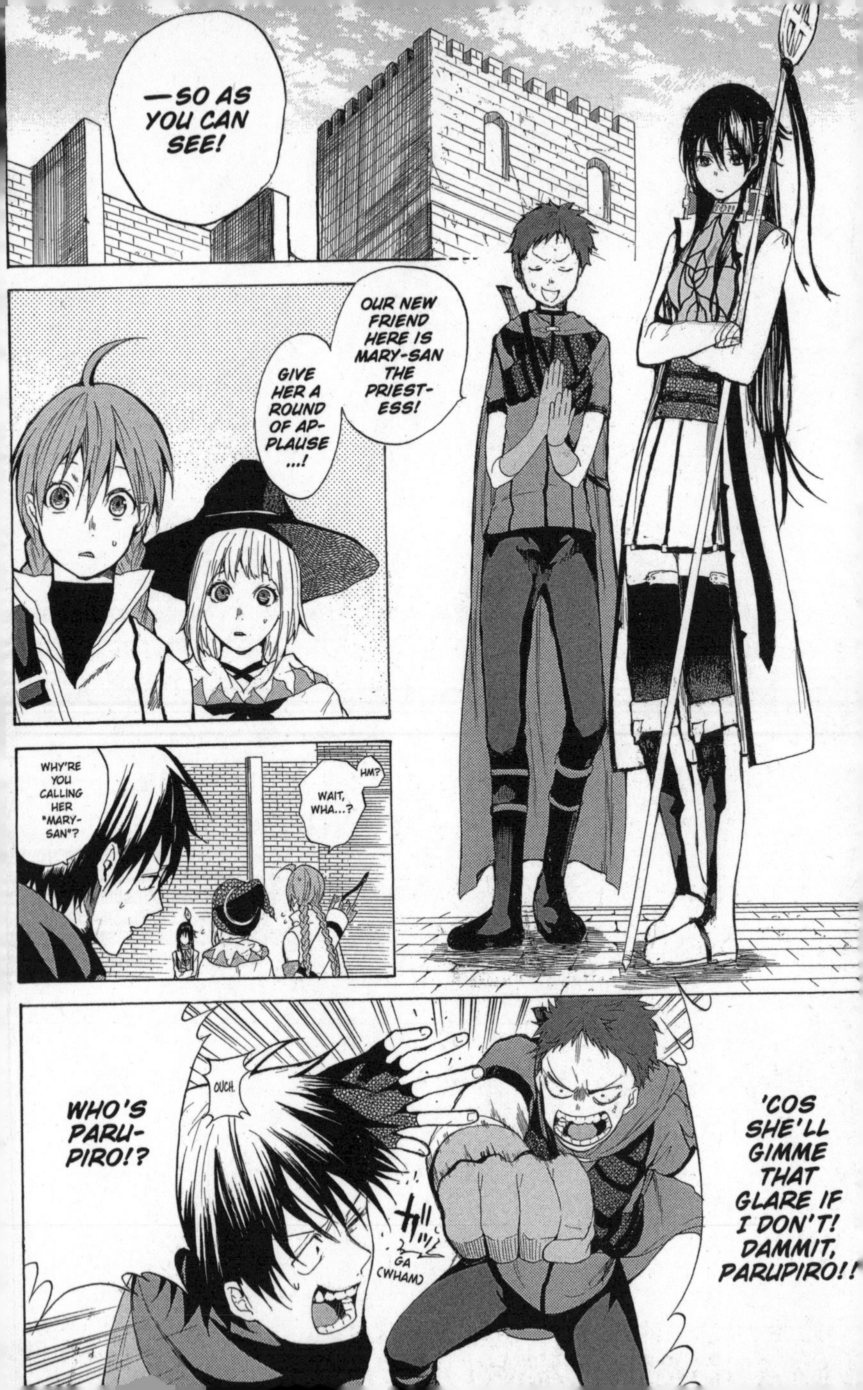
—SO AS YOU CAN SEE!
OUR NEW FRIEND HERE IS MARY-SAN THE PRIEST-ESS!
GIVE HER A ROUND OF AP-PLAUSE ...!
HM?
WAIT, WHA...?
WHY'RE YOU CALLING HER "MARY-SAN"?
'COS SHE'LL GIMME THAT GLARE IF I DON'T! DAMMIT, PARUPIRO!!
GA (WHAM)
OUCH.
WHO'S PARU-PIRO!?

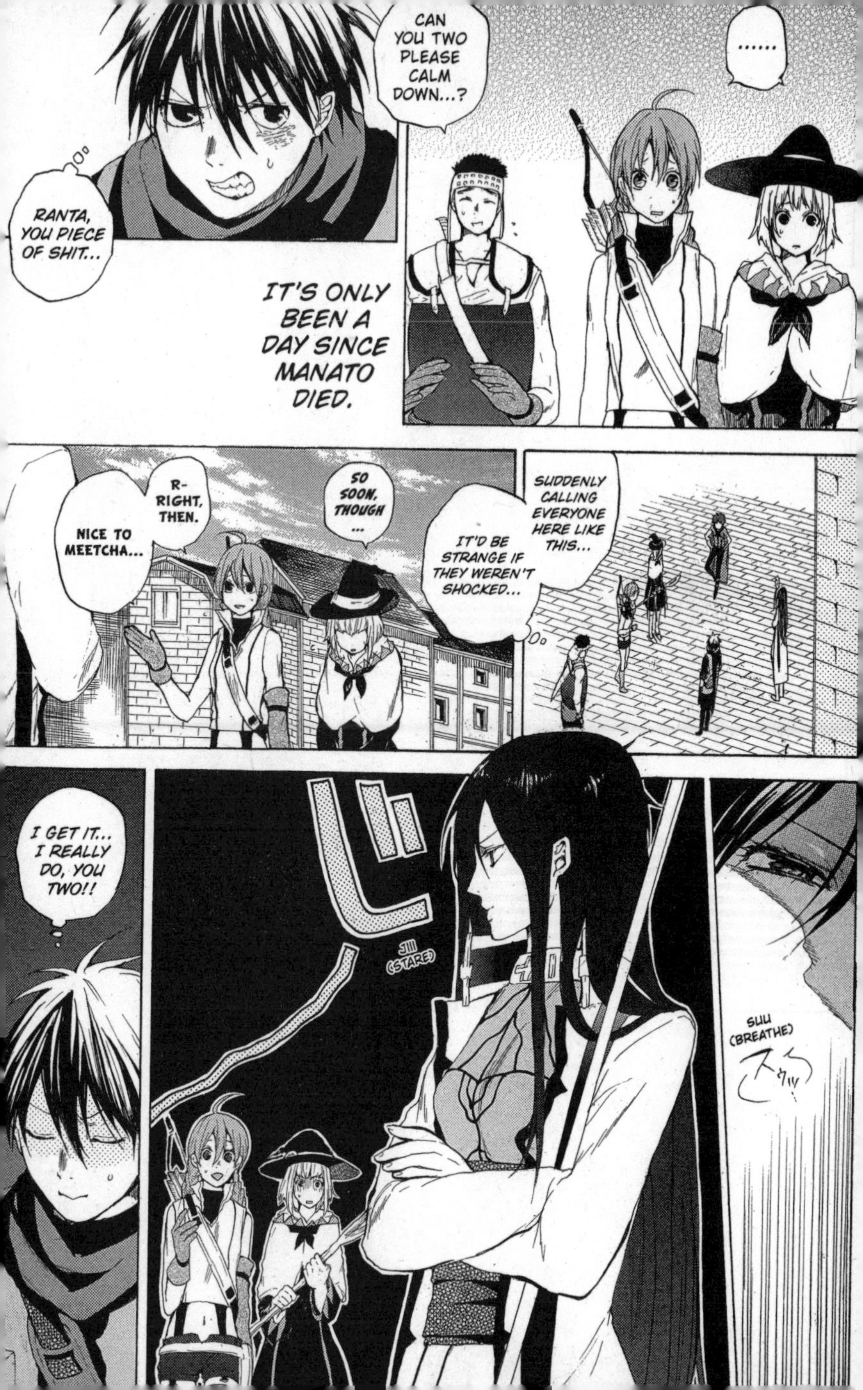
......
CAN YOU TWO PLEASE CALM DOWN...?
RANTA, YOU PIECE OF SHIT...
IT'S ONLY BEEN A DAY SINCE MANATO DIED.
SUDDENLY CALLING EVERYONE HERE LIKE THIS...
IT'D BE STRANGE IF THEY WEREN'T SHOCKED...
SO SOON, THOUGH...
R-RIGHT, THEN.
NICE TO MEETCHA...
SUU (BREATHE)
JIII (STARE)
I GET IT... I REALLY DO, YOU TWO!!

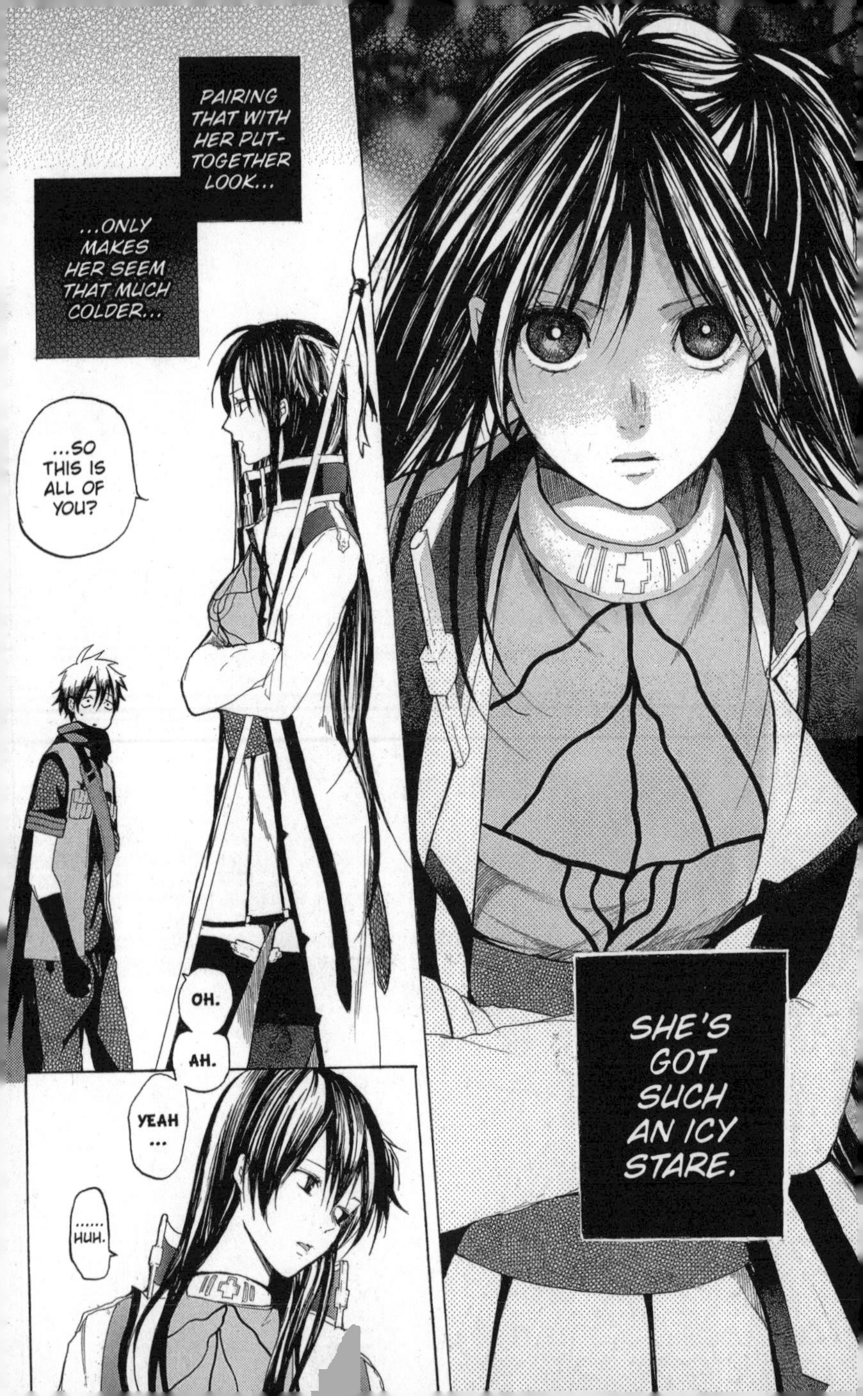
SHE'S GOT SUCH AN ICY STARE.
PAIRING THAT WITH HER PUT-TOGETHER LOOK...
...ONLY MAKES HER SEEM THAT MUCH COLDER...
...SO THIS IS ALL OF YOU?
OH.
AH.
YEAH...
......HUH.

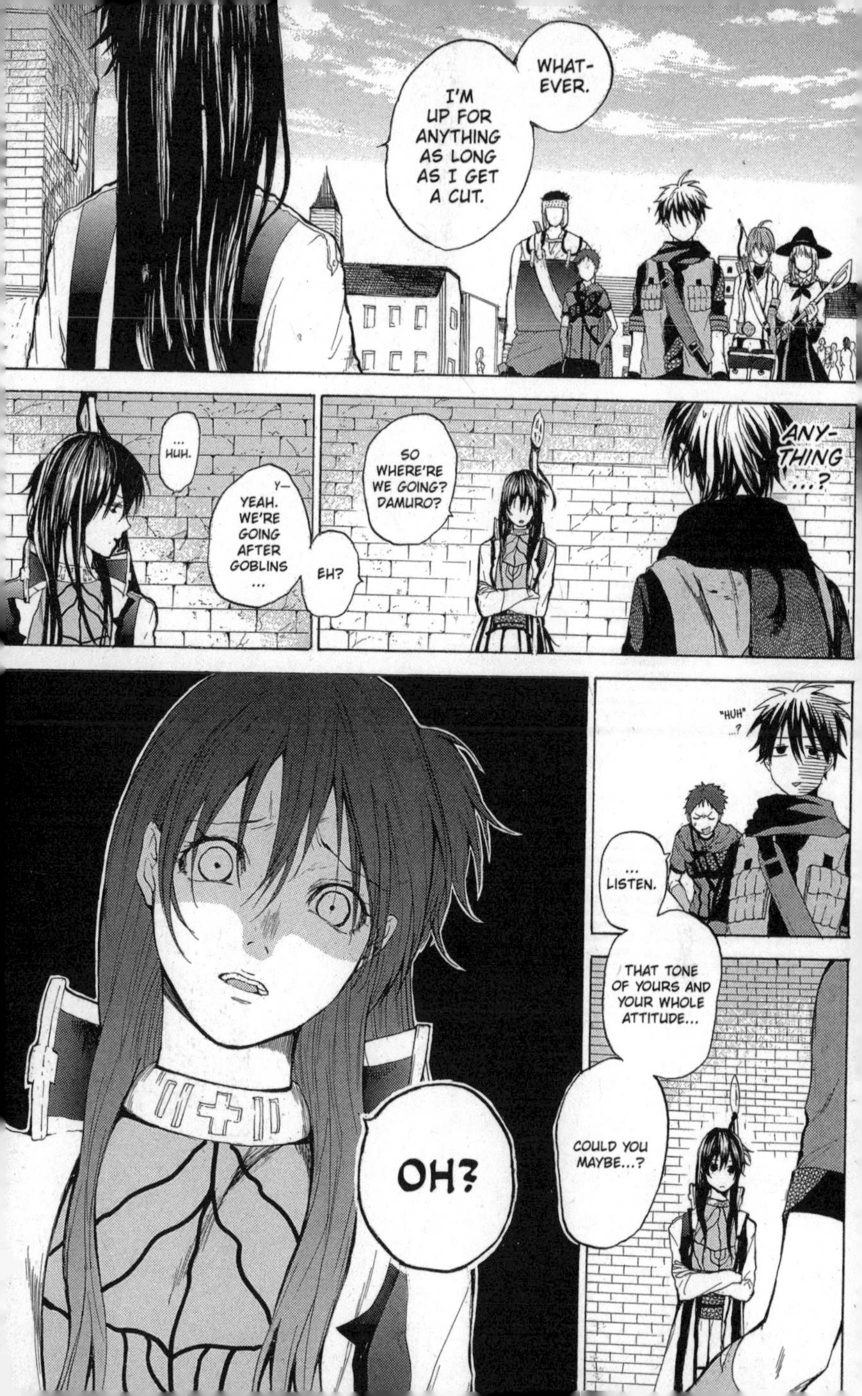
WHAT-EVER.
I'M UP FOR ANYTHING AS LONG AS I GET A CUT.
ANY-THING ...?
SO WHERE'RE WE GOING? DAMURO?
EH?
... HUH.
Y— YEAH. WE'RE GOING AFTER GOBLINS ...
"HUH" ...?
... LISTEN.
THAT TONE OF YOURS AND YOUR WHOLE ATTITUDE...
COULD YOU MAYBE...?
OH?

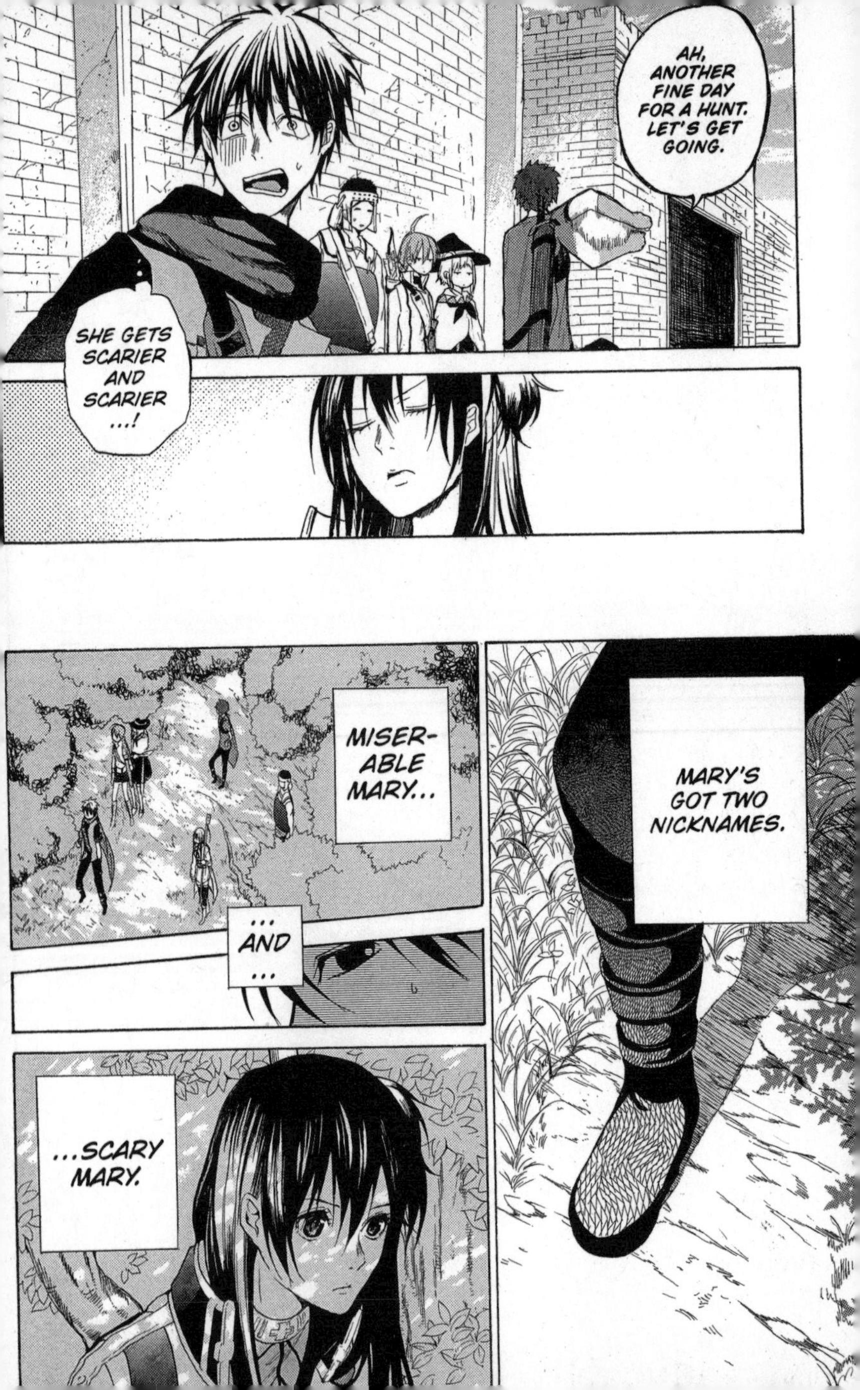
AH, ANOTHER FINE DAY FOR A HUNT. LET'S GET GOING.
SHE GETS SCARIER AND SCARIER ...!
MARY'S GOT TWO NICKNAMES.
MISER-ABLE MARY...
... AND ...
...SCARY MARY.

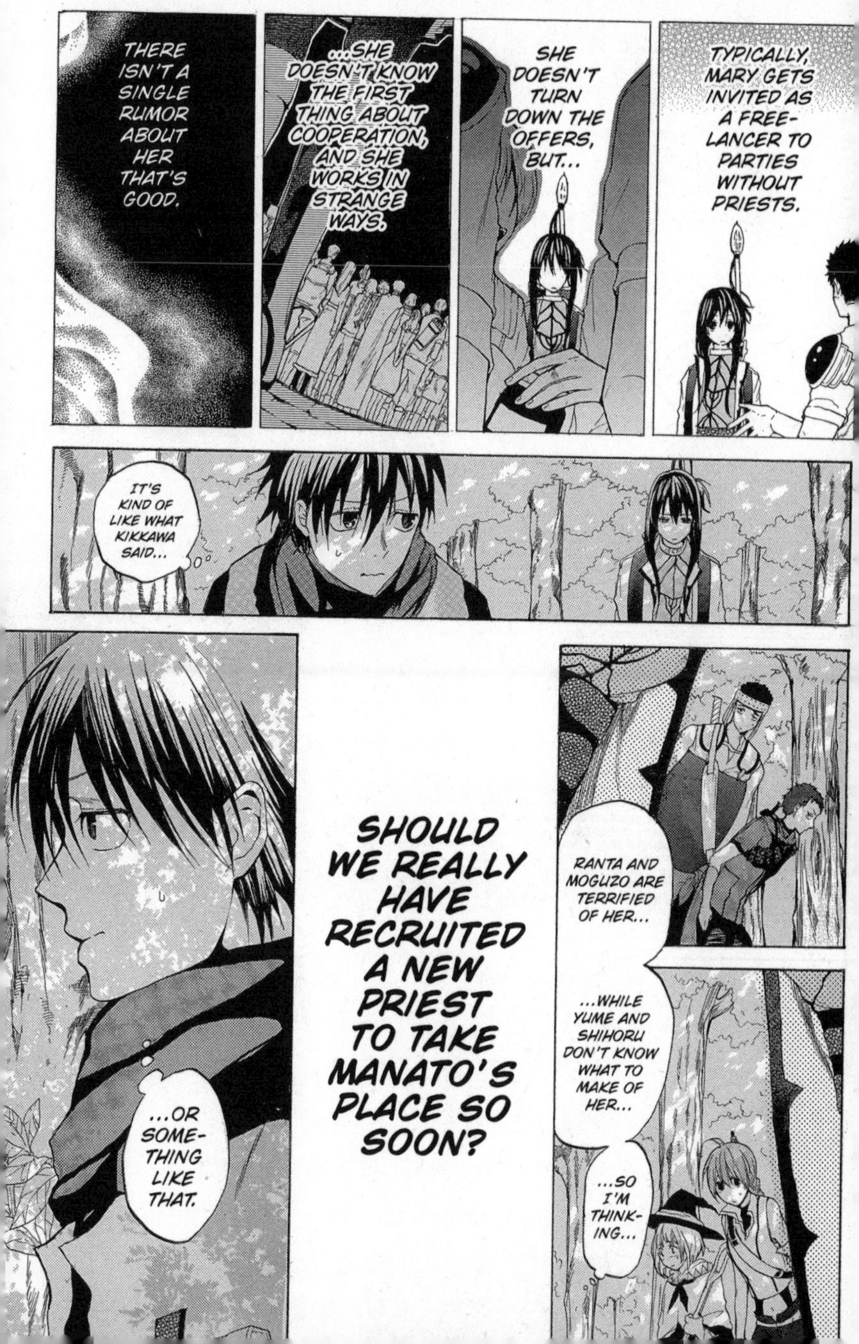
TYPICALLY, MARY GETS INVITED AS A FREELANCER TO PARTIES WITHOUT PRIESTS.
SHE DOESN'T TURN DOWN THE OFFERS, BUT...
...SHE DOESN'T KNOW THE FIRST THING ABOUT COOPERATION, AND SHE WORKS IN STRANGE WAYS.
THERE ISN'T A SINGLE RUMOR ABOUT HER THAT'S GOOD.
IT'S KIND OF LIKE WHAT KIKKAWA SAID...
RANTA AND MOGUZO ARE TERRIFIED OF HER...
...WHILE YUME AND SHIHORU DON'T KNOW WHAT TO MAKE OF HER...
...SO I'M THINKING...
SHOULD WE REALLY HAVE RECRUITED A NEW PRIEST TO TAKE MANATO'S PLACE SO SOON?
...OR SOMETHING LIKE THAT.

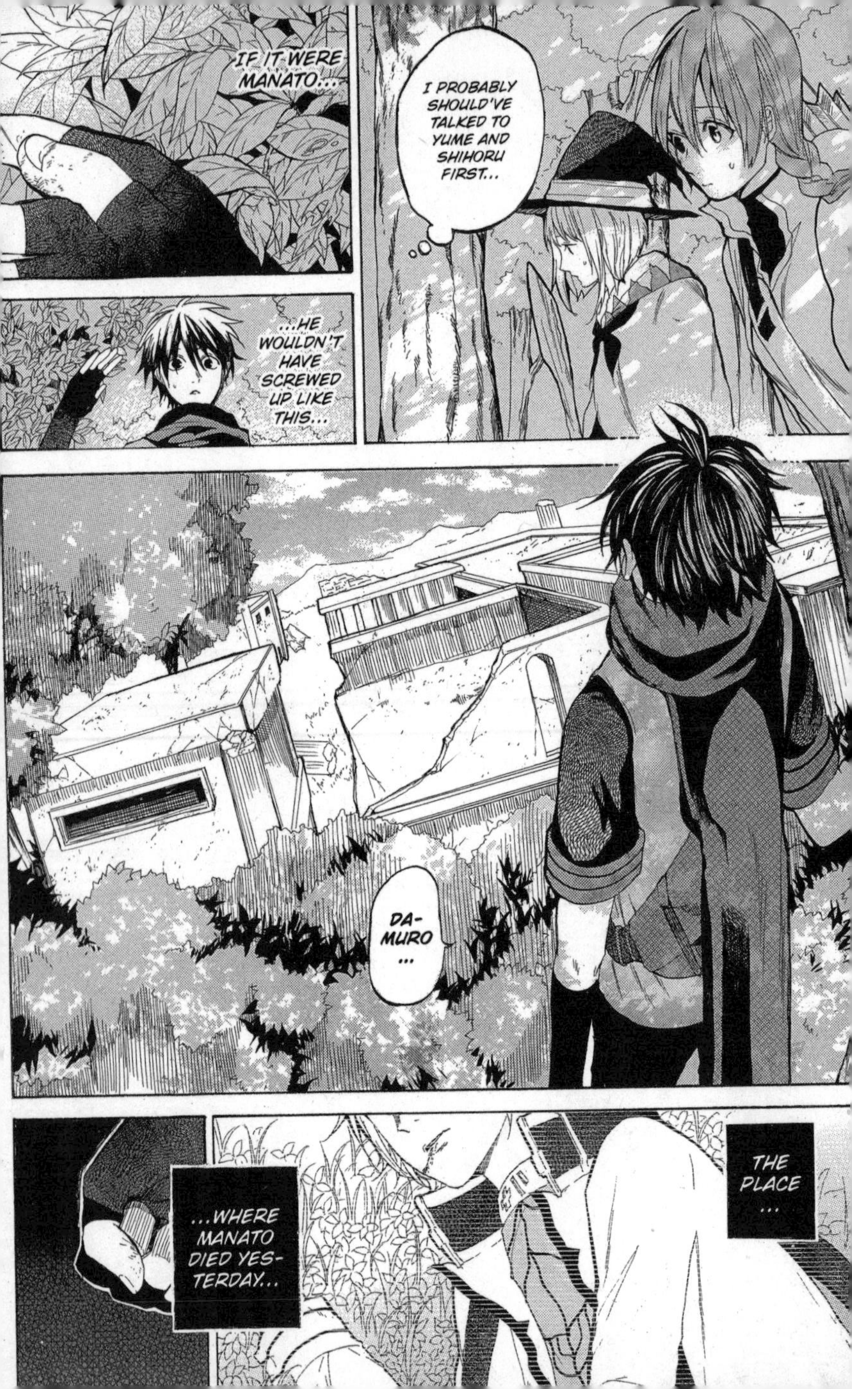
I PROBABLY SHOULD'VE TALKED TO YUME AND SHIHORU FIRST...
IF IT WERE MANATO...
...HE WOULDN'T HAVE SCREWED UP LIKE THIS...
DA-MURO ...
THE PLACE ...
...WHERE MANATO DIED YES-TERDAY...

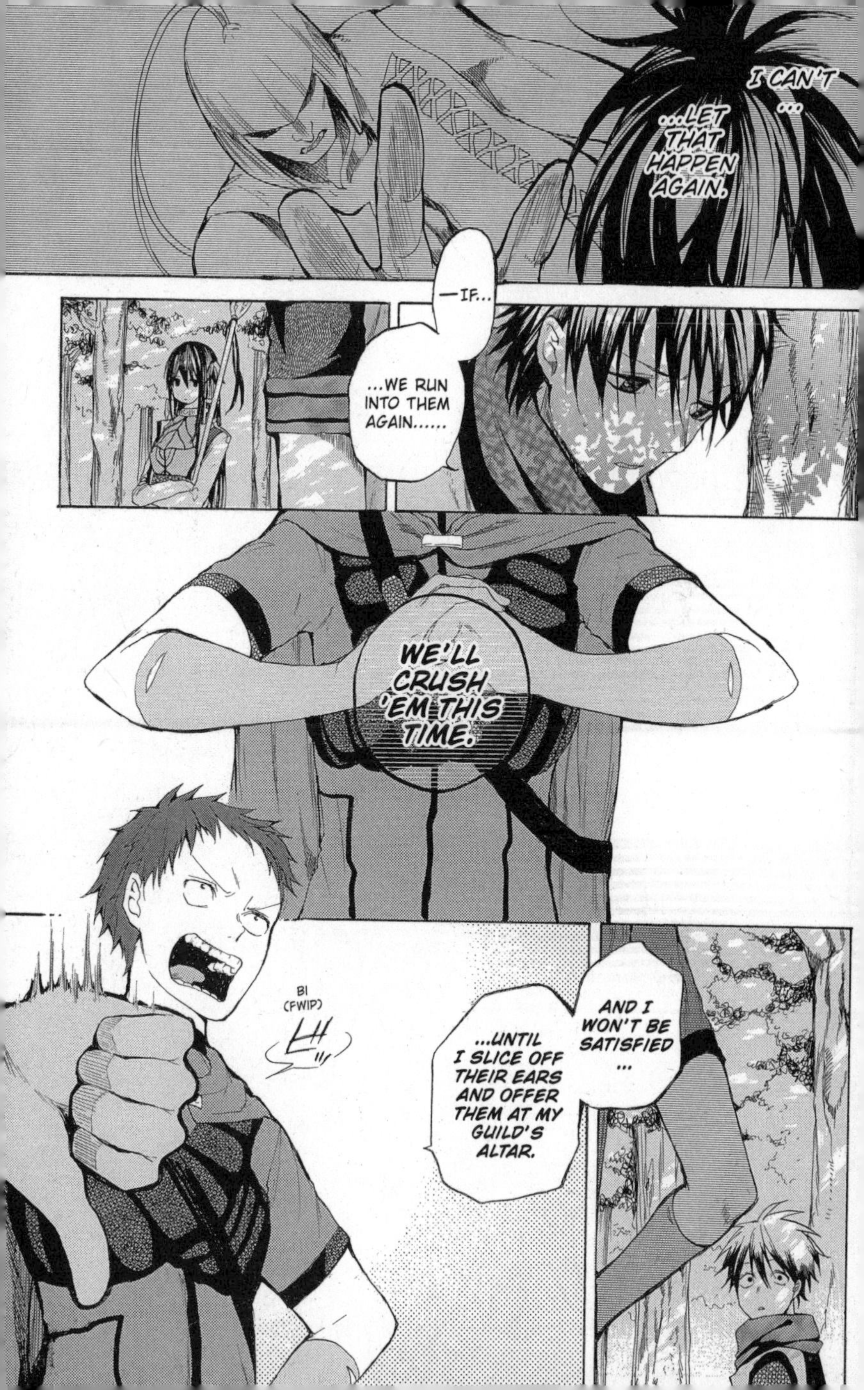
I CAN'T ...
...LET THAT HAPPEN AGAIN.
—IF...
...WE RUN INTO THEM AGAIN......
WE'LL CRUSH 'EM THIS TIME.
AND I WON'T BE SATISFIED ...
...UNTIL I SLICE OFF THEIR EARS AND OFFER THEM AT MY GUILD'S ALTAR.
BI (FWIP)

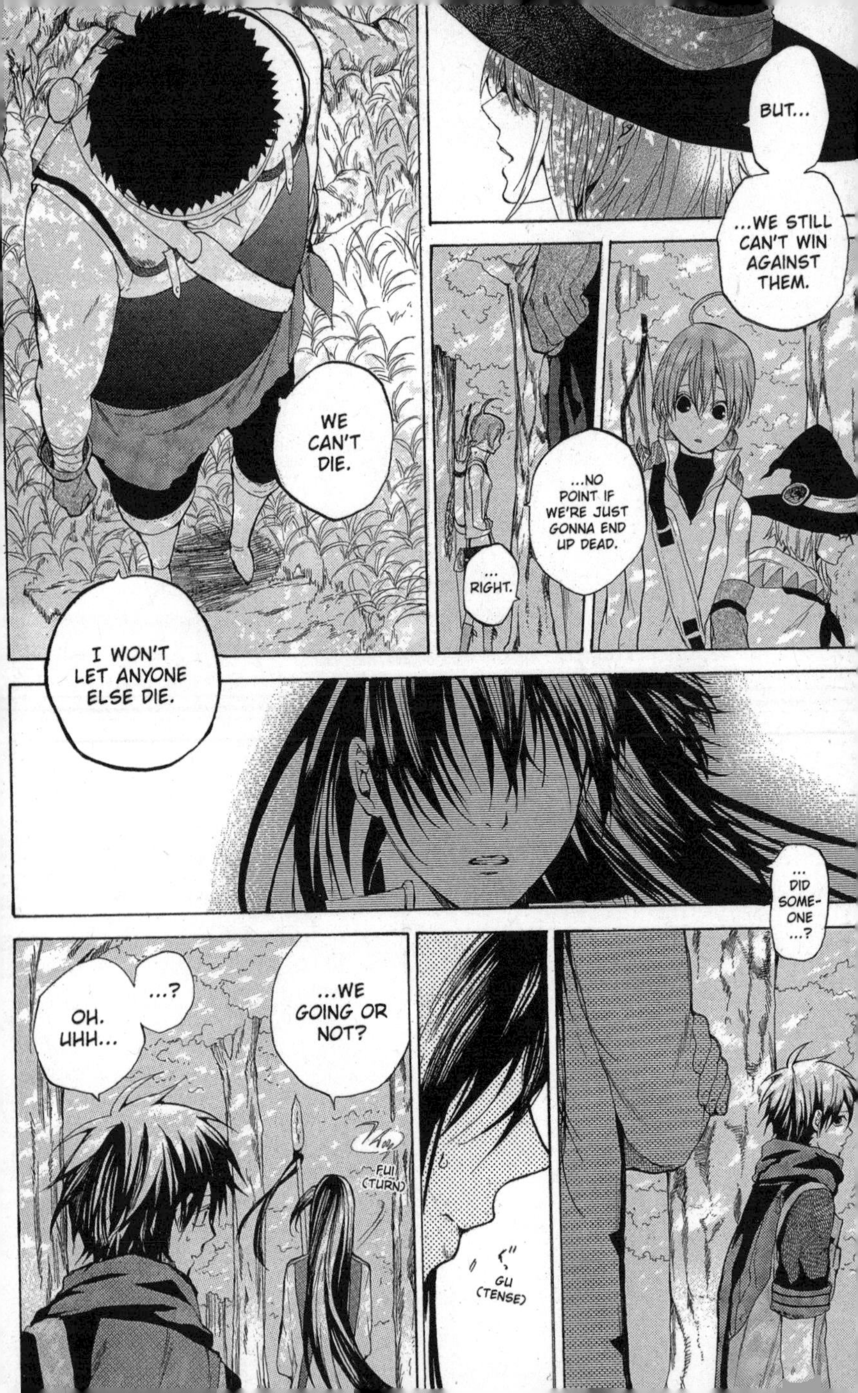
BUT...
...WE STILL CAN'T WIN AGAINST THEM.
...NO POINT IF WE'RE JUST GONNA END UP DEAD.
... RIGHT.
WE CAN'T DIE.
I WON'T LET ANYONE ELSE DIE.
... DID SOME-ONE ...?
GU (TENSE)
...WE GOING OR NOT?
FUI (TURN)
...?
OH. UHH...

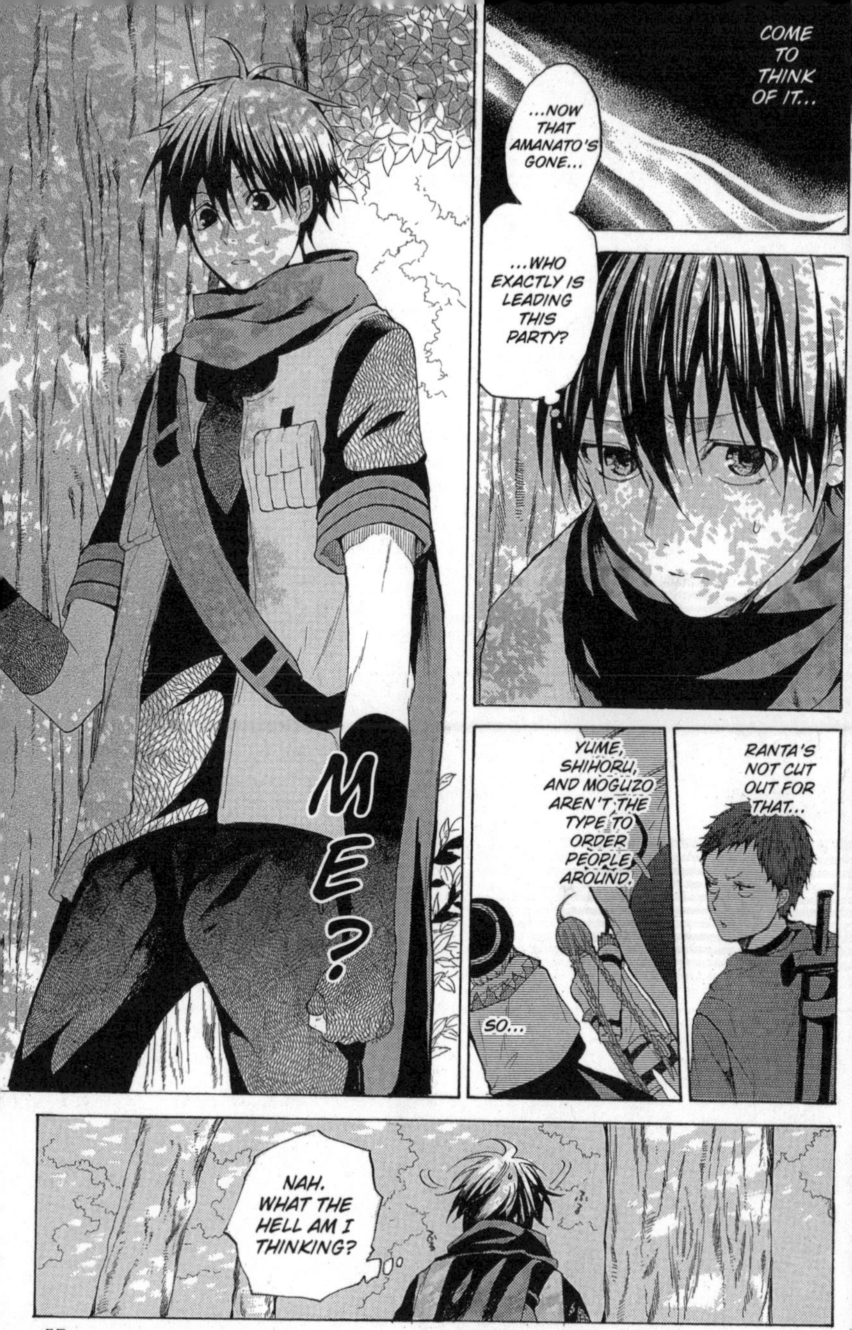
COME TO THINK OF IT...
...NOW THAT AMANATO'S GONE...
...WHO EXACTLY IS LEADING THIS PARTY?
RANTA'S NOT CUT OUT FOR THAT...
YUME, SHIHORU, AND MOGUZO AREN'T THE TYPE TO ORDER PEOPLE AROUND.
SO...
ME?
NAH. WHAT THE HELL AM I THINKING?

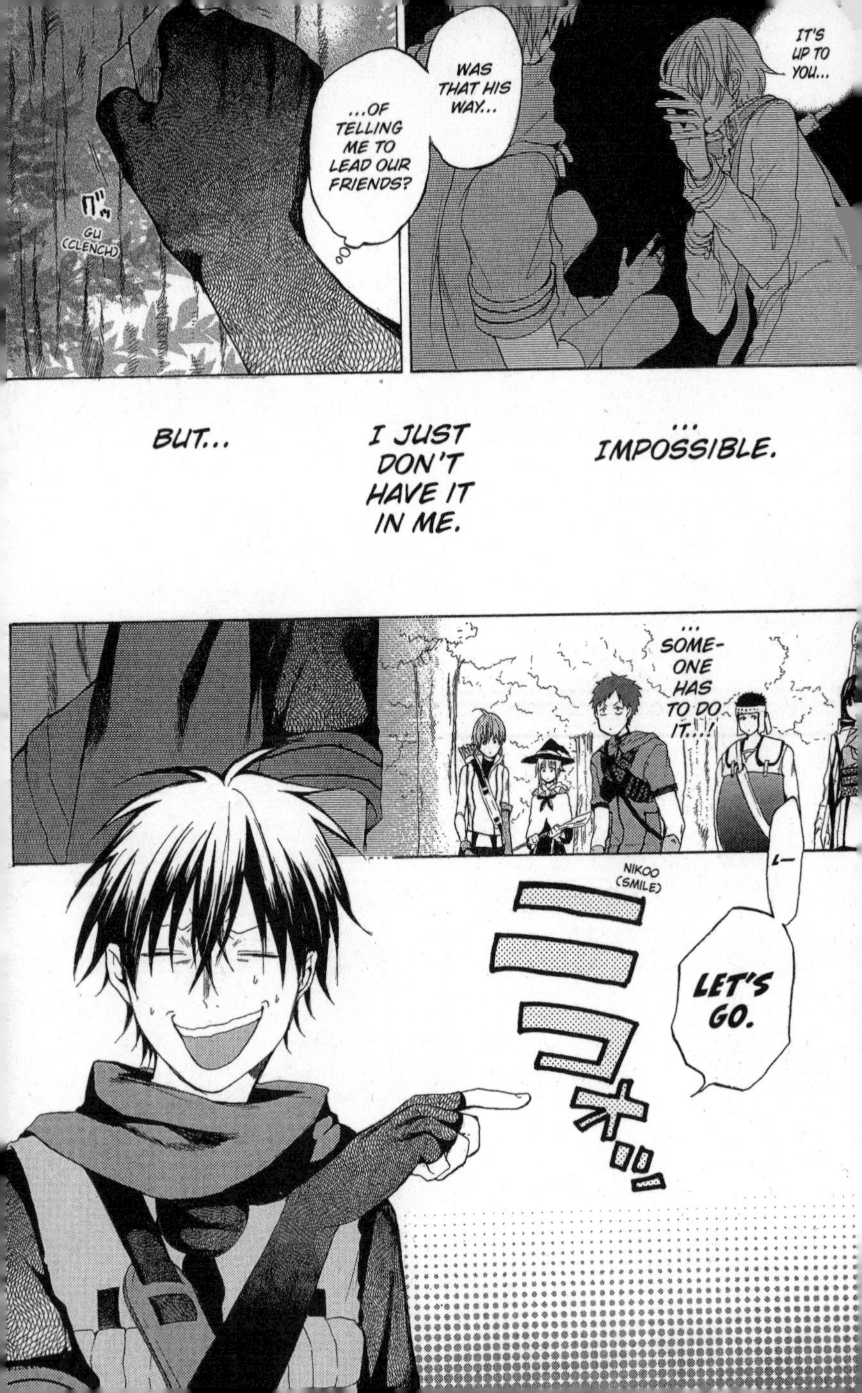
IT'S UP TO YOU...
WAS THAT HIS WAY...
...OF TELLING ME TO LEAD OUR FRIENDS?
GU (CLENCH)
...IMPOSSIBLE.
I JUST DON'T HAVE IT IN ME.
BUT...
...SOME-ONE HAS TO DO IT...!!
L—
LET'S GO.
NIKOO (SMILE)

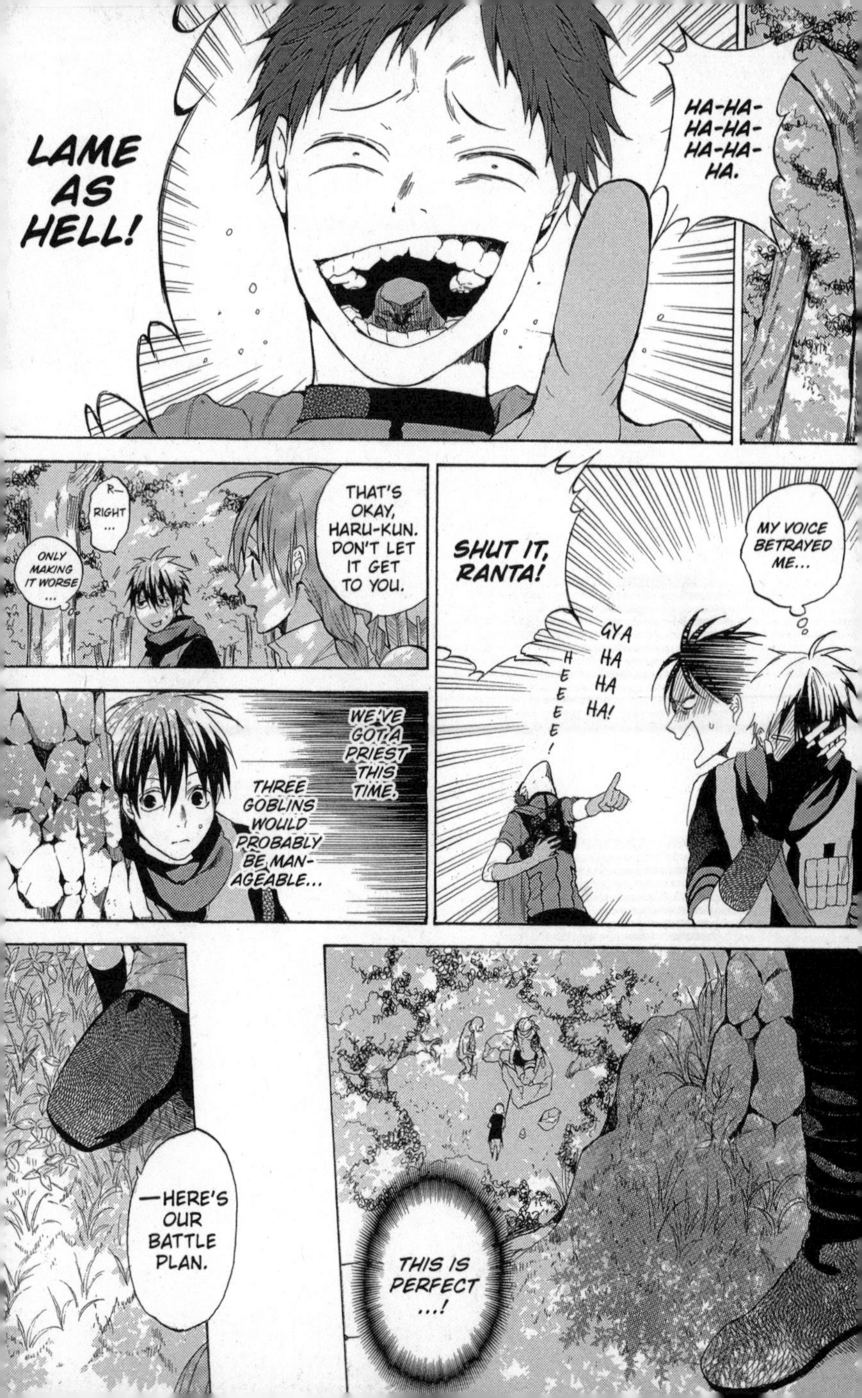
HA-HA-HA-HA-HA-HA-HA.
LAME AS HELL!
MY VOICE BETRAYED ME...
SHUT IT, RANTA!
GYA HA HA HA!
HEEEE!
THAT'S OKAY, HARU-KUN. DON'T LET IT GET TO YOU.
R—RIGHT...
ONLY MAKING IT WORSE...
WE'VE GOT A PRIEST THIS TIME.
THREE GOBLINS WOULD PROBABLY BE MANAGEABLE...
THIS IS PERFECT...!
—HERE'S OUR BATTLE PLAN.

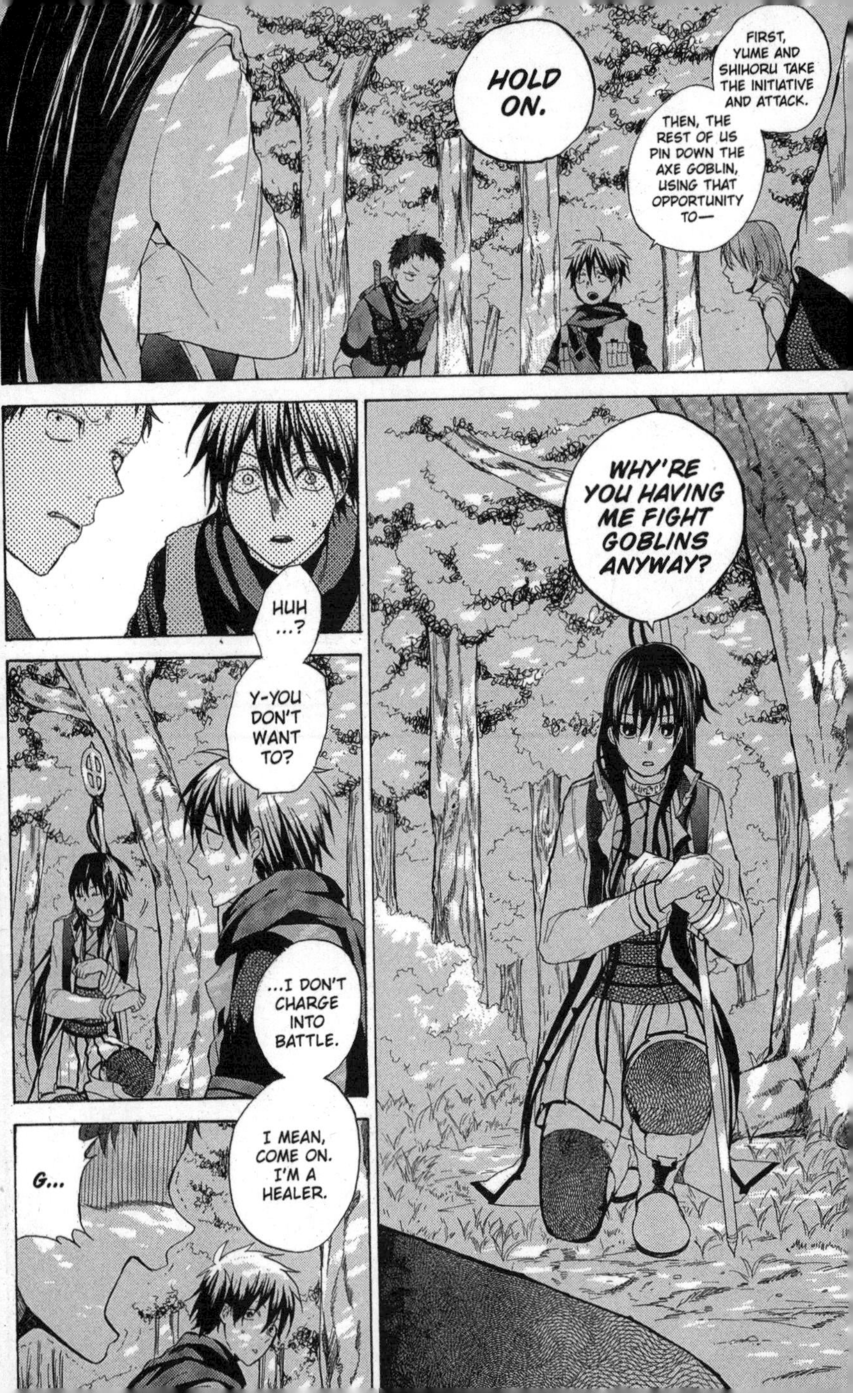
FIRST, YUME AND SHIHORU TAKE THE INITIATIVE AND ATTACK.
THEN, THE REST OF US PIN DOWN THE AXE GOBLIN, USING THAT OPPORTUNITY TO—
HOLD ON.
WHY'RE YOU HAVING ME FIGHT GOBLINS ANYWAY?
HUH ...?
Y-YOU DON'T WANT TO?
...I DON'T CHARGE INTO BATTLE.
I MEAN, COME ON. I'M A HEALER.
G...

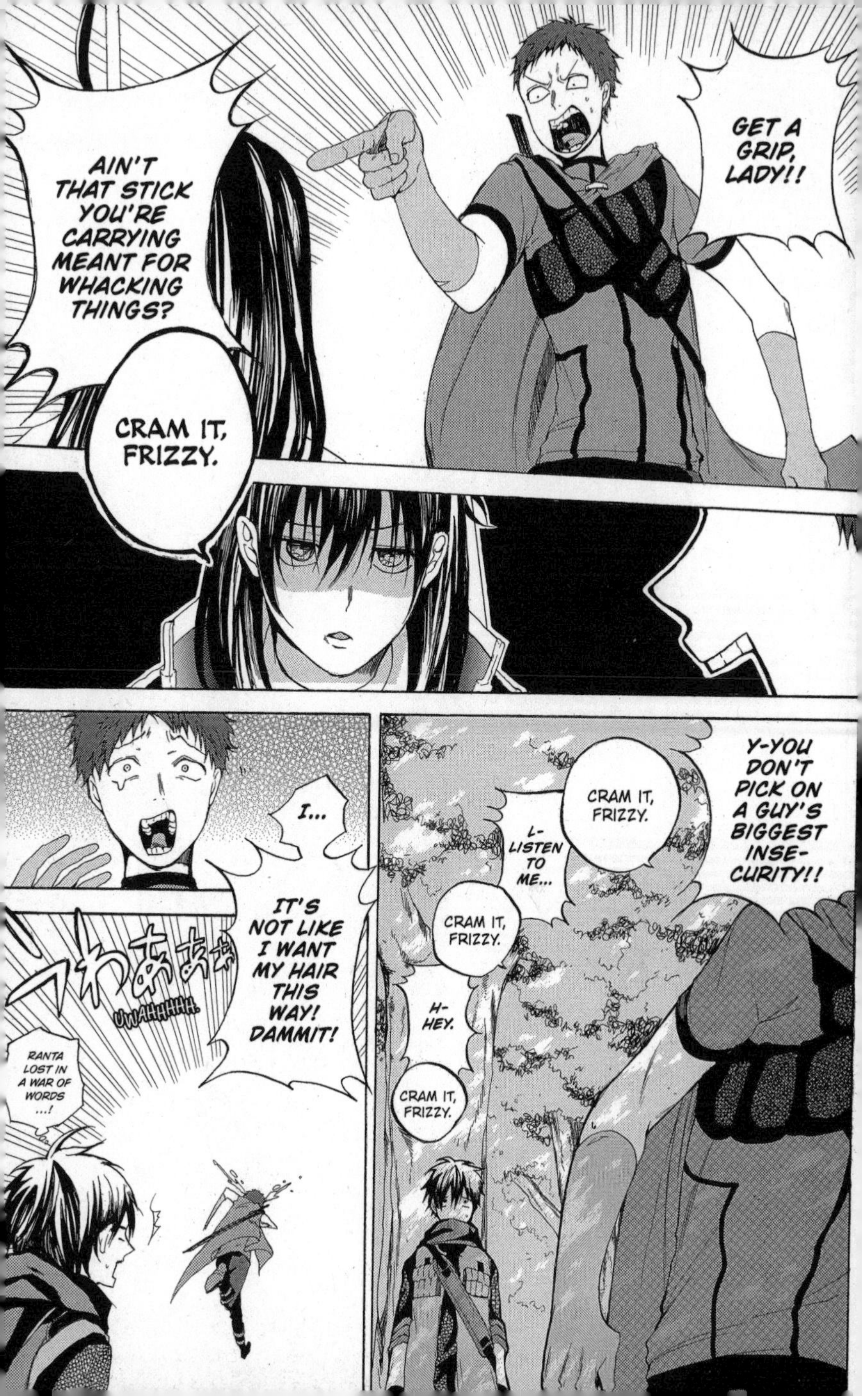
GET A GRIP, LADY!!
AIN'T THAT STICK YOU'RE CARRYING MEANT FOR WHACKING THINGS?
CRAM IT, FRIZZY.
Y-YOU DON'T PICK ON A GUY'S BIGGEST INSE-CURITY!!
CRAM IT, FRIZZY.
L-LISTEN TO ME...
CRAM IT, FRIZZY.
H-HEY.
CRAM IT, FRIZZY.
I...
IT'S NOT LIKE I WANT MY HAIR THIS WAY! DAMMIT!
わあああ
UWAHHHHH
RANTA LOST IN A WAR OF WORDS ...!

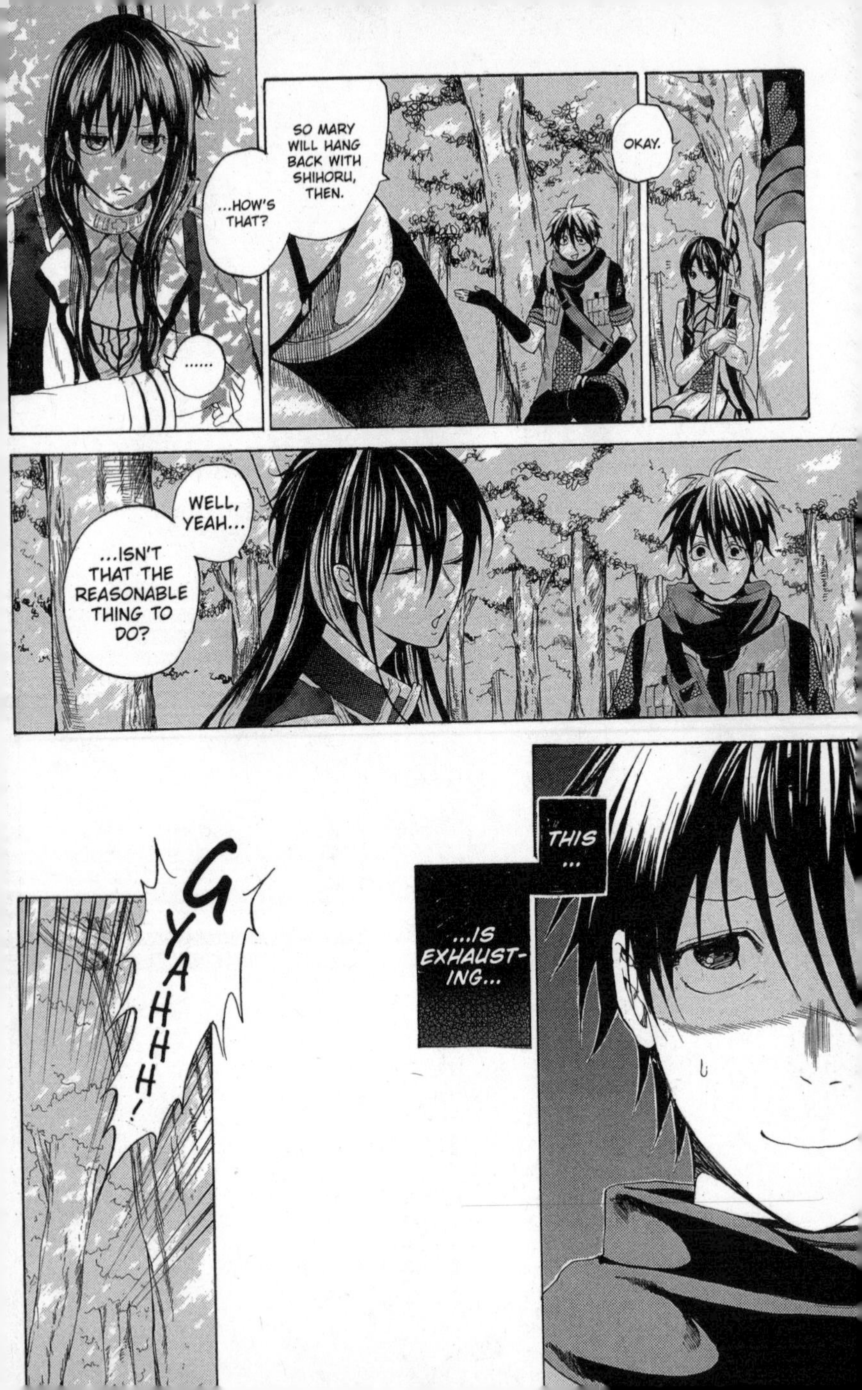
OKAY.
SO MARY WILL HANG BACK WITH SHIHORU, THEN.
...HOW'S THAT?
......
WELL, YEAH...
...ISN'T THAT THE REASONABLE THING TO DO?
THIS...
...IS EXHAUST-ING...
GYAHHH!

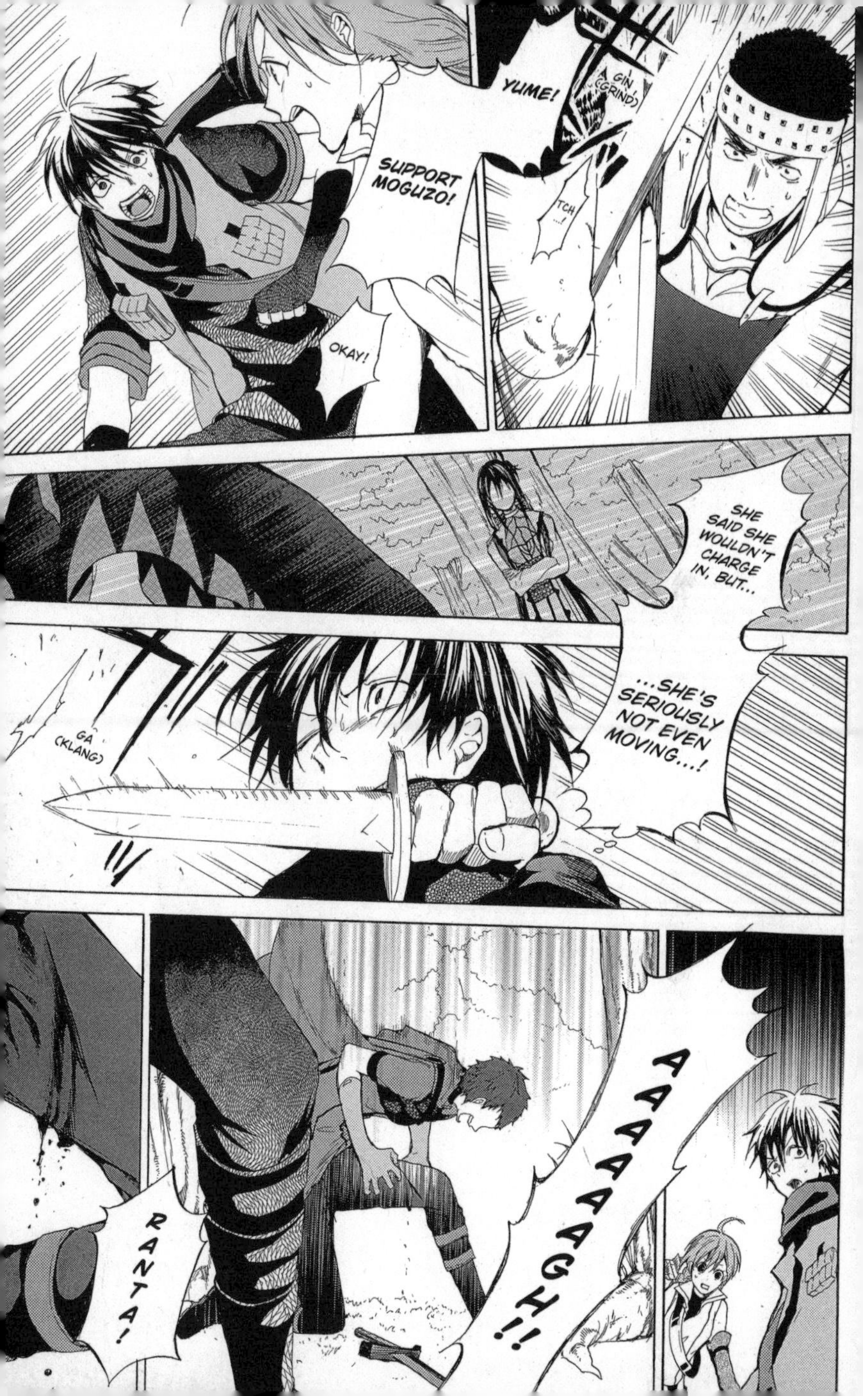
YUME!
A GIN (GRIND)
TCH ...!
SUPPORT MOGUZO!
OKAY!
SHE SAID SHE WOULDN'T CHARGE IN, BUT...
...SHE'S SERIOUSLY NOT EVEN MOVING...!
GA (KLANG)
AAAAAAAGH!!
RANTA!

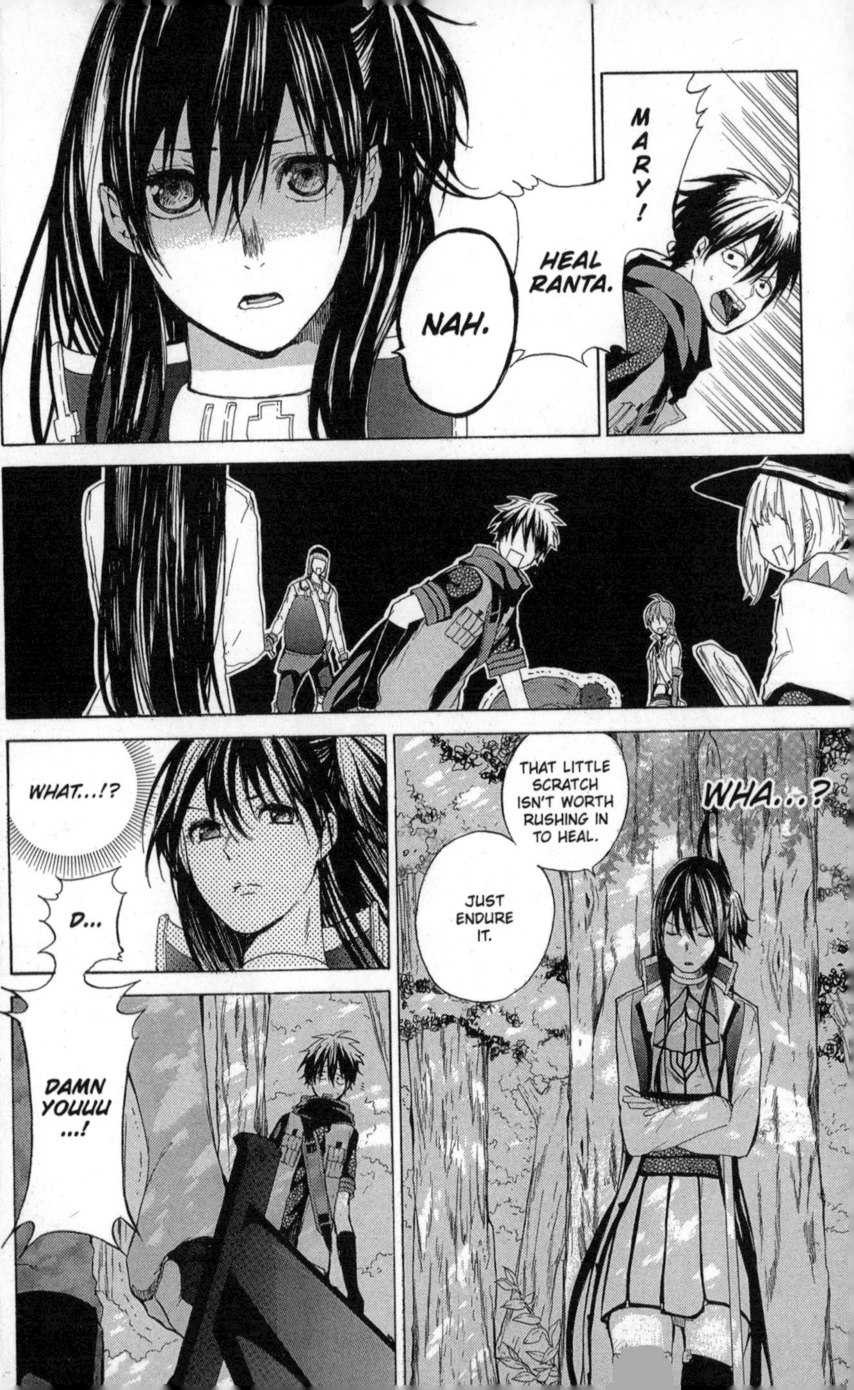
MARY!
HEAL RANTA.
NAH.
WHA...?
THAT LITTLE SCRATCH ISN'T WORTH RUSHING IN TO HEAL.
JUST ENDURE IT.
WHAT...!?
D...
DAMN YOUUU...!

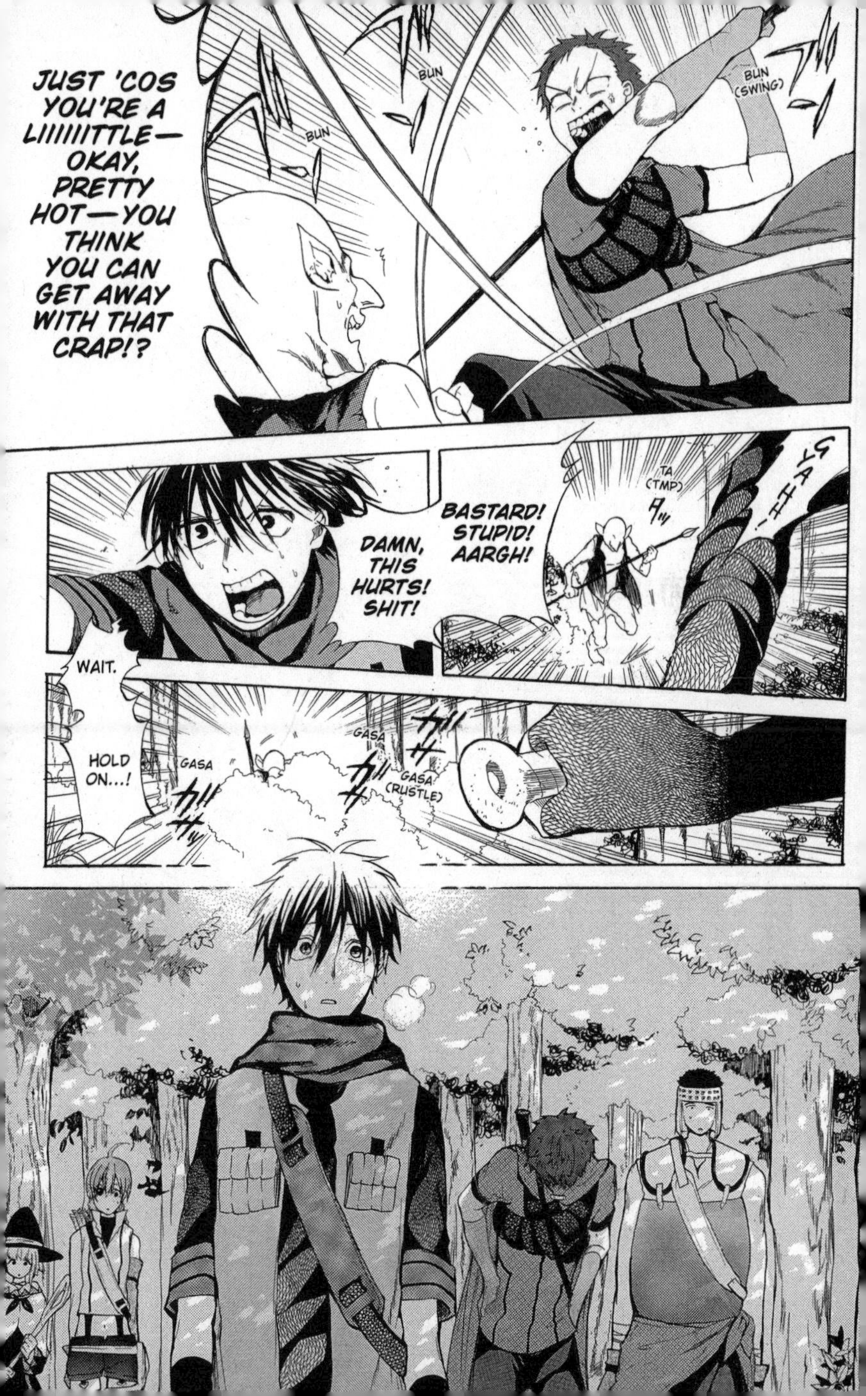
BUN (SWING)
BUN
BUN
JUST 'COS YOU'RE A LIIIIIIITTLE— OKAY, PRETTY HOT—YOU THINK YOU CAN GET AWAY WITH THAT CRAP!?
TA (TMP)
BASTARD! STUPID! AARGH!
DAMN, THIS HURTS! SHIT!
WAIT.
GASA
GASA (RUSTLE)
GASA
HOLD ON...!

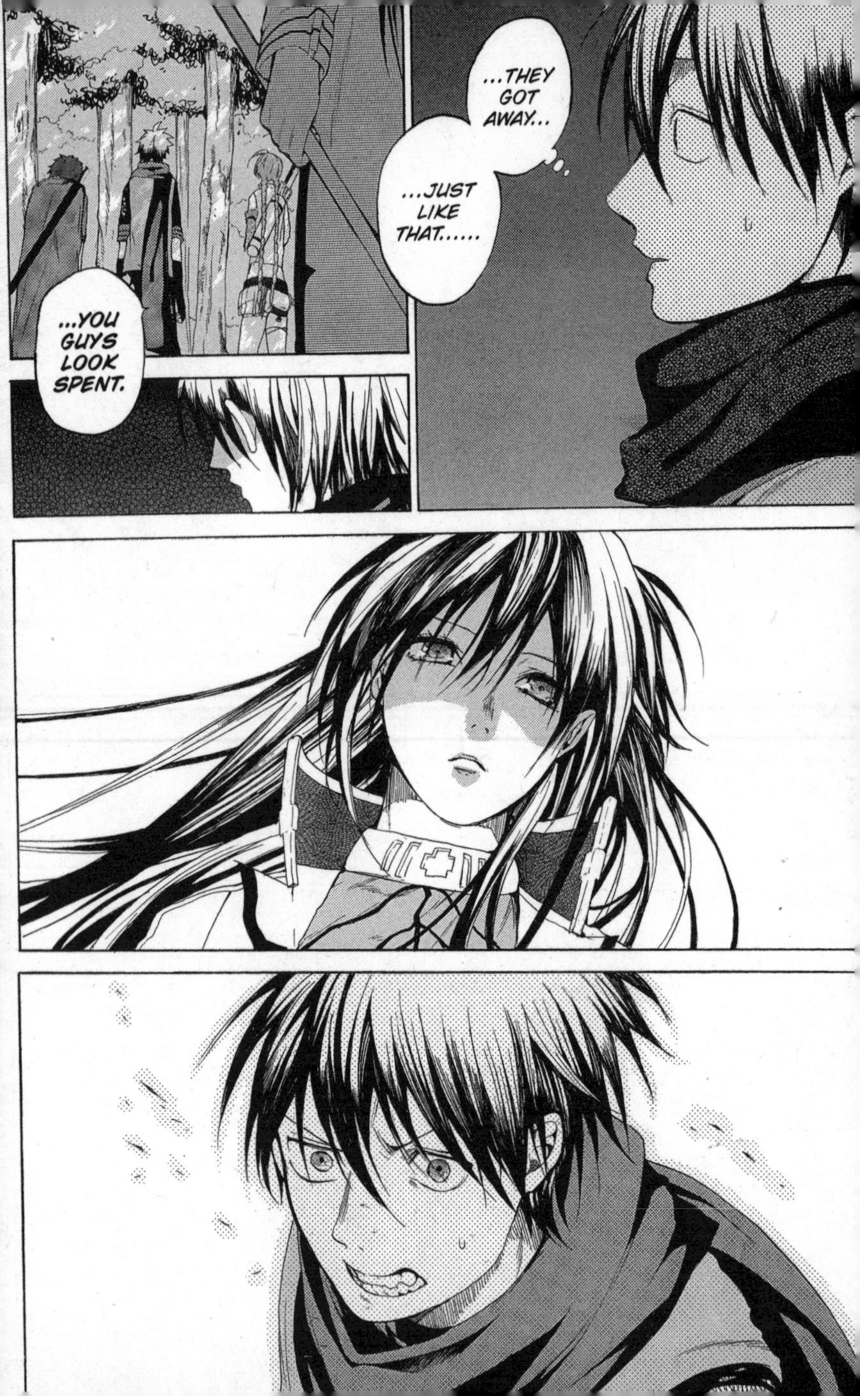
...THEY GOT AWAY...
...JUST LIKE THAT......
...YOU GUYS LOOK SPENT.

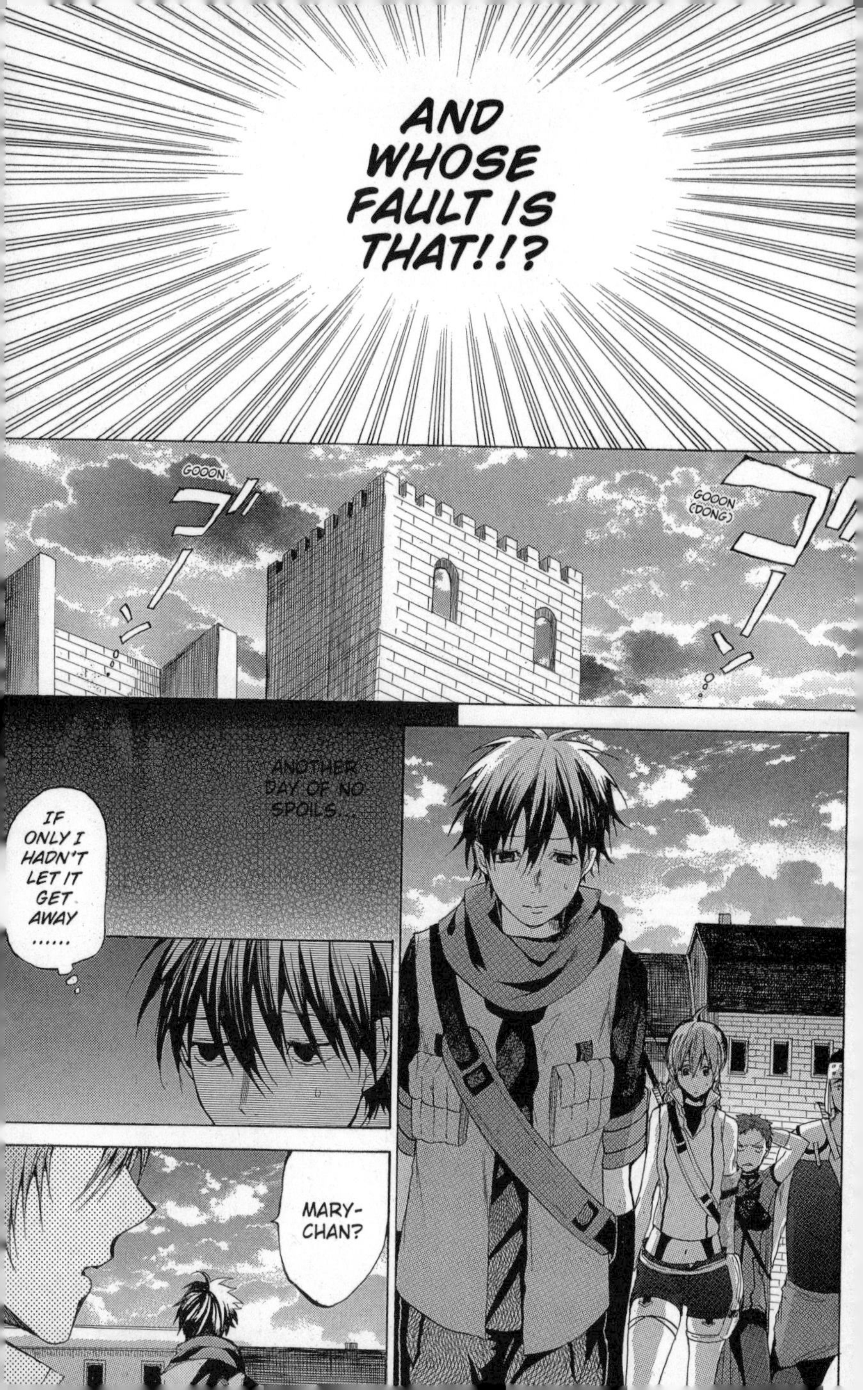
AND WHOSE FAULT IS THAT!!?
GOOON (DONG)
GOOON
ANOTHER DAY OF NO SPOILS...
IF ONLY I HADN'T LET IT GET AWAY......
MARY-CHAN?

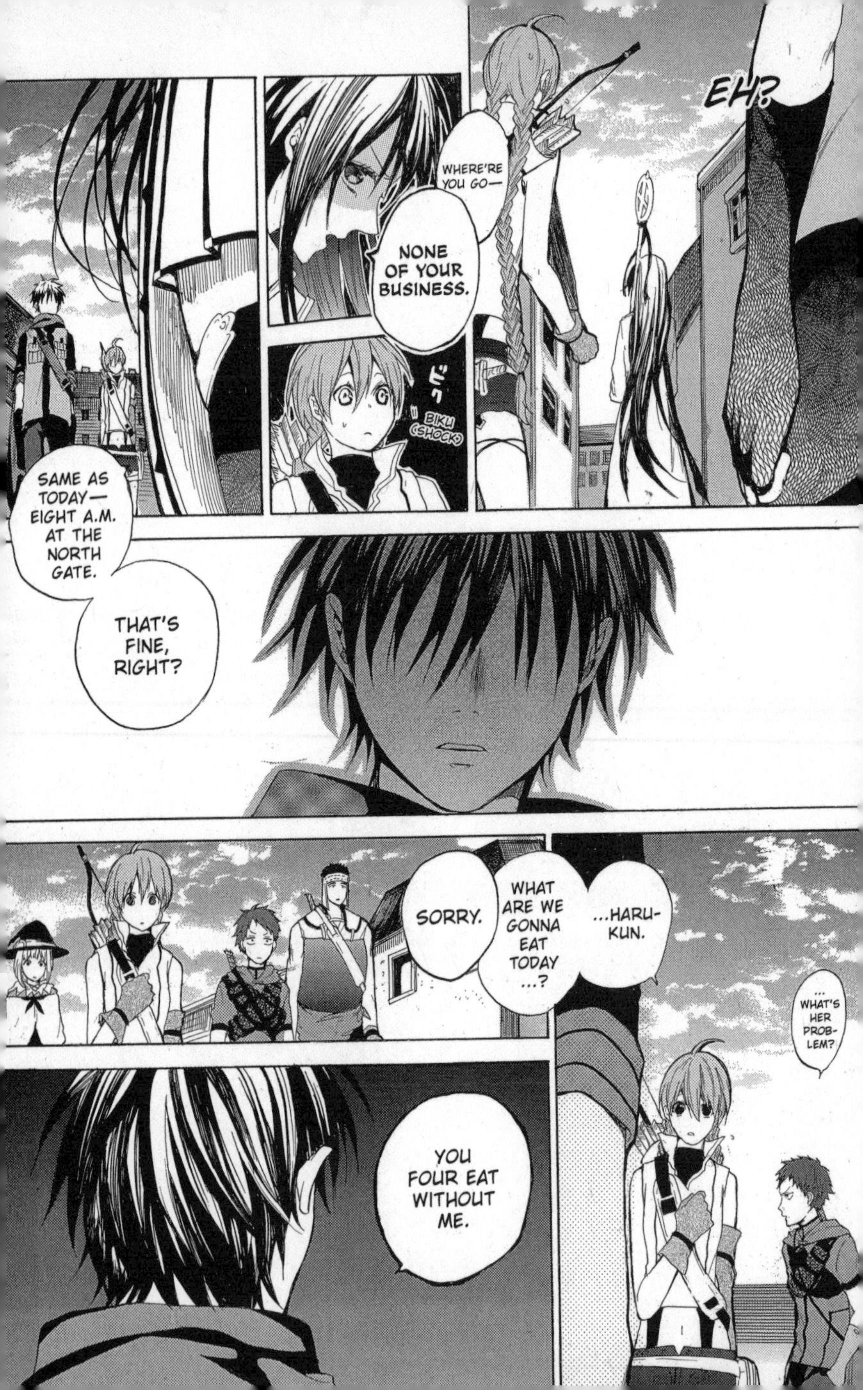
EH?
WHERE'RE YOU GO—
NONE OF YOUR BUSINESS.
ビク
BIKU (SHOCK)
SAME AS TODAY— EIGHT A.M. AT THE NORTH GATE.
THAT'S FINE, RIGHT?
...HARU-KUN.
WHAT ARE WE GONNA EAT TODAY ...?
...WHAT'S HER PROBLEM?
SORRY.
YOU FOUR EAT WITHOUT ME.

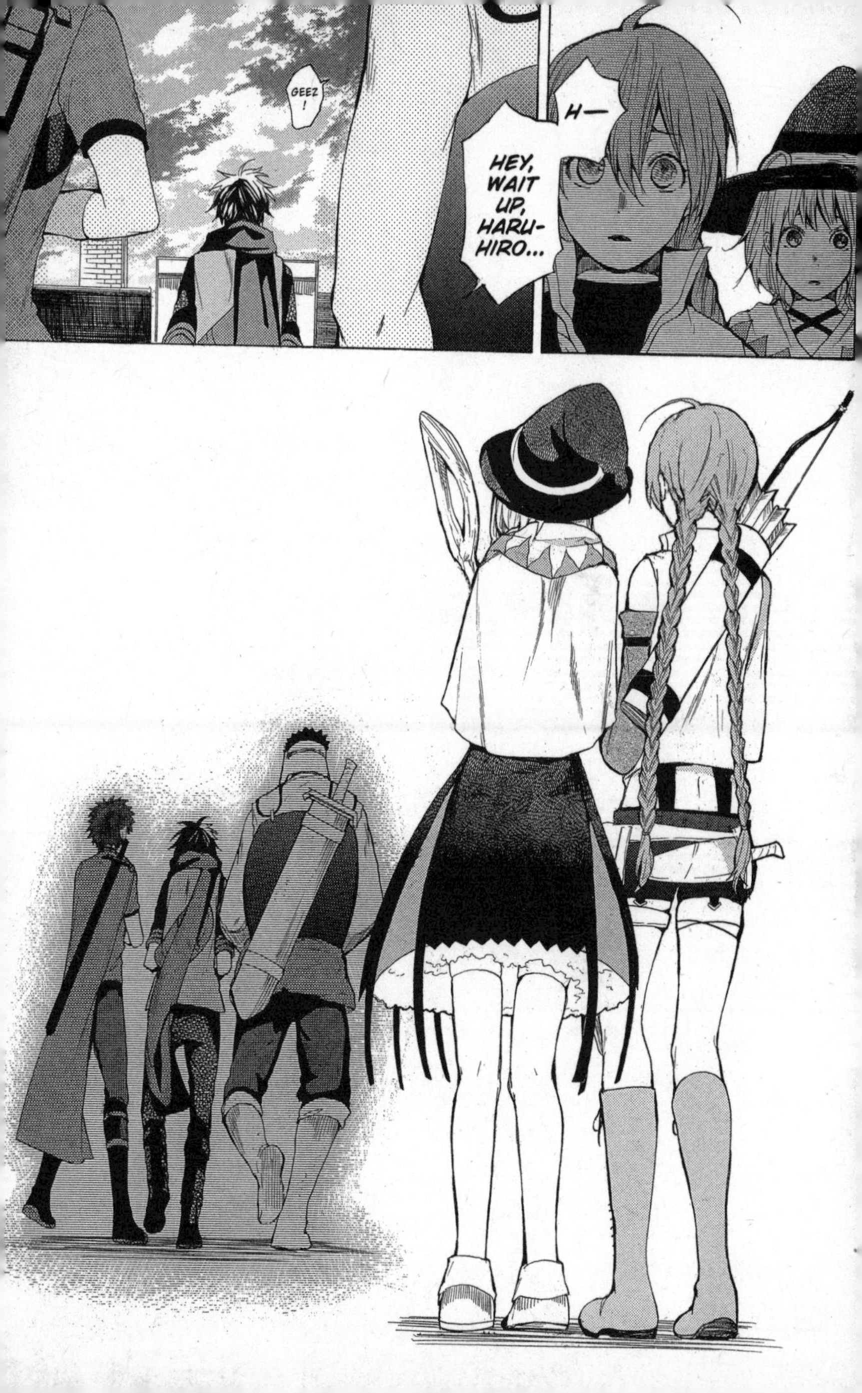
H—
HEY, WAIT UP, HARU-HIRO...
GEEZ!

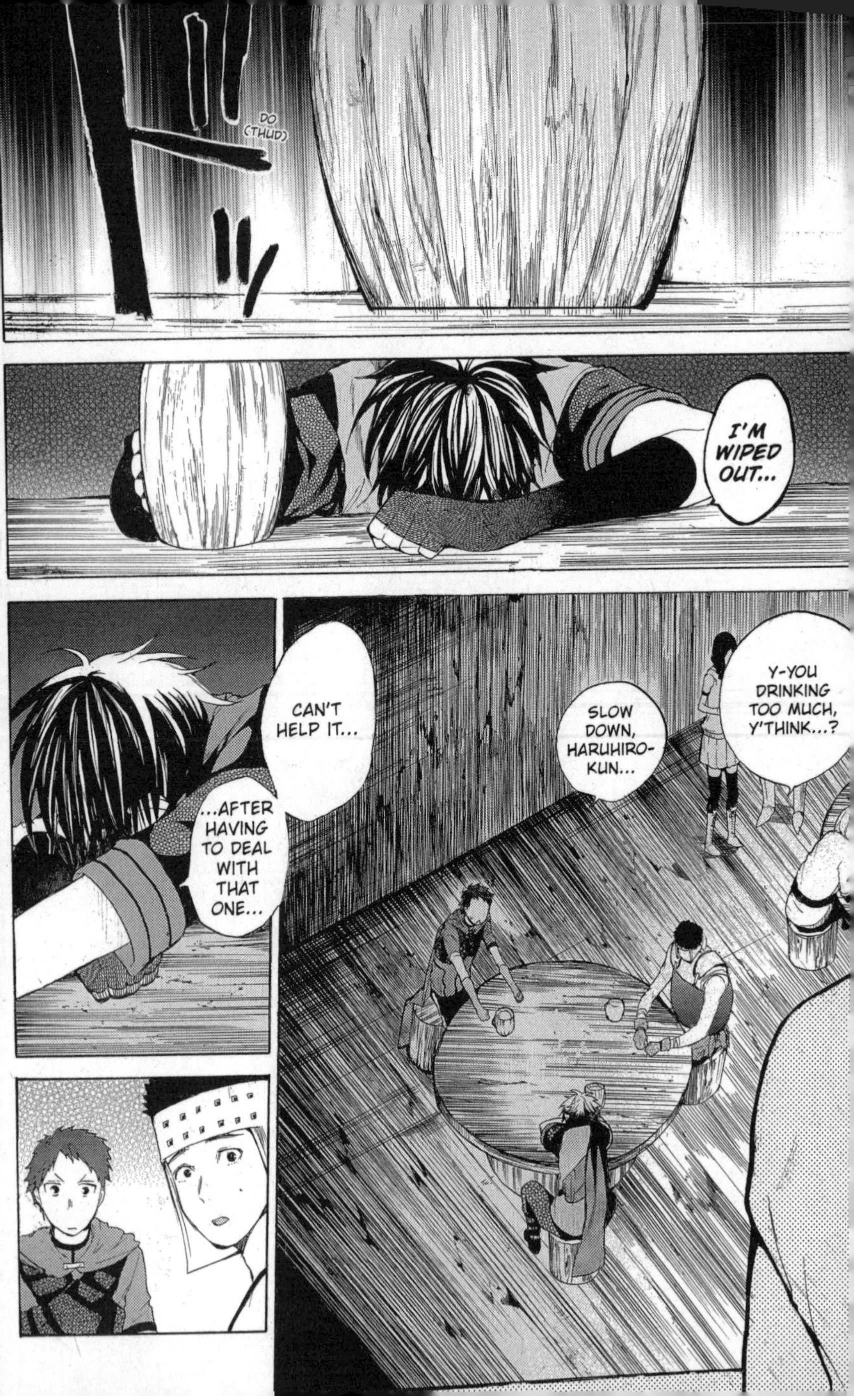
DO (THUD)
I'M WIPED OUT...
Y-YOU DRINKING TOO MUCH, Y'THINK...?
SLOW DOWN, HARUHIRO-KUN...
CAN'T HELP IT...
...AFTER HAVING TO DEAL WITH THAT ONE...

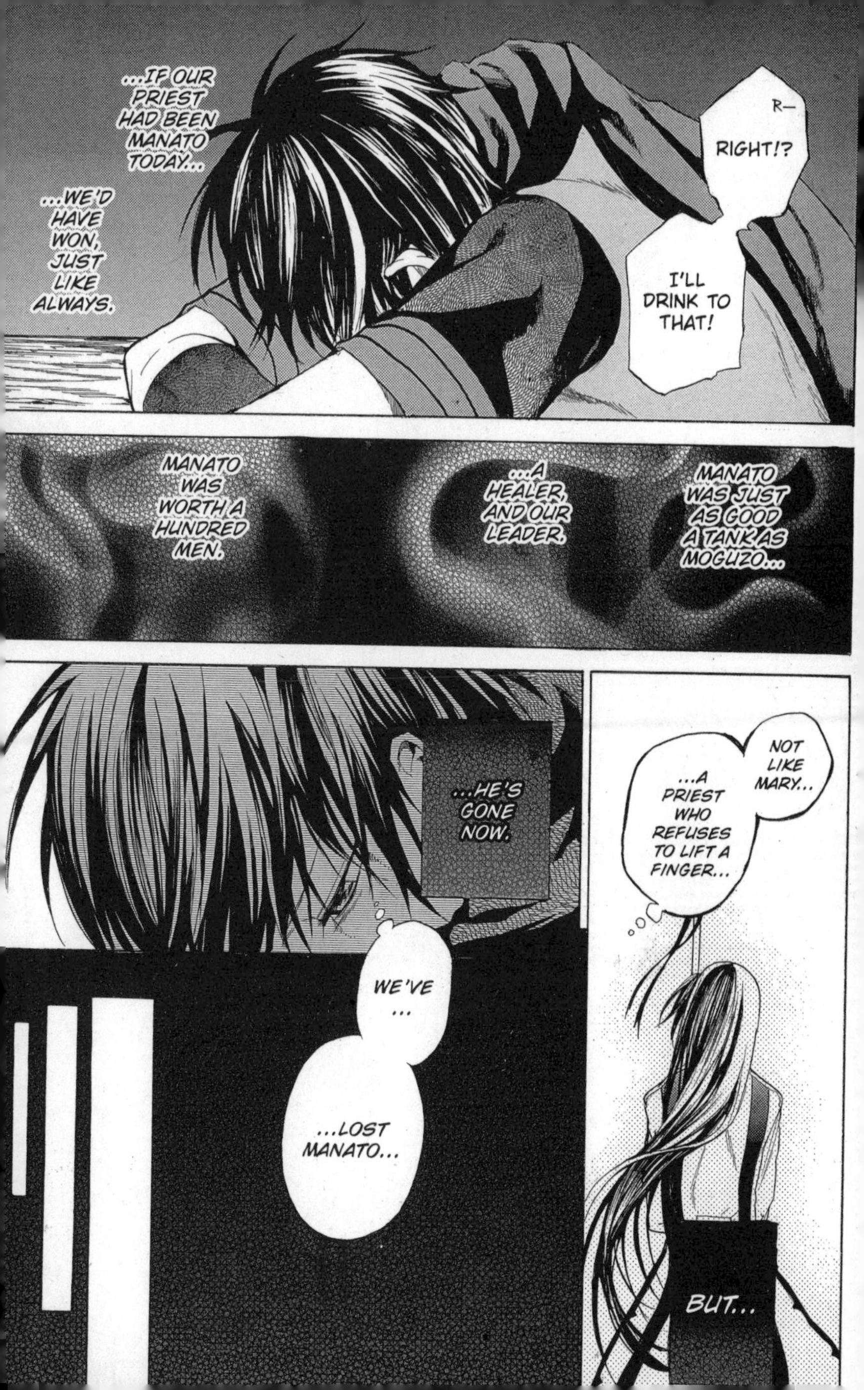
R— RIGHT!?
I'LL DRINK TO THAT!
...IF OUR PRIEST HAD BEEN MANATO TODAY...
...WE'D HAVE WON, JUST LIKE ALWAYS.
MANATO WAS JUST AS GOOD A TANK AS MOGUZO...
...A HEALER, AND OUR LEADER.
MANATO WAS WORTH A HUNDRED MEN.
NOT LIKE MARY...
...A PRIEST WHO REFUSES TO LIFT A FINGER...
BUT...
...HE'S GONE NOW.
WE'VE...
...LOST MANATO...

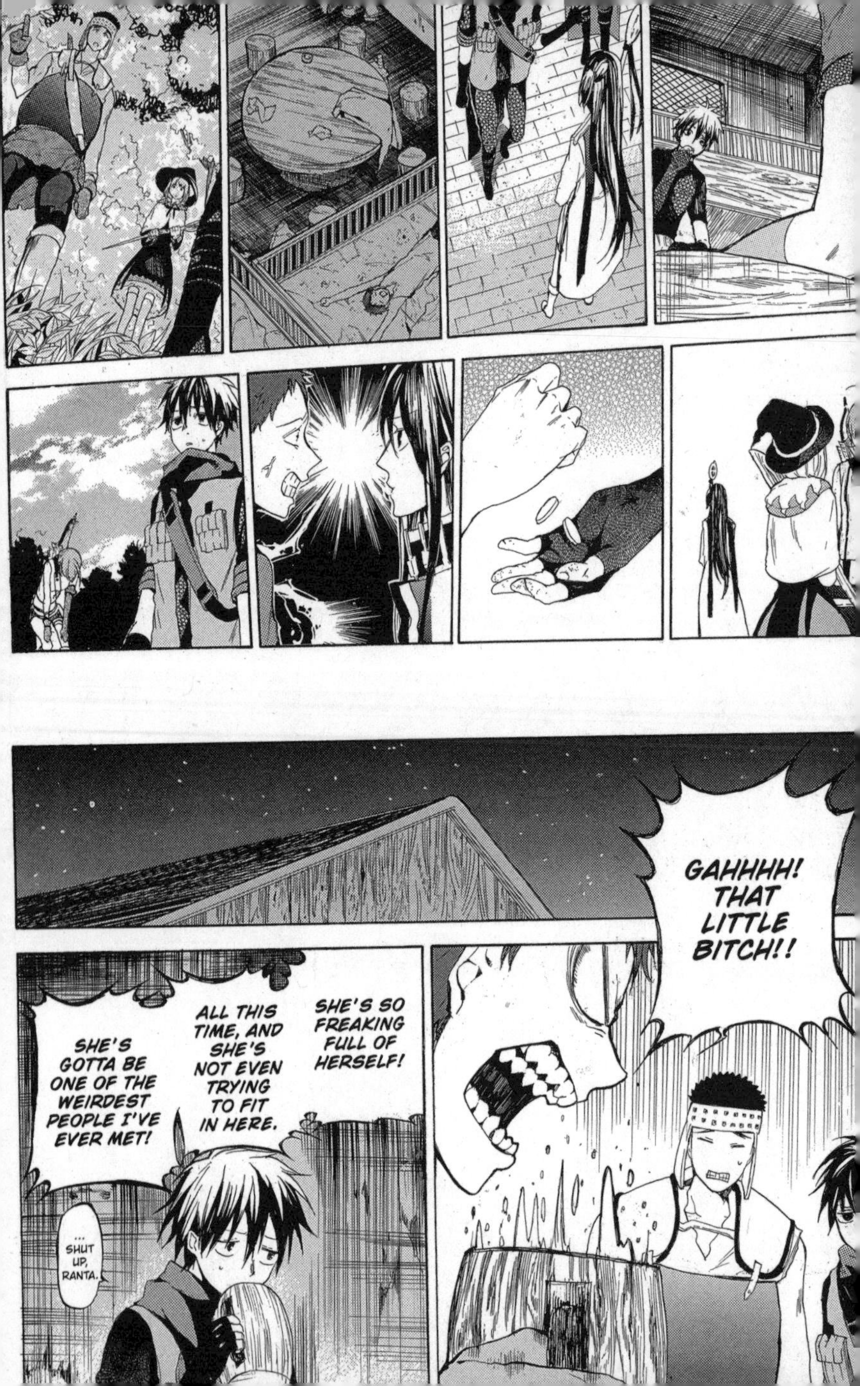
GAHHHH! THAT LITTLE BITCH!!
SHE'S SO FREAKING FULL OF HERSELF!
ALL THIS TIME, AND SHE'S NOT EVEN TRYING TO FIT IN HERE.
SHE'S GOTTA BE ONE OF THE WEIRDEST PEOPLE I'VE EVER MET!
... SHUT UP, RANTA.

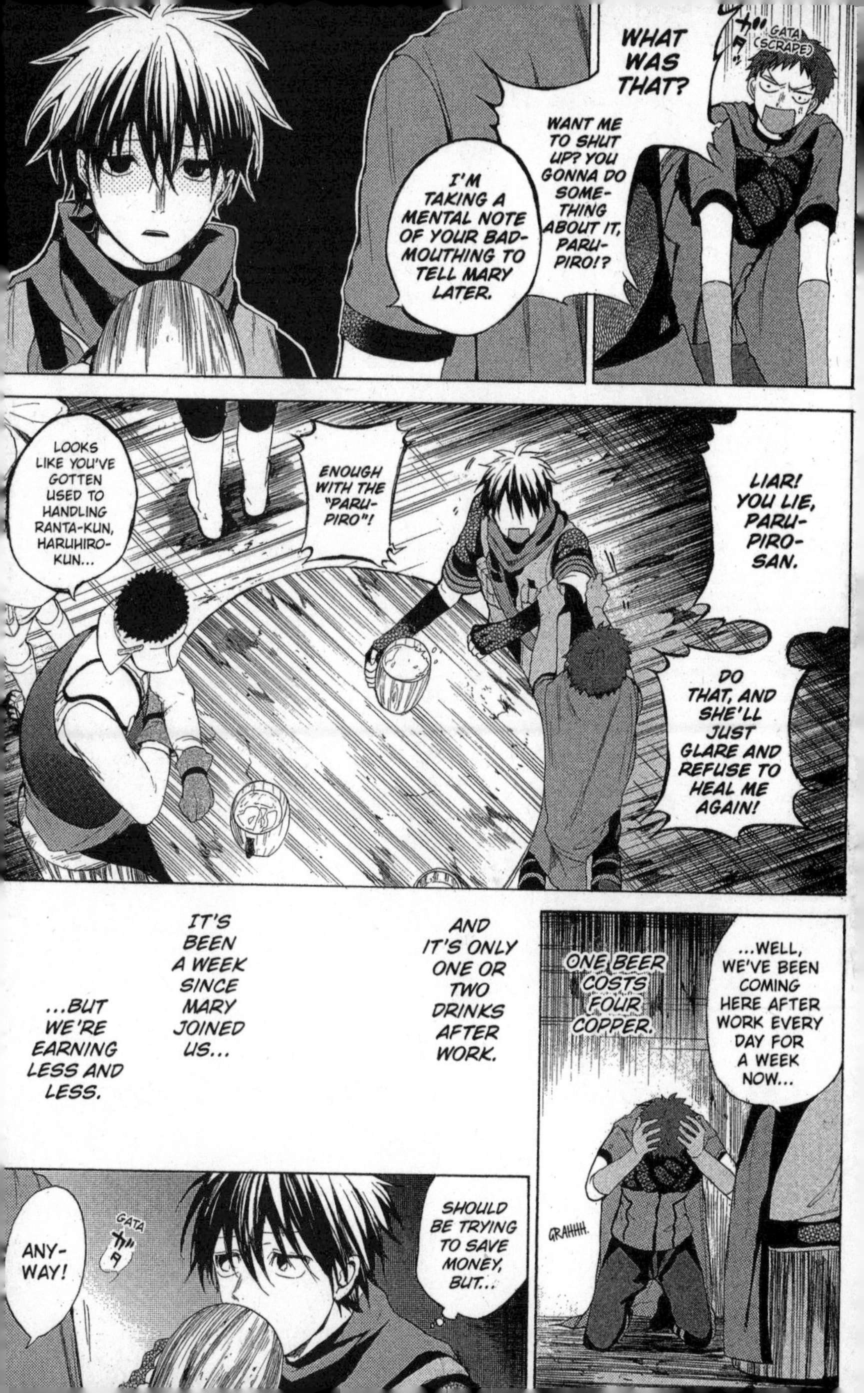
GATA (SCRAPE)
WHAT WAS THAT?
WANT ME TO SHUT UP? YOU GONNA DO SOMETHING ABOUT IT, PARU-PIRO!?
I'M TAKING A MENTAL NOTE OF YOUR BAD-MOUTHING TO TELL MARY LATER.
LIAR! YOU LIE, PARU-PIRO-SAN.
DO THAT, AND SHE'LL JUST GLARE AND REFUSE TO HEAL ME AGAIN!
ENOUGH WITH THE "PARU-PIRO"!
LOOKS LIKE YOU'VE GOTTEN USED TO HANDLING RANTA-KUN, HARUHIRO-KUN...
...WELL, WE'VE BEEN COMING HERE AFTER WORK EVERY DAY FOR A WEEK NOW...
ONE BEER COSTS FOUR COPPER.
GRAHHH.
AND IT'S ONLY ONE OR TWO DRINKS AFTER WORK.
IT'S BEEN A WEEK SINCE MARY JOINED US...
...BUT WE'RE EARNING LESS AND LESS.
SHOULD BE TRYING TO SAVE MONEY, BUT...
GATA
ANY-WAY!

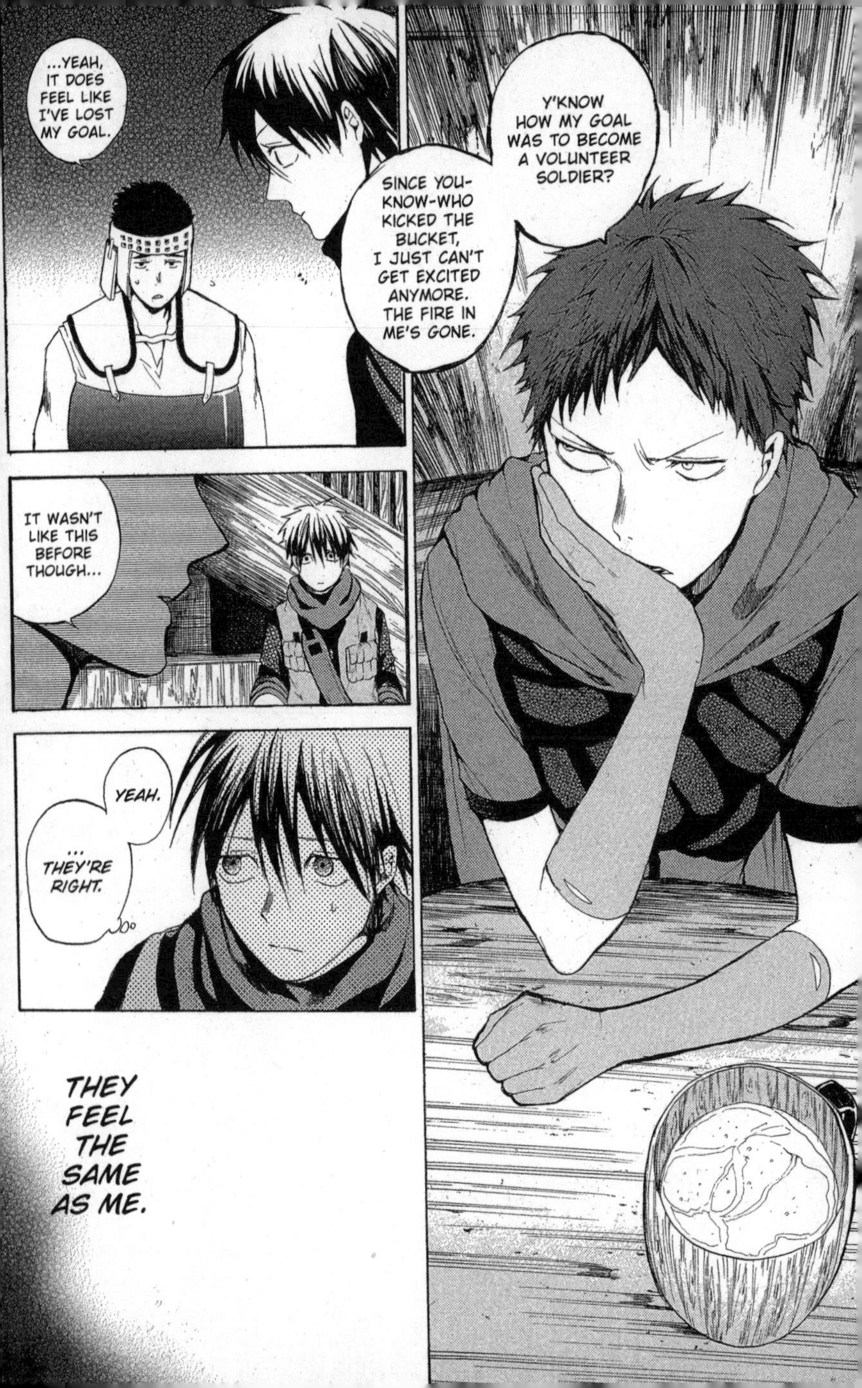
Y'KNOW HOW MY GOAL WAS TO BECOME A VOLUNTEER SOLDIER?
SINCE YOU-KNOW-WHO KICKED THE BUCKET, I JUST CAN'T GET EXCITED ANYMORE. THE FIRE IN ME'S GONE.
...YEAH, IT DOES FEEL LIKE I'VE LOST MY GOAL.
IT WASN'T LIKE THIS BEFORE THOUGH...
YEAH.
...THEY'RE RIGHT.
THEY FEEL THE SAME AS ME.

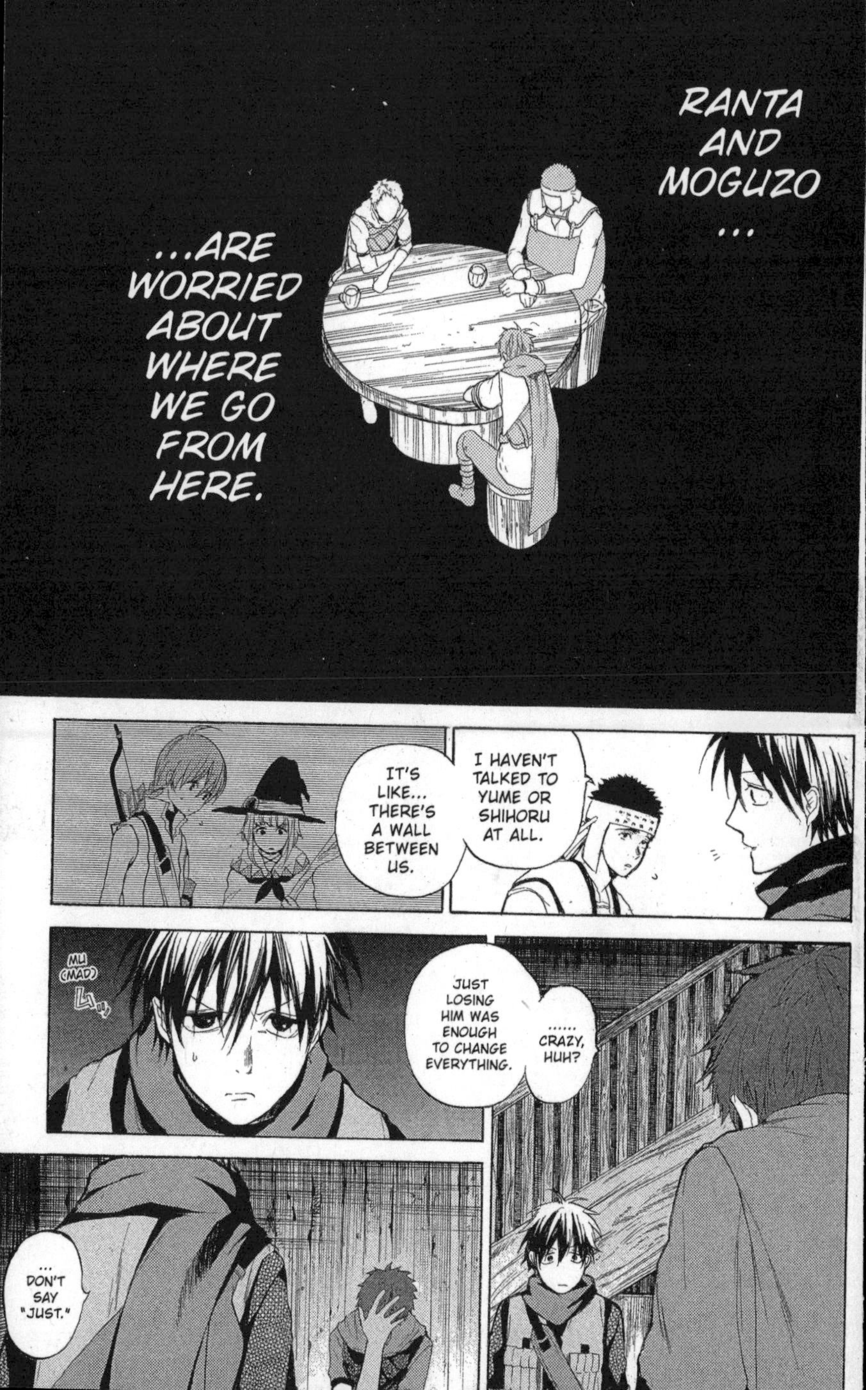
RANTA AND MOGUZO...
...ARE WORRIED ABOUT WHERE WE GO FROM HERE.
I HAVEN'T TALKED TO YUME OR SHIHORU AT ALL.
IT'S LIKE... THERE'S A WALL BETWEEN US.
JUST LOSING HIM WAS ENOUGH TO CHANGE EVERYTHING.
......CRAZY, HUH?
MU (MAD)
... DON'T SAY "JUST."

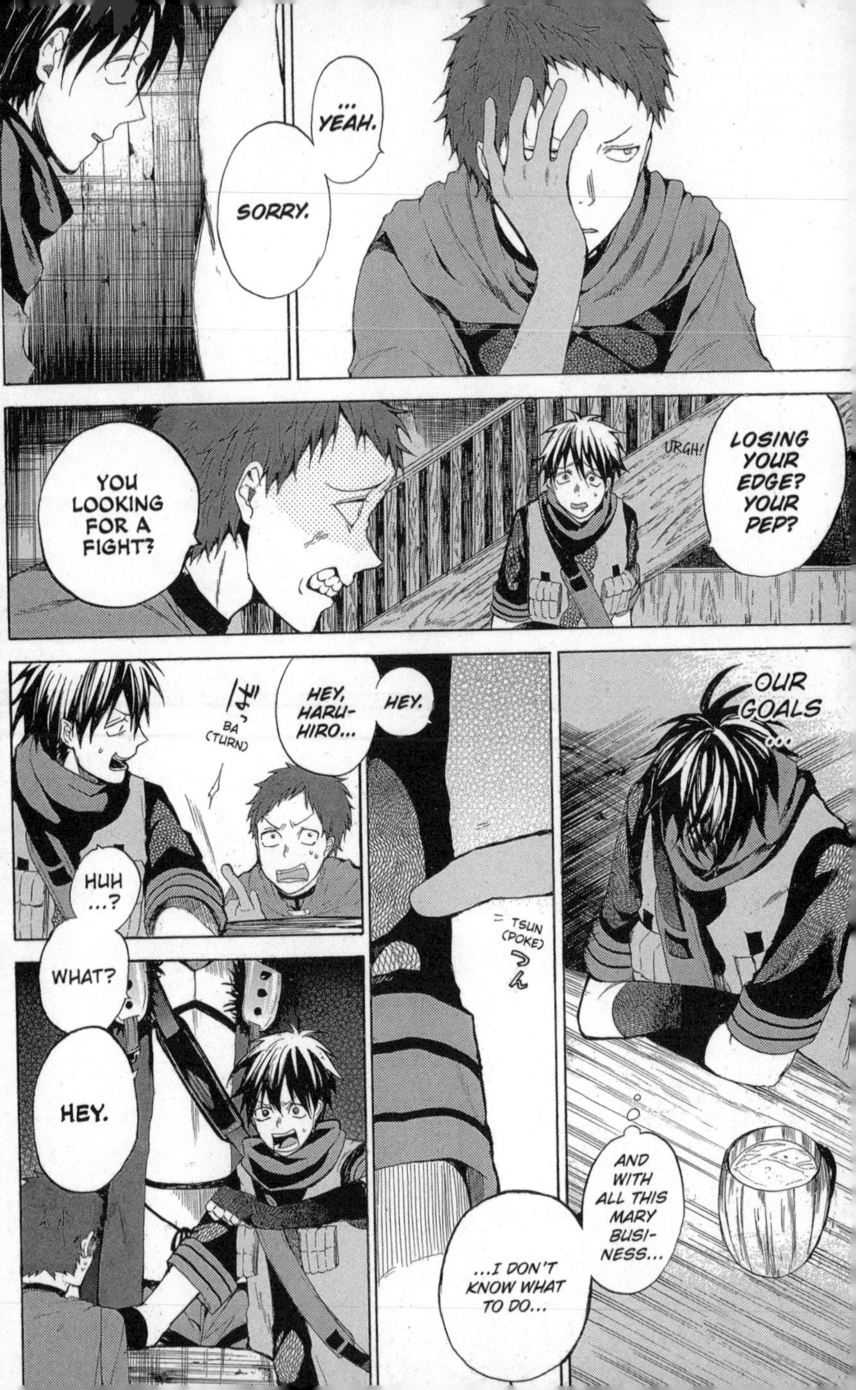
...YEAH.
SORRY.
LOSING YOUR EDGE? YOUR PEP?
URGH!
YOU LOOKING FOR A FIGHT?
OUR GOALS...
AND WITH ALL THIS MARY BUSINESS...
...I DON'T KNOW WHAT TO DO...
つん
= TSUN (POKE)
HEY.
HEY, HARUHIRO...
ばっ
BA (TURN)
HUH ...?
WHAT?
HEY.

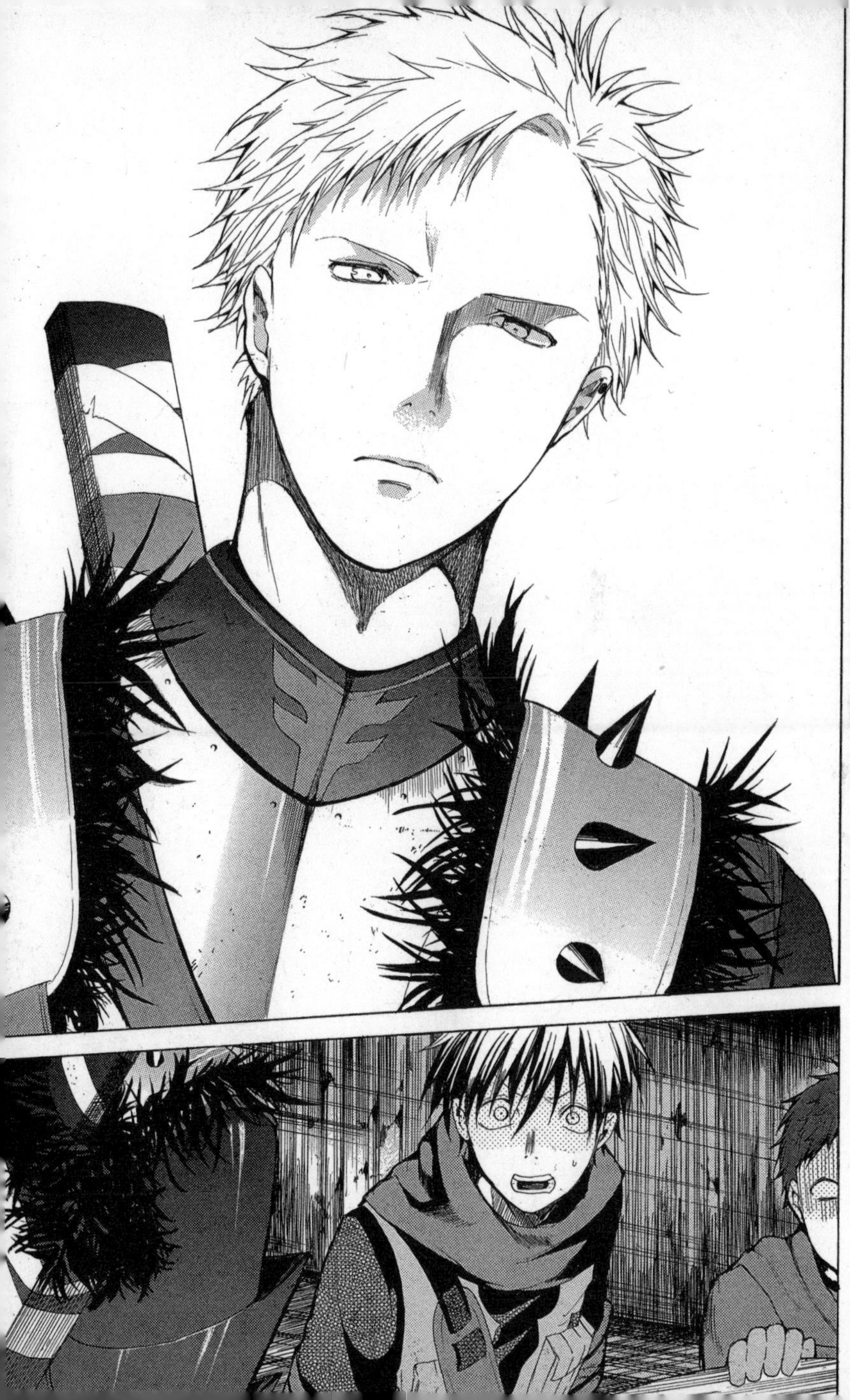

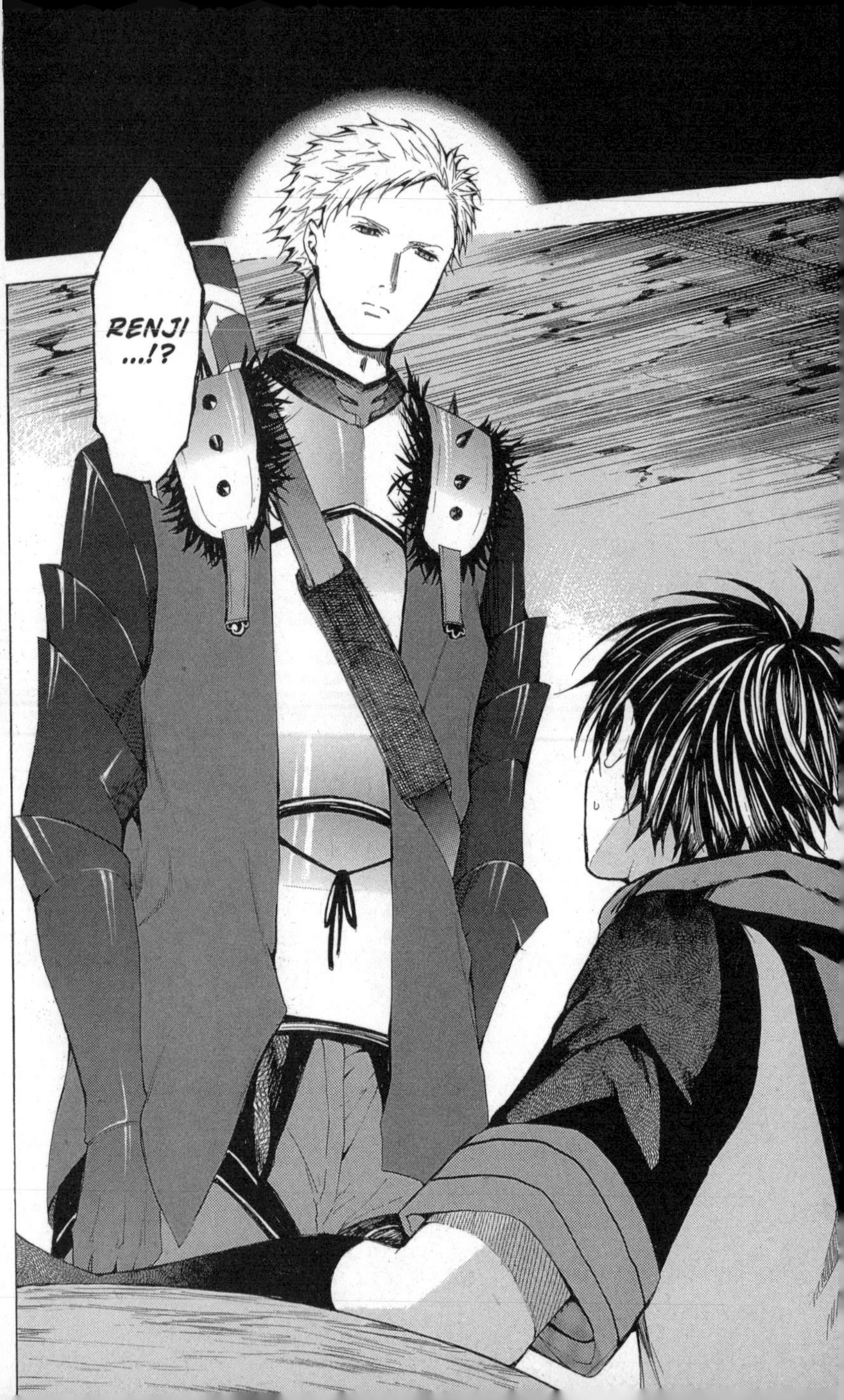
RENJI ...!?

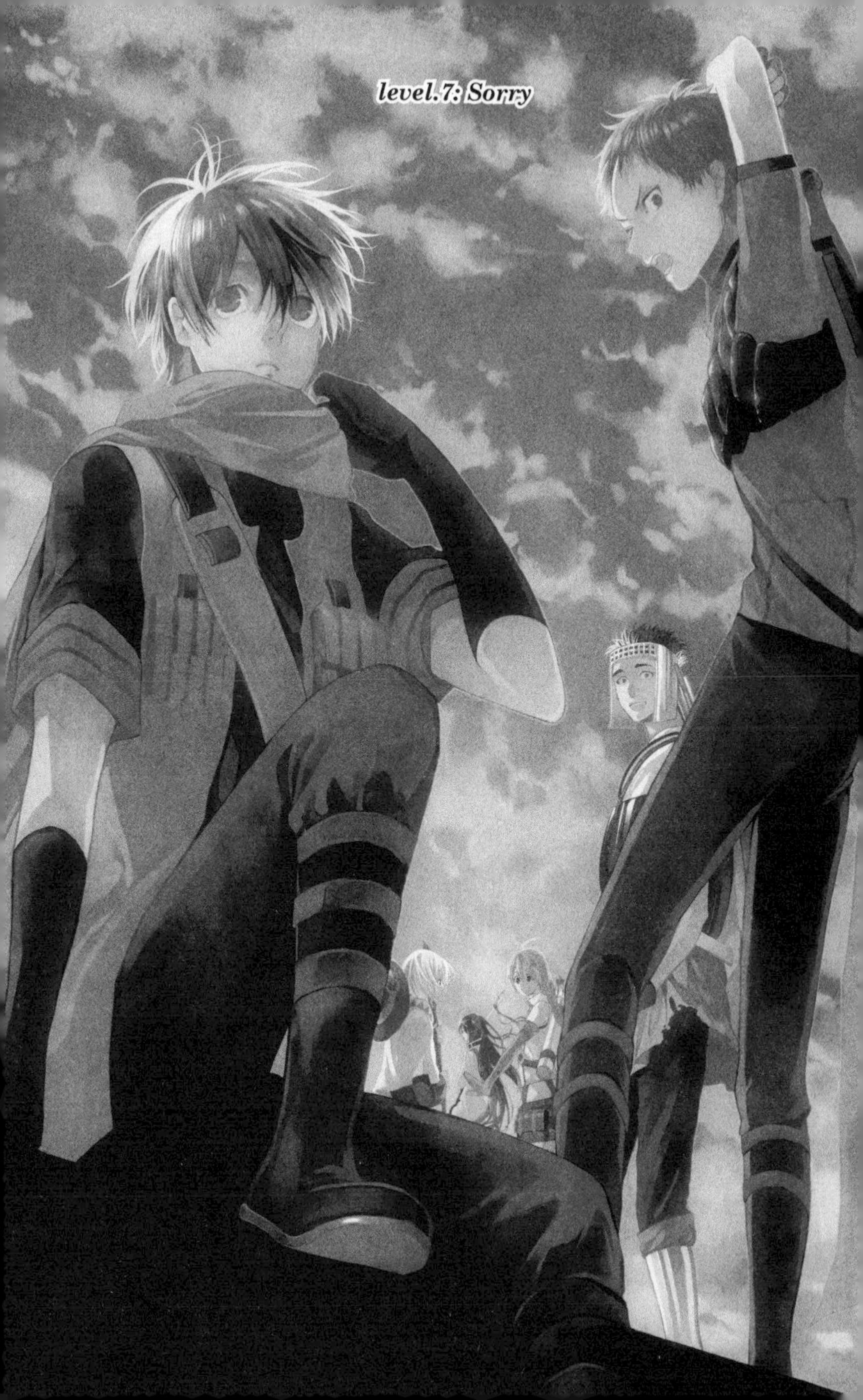
level.7: Sorry

TRAVELING GOBS— STRANGE TALES FROM GRIMGAR OF FANTASY AND ASH

EARRING

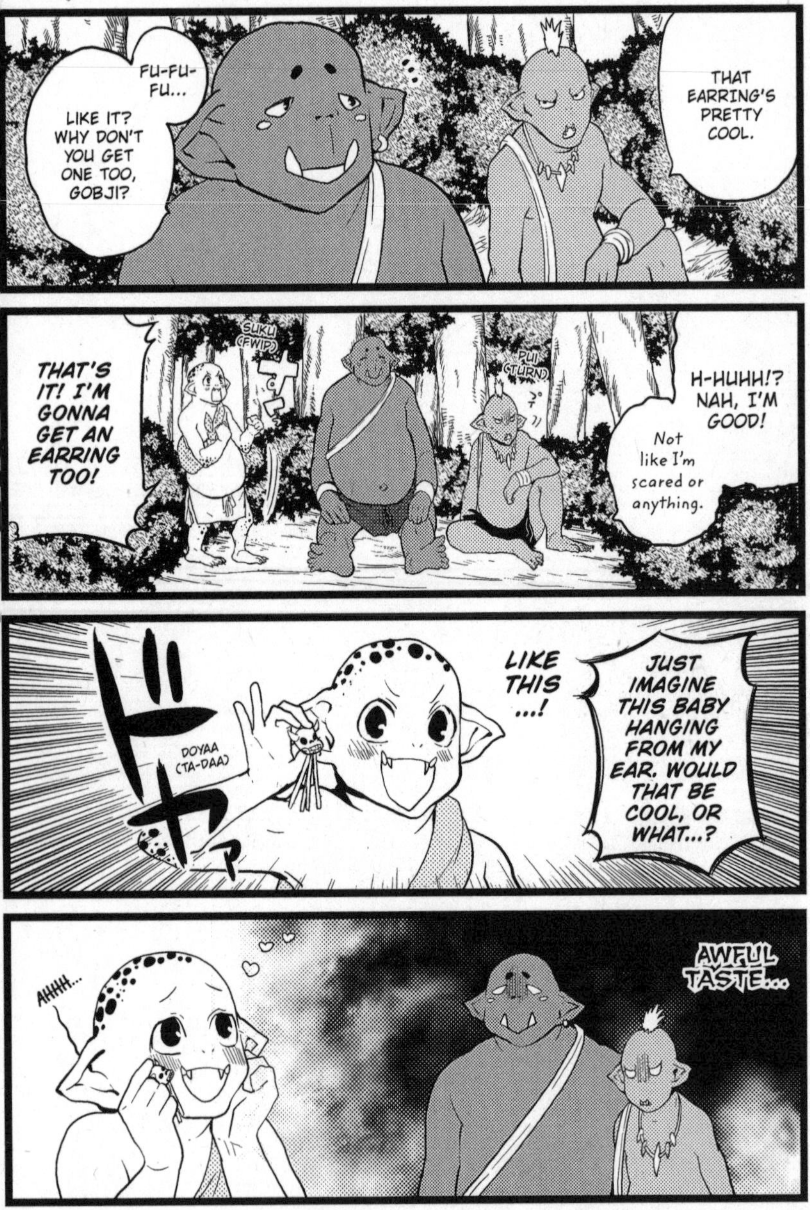
THAT EARRING'S PRETTY COOL.
FU-FU-FU...
LIKE IT? WHY DON'T YOU GET ONE TOO, GOBJI?
H-HUHH!? NAH, I'M GOOD!
Not like I'm scared or anything.
PUI (TURN)
SUKU (FWIP)
THAT'S IT! I'M GONNA GET AN EARRING TOO!
JUST IMAGINE THIS BABY HANGING FROM MY EAR. WOULD THAT BE COOL, OR WHAT...?
LIKE THIS ...!
DOYAA (TA-DAA)
AWFUL TASTE...
AHHH...

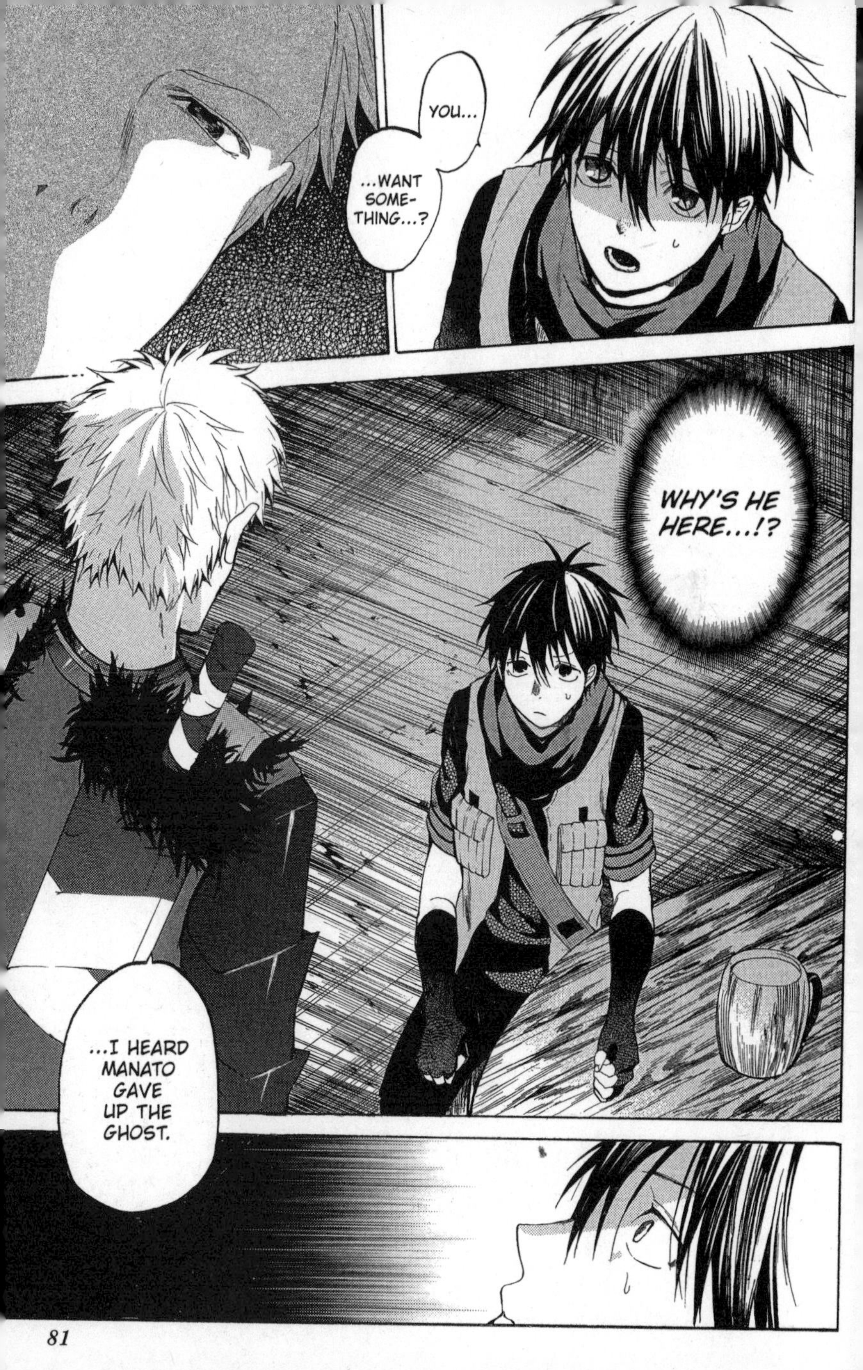
YOU...
...WANT SOME-THING...?
WHY'S HE HERE...!?
...I HEARD MANATO GAVE UP THE GHOST.

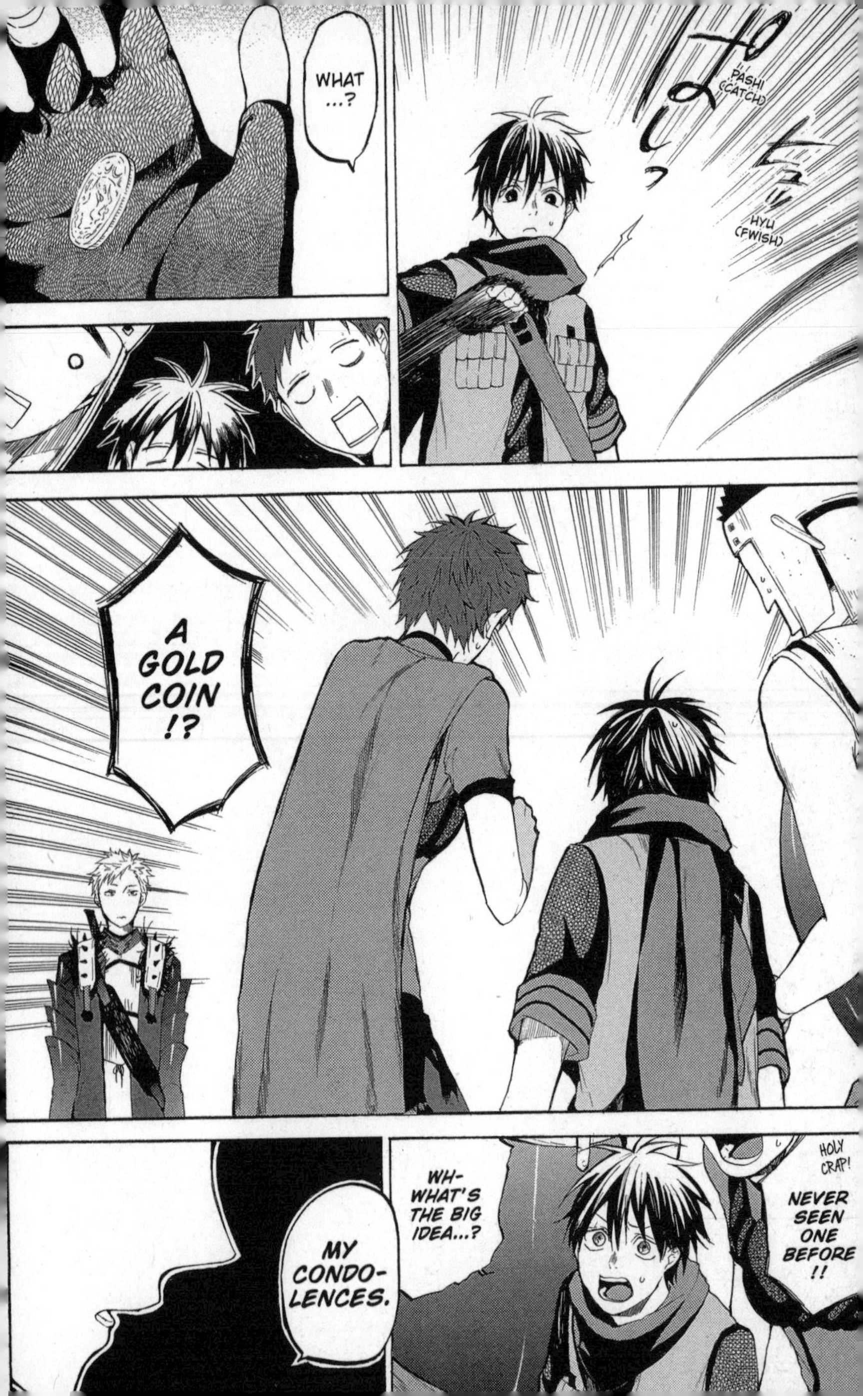
PASHI (CATCH)
HYU (FWISH)
WHAT ...?
A GOLD COIN !?
HOLY CRAP!
NEVER SEEN ONE BEFORE !!
WH- WHAT'S THE BIG IDEA...?
MY CONDO-LENCES.

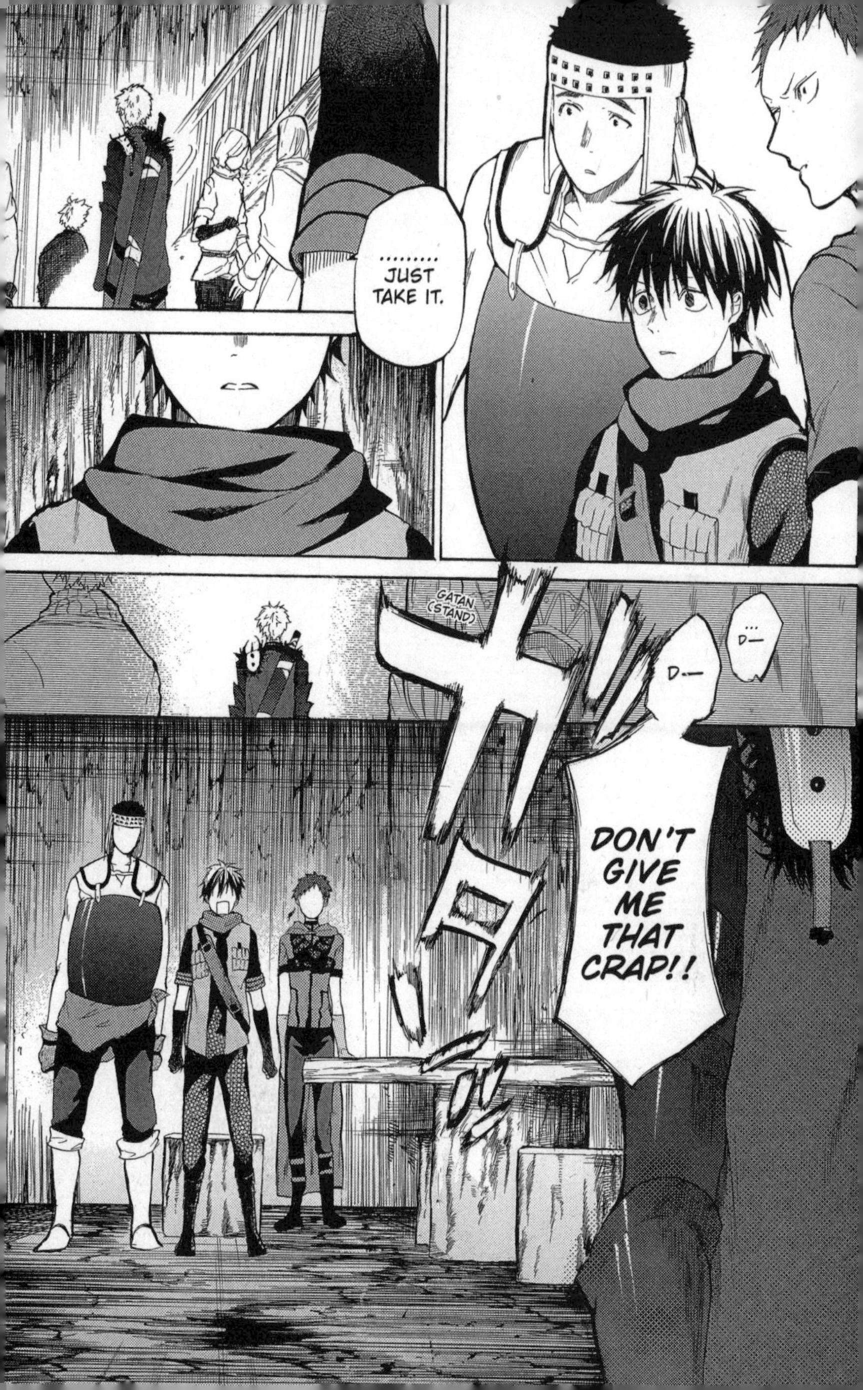

.... JUST TAKE IT.
... D—
D—
GATAN (STAND)
DON'T GIVE ME THAT CRAP!!

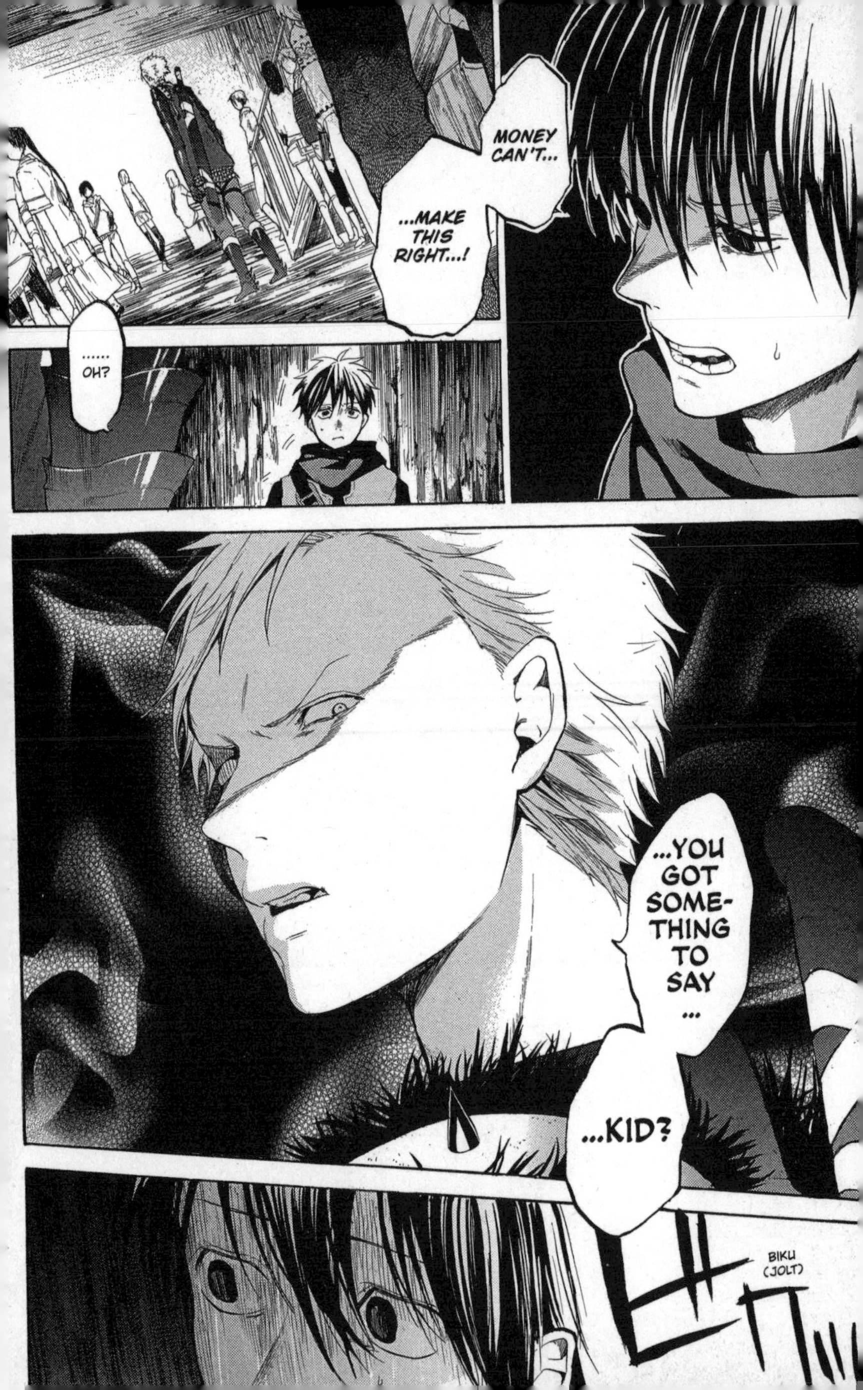

MONEY CAN'T...
...MAKE THIS RIGHT...!
......OH?
...YOU GOT SOME-THING TO SAY...
...KID?
BIKU (JOLT)

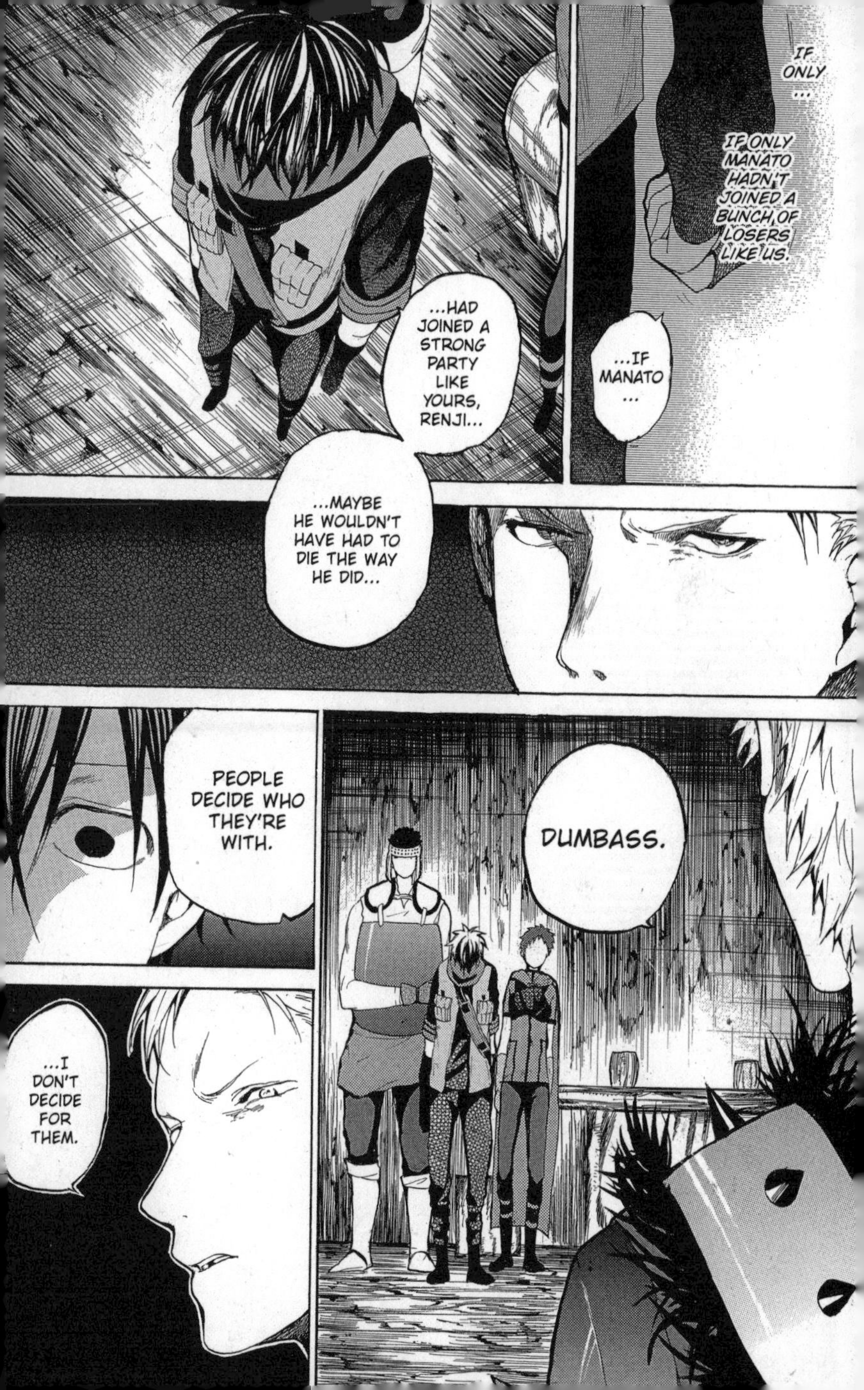
IF ONLY ...
IF ONLY MANATO HADN'T JOINED A BUNCH OF LOSERS LIKE US.
...IF MANATO ...
...HAD JOINED A STRONG PARTY LIKE YOURS, RENJI...
...MAYBE HE WOULDN'T HAVE HAD TO DIE THE WAY HE DID...
DUMBASS.
PEOPLE DECIDE WHO THEY'RE WITH.
...I DON'T DECIDE FOR THEM.

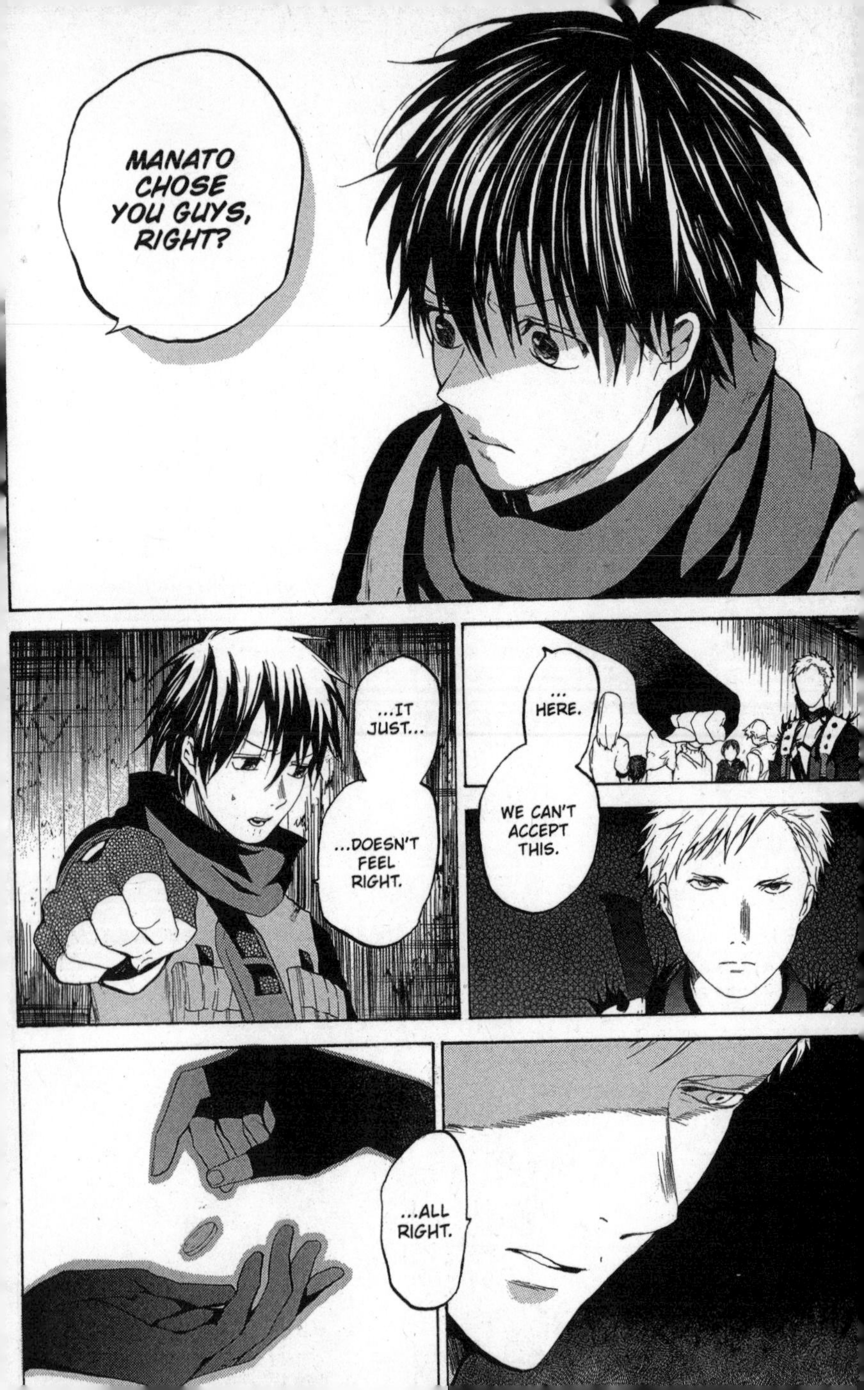
MANATO CHOSE YOU GUYS, RIGHT?
...HERE.
WE CAN'T ACCEPT THIS.
...IT JUST...
...DOESN'T FEEL RIGHT.
...ALL RIGHT.

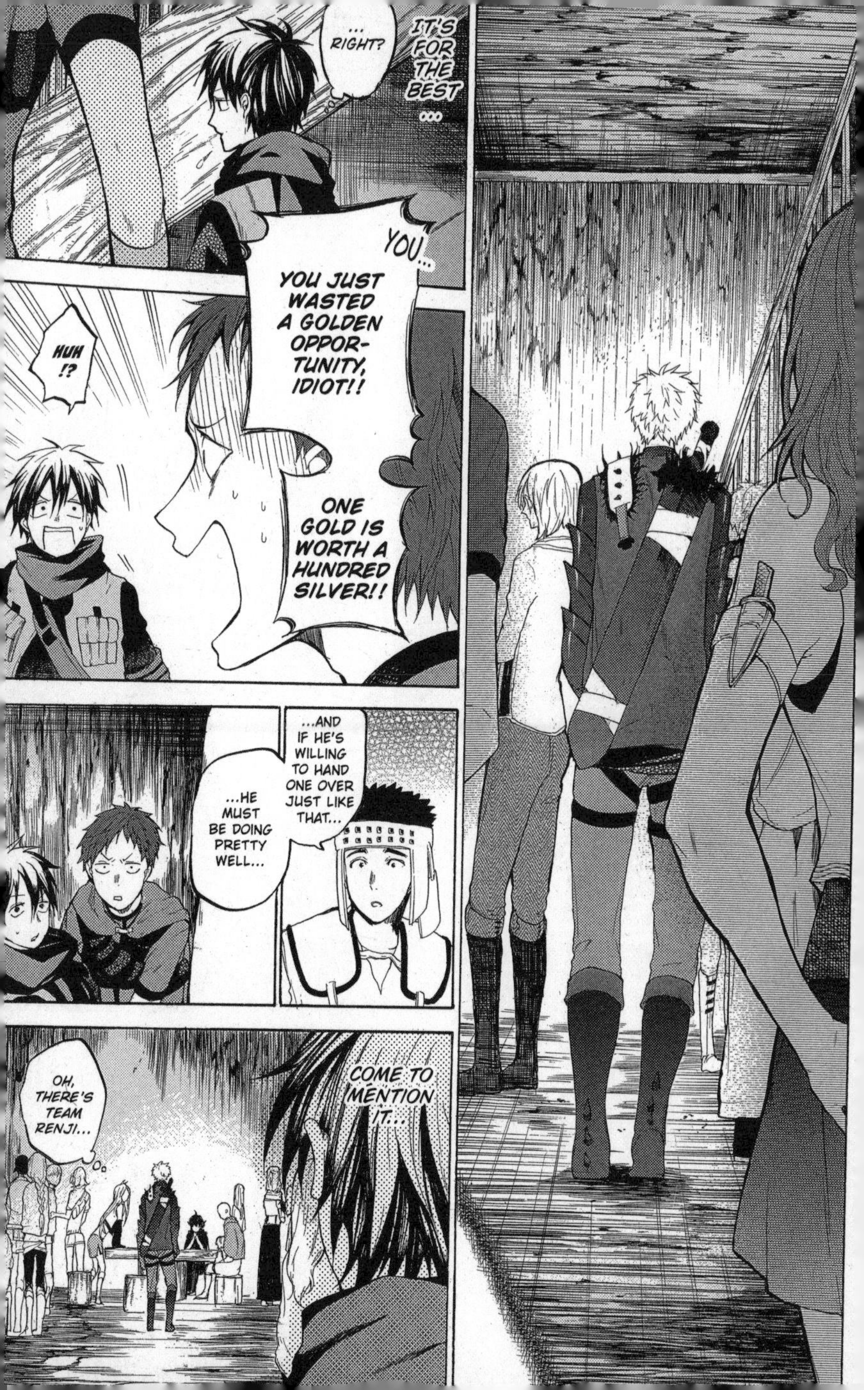
IT'S FOR THE BEST...
...RIGHT?
YOU...
YOU JUST WASTED A GOLDEN OPPOR-TUNITY, IDIOT!!
ONE GOLD IS WORTH A HUNDRED SILVER!!
HUH!?
...AND IF HE'S WILLING TO HAND ONE OVER JUST LIKE THAT...
...HE MUST BE DOING PRETTY WELL...
COME TO MENTION IT...
OH, THERE'S TEAM RENJI...

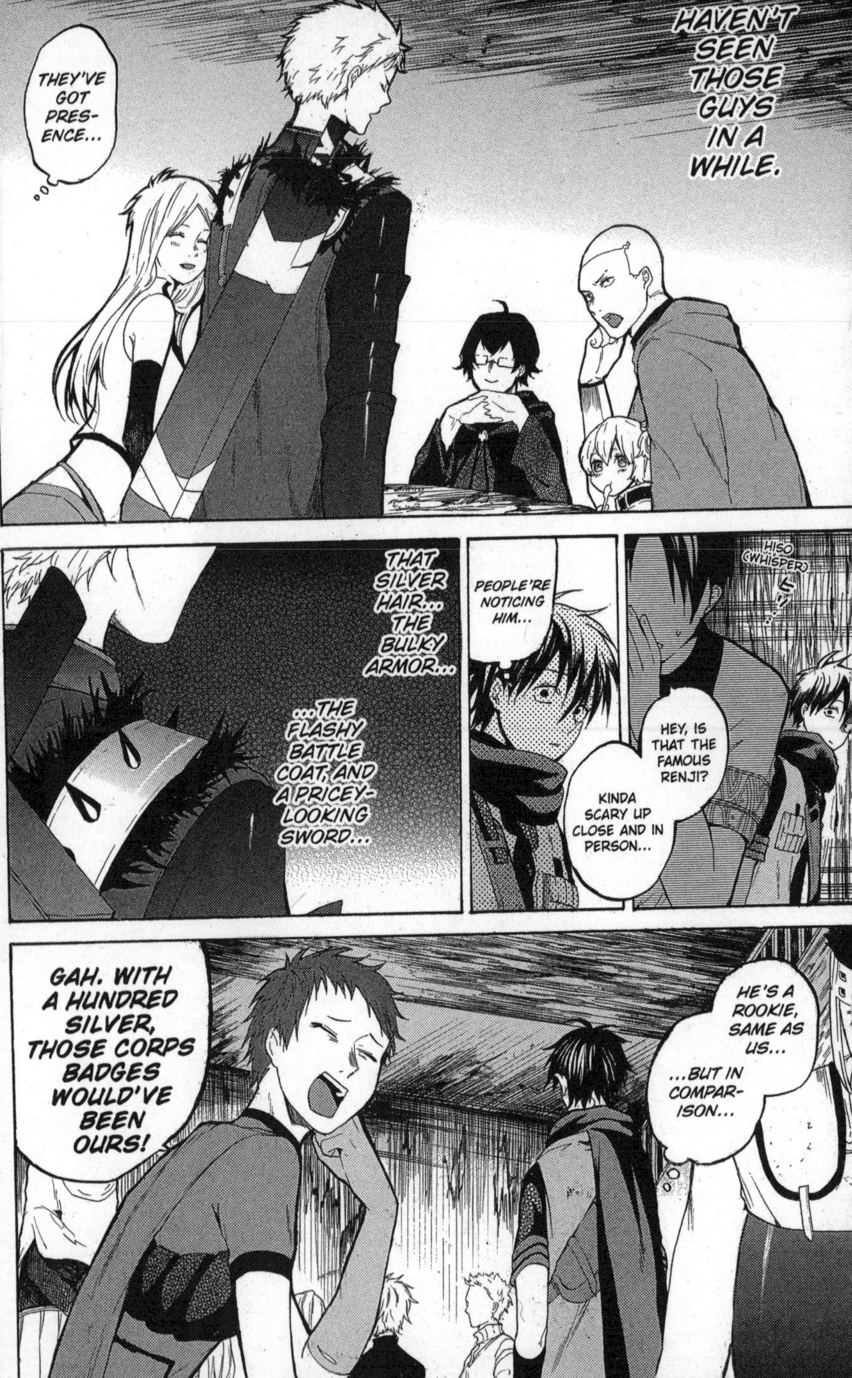
HAVEN'T SEEN THOSE GUYS IN A WHILE.
THEY'VE GOT PRES-ENCE...
HISO (WHISPER)
HEY, IS THAT THE FAMOUS RENJI?
KINDA SCARY UP CLOSE AND IN PERSON...
PEOPLE'RE NOTICING HIM...
THAT SILVER HAIR... THE BULKY ARMOR...
...THE FLASHY BATTLE COAT, AND A PRICEY-LOOKING SWORD...
HE'S A ROOKIE, SAME AS US...
...BUT IN COMPAR-ISON...
GAH. WITH A HUNDRED SILVER, THOSE CORPS BADGES WOULD'VE BEEN OURS!

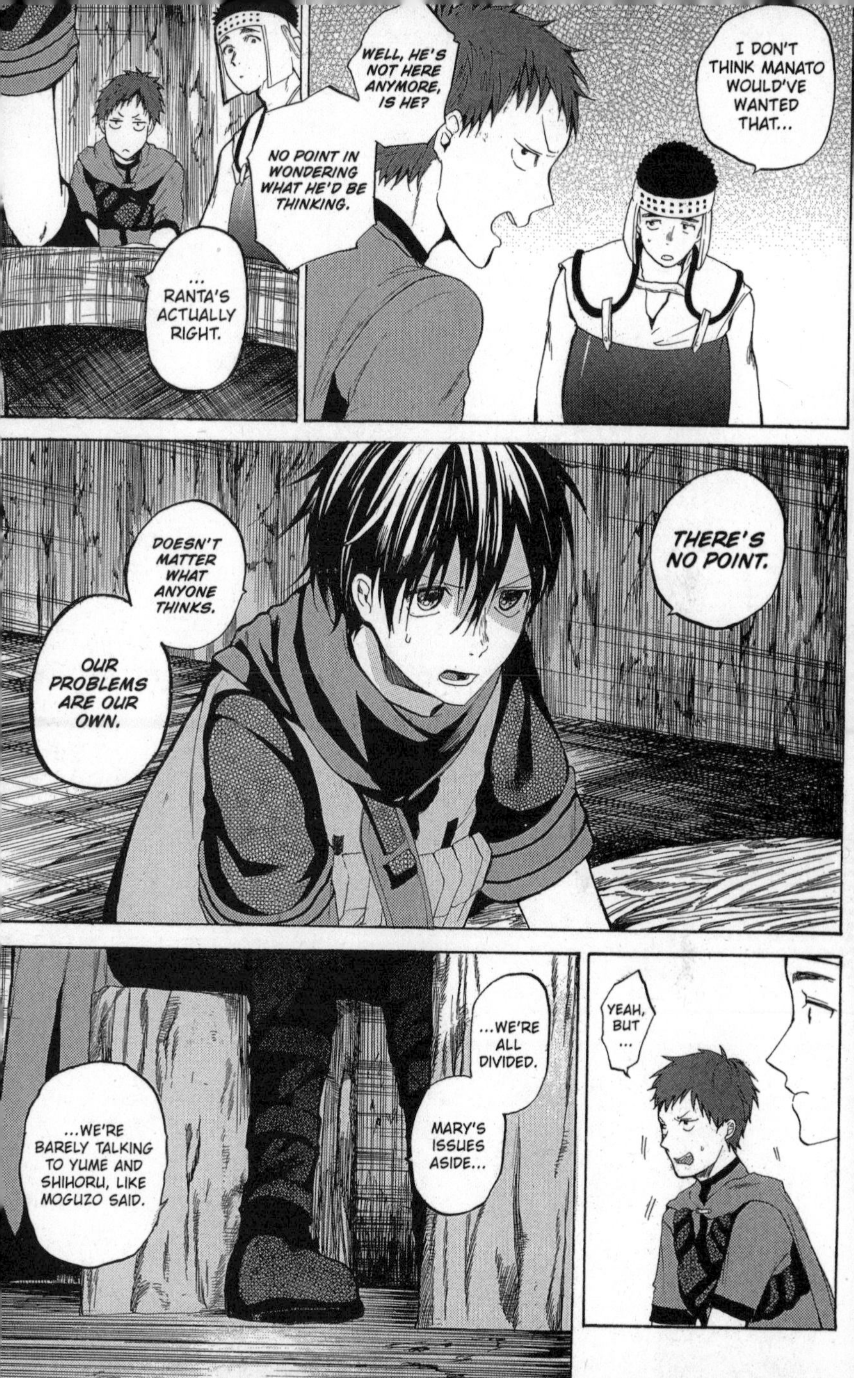
I DON'T THINK MANATO WOULD'VE WANTED THAT...
WELL, HE'S NOT HERE ANYMORE, IS HE?
NO POINT IN WONDERING WHAT HE'D BE THINKING.
...RANTA'S ACTUALLY RIGHT.
THERE'S NO POINT.
DOESN'T MATTER WHAT ANYONE THINKS.
OUR PROBLEMS ARE OUR OWN.
YEAH, BUT ...
...WE'RE ALL DIVIDED.
MARY'S ISSUES ASIDE...
...WE'RE BARELY TALKING TO YUME AND SHIHORU, LIKE MOGUZO SAID.

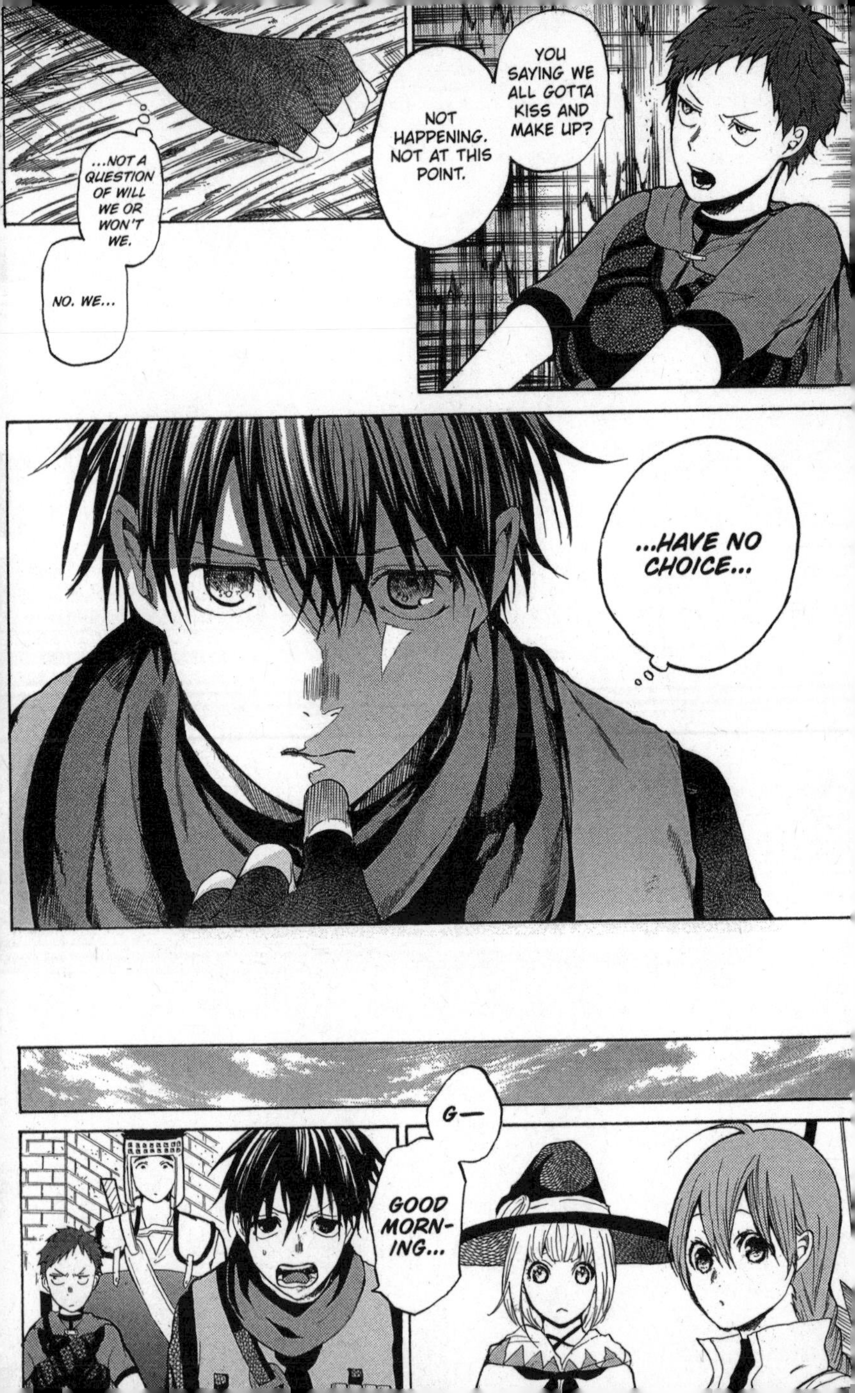
YOU SAYING WE ALL GOTTA KISS AND MAKE UP?
NOT HAPPENING. NOT AT THIS POINT.
...NOT A QUESTION OF WILL WE OR WON'T WE.
NO. WE...
...HAVE NO CHOICE...
G—
GOOD MORNING...

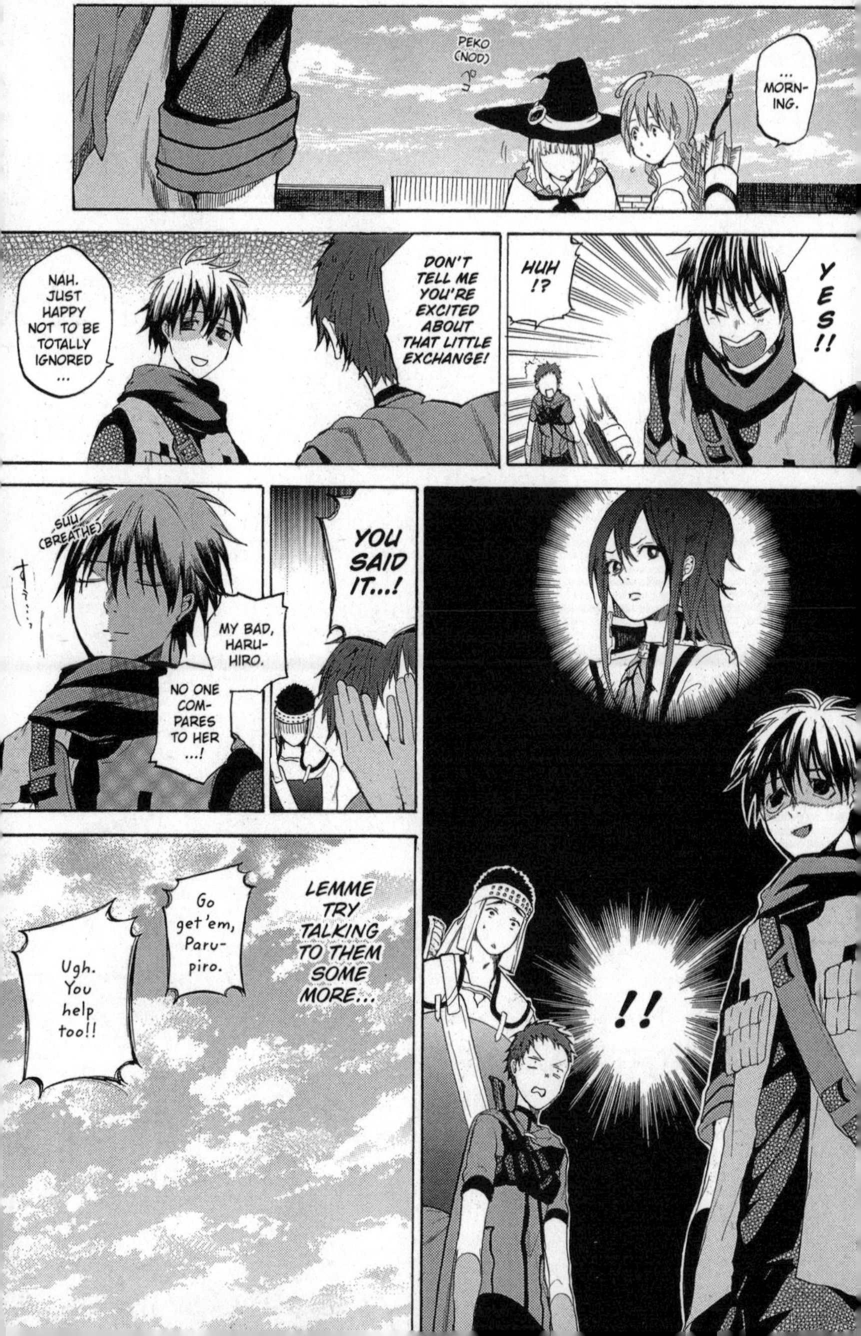

... MORN-ING.
PEKO (NOD)
YES!!
HUH!?
DON'T TELL ME YOU'RE EXCITED ABOUT THAT LITTLE EXCHANGE!
NAH. JUST HAPPY NOT TO BE TOTALLY IGNORED ...
!!
YOU SAID IT...!
SUU (BREATHE)
MY BAD, HARU-HIRO.
NO ONE COM-PARES TO HER ...!
LEMME TRY TALKING TO THEM SOME MORE...
Go get 'em, Paru-piro.
Ugh. You help too!!

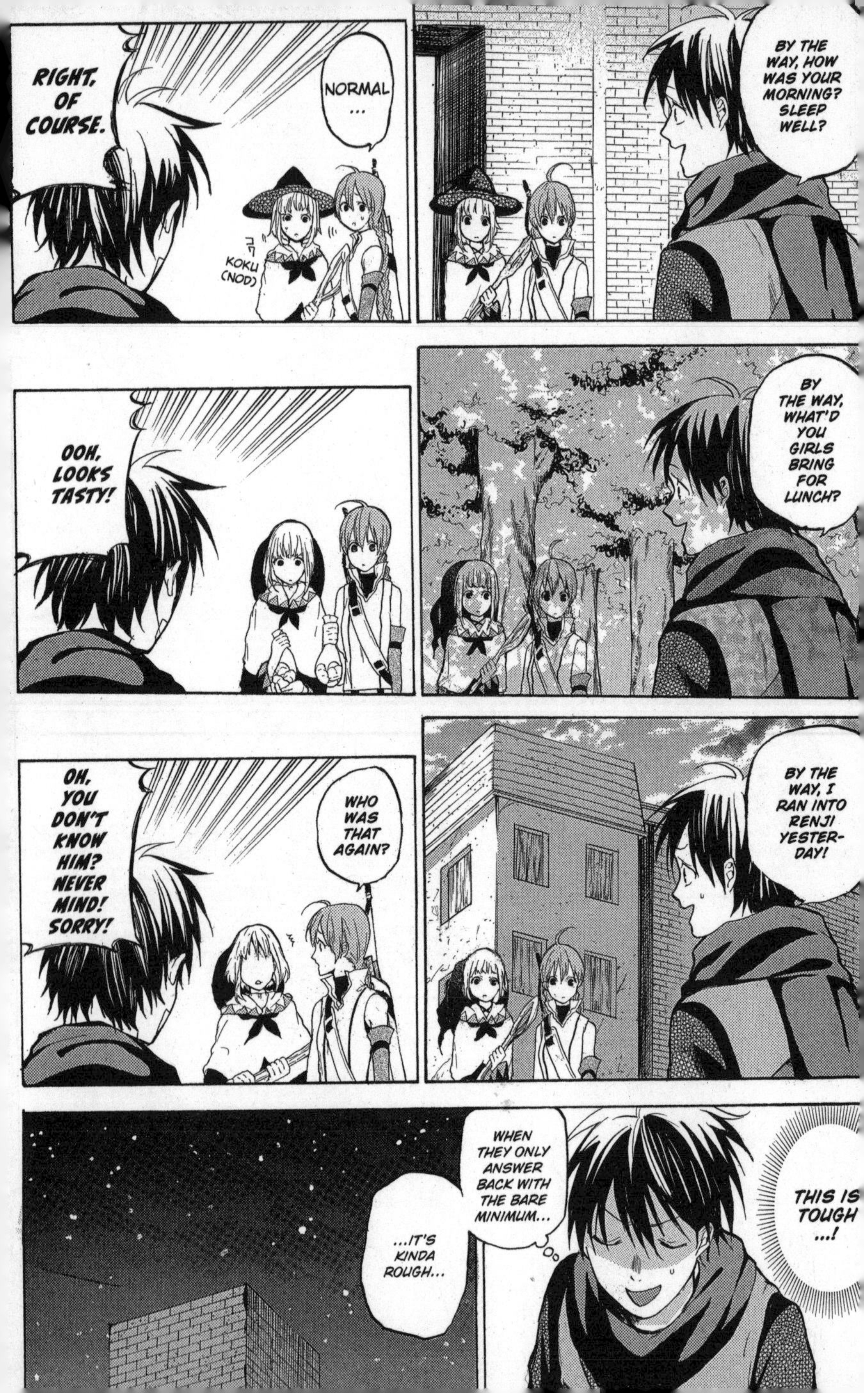
BY THE WAY, HOW WAS YOUR MORNING? SLEEP WELL?
NORMAL...
コク
KOKU (NOD)
RIGHT, OF COURSE.
BY THE WAY, WHAT'D YOU GIRLS BRING FOR LUNCH?
OOH, LOOKS TASTY!
BY THE WAY, I RAN INTO RENJI YESTER-DAY!
WHO WAS THAT AGAIN?
OH, YOU DON'T KNOW HIM? NEVER MIND! SORRY!
THIS IS TOUGH ...!
WHEN THEY ONLY ANSWER BACK WITH THE BARE MINIMUM...
...IT'S KINDA ROUGH...

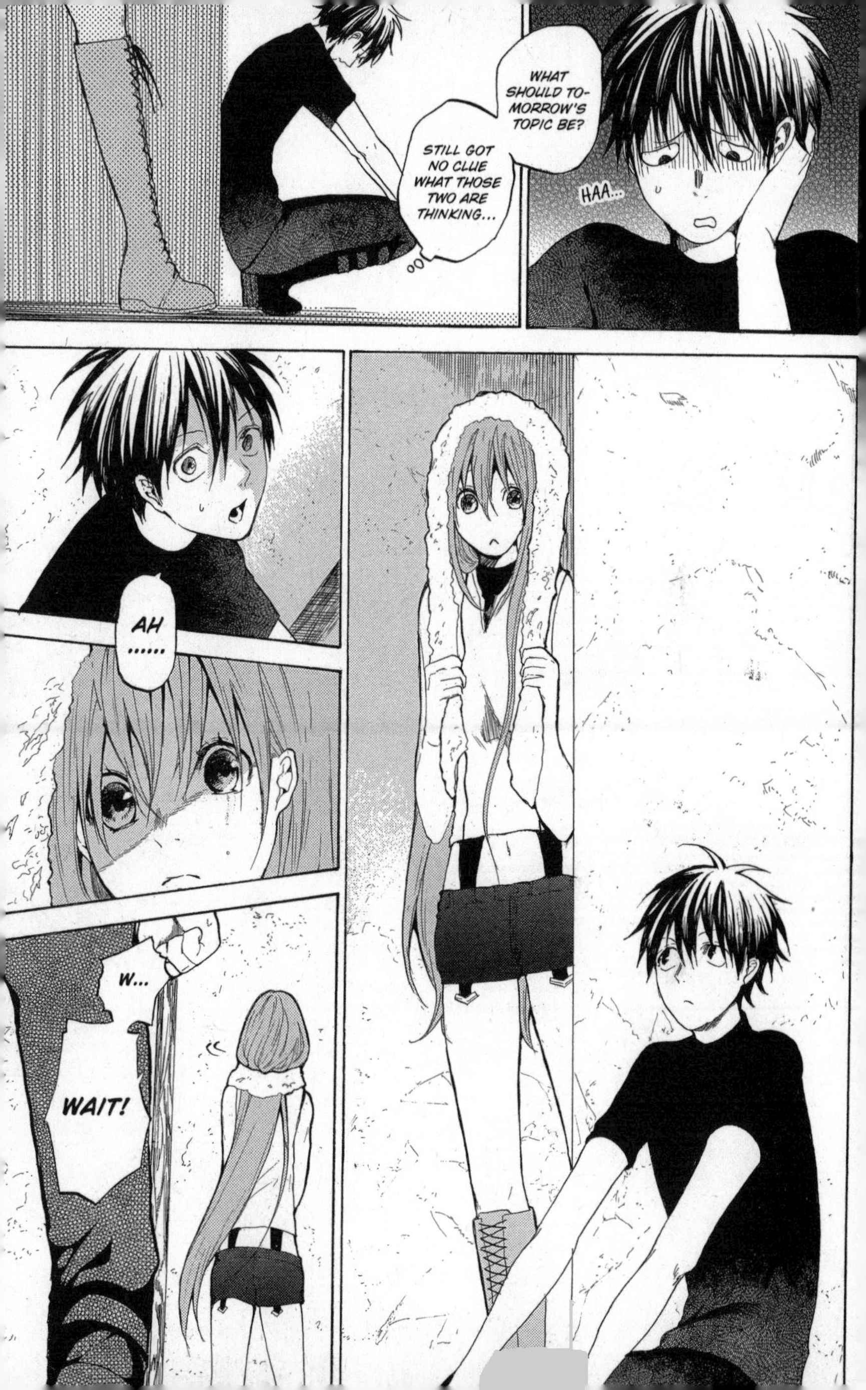
WHAT SHOULD TO-MORROW'S TOPIC BE?
HAA...
STILL GOT NO CLUE WHAT THOSE TWO ARE THINKING...
AH ......
W...
WAIT!

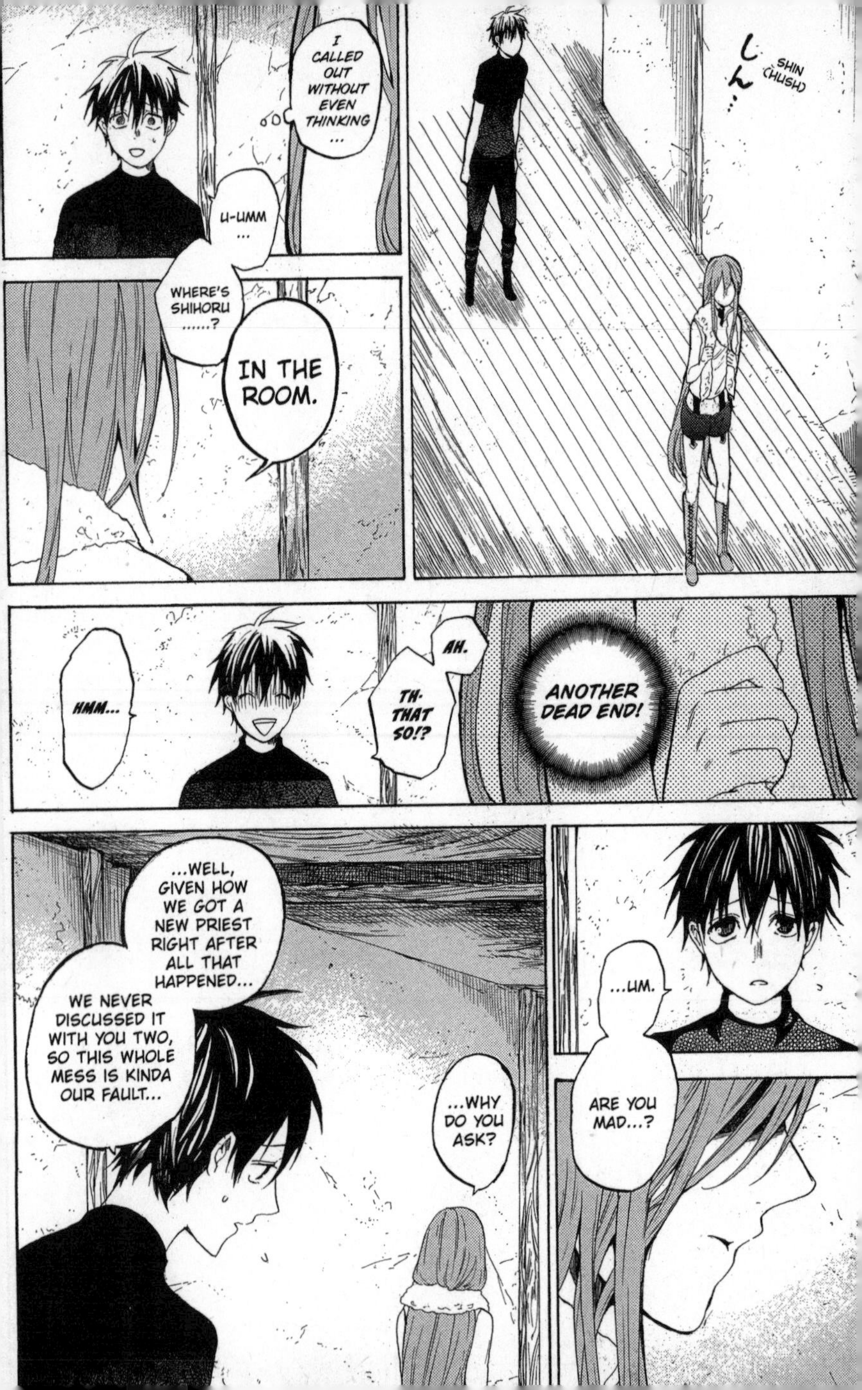
しん…
SHIN (HUSH)
I CALLED OUT WITHOUT EVEN THINKING ...
U-UMM ...
WHERE'S SHIHORU ......?
IN THE ROOM.
ANOTHER DEAD END!
AH.
TH-THAT SO!?
HMM...
...UM.
ARE YOU MAD...?
...WHY DO YOU ASK?
...WELL, GIVEN HOW WE GOT A NEW PRIEST RIGHT AFTER ALL THAT HAPPENED...
WE NEVER DISCUSSED IT WITH YOU TWO, SO THIS WHOLE MESS IS KINDA OUR FAULT...

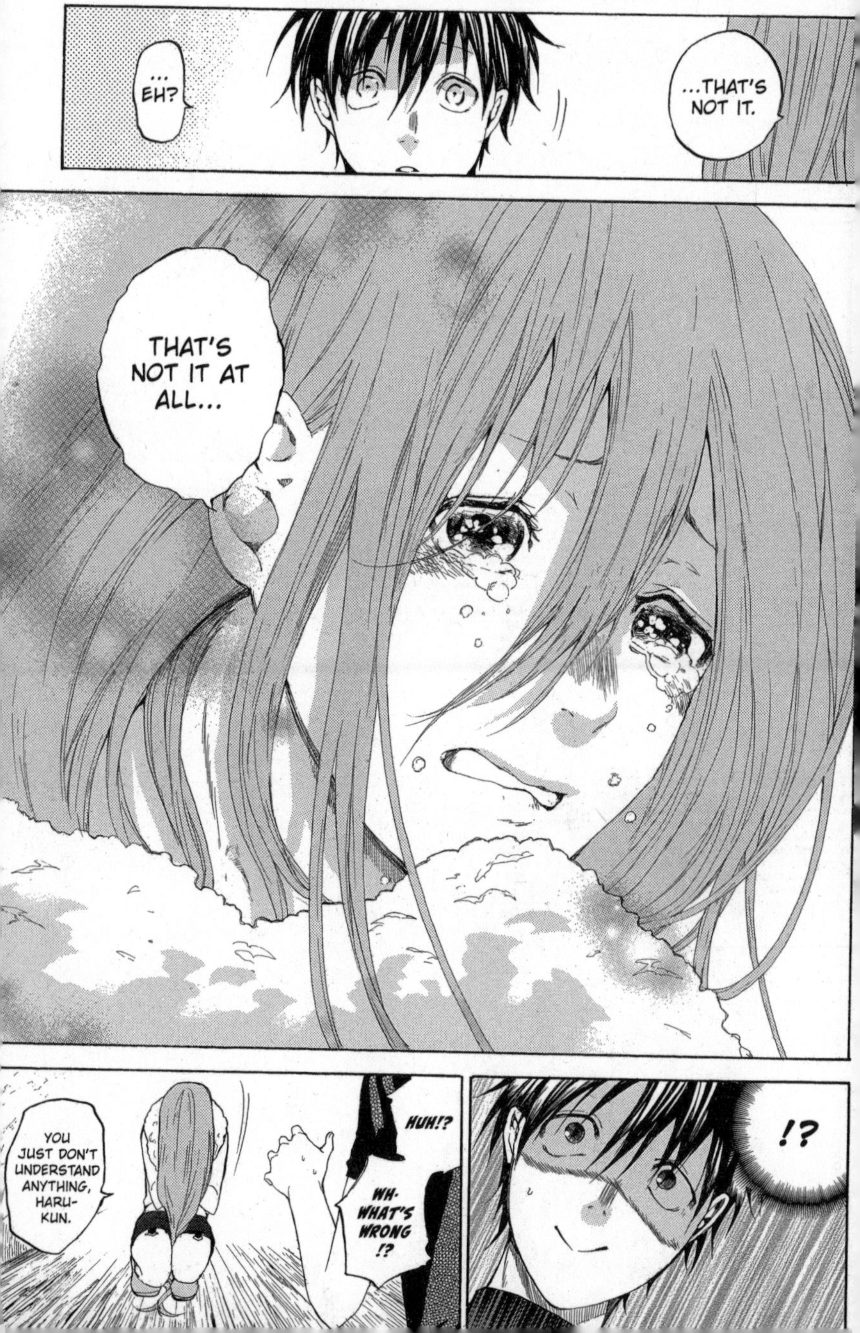
...THAT'S NOT IT.
... EH?
THAT'S NOT IT AT ALL...
!?
HUH!?
WH-WHAT'S WRONG!?
YOU JUST DON'T UNDERSTAND ANYTHING, HARU-KUN.

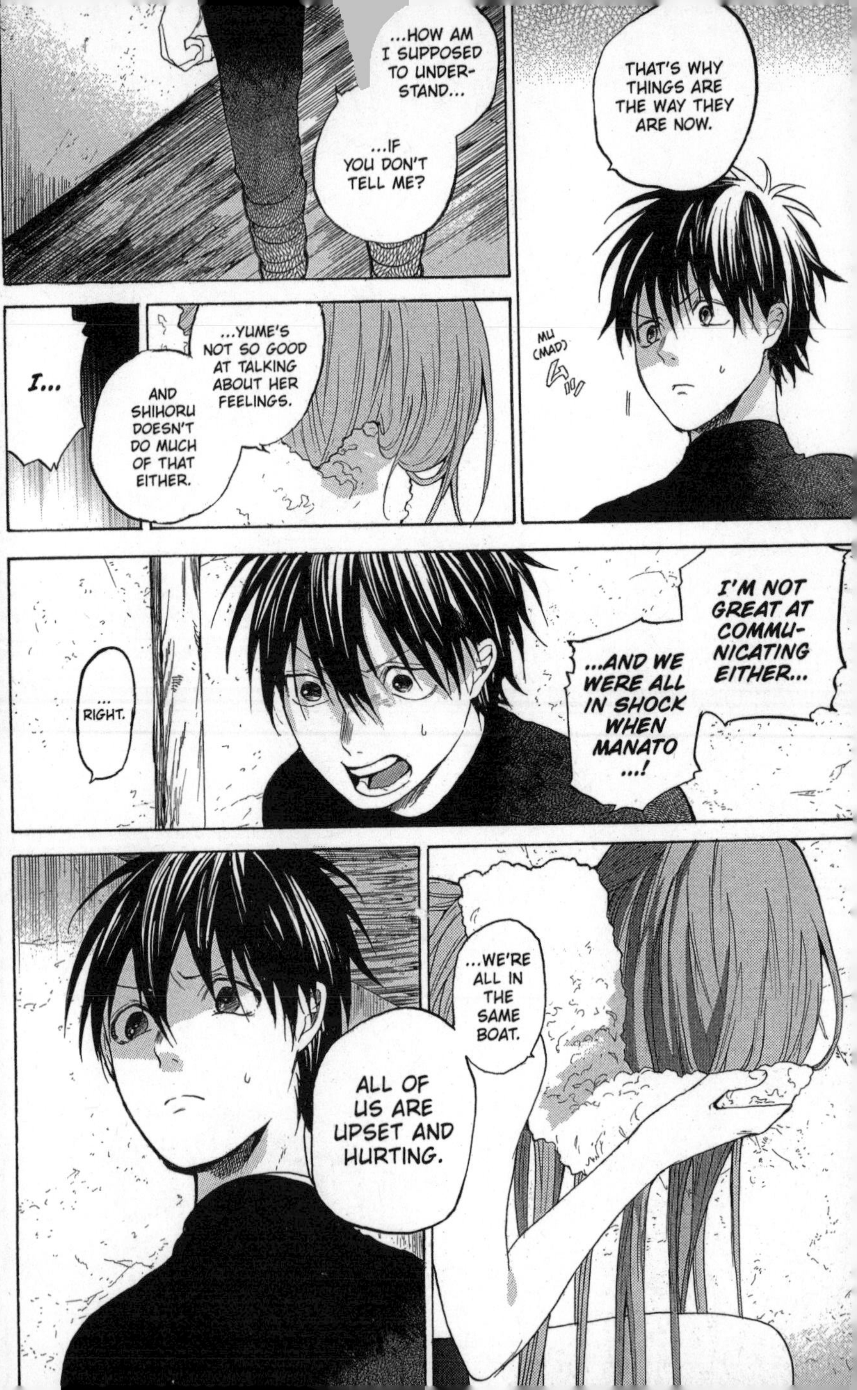
THAT'S WHY THINGS ARE THE WAY THEY ARE NOW.
MU (MAD)
...HOW AM I SUPPOSED TO UNDER-STAND...
...IF YOU DON'T TELL ME?
...YUME'S NOT SO GOOD AT TALKING ABOUT HER FEELINGS.
AND SHIHORU DOESN'T DO MUCH OF THAT EITHER.
I...
I'M NOT GREAT AT COMMU-NICATING EITHER...
...AND WE WERE ALL IN SHOCK WHEN MANATO ...!
... RIGHT.
...WE'RE ALL IN THE SAME BOAT.
ALL OF US ARE UPSET AND HURTING.

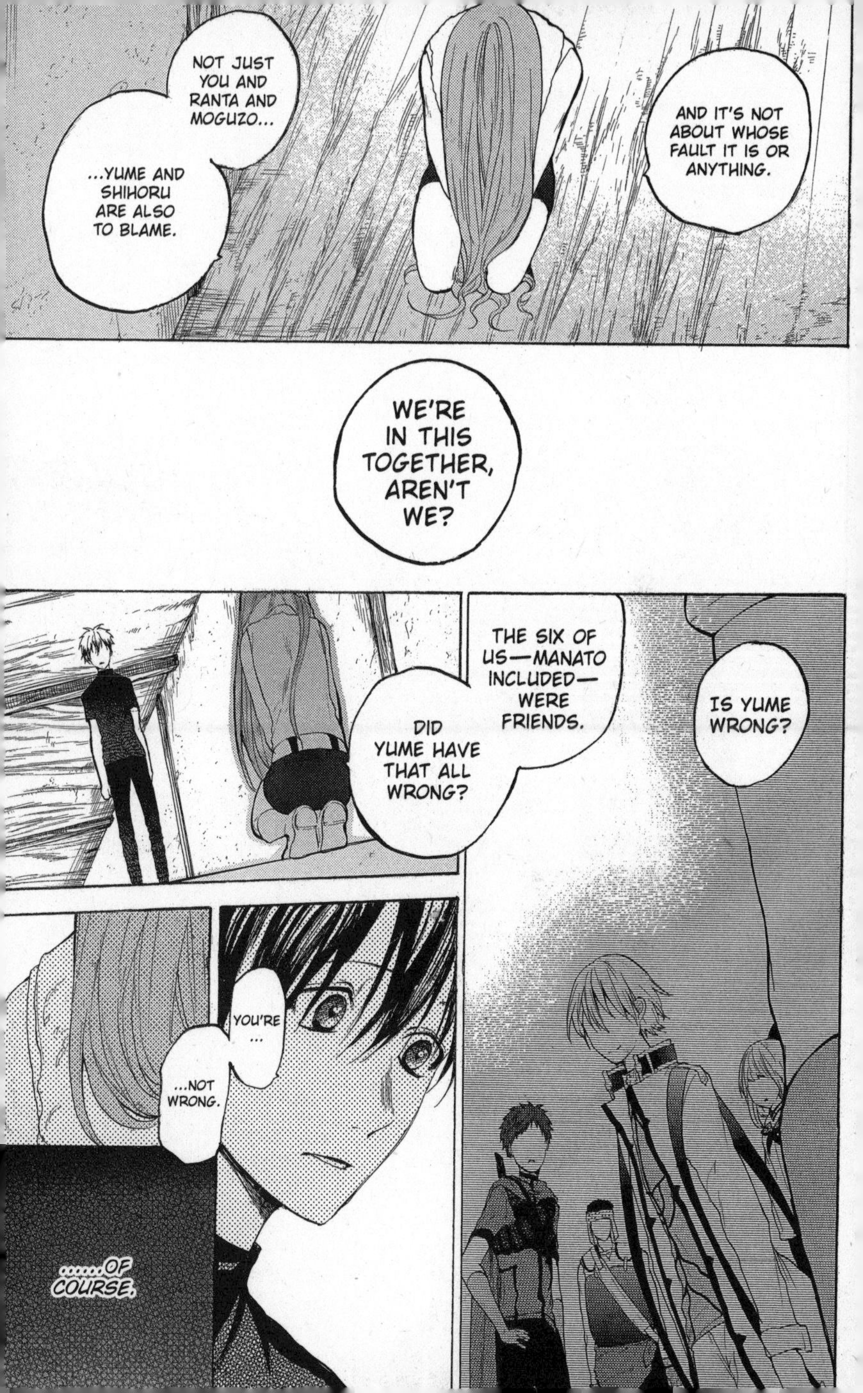

AND IT'S NOT ABOUT WHOSE FAULT IT IS OR ANYTHING.
NOT JUST YOU AND RANTA AND MOGUZO...
...YUME AND SHIHORU ARE ALSO TO BLAME.
WE'RE IN THIS TOGETHER, AREN'T WE?
IS YUME WRONG?
THE SIX OF US—MANATO INCLUDED—WERE FRIENDS.
DID YUME HAVE THAT ALL WRONG?
YOU'RE...
...NOT WRONG.
......OF COURSE.

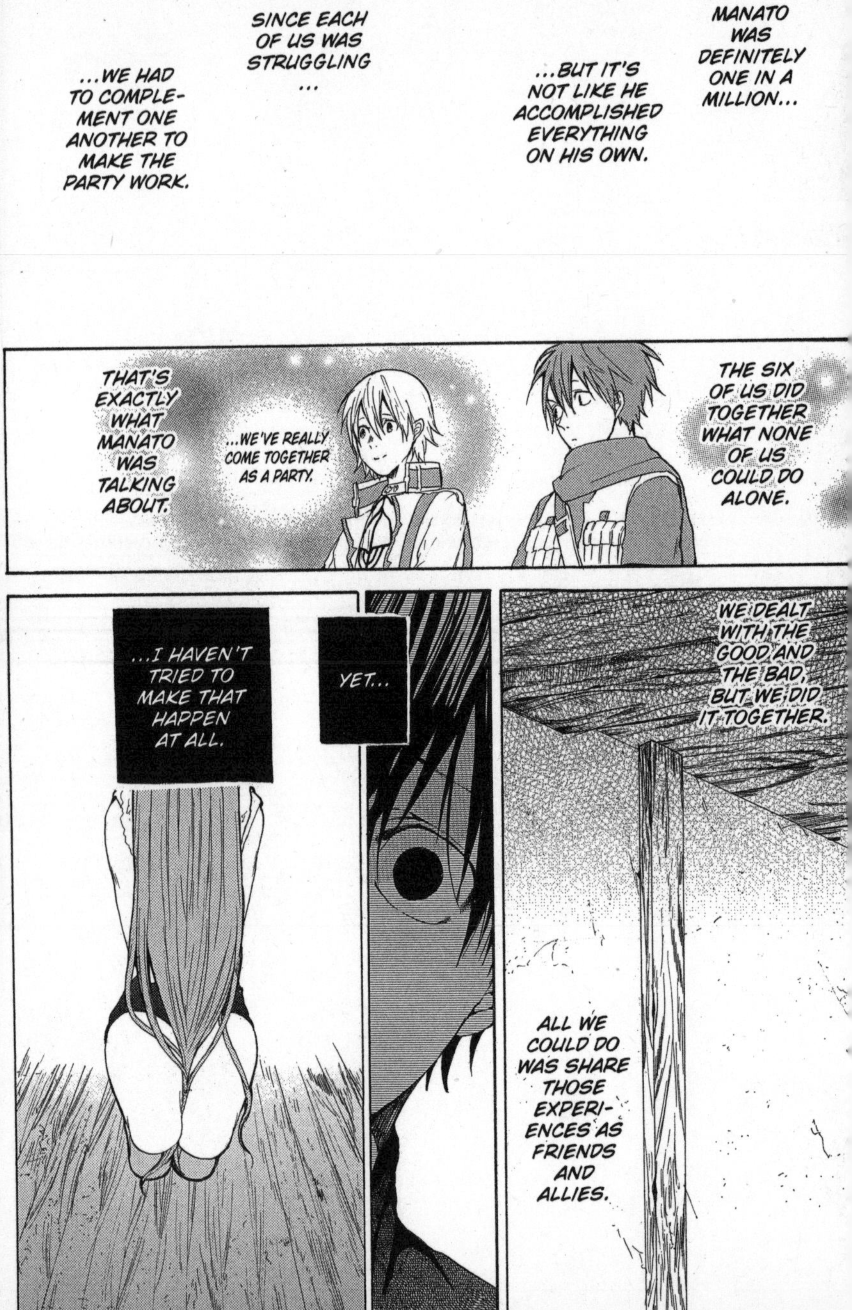
MANATO WAS DEFINITELY ONE IN A MILLION...
...BUT IT'S NOT LIKE HE ACCOMPLISHED EVERYTHING ON HIS OWN.
SINCE EACH OF US WAS STRUGGLING...
...WE HAD TO COMPLE-MENT ONE ANOTHER TO MAKE THE PARTY WORK.
THE SIX OF US DID TOGETHER WHAT NONE OF US COULD DO ALONE.
...WE'VE REALLY COME TOGETHER AS A PARTY.
THAT'S EXACTLY WHAT MANATO WAS TALKING ABOUT.
WE DEALT WITH THE GOOD AND THE BAD, BUT WE DID IT TOGETHER.
ALL WE COULD DO WAS SHARE THOSE EXPERI-ENCES AS FRIENDS AND ALLIES.
YET...
...I HAVEN'T TRIED TO MAKE THAT HAPPEN AT ALL.

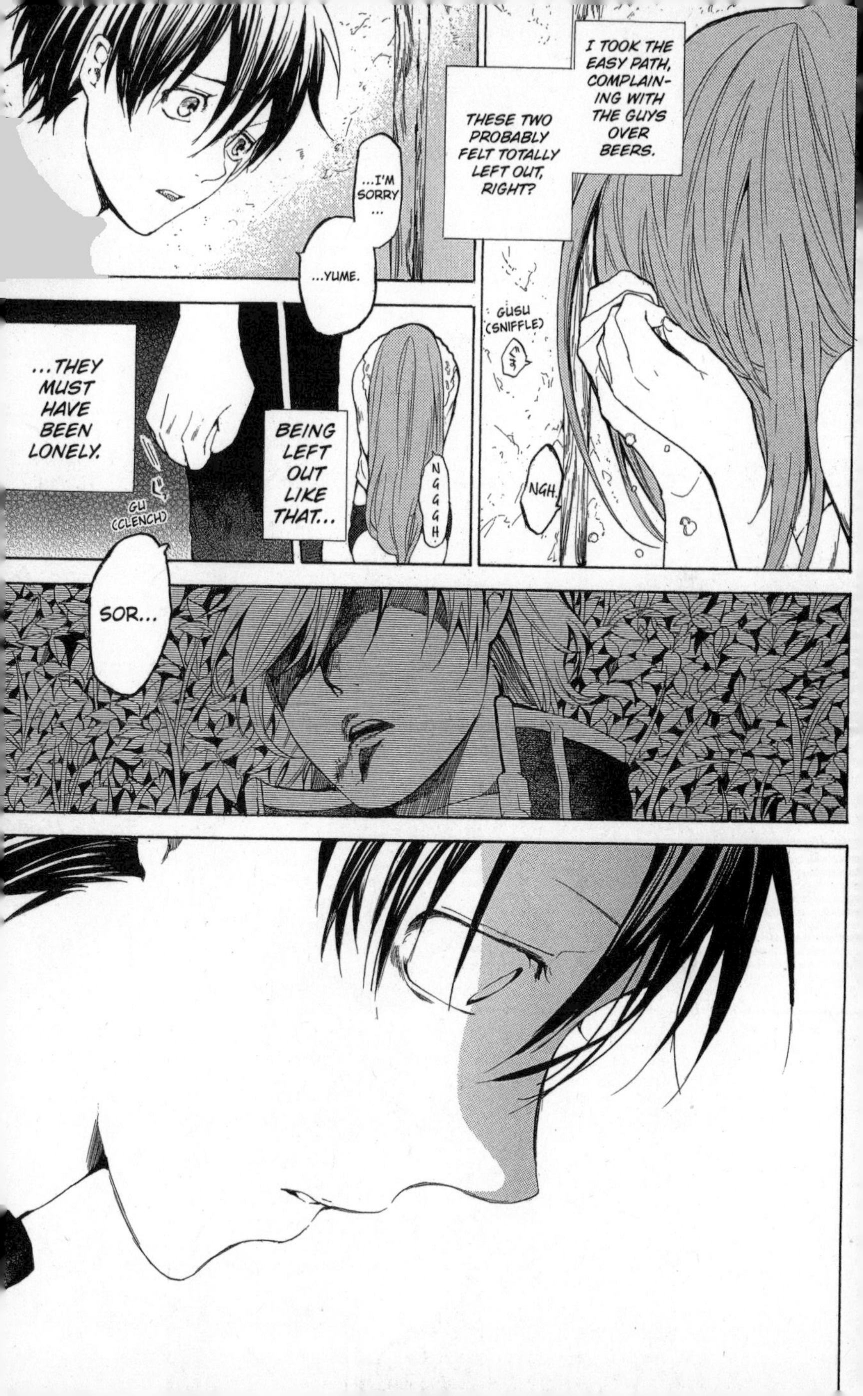
I TOOK THE EASY PATH, COMPLAINING WITH THE GUYS OVER BEERS.
THESE TWO PROBABLY FELT TOTALLY LEFT OUT, RIGHT?
...I'M SORRY...
...YUME.
GUSU (SNIFFLE)
NGH.
BEING LEFT OUT LIKE THAT...
NGGGH.
...THEY MUST HAVE BEEN LONELY.
GU (CLENCH)
SOR...

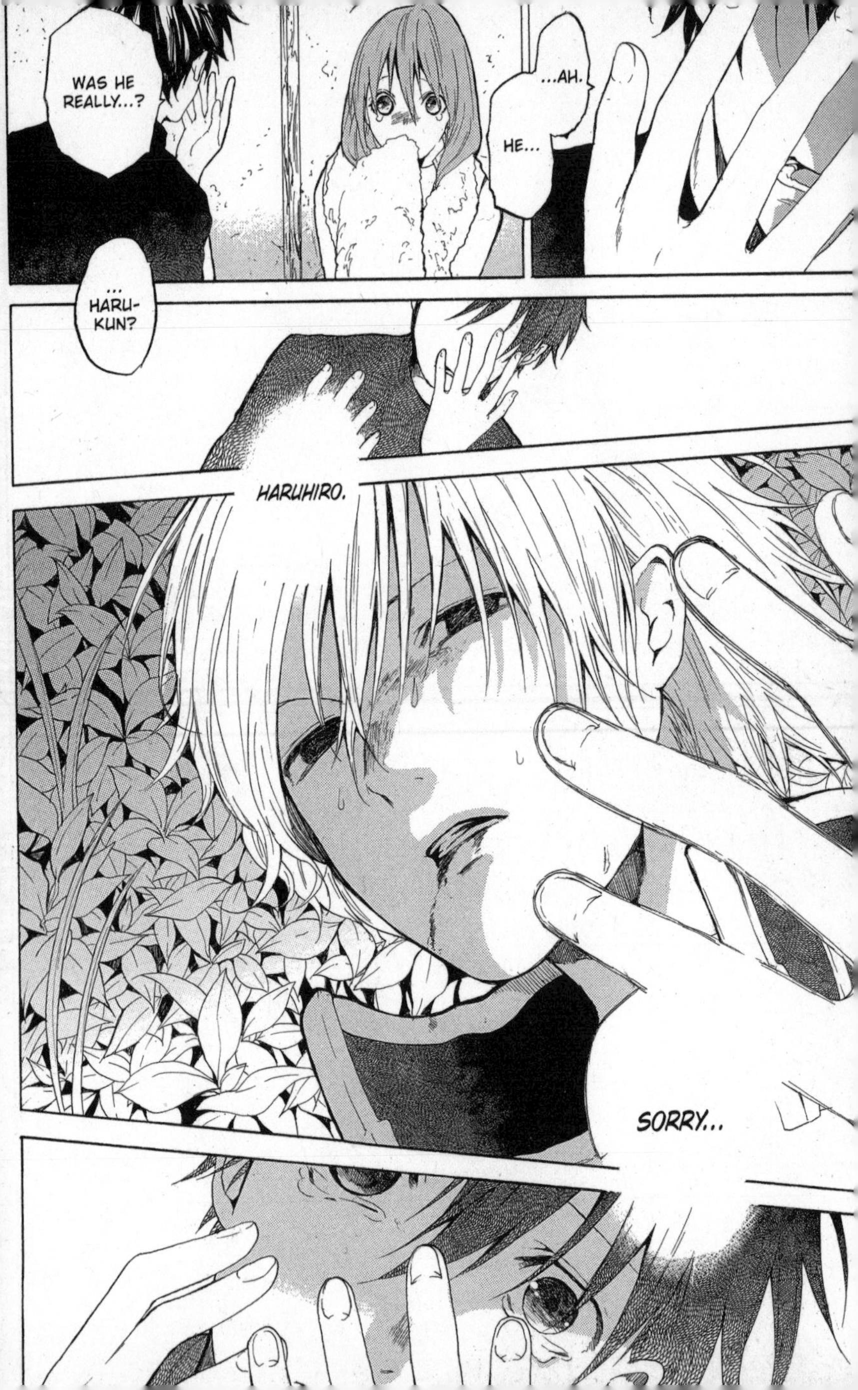
...AH.
HE...
WAS HE REALLY...?
... HARU-KUN?
HARUHIRO.
SORRY...

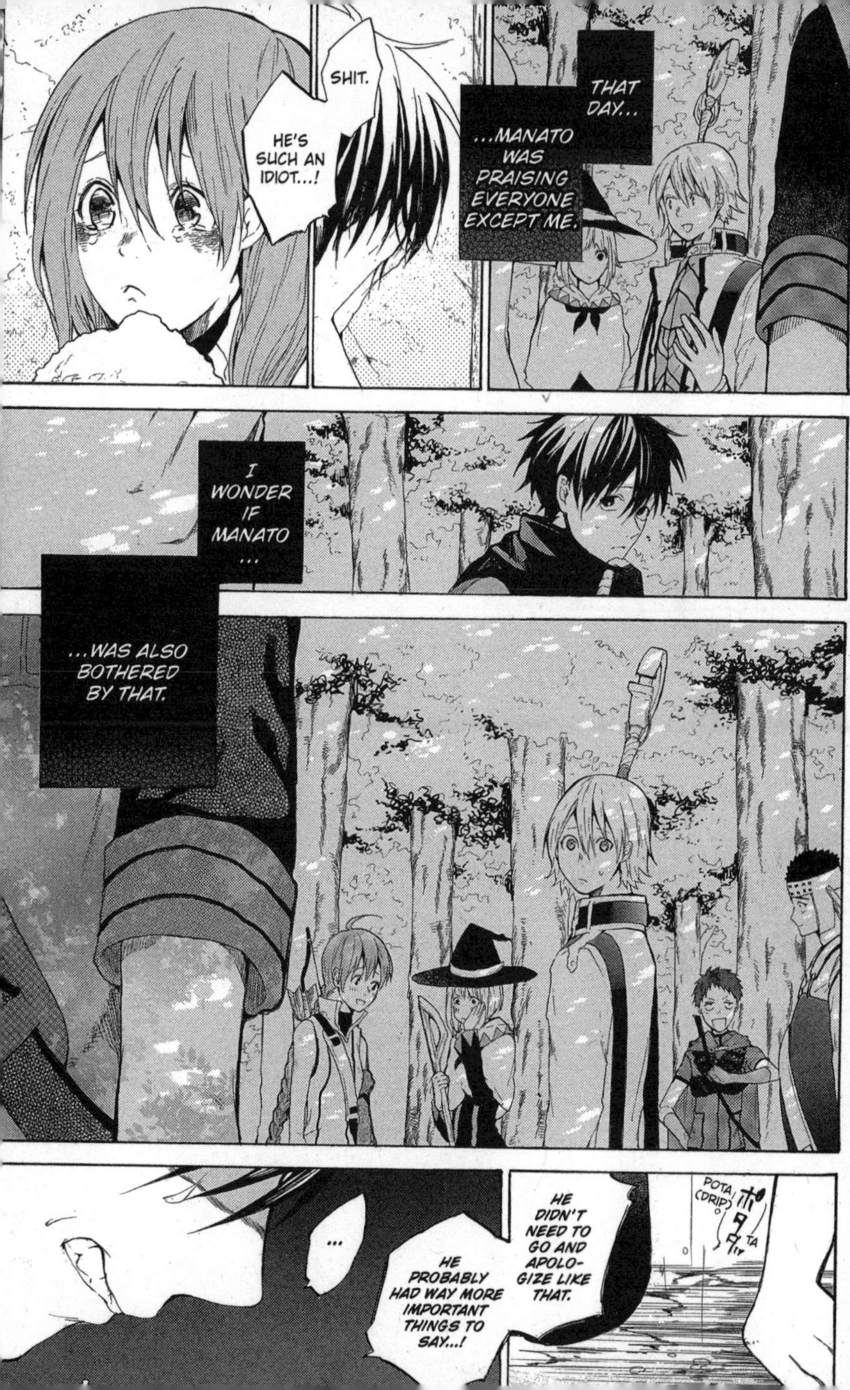
THAT DAY...
...MANATO WAS PRAISING EVERYONE EXCEPT ME.
SHIT.
HE'S SUCH AN IDIOT...!
I WONDER IF MANATO ...
...WAS ALSO BOTHERED BY THAT.
POTA (DRIP)
TA
HE DIDN'T NEED TO GO AND APOLOGIZE LIKE THAT.
...
HE PROBABLY HAD WAY MORE IMPORTANT THINGS TO SAY...!

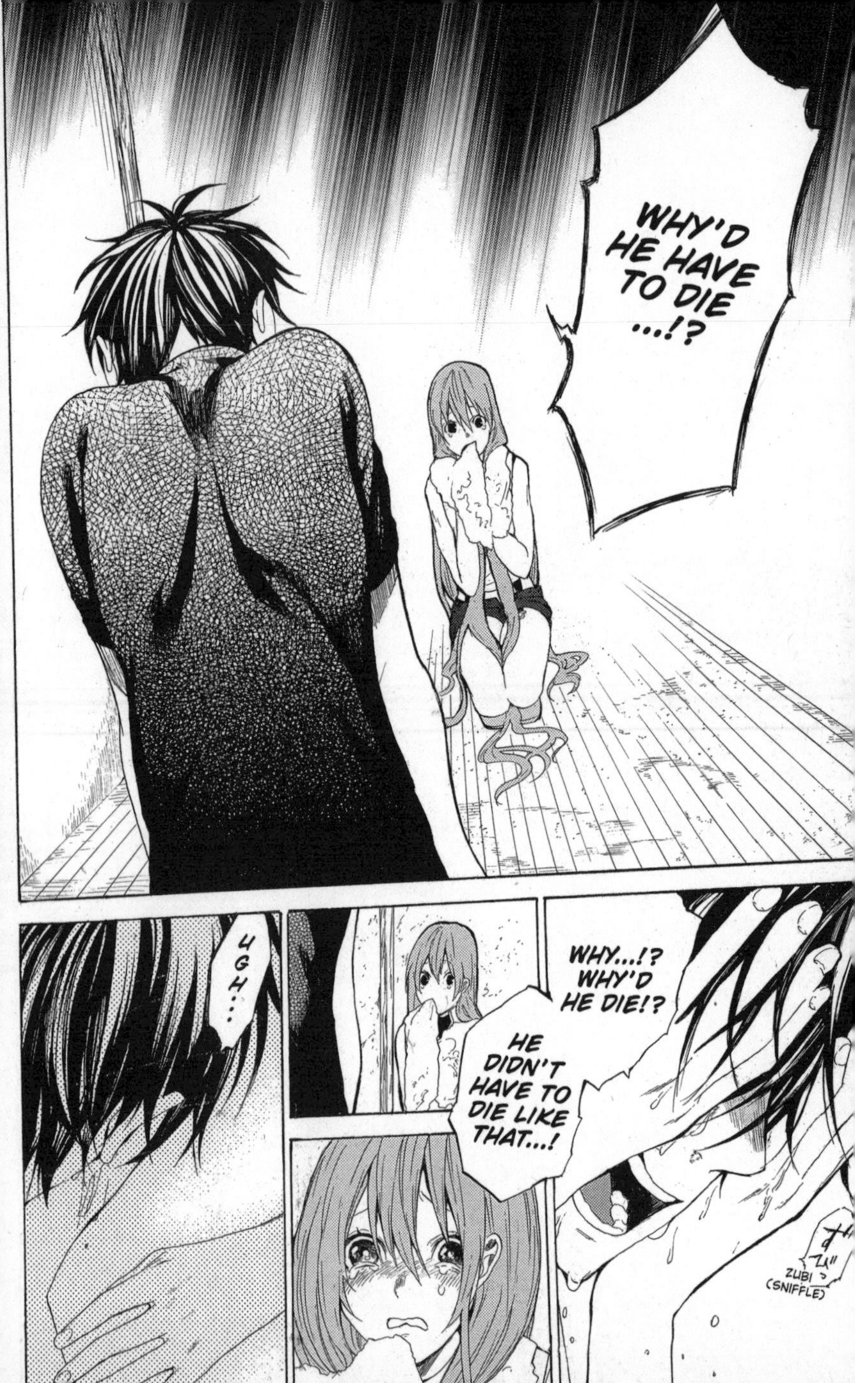
WHY'D HE HAVE TO DIE ...!?
WHY...!? WHY'D HE DIE!?
HE DIDN'T HAVE TO DIE LIKE THAT...!
ZUBI (SNIFFLE)
UGH...

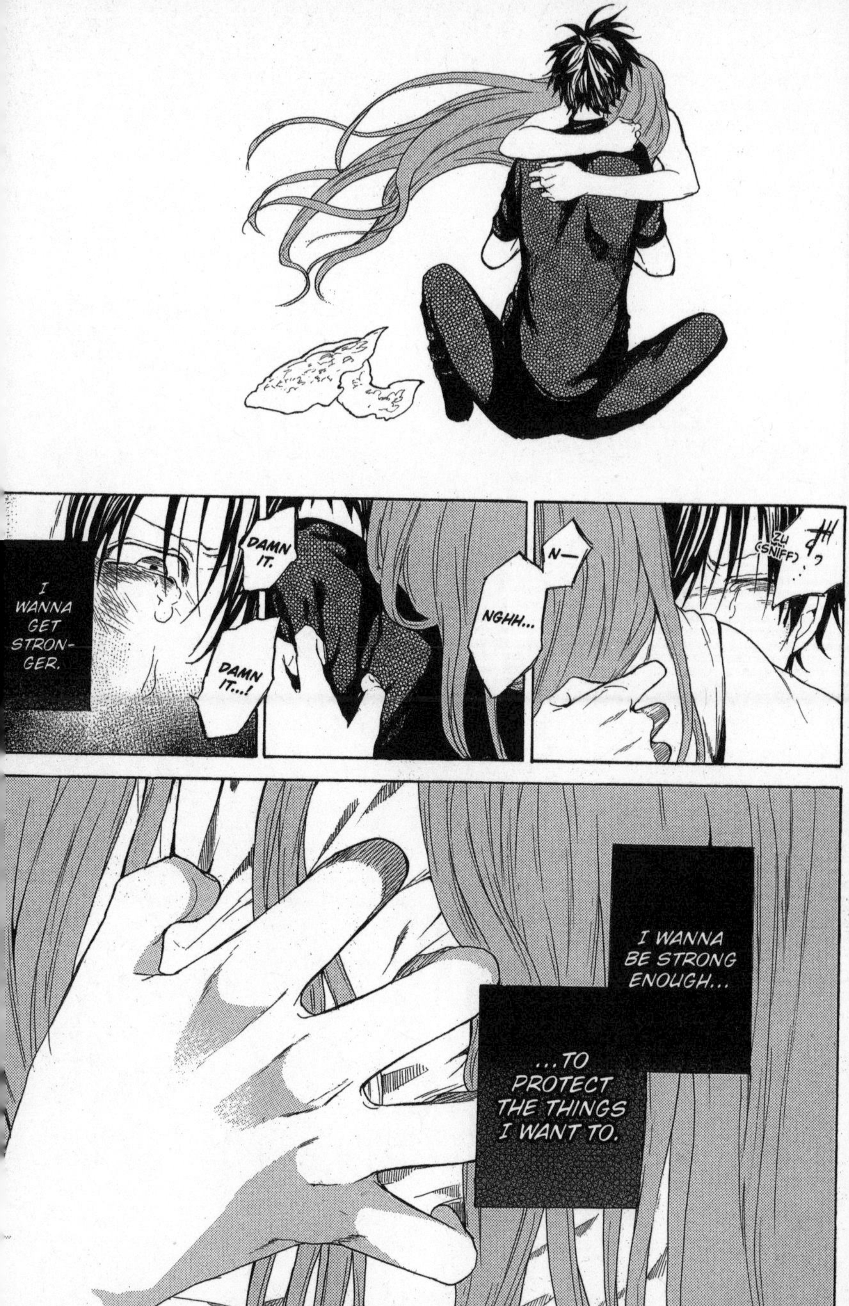
ZU (SNIFF)
N—
NGHH...
DAMN IT.
DAMN IT...!
I WANNA GET STRON-GER.
I WANNA BE STRONG ENOUGH...
...TO PROTECT THE THINGS I WANT TO.

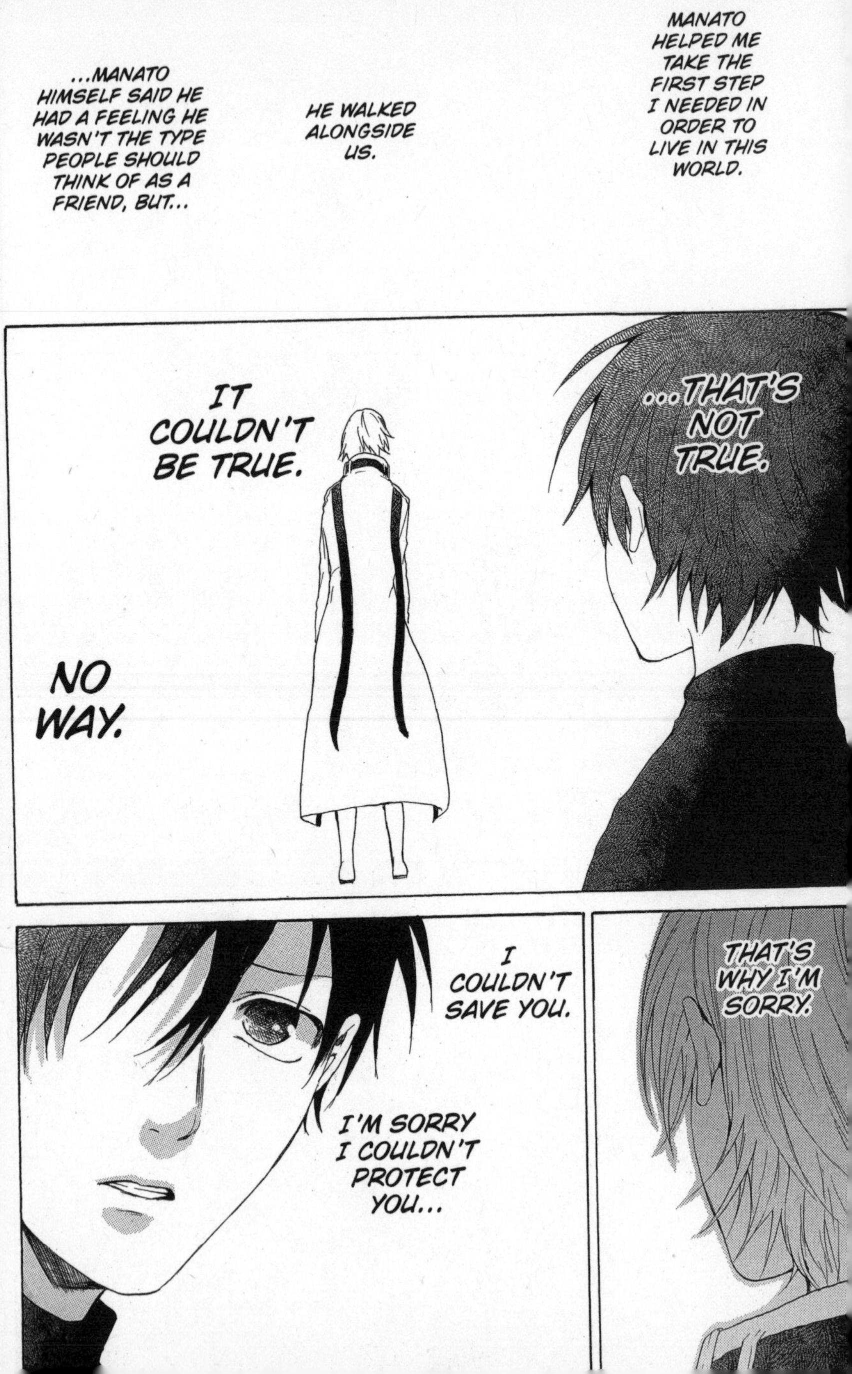
MANATO HELPED ME TAKE THE FIRST STEP I NEEDED IN ORDER TO LIVE IN THIS WORLD.
HE WALKED ALONGSIDE US.
...MANATO HIMSELF SAID HE HAD A FEELING HE WASN'T THE TYPE PEOPLE SHOULD THINK OF AS A FRIEND, BUT...
...THAT'S NOT TRUE.
IT COULDN'T BE TRUE.
NO WAY.
THAT'S WHY I'M SORRY.
I COULDN'T SAVE YOU.
I'M SORRY I COULDN'T PROTECT YOU...

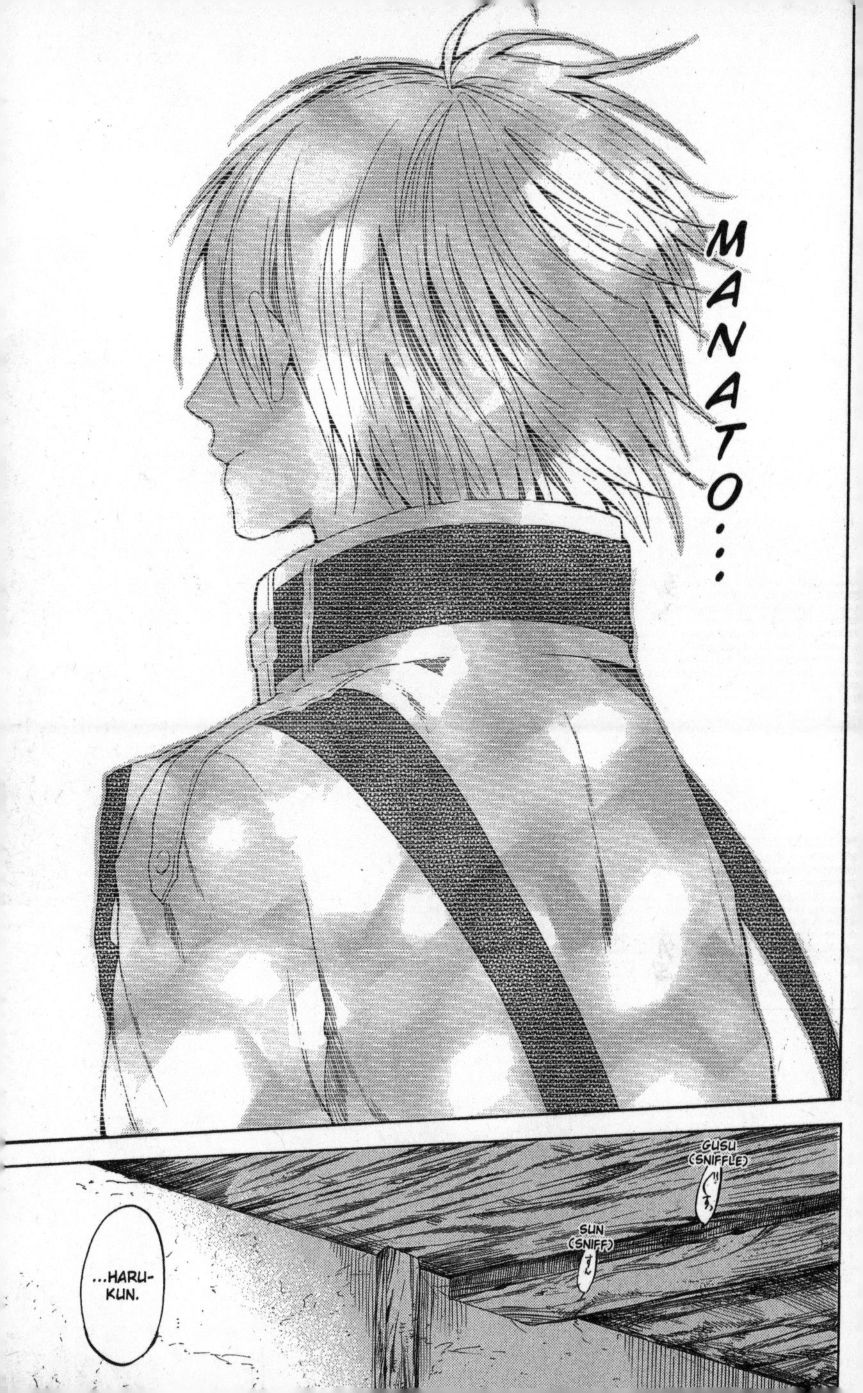
MANATO...
GUSU (SNIFFLE)
SUN (SNIFF)
...HARU-KUN.

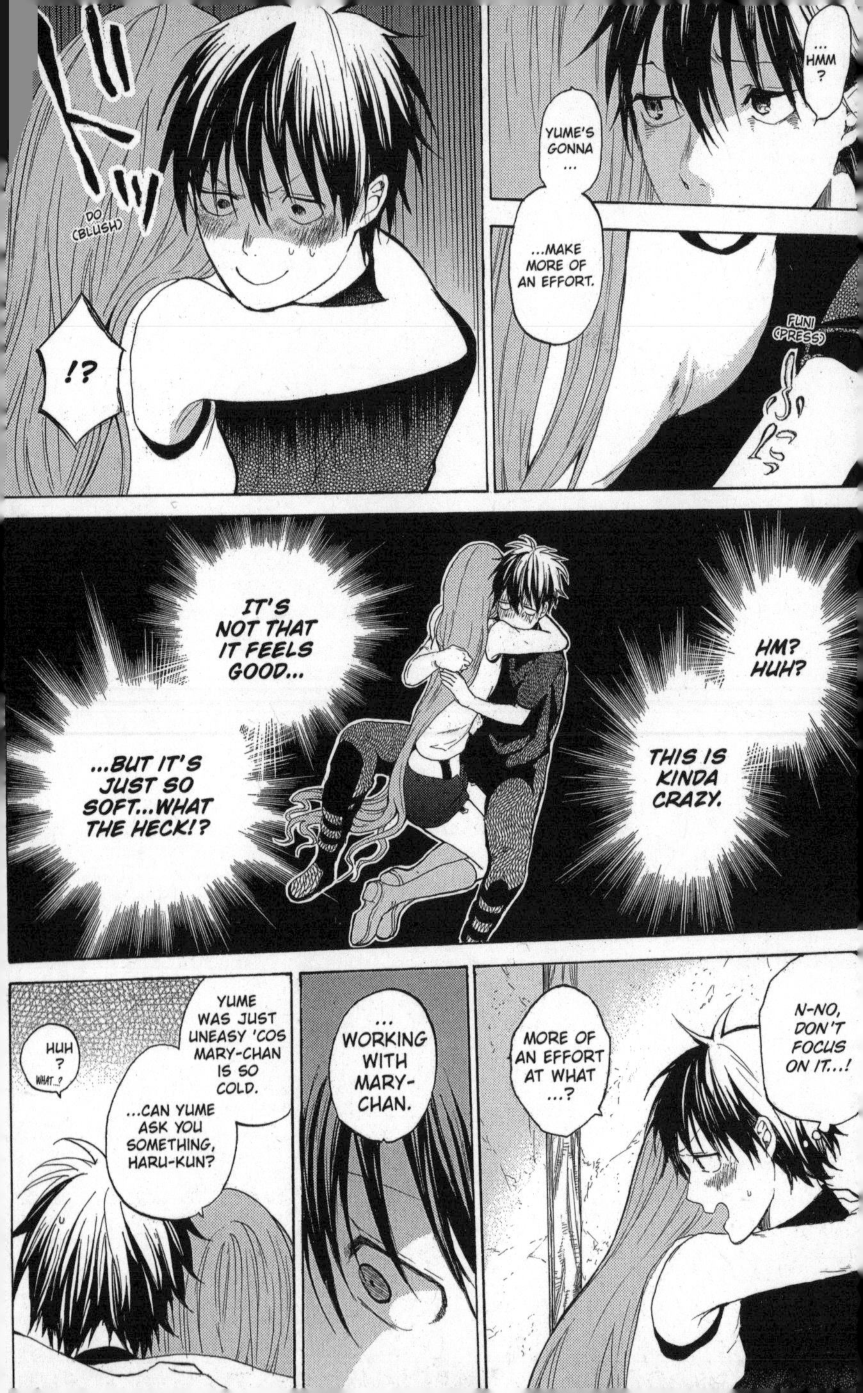
...HMM?
YUME'S GONNA...
...MAKE MORE OF AN EFFORT.
FUNI (PRESS)
DO (BLUSH)
!?
HM? HUH?
THIS IS KINDA CRAZY.
IT'S NOT THAT IT FEELS GOOD...
...BUT IT'S JUST SO SOFT...WHAT THE HECK!?
N-NO, DON'T FOCUS ON IT...!
MORE OF AN EFFORT AT WHAT...?
...WORKING WITH MARY-CHAN.
YUME WAS JUST UNEASY 'COS MARY-CHAN IS SO COLD.
HUH? WHAT...?
...CAN YUME ASK YOU SOMETHING, HARU-KUN?

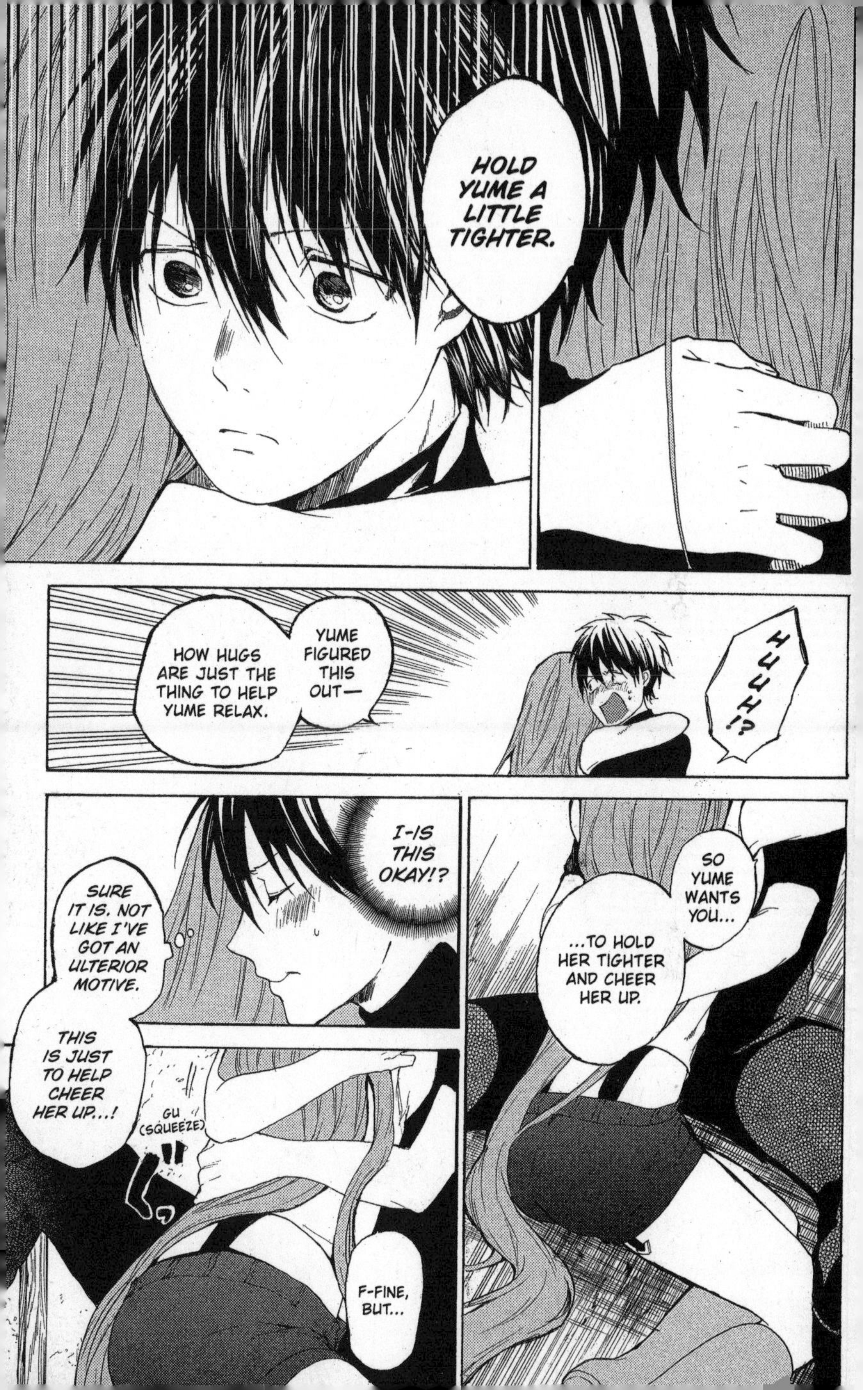
HOLD YUME A LITTLE TIGHTER.
HUUUH!?
YUME FIGURED THIS OUT—
HOW HUGS ARE JUST THE THING TO HELP YUME RELAX.
SO YUME WANTS YOU...
...TO HOLD HER TIGHTER AND CHEER HER UP.
I-IS THIS OKAY!?
SURE IT IS. NOT LIKE I'VE GOT AN ULTERIOR MOTIVE.
THIS IS JUST TO HELP CHEER HER UP...!
GU (SQUEEZE)
F-FINE, BUT...

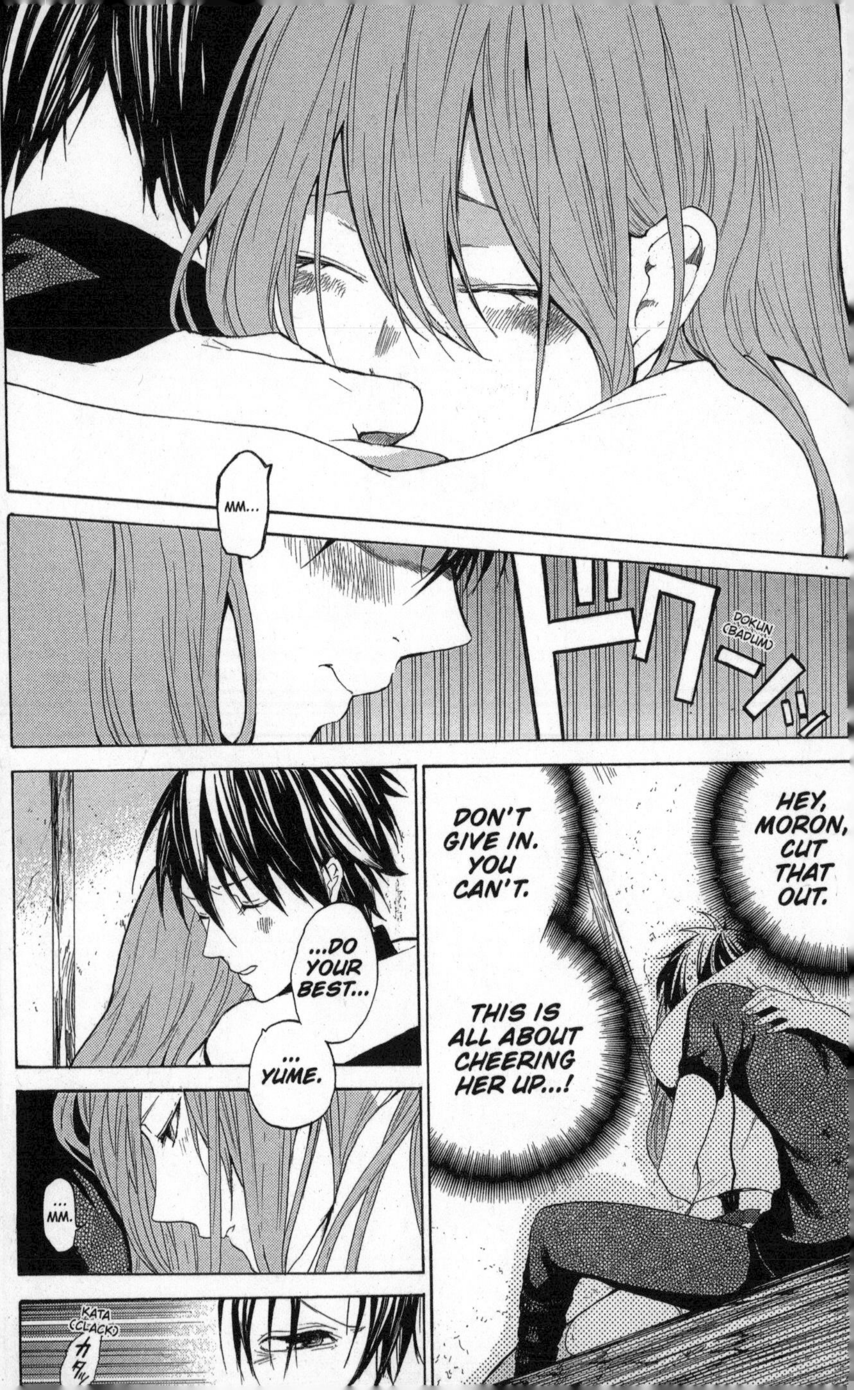
MM...
DOKUN (BADUM)
HEY, MORON, CUT THAT OUT.
DON'T GIVE IN. YOU CAN'T.
THIS IS ALL ABOUT CHEERING HER UP...!
...DO YOUR BEST...
... YUME.
... MM.
KATA (CLACK)

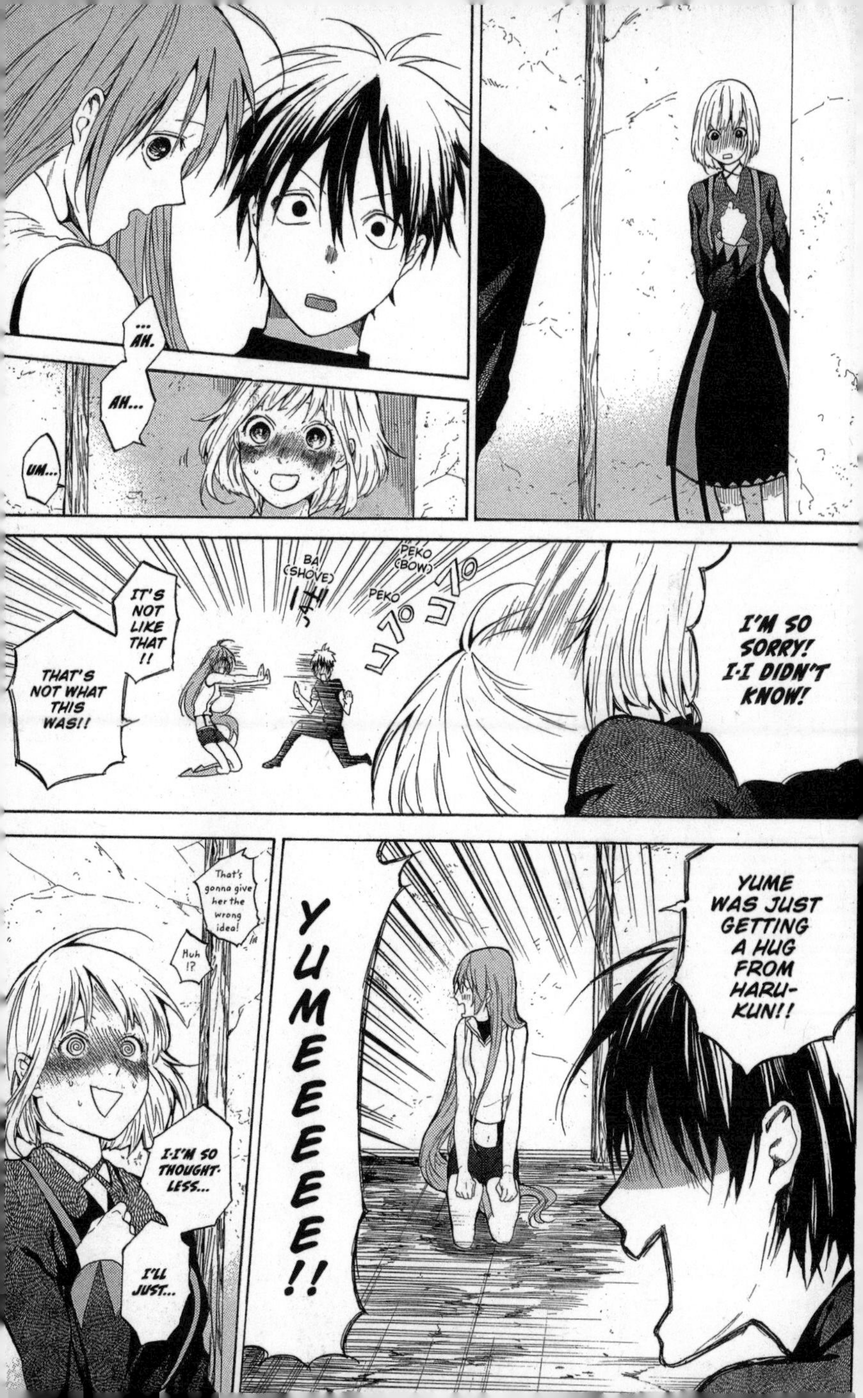

... AH.
AH...
UM...
I'M SO SORRY! I-I DIDN'T KNOW!
PEKO (BOW)
PEKO
BA (SHOVE)
IT'S NOT LIKE THAT!!
THAT'S NOT WHAT THIS WAS!!
YUME WAS JUST GETTING A HUG FROM HARU-KUN!!
YUMEEEEEEE!!
That's gonna give her the wrong idea!
Huh!?
I-I'M SO THOUGHTLESS...
I'LL JUST...

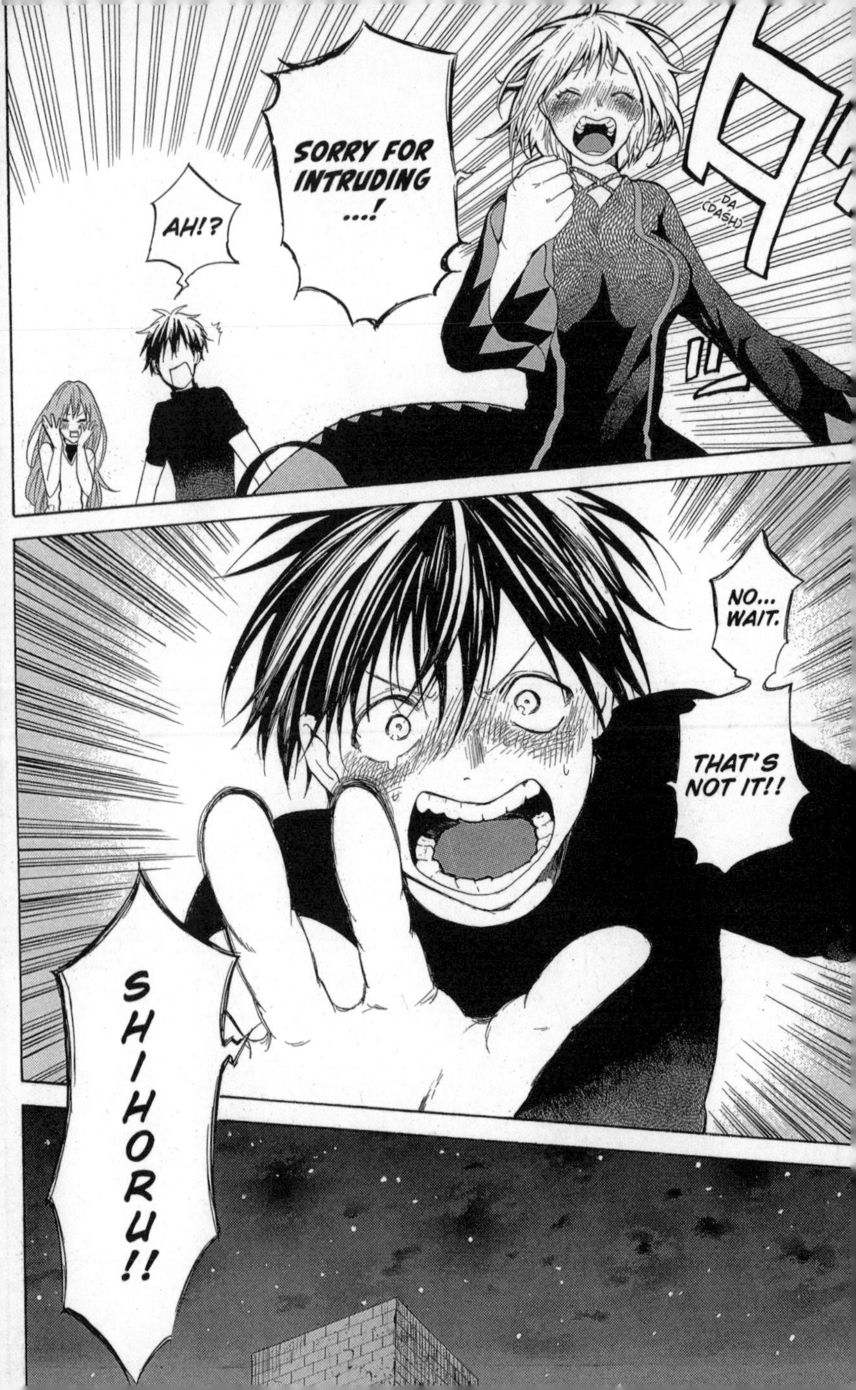
DA (DASH)
SORRY FOR INTRUDING ...!
AH!?
NO... WAIT.
THAT'S NOT IT!!
SHIHORU!!

level.8: Aim for the Top, and...

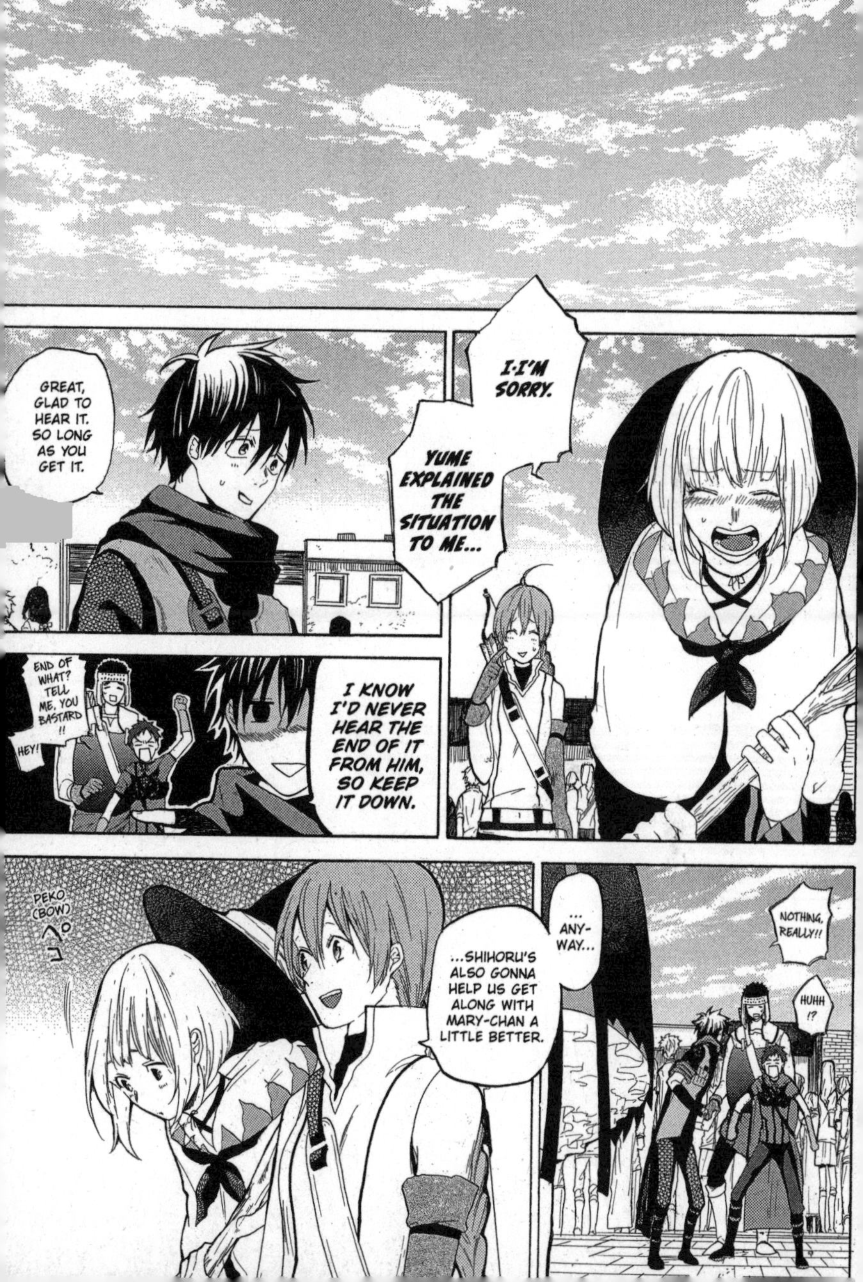
I·I'M SORRY.
YUME EXPLAINED THE SITUATION TO ME...
GREAT, GLAD TO HEAR IT. SO LONG AS YOU GET IT.
I KNOW I'D NEVER HEAR THE END OF IT FROM HIM, SO KEEP IT DOWN.
END OF WHAT? TELL ME, YOU BASTARD!!
HEY!
NOTHING, REALLY!!
HUHH!?
...ANYWAY...
...SHIHORU'S ALSO GONNA HELP US GET ALONG WITH MARY-CHAN A LITTLE BETTER.
PEKO (BOW)

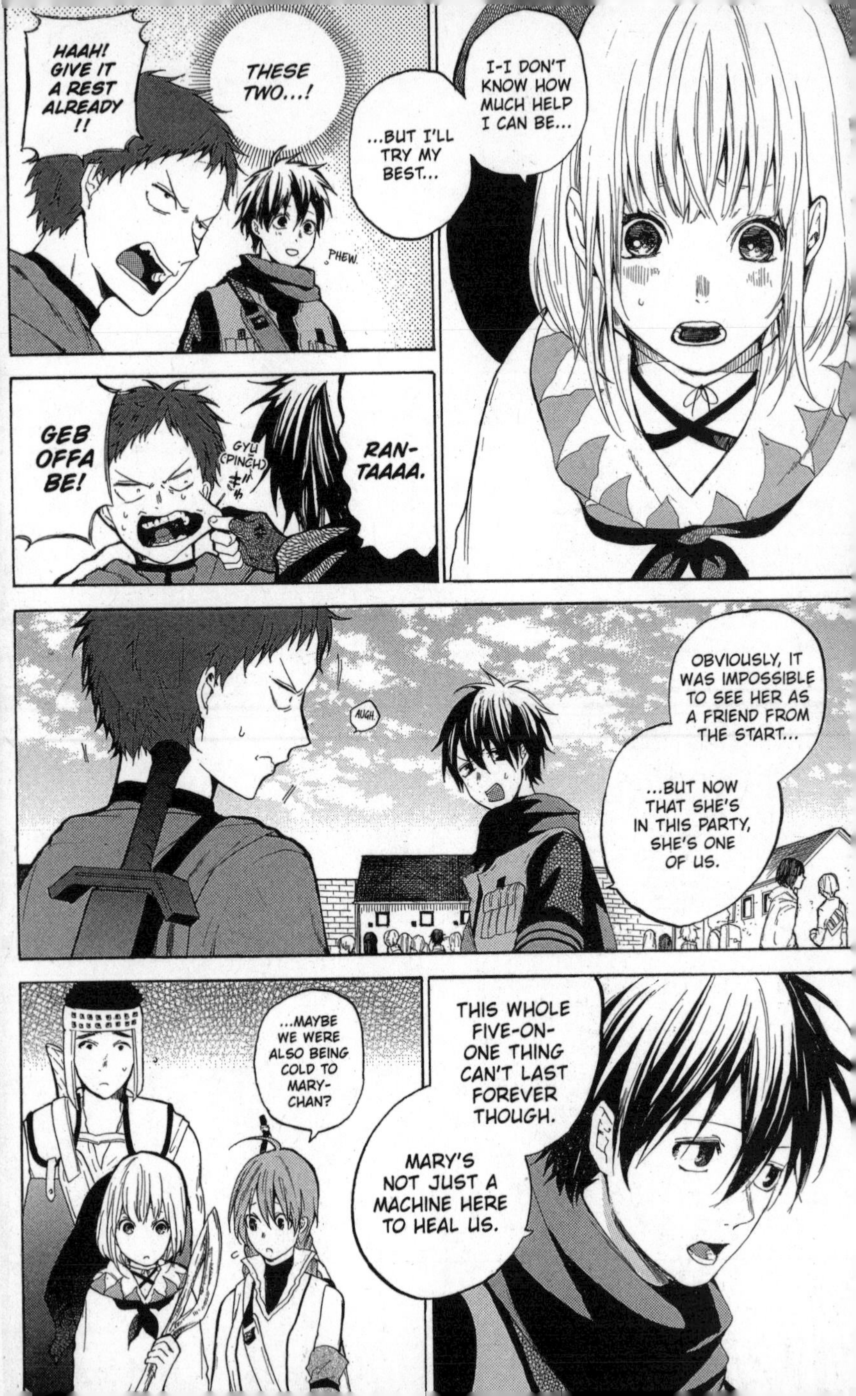
I-I DON'T KNOW HOW MUCH HELP I CAN BE...
...BUT I'LL TRY MY BEST...
THESE TWO...!
HAAH! GIVE IT A REST ALREADY!!
PHEW.
RAN-TAAAA.
GYU (PINCH)
GEB OFFA BE!
OBVIOUSLY, IT WAS IMPOSSIBLE TO SEE HER AS A FRIEND FROM THE START...
...BUT NOW THAT SHE'S IN THIS PARTY, SHE'S ONE OF US.
AUGH.
THIS WHOLE FIVE-ON-ONE THING CAN'T LAST FOREVER THOUGH.
MARY'S NOT JUST A MACHINE HERE TO HEAL US.
...MAYBE WE WERE ALSO BEING COLD TO MARY-CHAN?

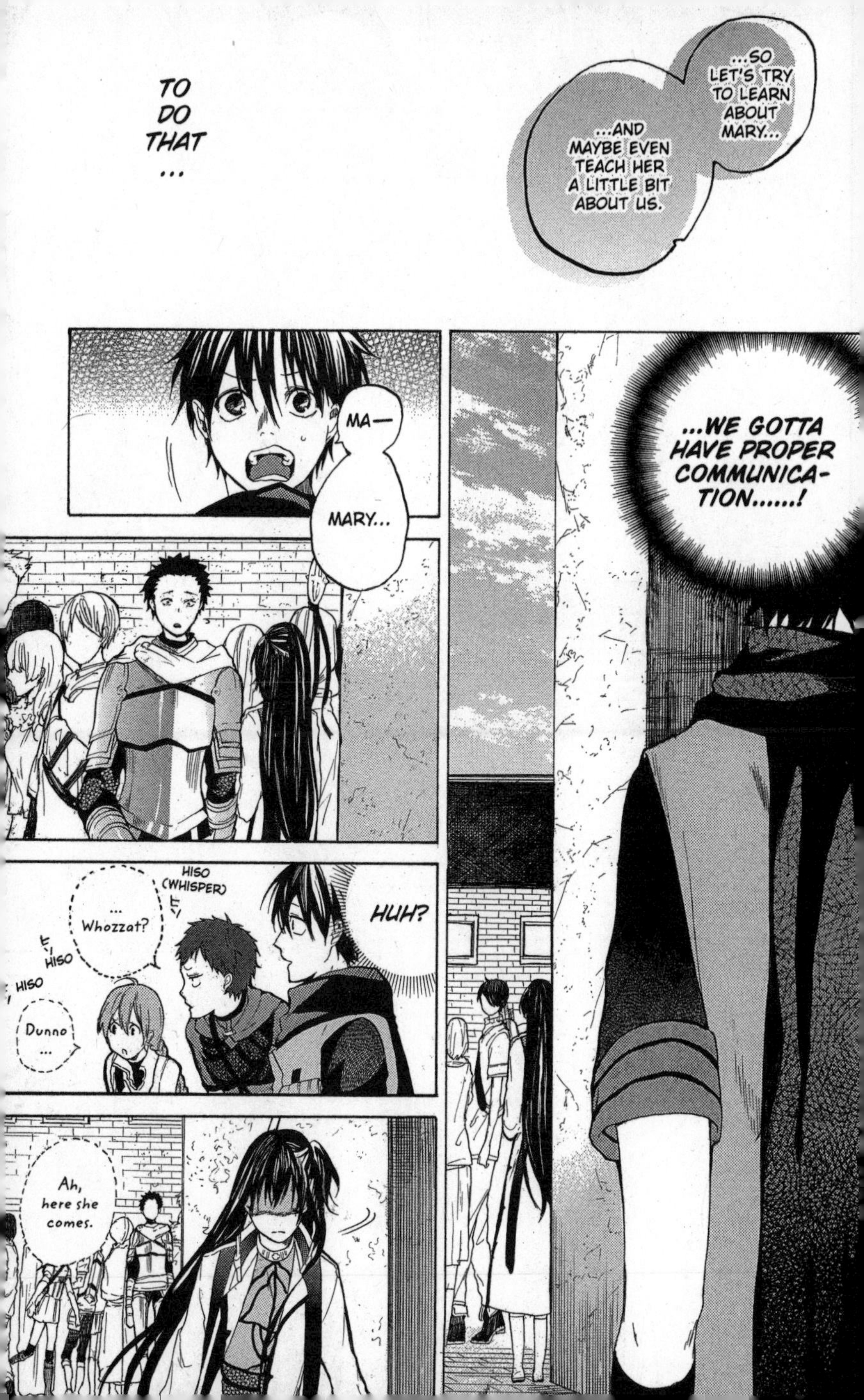
...SO LET'S TRY TO LEARN ABOUT MARY...
...AND MAYBE EVEN TEACH HER A LITTLE BIT ABOUT US.
TO DO THAT ...
...WE GOTTA HAVE PROPER COMMUNICATION......!
MA—
MARY...
HUH?
HISO (WHISPER)
... Whozzat?
HISO
HISO
Dunno ...
Ah, here she comes.

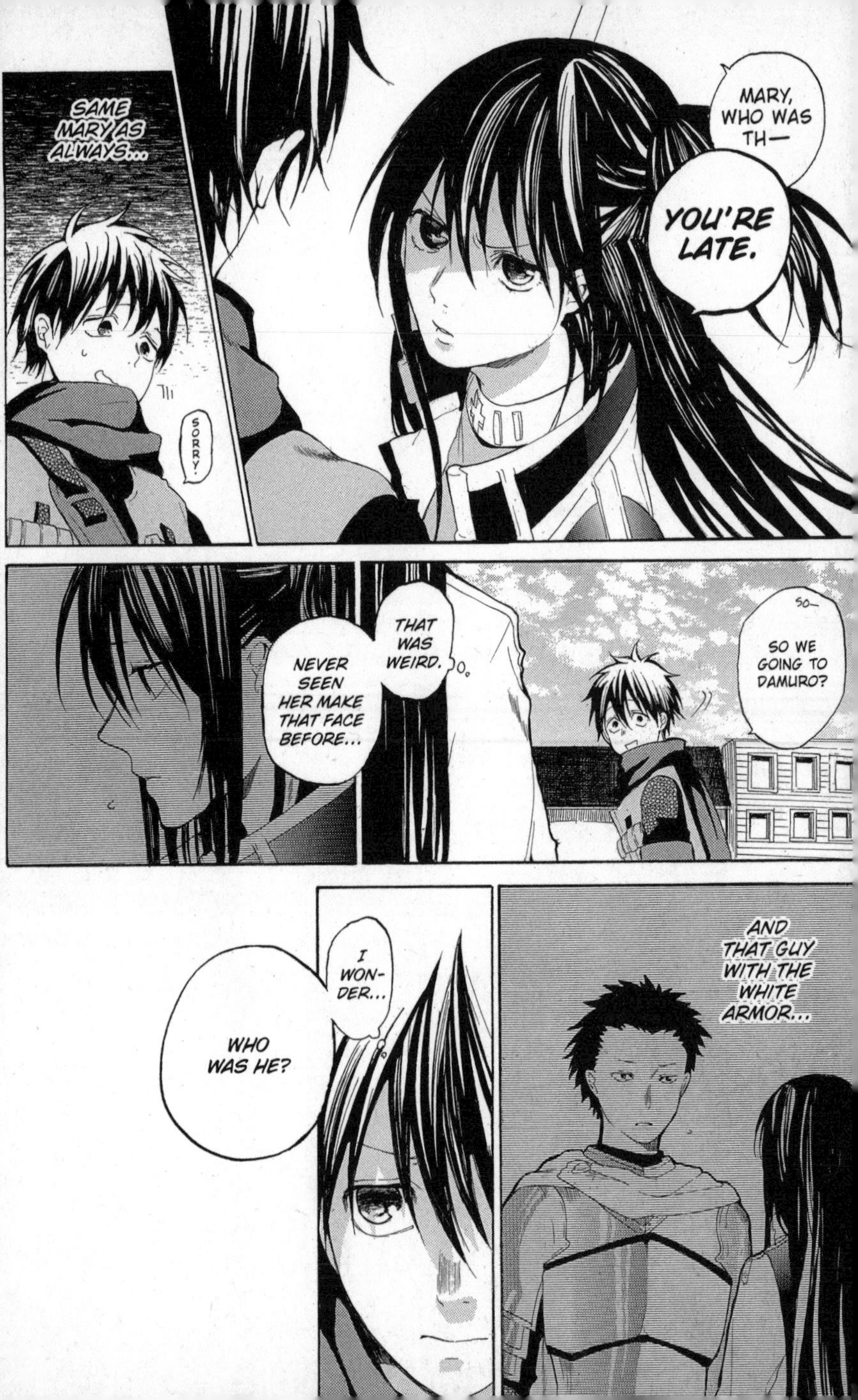
MARY, WHO WAS TH—
YOU'RE LATE.
SAME MARY AS ALWAYS...
SORRY.
SO—
SO WE GOING TO DAMURO?
THAT WAS WEIRD.
NEVER SEEN HER MAKE THAT FACE BEFORE...
AND THAT GUY WITH THE WHITE ARMOR...
I WONDER...
WHO WAS HE?

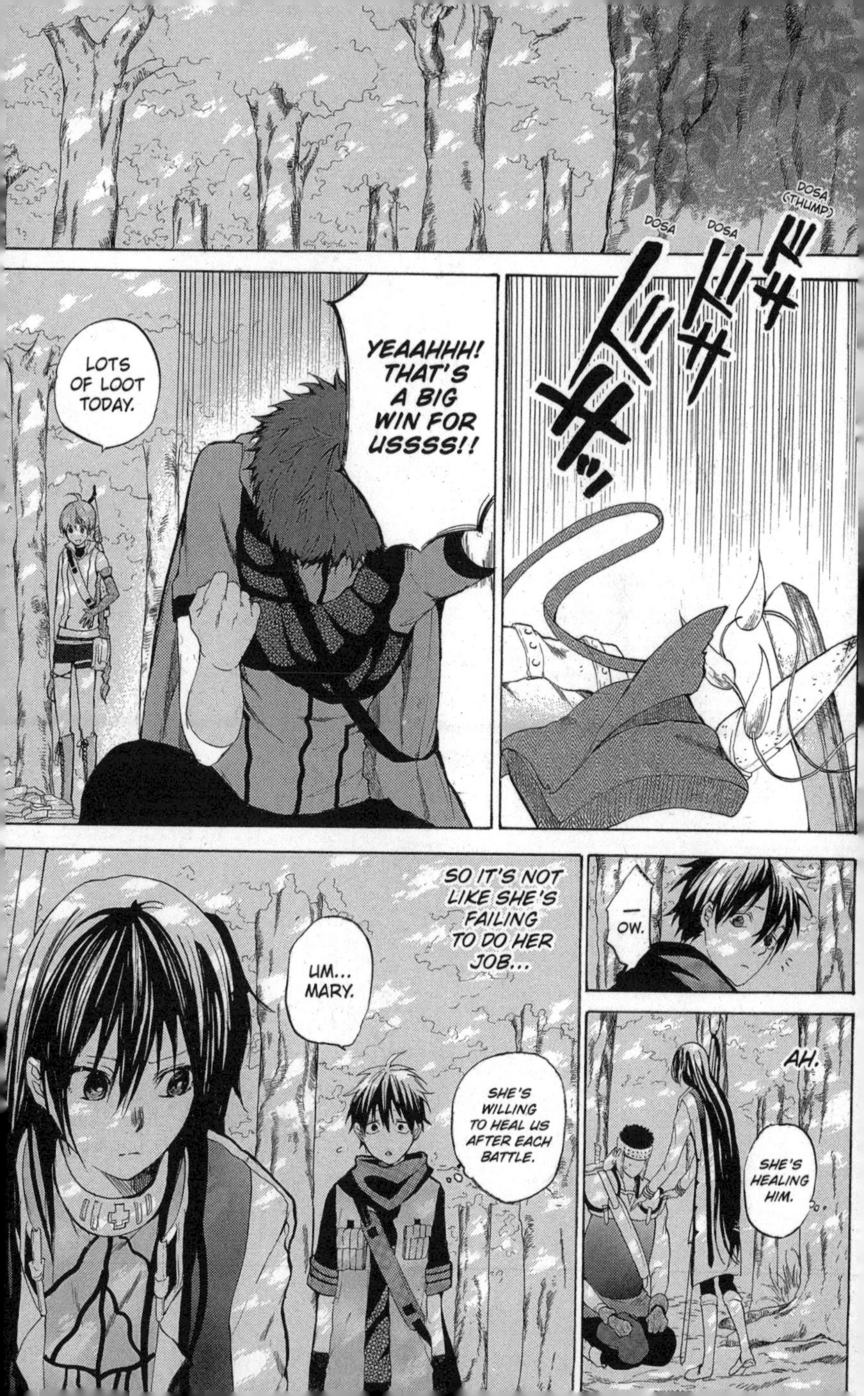
DOSA (THUMP)
DOSA
DOSA
YEAAHHH! THAT'S A BIG WIN FOR USSSS!!
LOTS OF LOOT TODAY.
—OW.
AH.
SHE'S HEALING HIM.
SO IT'S NOT LIKE SHE'S FAILING TO DO HER JOB...
SHE'S WILLING TO HEAL US AFTER EACH BATTLE.
UM... MARY.

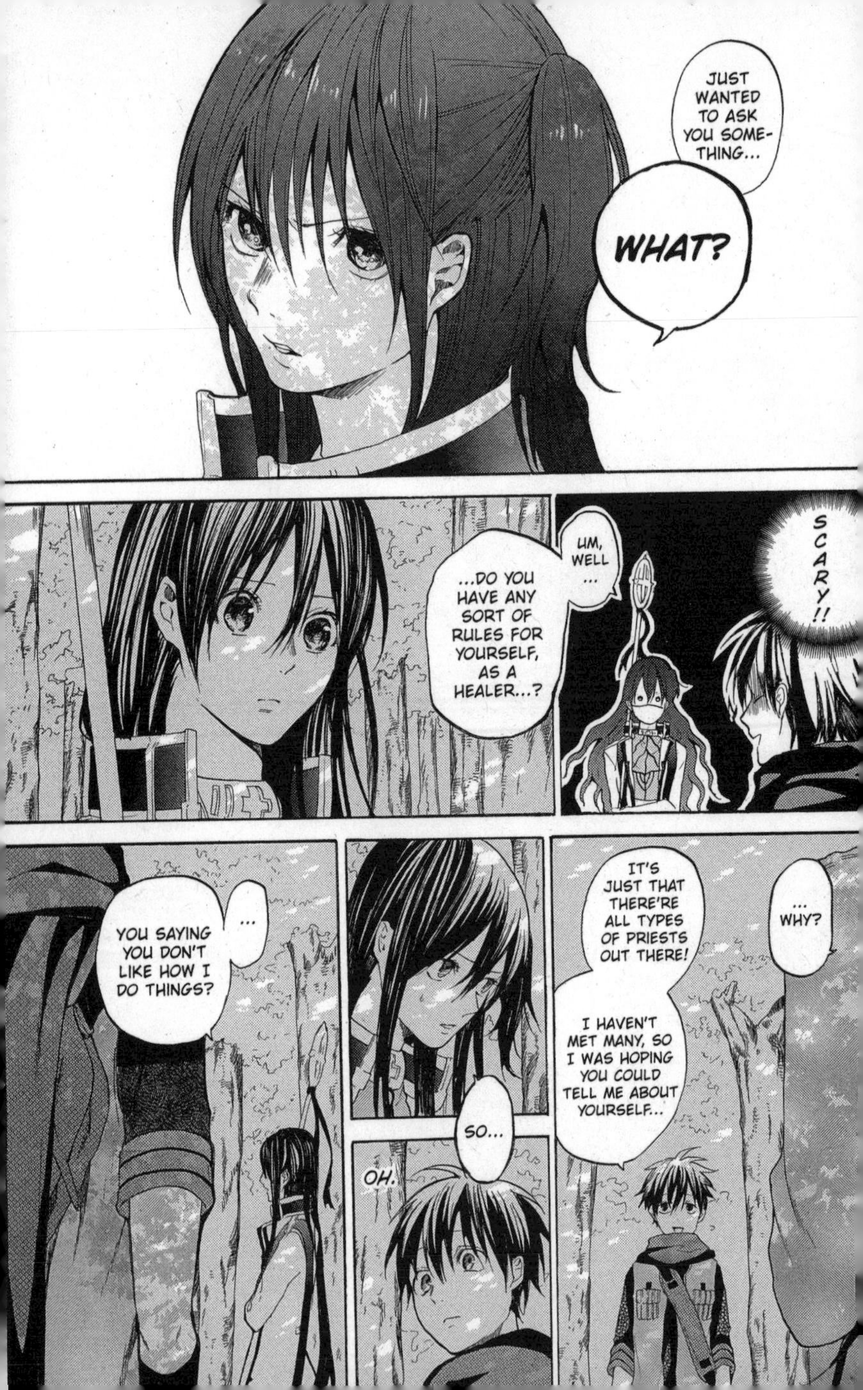
JUST WANTED TO ASK YOU SOME-THING...
WHAT?
SCARY!!
UM, WELL ...
...DO YOU HAVE ANY SORT OF RULES FOR YOURSELF, AS A HEALER...?
... WHY?
IT'S JUST THAT THERE'RE ALL TYPES OF PRIESTS OUT THERE!
I HAVEN'T MET MANY, SO I WAS HOPING YOU COULD TELL ME ABOUT YOURSELF...
SO...
OH.
...
YOU SAYING YOU DON'T LIKE HOW I DO THINGS?

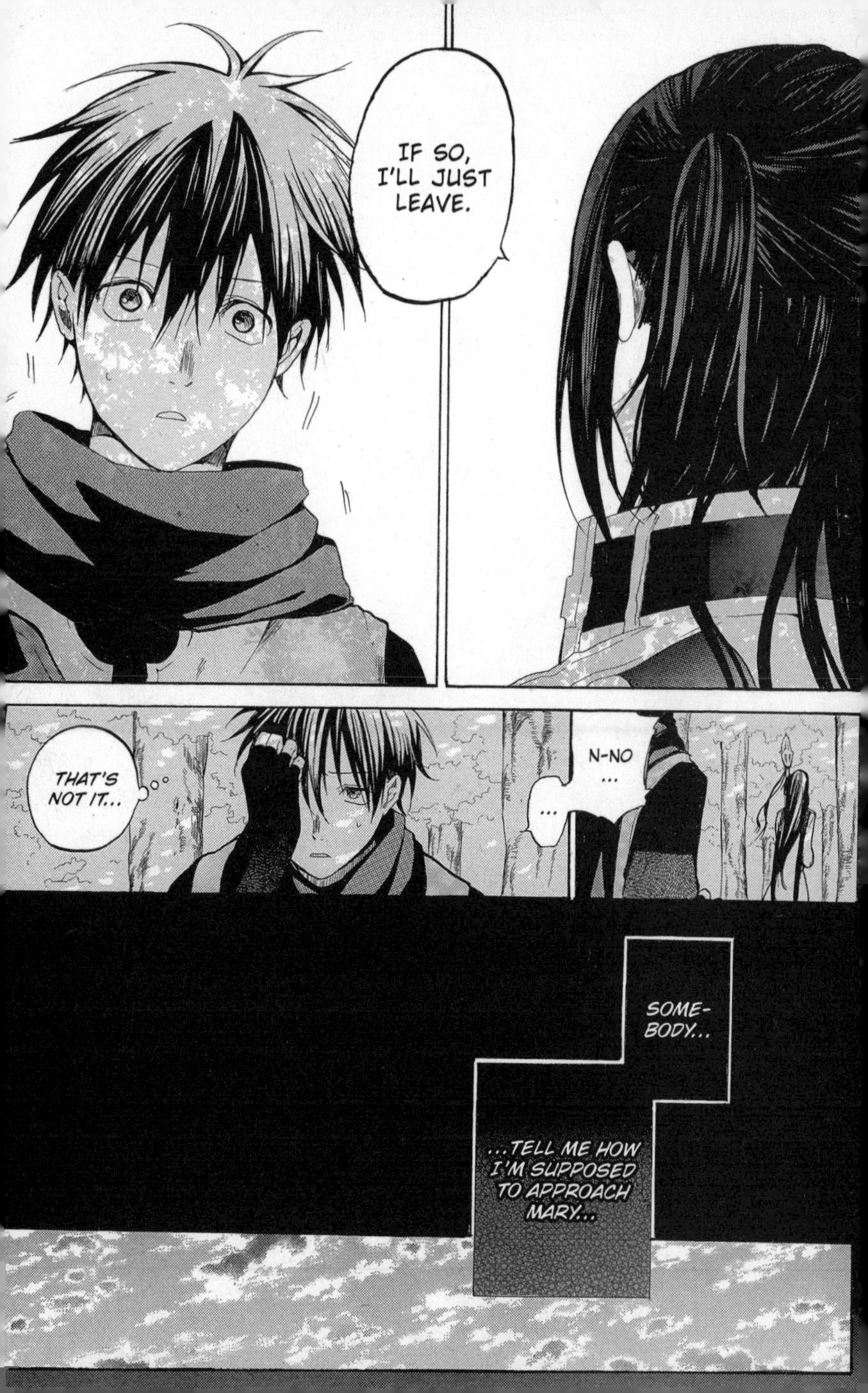
IF SO, I'LL JUST LEAVE.
N-NO ... ...
THAT'S NOT IT...
SOME-BODY...
...TELL ME HOW I'M SUPPOSED TO APPROACH MARY...

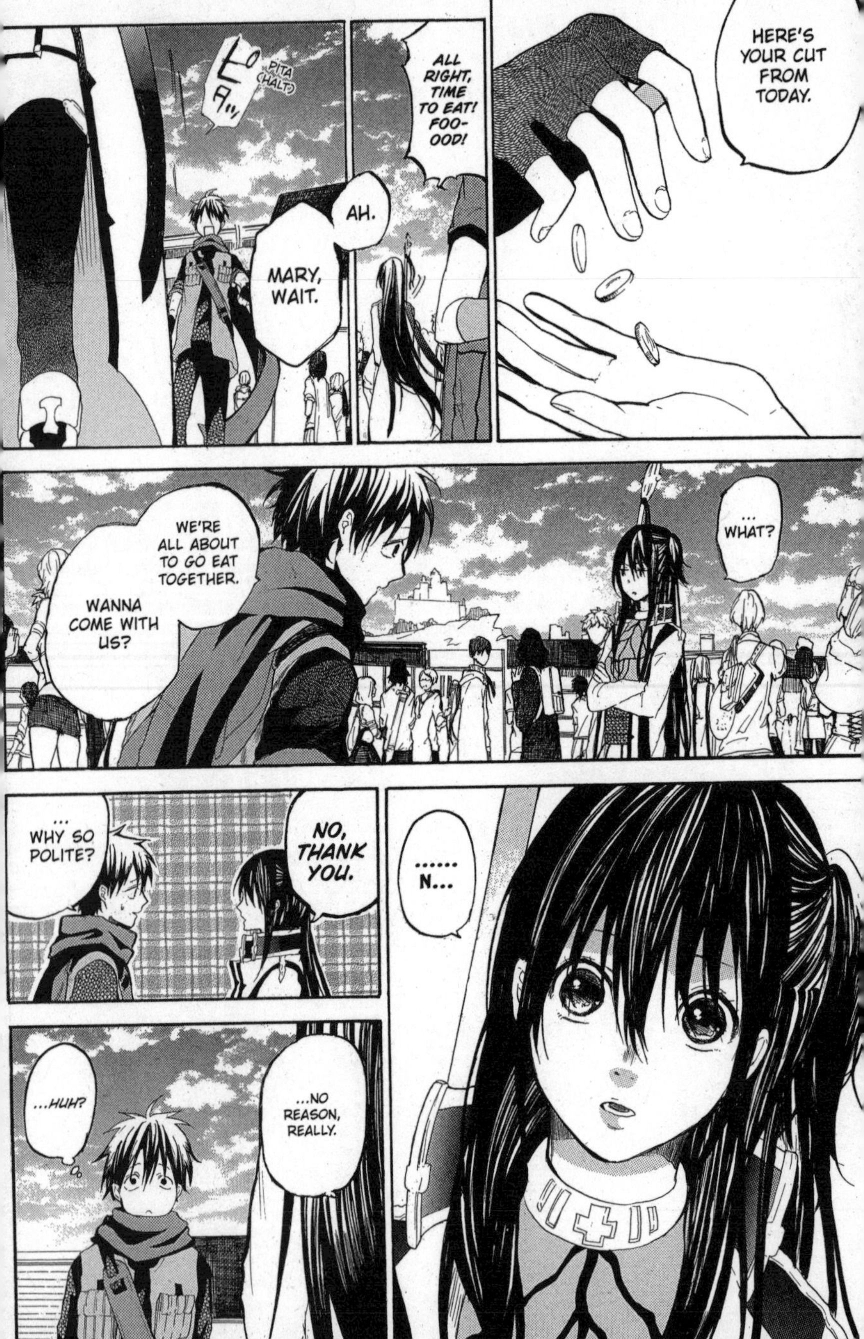
HERE'S YOUR CUT FROM TODAY.
ALL RIGHT, TIME TO EAT! FOOO-OOD!
AH.
MARY, WAIT.
PITA (HALT)
... WHAT?
WE'RE ALL ABOUT TO GO EAT TOGETHER.
WANNA COME WITH US?
...... N...
NO, THANK YOU.
... WHY SO POLITE?
...NO REASON, REALLY.
...HUH?

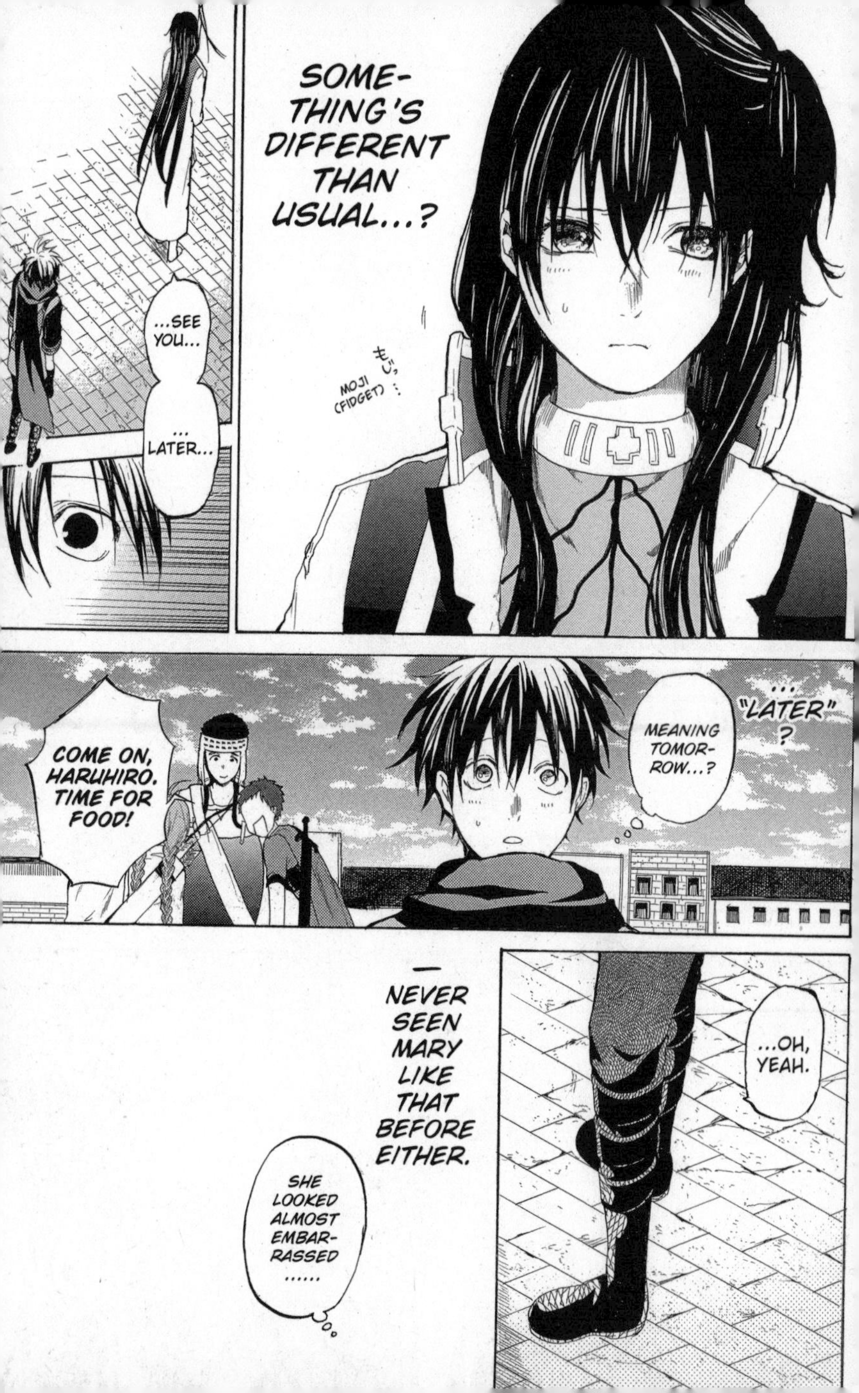
SOMETHING'S DIFFERENT THAN USUAL...?
もじっ
MOJI (FIDGET)
...SEE YOU...
... LATER...
... "LATER"?
MEANING TOMORROW...?
COME ON, HARUHIRO. TIME FOR FOOD!
...OH, YEAH.
—NEVER SEEN MARY LIKE THAT BEFORE EITHER.
SHE LOOKED ALMOST EMBARRASSED ......

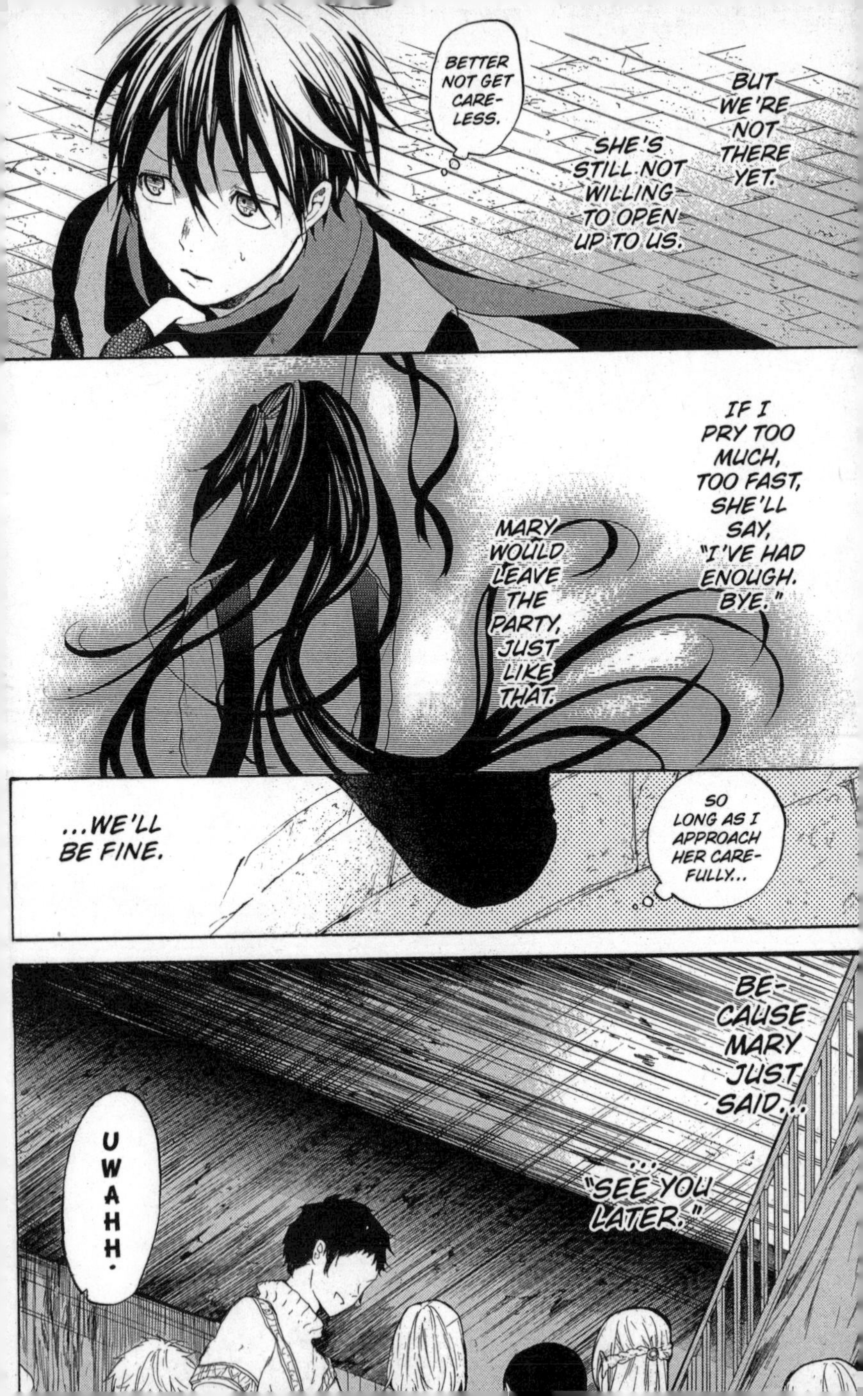
BUT WE'RE NOT THERE YET.
SHE'S STILL NOT WILLING TO OPEN UP TO US.
BETTER NOT GET CARE-LESS.
IF I PRY TOO MUCH, TOO FAST, SHE'LL SAY, "I'VE HAD ENOUGH. BYE."
MARY WOULD LEAVE THE PARTY, JUST LIKE THAT.
SO LONG AS I APPROACH HER CARE-FULLY...
...WE'LL BE FINE.
BE-CAUSE MARY JUST SAID...
..."SEE YOU LATER."
UWAHH.

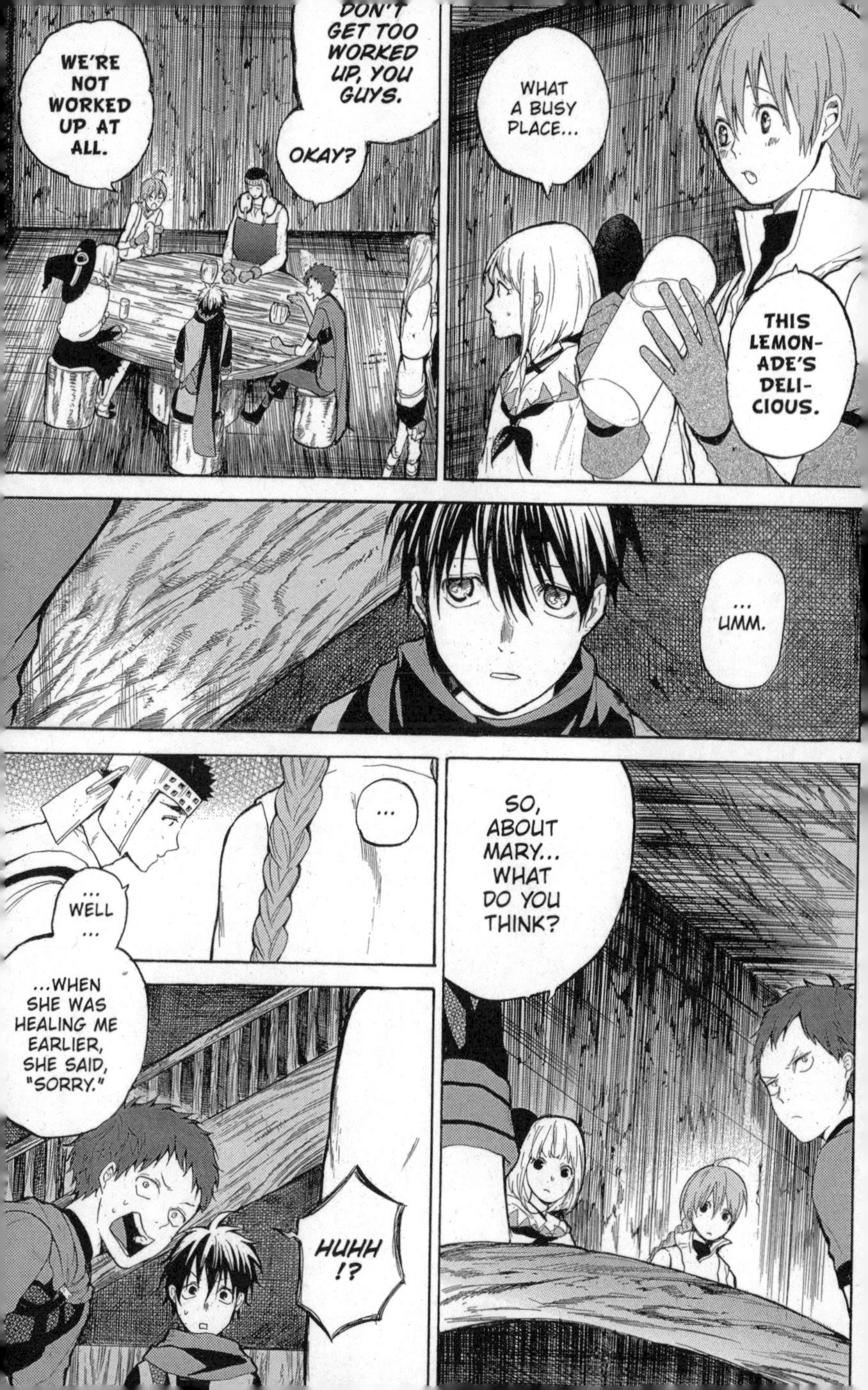
WHAT A BUSY PLACE...
THIS LEMONADE'S DELICIOUS.
DON'T GET TOO WORKED UP, YOU GUYS.
OKAY?
WE'RE NOT WORKED UP AT ALL.
... UMM.
SO, ABOUT MARY... WHAT DO YOU THINK?
...
... WELL ...
...WHEN SHE WAS HEALING ME EARLIER, SHE SAID, "SORRY."
HUHH !?

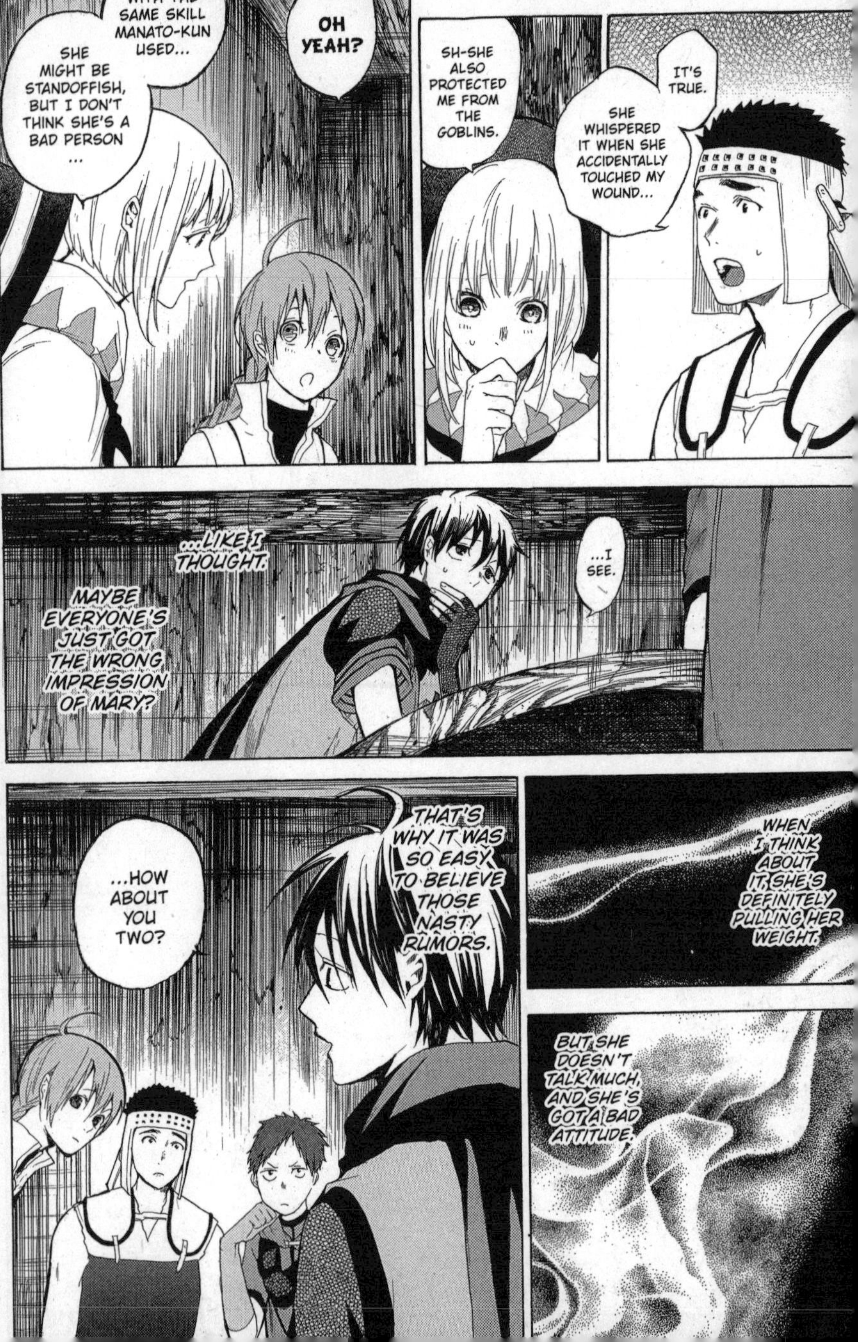
IT'S TRUE.
SHE WHISPERED IT WHEN SHE ACCIDENTALLY TOUCHED MY WOUND...
SH-SHE ALSO PROTECTED ME FROM THE GOBLINS.
OH YEAH?
YES, WITH THE SAME SKILL MANATO-KUN USED...
SHE MIGHT BE STANDOFFISH, BUT I DON'T THINK SHE'S A BAD PERSON...
...I SEE.
...LIKE I THOUGHT.
MAYBE EVERYONE'S JUST GOT THE WRONG IMPRESSION OF MARY?
WHEN I THINK ABOUT IT, SHE'S DEFINITELY PULLING HER WEIGHT.
BUT SHE DOESN'T TALK MUCH, AND SHE'S GOT A BAD ATTITUDE.
THAT'S WHY IT WAS SO EASY TO BELIEVE THOSE NASTY RUMORS.
...HOW ABOUT YOU TWO?

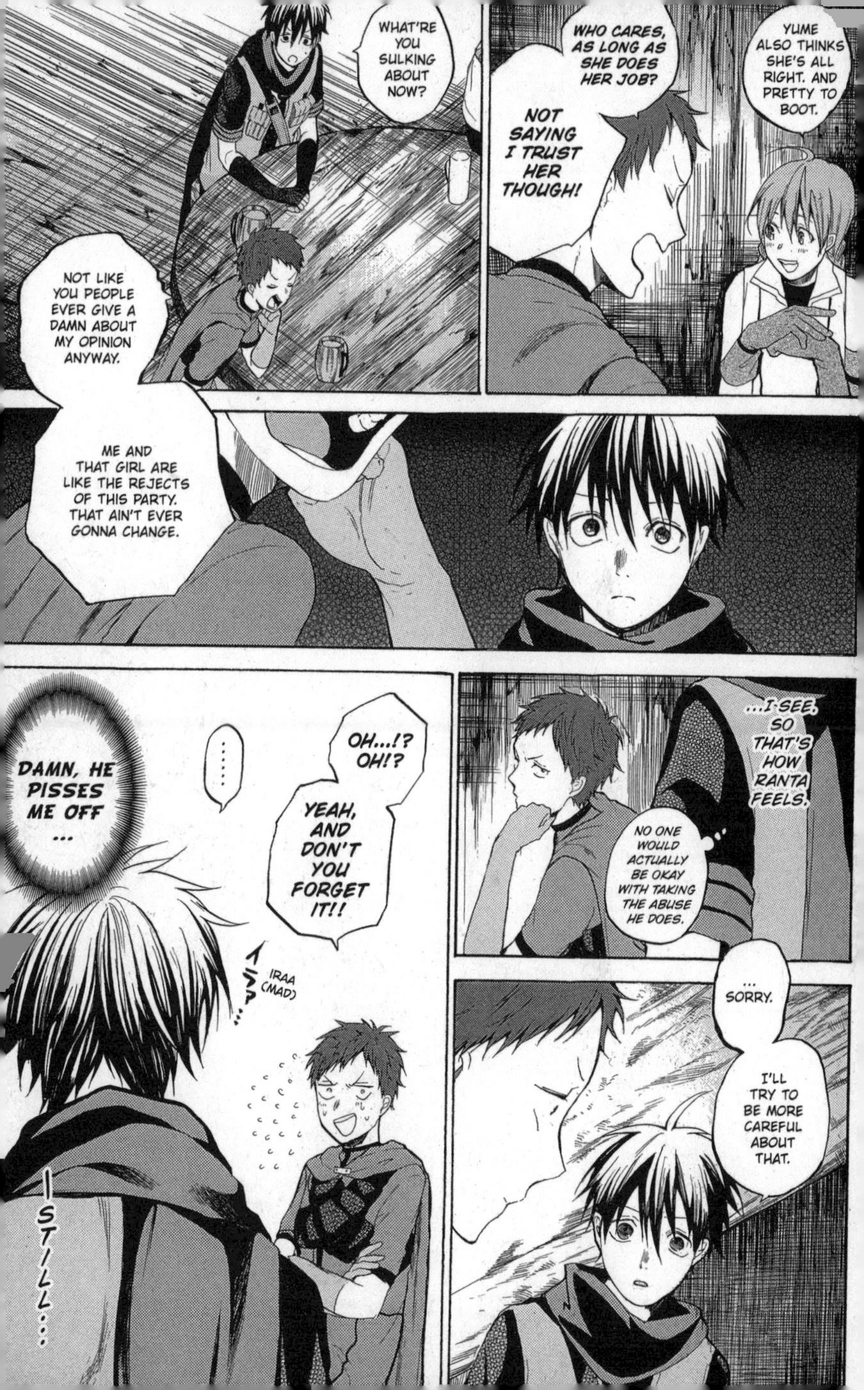
YUME ALSO THINKS SHE'S ALL RIGHT. AND PRETTY TO BOOT.
WHO CARES, AS LONG AS SHE DOES HER JOB?
NOT SAYING I TRUST HER THOUGH!
WHAT'RE YOU SULKING ABOUT NOW?
NOT LIKE YOU PEOPLE EVER GIVE A DAMN ABOUT MY OPINION ANYWAY.
ME AND THAT GIRL ARE LIKE THE REJECTS OF THIS PARTY. THAT AIN'T EVER GONNA CHANGE.
...I SEE. SO THAT'S HOW RANTA FEELS.
NO ONE WOULD ACTUALLY BE OKAY WITH TAKING THE ABUSE HE DOES.
... SORRY.
I'LL TRY TO BE MORE CAREFUL ABOUT THAT.
OH...!? OH!?
......
DAMN, HE PISSES ME OFF ...
YEAH, AND DON'T YOU FORGET IT!!
イラァ...
IRAA (MAD)
STILL...

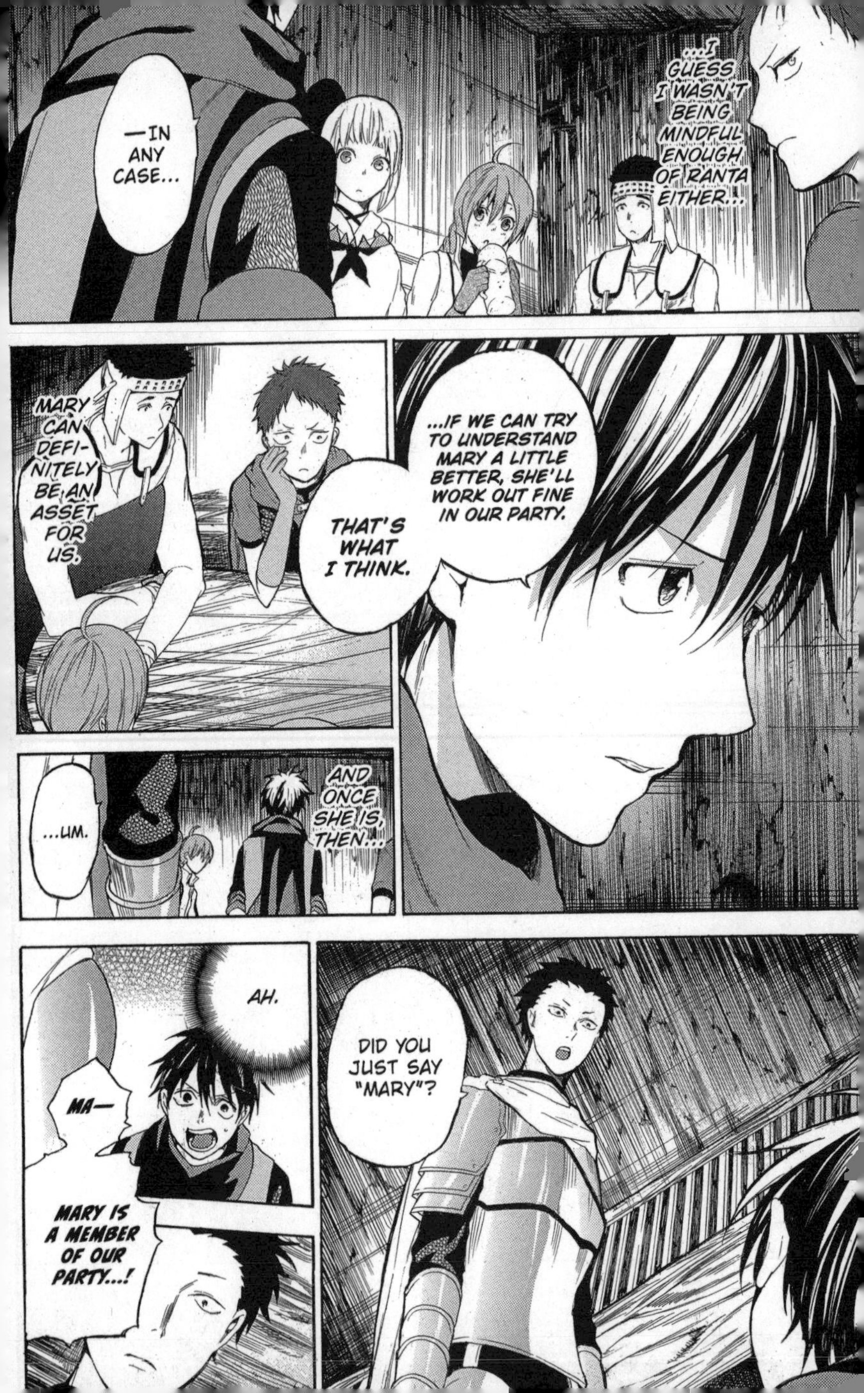
...I GUESS I WASN'T BEING MINDFUL ENOUGH OF RANTA EITHER...
—IN ANY CASE...
...IF WE CAN TRY TO UNDERSTAND MARY A LITTLE BETTER, SHE'LL WORK OUT FINE IN OUR PARTY.
THAT'S WHAT I THINK.
MARY CAN DEFINITELY BE AN ASSET FOR US.
AND ONCE SHE IS, THEN...
...UM.
DID YOU JUST SAY "MARY"?
AH.
MA—
MARY IS A MEMBER OF OUR PARTY...!

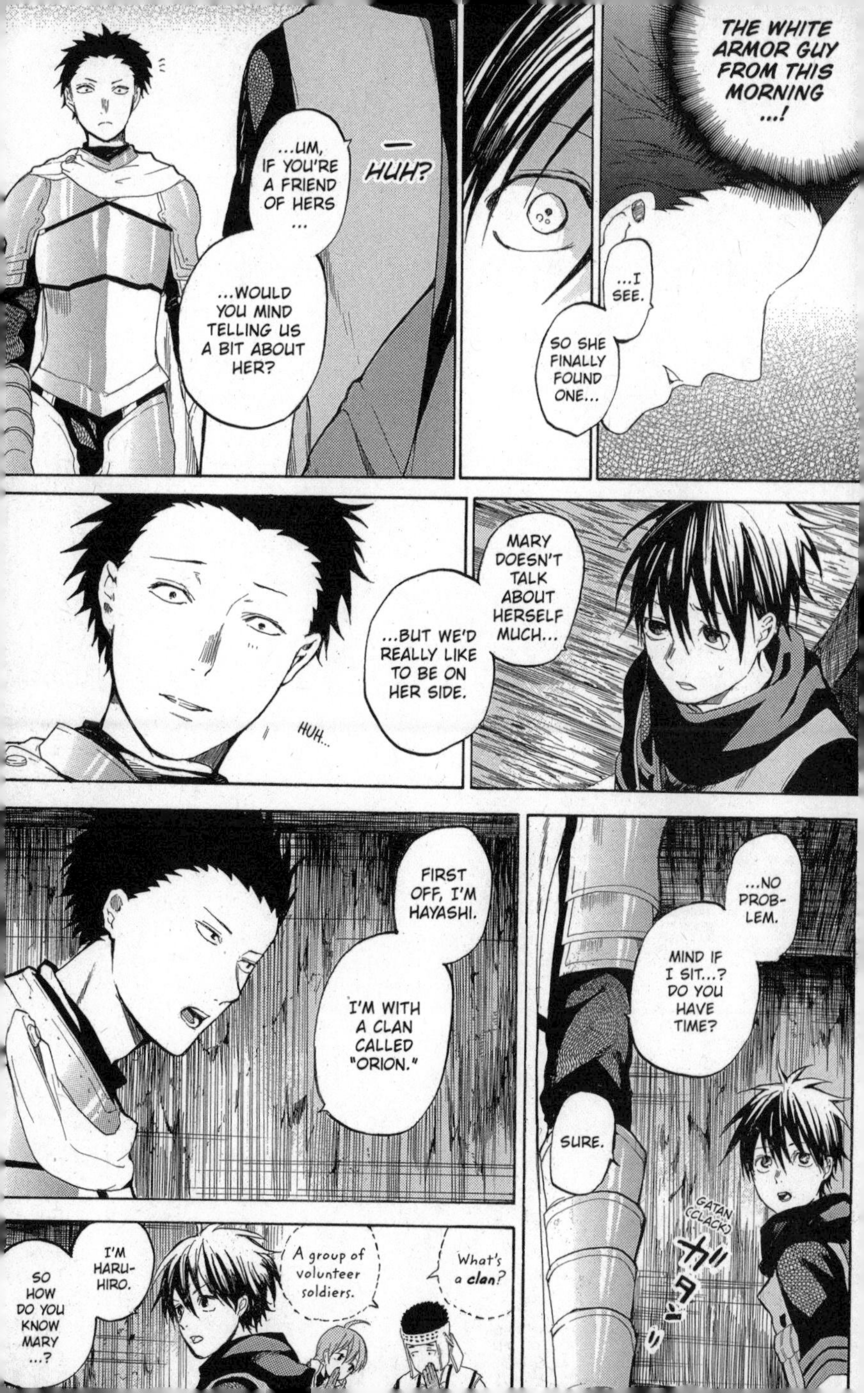
THE WHITE ARMOR GUY FROM THIS MORNING ...!
...I SEE.
SO SHE FINALLY FOUND ONE...
—HUH?
...UM, IF YOU'RE A FRIEND OF HERS ...
...WOULD YOU MIND TELLING US A BIT ABOUT HER?
MARY DOESN'T TALK ABOUT HERSELF MUCH...
...BUT WE'D REALLY LIKE TO BE ON HER SIDE.
HUH...
...NO PROB-LEM.
MIND IF I SIT...? DO YOU HAVE TIME?
SURE.
GATAN (CLACK)
FIRST OFF, I'M HAYASHI.
I'M WITH A CLAN CALLED "ORION."
What's a clan?
A group of volunteer soldiers.
I'M HARU-HIRO.
SO HOW DO YOU KNOW MARY ...?

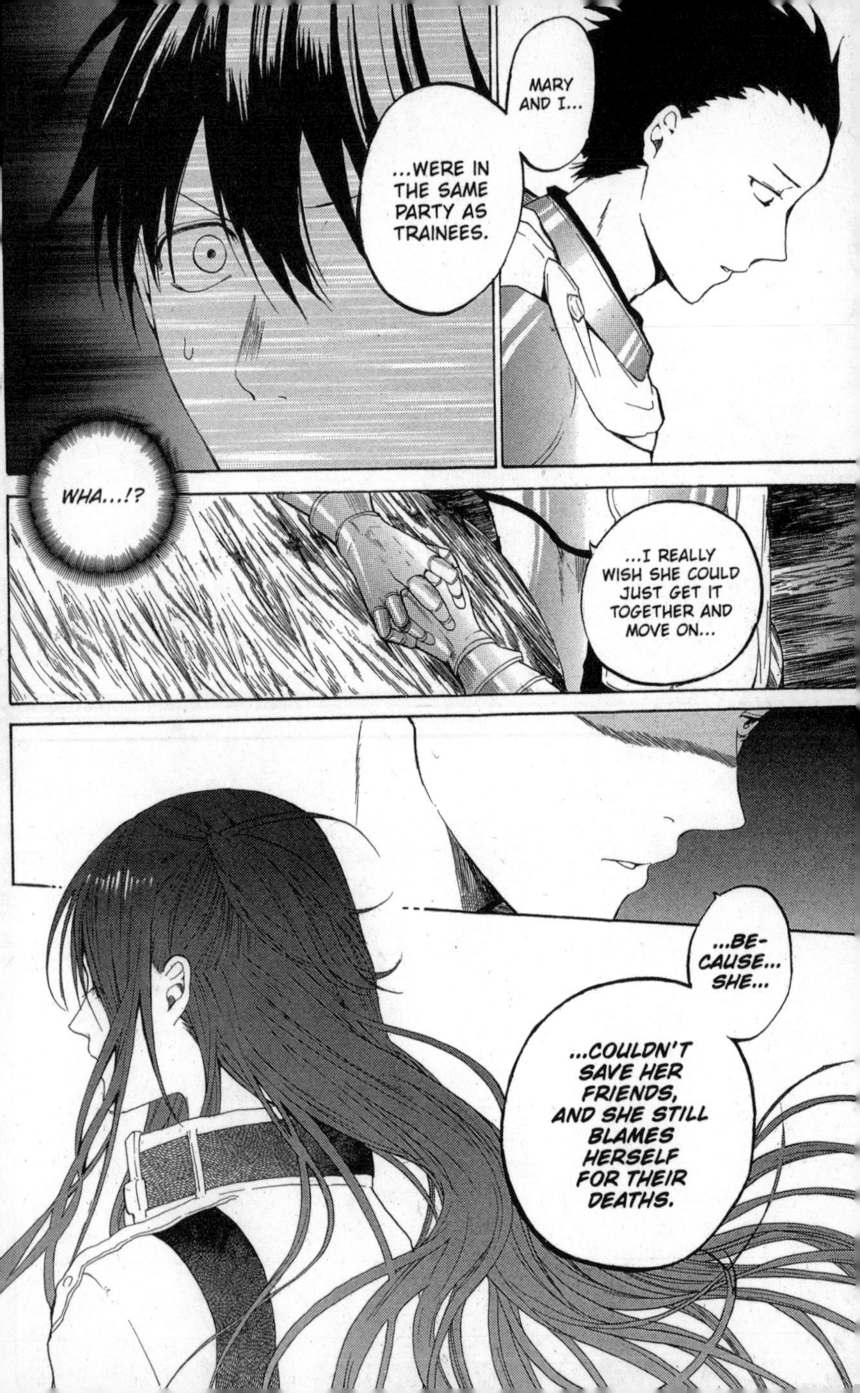
MARY AND I...
...WERE IN THE SAME PARTY AS TRAINEES.
WHA...!?
...I REALLY WISH SHE COULD JUST GET IT TOGETHER AND MOVE ON...
...BE-CAUSE... SHE...
...COULDN'T SAVE HER FRIENDS, AND SHE STILL BLAMES HERSELF FOR THEIR DEATHS.

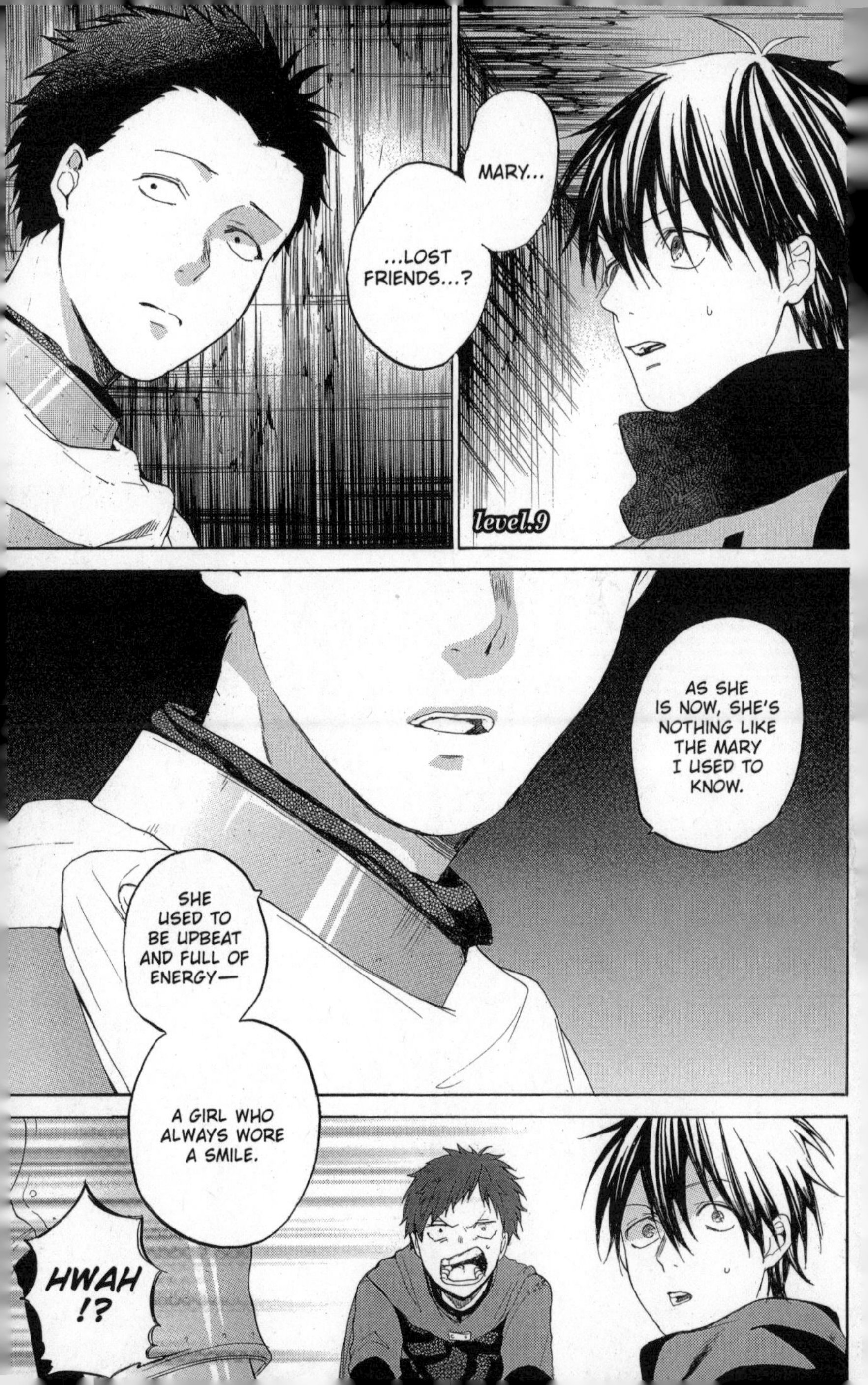
level.9
MARY...
...LOST FRIENDS...?
AS SHE IS NOW, SHE'S NOTHING LIKE THE MARY I USED TO KNOW.
SHE USED TO BE UPBEAT AND FULL OF ENERGY—
A GIRL WHO ALWAYS WORE A SMILE.
HWAH!?

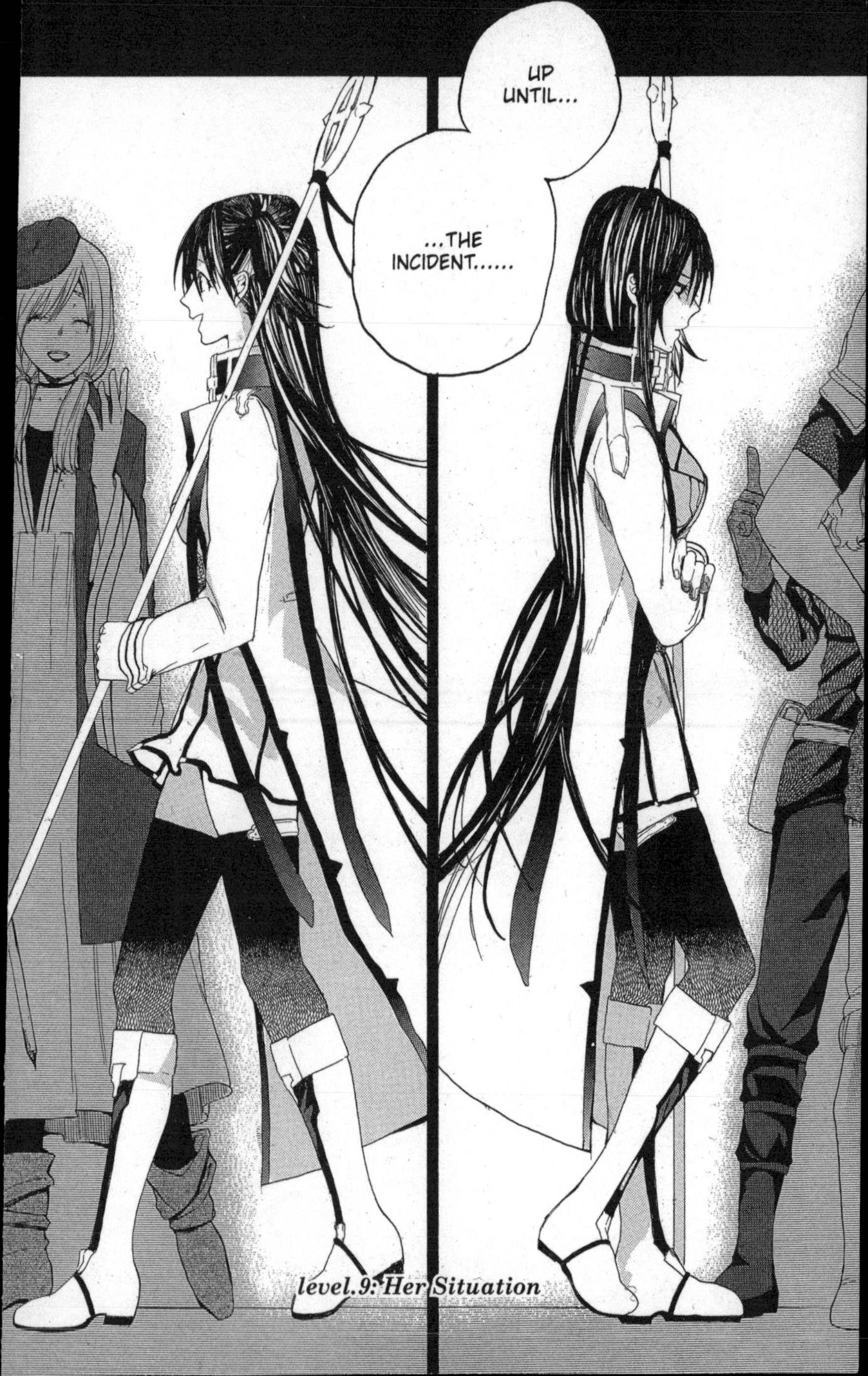
UP UNTIL...
...THE INCIDENT......
level.9: Her Situation

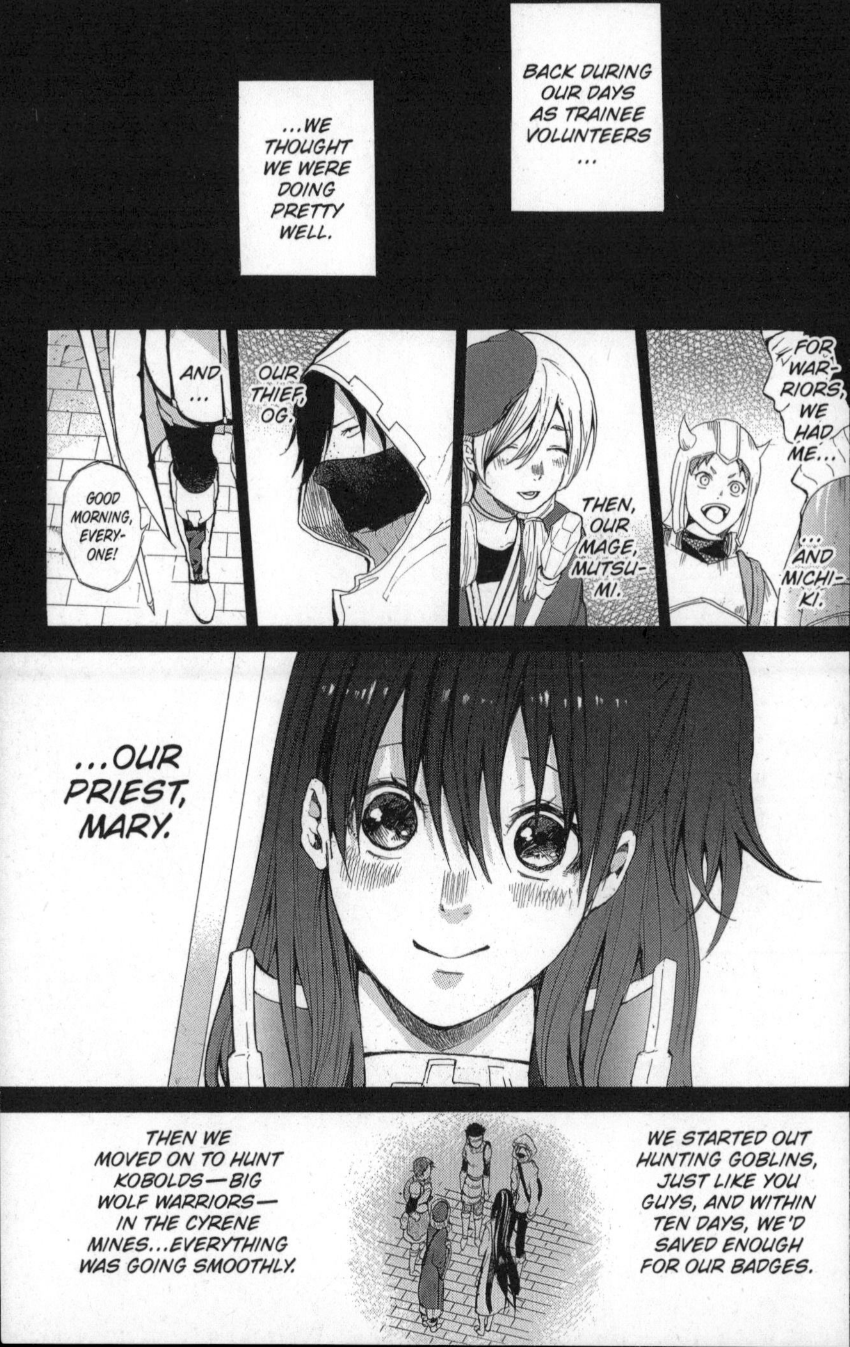
BACK DURING OUR DAYS AS TRAINEE VOLUNTEERS...
...WE THOUGHT WE WERE DOING PRETTY WELL.
FOR WARRIORS, WE HAD ME...
...AND MICHIKI.
THEN, OUR MAGE, MUTSUMI.
OUR THIEF, OG.
AND...
GOOD MORNING, EVERYONE!
...OUR PRIEST, MARY.
WE STARTED OUT HUNTING GOBLINS, JUST LIKE YOU GUYS, AND WITHIN TEN DAYS, WE'D SAVED ENOUGH FOR OUR BADGES.
THEN WE MOVED ON TO HUNT KOBOLDS—BIG WOLF WARRIORS—IN THE CYRENE MINES...EVERYTHING WAS GOING SMOOTHLY.

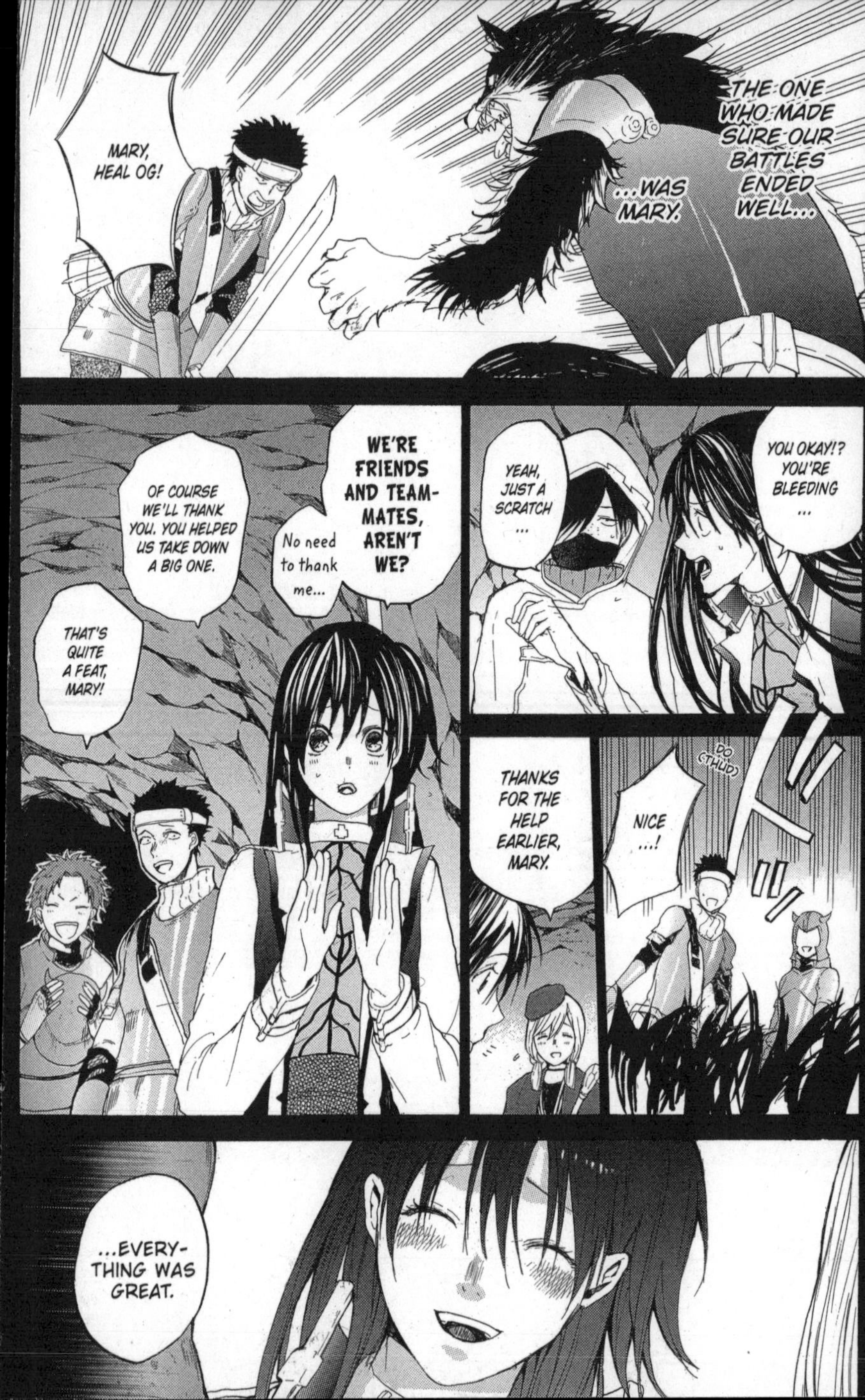
THE ONE WHO MADE SURE OUR BATTLES ENDED WELL...
...WAS MARY.
MARY, HEAL OG!
YOU OKAY!? YOU'RE BLEEDING...
YEAH, JUST A SCRATCH...
DO (THUD)
NICE...!
THANKS FOR THE HELP EARLIER, MARY.
WE'RE FRIENDS AND TEAM-MATES, AREN'T WE?
No need to thank me...
OF COURSE WE'LL THANK YOU. YOU HELPED US TAKE DOWN A BIG ONE.
THAT'S QUITE A FEAT, MARY!
...EVERY-THING WAS GREAT.

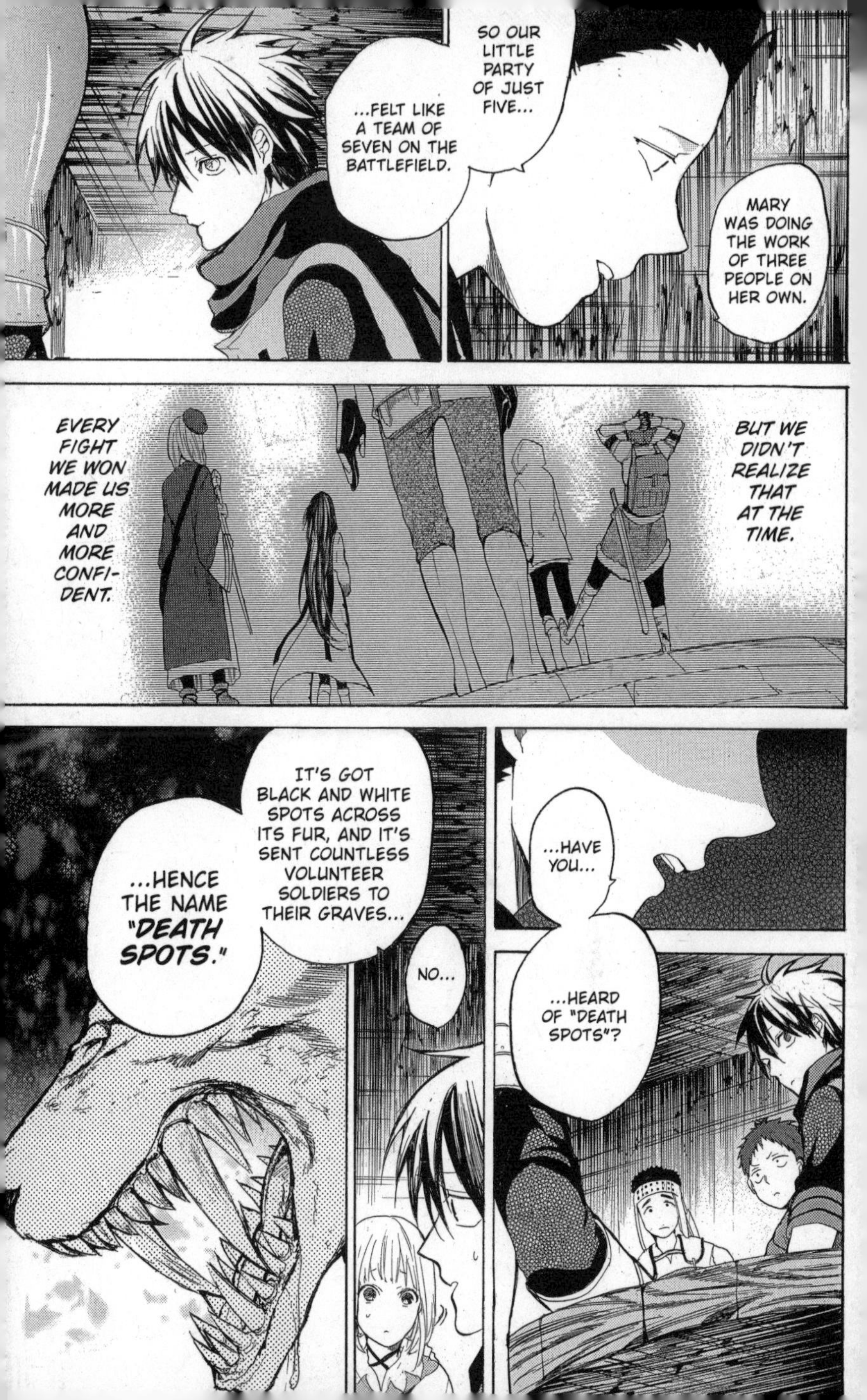
MARY WAS DOING THE WORK OF THREE PEOPLE ON HER OWN.
SO OUR LITTLE PARTY OF JUST FIVE...
...FELT LIKE A TEAM OF SEVEN ON THE BATTLEFIELD.
BUT WE DIDN'T REALIZE THAT AT THE TIME.
EVERY FIGHT WE WON MADE US MORE AND MORE CONFIDENT.
...HAVE YOU...
...HEARD OF "DEATH SPOTS"?
NO...
IT'S GOT BLACK AND WHITE SPOTS ACROSS ITS FUR, AND IT'S SENT COUNTLESS VOLUNTEER SOLDIERS TO THEIR GRAVES...
...HENCE THE NAME *"DEATH SPOTS."*

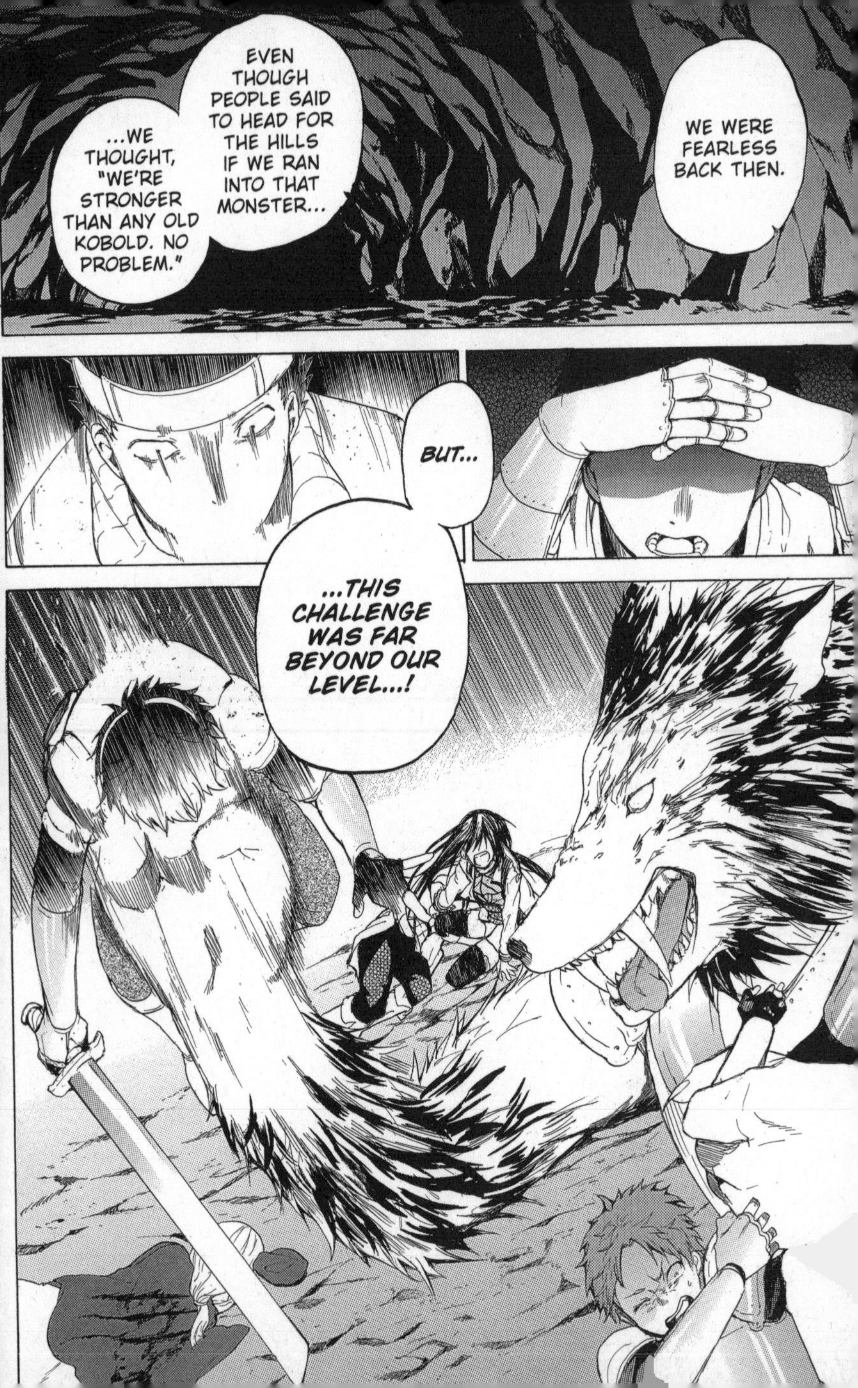
WE WERE FEARLESS BACK THEN.
EVEN THOUGH PEOPLE SAID TO HEAD FOR THE HILLS IF WE RAN INTO THAT MONSTER...
...WE THOUGHT, "WE'RE STRONGER THAN ANY OLD KOBOLD. NO PROBLEM."
BUT...
...THIS CHALLENGE WAS FAR BEYOND OUR LEVEL...!

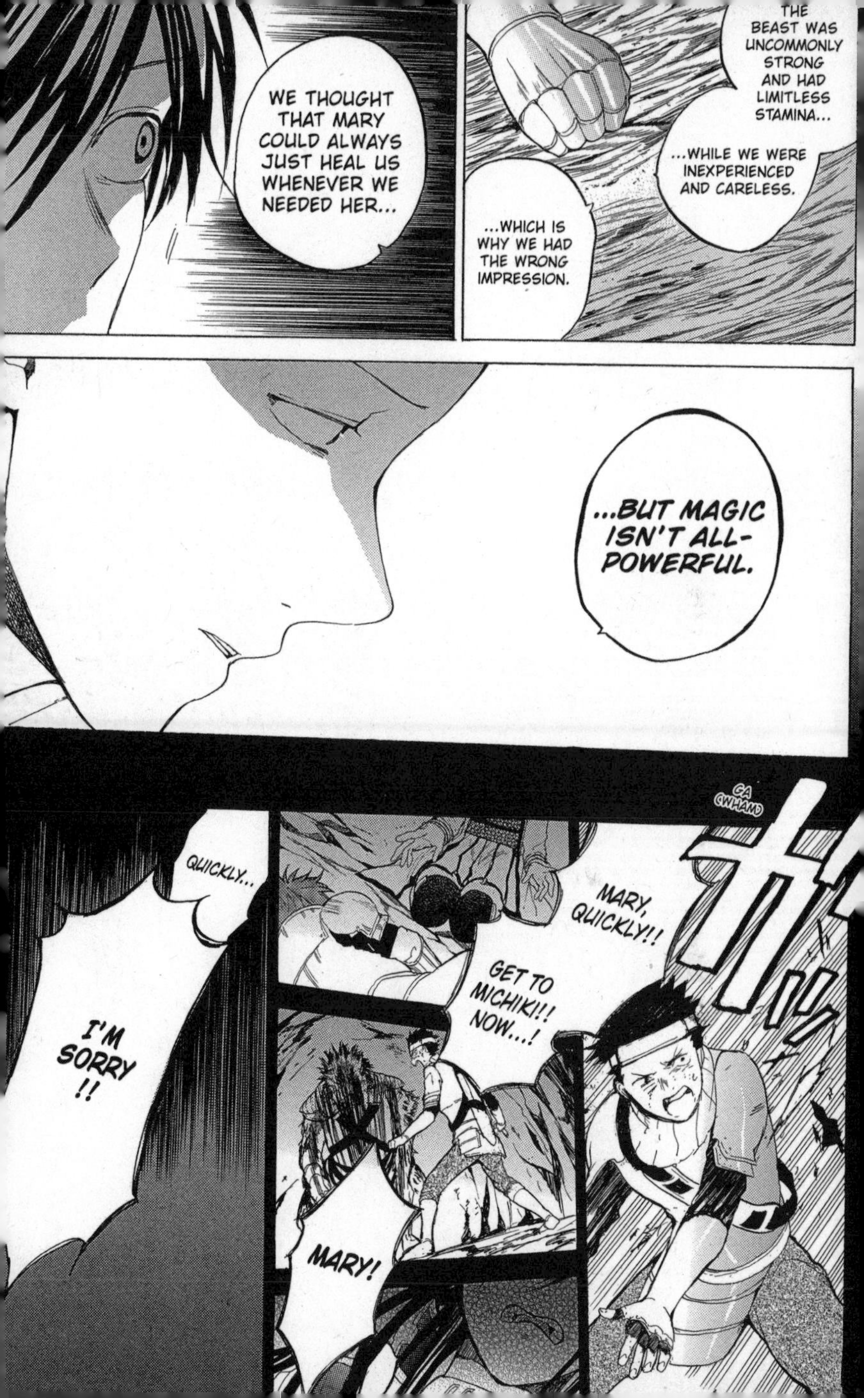
THE BEAST WAS UNCOMMONLY STRONG AND HAD LIMITLESS STAMINA...
...WHILE WE WERE INEXPERIENCED AND CARELESS.
...WHICH IS WHY WE HAD THE WRONG IMPRESSION.
WE THOUGHT THAT MARY COULD ALWAYS JUST HEAL US WHENEVER WE NEEDED HER...
...BUT MAGIC ISN'T ALL-POWERFUL.
GA (WHAM)
MARY, QUICKLY!!
GET TO MICHIKI!! NOW...!
MARY!
QUICKLY...
I'M SORRY!!

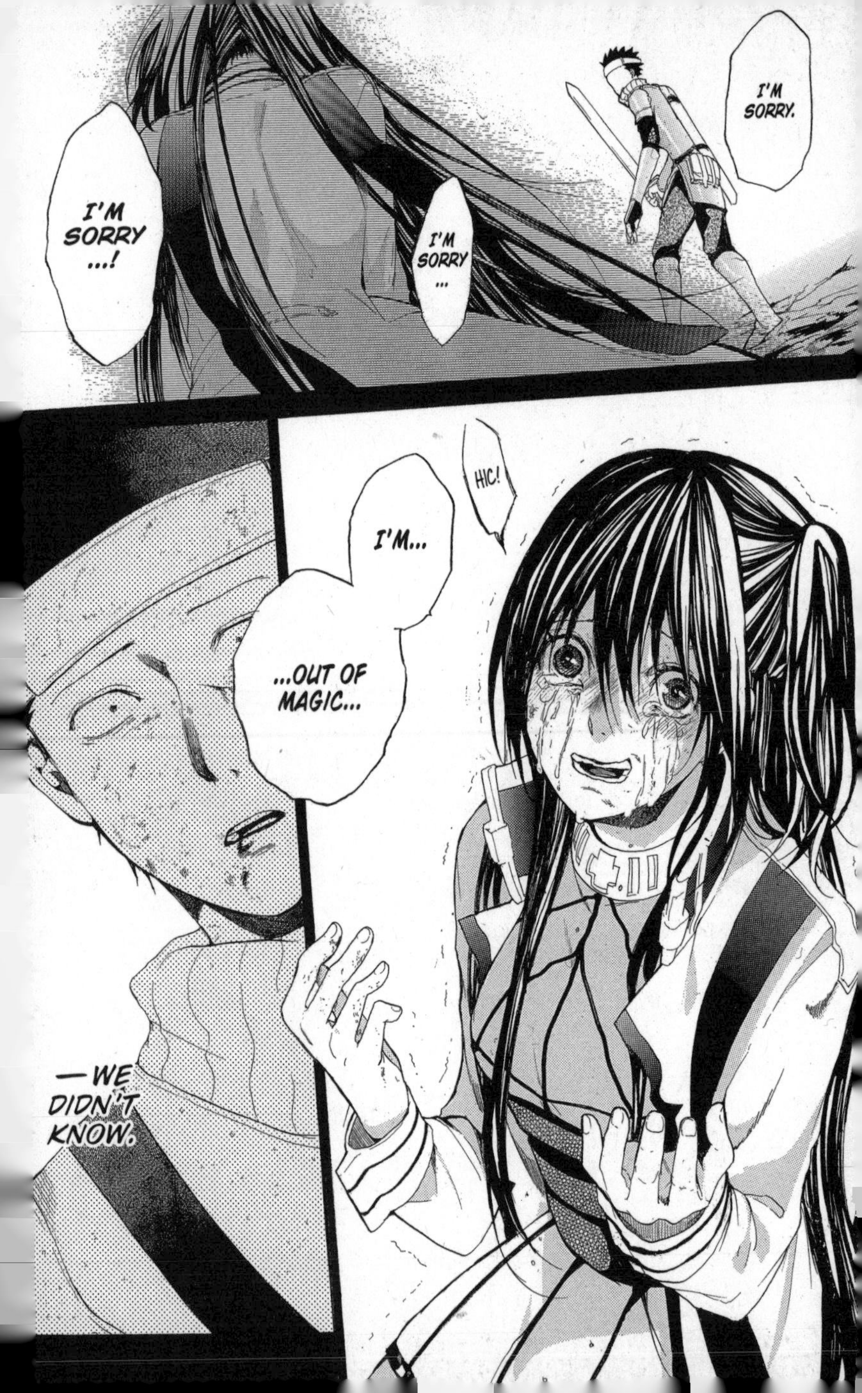
I'M SORRY.
I'M SORRY ...
I'M SORRY ...!
HIC!
I'M...
...OUT OF MAGIC...
—WE DIDN'T KNOW.

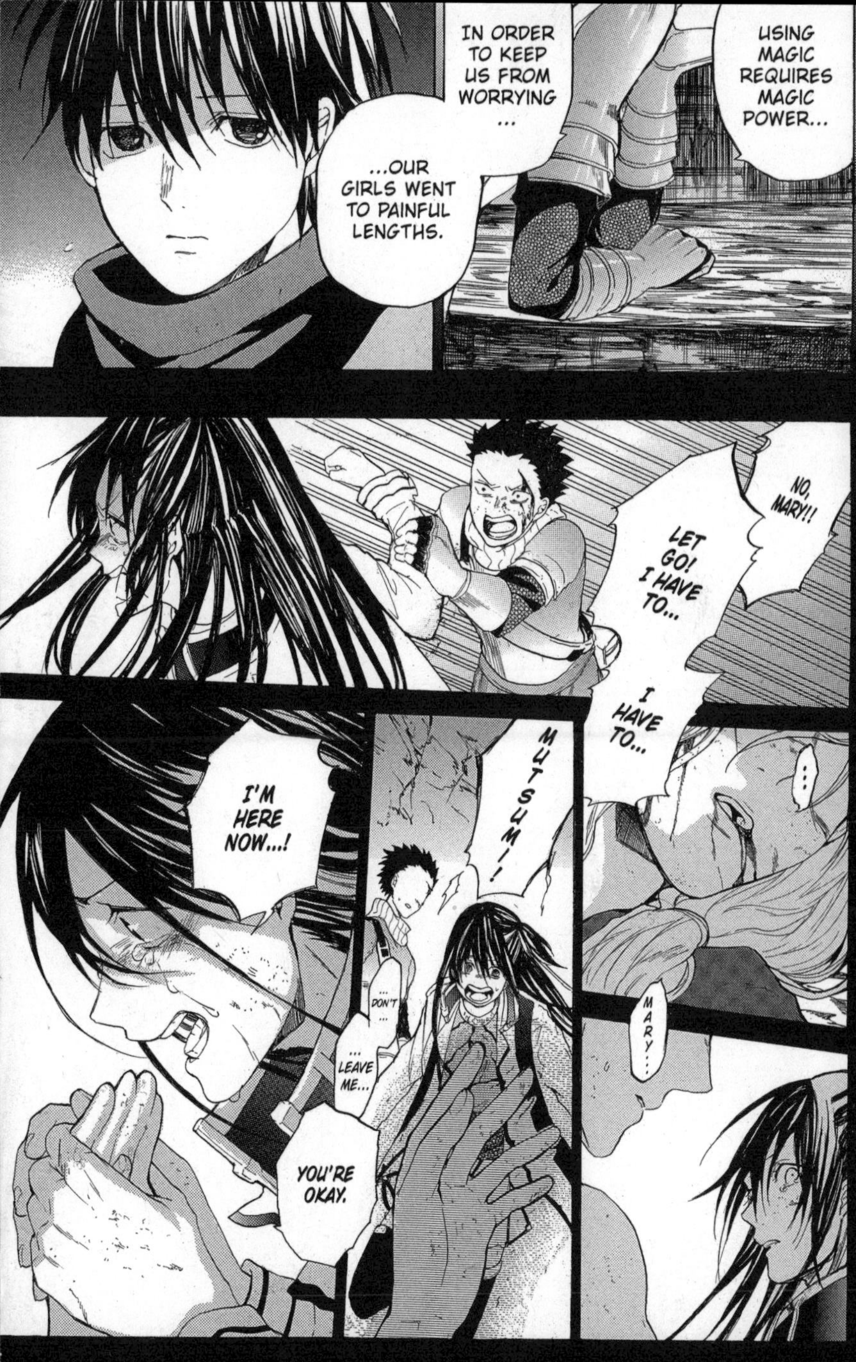
USING MAGIC REQUIRES MAGIC POWER...
IN ORDER TO KEEP US FROM WORRYING ...
...OUR GIRLS WENT TO PAINFUL LENGTHS.
NO, MARY!!
LET GO! I HAVE TO...
I HAVE TO...
...
MARY...
MUTSUMI!!
...DON'T...
...LEAVE ME...
I'M HERE NOW...!
YOU'RE OKAY.

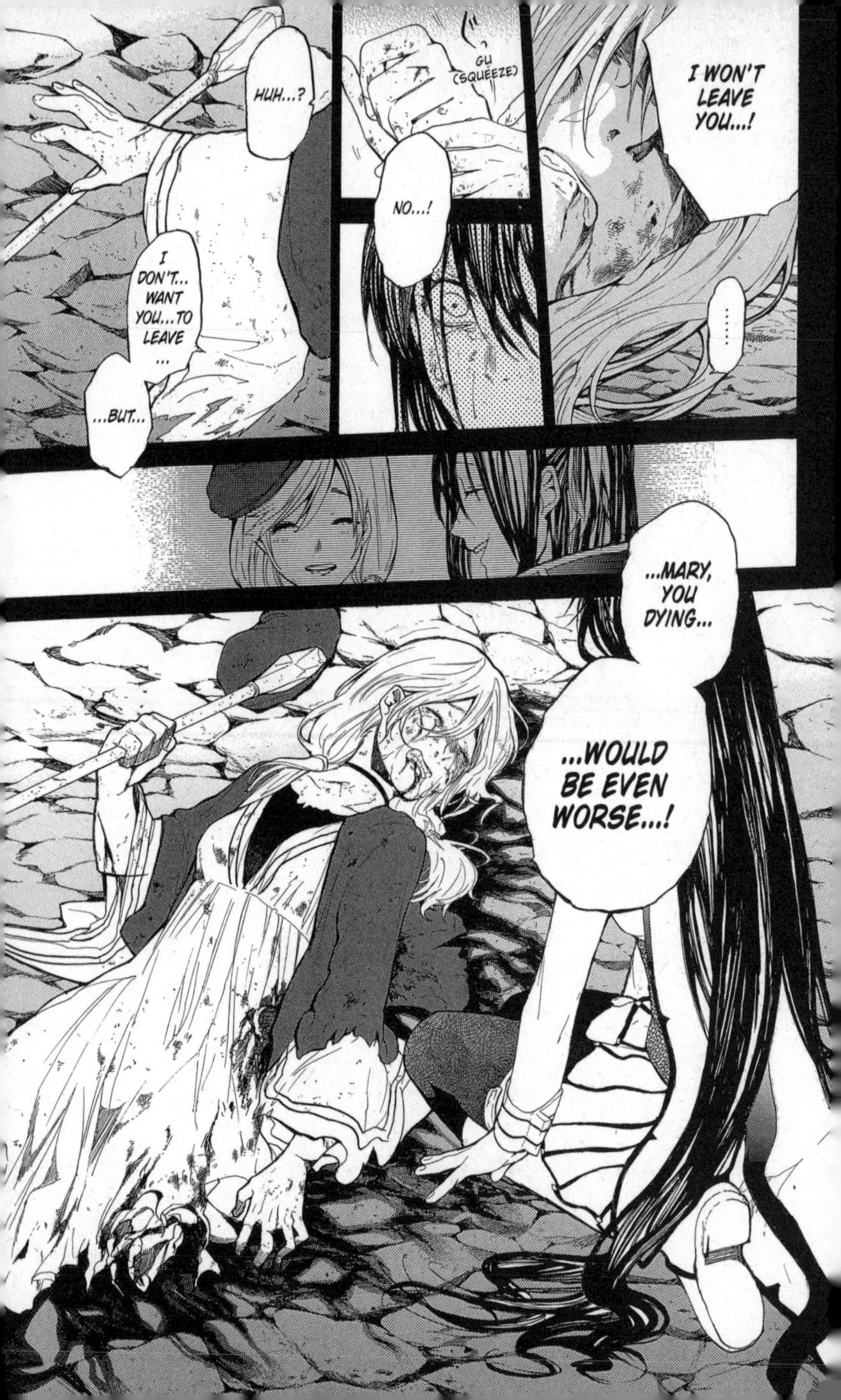
I WON'T LEAVE YOU...!
......
GU (SQUEEZE)
NO...!
HUH...?
I DON'T... WANT YOU...TO LEAVE ...
...BUT...
...MARY, YOU DYING...
...WOULD BE EVEN WORSE...!

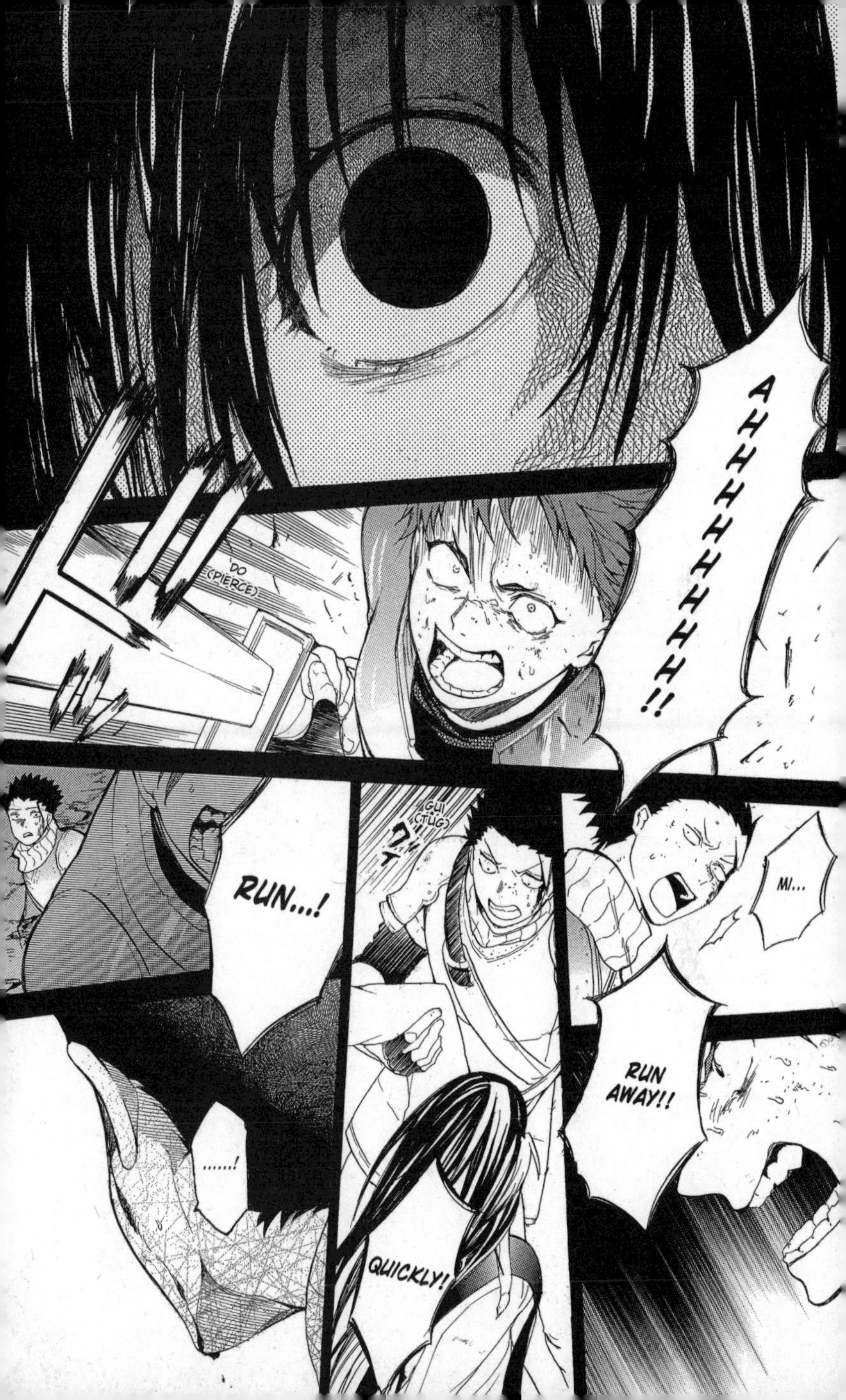
AHHHHHHHHHH!!
DO (PIERCE)
MI...
GUI (TUG)
RUN...!
RUN AWAY!!
QUICKLY!
......!

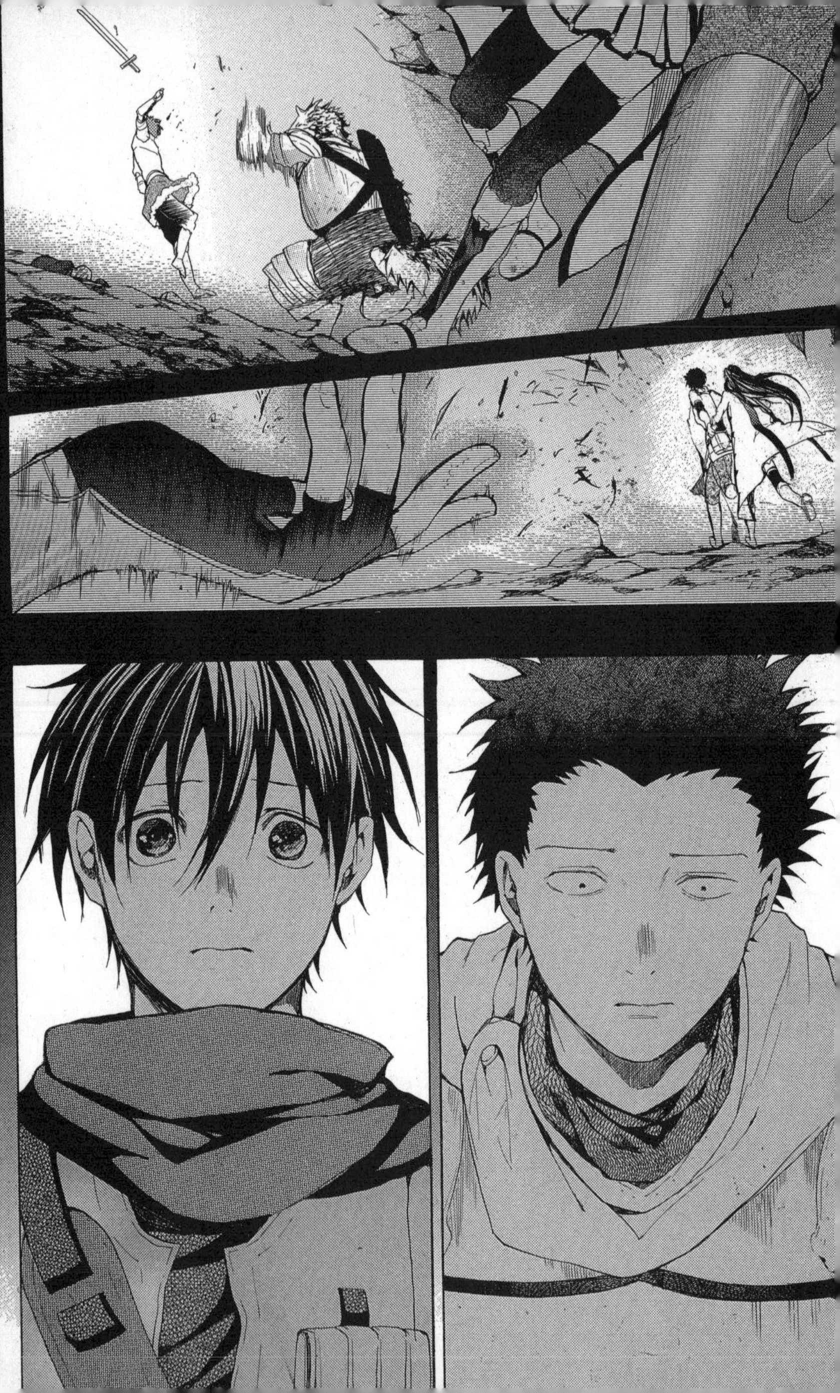

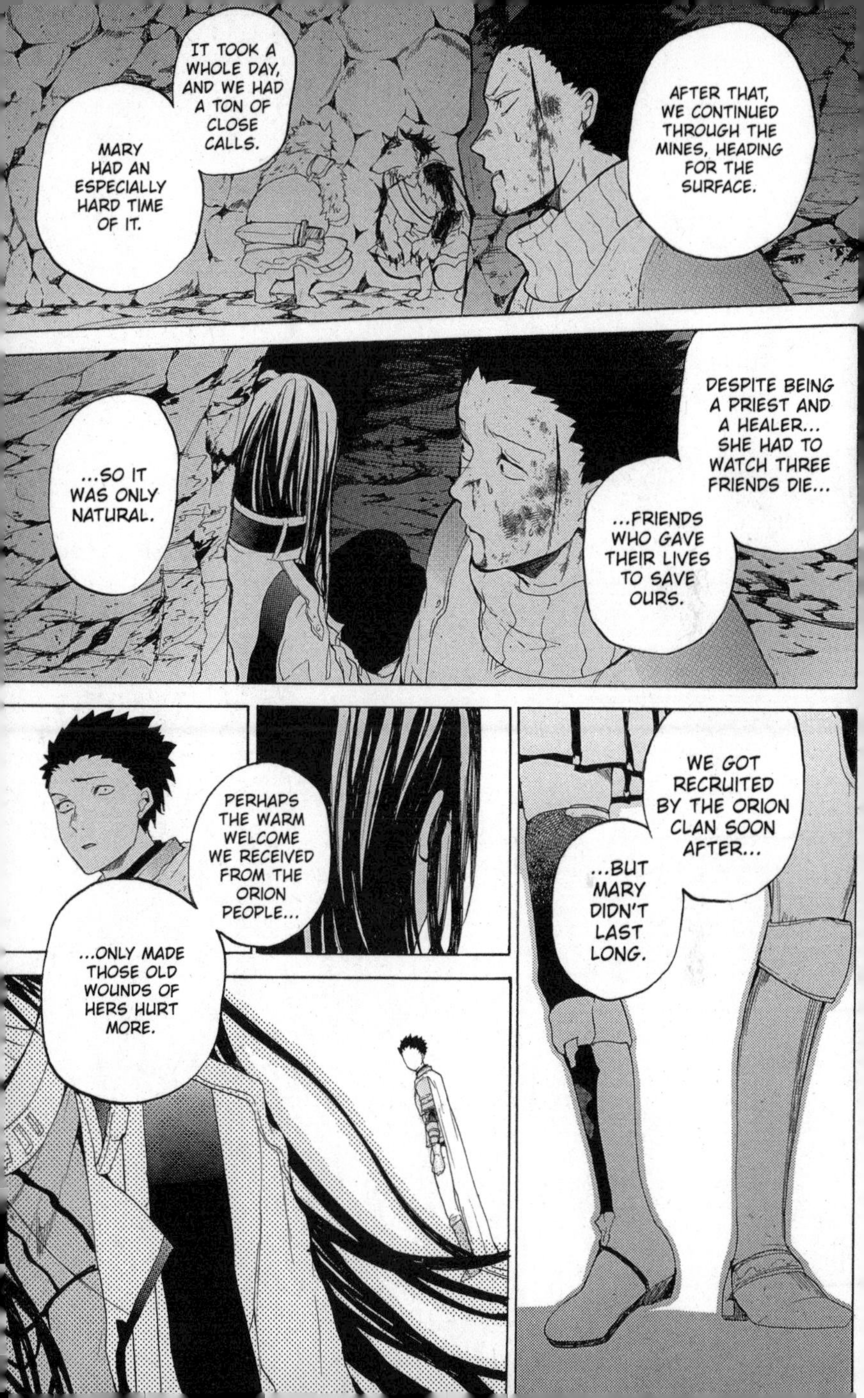
AFTER THAT, WE CONTINUED THROUGH THE MINES, HEADING FOR THE SURFACE.
IT TOOK A WHOLE DAY, AND WE HAD A TON OF CLOSE CALLS.
MARY HAD AN ESPECIALLY HARD TIME OF IT.
DESPITE BEING A PRIEST AND A HEALER... SHE HAD TO WATCH THREE FRIENDS DIE...
...FRIENDS WHO GAVE THEIR LIVES TO SAVE OURS.
...SO IT WAS ONLY NATURAL.
WE GOT RECRUITED BY THE ORION CLAN SOON AFTER...
...BUT MARY DIDN'T LAST LONG.
PERHAPS THE WARM WELCOME WE RECEIVED FROM THE ORION PEOPLE...
...ONLY MADE THOSE OLD WOUNDS OF HERS HURT MORE.

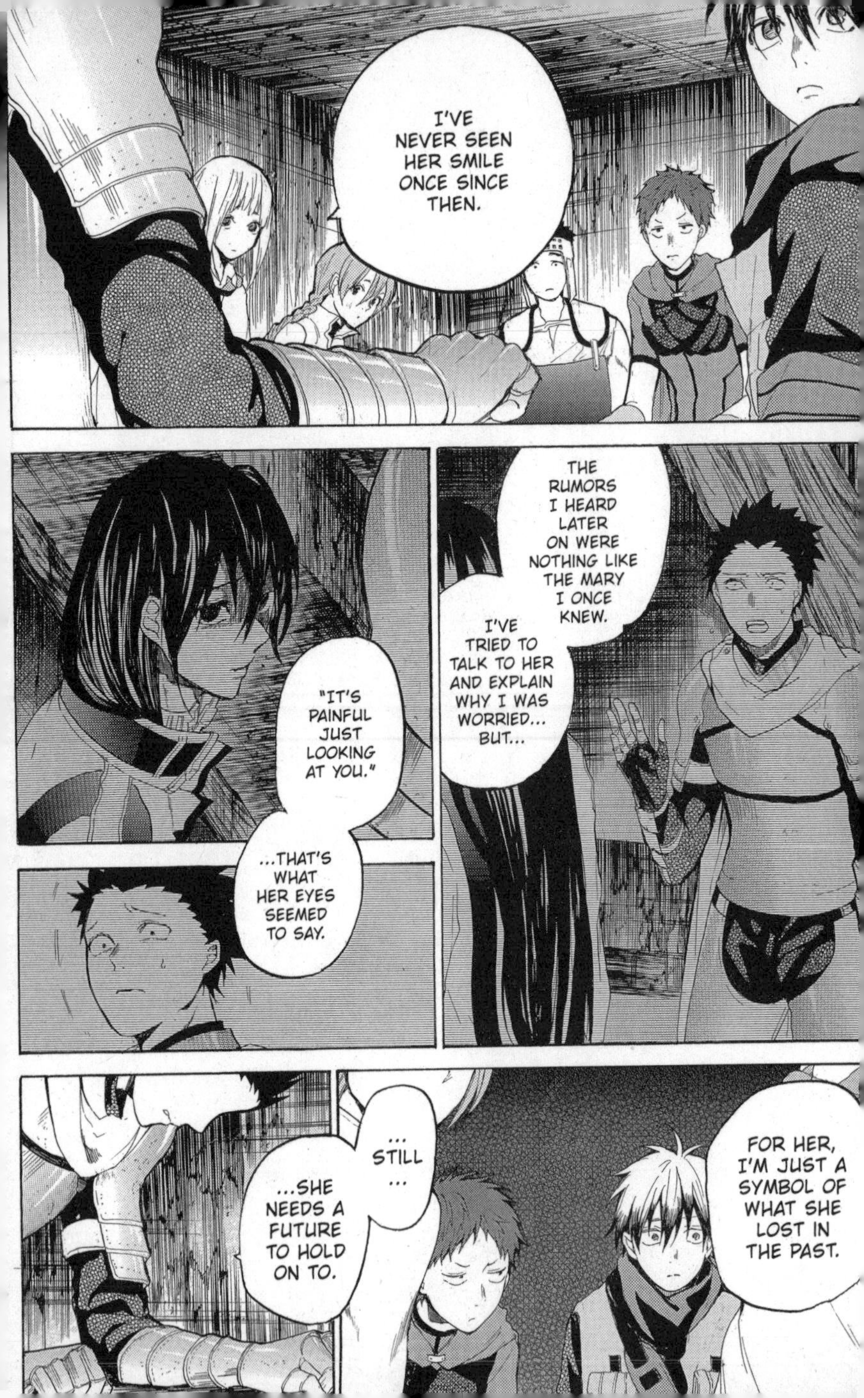
I'VE NEVER SEEN HER SMILE ONCE SINCE THEN.
THE RUMORS I HEARD LATER ON WERE NOTHING LIKE THE MARY I ONCE KNEW.
I'VE TRIED TO TALK TO HER AND EXPLAIN WHY I WAS WORRIED... BUT...
"IT'S PAINFUL JUST LOOKING AT YOU."
...THAT'S WHAT HER EYES SEEMED TO SAY.
FOR HER, I'M JUST A SYMBOL OF WHAT SHE LOST IN THE PAST.
...STILL...
...SHE NEEDS A FUTURE TO HOLD ON TO.

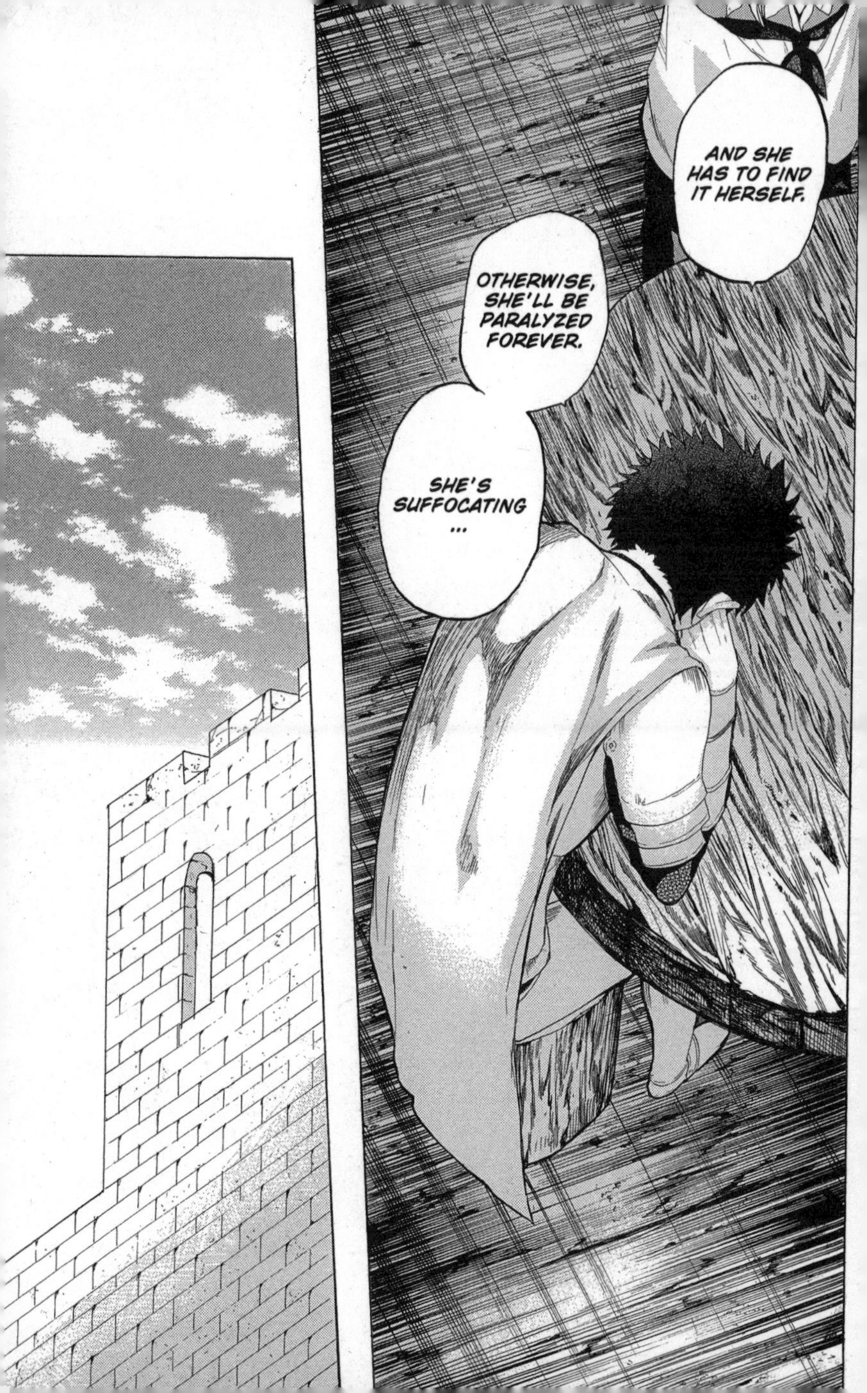
AND SHE HAS TO FIND IT HERSELF.
OTHERWISE, SHE'LL BE PARALYZED FOREVER.
SHE'S SUFFOCATING ...

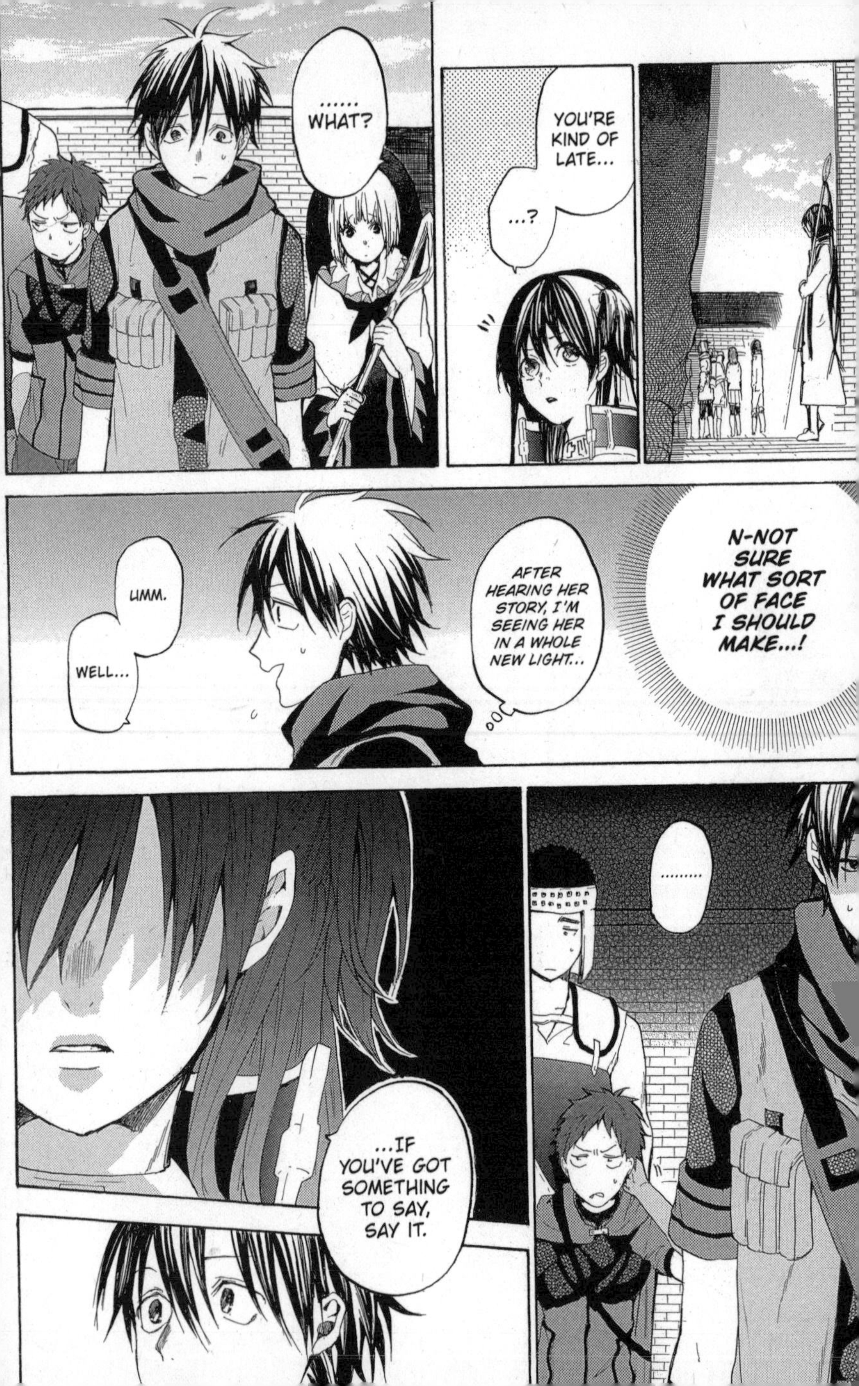
YOU'RE KIND OF LATE...
...?
...... WHAT?
N-NOT SURE WHAT SORT OF FACE I SHOULD MAKE...!
AFTER HEARING HER STORY, I'M SEEING HER IN A WHOLE NEW LIGHT...
UMM.
WELL...
....
...IF YOU'VE GOT SOMETHING TO SAY, SAY IT.

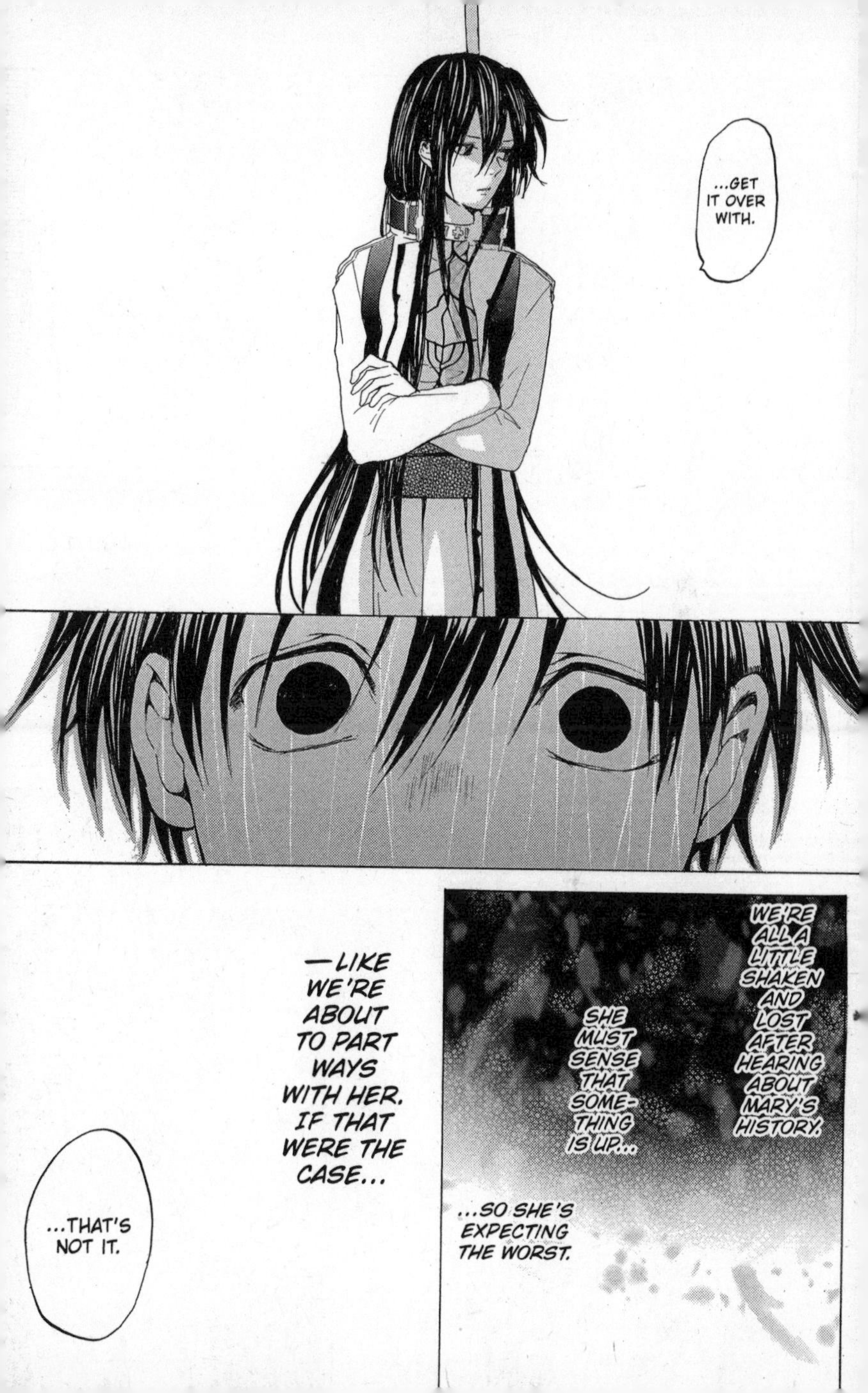
...GET IT OVER WITH.
WE'RE ALL A LITTLE SHAKEN AND LOST AFTER HEARING ABOUT MARY'S HISTORY.
SHE MUST SENSE THAT SOME-THING IS UP...
...SO SHE'S EXPECTING THE WORST.
—LIKE WE'RE ABOUT TO PART WAYS WITH HER. IF THAT WERE THE CASE...
...THAT'S NOT IT.

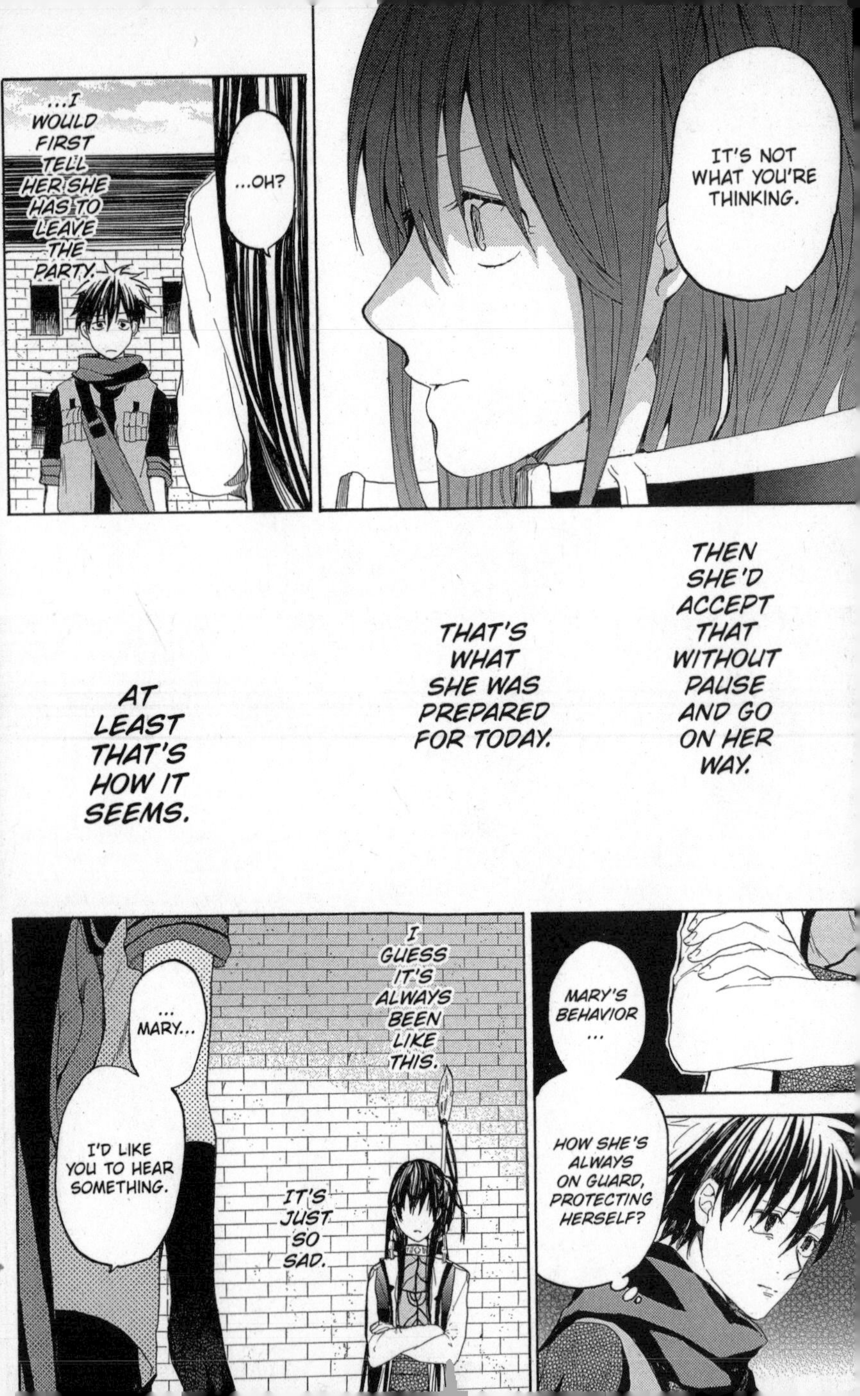
IT'S NOT WHAT YOU'RE THINKING.
...OH?
...I WOULD FIRST TELL HER SHE HAS TO LEAVE THE PARTY.
THEN SHE'D ACCEPT THAT WITHOUT PAUSE AND GO ON HER WAY.
THAT'S WHAT SHE WAS PREPARED FOR TODAY.
AT LEAST THAT'S HOW IT SEEMS.
MARY'S BEHAVIOR...
HOW SHE'S ALWAYS ON GUARD, PROTECTING HERSELF?
I GUESS IT'S ALWAYS BEEN LIKE THIS.
...MARY...
I'D LIKE YOU TO HEAR SOMETHING.
IT'S JUST SO SAD.

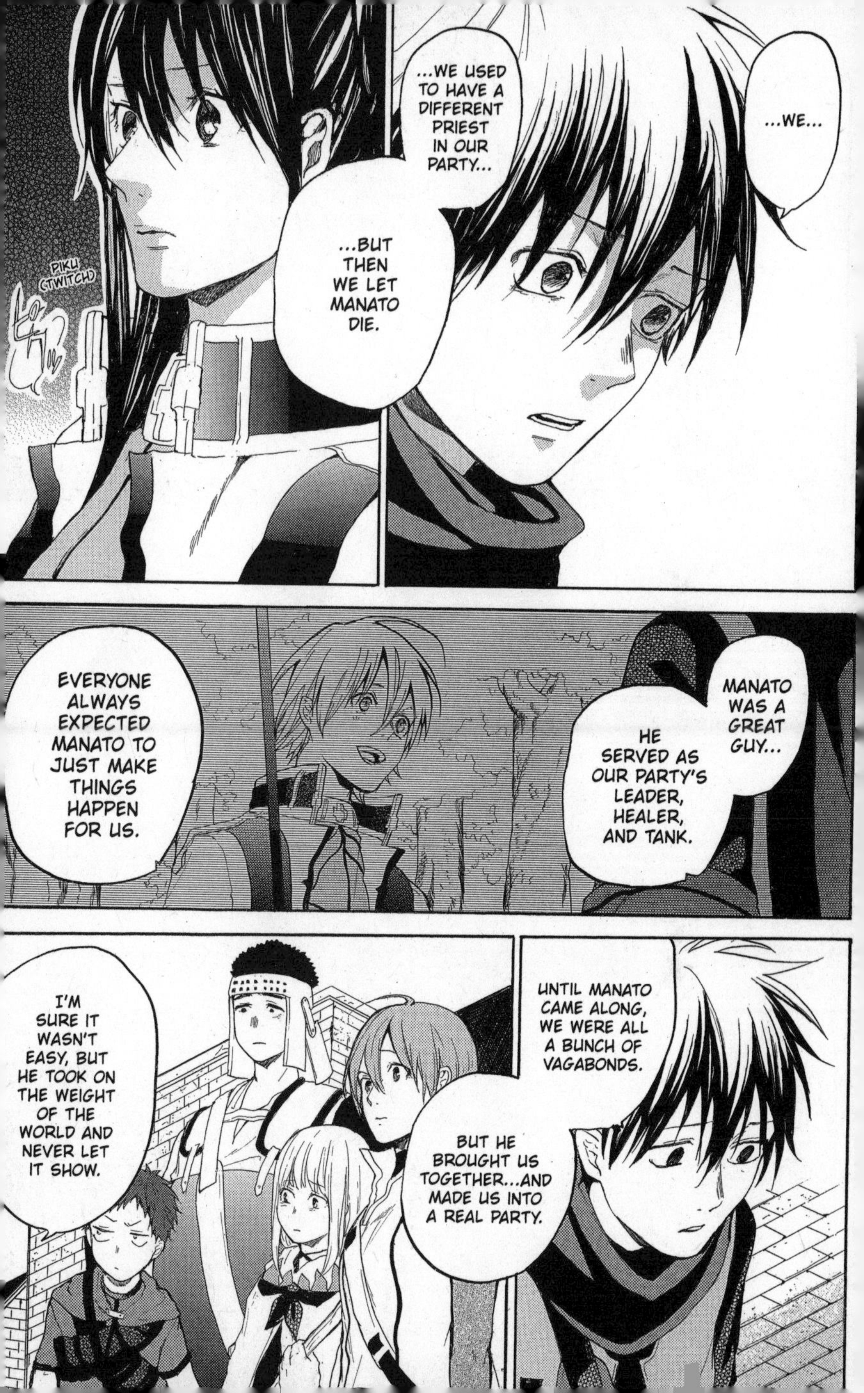
...WE...
...WE USED TO HAVE A DIFFERENT PRIEST IN OUR PARTY...
...BUT THEN WE LET MANATO DIE.
PIKU (TWITCH)
MANATO WAS A GREAT GUY...
HE SERVED AS OUR PARTY'S LEADER, HEALER, AND TANK.
EVERYONE ALWAYS EXPECTED MANATO TO JUST MAKE THINGS HAPPEN FOR US.
UNTIL MANATO CAME ALONG, WE WERE ALL A BUNCH OF VAGABONDS.
BUT HE BROUGHT US TOGETHER...AND MADE US INTO A REAL PARTY.
I'M SURE IT WASN'T EASY, BUT HE TOOK ON THE WEIGHT OF THE WORLD AND NEVER LET IT SHOW.

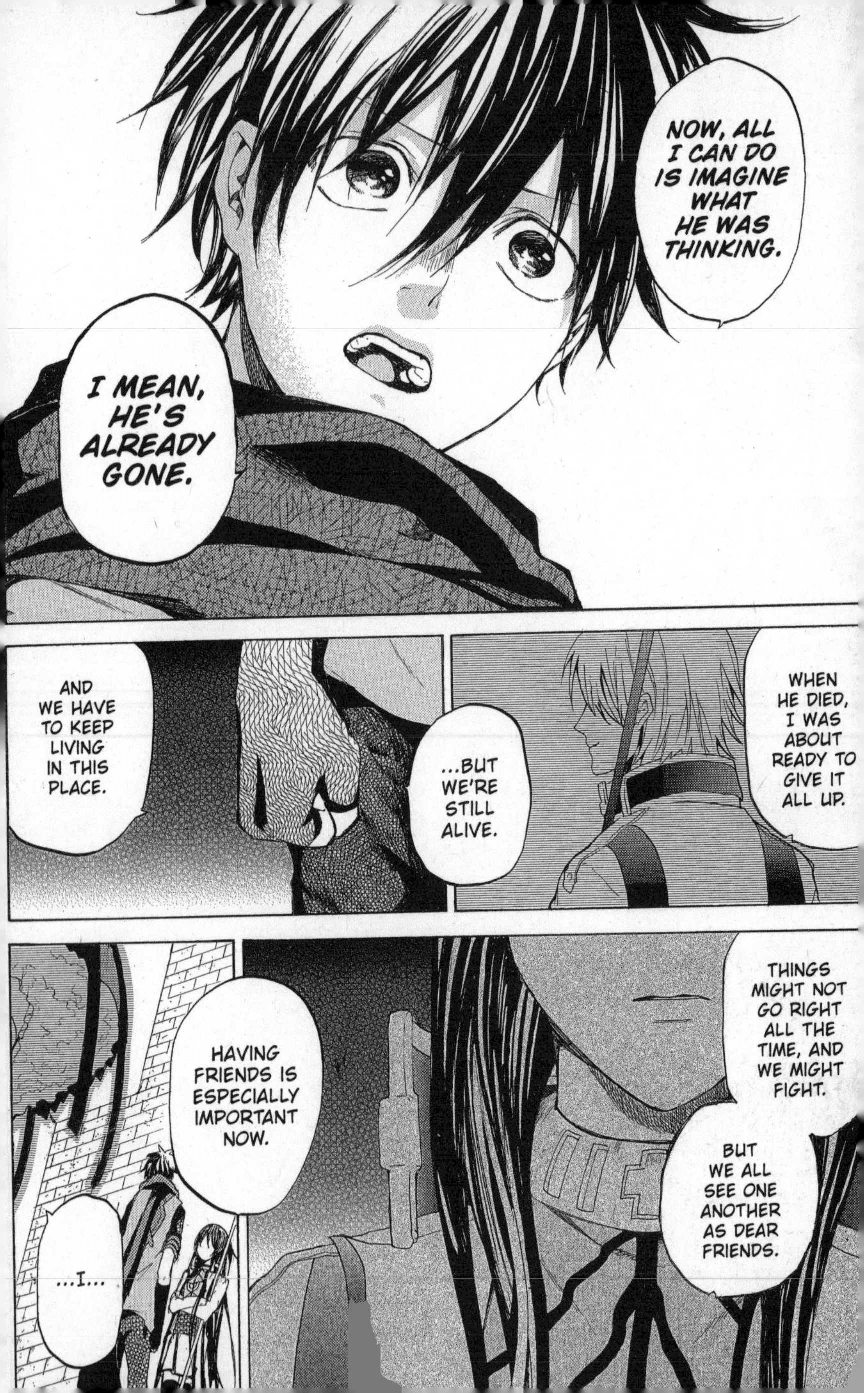
NOW, ALL I CAN DO IS IMAGINE WHAT HE WAS THINKING.
I MEAN, HE'S ALREADY GONE.
WHEN HE DIED, I WAS ABOUT READY TO GIVE IT ALL UP.
...BUT WE'RE STILL ALIVE.
AND WE HAVE TO KEEP LIVING IN THIS PLACE.
THINGS MIGHT NOT GO RIGHT ALL THE TIME, AND WE MIGHT FIGHT.
BUT WE ALL SEE ONE ANOTHER AS DEAR FRIENDS.
HAVING FRIENDS IS ESPECIALLY IMPORTANT NOW.
...I...

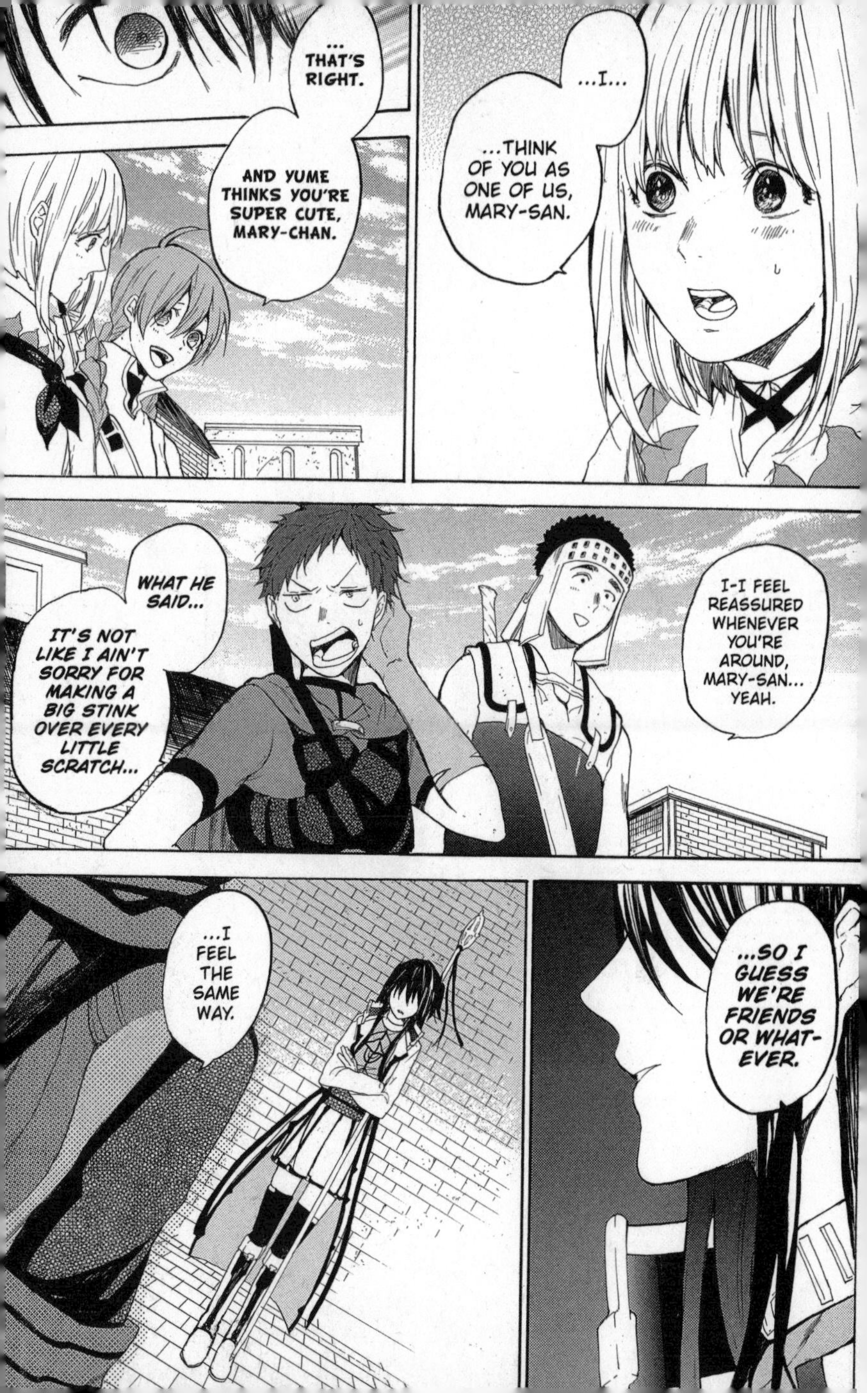
...I...
...THINK OF YOU AS ONE OF US, MARY-SAN.
... THAT'S RIGHT.
AND YUME THINKS YOU'RE SUPER CUTE, MARY-CHAN.
I-I FEEL REASSURED WHENEVER YOU'RE AROUND, MARY-SAN... YEAH.
WHAT HE SAID...
IT'S NOT LIKE I AIN'T SORRY FOR MAKING A BIG STINK OVER EVERY LITTLE SCRATCH...
...SO I GUESS WE'RE FRIENDS OR WHAT-EVER.
...I FEEL THE SAME WAY.

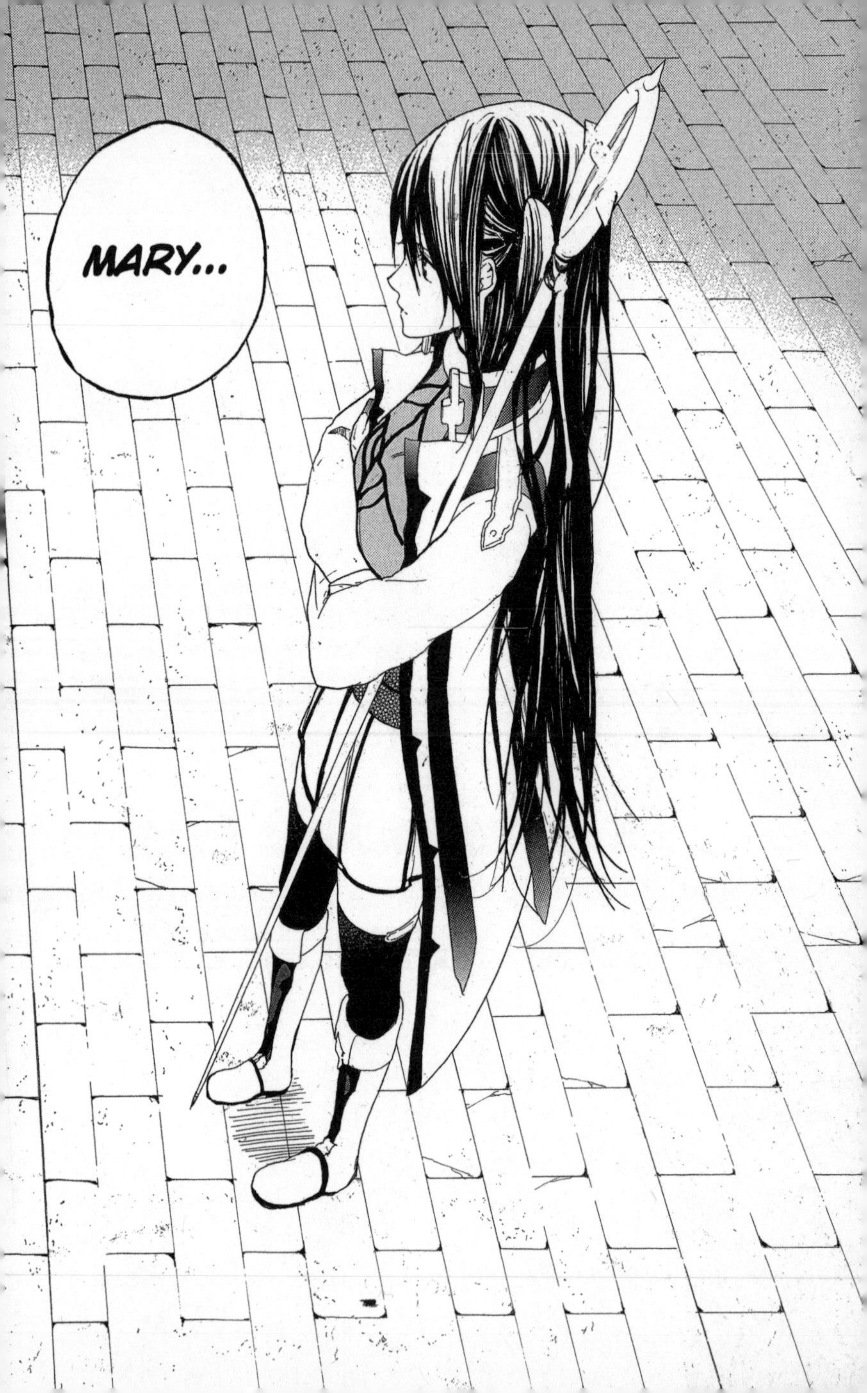
MARY...

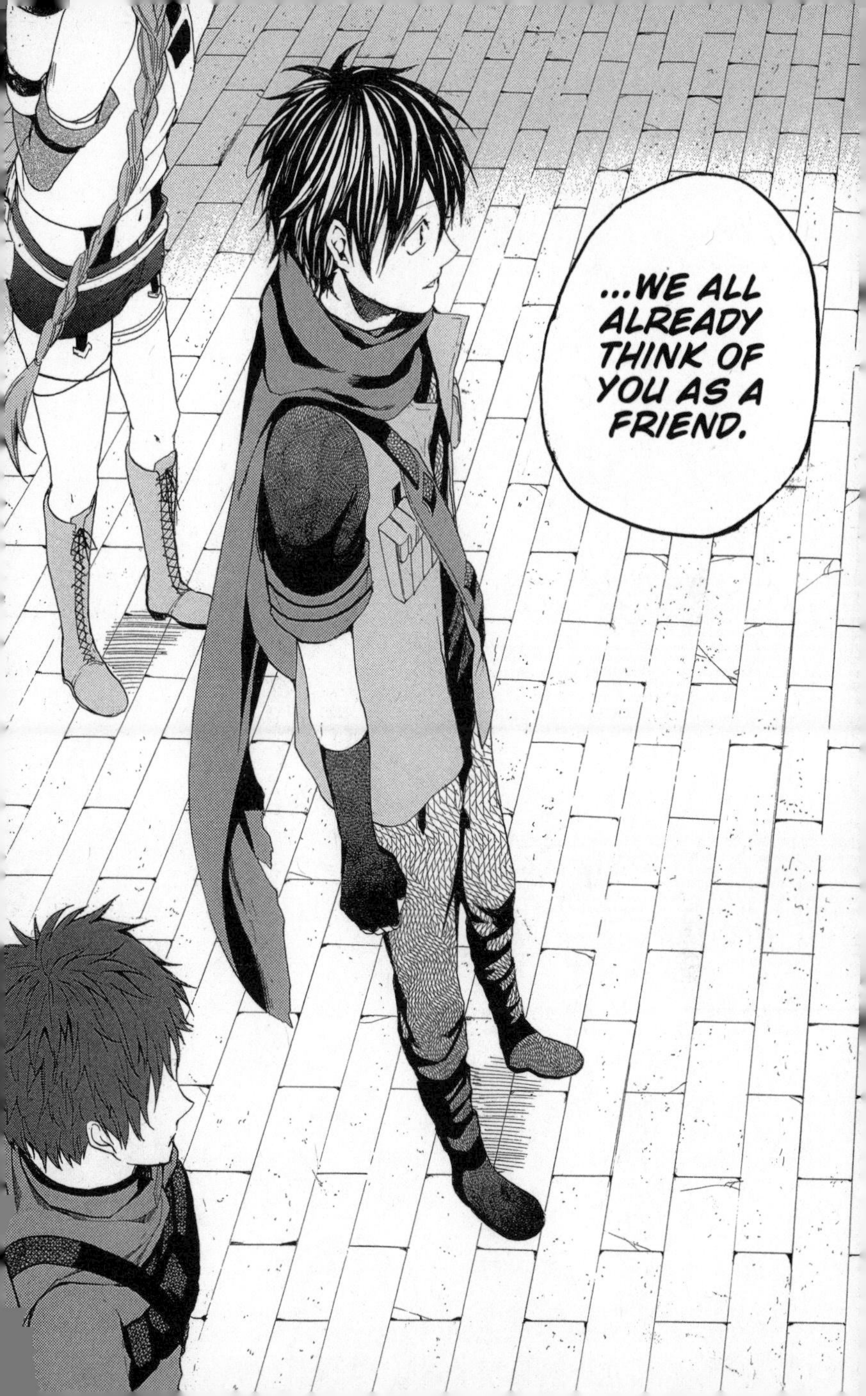
...WE ALL ALREADY THINK OF YOU AS A FRIEND.

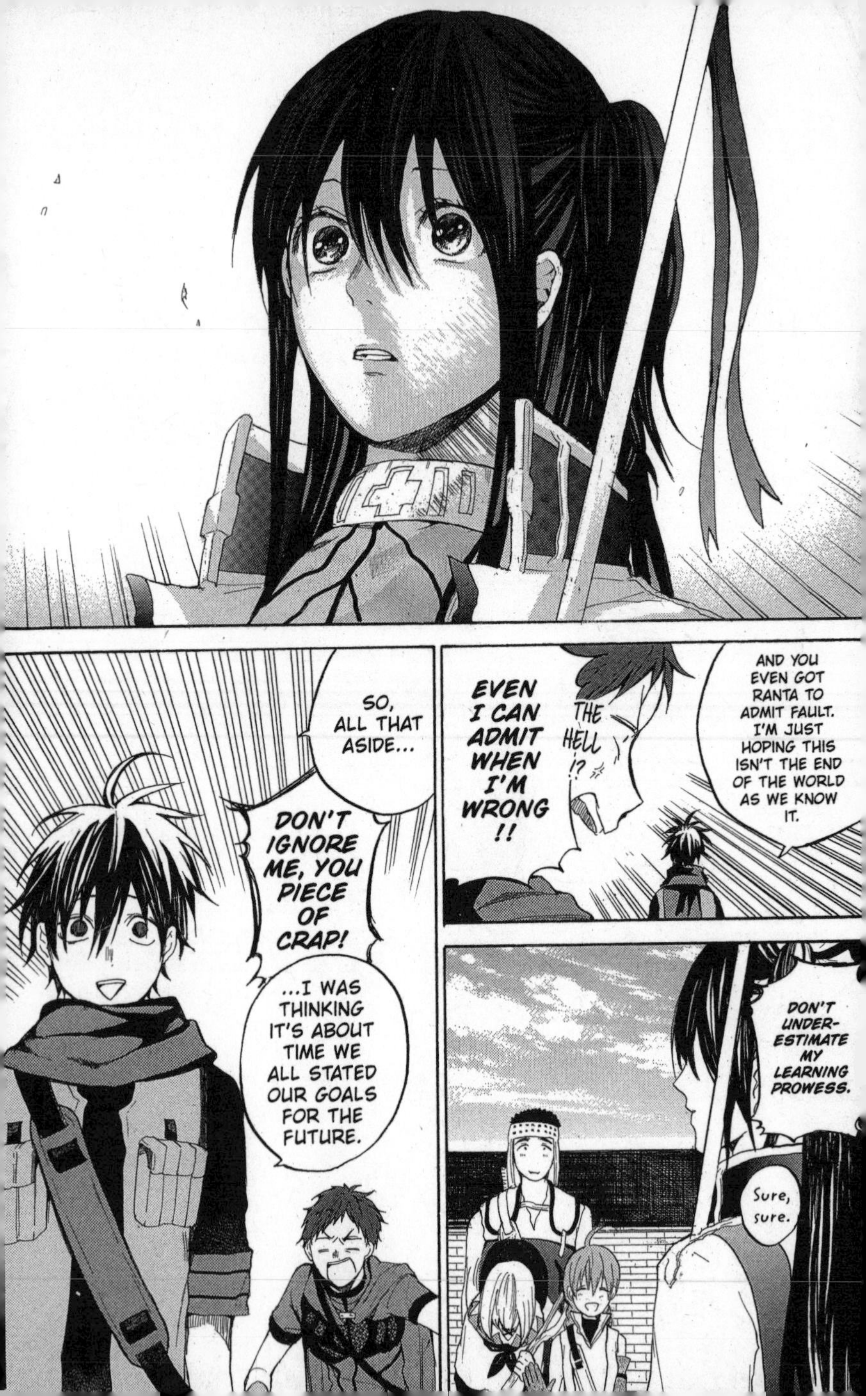
AND YOU EVEN GOT RANTA TO ADMIT FAULT. I'M JUST HOPING THIS ISN'T THE END OF THE WORLD AS WE KNOW IT.
THE HELL!?
EVEN I CAN ADMIT WHEN I'M WRONG!!
DON'T UNDER-ESTIMATE MY LEARNING PROWESS.
Sure, sure.
SO, ALL THAT ASIDE...
DON'T IGNORE ME, YOU PIECE OF CRAP!
...I WAS THINKING IT'S ABOUT TIME WE ALL STATED OUR GOALS FOR THE FUTURE.

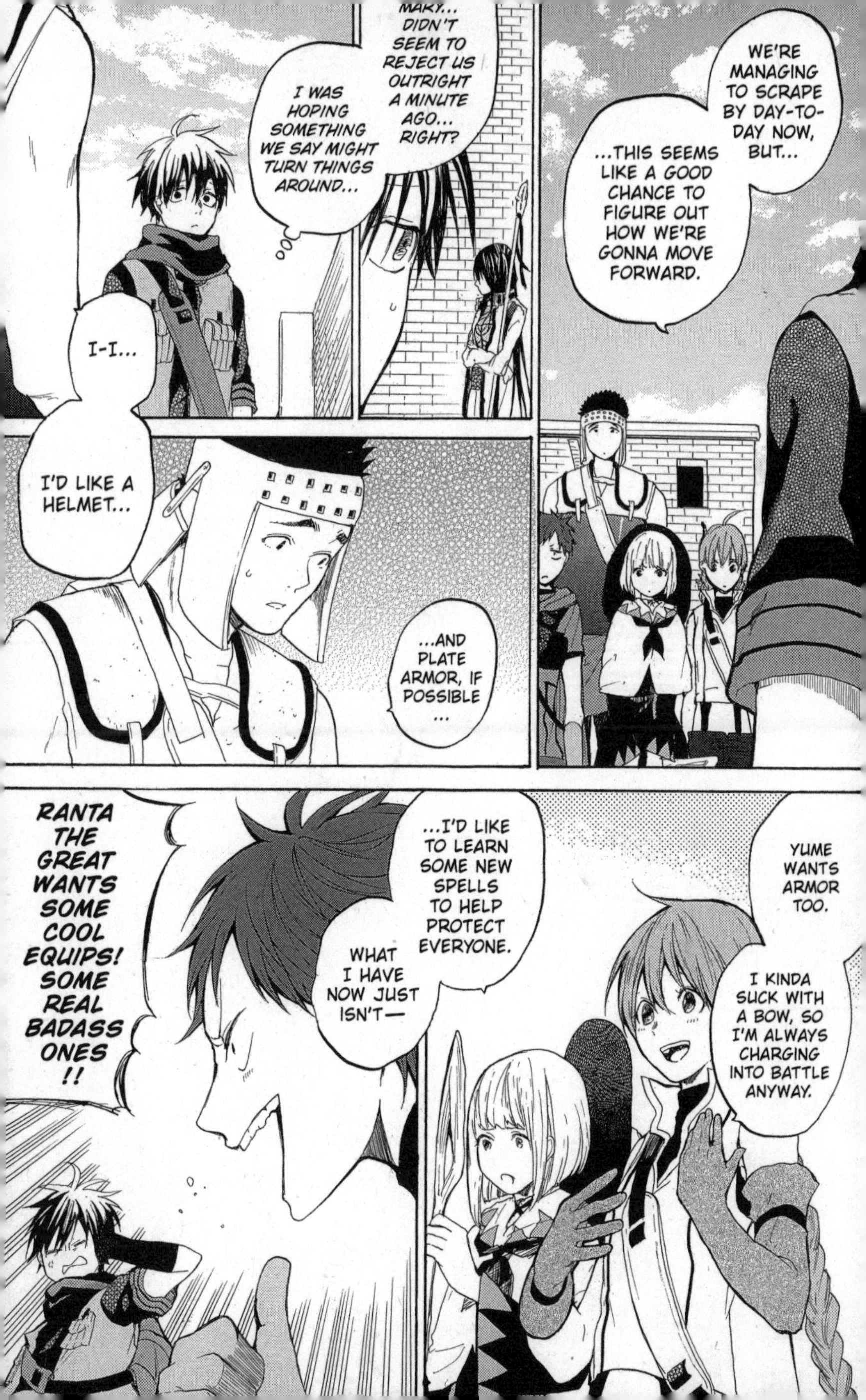
WE'RE MANAGING TO SCRAPE BY DAY-TO-DAY NOW, BUT...
...THIS SEEMS LIKE A GOOD CHANCE TO FIGURE OUT HOW WE'RE GONNA MOVE FORWARD.
MARY... DIDN'T SEEM TO REJECT US OUTRIGHT A MINUTE AGO... RIGHT?
I WAS HOPING SOMETHING WE SAY MIGHT TURN THINGS AROUND...
I-I...
I'D LIKE A HELMET...
...AND PLATE ARMOR, IF POSSIBLE...
YUME WANTS ARMOR TOO.
I KINDA SUCK WITH A BOW, SO I'M ALWAYS CHARGING INTO BATTLE ANYWAY.
...I'D LIKE TO LEARN SOME NEW SPELLS TO HELP PROTECT EVERYONE.
WHAT I HAVE NOW JUST ISN'T—
RANTA THE GREAT WANTS SOME COOL EQUIPS! SOME REAL BADASS ONES!!

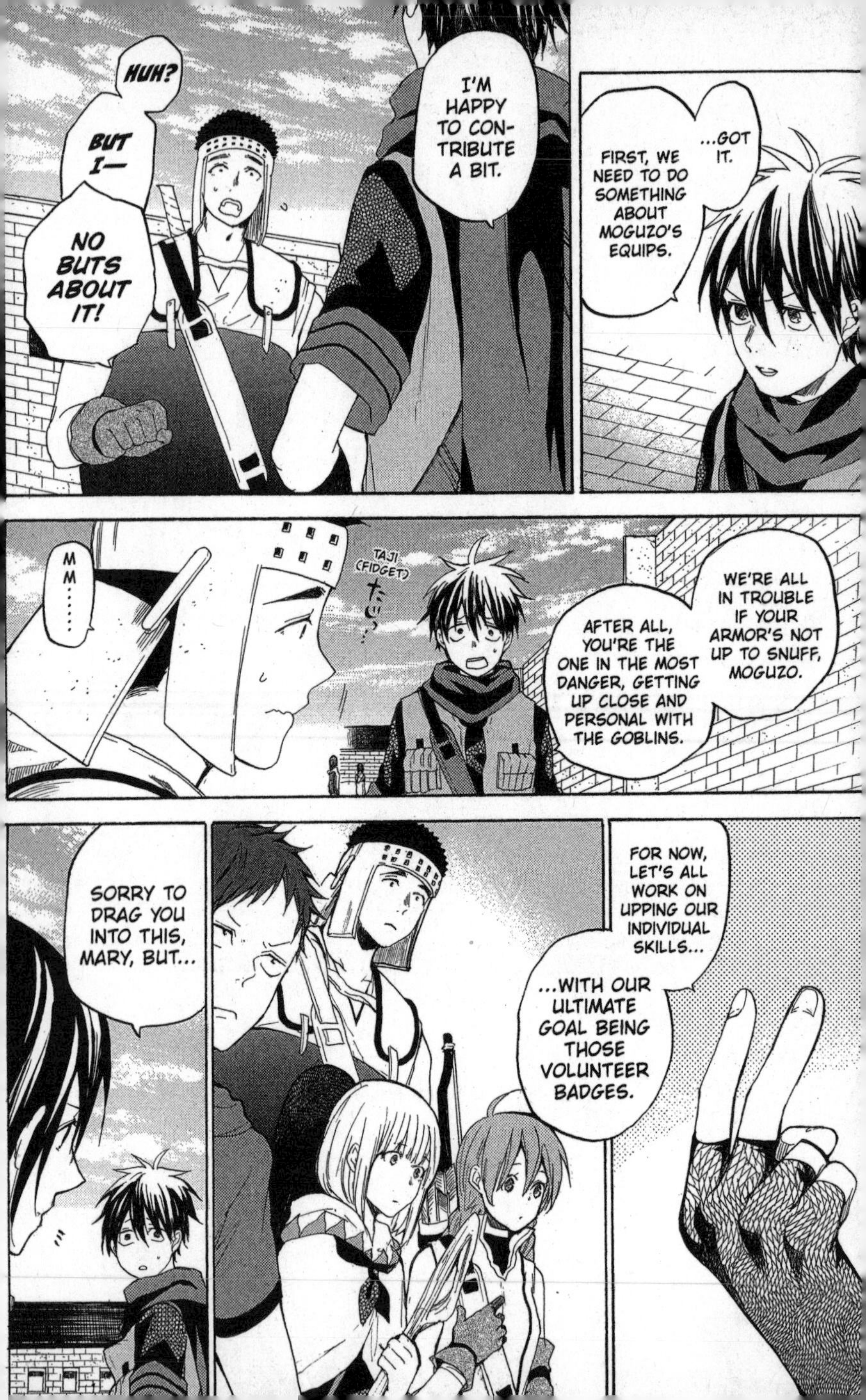
...GOT IT.
FIRST, WE NEED TO DO SOMETHING ABOUT MOGUZO'S EQUIPS.
I'M HAPPY TO CONTRIBUTE A BIT.
HUH?
BUT I—
NO BUTS ABOUT IT!
WE'RE ALL IN TROUBLE IF YOUR ARMOR'S NOT UP TO SNUFF, MOGUZO.
AFTER ALL, YOU'RE THE ONE IN THE MOST DANGER, GETTING UP CLOSE AND PERSONAL WITH THE GOBLINS.
TAJI (FIDGET)
MM......
FOR NOW, LET'S ALL WORK ON UPPING OUR INDIVIDUAL SKILLS...
...WITH OUR ULTIMATE GOAL BEING THOSE VOLUNTEER BADGES.
SORRY TO DRAG YOU INTO THIS, MARY, BUT...
!!

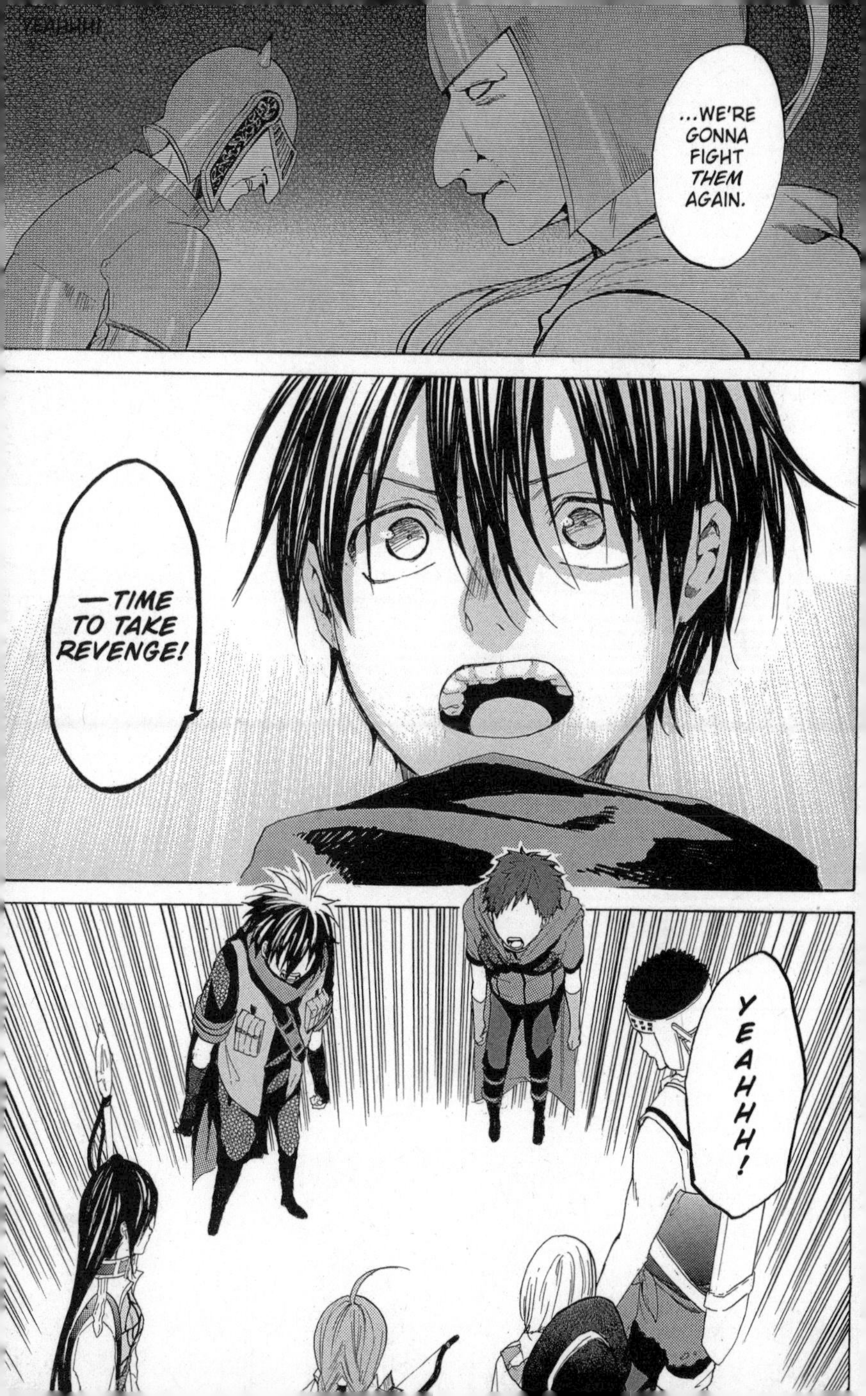
...WE'RE GONNA FIGHT THEM AGAIN.
—TIME TO TAKE REVENGE!
YEAHHH!

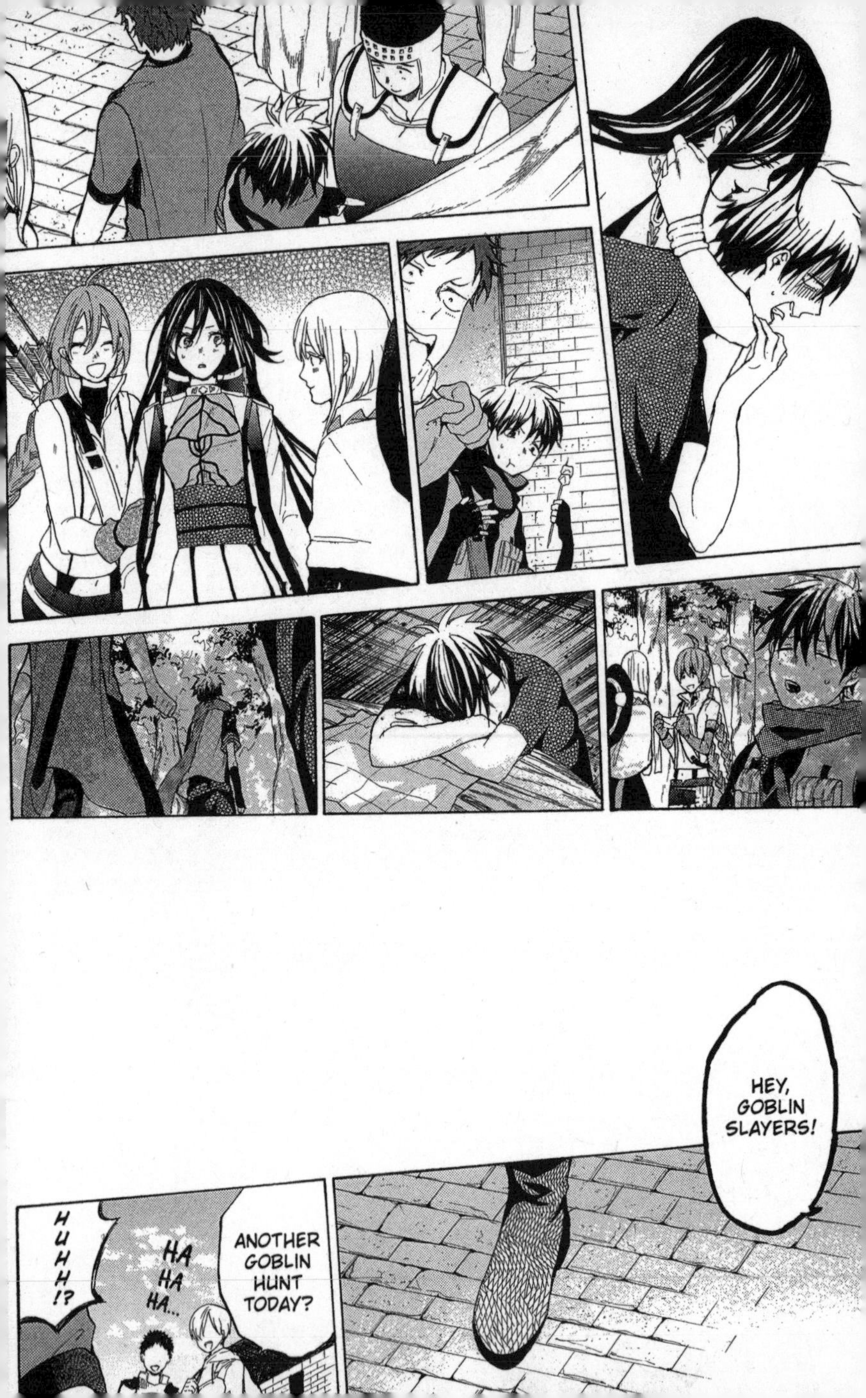
HEY, GOBLIN SLAYERS!
ANOTHER GOBLIN HUNT TODAY?
HA HA HA...
HUHH!?

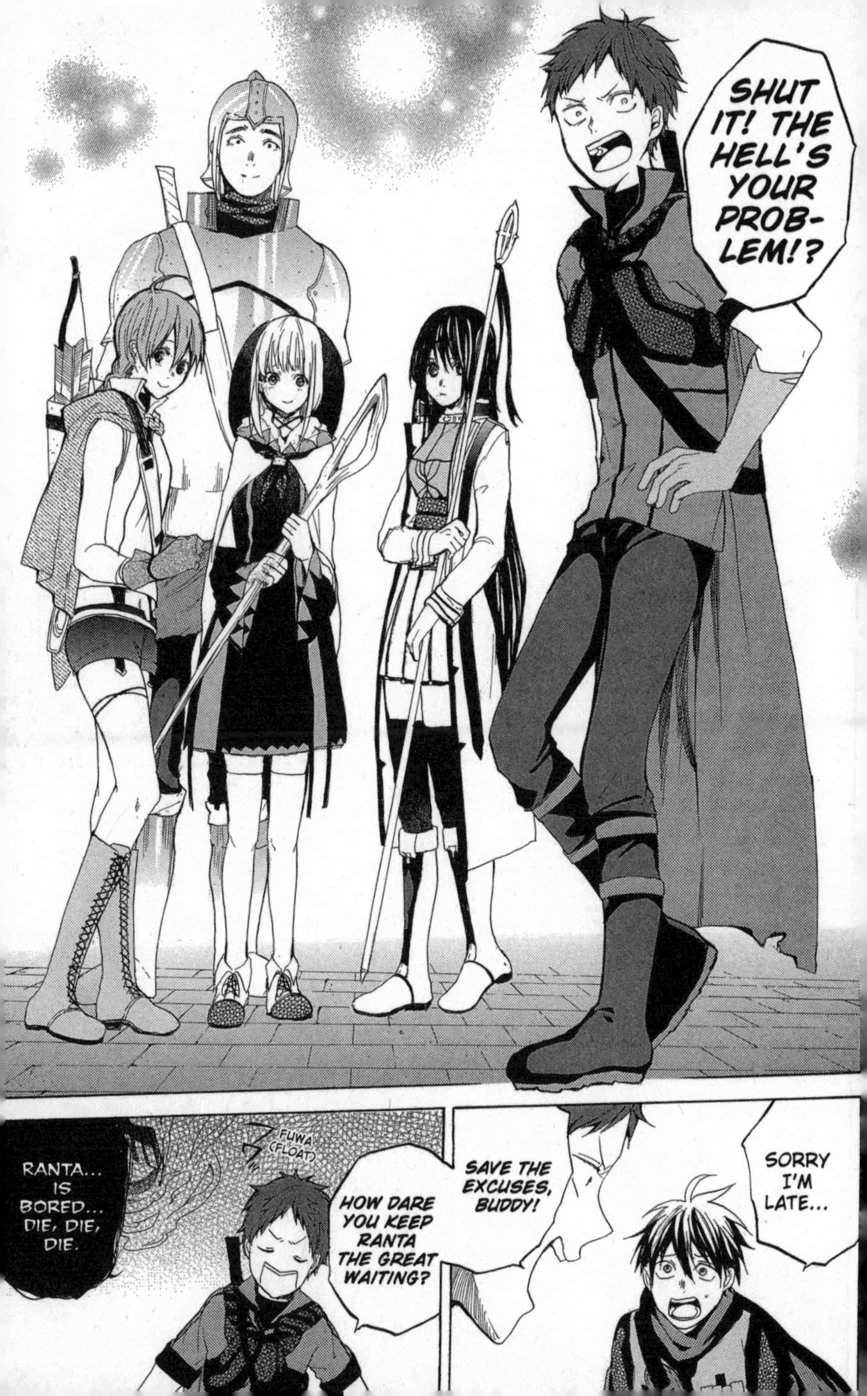
SHUT IT! THE HELL'S YOUR PROB-LEM!?
SORRY I'M LATE...
SAVE THE EXCUSES, BUDDY!
HOW DARE YOU KEEP RANTA THE GREAT WAITING?
FUWA (FLOAT)
RANTA... IS BORED... DIE, DIE, DIE.

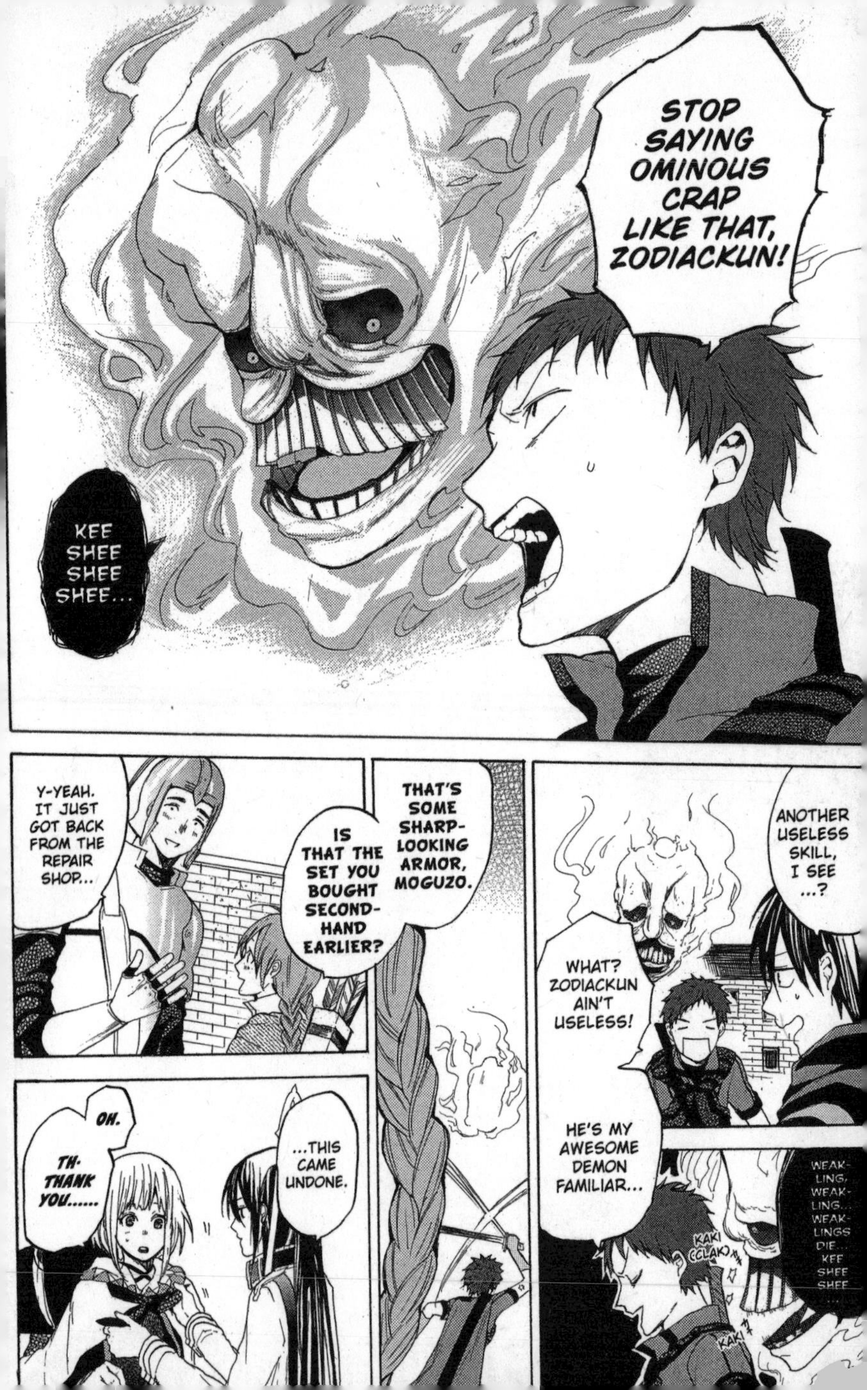
STOP SAYING OMINOUS CRAP LIKE THAT, ZODIACKUN!
KEE SHEE SHEE SHEE...
ANOTHER USELESS SKILL, I SEE ...?
WHAT? ZODIACKUN AIN'T USELESS!
HE'S MY AWESOME DEMON FAMILIAR...
WEAK-LING, WEAK-LING... WEAK-LINGS DIE... KEE SHEE SHEE...
KAKI (CLAK)
KAKI
THAT'S SOME SHARP-LOOKING ARMOR, MOGUZO.
IS THAT THE SET YOU BOUGHT SECOND-HAND EARLIER?
Y-YEAH. IT JUST GOT BACK FROM THE REPAIR SHOP...
...THIS CAME UNDONE.
OH.
TH-THANK YOU......

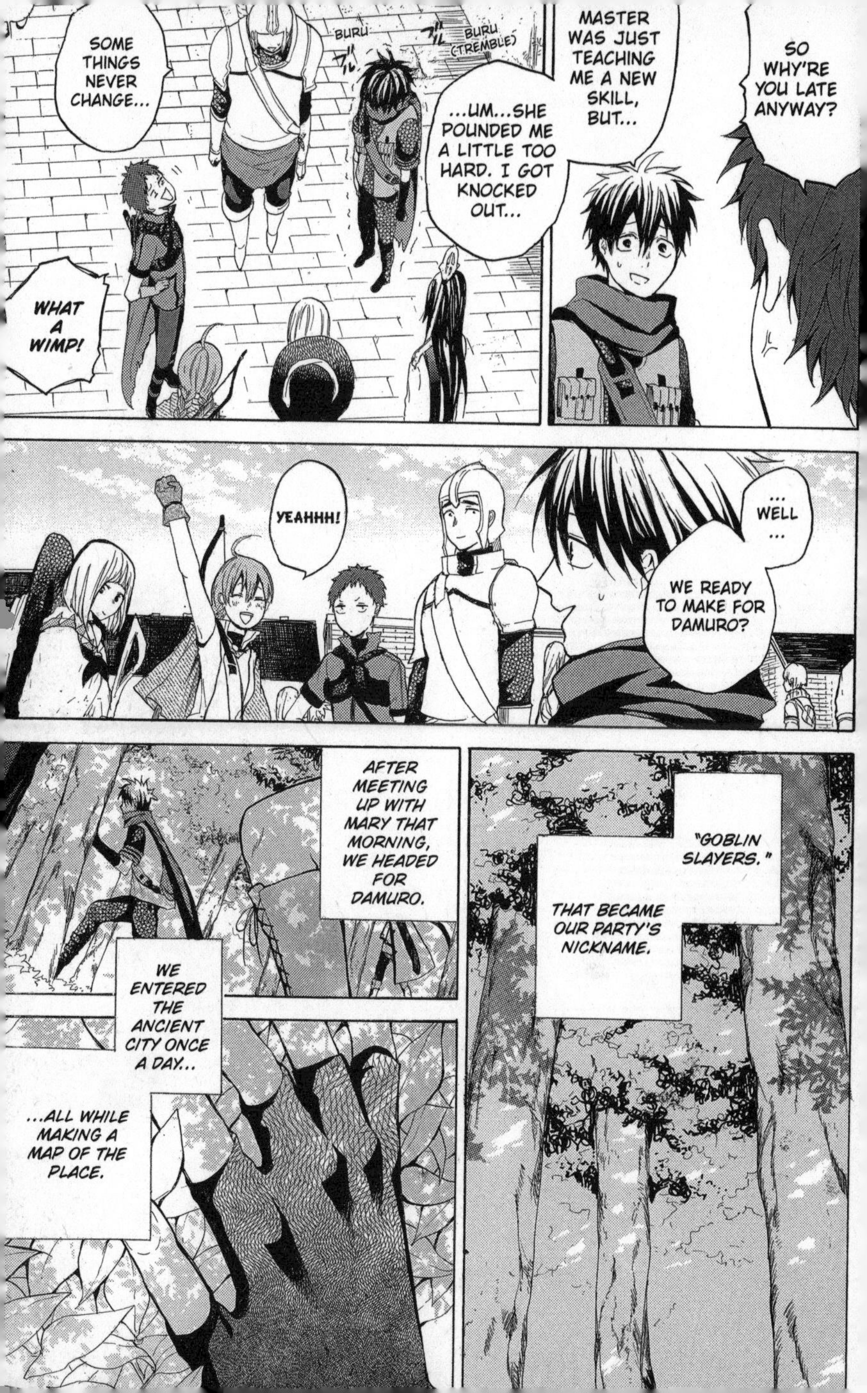
SO WHY'RE YOU LATE ANYWAY?
MASTER WAS JUST TEACHING ME A NEW SKILL, BUT...
...UM...SHE POUNDED ME A LITTLE TOO HARD. I GOT KNOCKED OUT...
BURU BURU (TREMBLE)
SOME THINGS NEVER CHANGE...
WHAT A WIMP!
...WELL...
WE READY TO MAKE FOR DAMURO?
YEAHHH!
"GOBLIN SLAYERS."
THAT BECAME OUR PARTY'S NICKNAME.
AFTER MEETING UP WITH MARY THAT MORNING, WE HEADED FOR DAMURO.
WE ENTERED THE ANCIENT CITY ONCE A DAY...
...ALL WHILE MAKING A MAP OF THE PLACE.

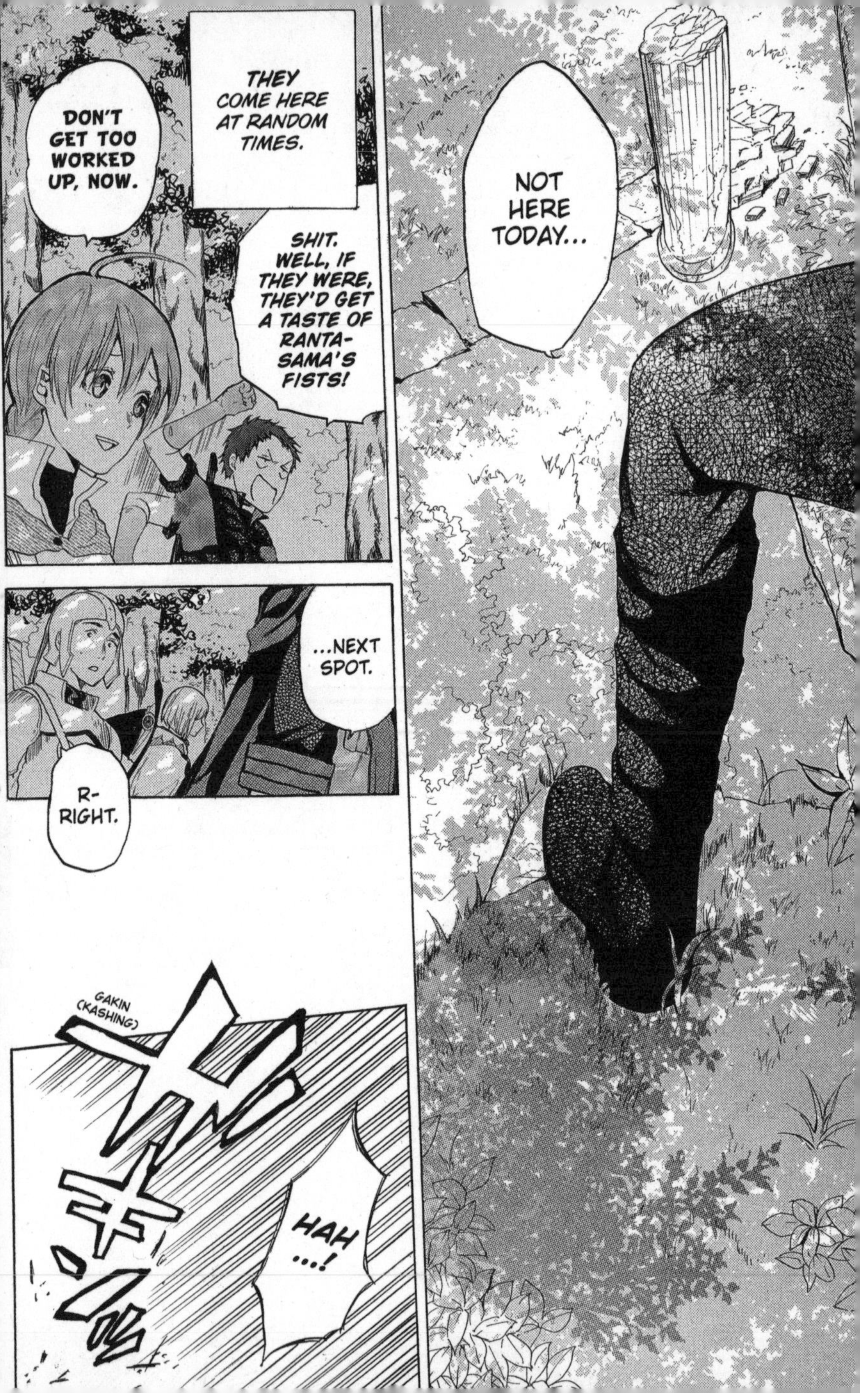
NOT HERE TODAY...
THEY COME HERE AT RANDOM TIMES.
SHIT. WELL, IF THEY WERE, THEY'D GET A TASTE OF RANTA-SAMA'S FISTS!
DON'T GET TOO WORKED UP, NOW.
...NEXT SPOT.
R-RIGHT.
GAKIN (KASHING)
HAH...!

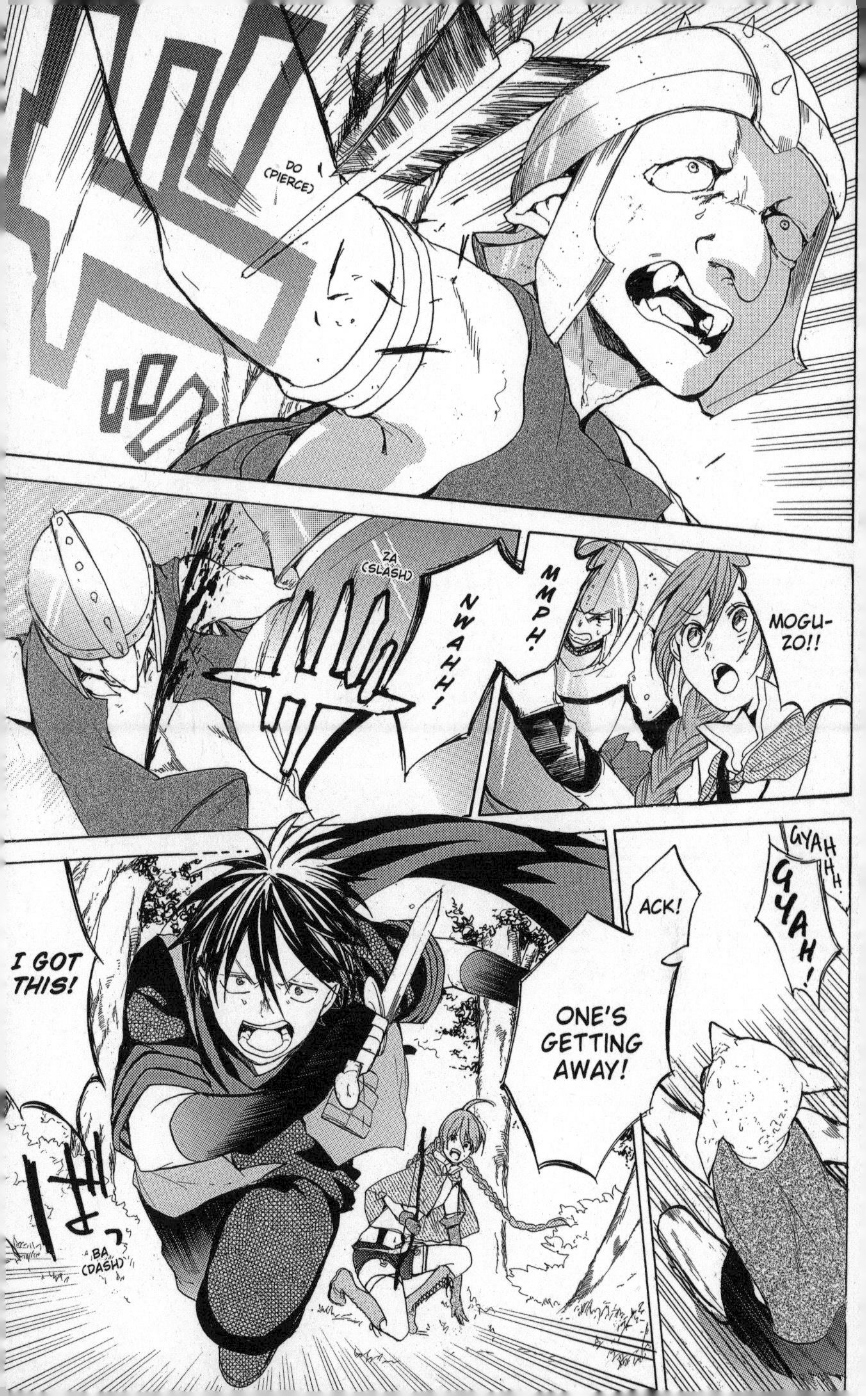
DO
(PIERCE)
MOGU-ZO!!
MMPH!
NWAHH!
ZA
(SLASH)
GYAHHHH!
GYAHH!
ACK!
ONE'S GETTING AWAY!
I GOT THIS!
BA
(DASH)

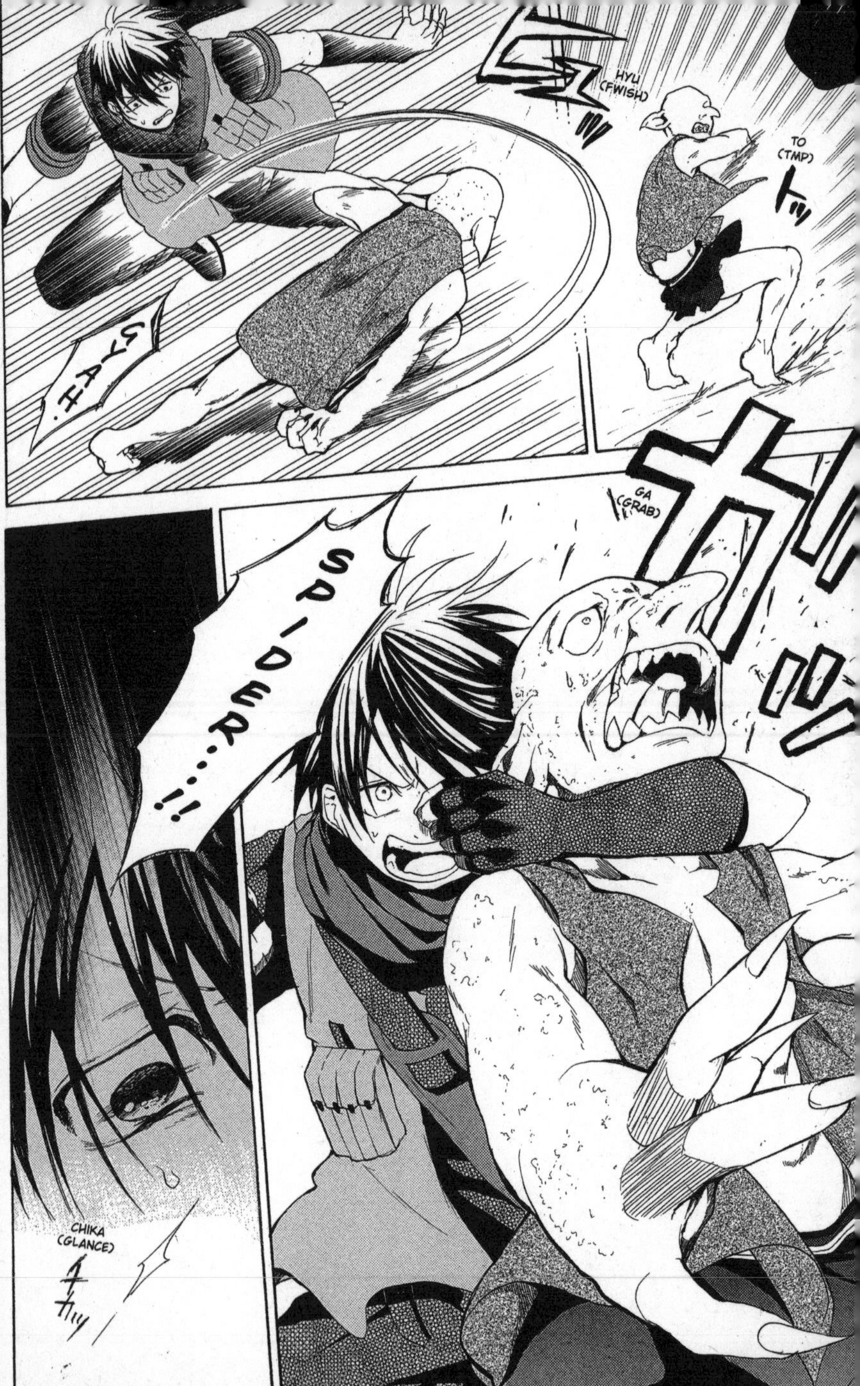
HYU
(FWISH)
TO
(TMP)
GYAH!
GA
(GRAB)
SPIDER...!!
CHIKA
(GLANCE)

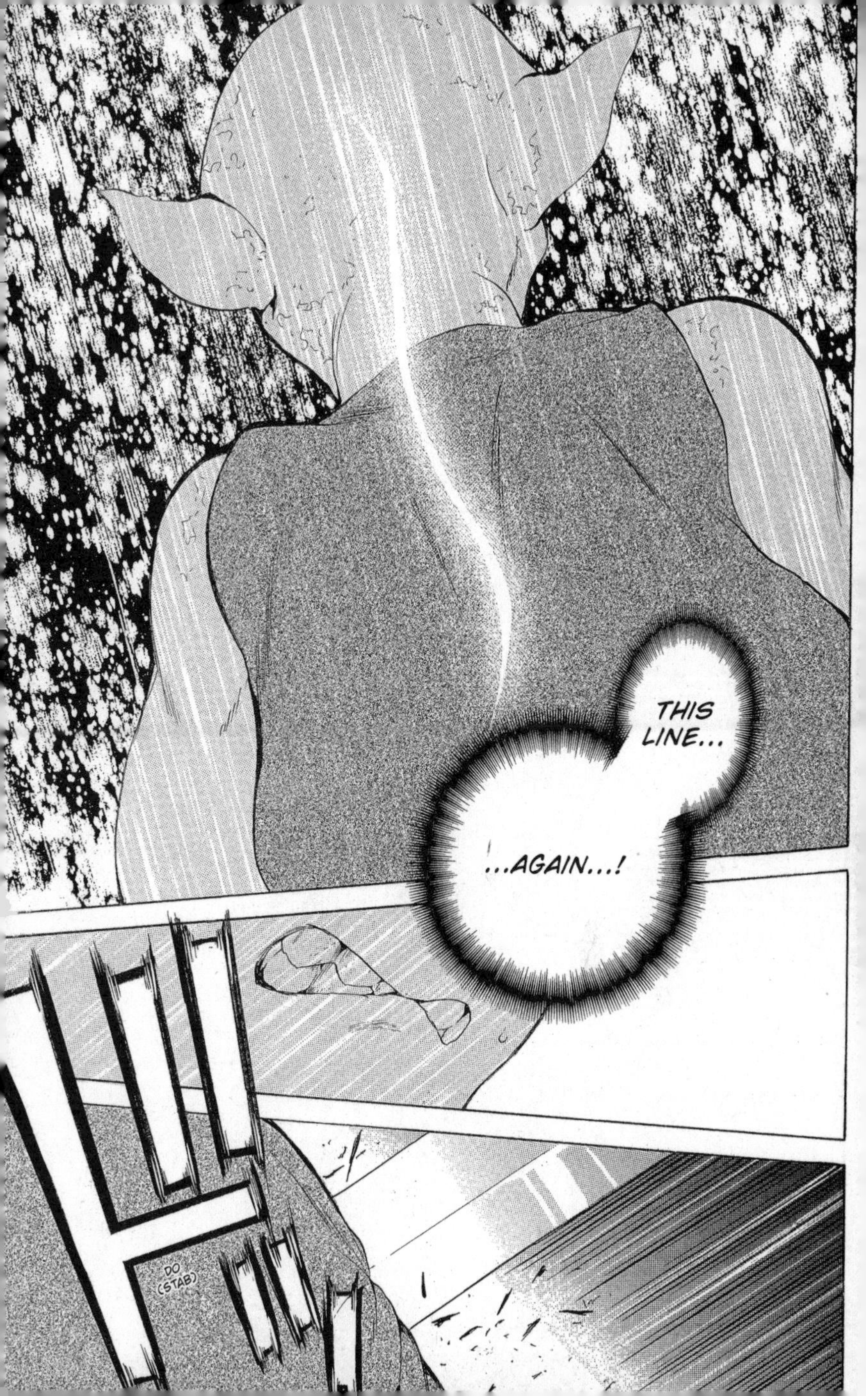

THIS LINE...
...AGAIN...!
DO (STAB)

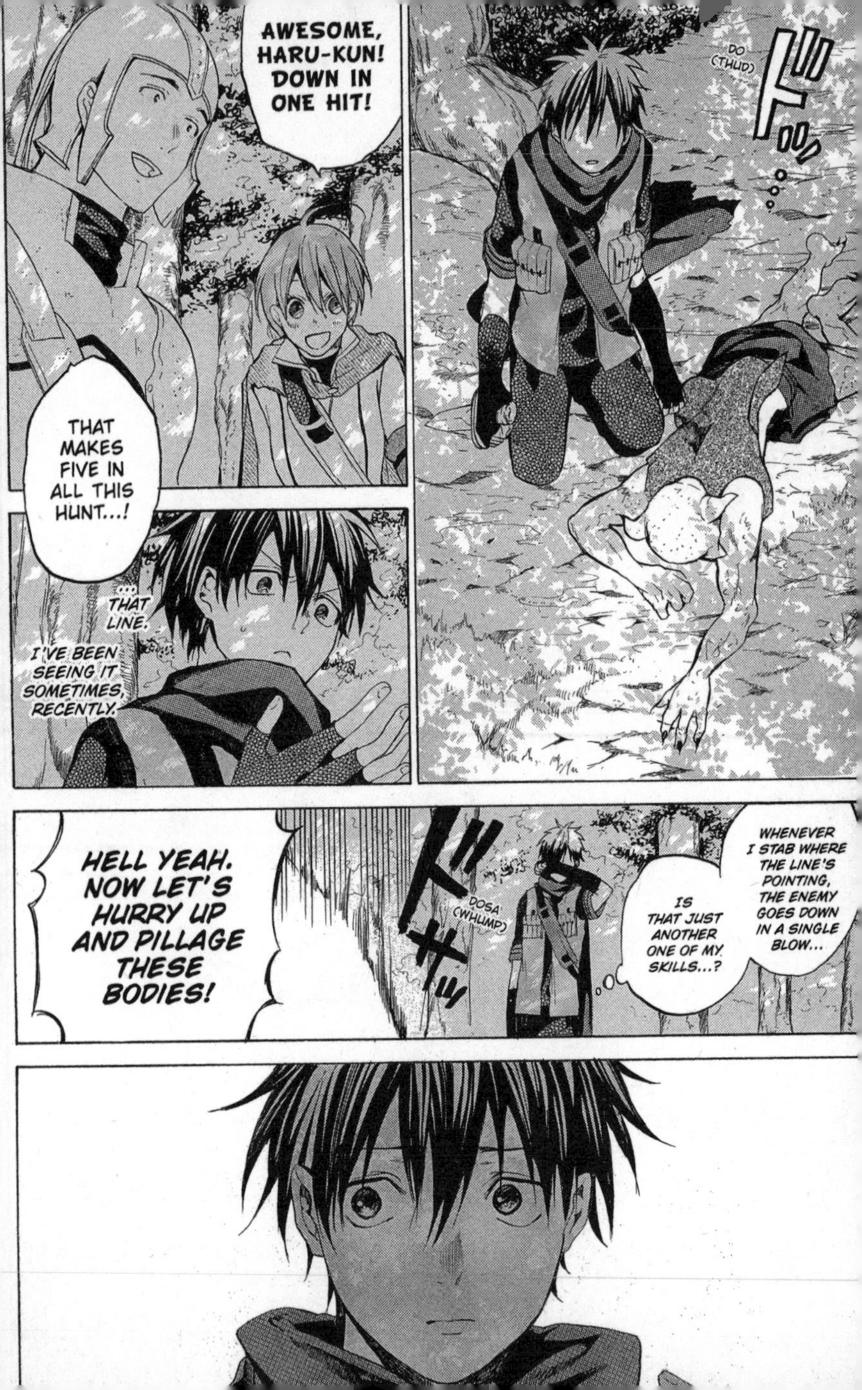
DO (THUD)
AWESOME, HARU-KUN! DOWN IN ONE HIT!
THAT MAKES FIVE IN ALL THIS HUNT...!
...THAT LINE.
I'VE BEEN SEEING IT SOMETIMES, RECENTLY.
WHENEVER I STAB WHERE THE LINE'S POINTING, THE ENEMY GOES DOWN IN A SINGLE BLOW...
IS THAT JUST ANOTHER ONE OF MY SKILLS...?
DOSA (WHUMP)
HELL YEAH. NOW LET'S HURRY UP AND PILLAGE THESE BODIES!

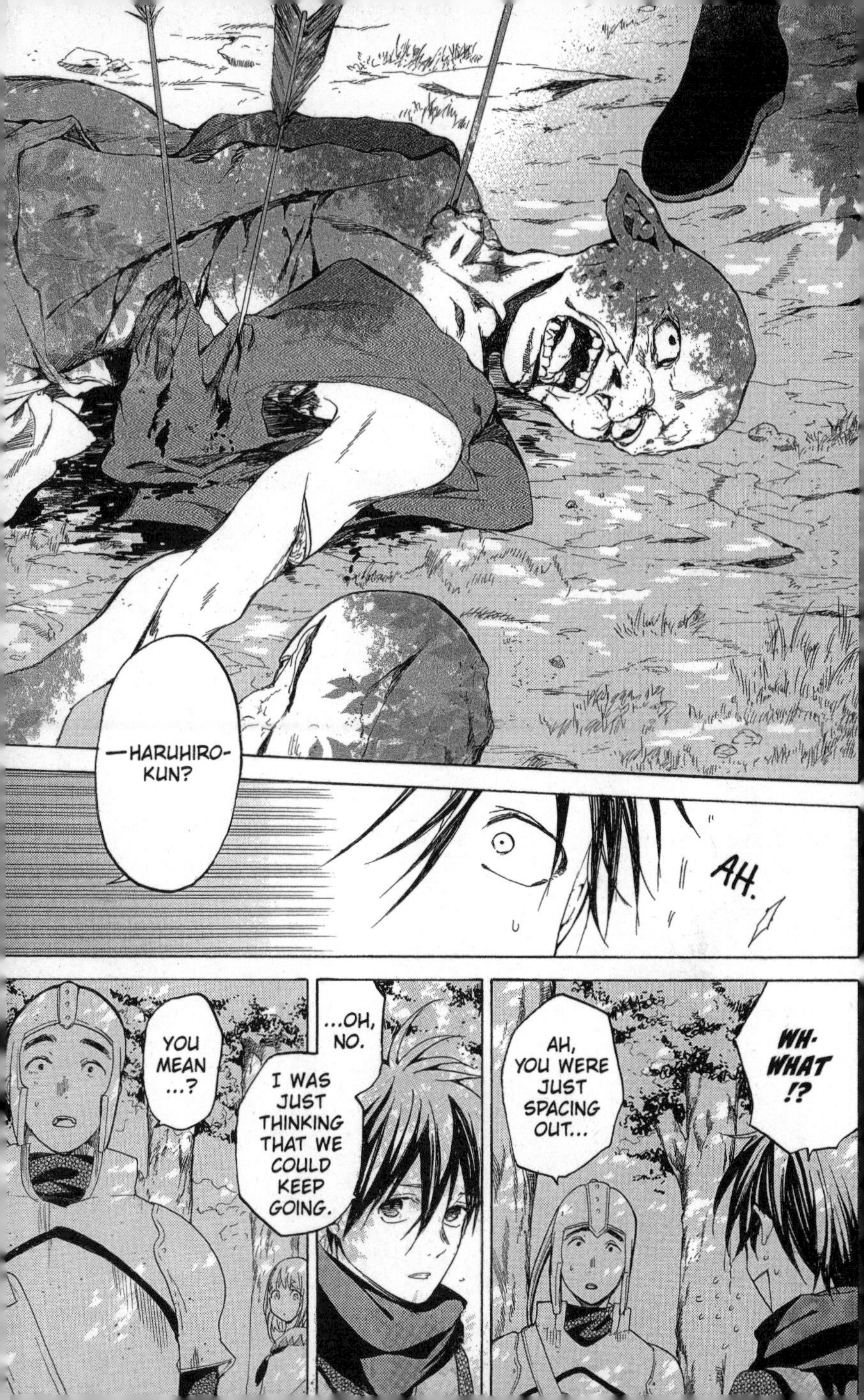
—HARUHIRO-KUN?
AH.
WH-WHAT!?
AH, YOU WERE JUST SPACING OUT...
...OH, NO.
I WAS JUST THINKING THAT WE COULD KEEP GOING.
YOU MEAN ...?

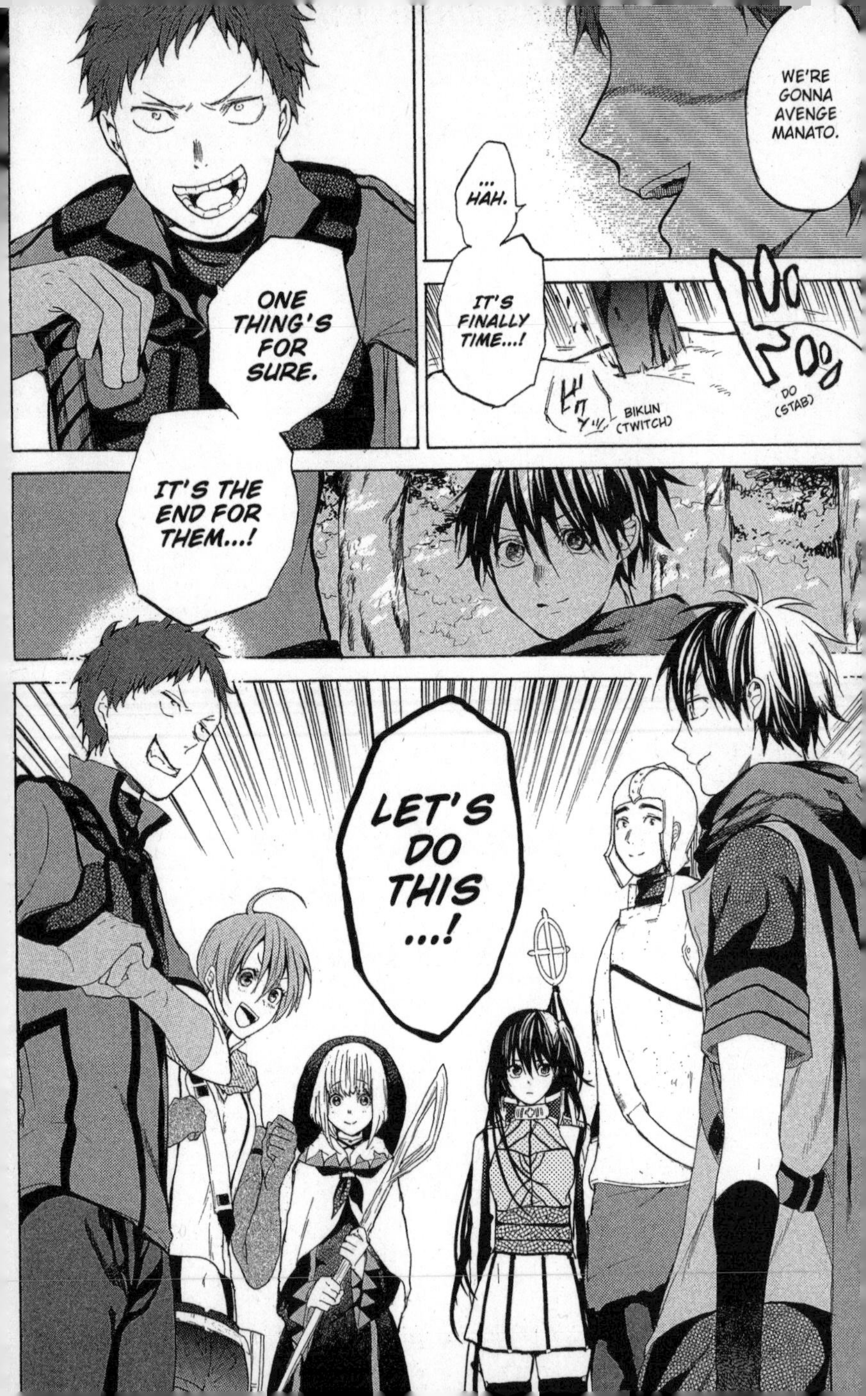
WE'RE GONNA AVENGE MANATO.
...HÄH.
DO (STAB)
IT'S FINALLY TIME...!
BIKUN (TWITCH)
ONE THING'S FOR SURE.
IT'S THE END FOR THEM...!
LET'S DO THIS...!

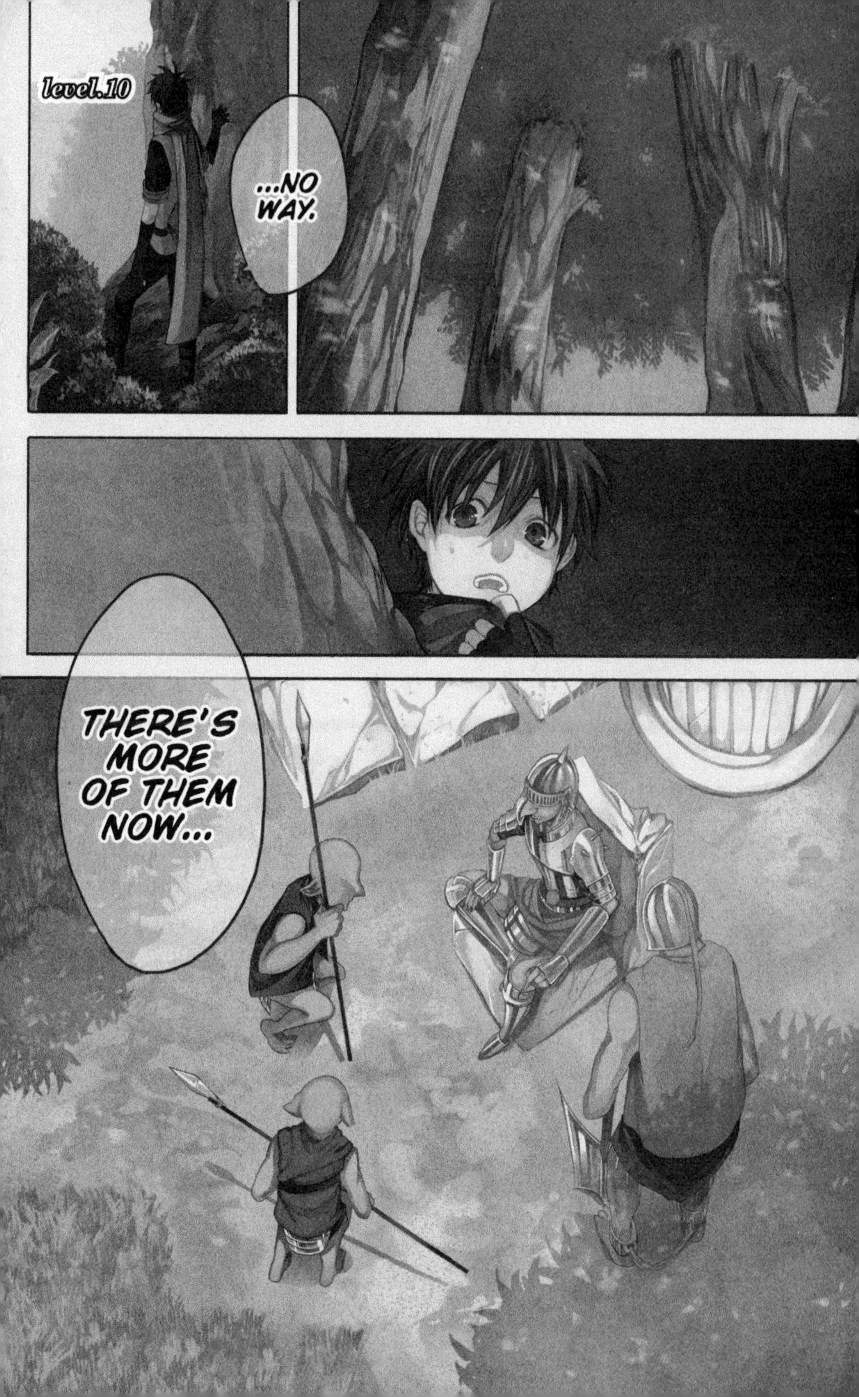
...NO WAY.
level.10
THERE'S MORE OF THEM NOW...

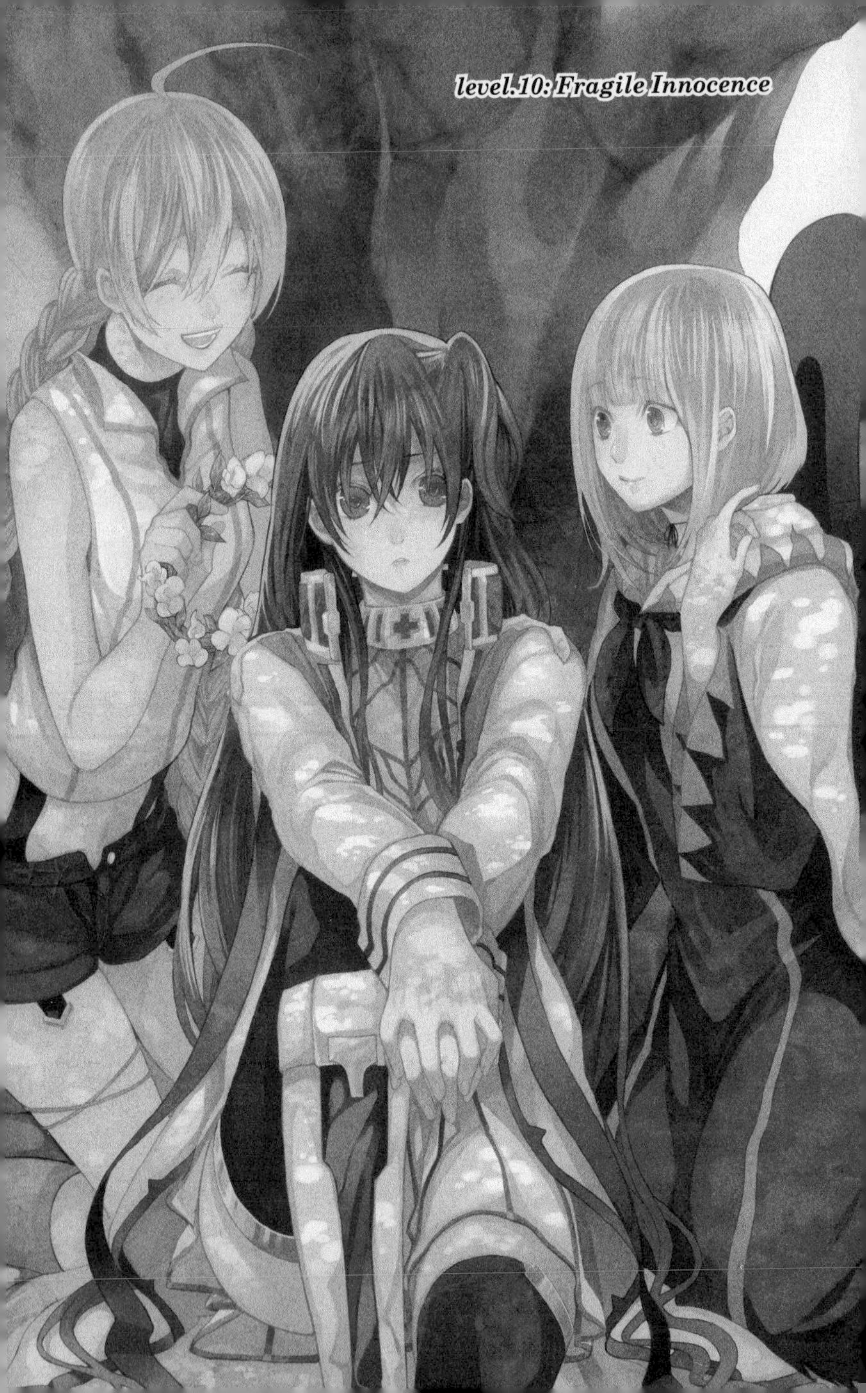
level.10: Fragile Innocence

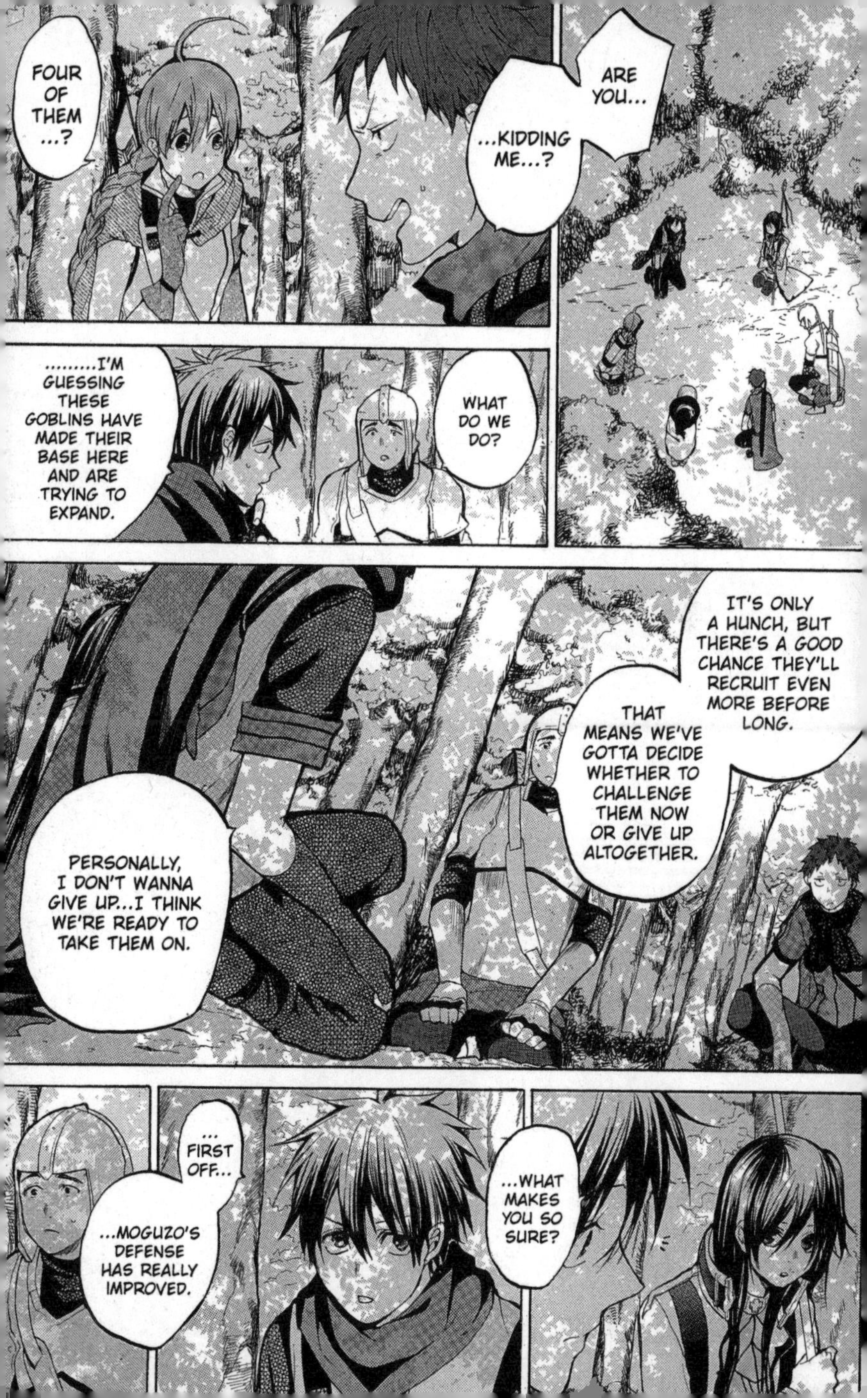
ARE YOU...
...KIDDING ME...?
FOUR OF THEM ...?
WHAT DO WE DO?
.........I'M GUESSING THESE GOBLINS HAVE MADE THEIR BASE HERE AND ARE TRYING TO EXPAND.
IT'S ONLY A HUNCH, BUT THERE'S A GOOD CHANCE THEY'LL RECRUIT EVEN MORE BEFORE LONG.
THAT MEANS WE'VE GOTTA DECIDE WHETHER TO CHALLENGE THEM NOW OR GIVE UP ALTOGETHER.
PERSONALLY, I DON'T WANNA GIVE UP...I THINK WE'RE READY TO TAKE THEM ON.
...WHAT MAKES YOU SO SURE?
... FIRST OFF...
...MOGUZO'S DEFENSE HAS REALLY IMPROVED.

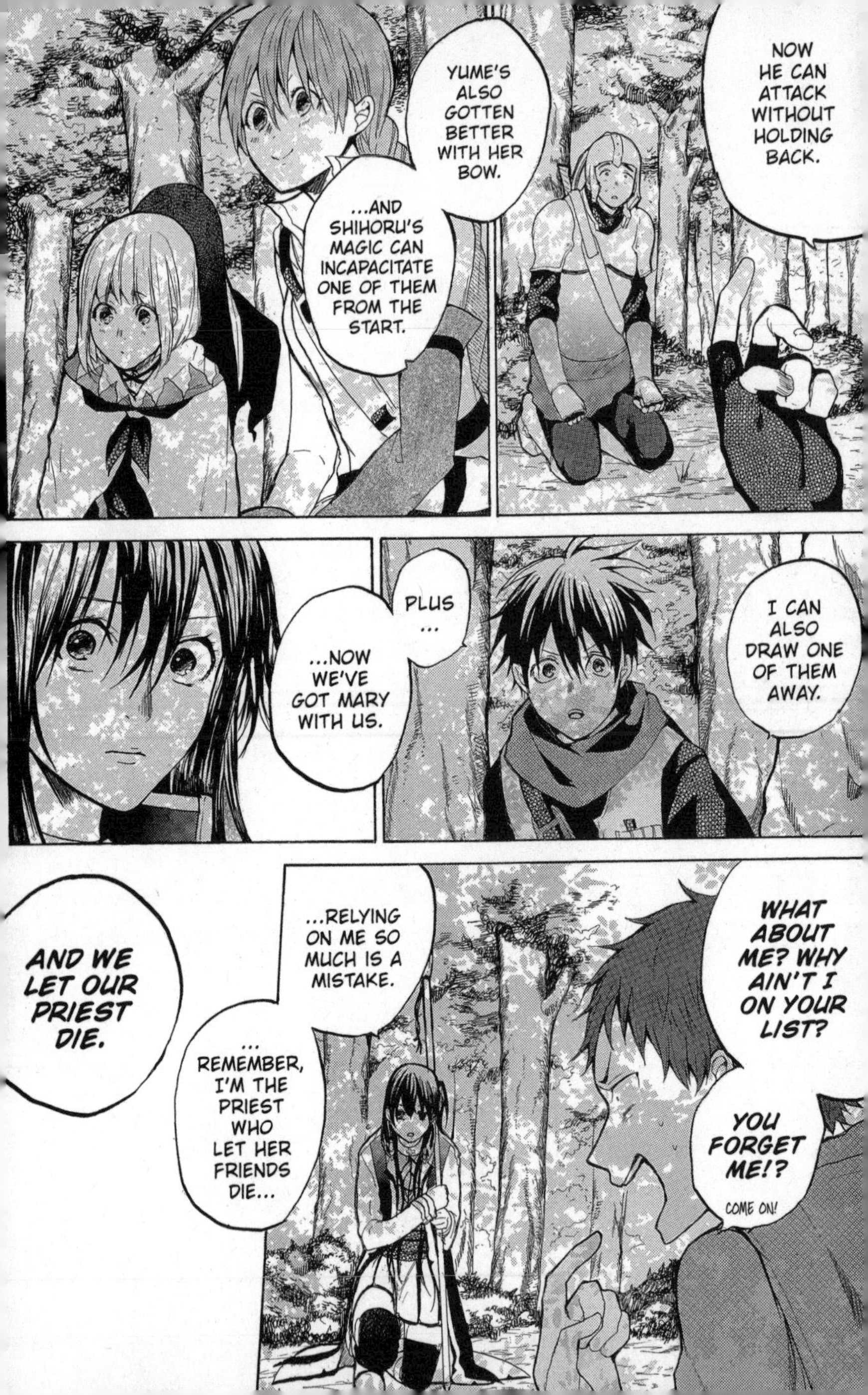

NOW HE CAN ATTACK WITHOUT HOLDING BACK.
YUME'S ALSO GOTTEN BETTER WITH HER BOW.
...AND SHIHORU'S MAGIC CAN INCAPACITATE ONE OF THEM FROM THE START.
I CAN ALSO DRAW ONE OF THEM AWAY.
PLUS ...
...NOW WE'VE GOT MARY WITH US.
WHAT ABOUT ME? WHY AIN'T I ON YOUR LIST?
YOU FORGET ME!?
COME ON!
...RELYING ON ME SO MUCH IS A MISTAKE.
... REMEMBER, I'M THE PRIEST WHO LET HER FRIENDS DIE...
AND WE LET OUR PRIEST DIE.

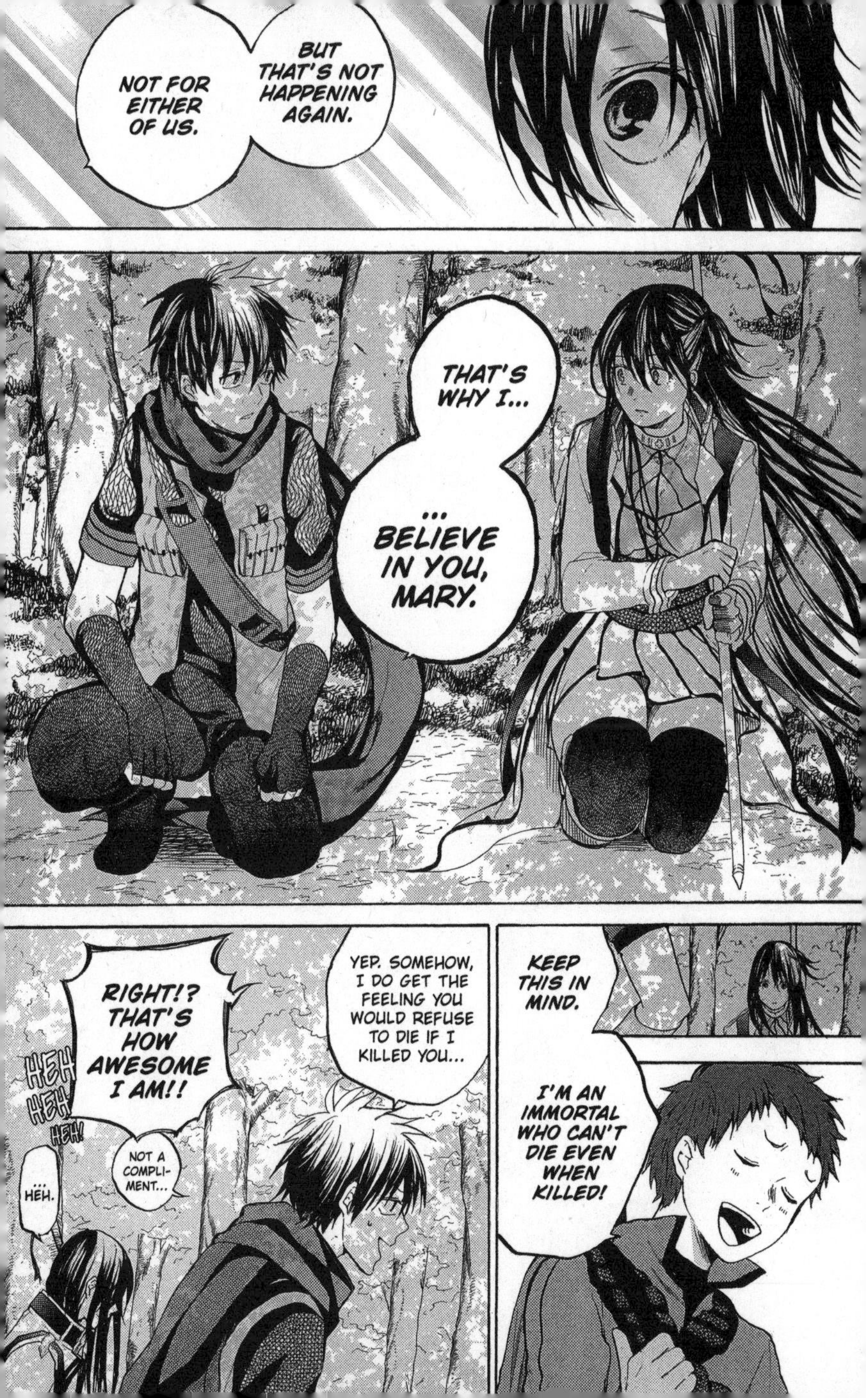
BUT THAT'S NOT HAPPENING AGAIN.
NOT FOR EITHER OF US.
THAT'S WHY I...
... BELIEVE IN YOU, MARY.
KEEP THIS IN MIND.
I'M AN IMMORTAL WHO CAN'T DIE EVEN WHEN KILLED!
YEP. SOMEHOW, I DO GET THE FEELING YOU WOULD REFUSE TO DIE IF I KILLED YOU...
RIGHT!? THAT'S HOW AWESOME I AM!!
HEH HEH HEH!
NOT A COMPLI-MENT...
... HEH.

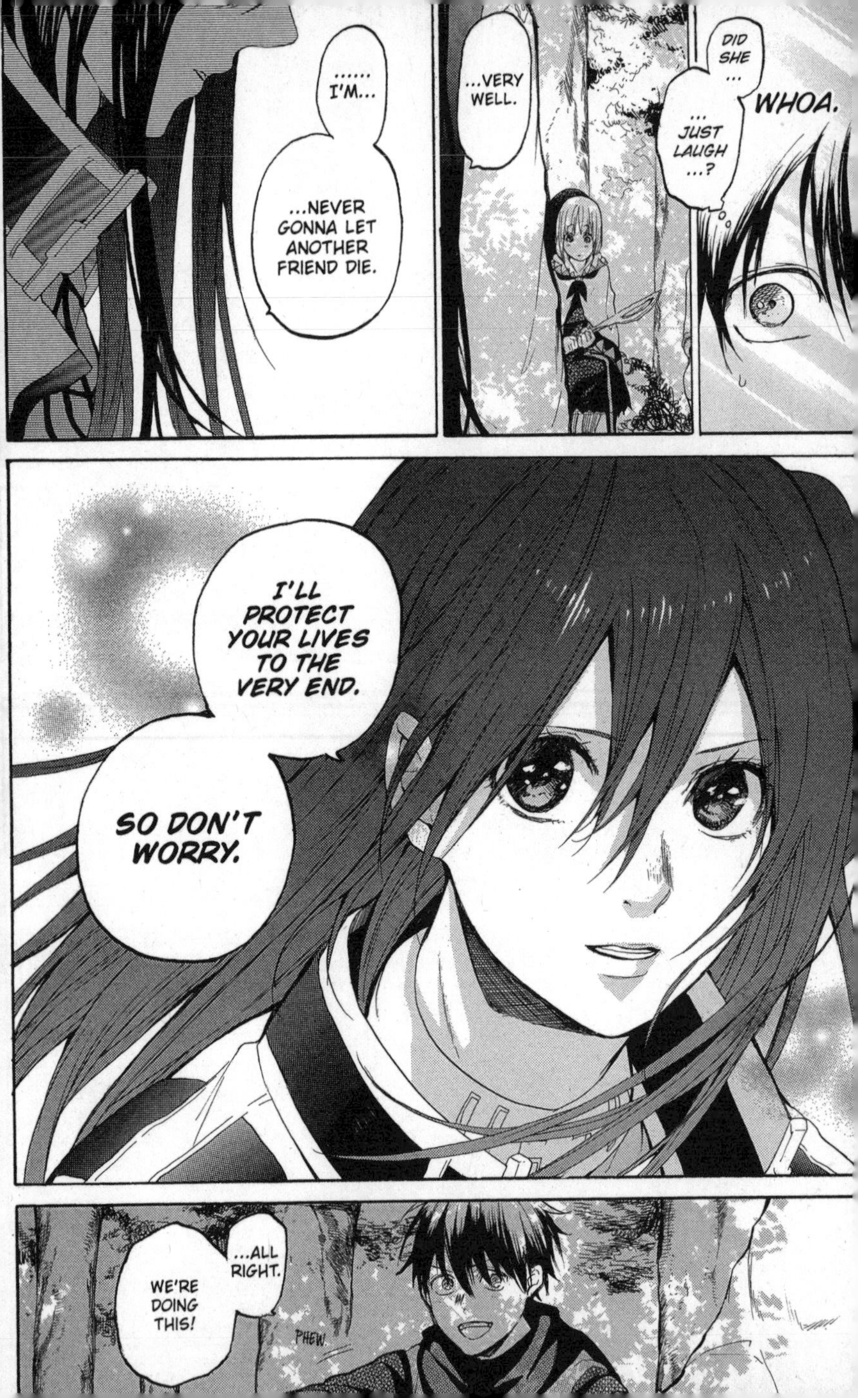
DID SHE ... ... JUST LAUGH ...?
WHOA.
...VERY WELL.
...... I'M...
...NEVER GONNA LET ANOTHER FRIEND DIE.
I'LL PROTECT YOUR LIVES TO THE VERY END.
SO DON'T WORRY.
...ALL RIGHT.
WE'RE DOING THIS!
PHEW.

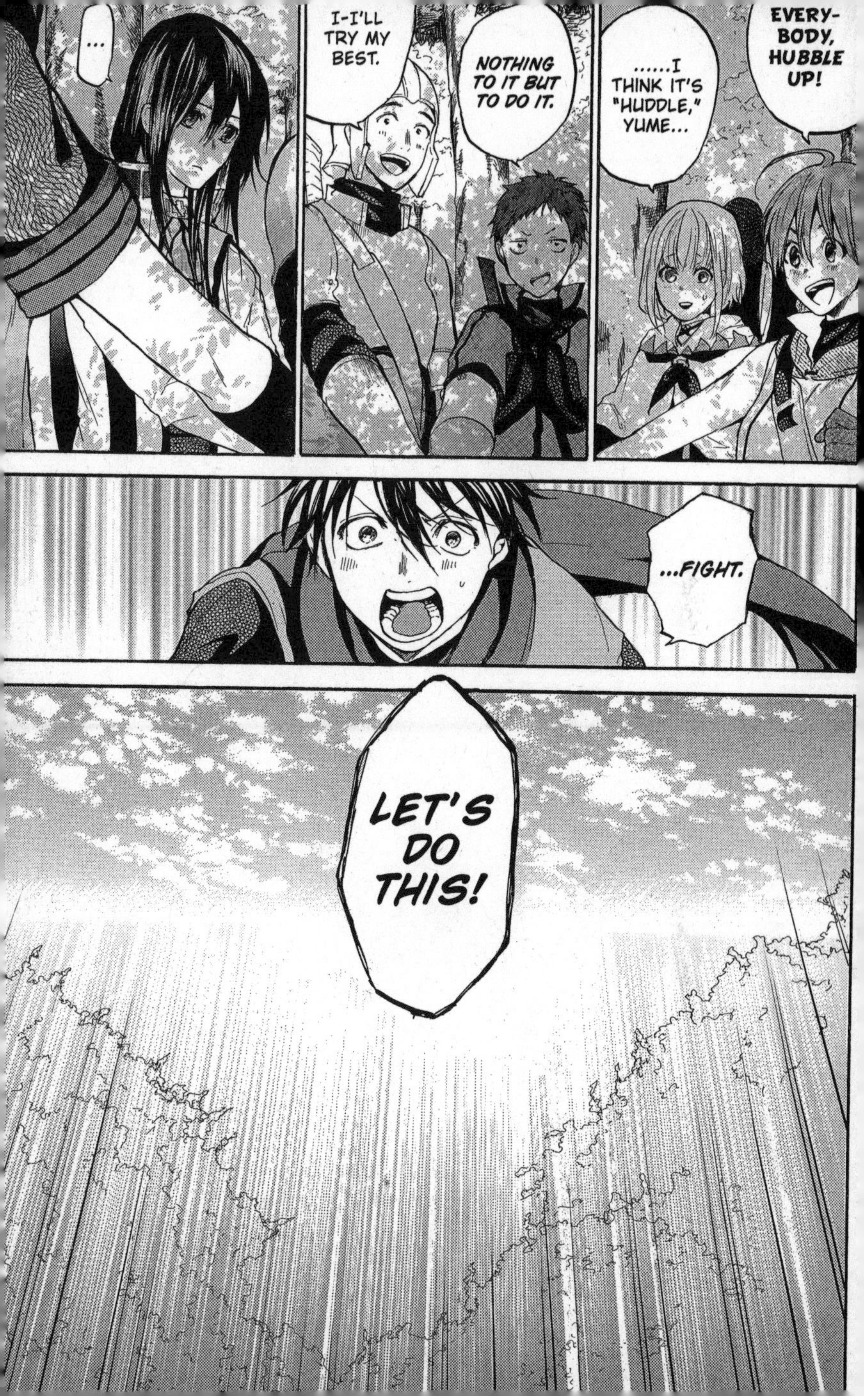
EVERY-BODY, HUBBLE UP!
......I THINK IT'S "HUDDLE," YUME...
NOTHING TO IT BUT TO DO IT.
I-I'LL TRY MY BEST.
...
...FIGHT.
LET'S DO THIS!

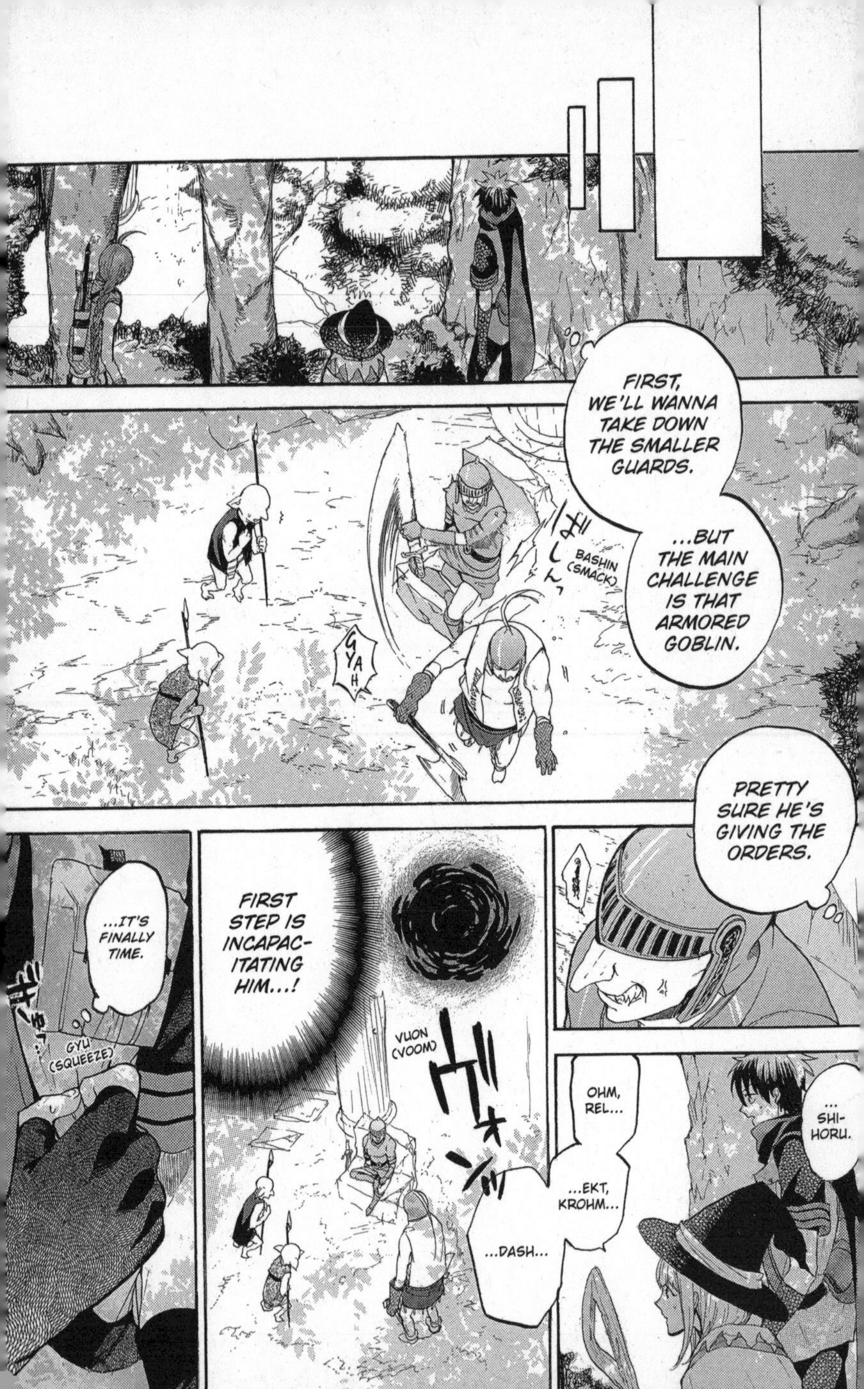
FIRST, WE'LL WANNA TAKE DOWN THE SMALLER GUARDS.
BASHIN (SMACK)
...BUT THE MAIN CHALLENGE IS THAT ARMORED GOBLIN.
GYAH!
PRETTY SURE HE'S GIVING THE ORDERS.
...SHIHORU.
OHM, REL...
...EKT, KROHM...
...DASH...
FIRST STEP IS INCAPACITATING HIM...!
VUON (VOOM)
...IT'S FINALLY TIME.
GYU (SQUEEZE)

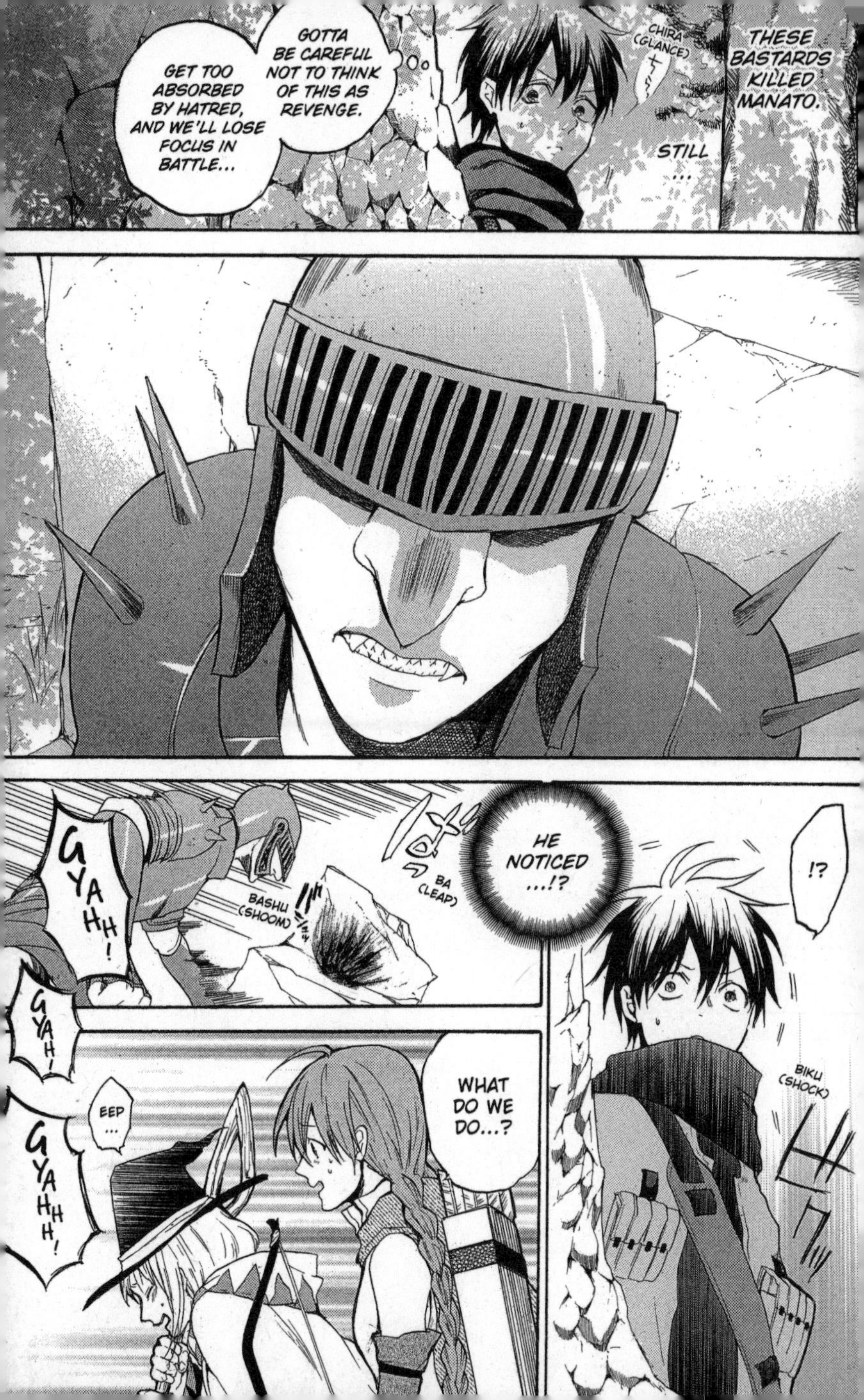

THESE BASTARDS KILLED MANATO.
CHIRA (GLANCE)
STILL...
GOTTA BE CAREFUL NOT TO THINK OF THIS AS REVENGE.
GET TOO ABSORBED BY HATRED, AND WE'LL LOSE FOCUS IN BATTLE...
!?
BIKU (SHOCK)
HE NOTICED ...!?
BA (LEAP)
BASHU (SHOOM)
GYAHH!
WHAT DO WE DO...?
EEP ...
GYAH!
GYAHHH!

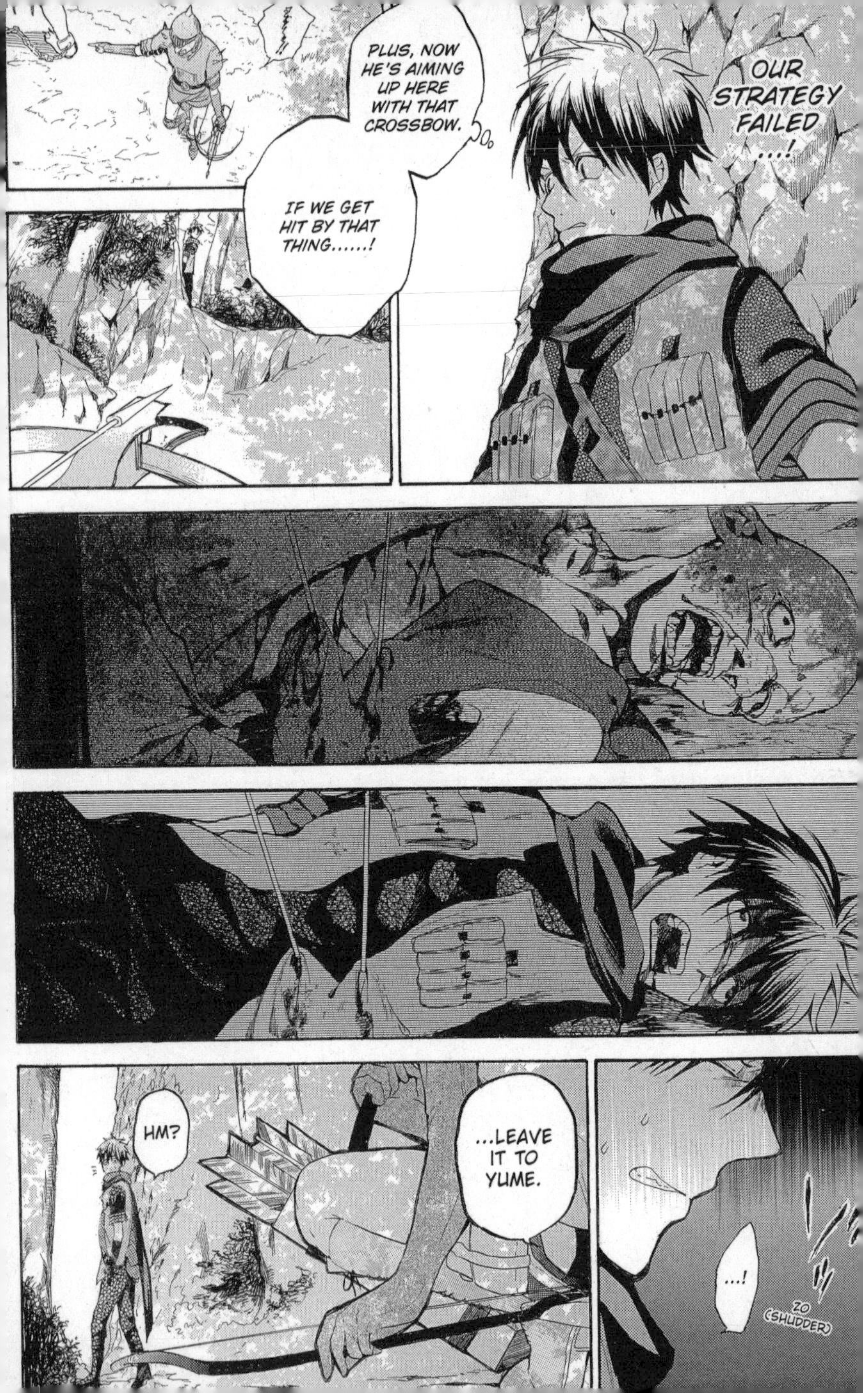
OUR STRATEGY FAILED ....!
PLUS, NOW HE'S AIMING UP HERE WITH THAT CROSSBOW.
IF WE GET HIT BY THAT THING......!
...!
ZO (SHUDDER)
...LEAVE IT TO YUME.
HM?

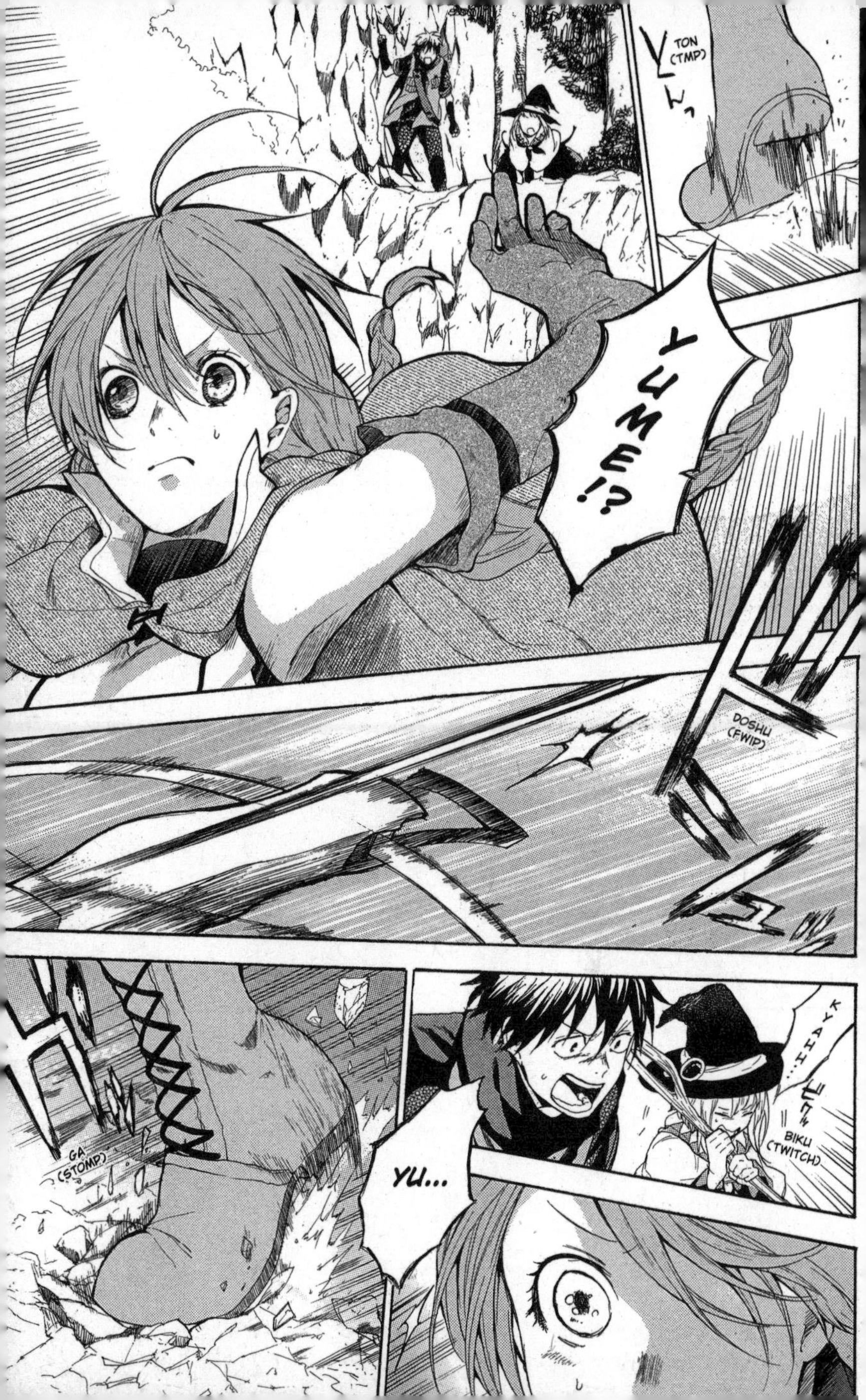
TON (TMP)
YUME!?
DOSHU (FWIP)
KYAHHH...!!
BIKU (TWITCH)
YU...
GA (STOMP)

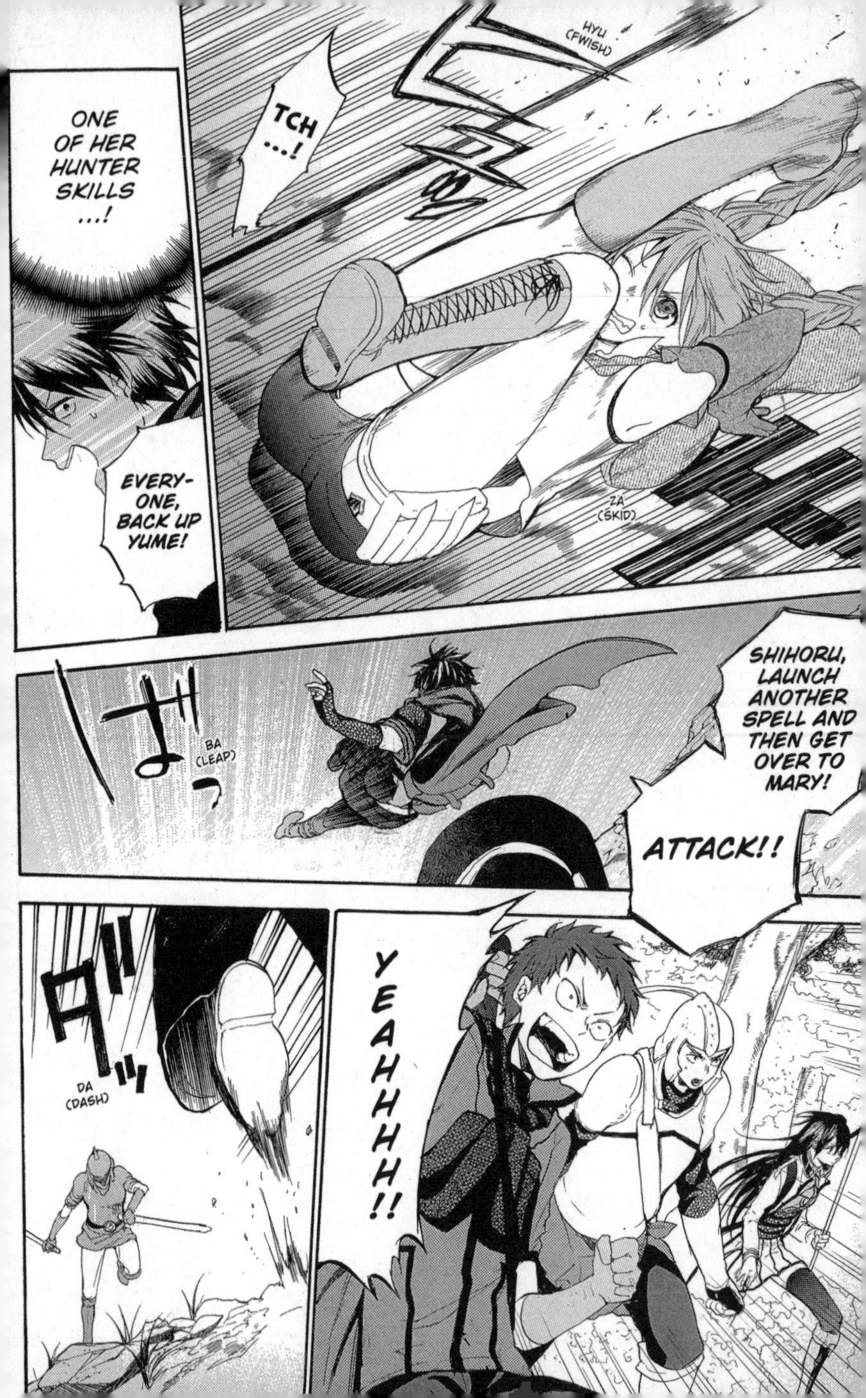
HYU (FWISH)
TCH ...!
ZA (SKID)
ONE OF HER HUNTER SKILLS ...!
EVERY-ONE, BACK UP YUME!
SHIHORU, LAUNCH ANOTHER SPELL AND THEN GET OVER TO MARY!
ATTACK!!
BA (LEAP)
YEAHHHHH!!
DA (DASH)

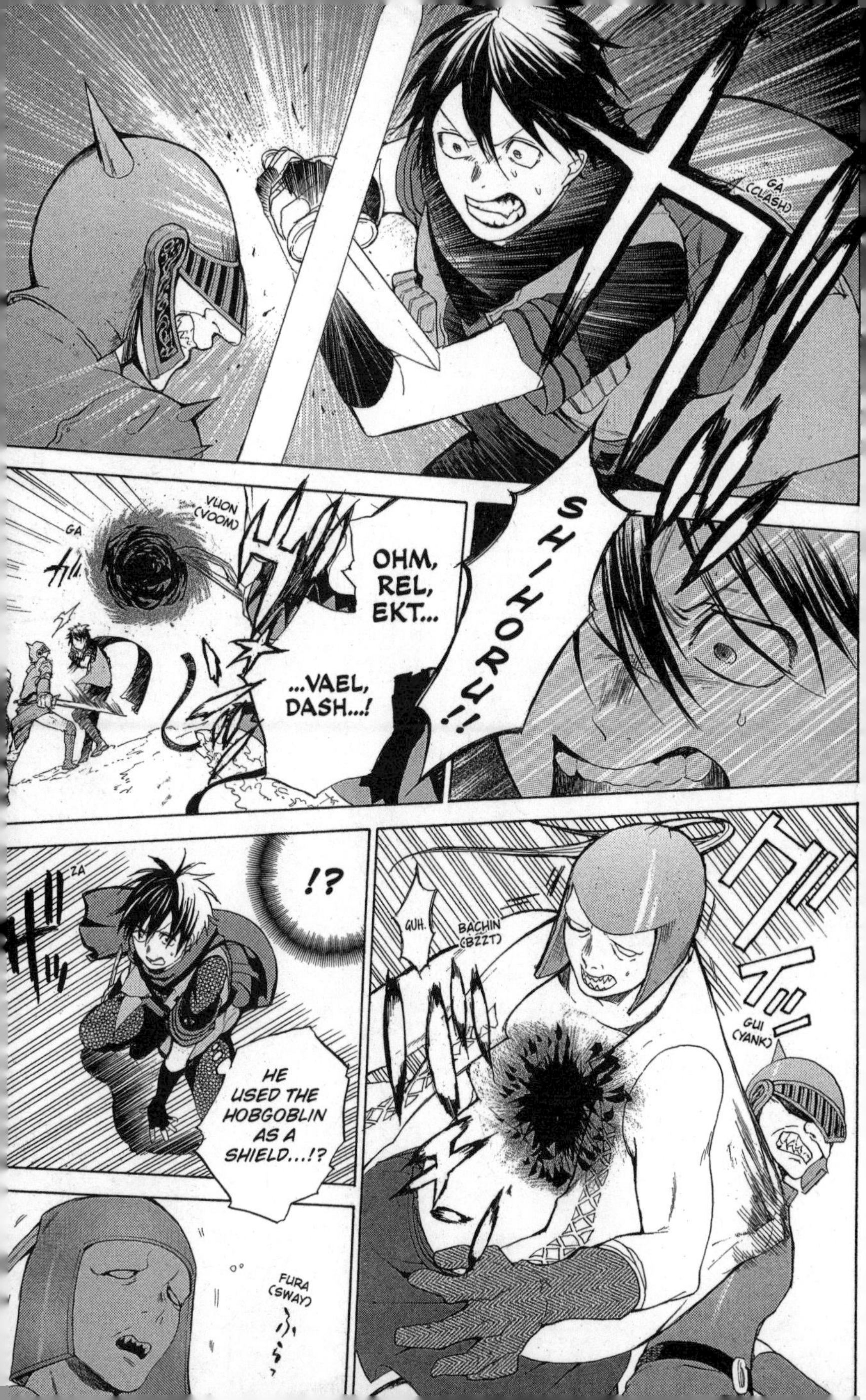
GA (CLASH)
SHI-HORU!!
OHM, REL, EKT...
VUON (VOOM)
GA
...VAEL, DASH...!
GUI (YANK)
BACHIN (BZZT)
GUH.
!?
ZA
HE USED THE HOBGOBLIN AS A SHIELD...!?
FURA (SWAY)

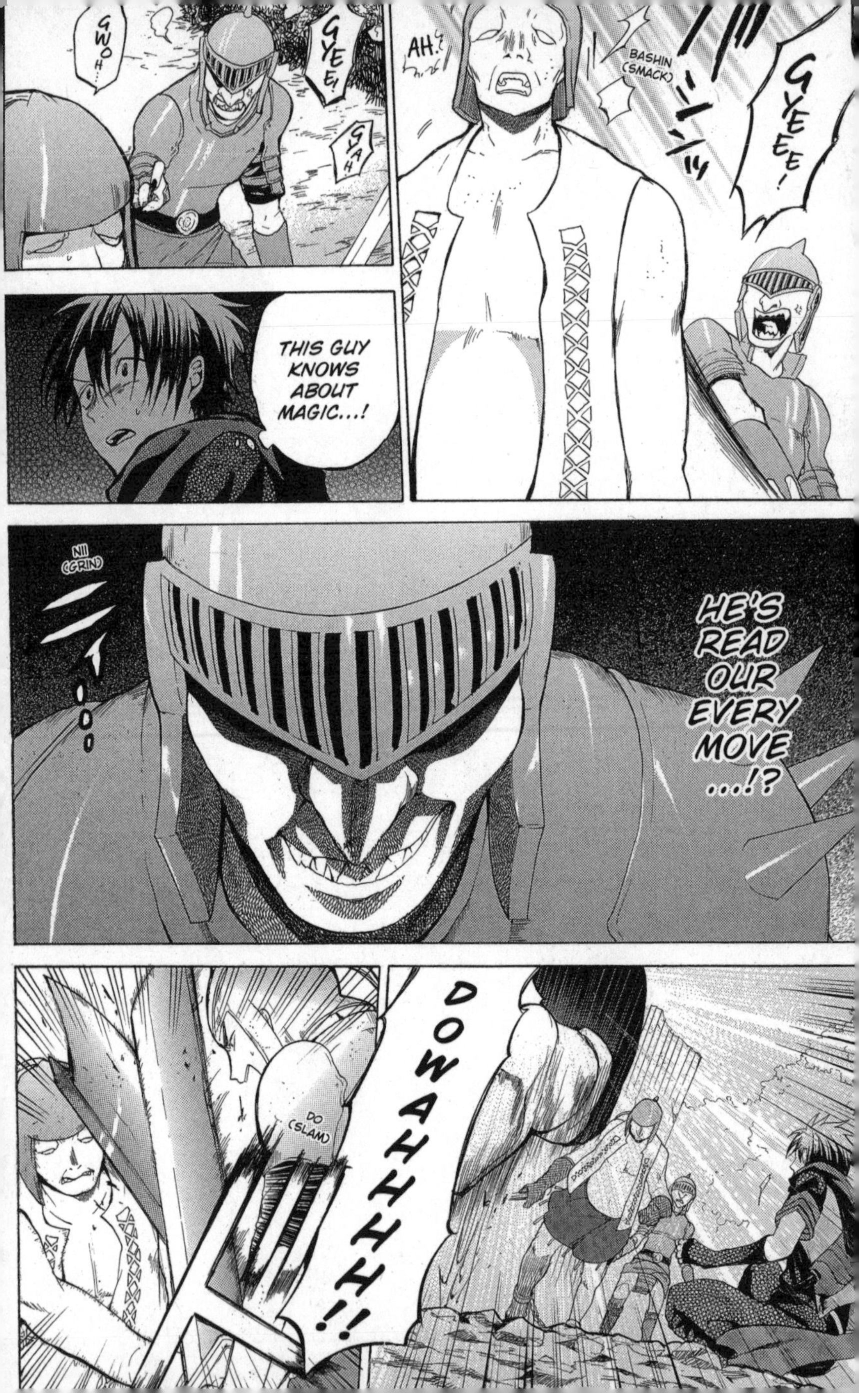
AH!?
BASHIN (SMACK)
GYEEEE!
GYEE!
GWOH...
GYAH
THIS GUY KNOWS ABOUT MAGIC...!
HE'S READ OUR EVERY MOVE...!?
NII (GRIND)
DOWAHHHHH!!
DO (SLAM)

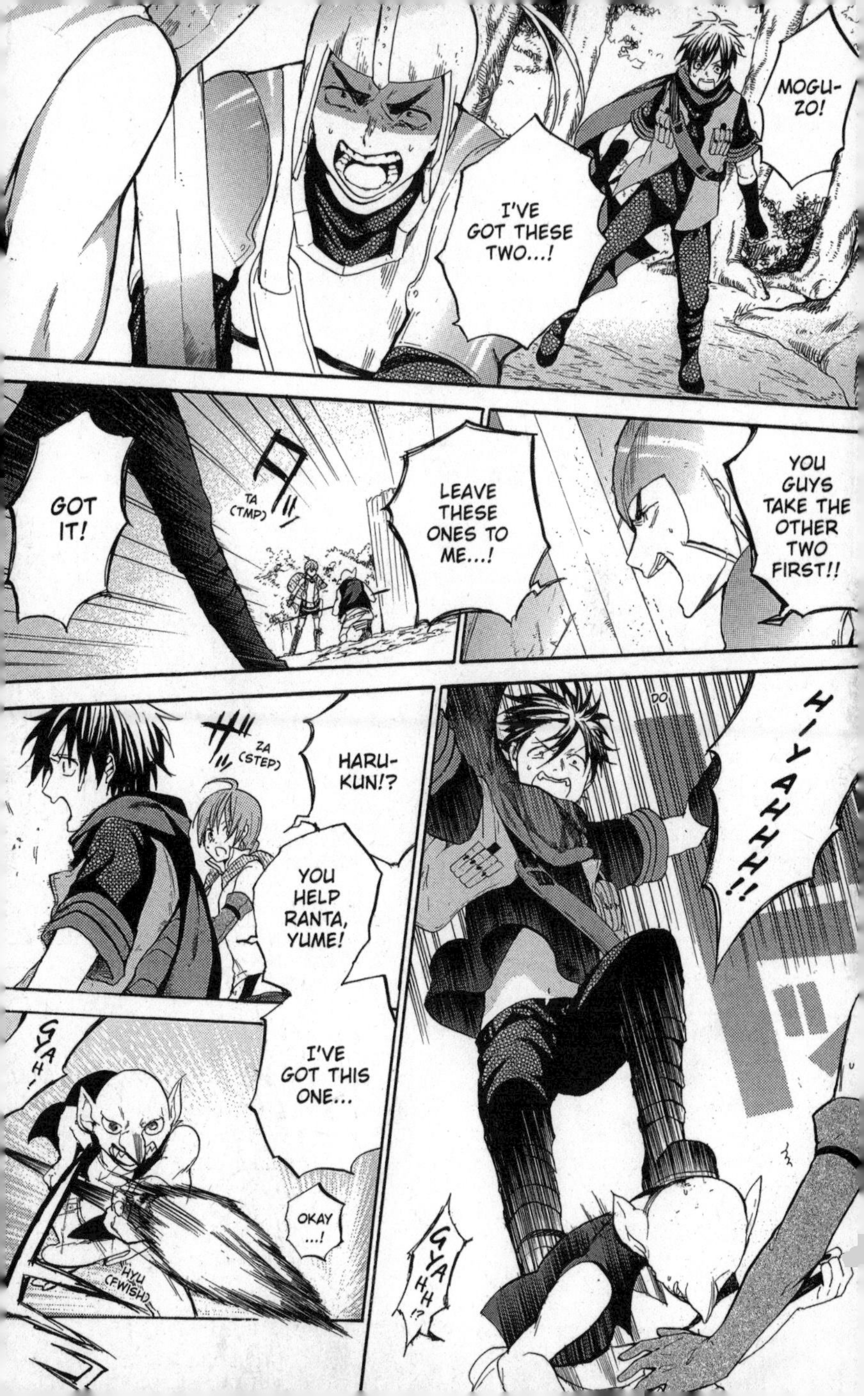
MOGU-ZO!
I'VE GOT THESE TWO...!
YOU GUYS TAKE THE OTHER TWO FIRST!!
LEAVE THESE ONES TO ME...!
TA (TMP)
GOT IT!
HIYAHHH!!
DO
GYAHH!?
HARU-KUN!?
ZA (STEP)
YOU HELP RANTA, YUME!
I'VE GOT THIS ONE...
GYAH!
OKAY...!
HYU (FWISH)

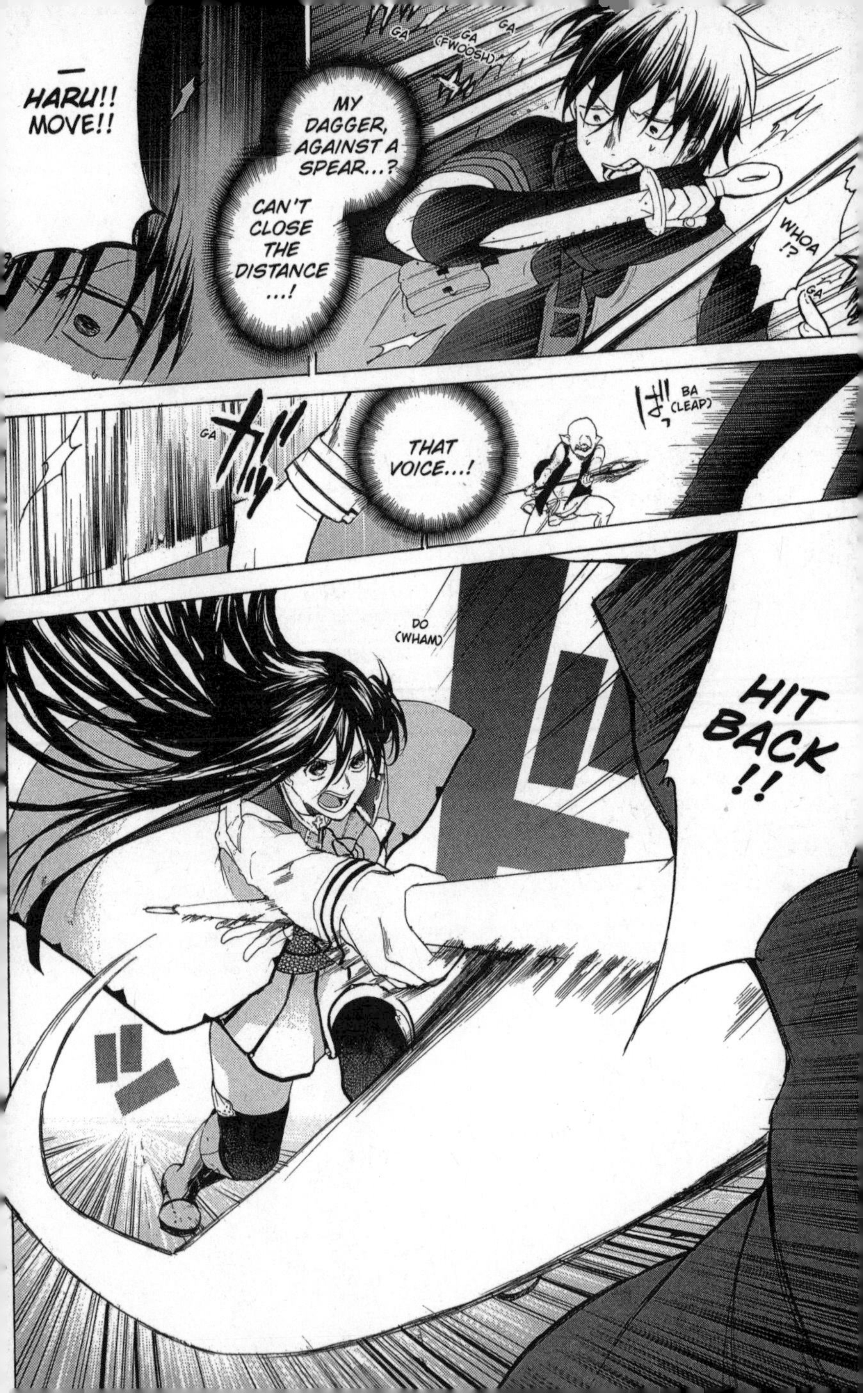
WHOA!?
GA
GA
GA
GA (FWOOSH)
MY DAGGER, AGAINST A SPEAR...?
CAN'T CLOSE THE DISTANCE...!
—HARU!! MOVE!!
BA (LEAP)
THAT VOICE...!
GA
HIT BACK!!
DO (WHAM)

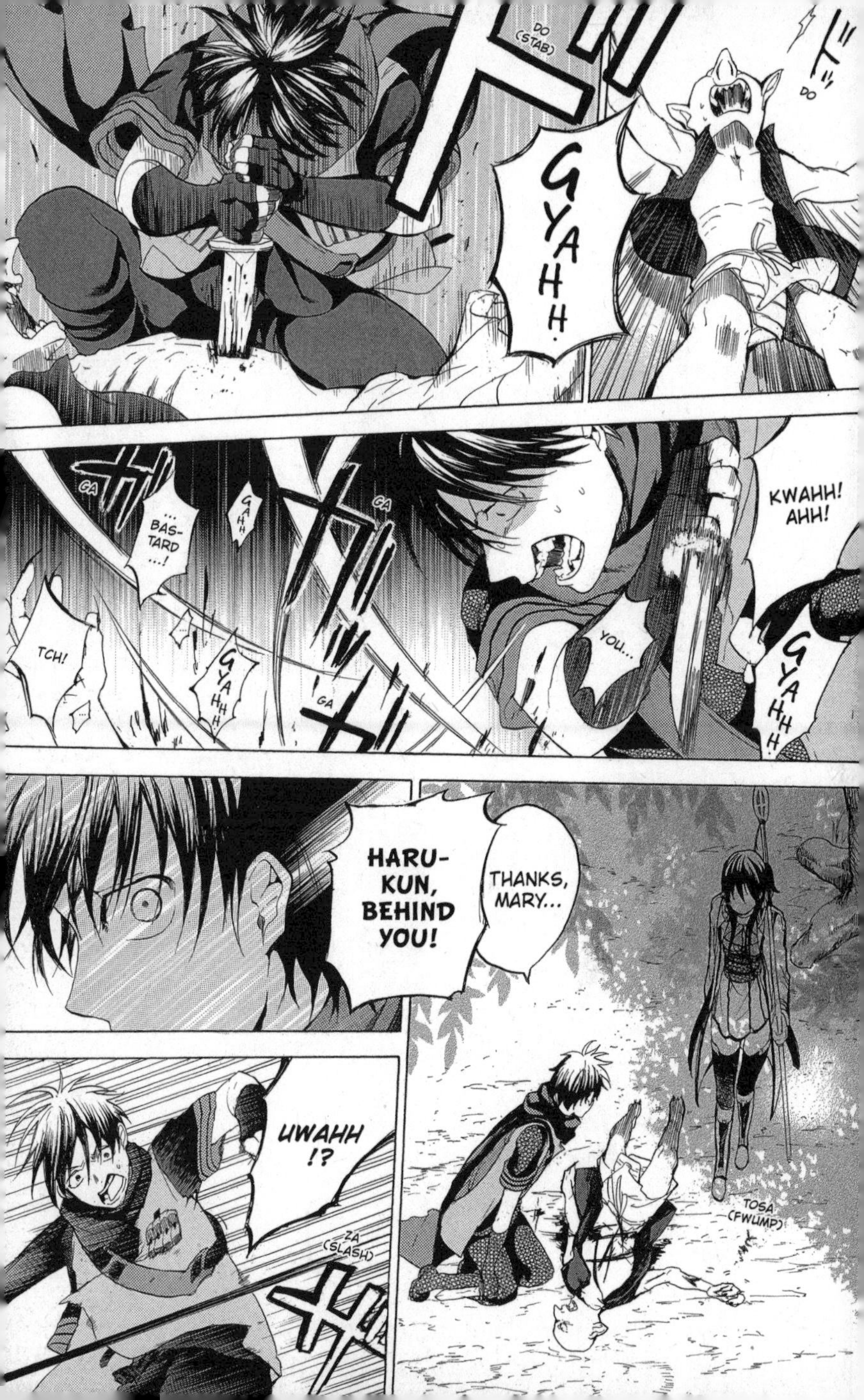
DO
DO (STAB)
GYAHH!
KWAHH! AHH!
GYAHHH
YOU...
GA
GAHH
GA
...BASTARD...!
GYAHHH
GA
TCH!
...
THANKS, MARY...
TOSA (FWUMP)
HARU-KUN, BEHIND YOU!
UWAHH!?
ZA (SLASH)

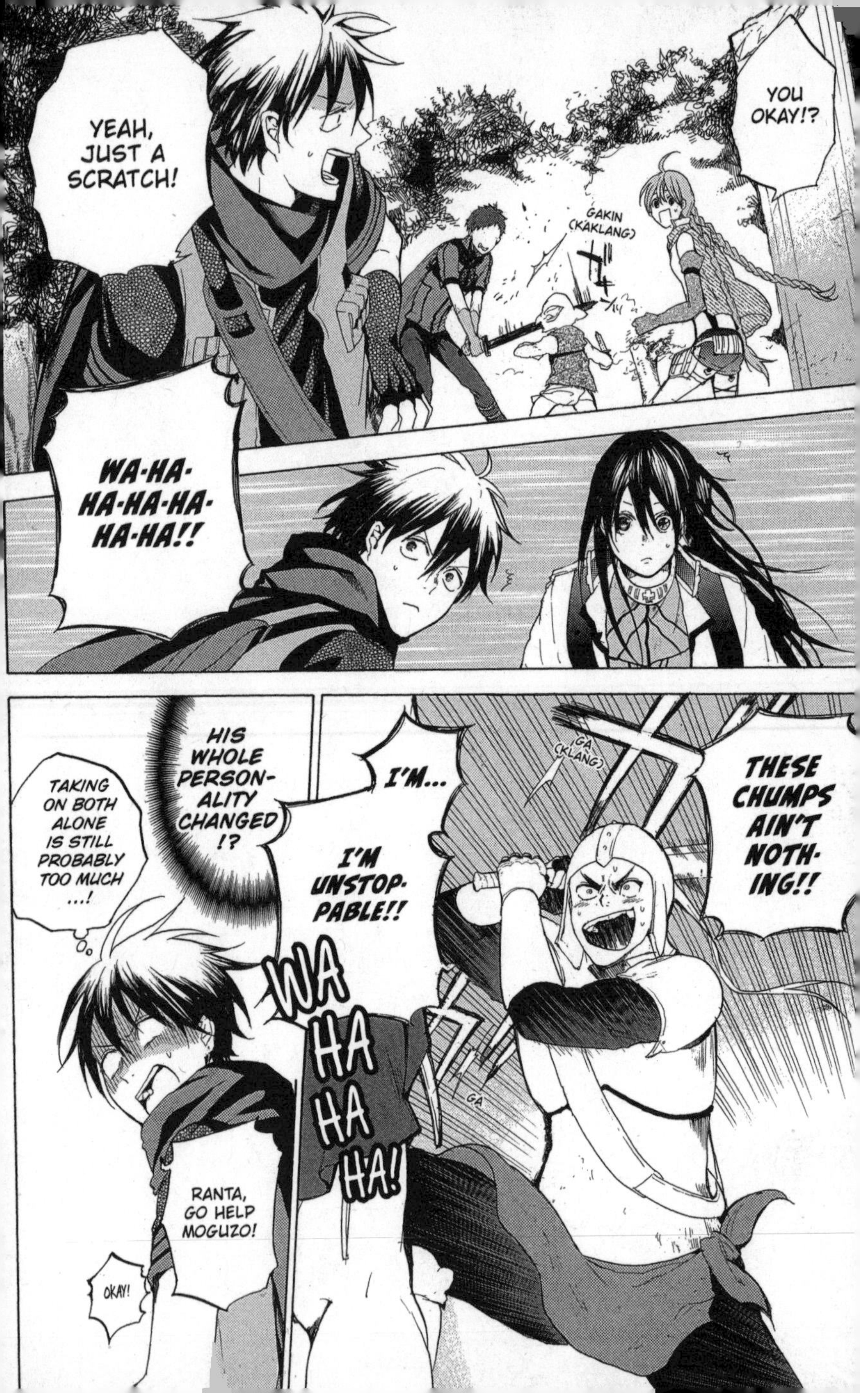
YOU OKAY!?
GAKIN (KAKLANG)
YEAH, JUST A SCRATCH!
WA-HA-HA-HA-HA-HA-HA!!
THESE CHUMPS AIN'T NOTHING!!
GA (KLANG)
I'M...
I'M UNSTOPPABLE!!
WA HA HA HA!
GA
HIS WHOLE PERSONALITY CHANGED!?
TAKING ON BOTH ALONE IS STILL PROBABLY TOO MUCH...!
RANTA, GO HELP MOGUZO!
OKAY!

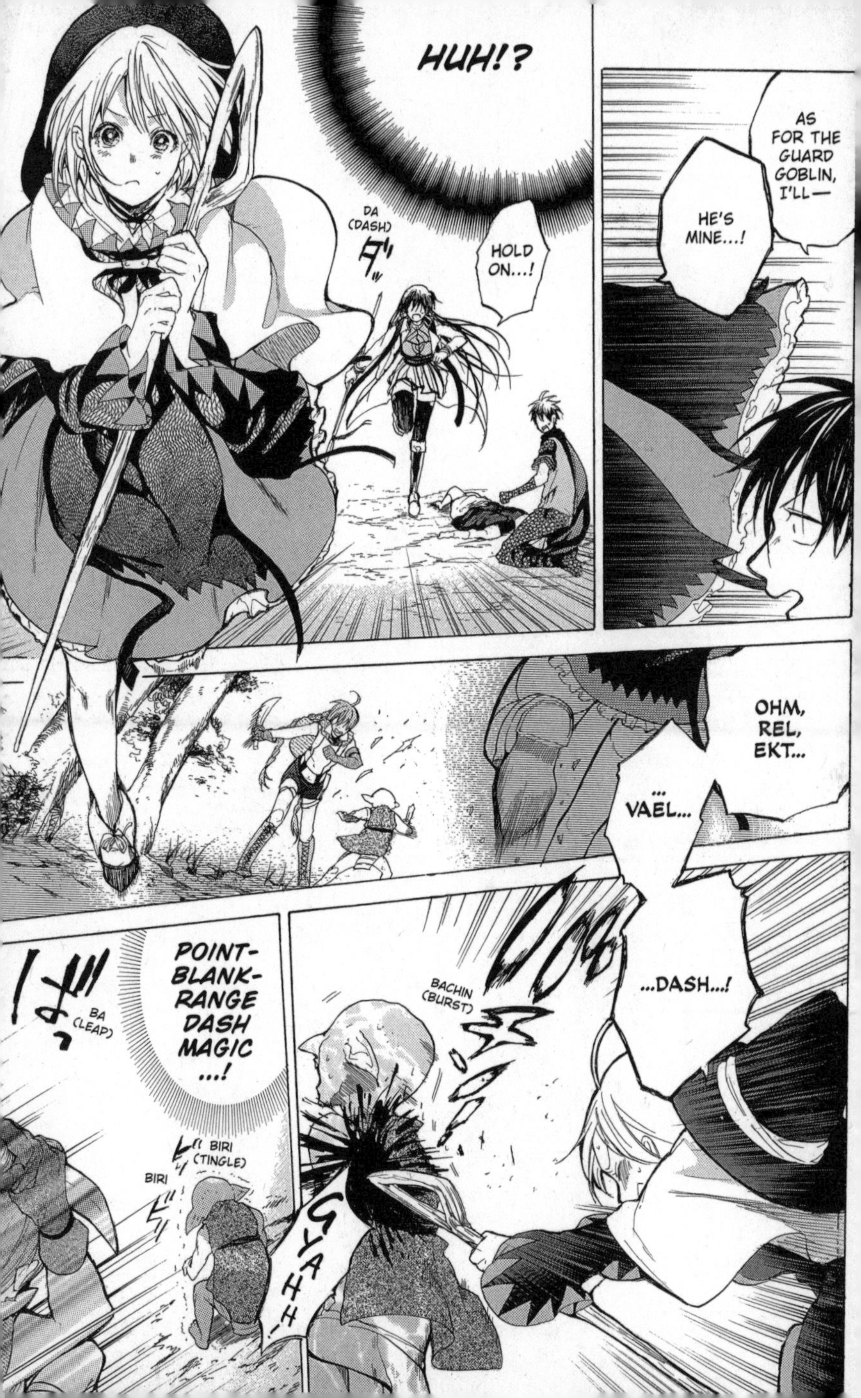
AS FOR THE GUARD GOBLIN, I'LL—
HE'S MINE...!
HUH!?
HOLD ON...!
DA (DASH)
OHM, REL, EKT...
... VAËL...
...DASH...!
BACHIN (BURST)
GYAHH!
POINT-BLANK-RANGE DASH MAGIC...!
BA (LEAP)
BIRI (TINGLE)
BIRI

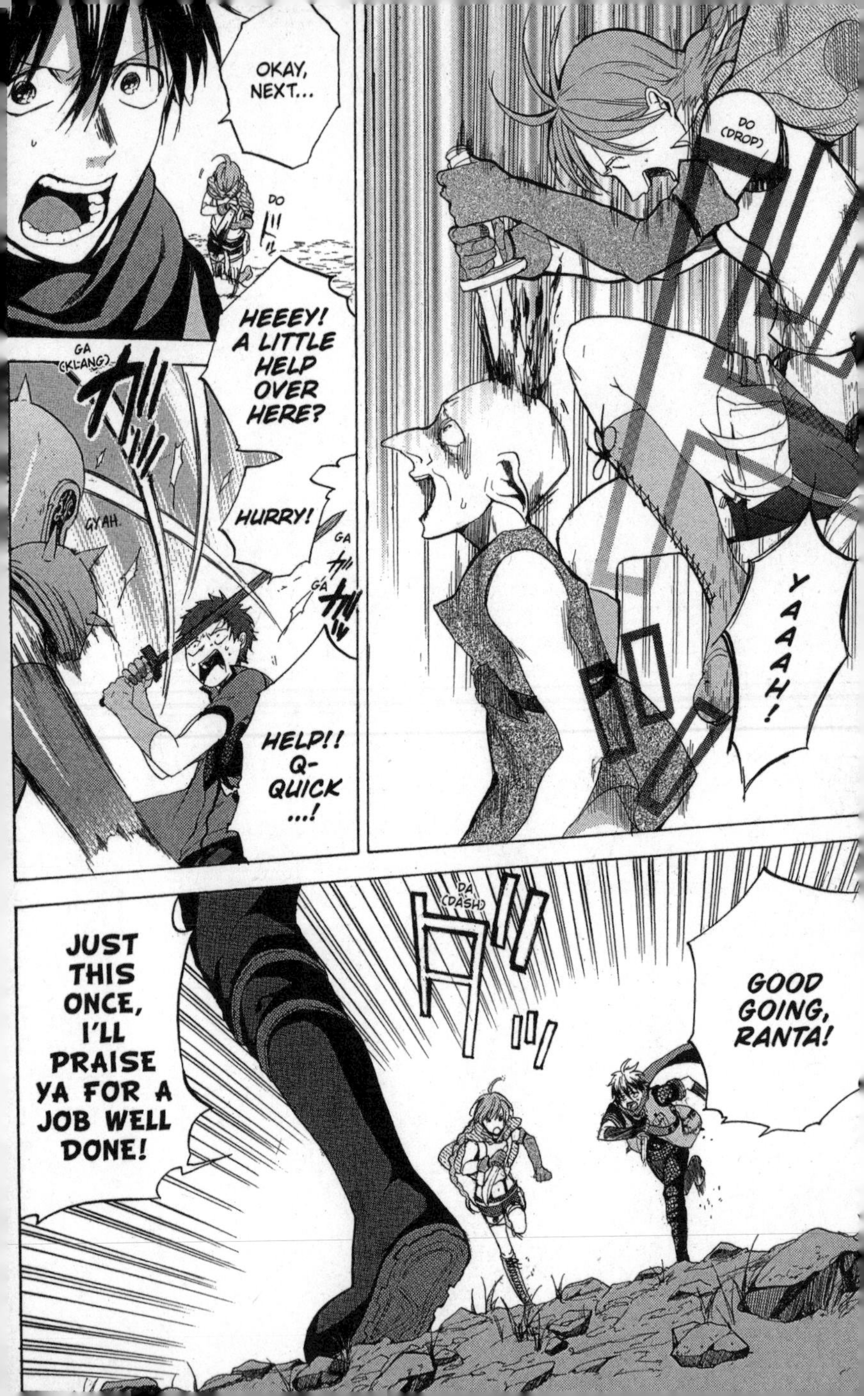
DO (DROP)
YAAAAH!
OKAY, NEXT...
DO
HEEEY! A LITTLE HELP OVER HERE?
GA (KLANG)
HURRY!
GA
GA
GYAH
HELP!! Q-QUICK ...!
GOOD GOING, RANTA!
DA (DASH)
JUST THIS ONCE, I'LL PRAISE YA FOR A JOB WELL DONE!

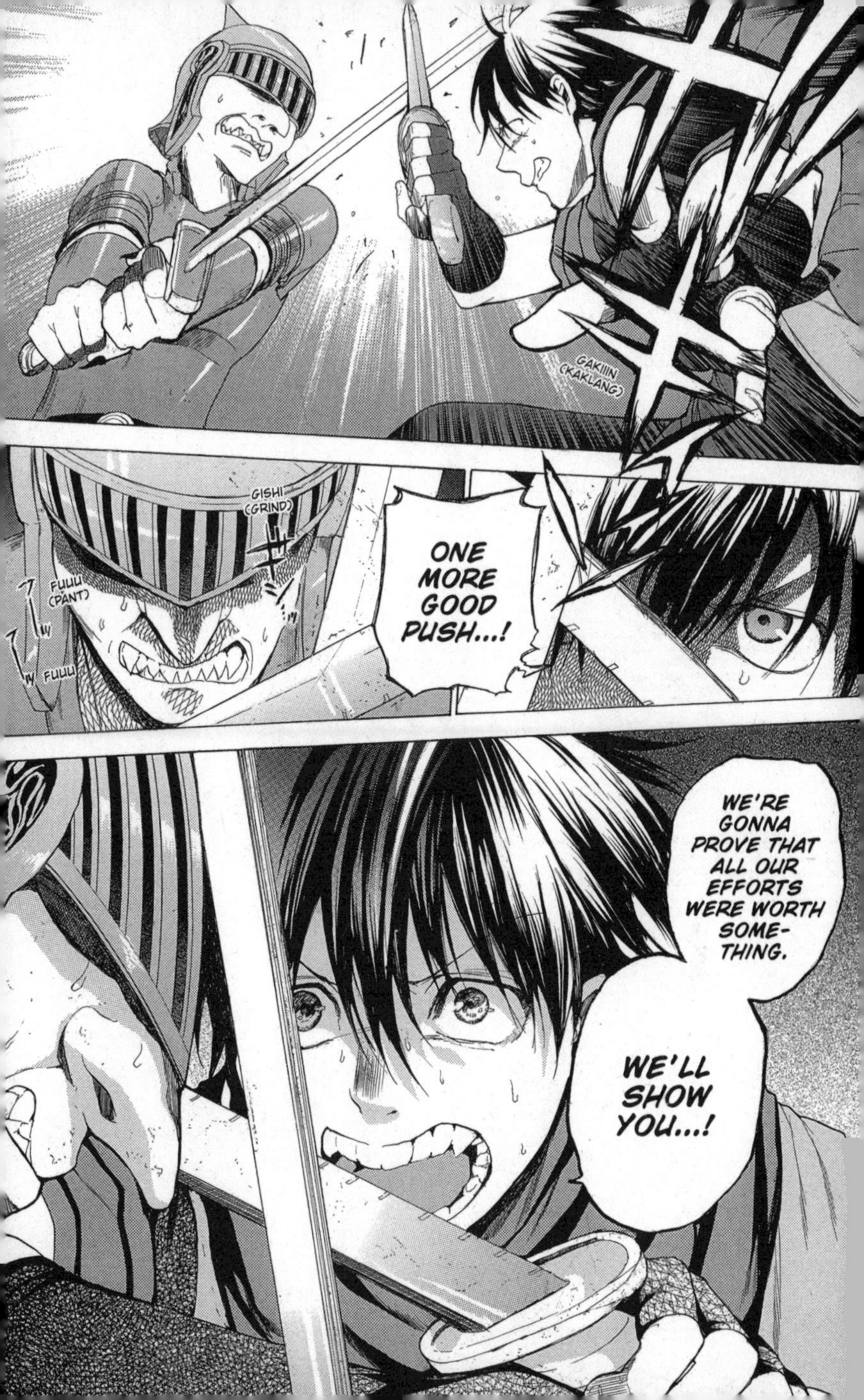
GAKIIN (KAKLANG)
ONE MORE GOOD PUSH...!
GISHI (GRIND)
FUUU (PANT)
FUUU
WE'RE GONNA PROVE THAT ALL OUR EFFORTS WERE WORTH SOME-THING.
WE'LL SHOW YOU...!

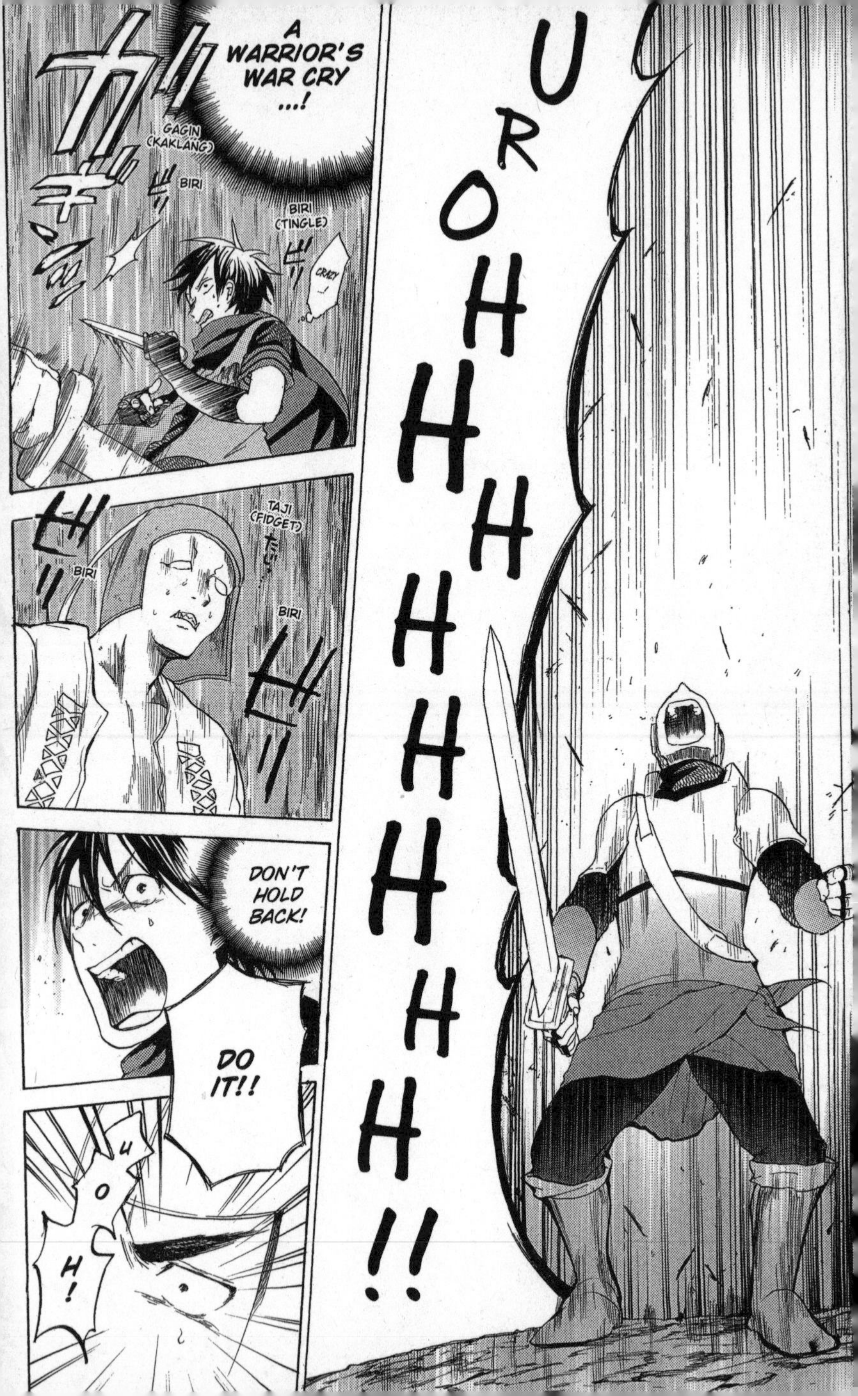
UROHHHHHHHHHH!!
A WARRIOR'S WAR CRY ...!
GAGIN (KAKLANG)
BIRI
BIRI (TINGLE)
CRAZY ...!
TAJI (FIDGET)
BIRI
BIRI
DON'T HOLD BACK!
DO IT!!
UOH!

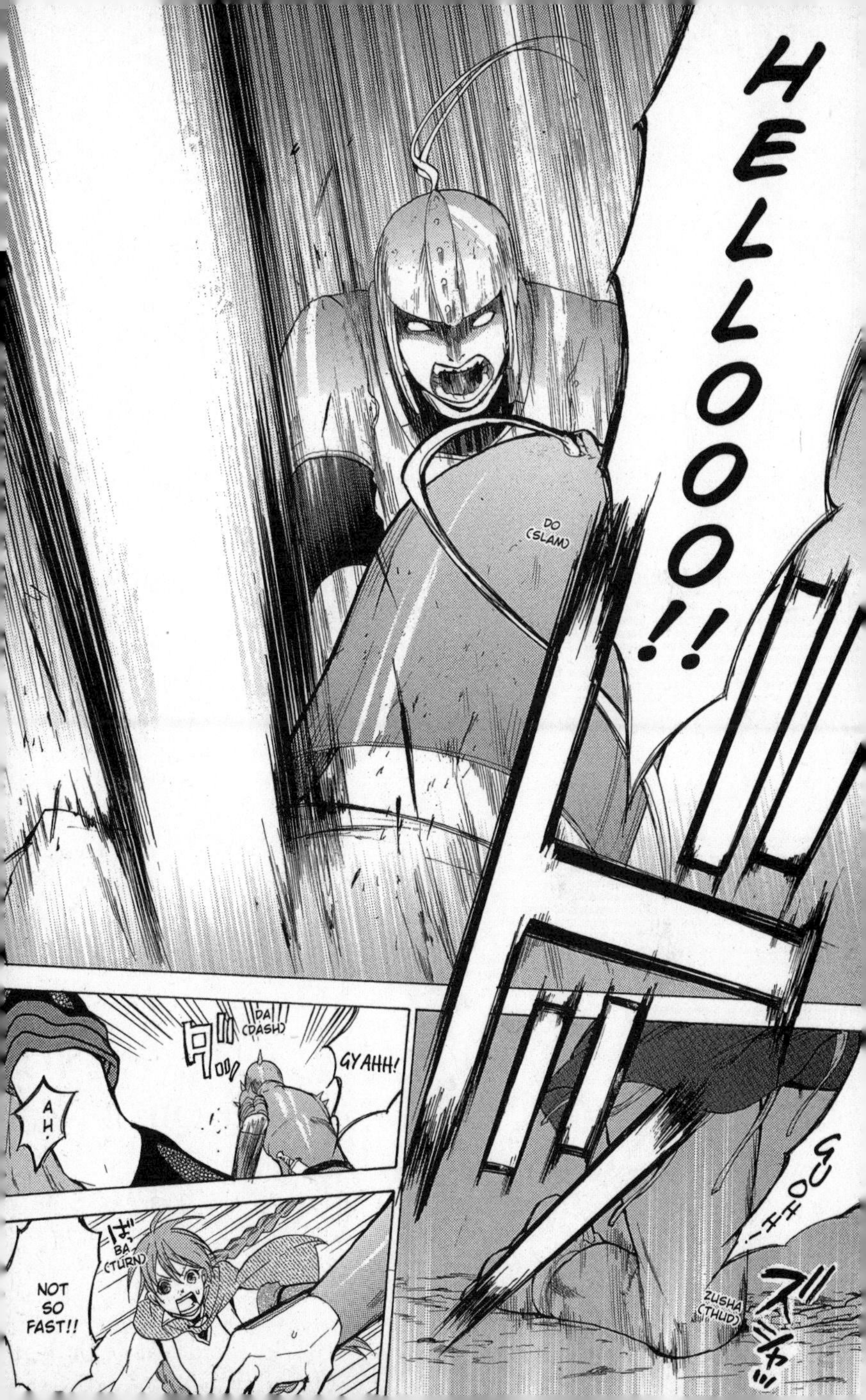
HELLOOOO!!
DO (SLAM)
GUOH—!
ズシャッ
ZUSHA (THUD)
ダッ
DA (DASH)
GYAHH!
AH!
ば
BA (TURN)
NOT SO FAST!!

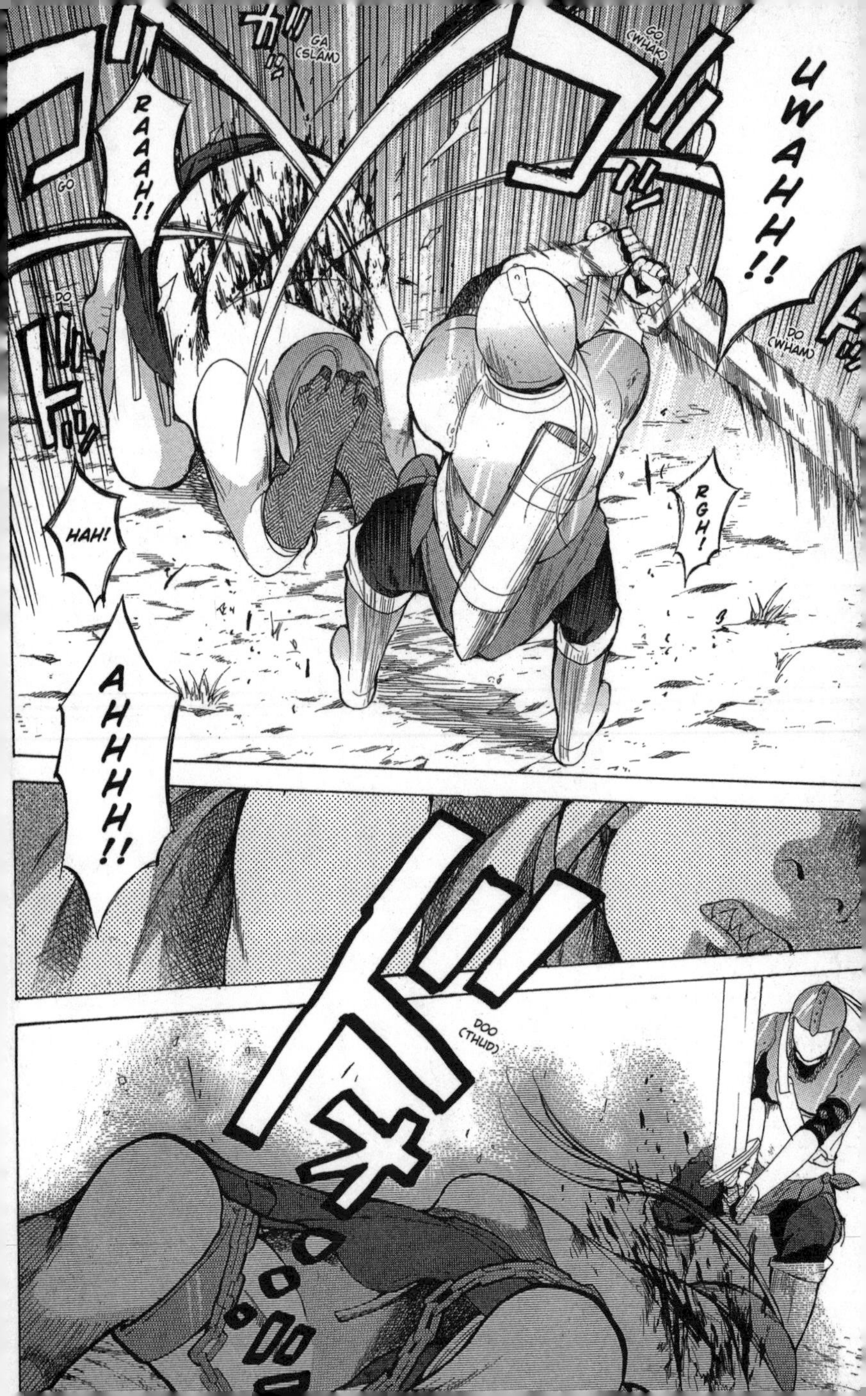
GO (WHAK)
UWAHHH!!
GA (SLAM)
RAAAAH!!
GO
DO (WHAM)
DO
RGH!
HAH!
AHHHHH!!
DOO (THUD)

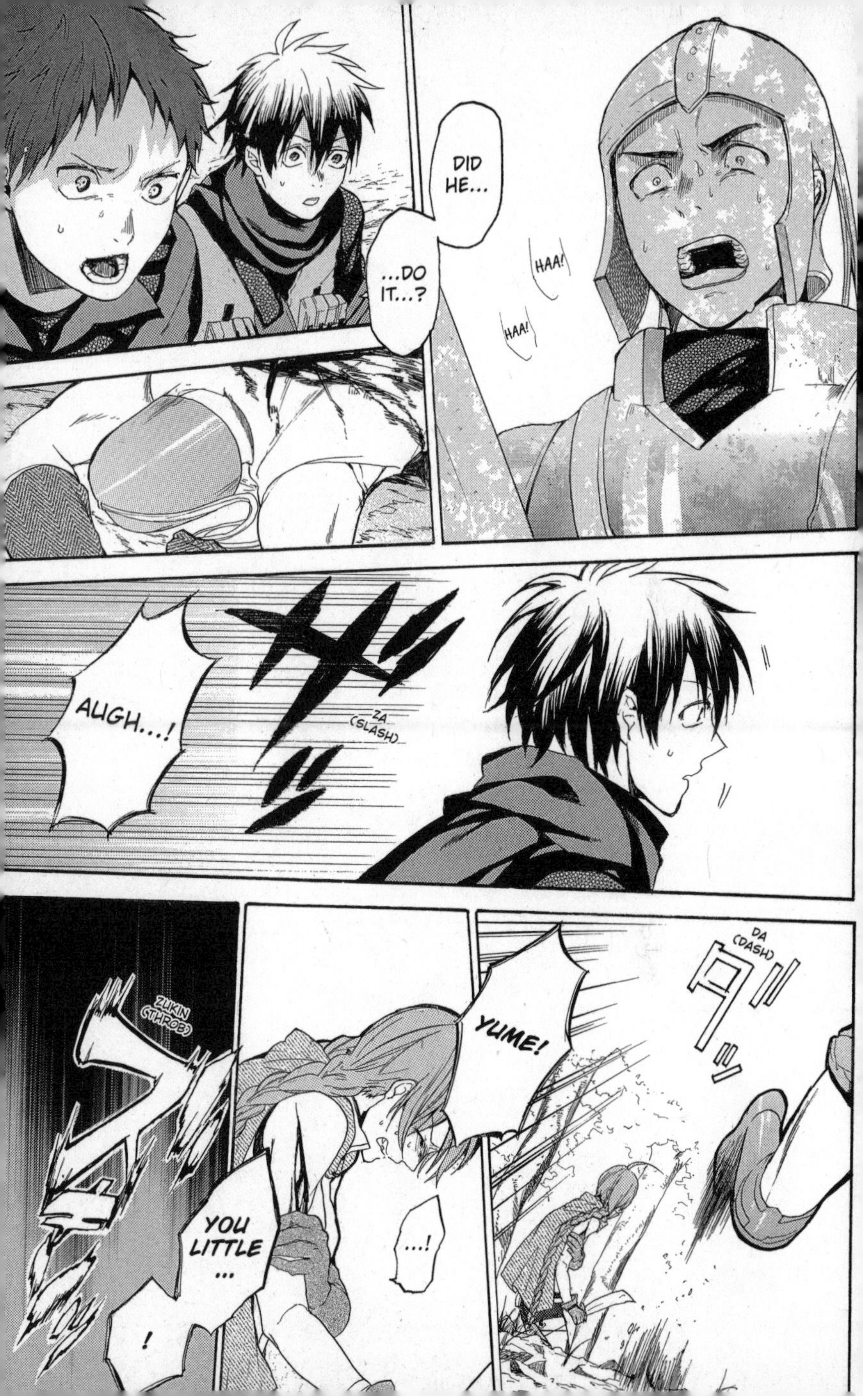
DID HE...
...DO IT...?
HAA!
HAA!
ZA (SLASH)
AUGH...!
DA (DASH)
YUME!
...!
YOU LITTLE ...
ZUKIN (THROB)
!

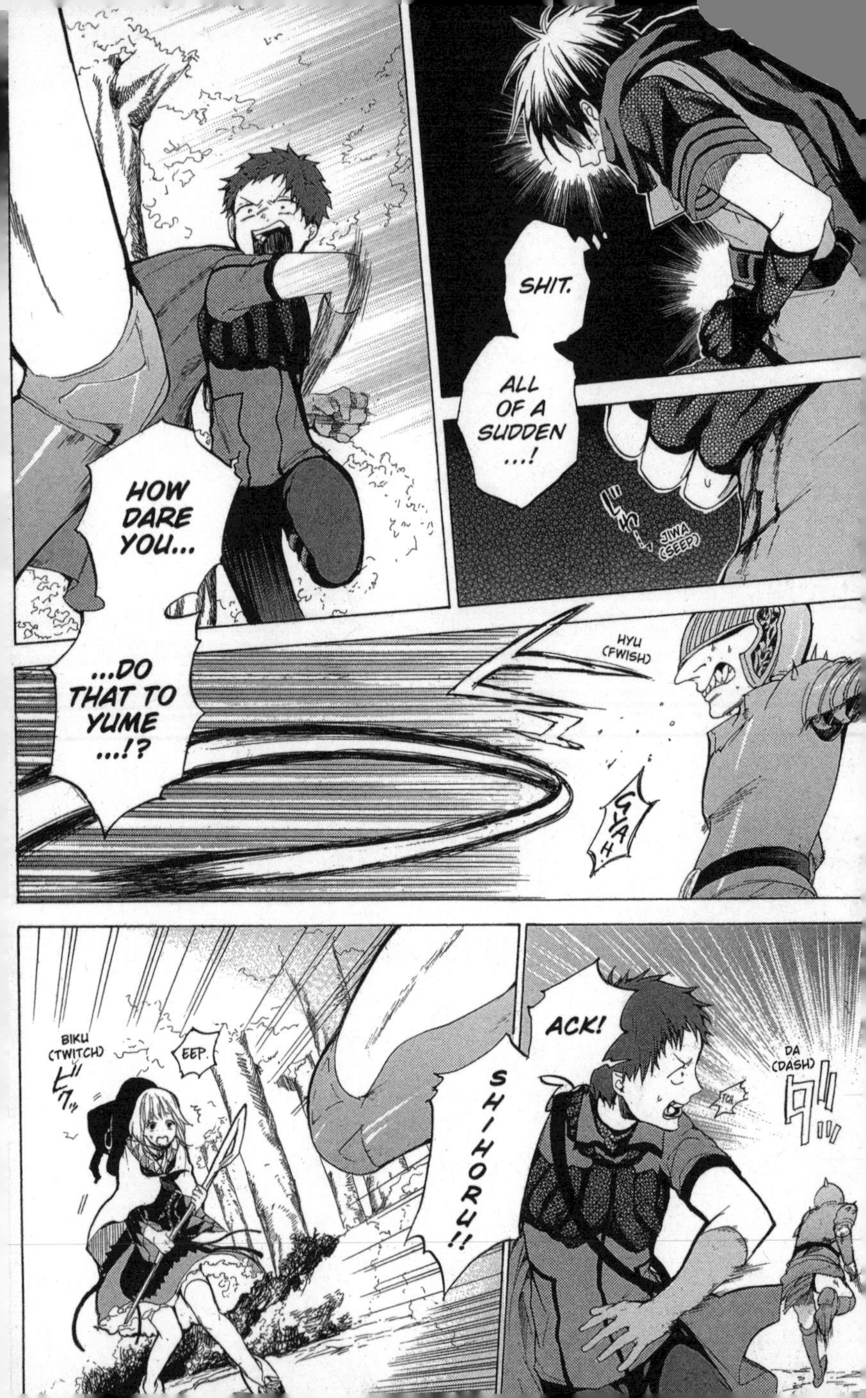
SHIT.
ALL OF A SUDDEN...!
JIWA (SEEP)
HOW DARE YOU...
HYU (FWISH)
GYAH
...DO THAT TO YUME...!?
DA (DASH)
ACK!
TCH
SHIHORU!!
EEP.
BIKU (TWITCH)

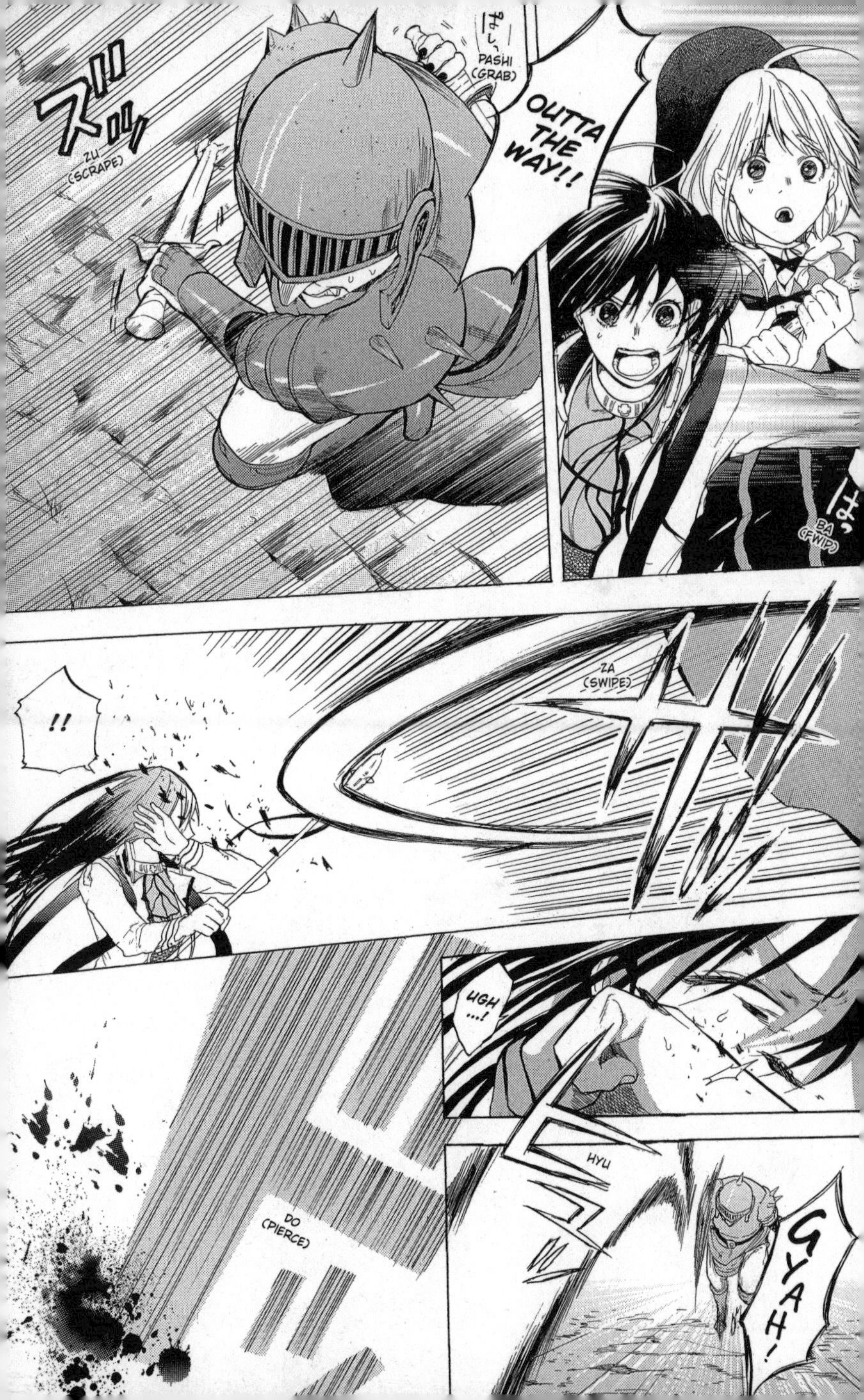
OUTTA THE WAY!!
はっ
BA (FWIP)
ぱしっ
PASHI (GRAB)
ズッ
ZU (SCRAPE)
ZA (SWIPE)
!!
UGH ...!
HYU
GYAH!
DO (PIERCE)

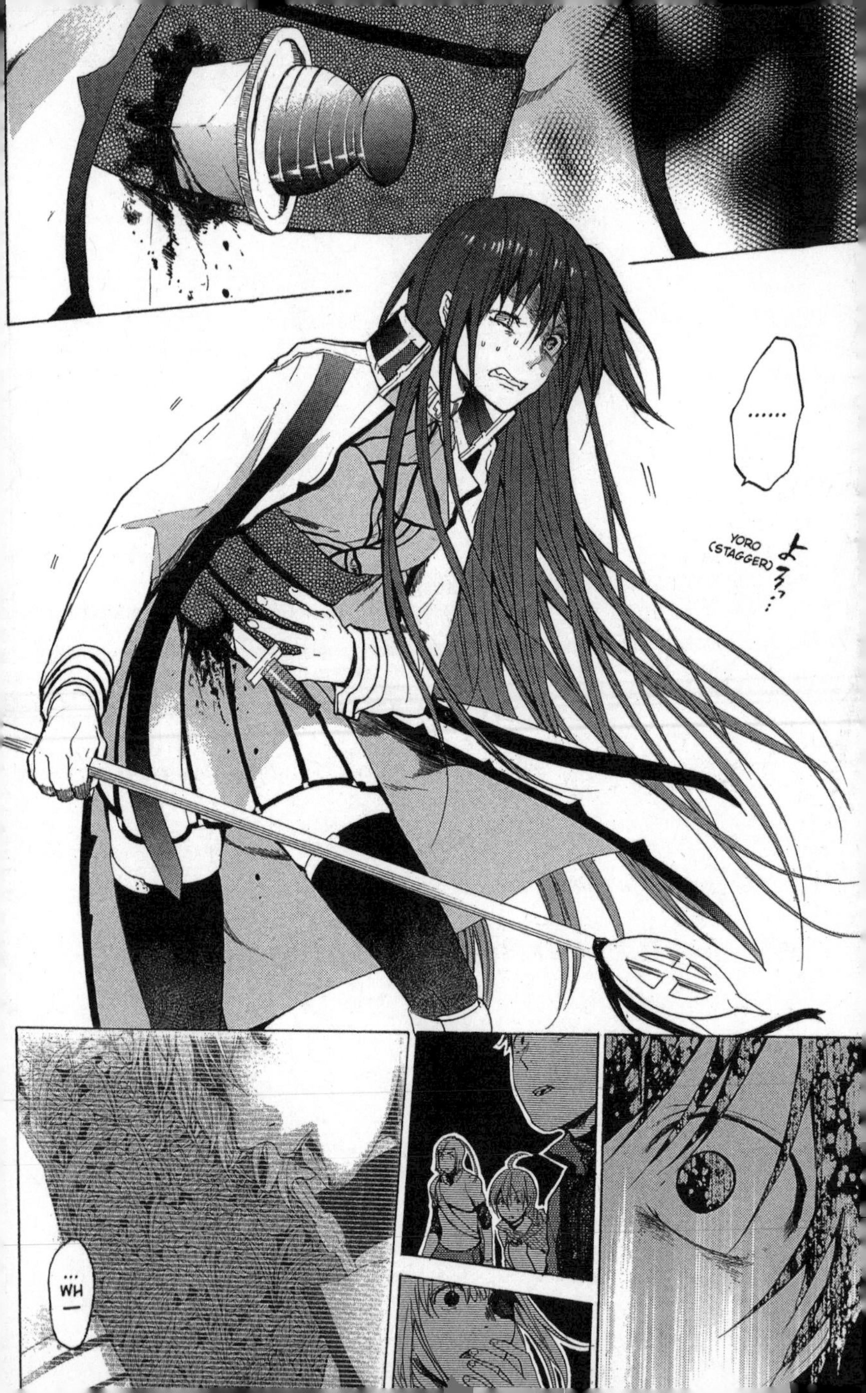
......
よろっ…
YORO (STAGGER)
...WH—

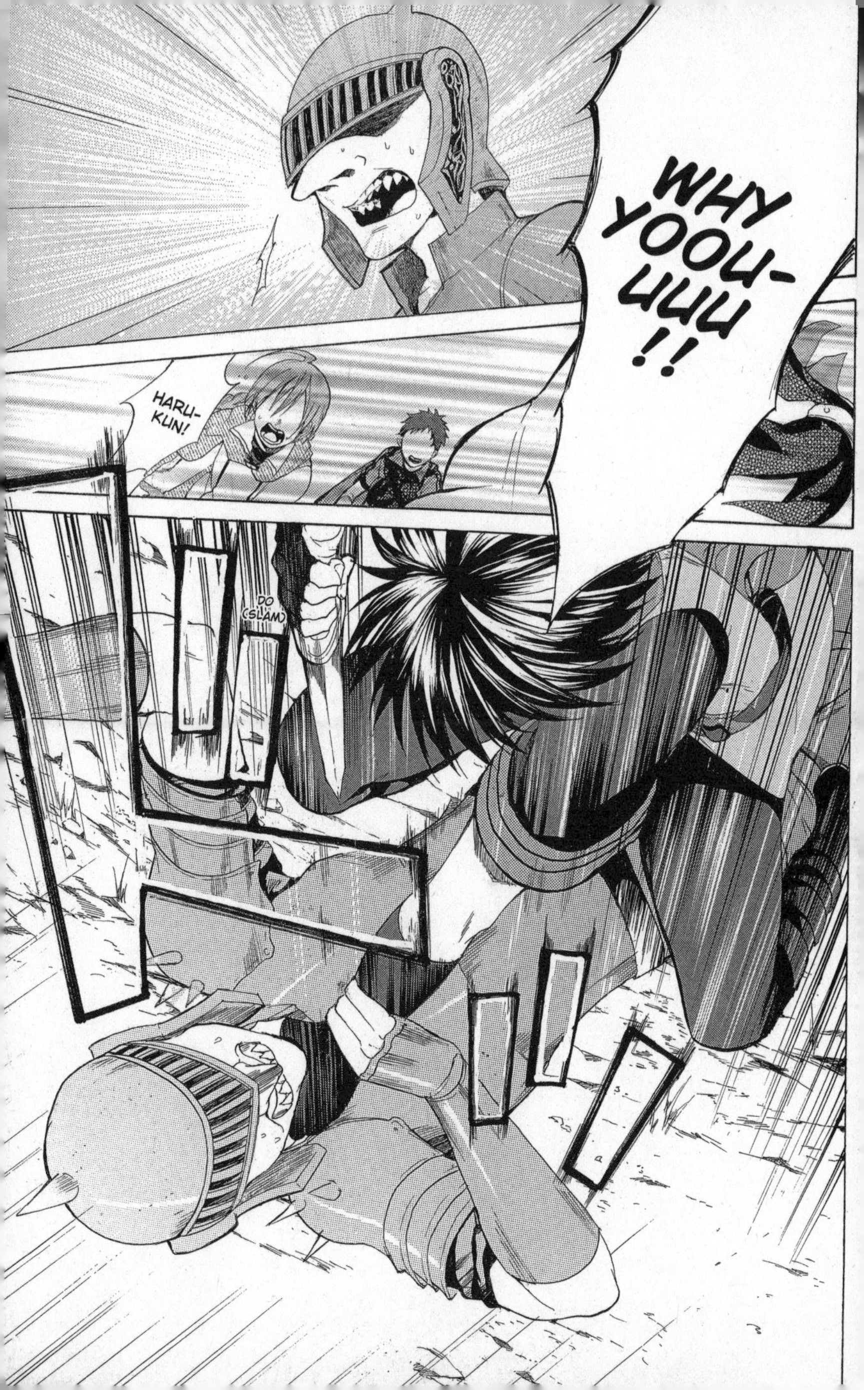
WHY YOOU-UUU!!
HARU-KUN!
DO (SLAM)

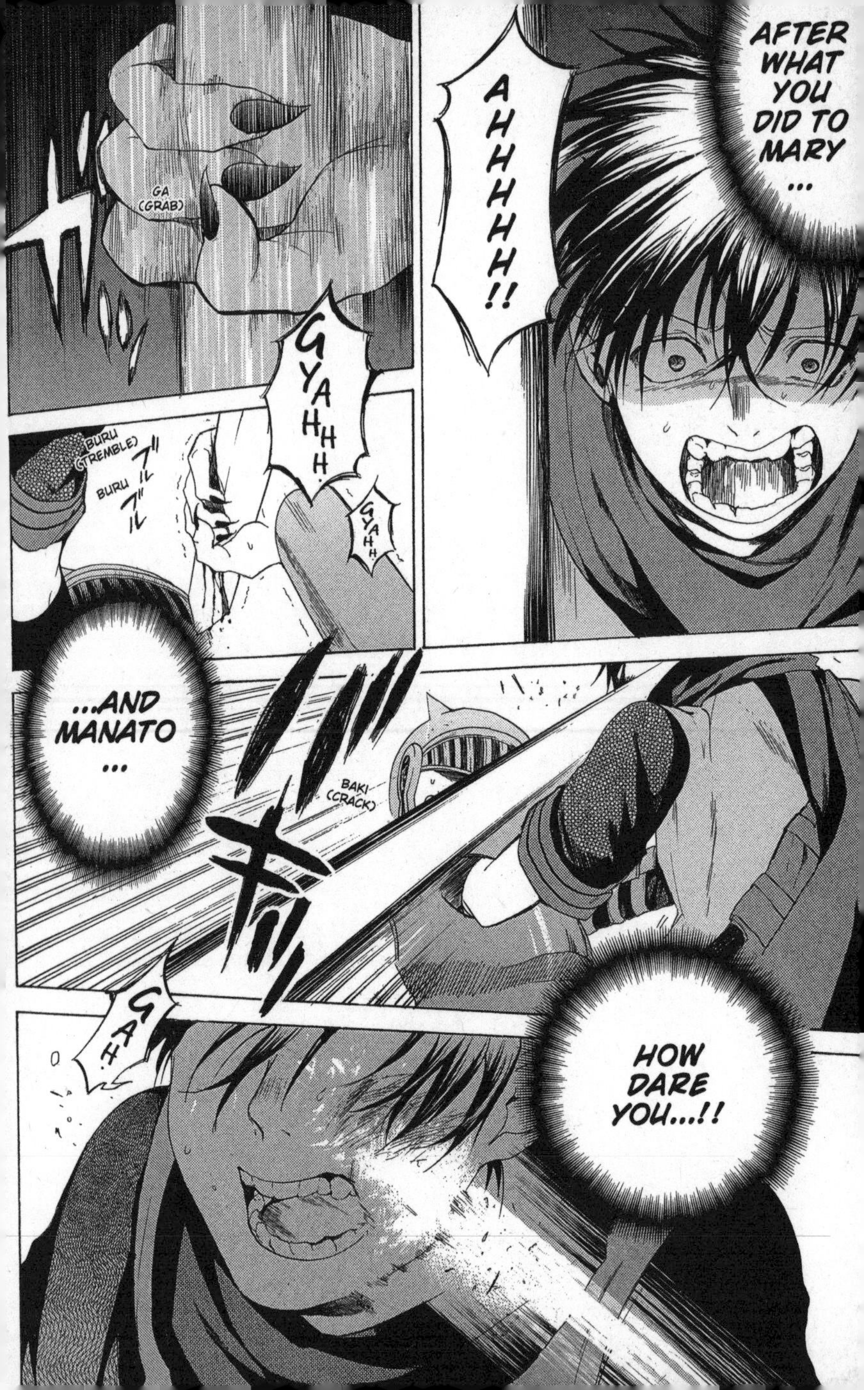
AFTER WHAT YOU DID TO MARY ...
AHHHHHH!!
GA (GRAB)
BURU (TREMBLE) BURU
GYAHHH
GYAHH
...AND MANATO ...
BAKI (CRACK)
HOW DARE YOU...!!
GAH

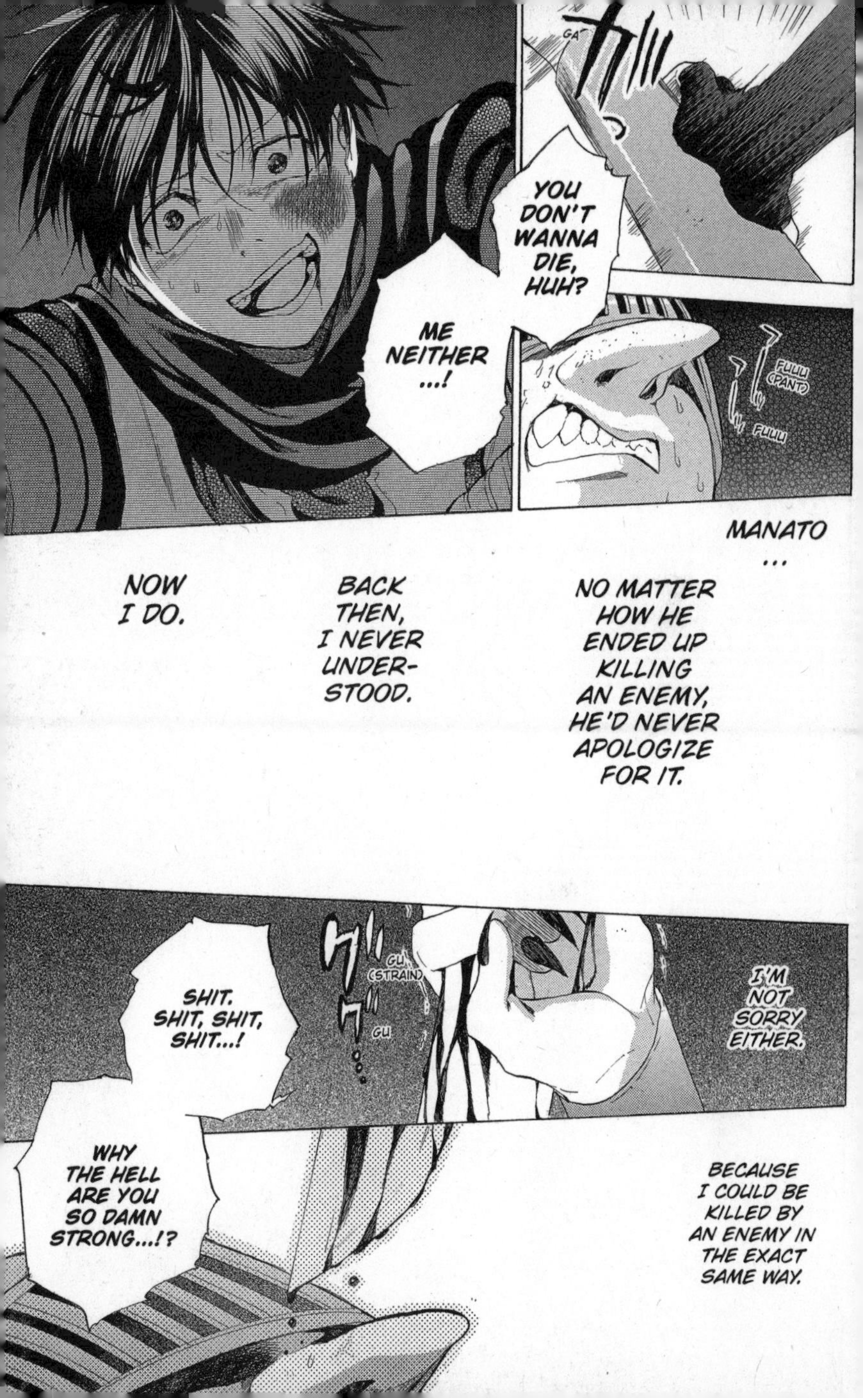
GA
YOU DON'T WANNA DIE, HUH?
FUUU (PANT)
FUUU
ME NEITHER ...!
MANATO ...
NO MATTER HOW HE ENDED UP KILLING AN ENEMY, HE'D NEVER APOLOGIZE FOR IT.
BACK THEN, I NEVER UNDER-STOOD.
NOW I DO.
I'M NOT SORRY EITHER.
GU (STRAIN)
GU
SHIT. SHIT, SHIT, SHIT...!
BECAUSE I COULD BE KILLED BY AN ENEMY IN THE EXACT SAME WAY.
WHY THE HELL ARE YOU SO DAMN STRONG...!?

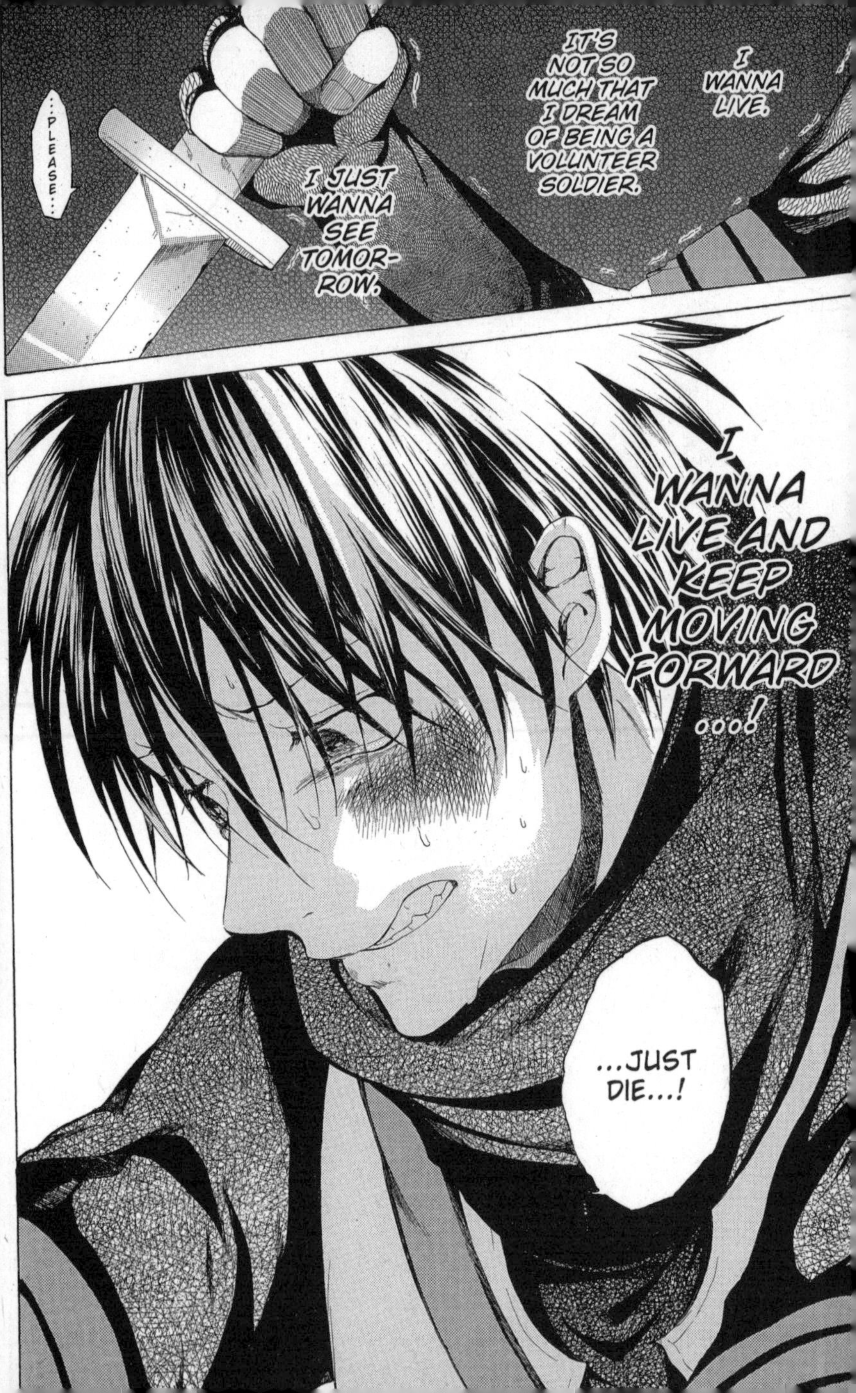
I WANNA LIVE.
IT'S NOT SO MUCH THAT I DREAM OF BEING A VOLUNTEER SOLDIER.
I JUST WANNA SEE TOMOR-ROW.
...PLEASE...
I WANNA LIVE AND KEEP MOVING FORWARD...!
...JUST DIE...!

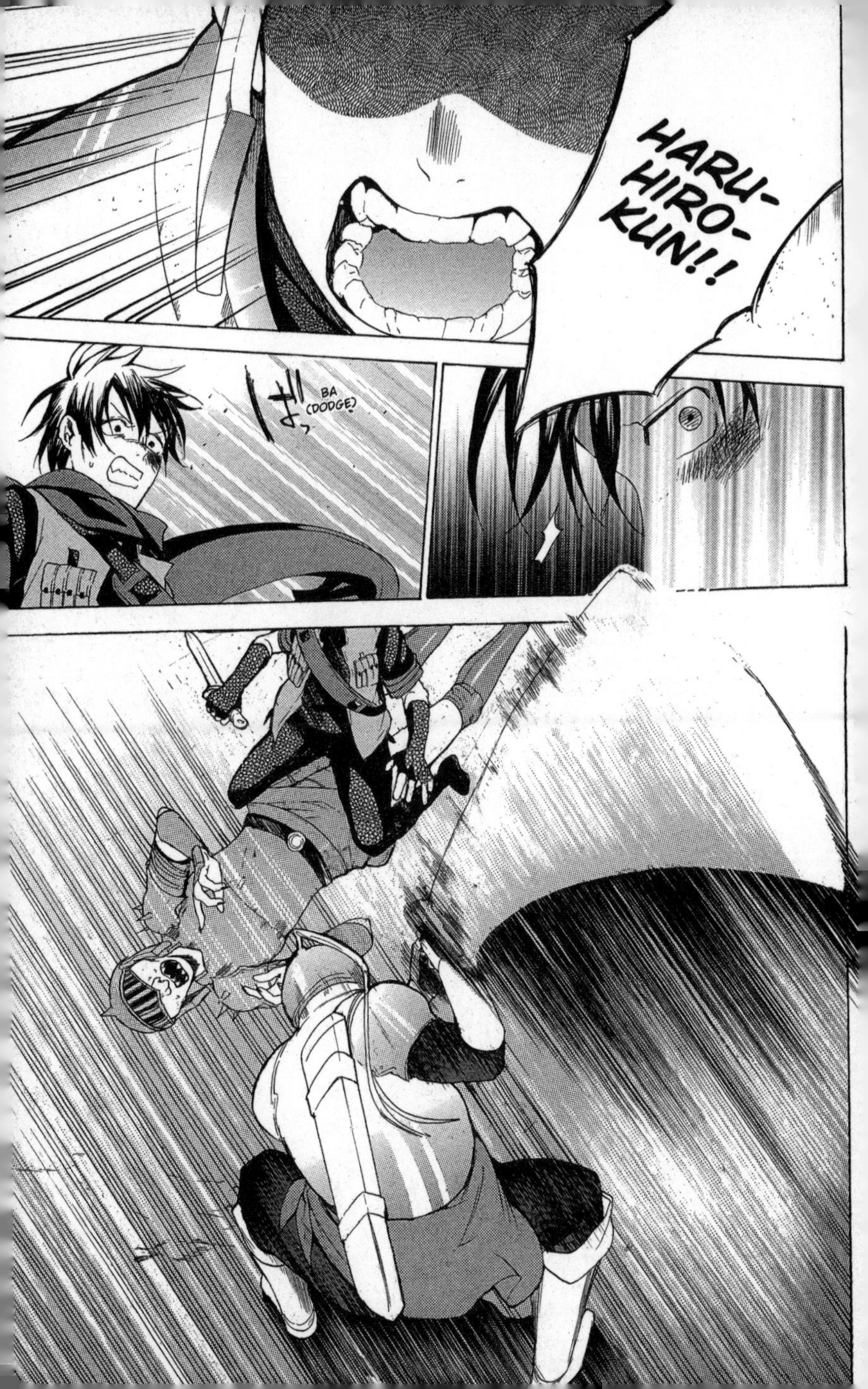
HARU-HIRO-KUN!!
BA (DODGE)

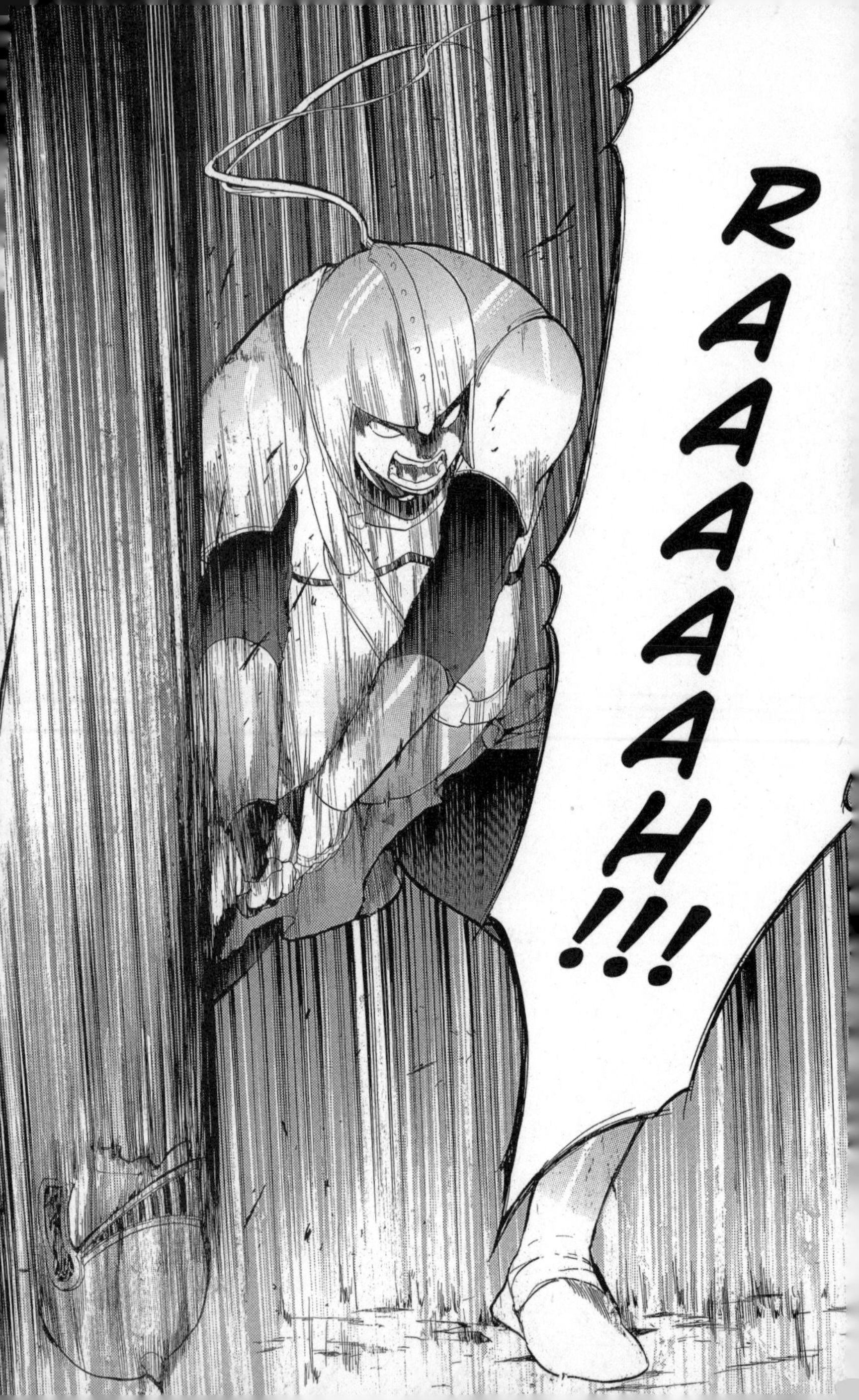
RAAAAAAH!!!

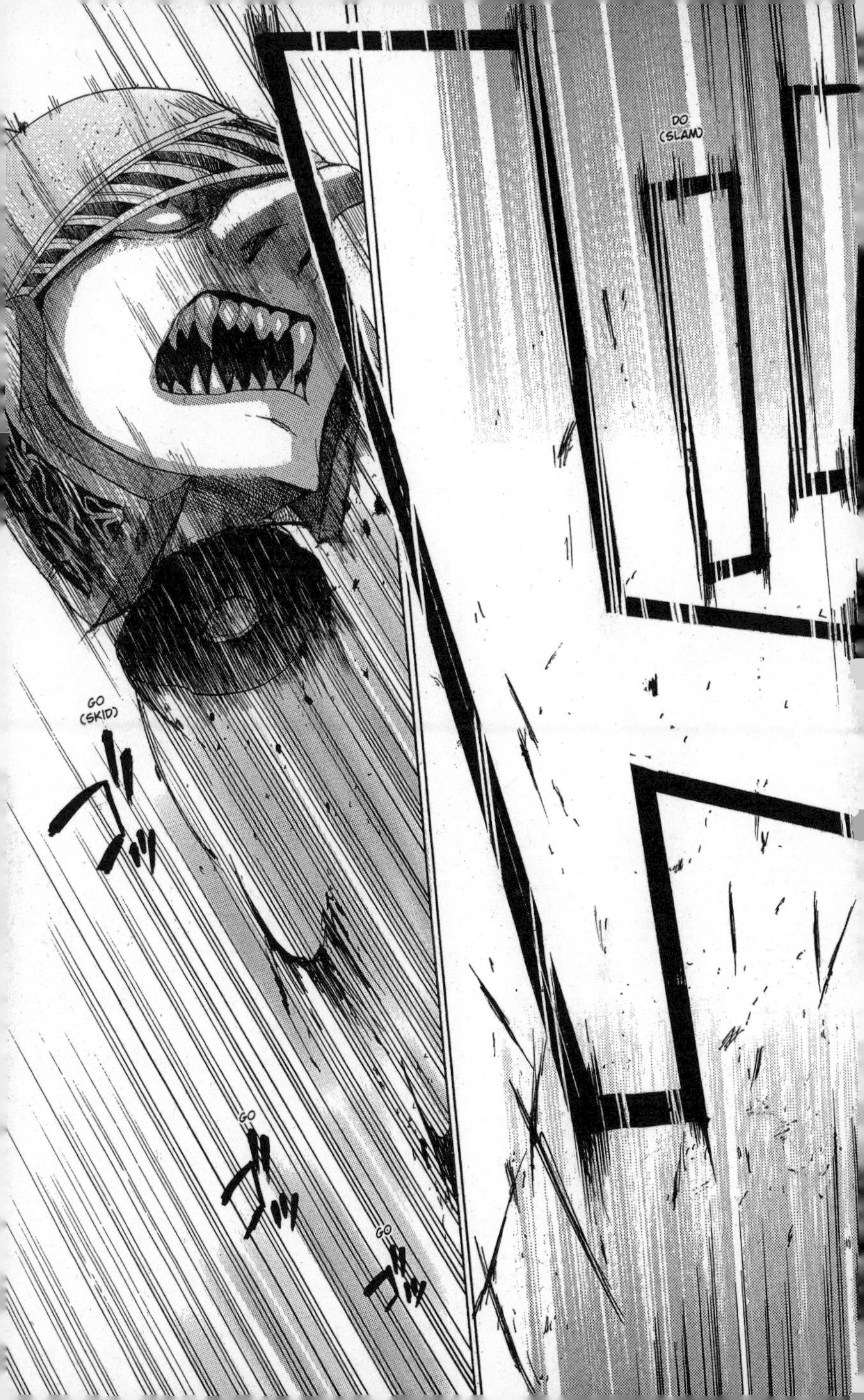
DO
(SLAM)
GO
(SKID)
GO
GO

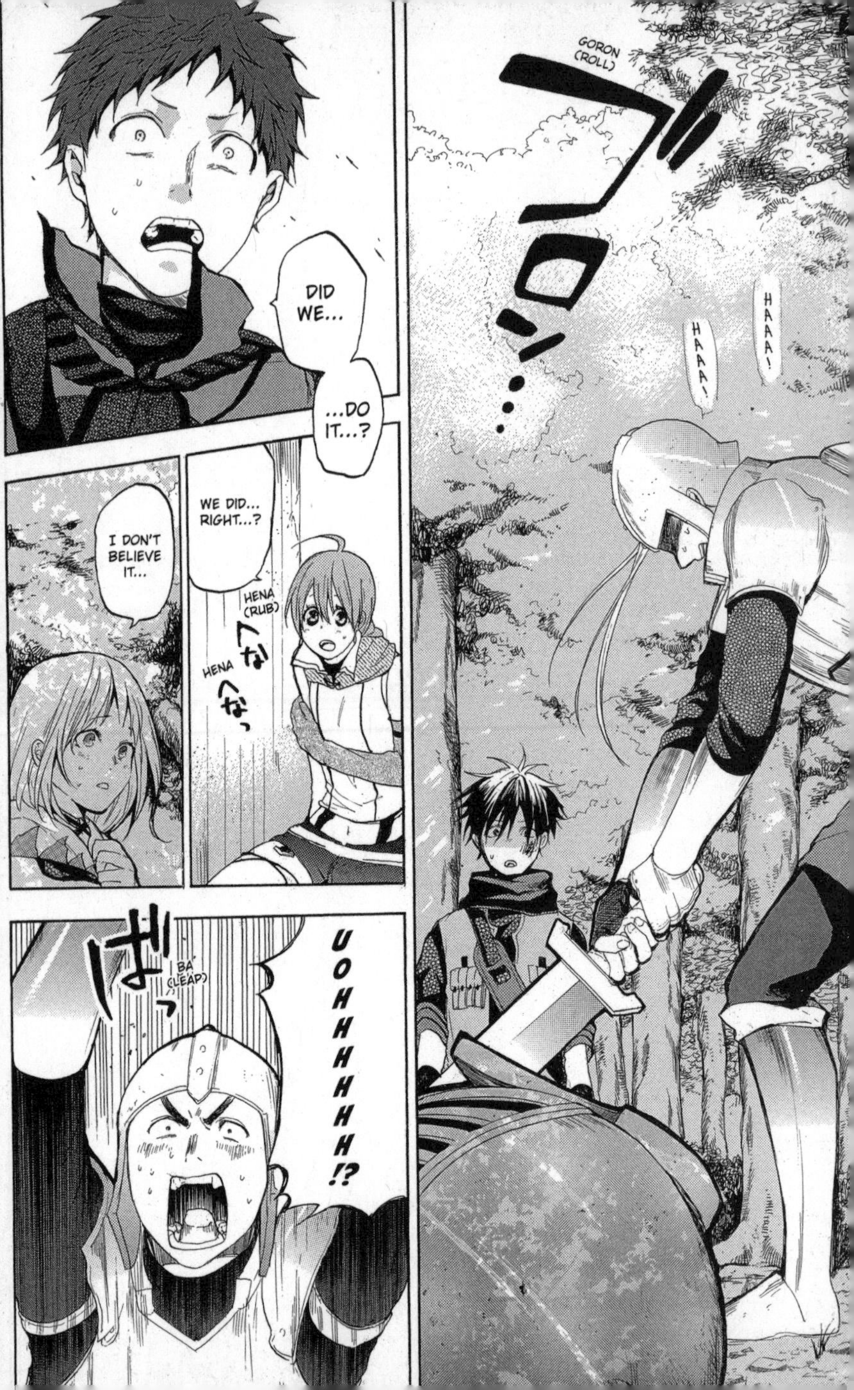
GORON (ROLL)
ゴロン…
HAAAA!
HAAA!
DID WE...
...DO IT...?
WE DID... RIGHT...?
HENA (RUB)
へな
HENA
へなっ
I DON'T BELIEVE IT...
UOHHHHHHHH!?
BA (LEAP)
ばっ

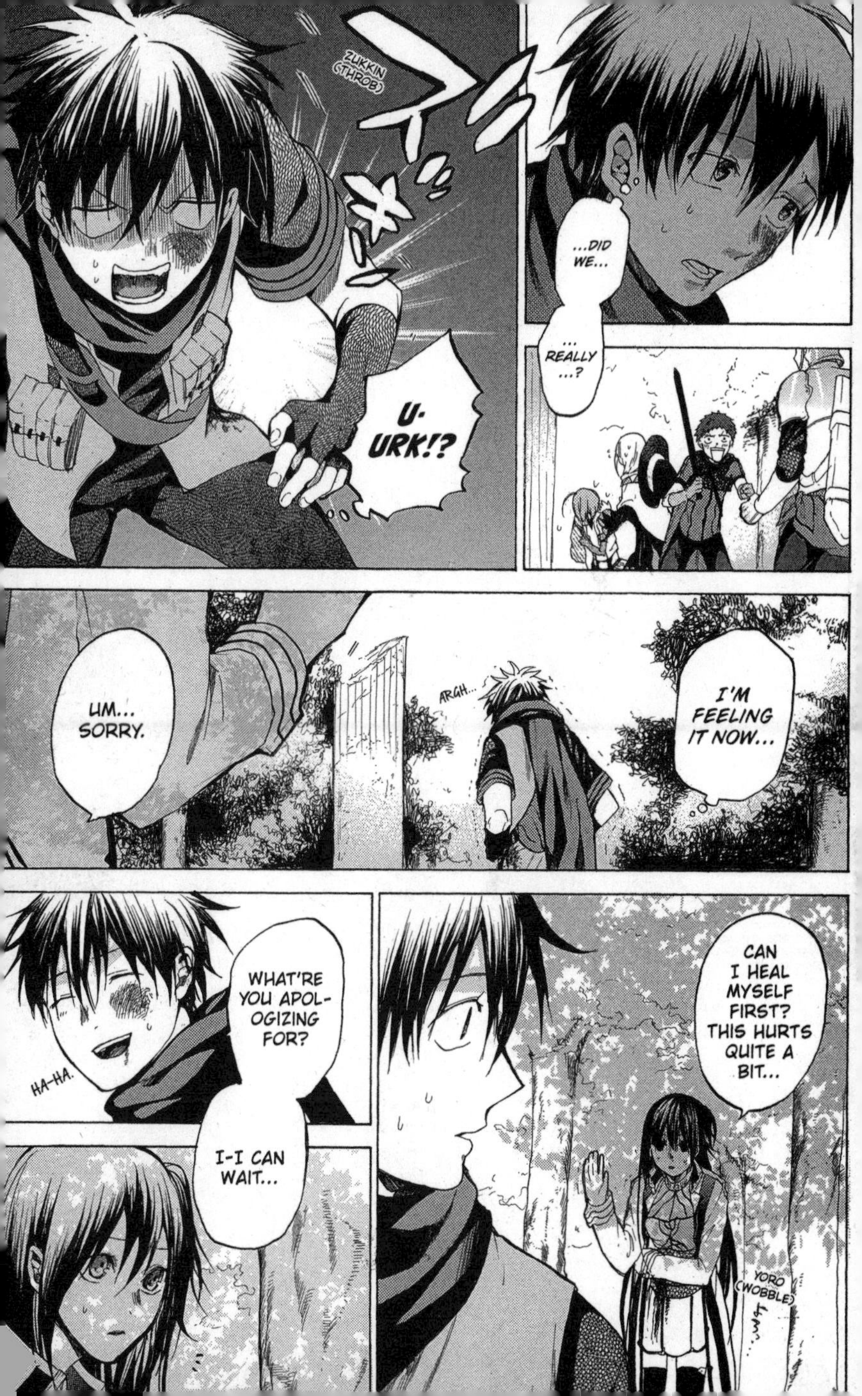
...DID WE...
... REALLY ...?
ZUKKIN (THROB)
U-URK!?
I'M FEELING IT NOW...
ARGH...
UM... SORRY.
CAN I HEAL MYSELF FIRST? THIS HURTS QUITE A BIT...
YORO (WOBBLE)
WHAT'RE YOU APOLOGIZING FOR?
HA-HA.
I-I CAN WAIT...

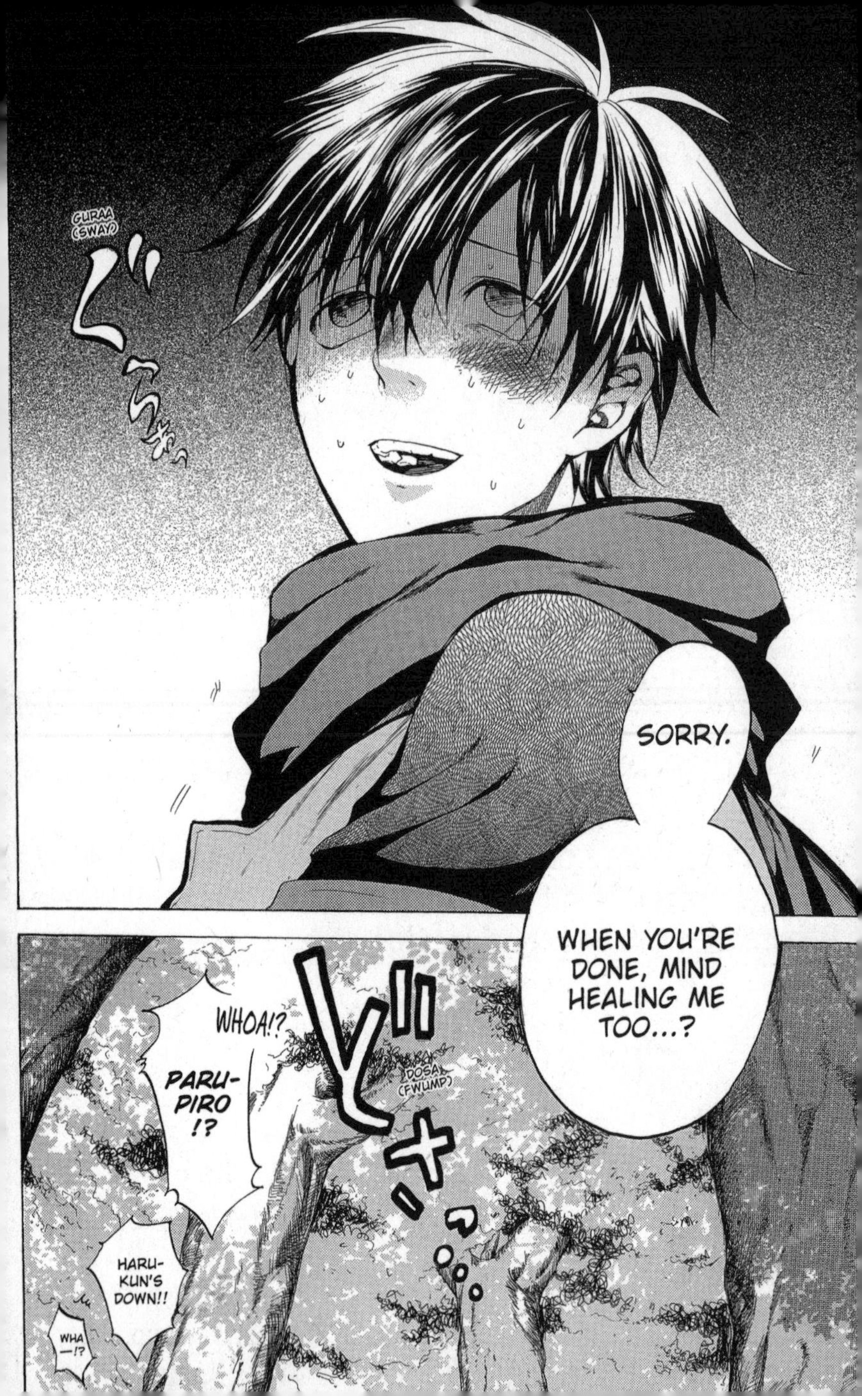
GURAA (SWAY)
SORRY.
WHEN YOU'RE DONE, MIND HEALING ME TOO...?
DOSA (FWUMP)
WHOA!?
PARU-PIRO!?
HARU-KUN'S DOWN!!
WHA—!?

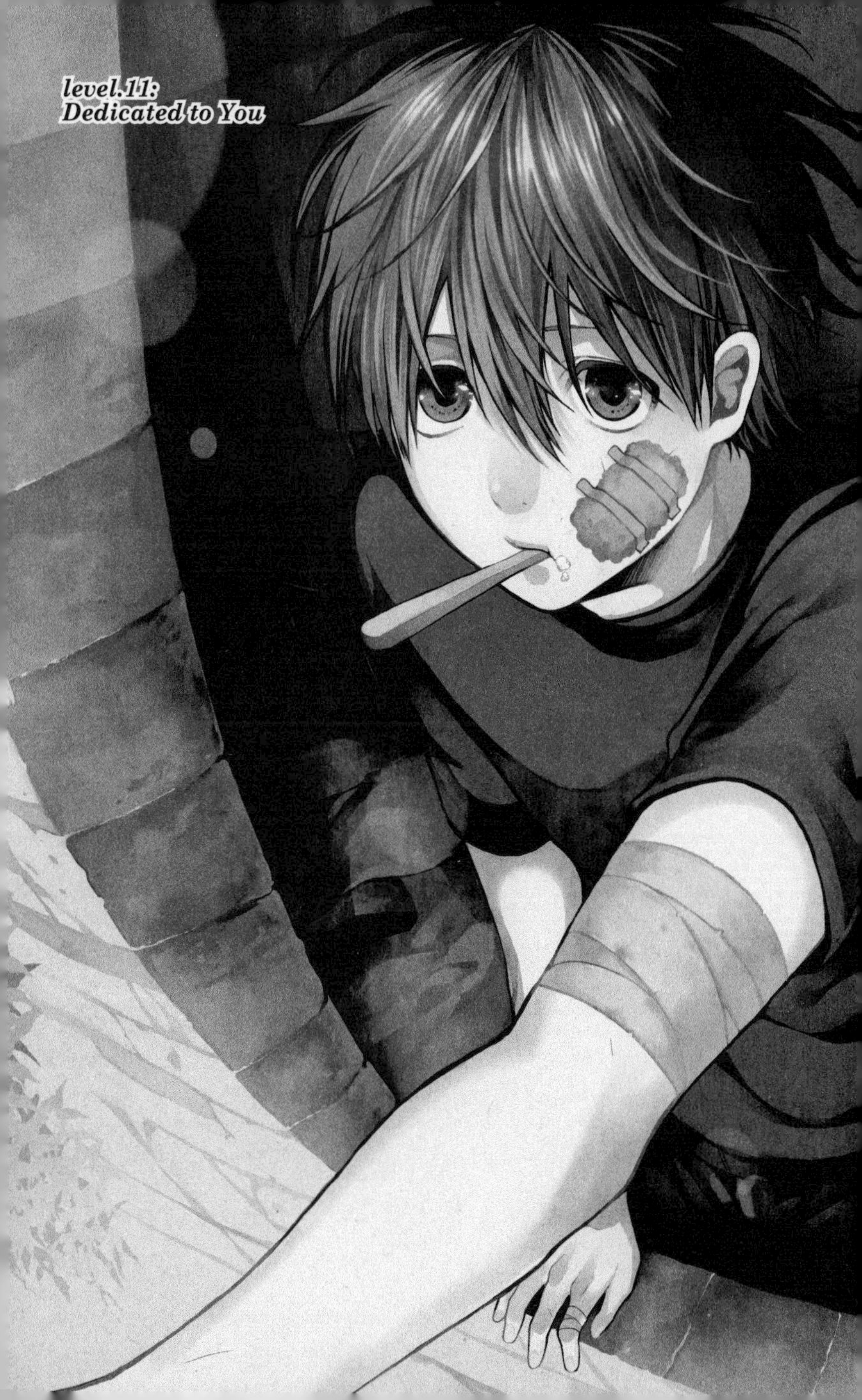
level.11:
Dedicated to You

TRAVELING GOBS—STRANGE TALES FROM GRIMGAR OF FANTASY AND ASH A MATTER OF PRIDE

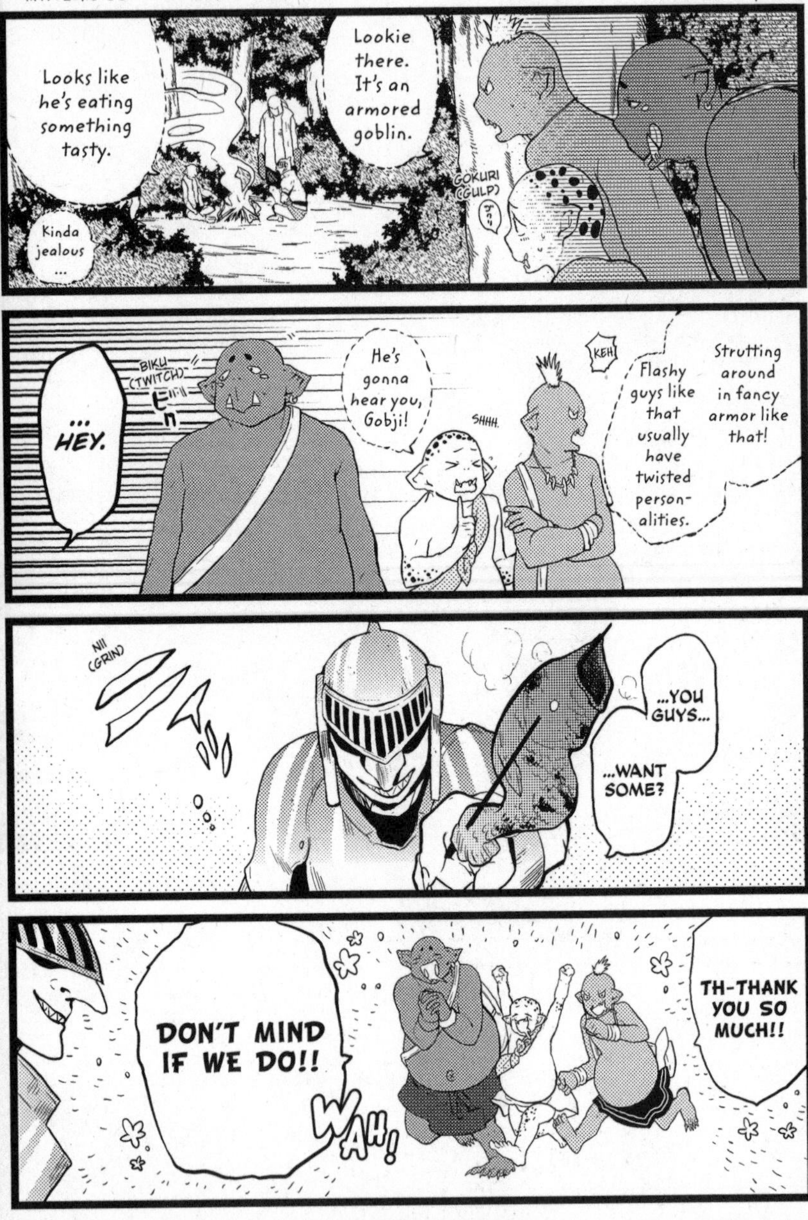
Lookie there. It's an armored goblin.
GOKURI (GULP)
Looks like he's eating something tasty.
Kinda jealous ...
KEH
Strutting around in fancy armor like that!
Flashy guys like that usually have twisted personalities.
SHHH.
He's gonna hear you, Gobji!
BIKU (TWITCH)
... HEY.
...YOU GUYS...
...WANT SOME?
NII (GRIN)
TH-THANK YOU SO MUCH!!
WAH!
DON'T MIND IF WE DO!!

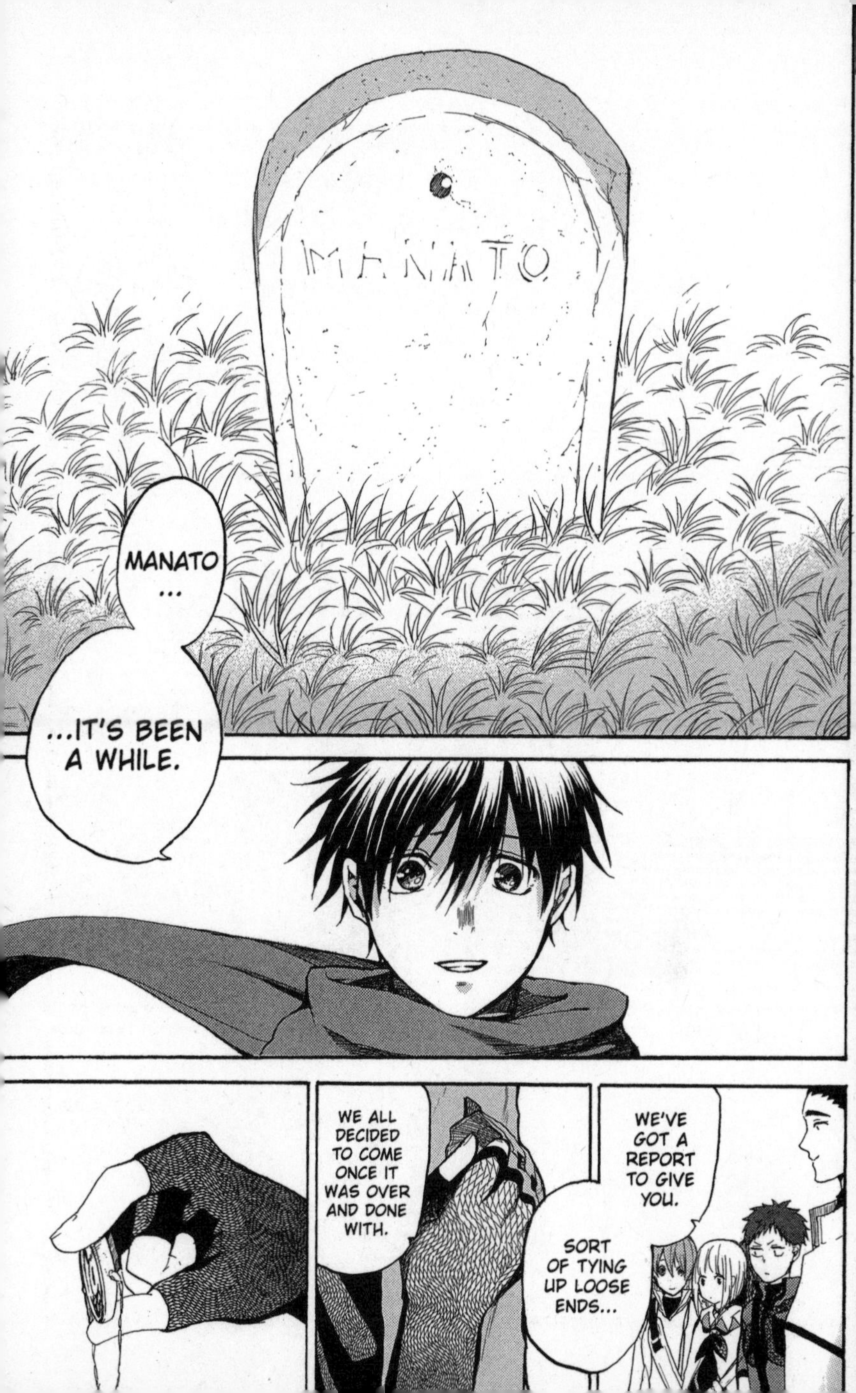
MANATO
MANATO ...
...IT'S BEEN A WHILE.
WE'VE GOT A REPORT TO GIVE YOU.
SORT OF TYING UP LOOSE ENDS...
WE ALL DECIDED TO COME ONCE IT WAS OVER AND DONE WITH.

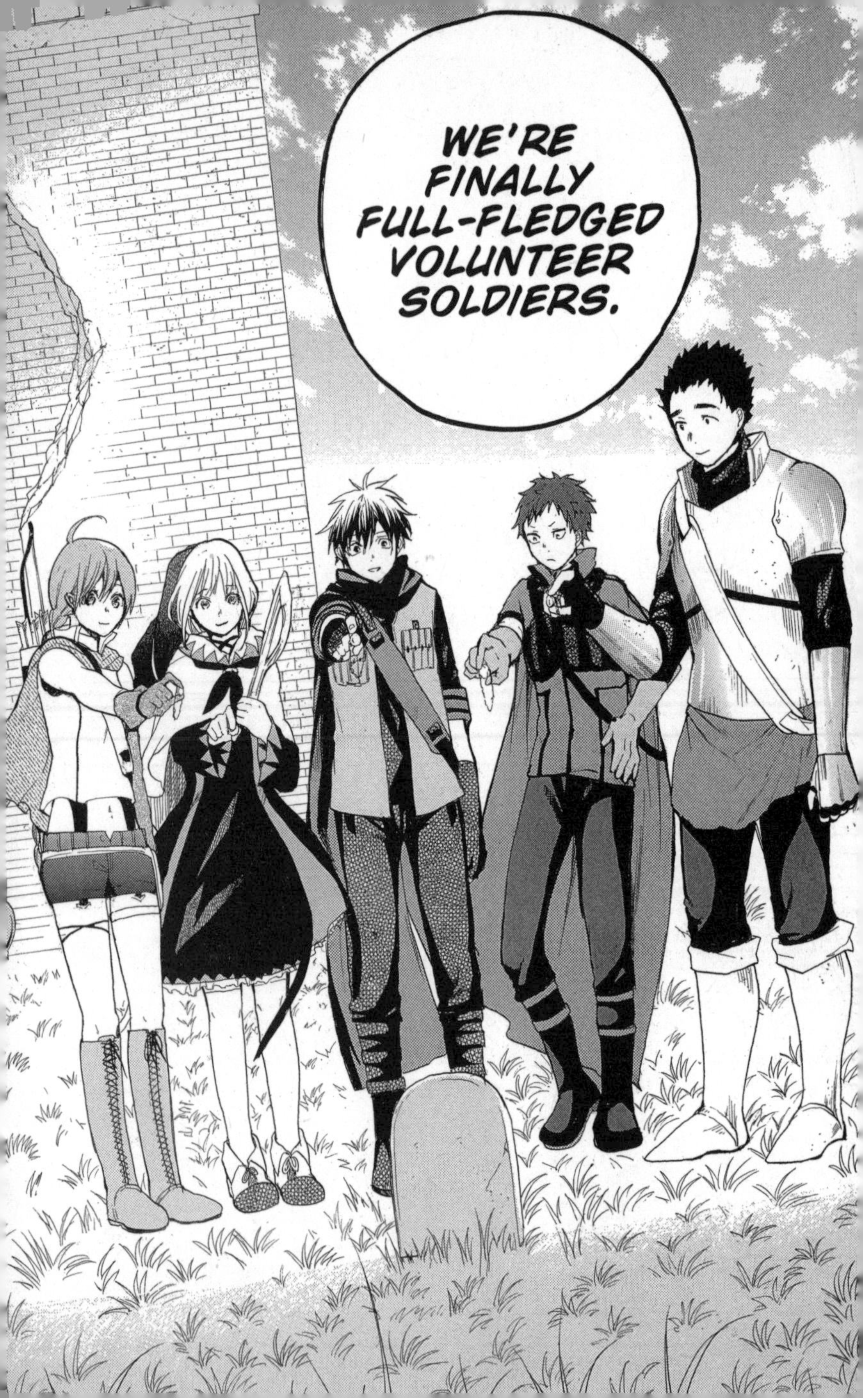
WE'RE FINALLY FULL-FLEDGED VOLUNTEER SOLDIERS.

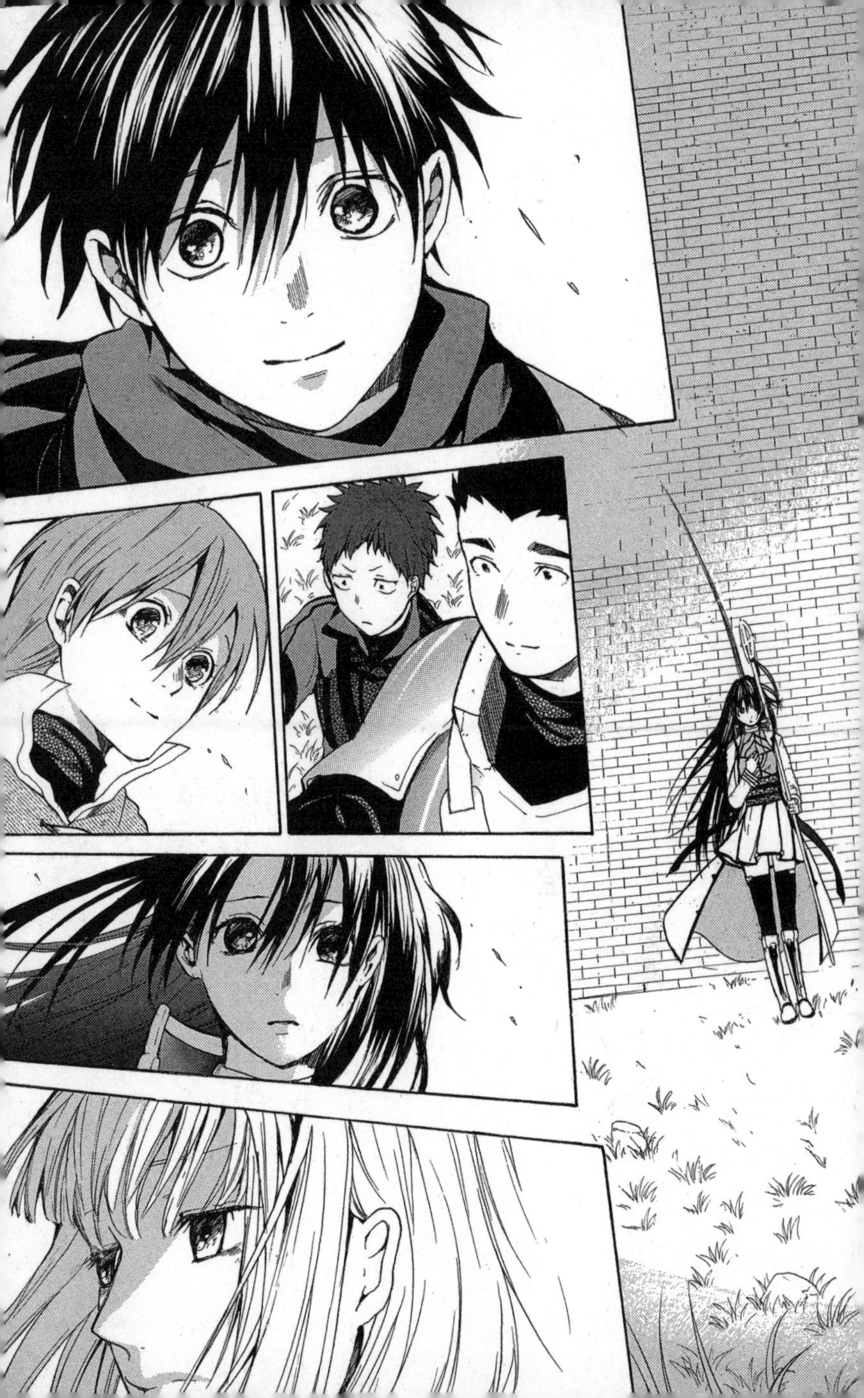

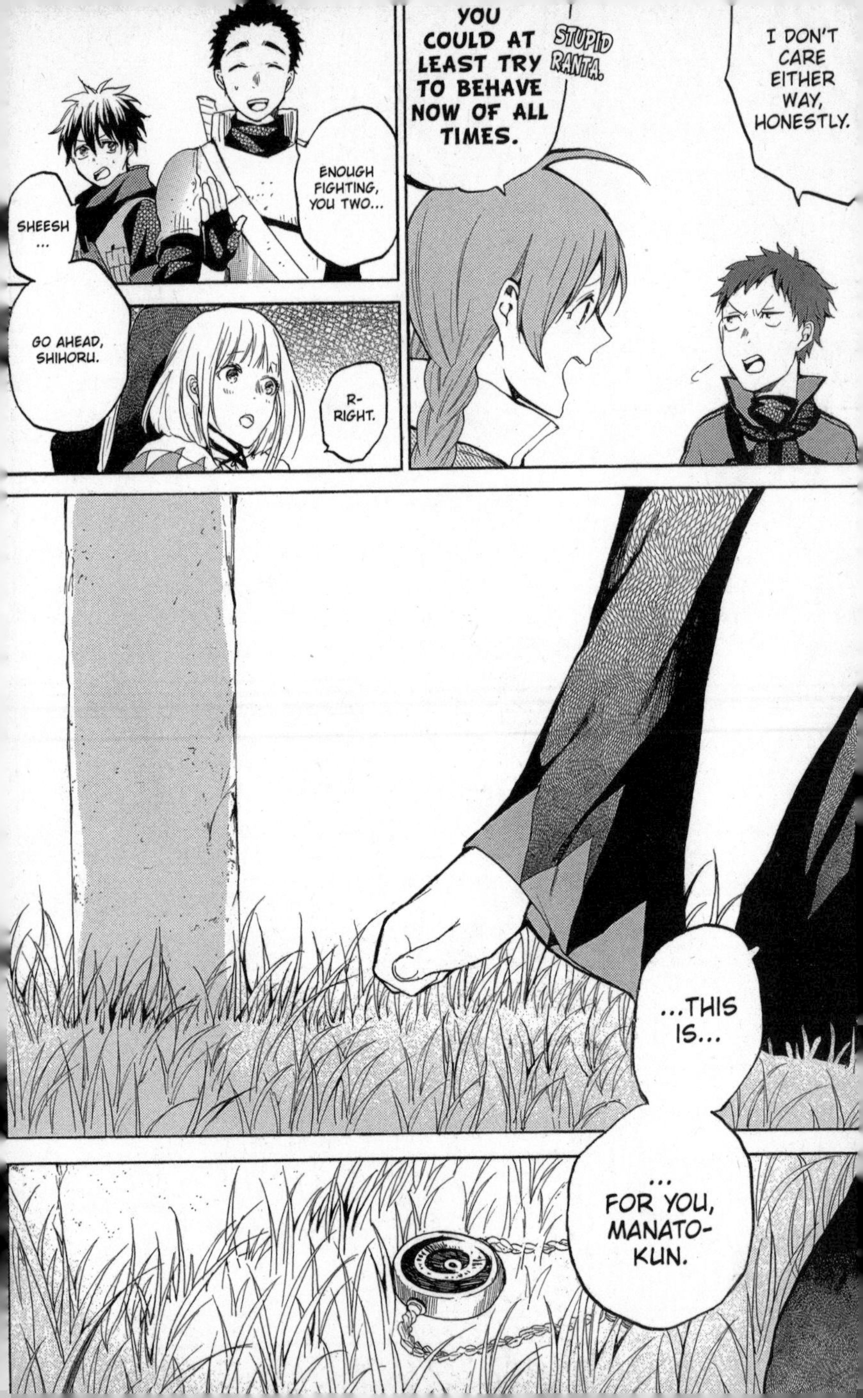
I DON'T CARE EITHER WAY, HONESTLY.
YOU COULD AT LEAST TRY TO BEHAVE NOW OF ALL TIMES.
STUPID RANTA.
ENOUGH FIGHTING, YOU TWO...
SHEESH ...
GO AHEAD, SHIHORU.
R- RIGHT.
...THIS IS...
... FOR YOU, MANATO-KUN.

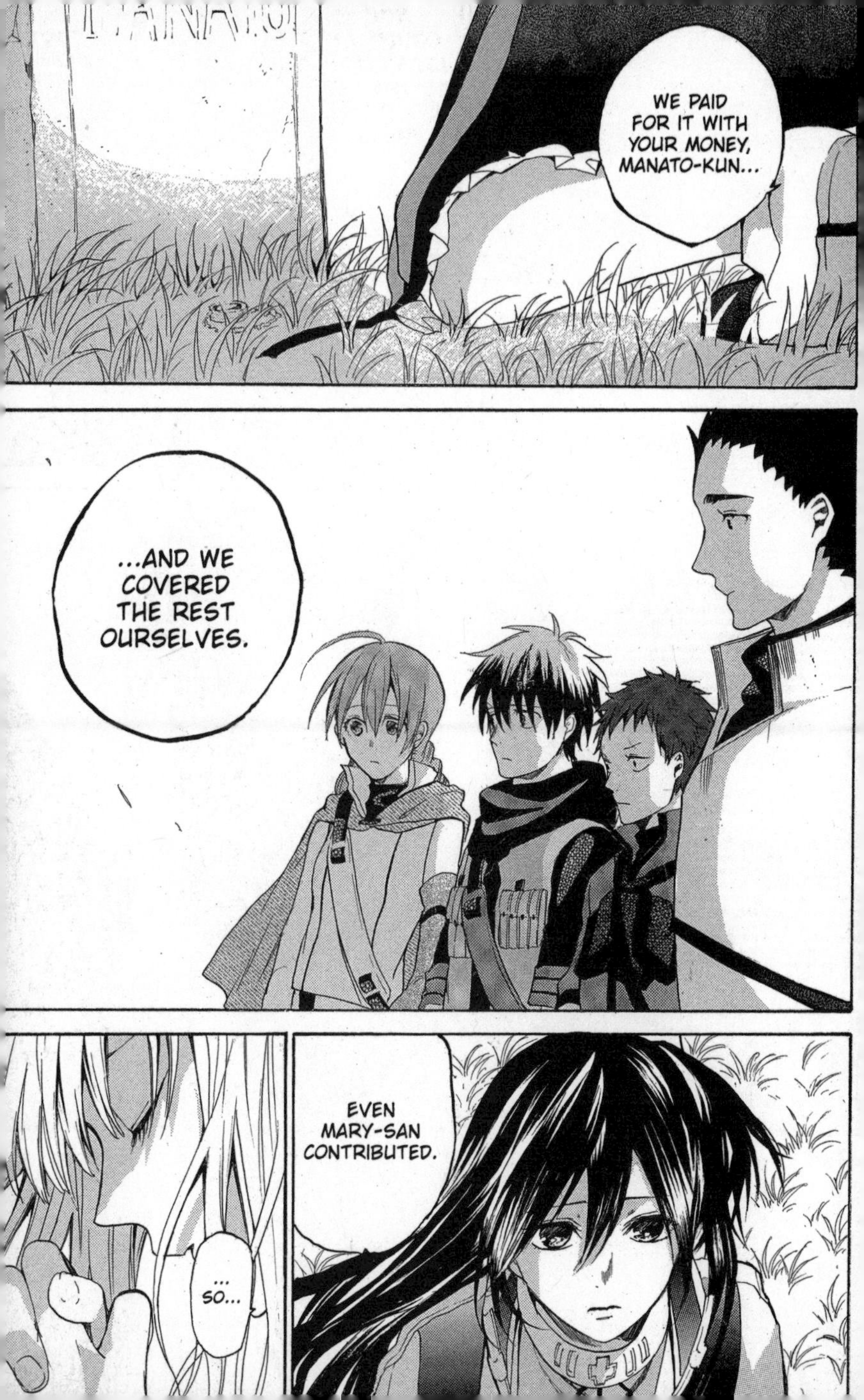
WE PAID FOR IT WITH YOUR MONEY, MANATO-KUN...
...AND WE COVERED THE REST OURSELVES.
EVEN MARY-SAN CONTRIBUTED.
... SO...

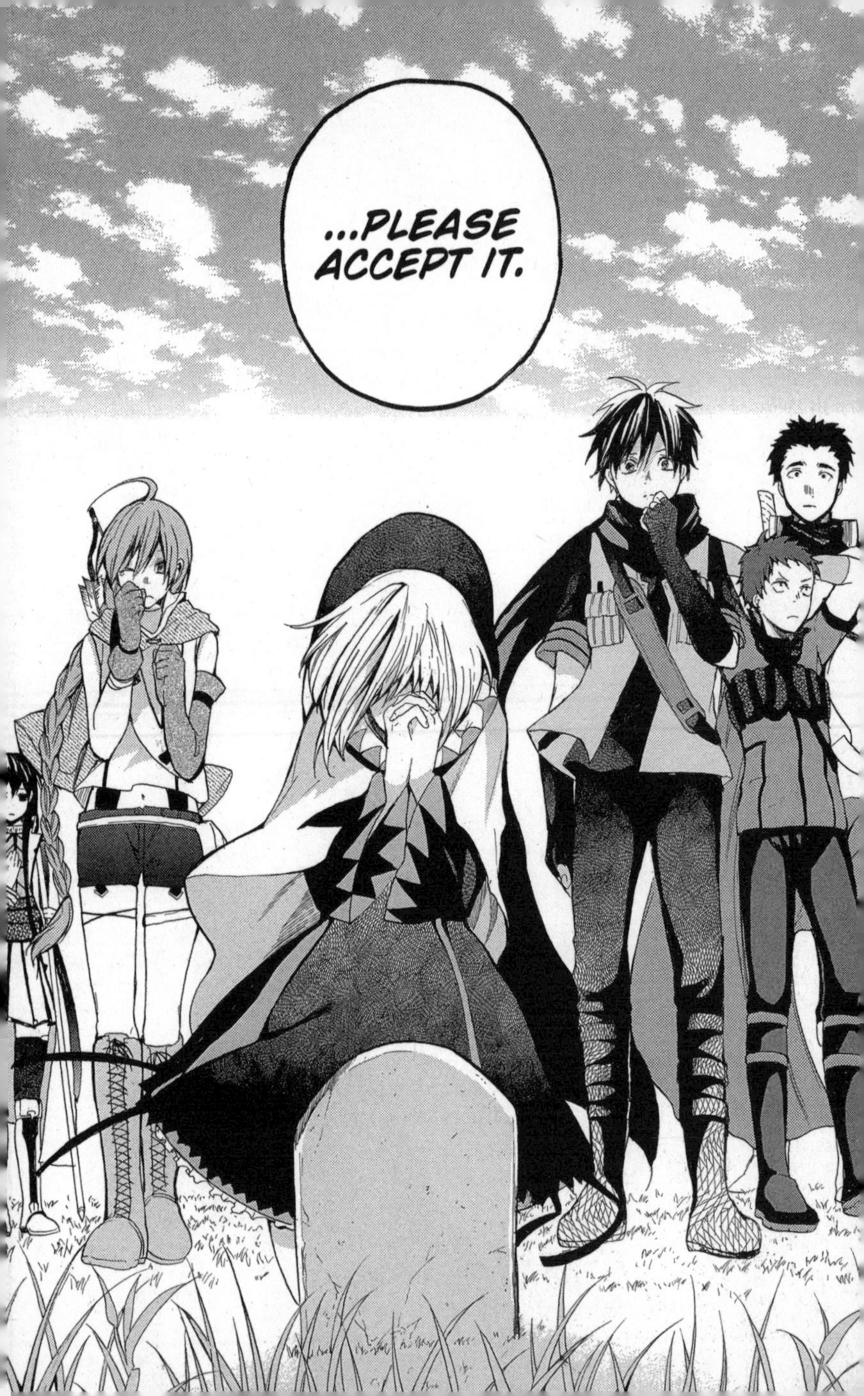
...PLEASE ACCEPT IT.

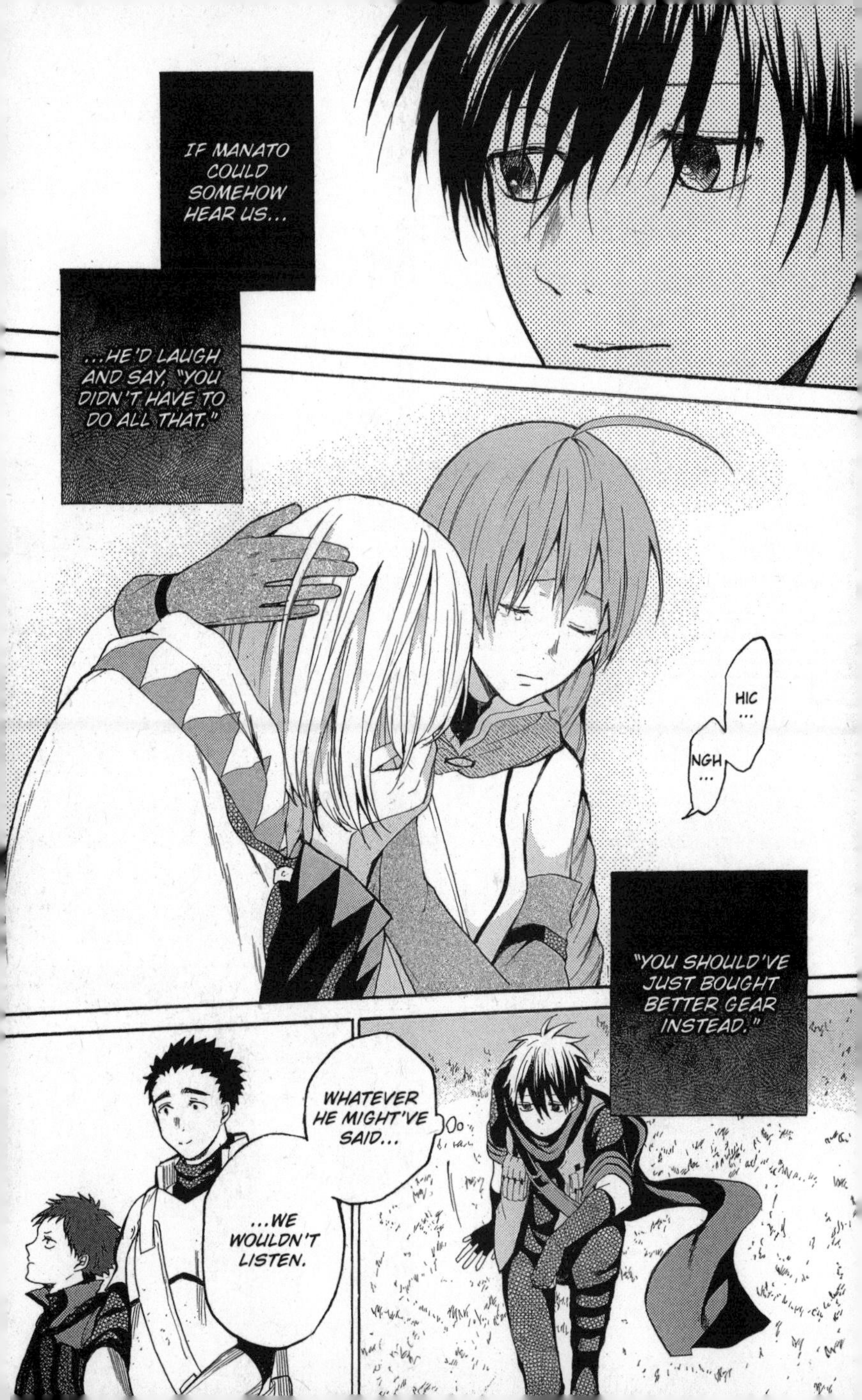
IF MANATO COULD SOMEHOW HEAR US...
...HE'D LAUGH AND SAY, "YOU DIDN'T HAVE TO DO ALL THAT."
HIC...
NGH...
"YOU SHOULD'VE JUST BOUGHT BETTER GEAR INSTEAD."
WHATEVER HE MIGHT'VE SAID...
...WE WOULDN'T LISTEN.

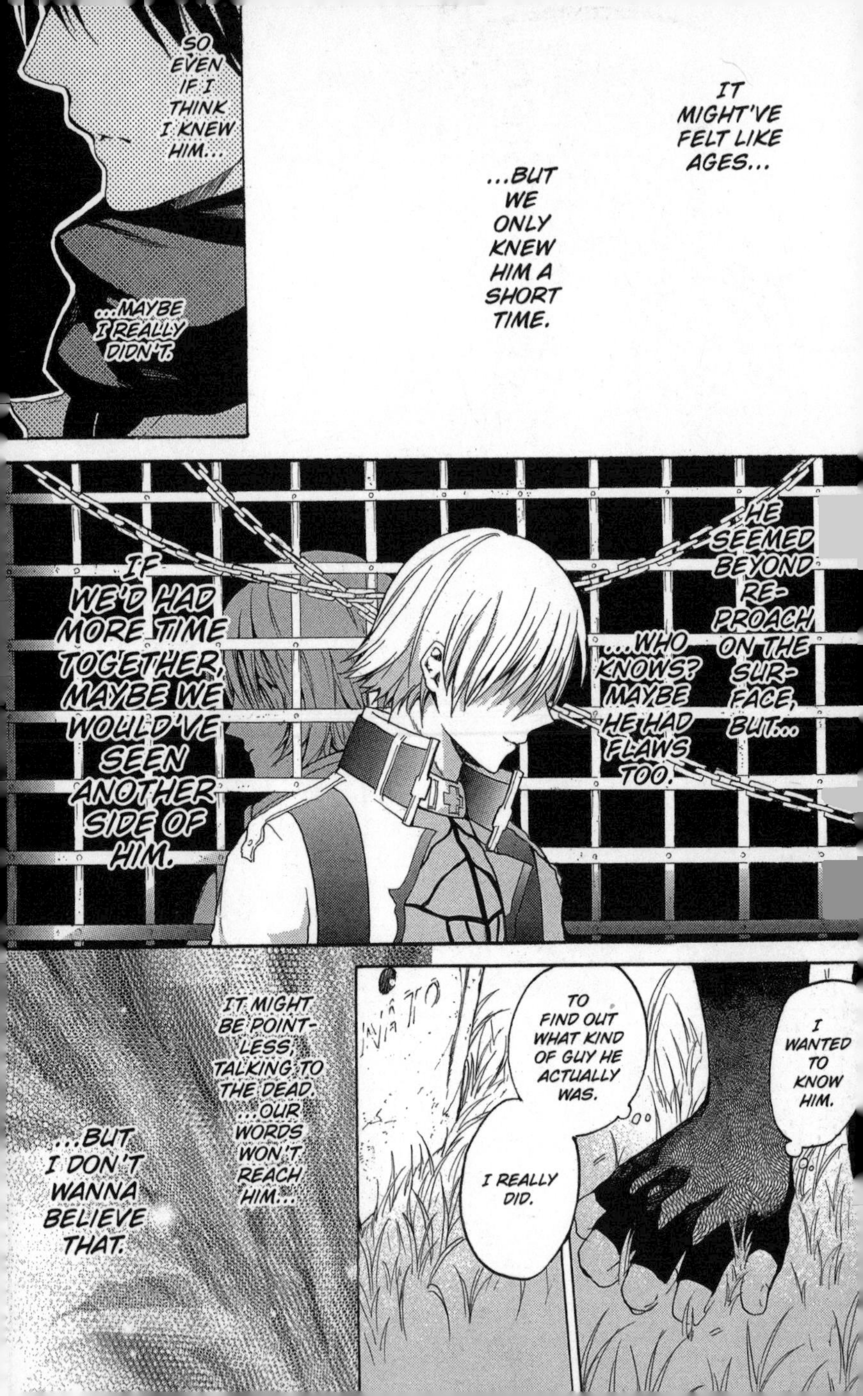
IT MIGHT'VE FELT LIKE AGES...
...BUT WE ONLY KNEW HIM A SHORT TIME.
SO EVEN IF I THINK I KNEW HIM...
...MAYBE I REALLY DIDN'T.
HE SEEMED BEYOND RE-PROACH ON THE SUR-FACE, BUT...
...WHO KNOWS? MAYBE HE HAD FLAWS TOO.
IF WE'D HAD MORE TIME TOGETHER, MAYBE WE WOULD'VE SEEN ANOTHER SIDE OF HIM.
I WANTED TO KNOW HIM.
TO FIND OUT WHAT KIND OF GUY HE ACTUALLY WAS.
I REALLY DID.
IT MIGHT BE POINT-LESS, TALKING TO THE DEAD. ...OUR WORDS WON'T REACH HIM...
...BUT I DON'T WANNA BELIEVE THAT.

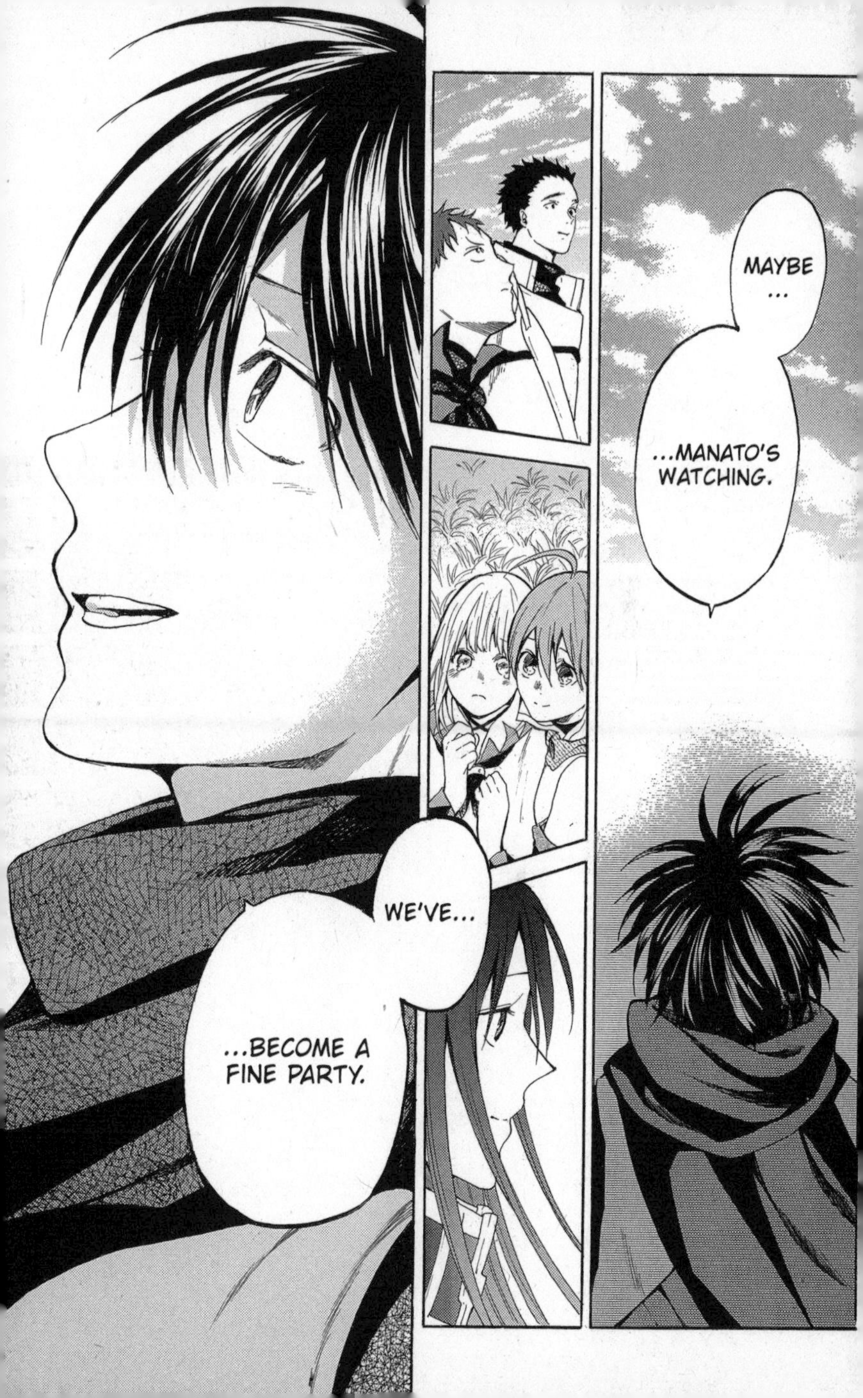
MAYBE ...
...MANATO'S WATCHING.
WE'VE...
...BECOME A FINE PARTY.

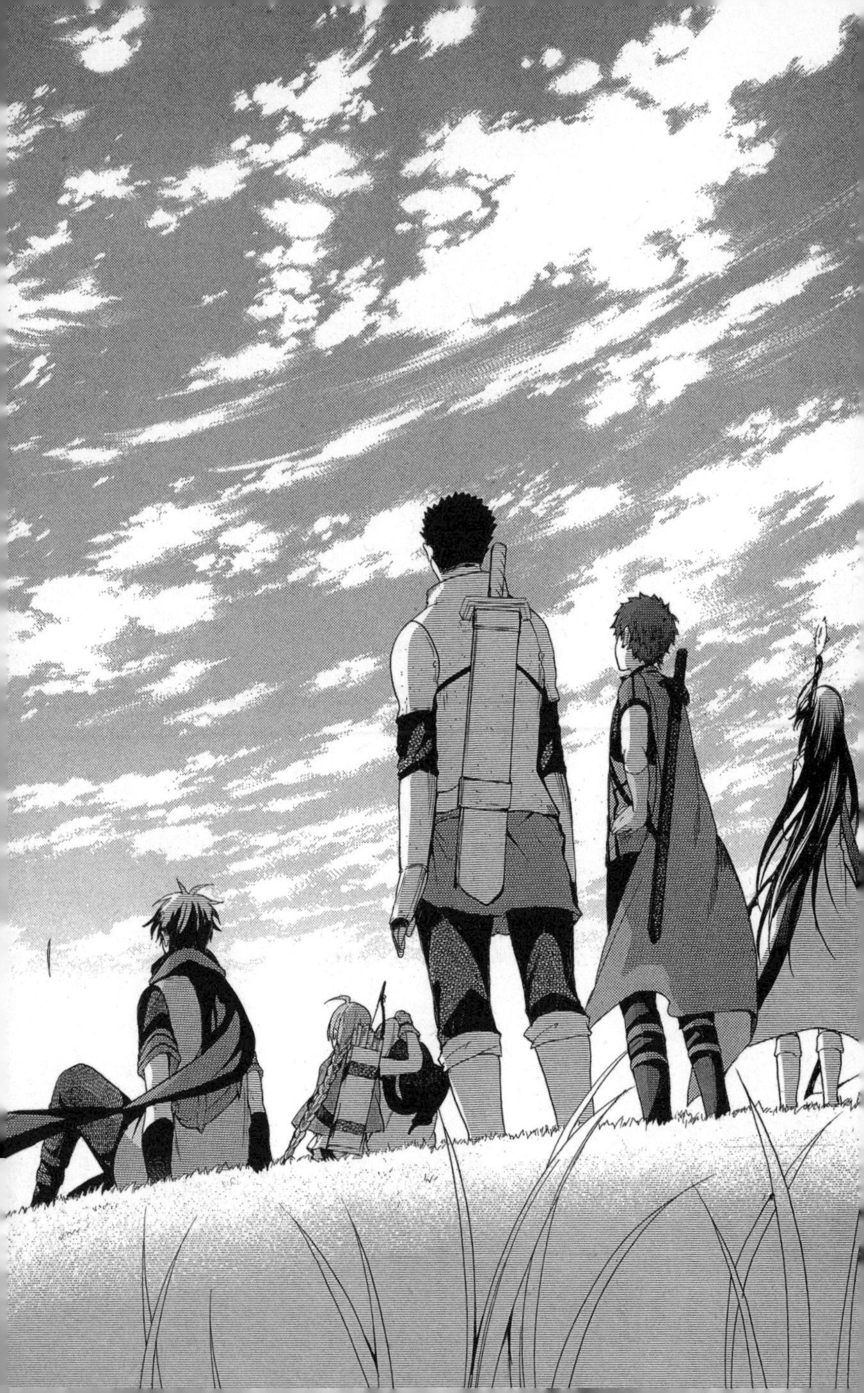

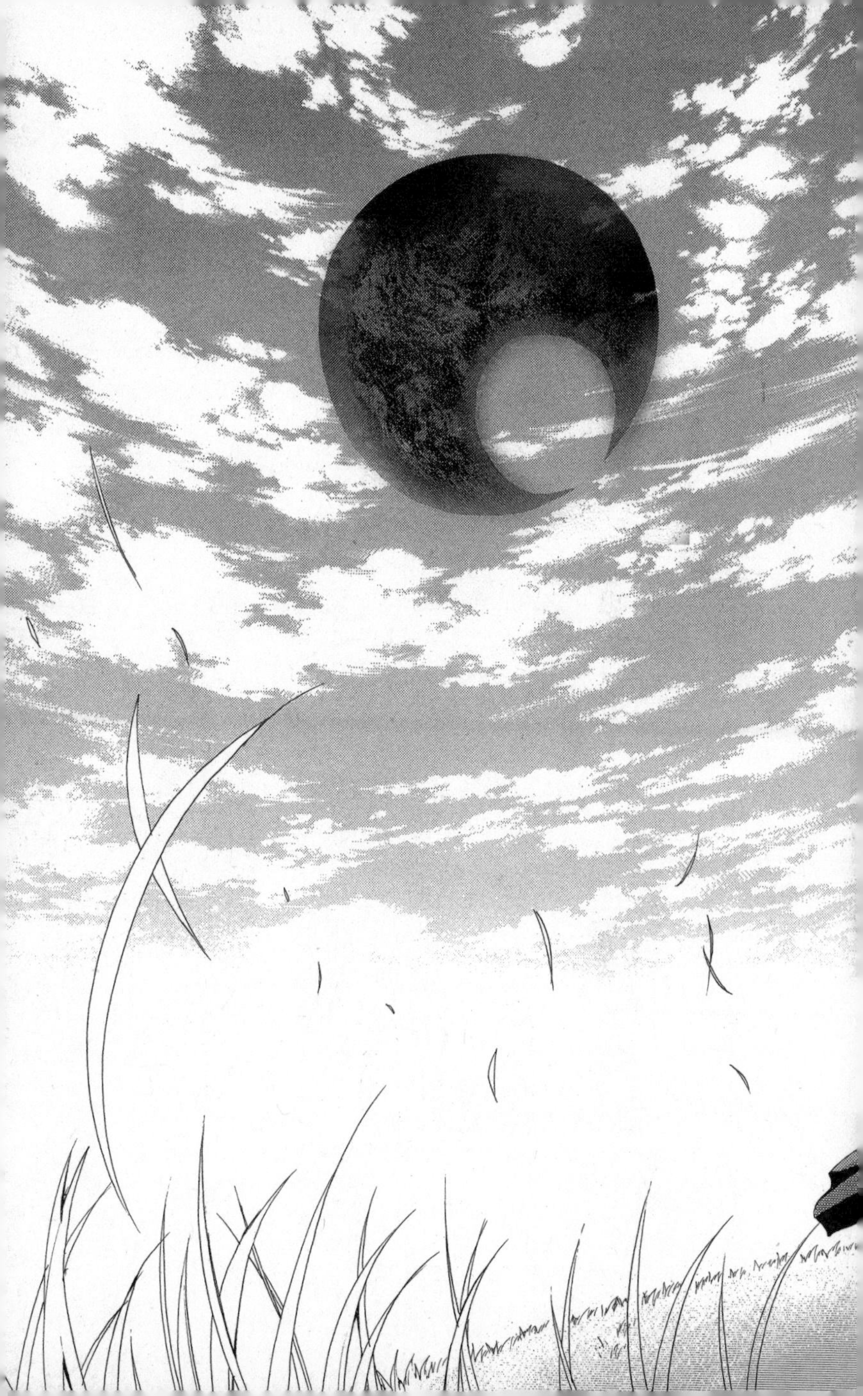

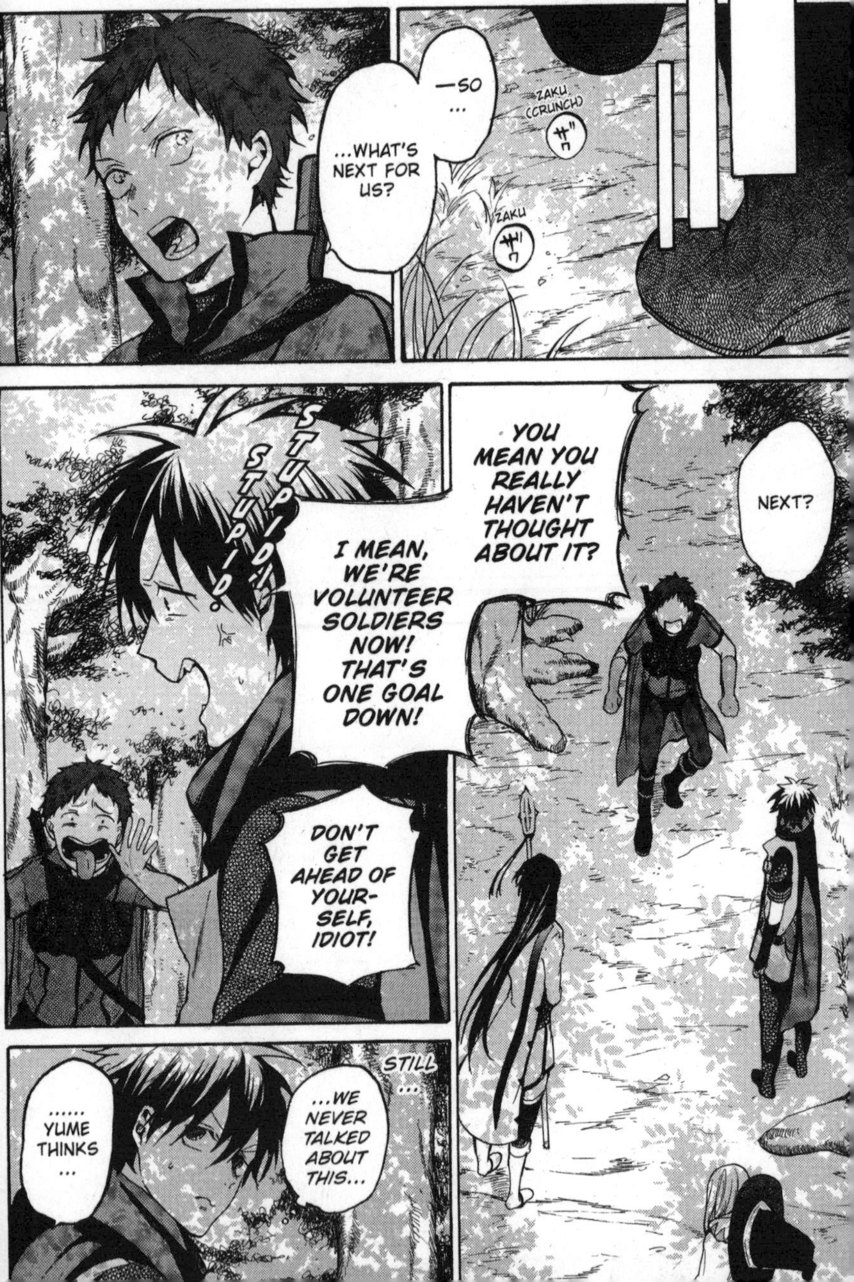
ザッ
ZAKU (CRUNCH)
ザッ
ZAKU
—SO ...
...WHAT'S NEXT FOR US?
NEXT?
YOU MEAN YOU REALLY HAVEN'T THOUGHT ABOUT IT?
I MEAN, WE'RE VOLUNTEER SOLDIERS NOW! THAT'S ONE GOAL DOWN!
STUPID STUPID
DON'T GET AHEAD OF YOUR-SELF, IDIOT!
STILL ...
...WE NEVER TALKED ABOUT THIS...
...... YUME THINKS ...

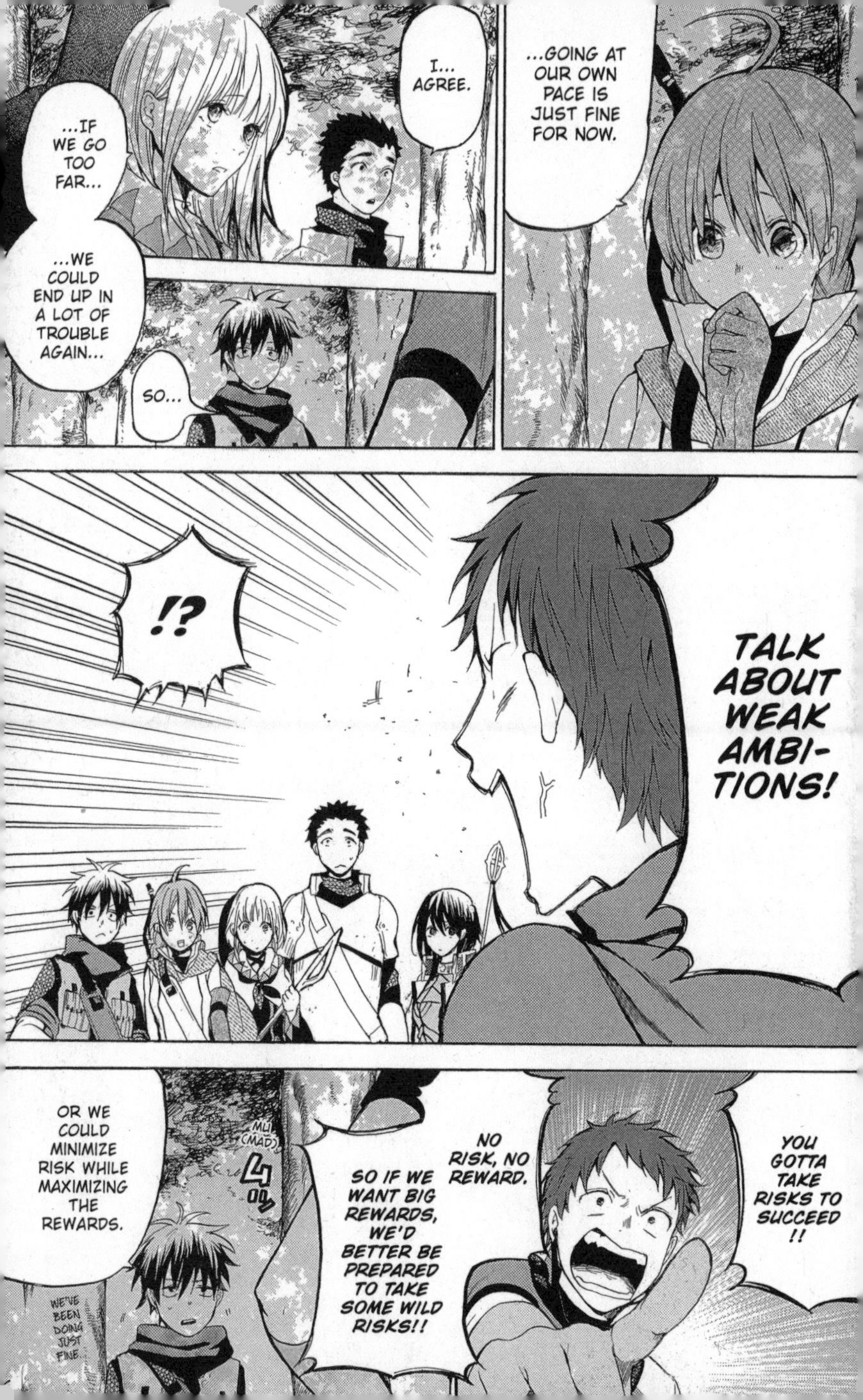
...GOING AT OUR OWN PACE IS JUST FINE FOR NOW.
I... AGREE.
...IF WE GO TOO FAR...
...WE COULD END UP IN A LOT OF TROUBLE AGAIN...
SO...
TALK ABOUT WEAK AMBI-TIONS!
!?
YOU GOTTA TAKE RISKS TO SUCCEED!!
NO RISK, NO REWARD.
SO IF WE WANT BIG REWARDS, WE'D BETTER BE PREPARED TO TAKE SOME WILD RISKS!!
MU (MAD)
OR WE COULD MINIMIZE RISK WHILE MAXIMIZING THE REWARDS.
WE'VE BEEN DOING JUST FINE.

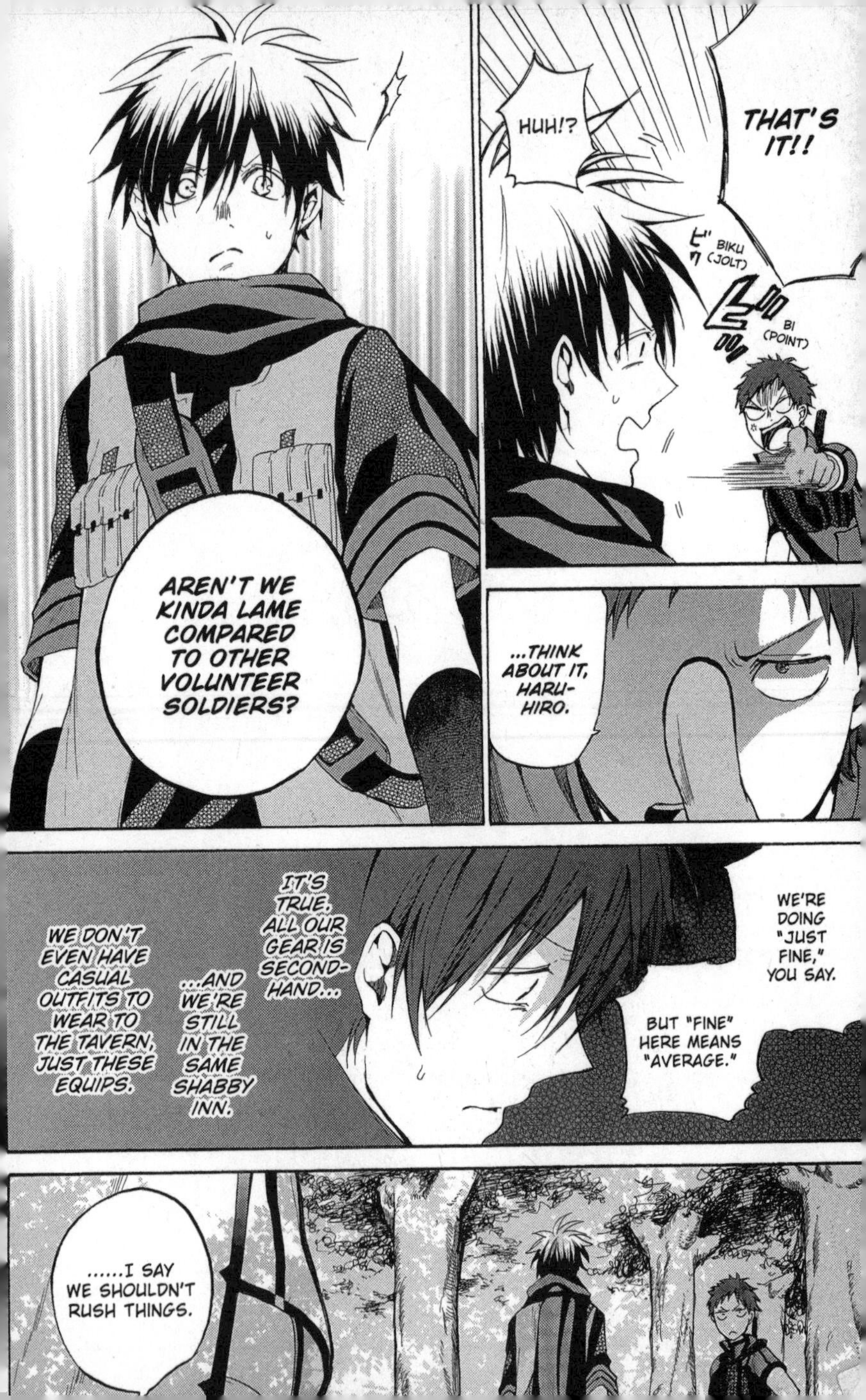
THAT'S IT!!
HUH!?
ビク BIKU (JOLT)
BI (POINT)
...THINK ABOUT IT, HARUHIRO.
AREN'T WE KINDA LAME COMPARED TO OTHER VOLUNTEER SOLDIERS?
WE'RE DOING "JUST FINE," YOU SAY.
BUT "FINE" HERE MEANS "AVERAGE."
IT'S TRUE. ALL OUR GEAR IS SECOND-HAND...
...AND WE'RE STILL IN THE SAME SHABBY INN.
WE DON'T EVEN HAVE CASUAL OUTFITS TO WEAR TO THE TAVERN, JUST THESE EQUIPS.
......I SAY WE SHOULDN'T RUSH THINGS.

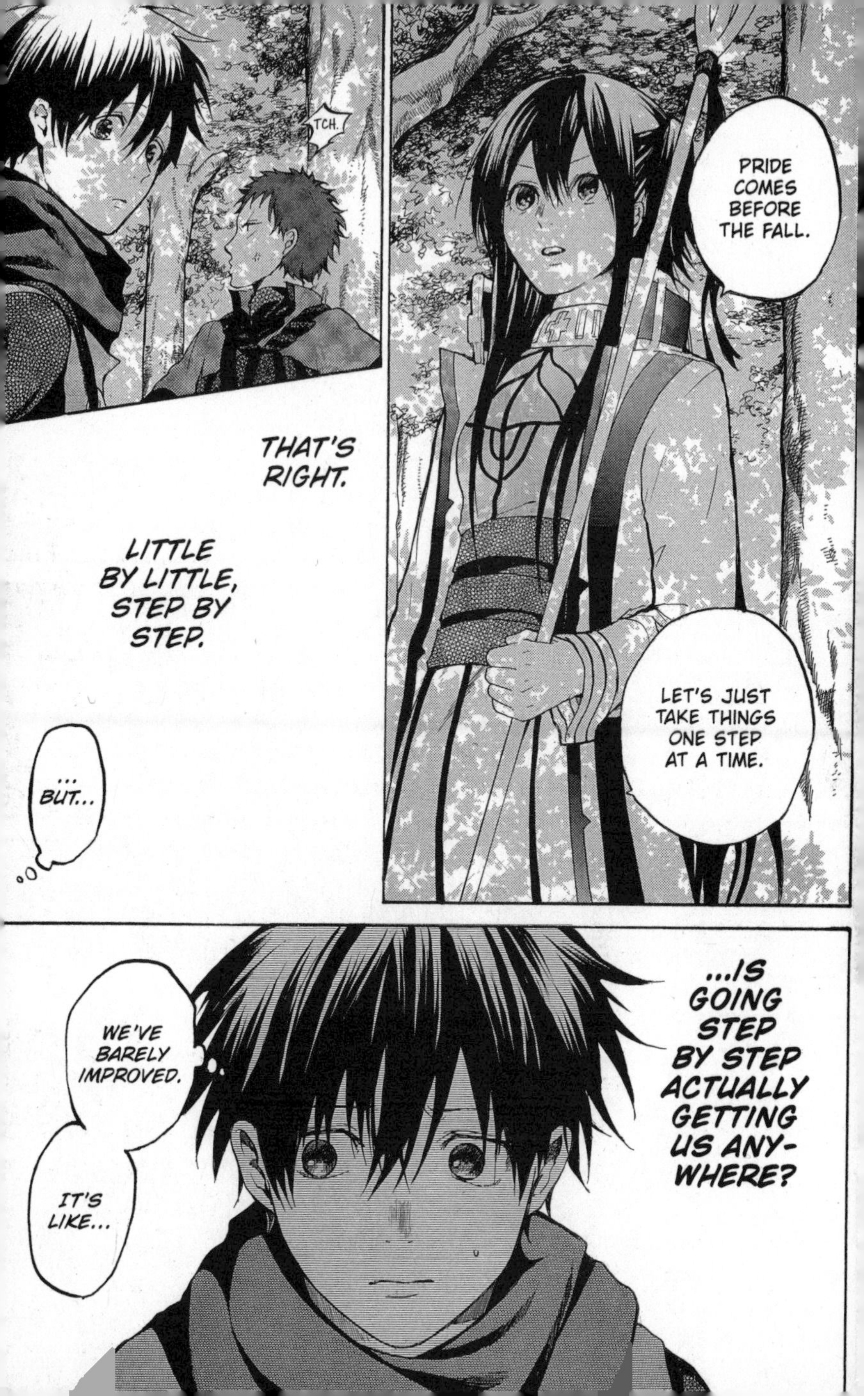
PRIDE COMES BEFORE THE FALL.
LET'S JUST TAKE THINGS ONE STEP AT A TIME.
TCH.
THAT'S RIGHT.
LITTLE BY LITTLE, STEP BY STEP.
... BUT...
...IS GOING STEP BY STEP ACTUALLY GETTING US ANY-WHERE?
WE'VE BARELY IMPROVED.
IT'S LIKE...

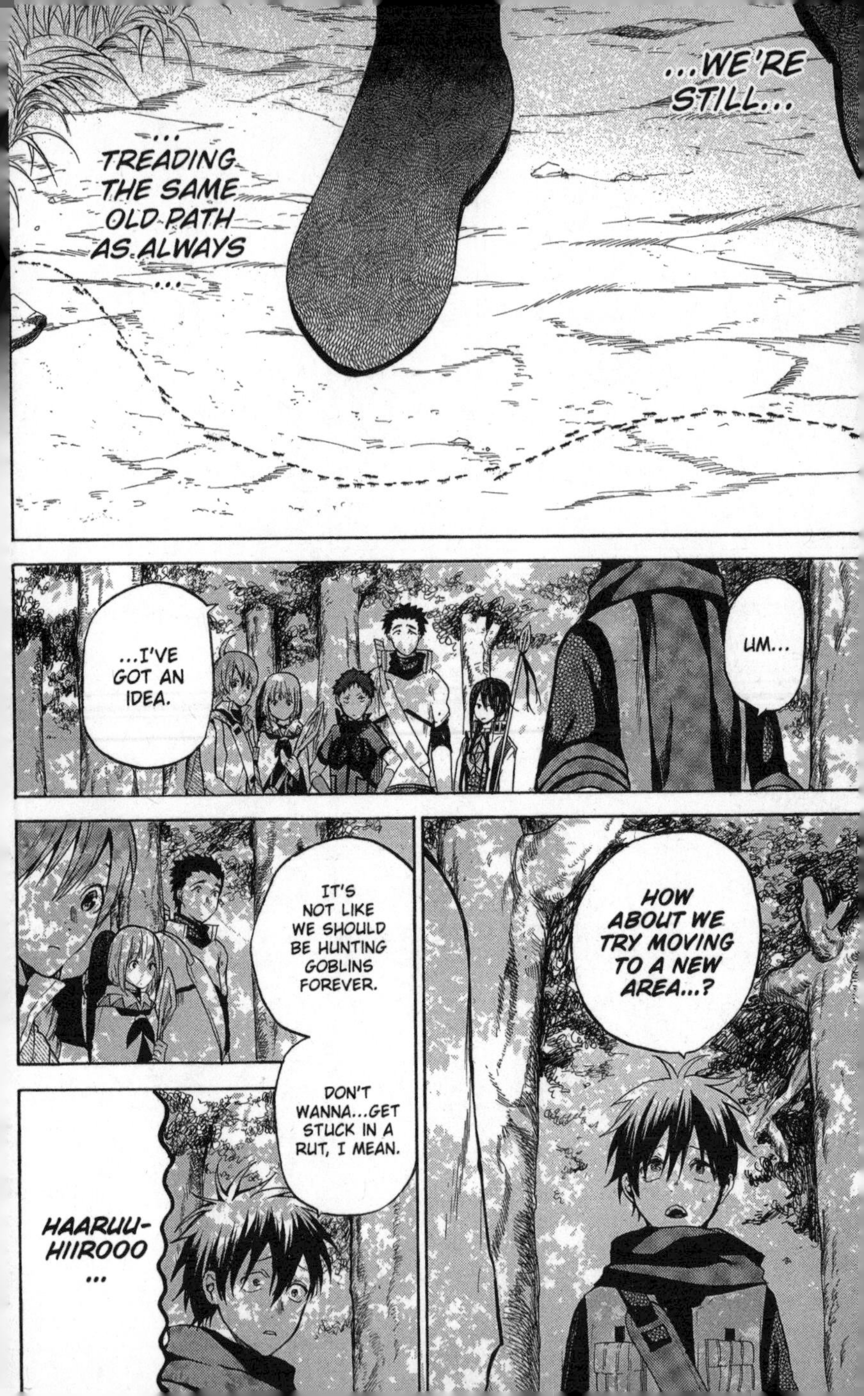
...WE'RE STILL...
...TREADING THE SAME OLD PATH AS ALWAYS...
UM...
...I'VE GOT AN IDEA.
HOW ABOUT WE TRY MOVING TO A NEW AREA...?
IT'S NOT LIKE WE SHOULD BE HUNTING GOBLINS FOREVER.
DON'T WANNA...GET STUCK IN A RUT, I MEAN.
HAARUU-HIIROOO...

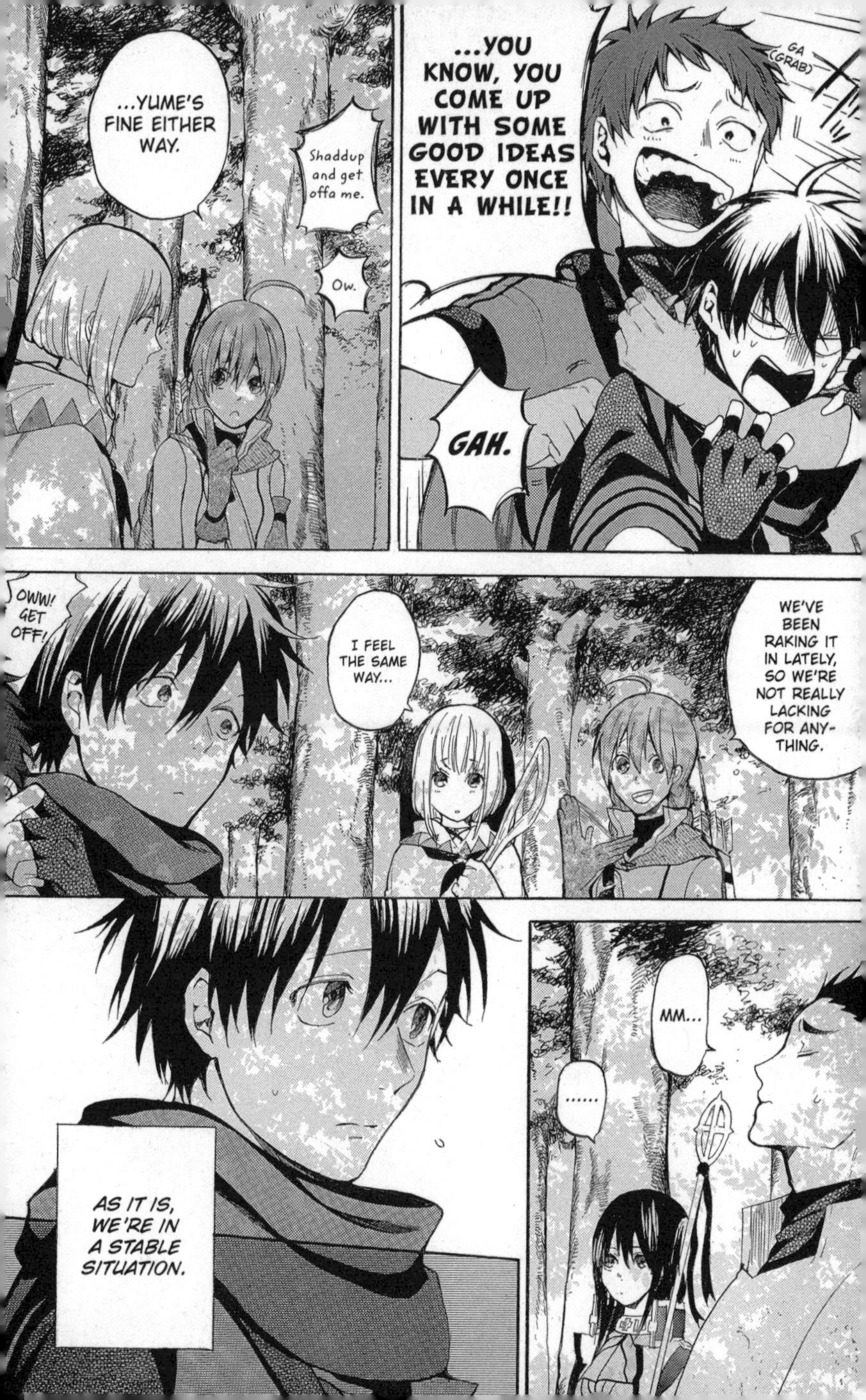
GA (GRAB)
...YOU KNOW, YOU COME UP WITH SOME GOOD IDEAS EVERY ONCE IN A WHILE!!
GAH.
Shaddup and get offa me.
Ow.
...YUME'S FINE EITHER WAY.
WE'VE BEEN RAKING IT IN LATELY, SO WE'RE NOT REALLY LACKING FOR ANY-THING.
I FEEL THE SAME WAY...
OWW! GET OFF!
MM...
......
AS IT IS, WE'RE IN A STABLE SITUATION.

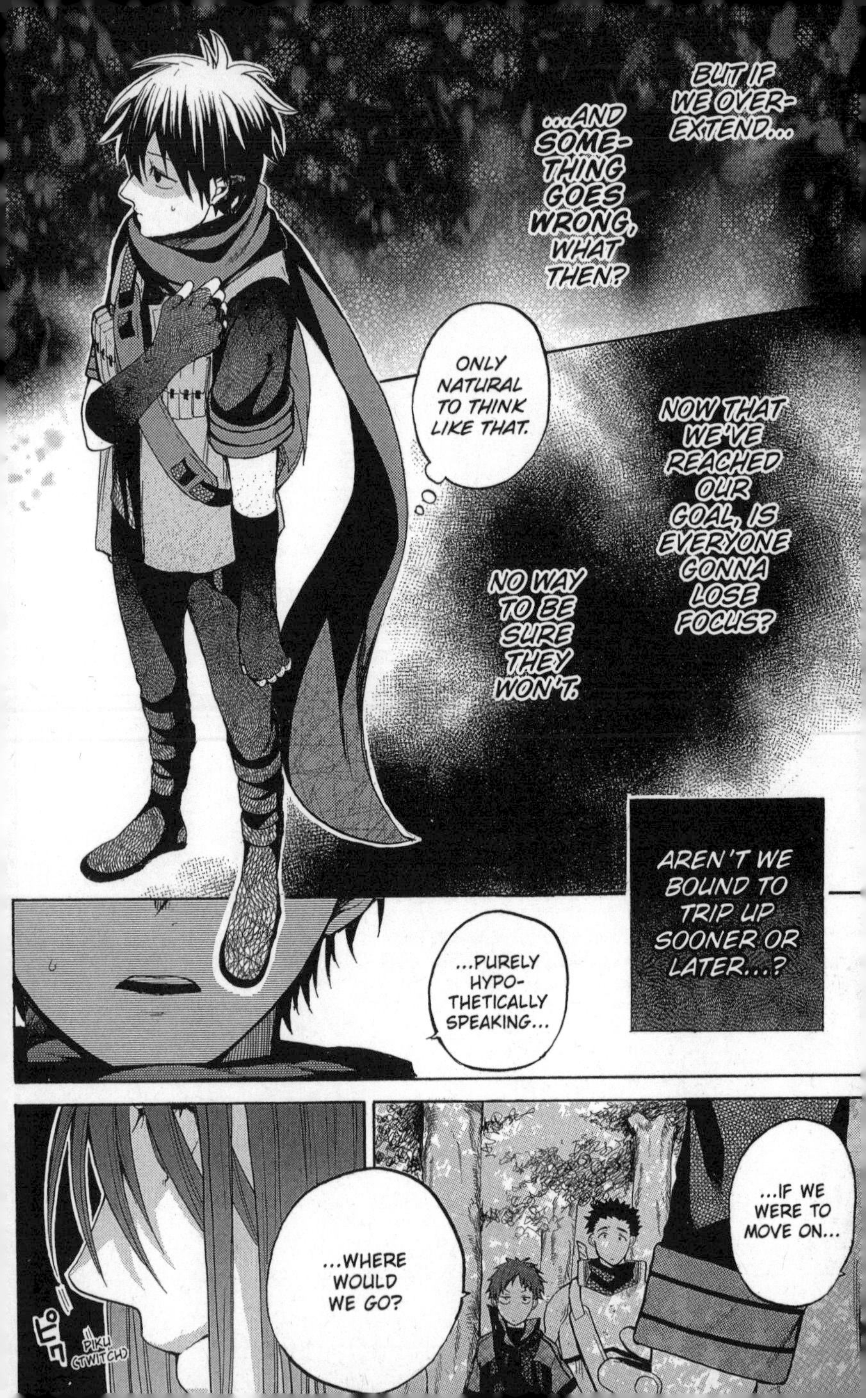

BUT IF WE OVER-EXTEND...
...AND SOMETHING GOES WRONG, WHAT THEN?
NOW THAT WE'VE REACHED OUR GOAL, IS EVERYONE GONNA LOSE FOCUS?
ONLY NATURAL TO THINK LIKE THAT.
NO WAY TO BE SURE THEY WON'T.
AREN'T WE BOUND TO TRIP UP SOONER OR LATER...?
...PURELY HYPOTHETICALLY SPEAKING...
...IF WE WERE TO MOVE ON...
...WHERE WOULD WE GO?
PIKU (TWITCH)

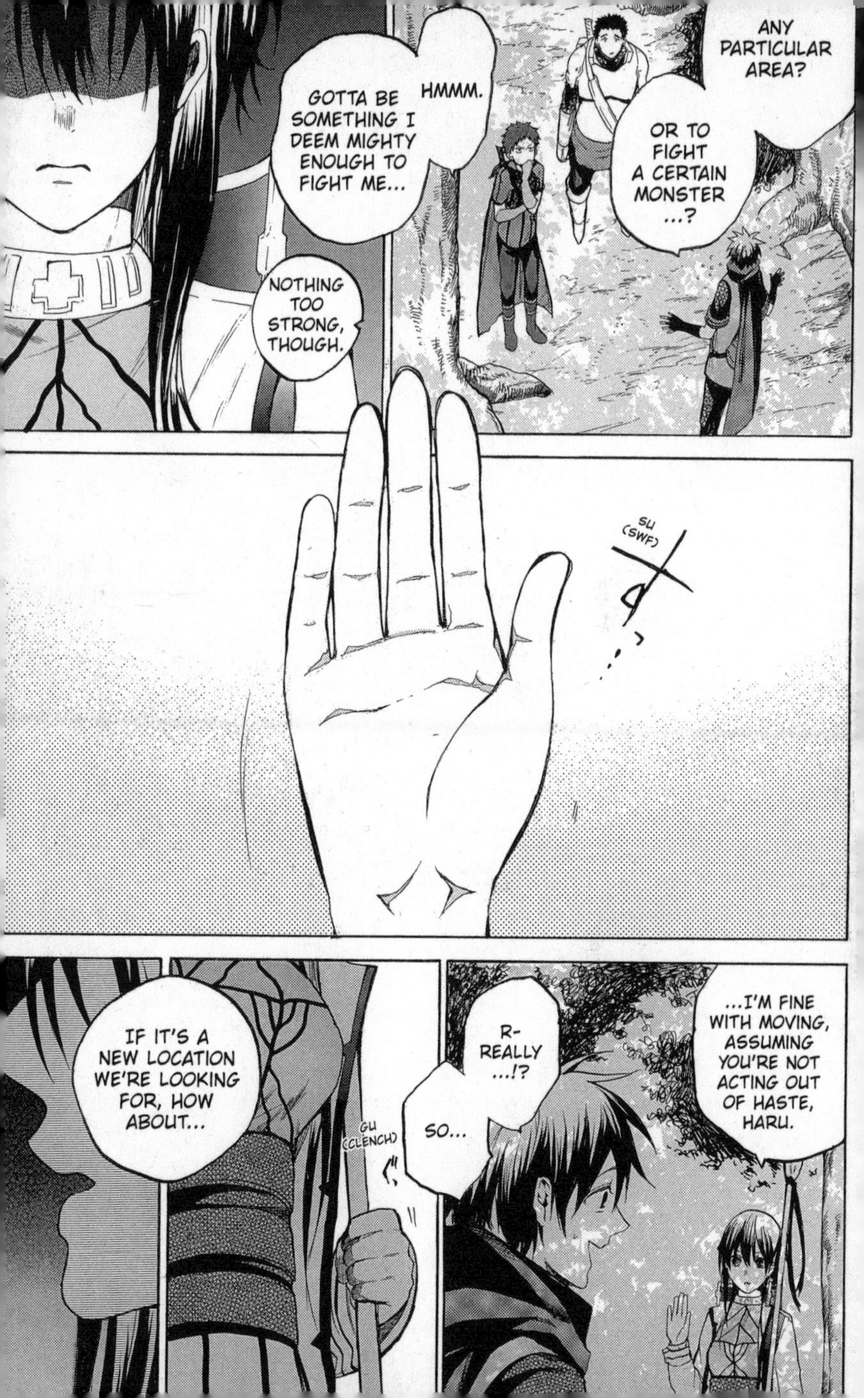
ANY PARTICULAR AREA?
OR TO FIGHT A CERTAIN MONSTER ...?
HMMM.
GOTTA BE SOMETHING I DEEM MIGHTY ENOUGH TO FIGHT ME...
NOTHING TOO STRONG, THOUGH.
SU (SWF)
...I'M FINE WITH MOVING, ASSUMING YOU'RE NOT ACTING OUT OF HASTE, HARU.
R-REALLY ...!?
SO...
GU (CLENCH)
IF IT'S A NEW LOCATION WE'RE LOOKING FOR, HOW ABOUT...

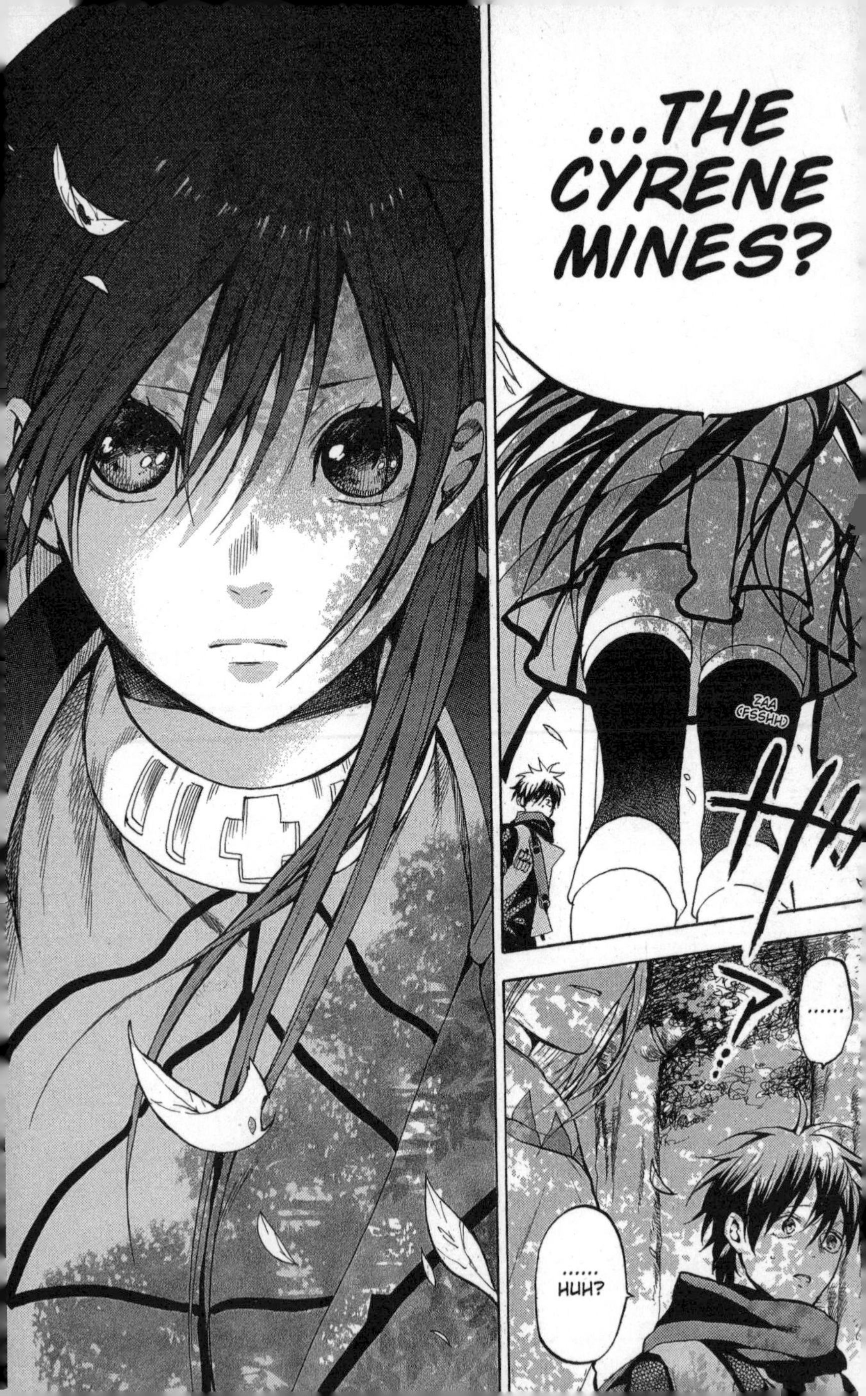
...THE CYRENE MINES?
ZAA (FSSHH)
......
......HUH?

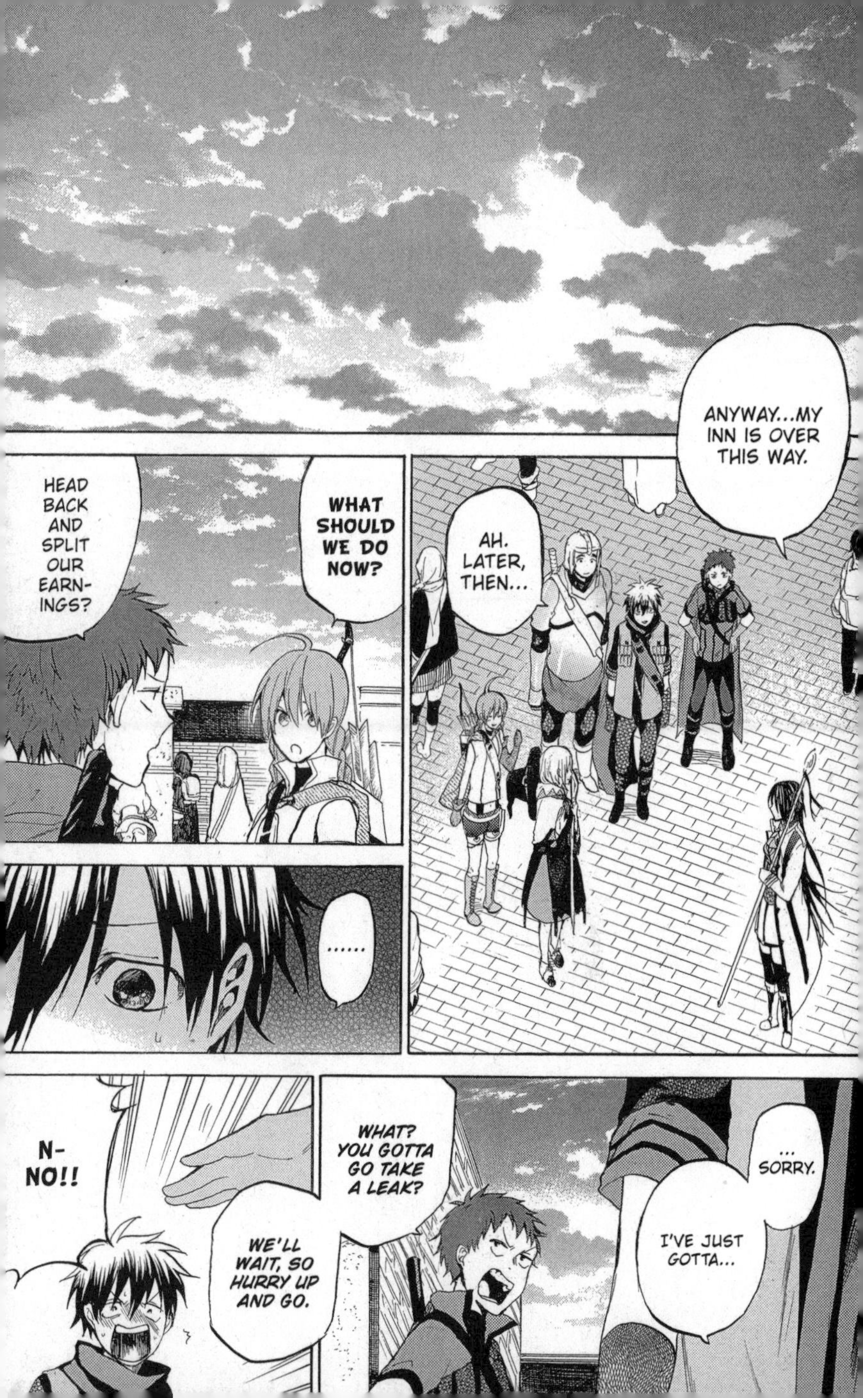
ANYWAY...MY INN IS OVER THIS WAY.
AH. LATER, THEN...
WHAT SHOULD WE DO NOW?
HEAD BACK AND SPLIT OUR EARNINGS?
......
... SORRY.
I'VE JUST GOTTA...
WHAT? YOU GOTTA GO TAKE A LEAK?
WE'LL WAIT, SO HURRY UP AND GO.
N- NO!!

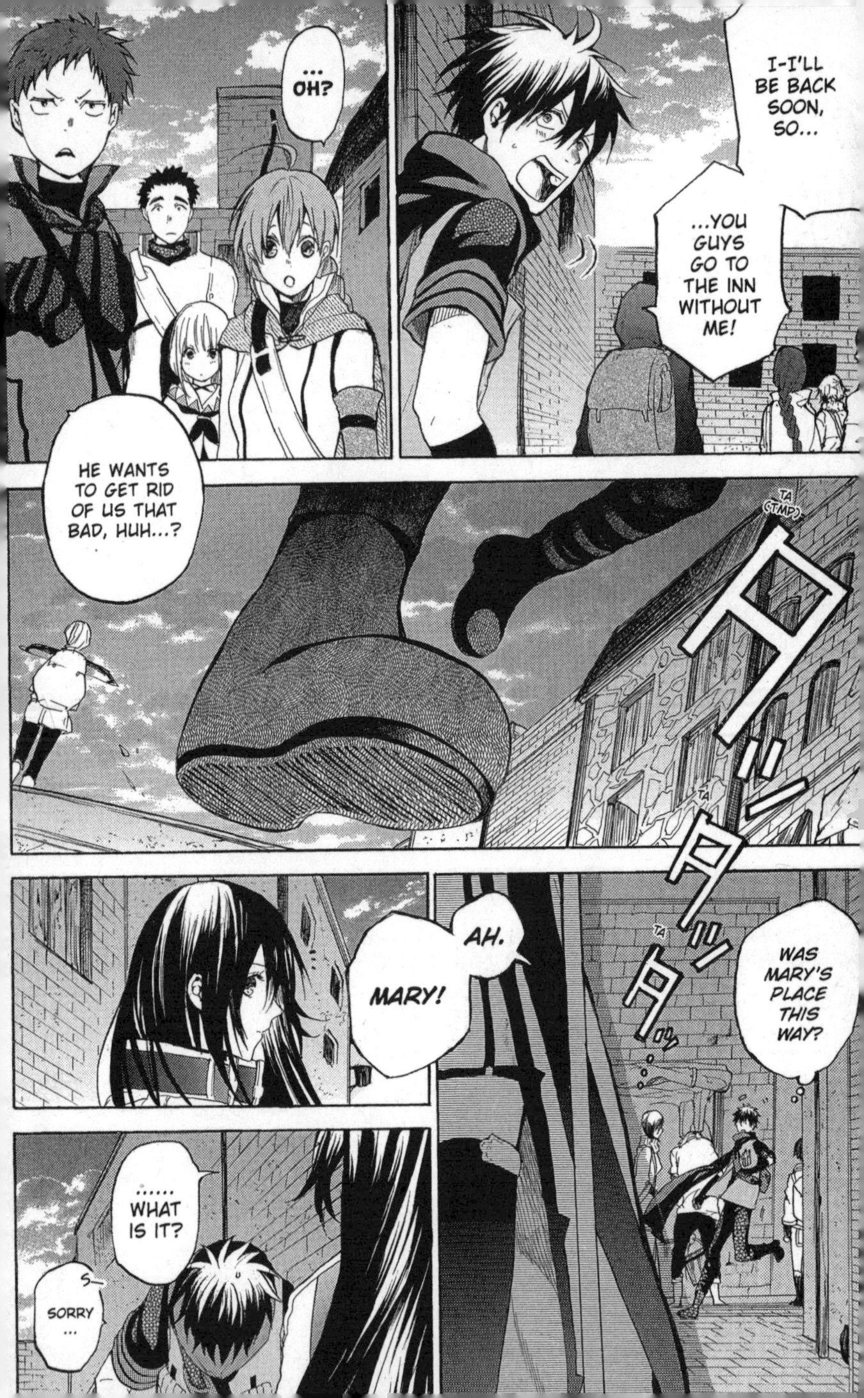
I-I'LL BE BACK SOON, SO...
...YOU GUYS GO TO THE INN WITHOUT ME!
... OH?
HE WANTS TO GET RID OF US THAT BAD, HUH...?
TA (TMP)
TA
TA
WAS MARY'S PLACE THIS WAY?
AH.
MARY!
...... WHAT IS IT?
S— SORRY ...

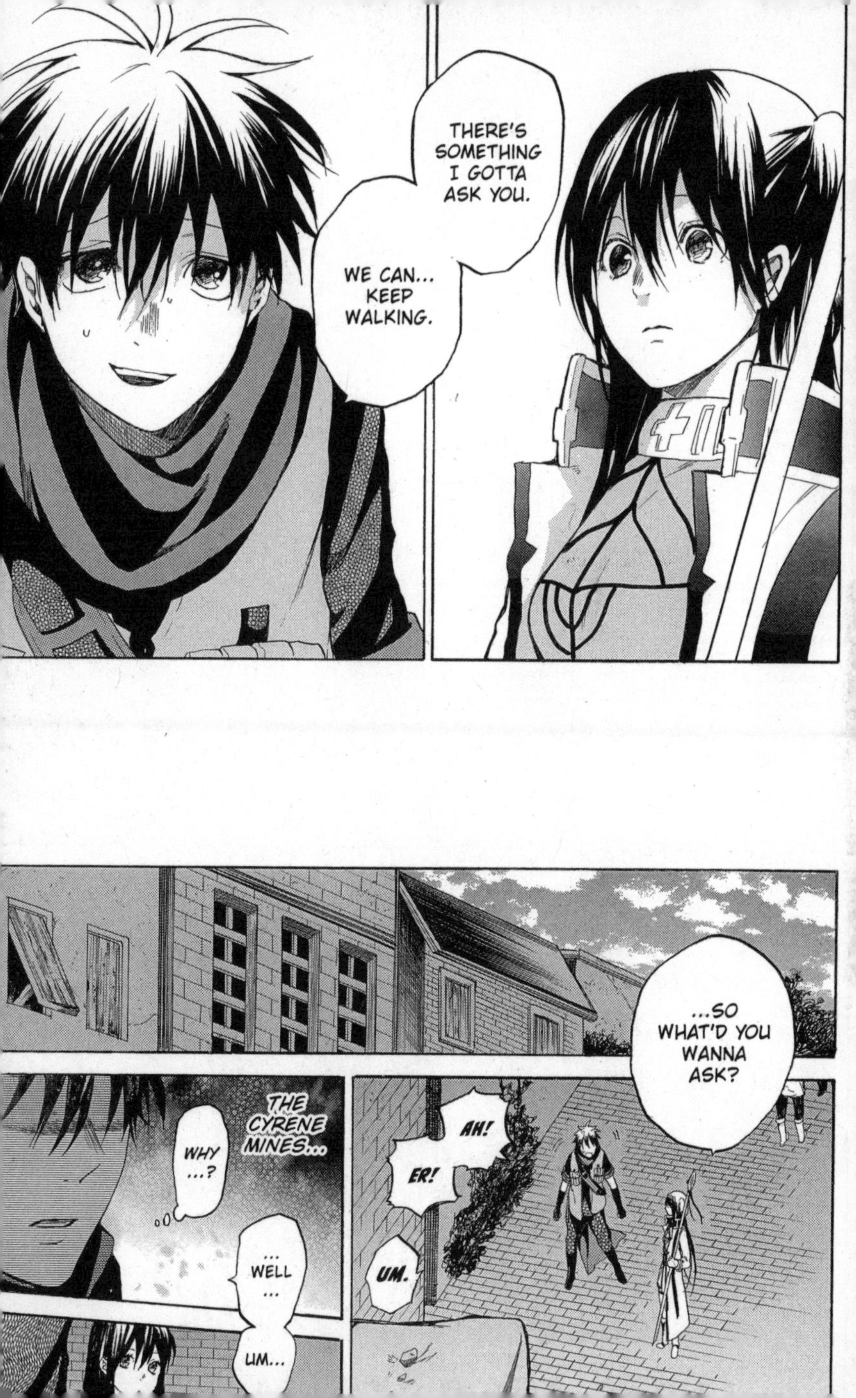
THERE'S SOMETHING I GOTTA ASK YOU.
WE CAN... KEEP WALKING.
...SO WHAT'D YOU WANNA ASK?
AH!
ER!
UM.
THE CYRENE MINES...
WHY ...?
... WELL ...
UM...

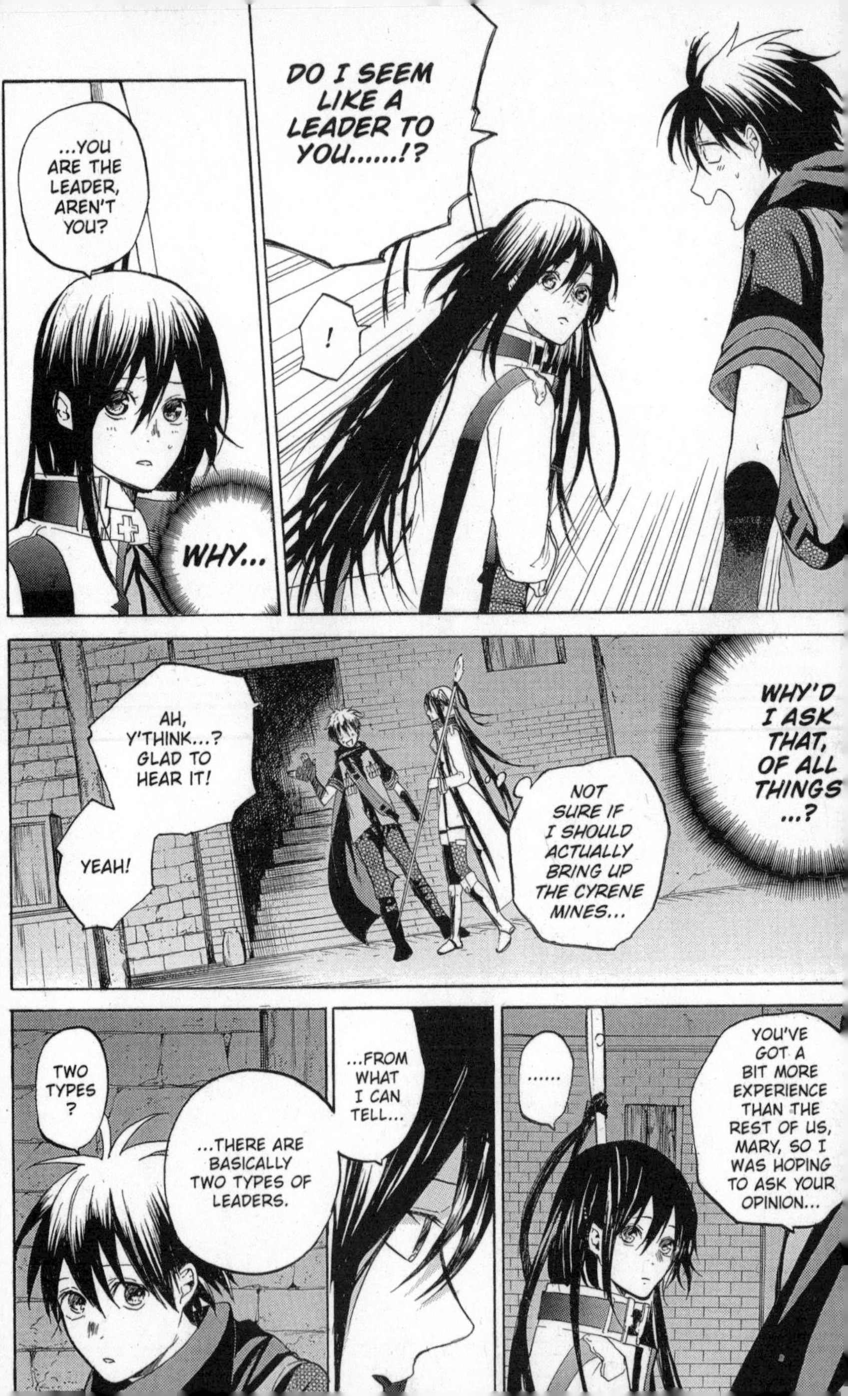
DO I SEEM LIKE A LEADER TO YOU......!?
!
...YOU ARE THE LEADER, AREN'T YOU?
WHY...
WHY'D I ASK THAT, OF ALL THINGS ...?
NOT SURE IF I SHOULD ACTUALLY BRING UP THE CYRENE MINES...
AH, Y'THINK...? GLAD TO HEAR IT!
YEAH!
YOU'VE GOT A BIT MORE EXPERIENCE THAN THE REST OF US, MARY, SO I WAS HOPING TO ASK YOUR OPINION...
......
...FROM WHAT I CAN TELL...
...THERE ARE BASICALLY TWO TYPES OF LEADERS.
TWO TYPES ?

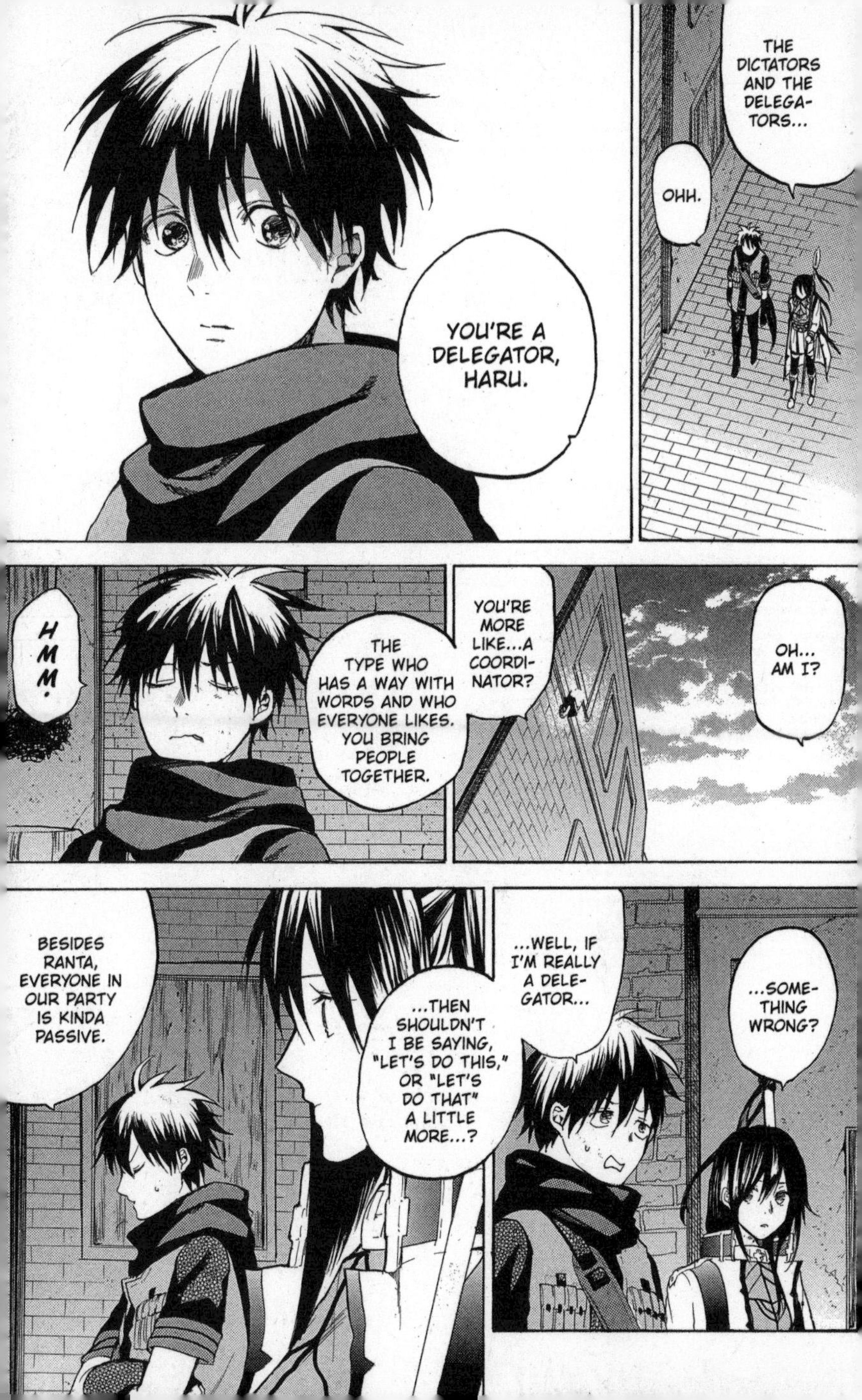
THE DICTATORS AND THE DELEGATORS...
OHH.
YOU'RE A DELEGATOR, HARU.
OH... AM I?
YOU'RE MORE LIKE...A COORDINATOR?
THE TYPE WHO HAS A WAY WITH WORDS AND WHO EVERYONE LIKES. YOU BRING PEOPLE TOGETHER.
HMM.
...SOMETHING WRONG?
...WELL, IF I'M REALLY A DELEGATOR...
...THEN SHOULDN'T I BE SAYING, "LET'S DO THIS," OR "LET'S DO THAT" A LITTLE MORE...?
BESIDES RANTA, EVERYONE IN OUR PARTY IS KINDA PASSIVE.

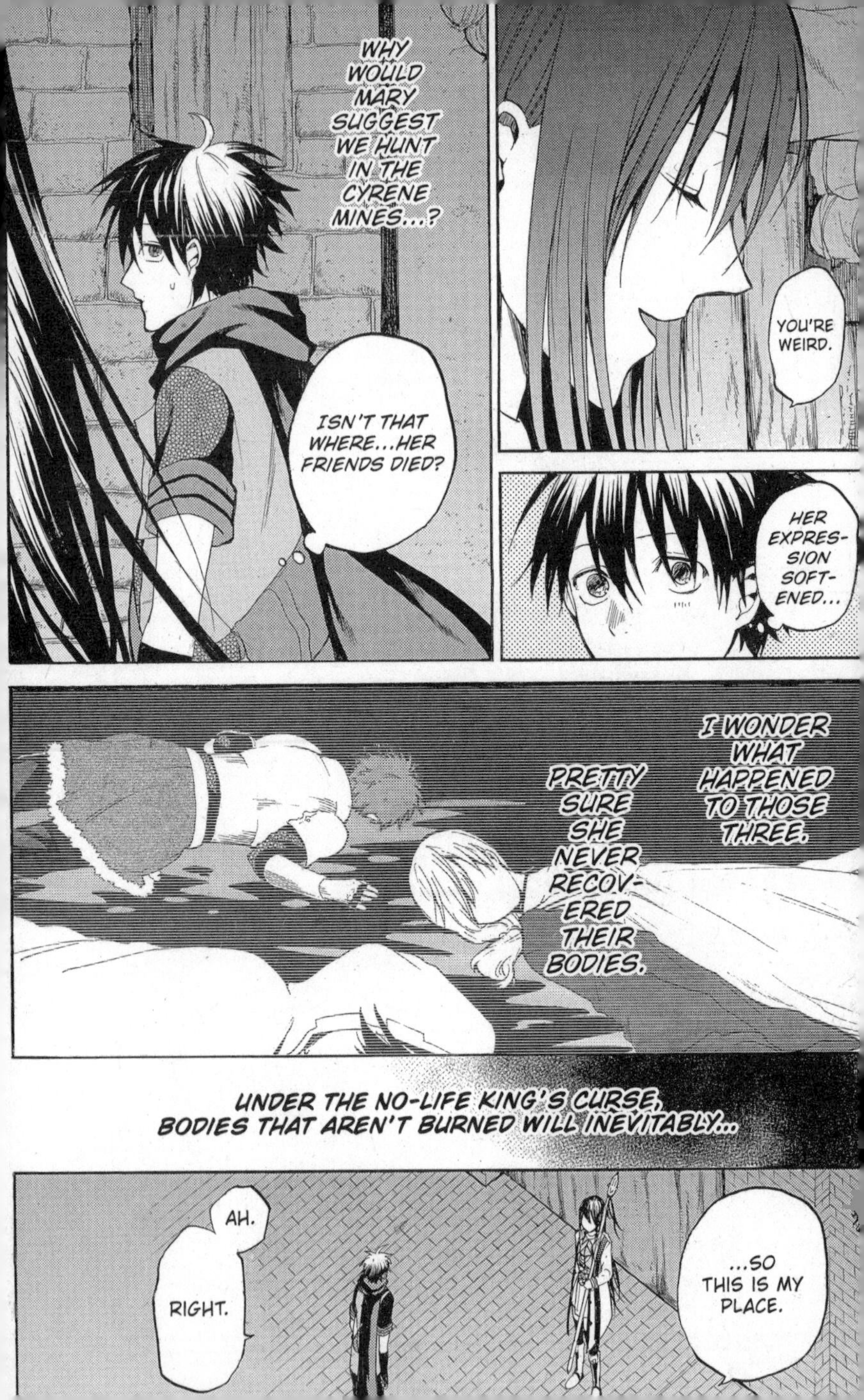
YOU'RE WEIRD.
HER EXPRES-SION SOFT-ENED...
WHY WOULD MARY SUGGEST WE HUNT IN THE CYRENE MINES...?
ISN'T THAT WHERE...HER FRIENDS DIED?
I WONDER WHAT HAPPENED TO THOSE THREE.
PRETTY SURE SHE NEVER RECOV-ERED THEIR BODIES.
UNDER THE NO-LIFE KING'S CURSE, BODIES THAT AREN'T BURNED WILL INEVITABLY...
...SO THIS IS MY PLACE.
AH.
RIGHT.

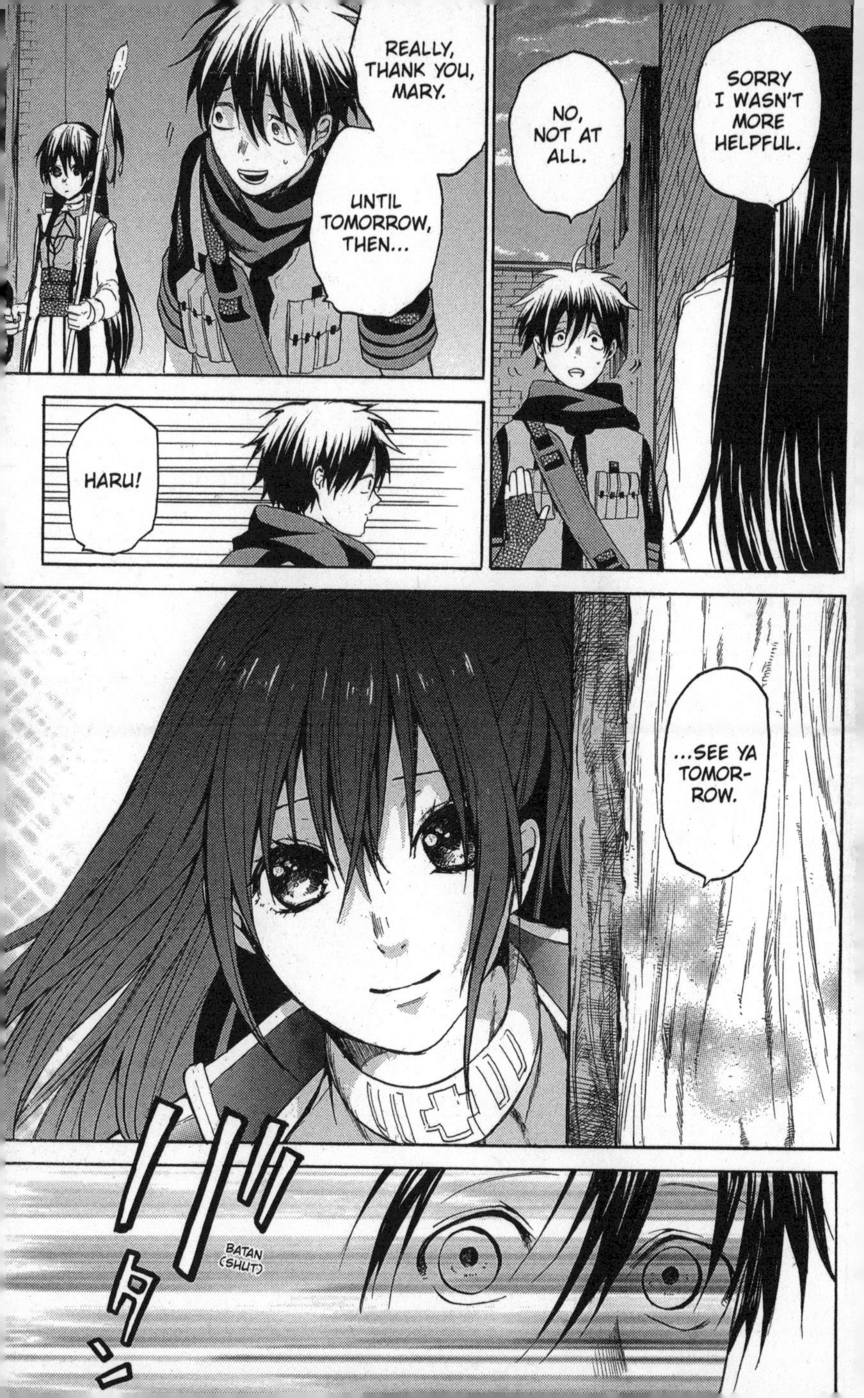
SORRY I WASN'T MORE HELPFUL.
NO, NOT AT ALL.
REALLY, THANK YOU, MARY.
UNTIL TOMORROW, THEN...
HARU!
...SEE YA TOMOR-ROW.
BATAN (SHUT)

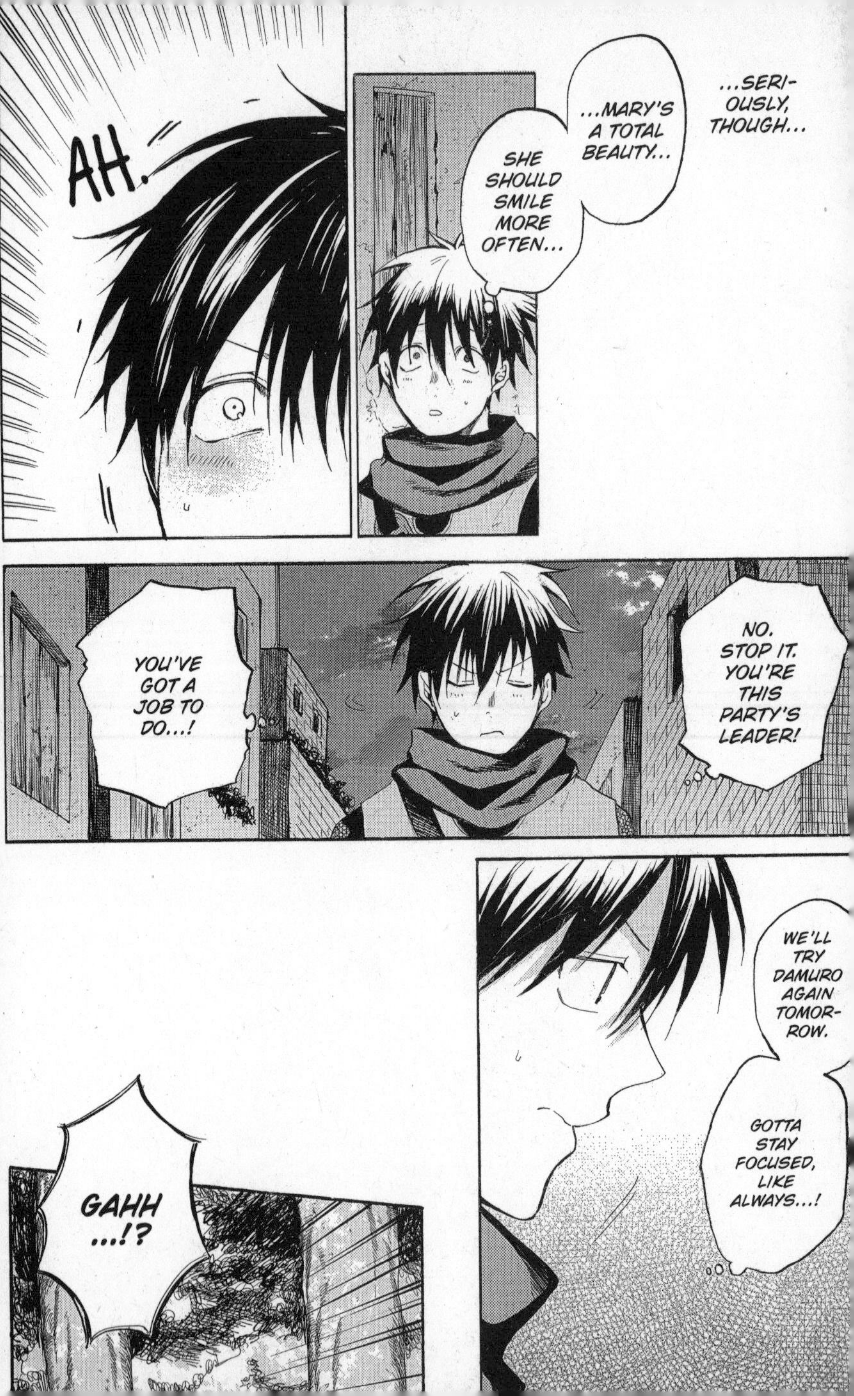
...SERIOUSLY, THOUGH...
...MARY'S A TOTAL BEAUTY...
SHE SHOULD SMILE MORE OFTEN...
AH.
NO. STOP IT. YOU'RE THIS PARTY'S LEADER!
YOU'VE GOT A JOB TO DO...!
WE'LL TRY DAMURO AGAIN TOMORROW.
GOTTA STAY FOCUSED, LIKE ALWAYS...!
GAHH ...!?

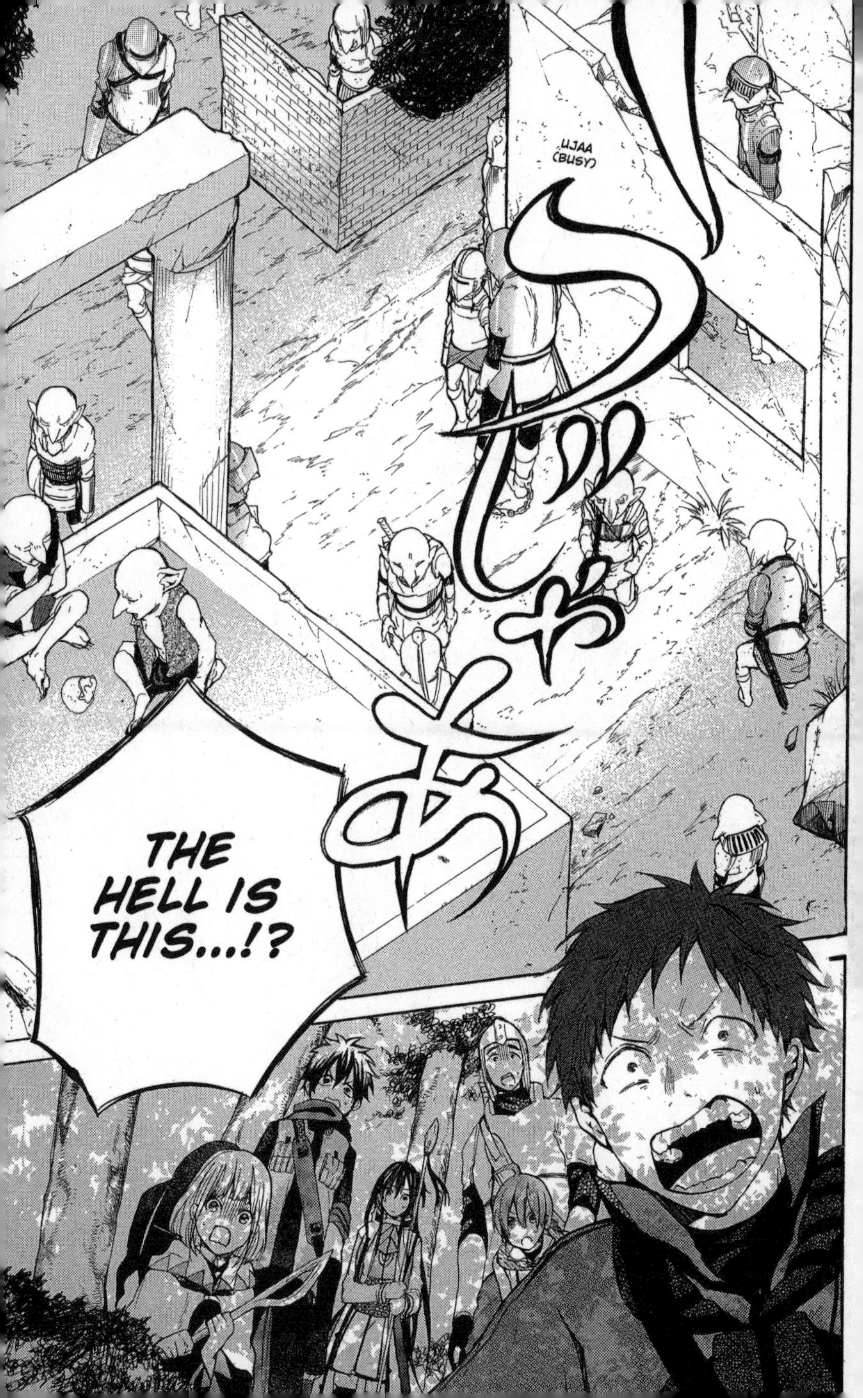

うじゃあ
UJAA
(BUSY)
THE HELL IS THIS...!?

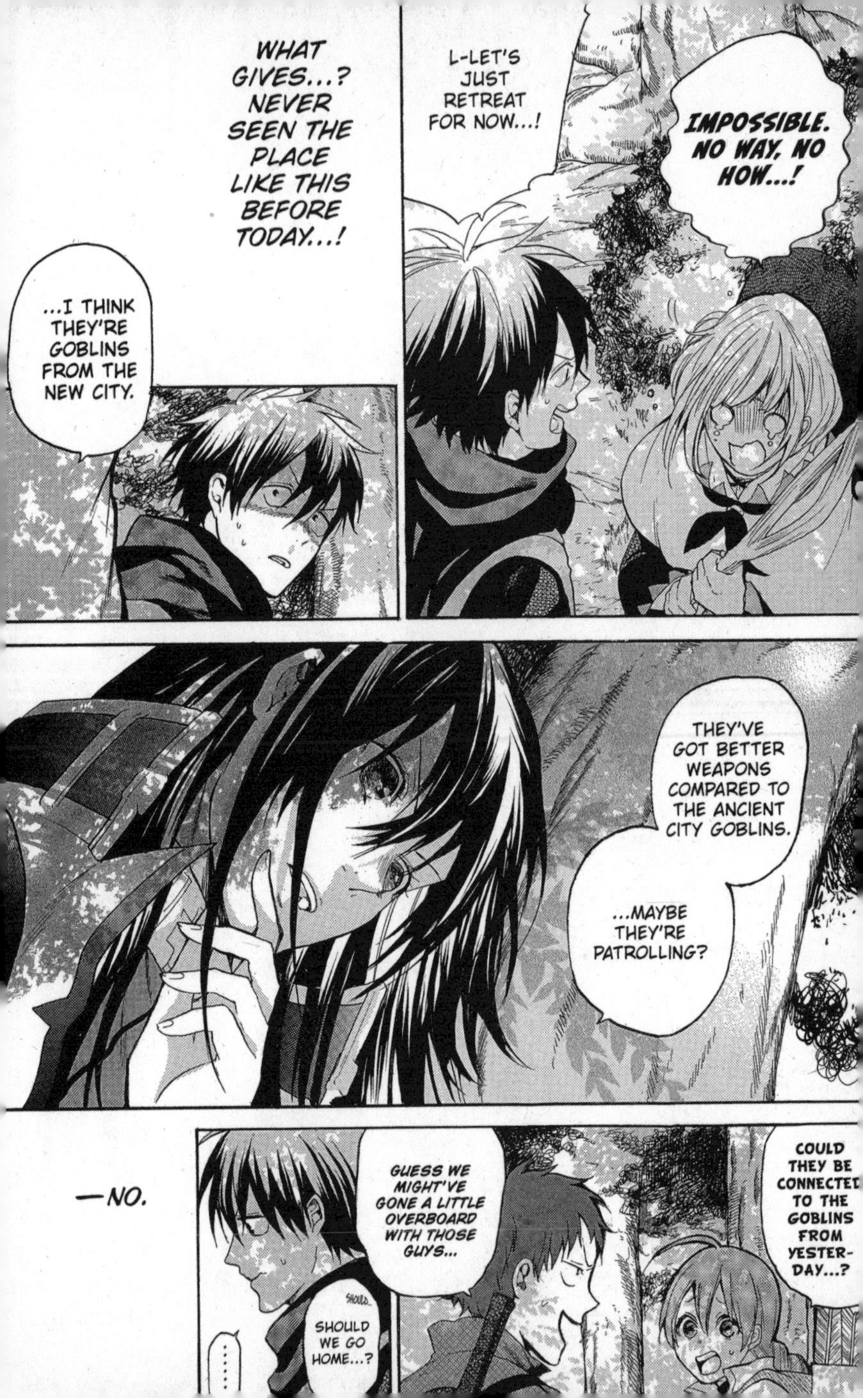
IMPOSSIBLE. NO WAY, NO HOW...!
L-LET'S JUST RETREAT FOR NOW...!
WHAT GIVES...? NEVER SEEN THE PLACE LIKE THIS BEFORE TODAY...!
...I THINK THEY'RE GOBLINS FROM THE NEW CITY.
THEY'VE GOT BETTER WEAPONS COMPARED TO THE ANCIENT CITY GOBLINS.
...MAYBE THEY'RE PATROLLING?
COULD THEY BE CONNECTED TO THE GOBLINS FROM YESTER-DAY...?
GUESS WE MIGHT'VE GONE A LITTLE OVERBOARD WITH THOSE GUYS...
SHOULD...
SHOULD WE GO HOME...?
......
—NO.

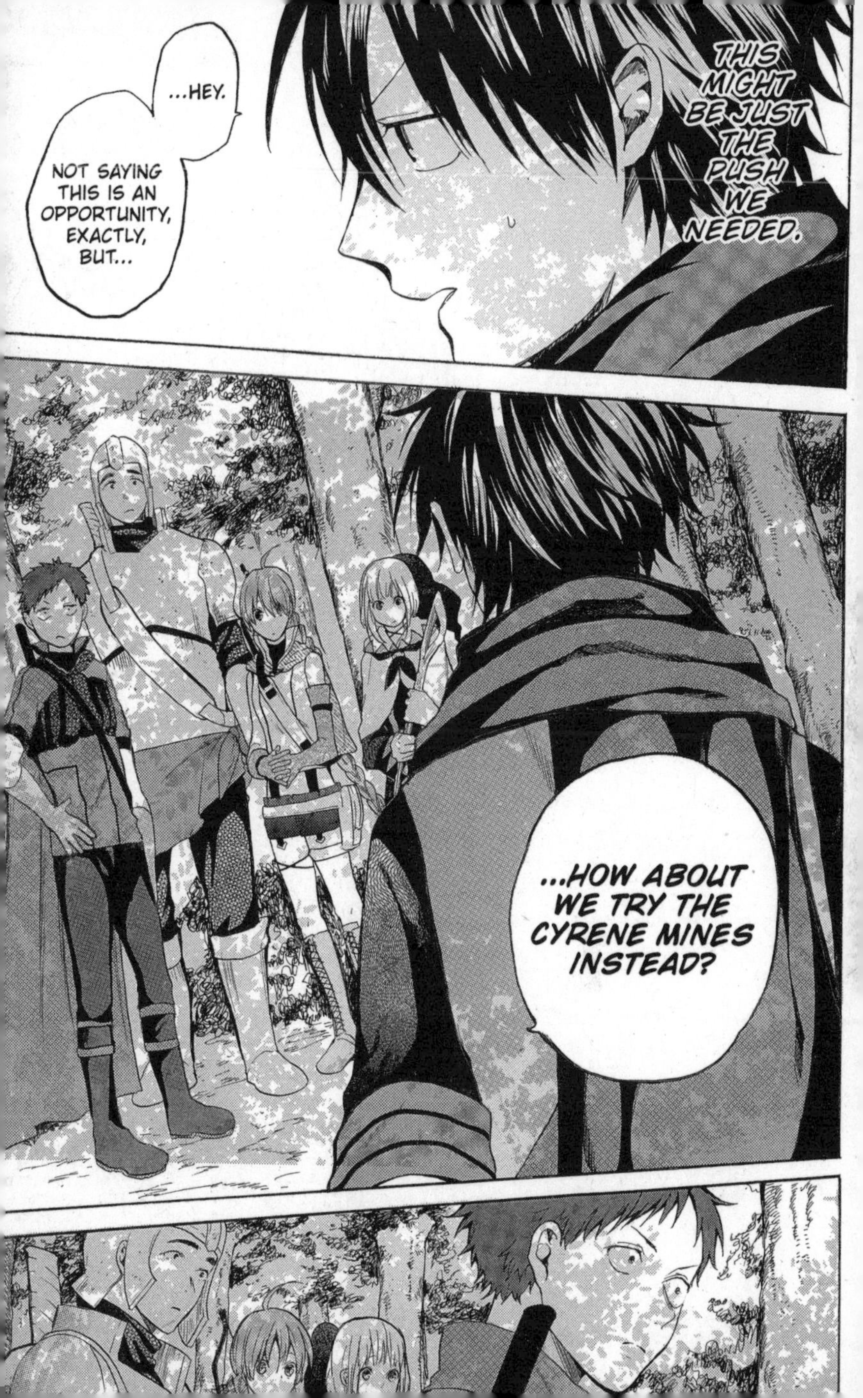
THIS MIGHT BE JUST THE PUSH WE NEEDED.
...HEY.
NOT SAYING THIS IS AN OPPORTUNITY, EXACTLY, BUT...
...HOW ABOUT WE TRY THE CYRENE MINES INSTEAD?

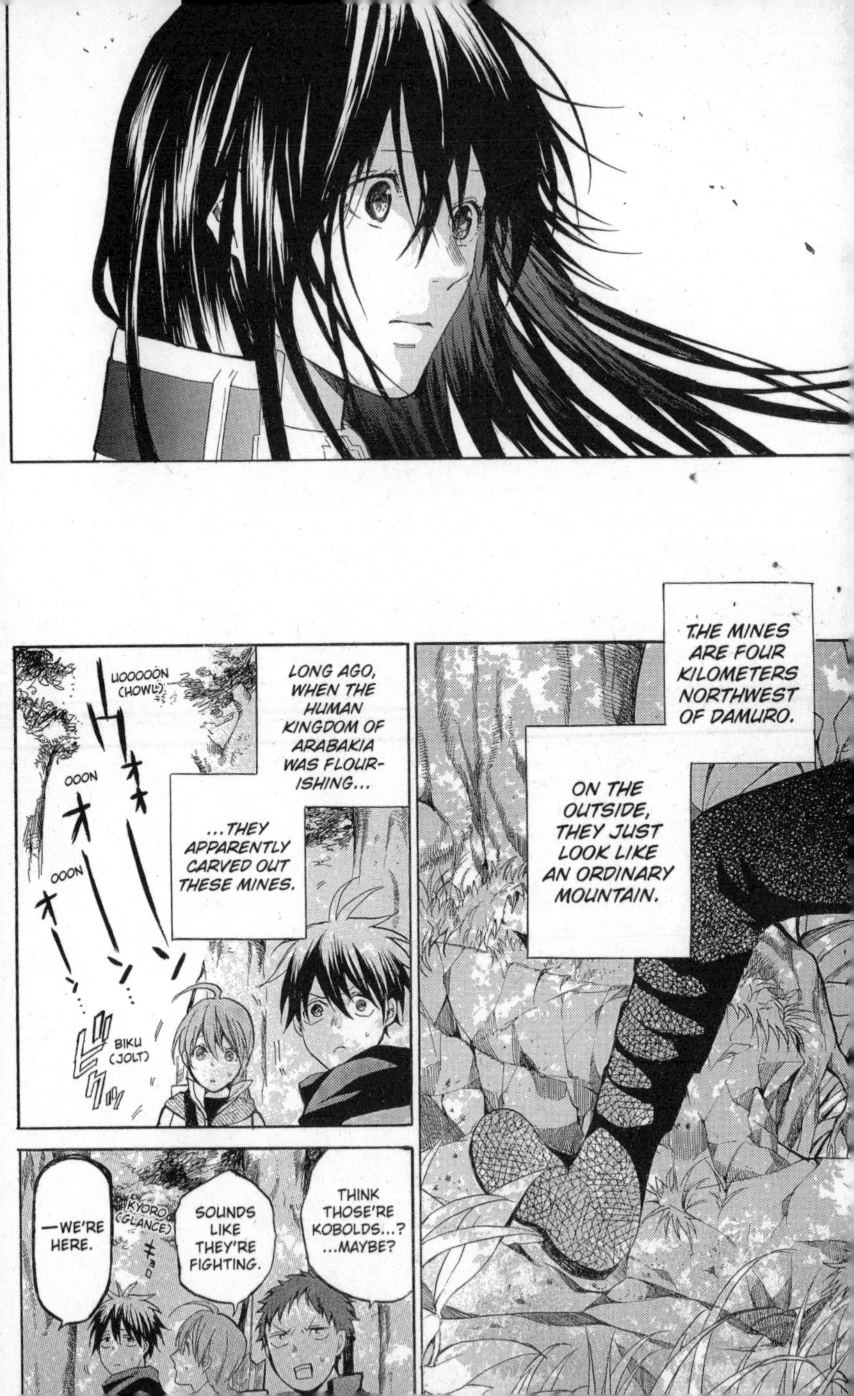
THE MINES ARE FOUR KILOMETERS NORTHWEST OF DAMURO.
ON THE OUTSIDE, THEY JUST LOOK LIKE AN ORDINARY MOUNTAIN.
LONG AGO, WHEN THE HUMAN KINGDOM OF ARABAKIA WAS FLOURISHING...
...THEY APPARENTLY CARVED OUT THESE MINES.
UOOOOON (HOWL)
OOON
OOON
BIKU (JOLT)
THINK THOSE'RE KOBOLDS...? ...MAYBE?
SOUNDS LIKE THEY'RE FIGHTING.
KYORO (GLANCE)
—WE'RE HERE.

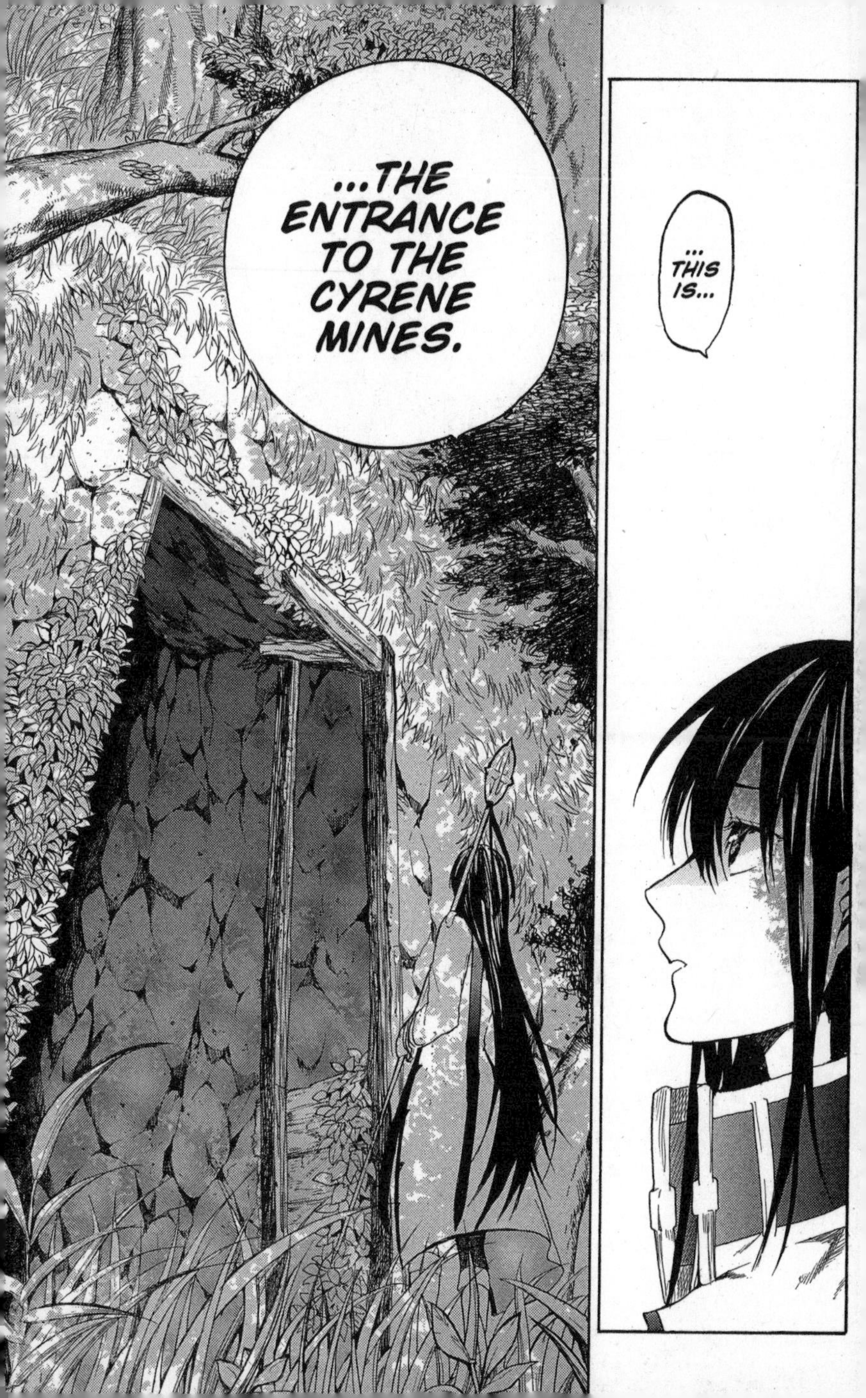
... THIS IS...
...THE ENTRANCE TO THE CYRENE MINES.

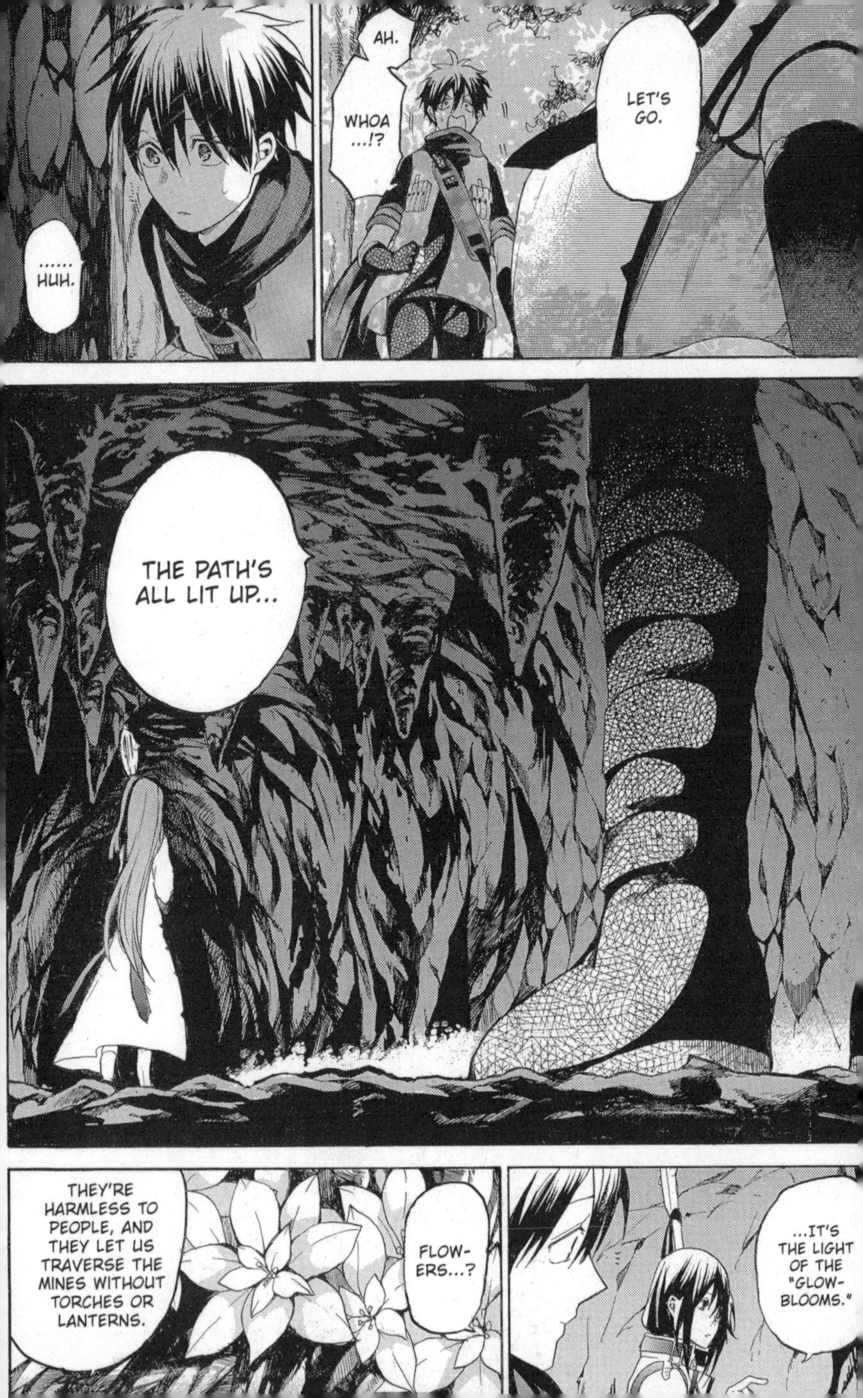
LET'S GO.
AH.
WHOA ...!?
...... HUH.
THE PATH'S ALL LIT UP...
...IT'S THE LIGHT OF THE "GLOW-BLOOMS."
FLOW-ERS...?
THEY'RE HARMLESS TO PEOPLE, AND THEY LET US TRAVERSE THE MINES WITHOUT TORCHES OR LANTERNS.

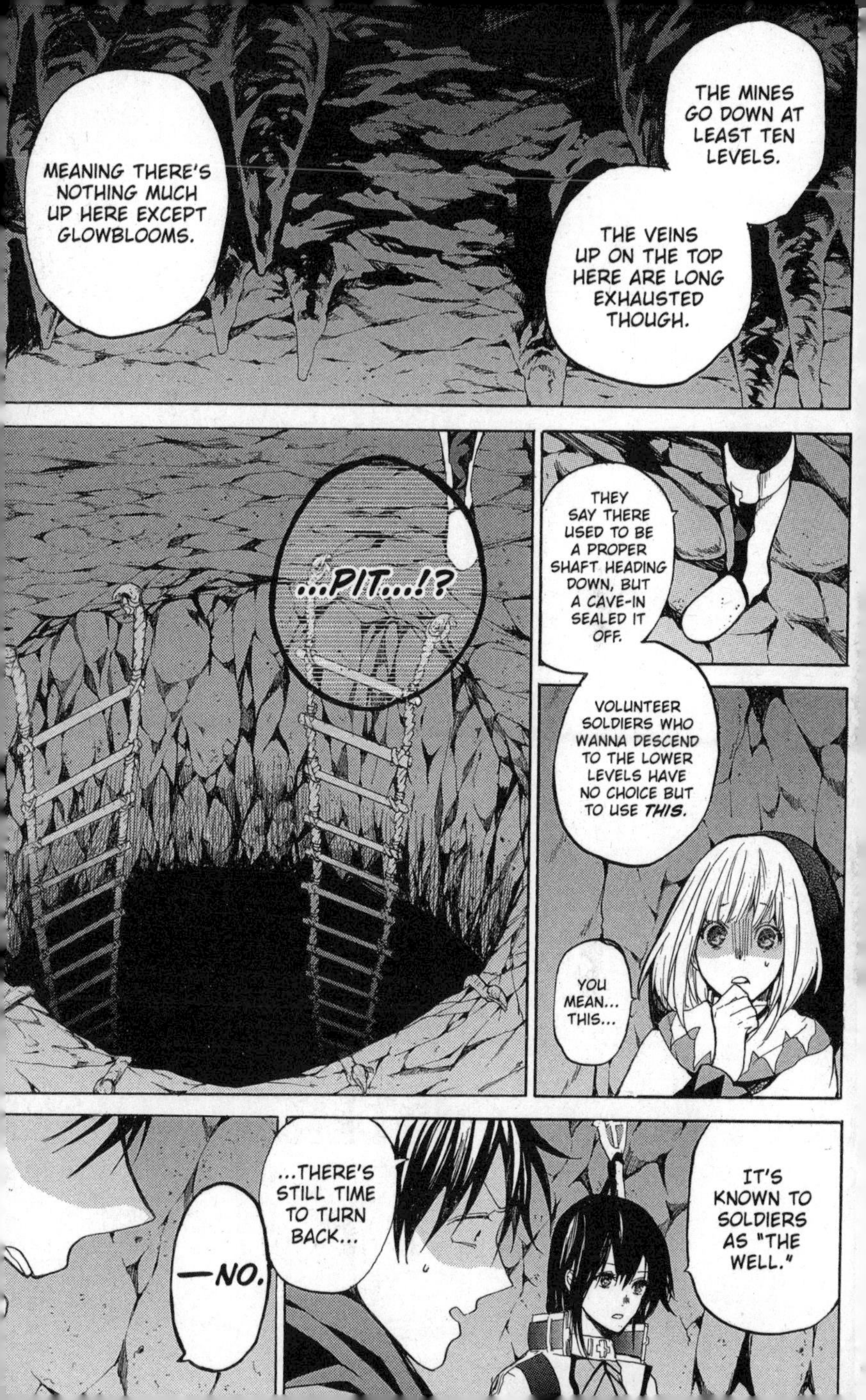
THE MINES GO DOWN AT LEAST TEN LEVELS.
THE VEINS UP ON THE TOP HERE ARE LONG EXHAUSTED THOUGH.
MEANING THERE'S NOTHING MUCH UP HERE EXCEPT GLOWBLOOMS.
THEY SAY THERE USED TO BE A PROPER SHAFT HEADING DOWN, BUT A CAVE-IN SEALED IT OFF.
VOLUNTEER SOLDIERS WHO WANNA DESCEND TO THE LOWER LEVELS HAVE NO CHOICE BUT TO USE *THIS.*
YOU MEAN... THIS...
...PIT...!?
IT'S KNOWN TO SOLDIERS AS "THE WELL."
...THERE'S STILL TIME TO TURN BACK...
—NO.

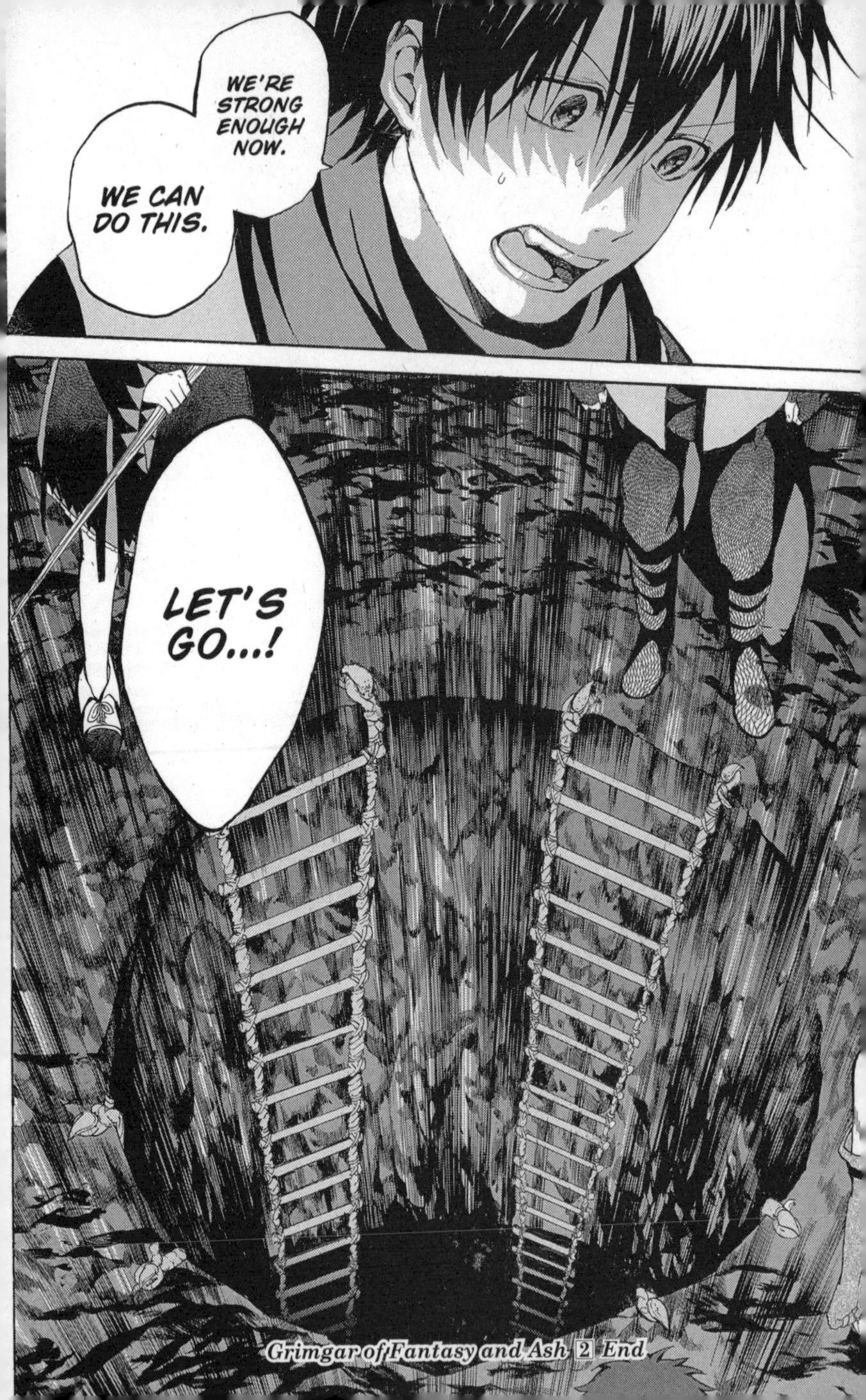
WE'RE STRONG ENOUGH NOW.
WE CAN DO THIS.
LET'S GO...!

Grimgar of Fantasy and Ash 2 End

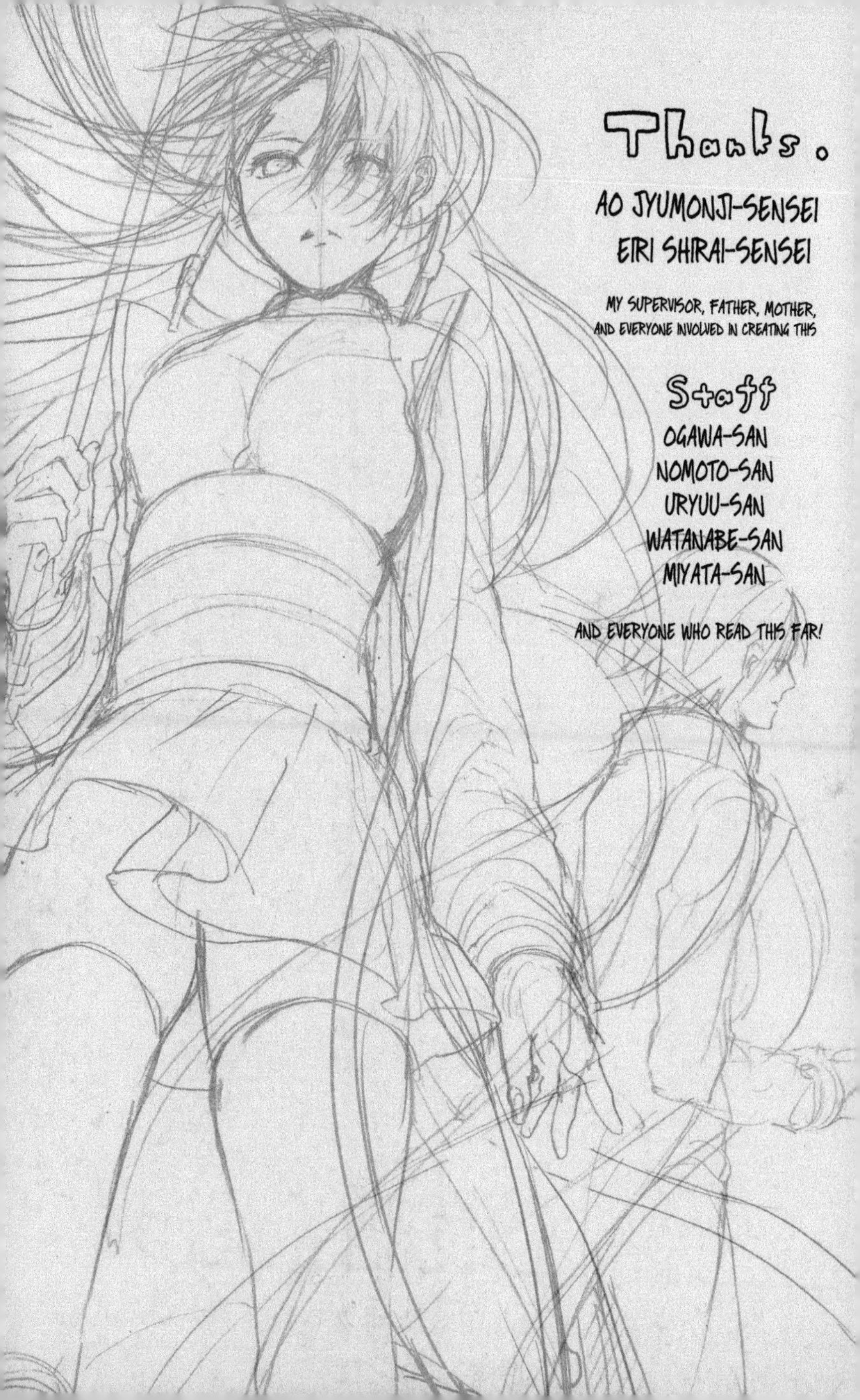
Thanks.
AO JYUMONJI-SENSEI
EIRI SHIRAI-SENSEI
MY SUPERVISOR, FATHER, MOTHER,
AND EVERYONE INVOLVED IN CREATING THIS
Staff
OGAWA-SAN
NOMOTO-SAN
URYUU-SAN
WATANABE-SAN
MIYATA-SAN
AND EVERYONE WHO READ THIS FAR!

Grimgar of Fantasy and Ash

STORY BY
Ao Jyumonji

ILLUSTRATION BY
Mutsumi Okubashi

ORIGINAL CHARACTER DESIGN BY
Eiri Shirai

TRANSLATION: **Caleb Cook**   LETTERING: **Phil Christie**

HAI TO GENSOU NO GRIMGAR Volume 2
©2016 Ao Jyumonji/OVERLAP
© 2016 Mutsumi Okubashi / SQUARE ENIX CO., LTD.
First published in Japan in 2016 by SQUARE ENIX CO., LTD. English translation rights arranged with Square Enix Co., Ltd. and Yen Press, LLC through Tuttle-Mori Agency, Inc.

English translation © 2017 by SQUARE ENIX CO., LTD.

Yen Press
1290 Avenue of the Americas
New York, NY 10104

Visit us at yenpress.com
facebook.com/yenpress
twitter.com/yenpress
yenpress.tumblr.com
instagram.com/yenpress

First Yen Press Edition: October 2017

Yen Press is an imprint of Yen Press, LLC.
The Yen Press name and logo are trademarks of Yen Press, LLC.

The publisher is not responsible for websites (or their content) that are not owned by the publisher.

Library of Congress Control Number: 2017933038

ISBNs: 978-0-316-44181-0 (paperback)
978-0-316-47996-7 (ebook)

10 9 8 7 6 5 4 3 2 1

BVG

Printed in the United States of America